QUEST FOR IDENTITY

Quest for Identity: America Since 1945 is a survey of the American experience from the close of World War II through the Cold War and 9/11 to the present. It helps students understand postwar American history through a seamless narrative punctuated with accessible analyses. Randall Bennett Woods addresses and explains the major themes that highlight the period: the Cold War, the civil rights and women's rights movements, and other great changes that led to major realignments of American life. While the narrative political history is featured, the book also fully discusses cultural matters and socioeconomic problems. Dramatic new patterns of immigration and migration characterized the period as much as the counterculture, the growth of television and the Internet, the interstate highway system, rock and roll, and the exploration of space. The pageantry, drama, irony, poignancy, and humor of the American journey since World War II are all here.

Randall Bennett Woods is John A. Cooper Distinguished Professor of History at the University of Arkansas. He has written widely on twentieth-century American history, including *Dawning of the Cold War* (1991), *Changing of the Guard* (1990), and *Fulbright: A Biography* (1995), which won both the Ferrell and Ledbetter Prizes. He was also editor of *Vietnam and the American Political Tradition: The Politics of Dissent* (Cambridge, 2003).

Quest for Identity

America Since 1945

Randall Bennett Woods

University of Arkansas

CAMBRIDGE
UNIVERSITY PRESS

CAMBRIDGE UNIVERSITY PRESS
Cambridge, New York, Melbourne, Madrid, Cape Town, Singapore, São Paulo

Cambridge University Press
40 West 20th Street, New York, NY 10011-4211, USA

www.cambridge.org
Information on this title: www.cambridge.org/9780521840651

First published 2005

Printed in the United States of America

A catalog record for this book is available from the British Library.

Library of Congress Cataloging in Publication Data
Woods, Randall Bennett, 1944–

    Quest for identity : America since 1945 / Randall Bennett Woods.

      p. cm.

    Includes bibliographical references and index.

    ISBN 0-521-84065-1 – ISBN 0-521-54997-3 (pbk.)

    1. United States – History – 1945–   2. United States – Social conditions – 1945–
   3. National characteristics, American.   I. Title.
E741.W88   2005
973.92 – dc22   2004025179

ISBN-13   978-0-521-84065-1 hardback
ISBN-10   0-521-84065-1 hardback

ISBN-13   978-0-521-54997-4 paperback
ISBN-10   0-521-54997-3 paperback

Contents

Preface

The study of any period in history is in part defined by what came before and by what came after. What makes an inquiry into postwar American life unique and somewhat problematic is that there is no postscript, no epilogue. Consequently, there is in such chronicles an inevitable lack of perspective. Nevertheless, the case for writing a history of the recent past is compelling. Students are fascinated by it; the half century since World War II is the frame of reference for their parents and grandparents. For many it will be the gateway to the study of history as a whole. It is the period that, for better or worse, is most likely to inform the present and the future. And surely, the recent era is as full of change, drama, and complexity as any other period in human history.

Perhaps the three most obvious themes for a book on postwar America are the Cold War, the struggle of nonwhite Americans for their full rights under the Constitution, and the women's movement. The fifty-year battle that the United States and its allies waged with the forces of international communism affected virtually every aspect of American life. Most obviously, it dominated foreign affairs, forcing policymakers to view every problem through its distorting prism. The East–West confrontation involved the United States in two hot wars, Korea and Vietnam. That latter conflict shattered the New Deal–Fair Deal–New Frontier–Great Society reform coalition, marking a break in a cycle of reform-consolidation-reform and introducing one of reaction-consolidation-reaction in domestic affairs. Because it seemed to many Americans that only a monolith could defeat the monolithic communist threat, the Cold War made change for women and minorities more difficult. At the same time, because the ongoing conflict with the Soviet Union and Communist China continually forced the nation to reexamine its values and identity, it actually facilitated change. The Cold War spawned the military–industrial complex and the national security state. And finally, it gave rise to periodic domestic witch hunts by extremists convinced that the greatest danger to the nation's survival was posed not by the threat of external communist aggression but by the threat of internal communist subversion. The resulting impact on the intellectual, cultural, and political life of the country was profound.

The half century following World War II was characterized by dramatic new patterns of immigration and migration. The country continued to be a magnet to the oppressed and poverty stricken of the world. Encouraged by more liberal immigration laws passed in the 1960s, by special provisions stemming from the Vietnam War, World War II, and the communization of Cuba, and by a relatively porous 2,000-mile border between the United States and Mexico, millions of immigrants, both legal and illegal, flooded into the country. One of the many effects of this inflow was to ensure that Hispanic Americans would become the largest ethnic minority in the United States sometime early in the twenty-first century. By the 1970s millions of Americans were abandoning the manufacturing regions of the North and Midwest for the more service- and high tech–oriented economies of the South and West: the "Sunbelt." This migration and its underlying causes gave rise to new pockets of poverty and prosperity and contributed to a major realignment in American political life.

Spurred by the changes wrought by World War II and by their own frustrations, African Americans and women made huge if uneven and painful strides toward full citizenship and self-realization. The civil rights and women's movements in turn forced the country to continually confront its democratic values and attempt to reconcile them with reality. It was a sign of how far things had progressed that by the 1990s the national debate was not over whether blacks and women ought to be accorded equal rights but whether through affirmative action they should be given preference in hiring and admission to educational institutions.

No period in American history witnessed greater cultural change than the years from 1945 to 2000. Sports, professional and amateur, increasingly integrated and became a national preoccupation and at times an obsession. The television, the interstate highway system, the credit card, and the computer changed the way Americans lived and thought. Exploration of space became more than just a dream of science fiction writers. The advent of rock and roll and the emergence of a counterculture during the 1960s highlighted the emergence of an increasingly self-conscious and assertive youth culture. High culture remained solidly entrenched in American life, but pop culture flourished. While highbrows reveled in postmodernist painting and the renderings of avant-garde composers, television, motion pictures, videos, and compact discs made Elvis and Madonna accessible to even the poorest Americans. By the 1990s the country was immersed in the so-called "culture wars" as advocates of change urged their fellow citizens to do nothing less than reject the until-then-accepted past as a contrivance of "dead white males." They were in turn denounced by traditionalists as "feminazis" and intellectual nihilists.

During the 1960s Americans "discovered" the culture of poverty. Liberals tried to change it while conservatives attempted either to ignore it or wait it out. Poverty, particularly in urban ghettos, in Appalachia, and in the rural South, persisted. As a result so did drugs and crime. It should be noted, however, that by the 1980s drug use and violence had become an affliction not just of the poor but of Americans of all classes, colors, and regions.

Americans also rediscovered the environment. By the late 1970s the drive to prevent pollution, limit population, and preserve at least part of nature in its natural state had become a movement that involved Americans of all political persuasions. Frequently they were pitted against advocates of "development" and economic progress who argued that providing jobs and the good life for all was more important than saving the spotted owl. An important part of environmentalism was population control but that movement aroused the fears of Catholics, Muslims, religious conservatives, and anti-abortionists in general.

Aside from the Cold War and other, lesser foreign crises, politics was dominated by the growth of the welfare state and the debate between conservatives and liberals (admittedly amorphous and uncertain terms) over the wisdom and implications of this phenomenon. In essence, what transpired was an ongoing struggle between two historical narratives: one featuring the doctrine of the free, self-reliant individual voluntarily associating in limited government for personal and collective benefit versus the concept of a benevolent state regulating society to ensure equality of opportunity and a safety net for those who could not fend for themselves. It was, of course, the age-old story of two competing views of human nature.

Quest for Identity is designed to meet the need of students of postwar America for a concise but full narrative encompassing the events, personalities, and conditions that shaped the national consciousness. It also includes analyses of the causes underlying the principal social, economic, political, and international problems of the era. The book is divided into 14 chapters. Chapter titles seem to indicate an emphasis on politics and foreign affairs, but far more than half of the material deals with cultural matters and socioeconomic problems which are, of course, the sources of all politics and diplomacy. I am acutely aware that history is made on shop floors, in rural church meetings, and in local coffee shops as well as in the West Wing, congressional caucuses, and corporate board rooms. Each chapter features an introduction and conclusion and is punctuated with maps designed to enhance the students' understanding of the content. A list of "Additional Readings" follows each installment except the last.

1   The Republic in Transition

Demobilization and Reconversion

$\mathbf{A}$s World War II came to a close, Americans were exhausted, numbed by four long years of war, but at the same time most were optimistic, and the country was remarkably united. A general agreement prevailed that the struggle against the Axis had been just. Germany, Japan, Italy, and their allies represented the forces of evil, and the United States had to intervene to save itself and mankind in general. As a result of this consensus, America was spared the isolationist backlash that had overwhelmed the Treaty of Versailles following World War I; nor was there a Red Scare similar to that which had swept the United States in 1919. Except for treatment of the nisei, Japanese Americans, and some 11,000 German aliens – unjustly interned by a government that confused ethnicity and nationality with treachery – violations of civil liberties did not compare with those committed during previous conflicts. Convinced that the struggle for democracy abroad would translate into equity under the law and nondiscrimination, African Americans experienced a rising level of expectations. Similar expectations arose among American women who had entered the workplace in droves during the war and who wanted the freedom to choose between a career inside and a career outside the home (although most, like returning male veterans, dreamed of marriage and children). The dawn of the atomic age created widespread anxiety, but for the time being, only the United States possessed the bomb. Clearly, the world was a dangerous place, but American hegemony seemed an adequate safeguard against another major war. In short, Americans no less than Britons were convinced that World War II had indeed been "a people's war" and that a new age of social justice and peace was in the offing.

The Heritage of War

As was true of the Civil War, World War II served as a great stimulus to the national economy. America truly became the "arsenal of democracy." By 1943, U.S. industrial output exceeded that for all of the Axis powers combined. Massive government spending produced a steady stream of guns, planes, tanks, and ships; stimulated the private sector; and laid the basis for postwar prosperity. So large were wartime expenditures that they twice exceeded all federal appropriations prior to 1941. Indeed, historians would later conclude that World War II rather than the New Deal pulled the United States out of the Great Depression. During the New Deal, the administration of Franklin D. Roosevelt experimented with Keynesian economics (government spending to stimulate the private sector), but the president's innate fiscal conservatism had kept government expenditures to a minimum. As a result, unemployment persisted. In forcing billions in federal expenditures, World War II had the effect of converting Roosevelt into a Keynesian. The war, moreover, contributed to consolidation in industry and labor: fewer corporations produced more goods more efficiently and employed more people. One hundred companies received $160 billion of the $240 billion spent on war contracts, and 10 companies received 30% of the total. New industries, such as those manufacturing synthetic rubber and, later in the war, jet aircraft engines, sprang up, and American chemical and electronics enterprises led the world in productivity and technological innovation.

Although the rich grew richer during World War II, working-class Americans prospered as well. In 1941, 53% of all families lived on less than $2,000 per year, while 24% lived on less than $1,000. During the war, average weekly incomes increased by 70%, more than enough to offset a 47% inflation rate. For the first and only time in the twentieth century, the United States experienced a downward redistribution of income. The share of the nation's wealth taken by the top 5% of the population declined from 22% to 17%, with most of the difference going to the bottom 40% of the population. Not coincidentally, trade unions flourished during the war. Encouraged by the prolabor stance of the Roosevelt administration and led by the Congress of Industrial Organizations (CIO), American workers in the 1930s had staged sit-down strikes and successfully organized the automobile, steel, and textile industries. Ordinary citizens appreciated the benevolent neutrality of the White House. One blue-collar citizen put it simply: "Mr. Roosevelt is the only man we ever had in the White House who is not a son of a bitch." During the war, the War Labor Board, committed to maintaining industrial peace, encouraged new workers to join unions where they immediately were eligible for benefits, including higher wages, better fringe benefits, and increased job security. From 1941 to 1945, union membership increased from 10.5 to 14.8 million.

Another enduring legacy of World War II was the growth of the federal government. Although free enterprise and civil liberties survived during the war, the government intervened into every walk of life, setting prices, allocating manpower, rationing tires and gasoline, and taxing on a massive scale. Franklin D. Roosevelt, who was elected to an unprecedented fourth term in 1944, symbolized the presence and grudging acceptance of this leviathan. Federal bureaucracies, already swollen by the New Deal, expanded still further under the impact of war. The War Production Board told industries what to manufacture and set quotas for them to meet. The Office of Price Administration set prices for virtually every commodity produced in America. The federal government determined the distribution of strategic raw materials – aluminum, rubber, and food – and classified jobs according to their contribution to the national defense.

The "Conservative Coalition"

Not surprisingly, the growth of the federal government during the New Deal and World War II, Roosevelt's election to four terms as president, and the return of prosperity produced a conservative reaction during and after the war. Indeed, sensing this trend, Roosevelt had rejected the notion of countercyclical deficit spending and promised to balance the budget before the war ended. Rationing and wartime controls generated resentment against big government, while a widespread desire to get back to "normal" life militated against social reform. Wartime prosperity had elevated millions of working-class Americans to the middle class, and in the process, dissipated much of the energy that had been responsible for the New Deal. President of the National Association of Manufacturers, anti–New Dealer, and anti-unionist Frederick Crawford argued for "jobs, freedom and opportunity" and "enterprise [that] must be free of restraint and government regulation." Congress fell under the sway of a "conservative coalition," consisting of Republicans and southern Democrats who championed the causes of states' rights and free enterprise and believed the federal government had no business interfering with the relationship between races and sexes, no matter how exploitive or oppressive. The midterm congressional elections in 1942 had produced marked Republican gains, and the conservative coalition had attacked hallowed New Deal programs such as the Works Progress Administration, the National Youth Administration, and the Farm Security Administration. The latter agency was virtually the only arm of government committed to defending the interests of poor farmers and sharecroppers.

The Melding of Isolationism and Internationalism

World War II had converted many former isolationists into aggressive nationalists. The Japanese attack on Pearl Harbor had destroyed the myth of impregnability that the America First movement had worked so assiduously to disseminate. The Atlantic and Pacific were not great barriers protecting "Fortress America" from attack as the isolationists had argued, but rather were highways across which hostile ships and airplanes could rain down destruction on the Western Hemisphere. Led by *Time-Life* publisher Henry Luce, old America Firsters decided that if America could not hide from the rest of the world, it must control it. The United States emerged from World War II as the most powerful nation in the world, both economically and militarily. It controlled most of the former Japanese islands in the Pacific, took an active role in the occupation of Germany and Japan, and by virtue of its massive gold reserves and industrial plants was in a position to act both as the world's banker and its chief supplier of manufactured goods.

Joining the neo-imperialists in pushing for an activist American role in world affairs were Wilsonian internationalists who believed that, if only the United States had joined the League of Nations and acted in concert with the western democracies, fascist aggression could have been nipped in the bud. In the spring of 1945, the United States led the way in establishing a new collective security organization, the United Nations, whose stated goals were the prevention of armed aggression and the promotion of prosperity and democracy throughout the world. Most Americans believed that the lessons of the past had been learned and that the world would never again have to confront a Hitler, Mussolini, or Tojo.

The Changing American Woman

The war changed the face of American society in numerous ways. Perhaps women were the group most affected by the global conflict. The Great Depression had erased many of the gains made by American women in the 1920s. Federal agencies, the popular print media, religious organizations, and even women's groups urged females to return to the home to make room in the workforce for men, still perceived to be the traditional heads of household. Federal legislation prohibited more than one member of the same family from working in the civil service.

All that changed with the coming of the war. The outbreak of hostilities created a huge labor shortage. In response, 6 million women entered the workforce, dramatically increasing the number of females employed outside the home. In 1940, 14.2 million women made up 25.2% of the workforce. Five years later, the 19.3 million employed females constituted 29.2% of employed Americans. Shortly after Pearl Harbor, the federal government and the mass media launched a campaign to convince women that their place was in the factory as well as in the kitchen. Women maintained roadbeds, operated giant cranes, and replaced lumberjacks in the forests of the great Northwest. But the most conspicuous workplace for the new woman was the defense industry. The head of the War Manpower Commission acknowledged that "getting women into industry is a tremendous sales proposition" and encouraged the defense industries to hire women workers. In 1941, a total of 36 women were employed in the ship construction business. By 1942, more than 160,000 were at work laying keels, welding hatches, and installing conning towers. Rosie the Riveter, the fictional defense plant worker created by government public relations experts, became a national heroine. However, the most important change wrought by the war on the working woman was demographic. From the beginning of the industrial era in America, the typical working female was single, young, and poor. But during World War II, almost 75% of those who took jobs for the first time were married, and 60% were older than 35. Two thirds of the women who joined the labor force during the war listed their previous occupation as housewife, and many had preschool-age children. Margaret Hickey, head of the Women's Advisory Committee to the War Manpower Commission, declared that "employers, like other individuals, are finding it necessary to weigh old values, old institutions, in terms of a world at war."

Prior to World War II, women had served in the Army and Navy Nurse Corps, but they had received neither military rank nor pay in return for their services. In the aftermath of Pearl Harbor, however, the War Department, at the prodding of Congresswoman Edith Nourse Rogers, backed legislation creating the Women's Army Auxiliary Corps, later changed to Women's Auxiliary Corps (WACS). Subsequent measures in 1942 and 1943 created a women's naval corps (WAVES), the Marine Corps Women's Reserve, and expanded versions of the nurses corps. The 350,000 women who served in the armed services during World War II were barred from combat but not immune to danger. The vast majority of those in uniform remained in the United States working primarily as communications, clerical, or health care experts. In France, Italy, and North Africa, however, Army and Navy nurses performed their duties close to the front lines, and more than 1,000 women flew planes in a noncombat capacity.

Ironically but not surprisingly, the new woman continued to encounter stereotyping and discriminatory treatment even in service to their country. Virtually without exception, females were excluded from top policy-making bodies charged with running the wartime economy. Although the National War Labor Board endorsed the principle of equal work for equal pay in 1942, it was never enforced. In 1945 as in 1940, women workers in the manufacturing sector made only 65% of what men earned. Although an estimated 2 million children were in need of child care services, federal and state governments proved extremely reluctant to provide them. The private sector was equally recalcitrant. The notion that "a mother's primary duty is to her home and children" and fears over the breakup of the nuclear family proved to be powerful inhibiting factors. Overall, the American woman's mass participation in the workforce did not significantly affect popular attitudes toward sexual equality. "Legal equality ... between the sexes is not possible," declared Secretary of Labor Francis Perkins, "because men and women are not identical in physical structure or social function."

African Americans on the Move
The period from 1941 to 1945 produced an acceleration of the great internal migration of African Americans that had begun during World War I. Conditions in the South made life well-nigh unbearable for the descendents

of slaves. One black man recalled being "born in poverty" in Georgia where "white people virtually owned black people." White farmers would not allow black farmers to raise tobacco, he said, "cause there's a lot of money in it." Two million blacks moved out of the former Confederacy, mostly to urban areas in the Midwest and Northeast. They were prodded by the persistence of lynching, disfranchisement, and discrimination in their native region and lured by the prospect of government and defense industry jobs. Overall, the number of African Americans employed in industry grew from 500,000 to 1.2 million.

In 1941, black activist and labor leader A. Philip Randolph called for "ten thousand Negroes [to] march on Washington" and "demand the right to work and fight for our country." He then founded the March on Washington Movement (MOWM). Prompted by the MOWM, his wife Eleanor, and other liberals, President Roosevelt at least paid lip service to equal rights. In 1941, he established the Fair Employment Practices Committee (FEPC) and encouraged African Americans to seek redress of their grievances in court. But as was true of women and other groups, the black experience was a case of small progress in the midst of mass discrimination. Most national trade unions excluded blacks from membership. The FEPC had only "persuasive" powers, and these were generally ignored. Despite some improvement in job opportunities, most openings were at low levels, with blacks hired primarily as laborers, janitors, and cleaning women. Although African Americans enlisted at a rate 60% higher than their proportion of the population, they encountered discrimination at every turn in the military. Segregation was still the official policy in the armed forces, and blacks had to struggle to persuade the Army and Air Force to allow them entry into combat units.

Yet, the war unquestionably brought about new opportunities and new freedoms for African Americans. The Army agreed to train black pilots, and some integration took place on an experimental basis. Thousands of African American servicemen experienced life without prejudice during their overseas tours of duty. Despite the fact that the multitudes of southern blacks who moved north to find positions in munitions industries found themselves living in squalid ghettos, they also enjoyed greater psychological and political freedom than they had in the South. Northern political machines sought their votes and granted favors in return. The very acts of physical mobility and enlistment contributed to a sense of control and generated a rising level of expectation. In the face of continuing oppression and even violence – the worst example of which was the Detroit race riot of 1943 – black protest mounted. During the war, membership in the National Association for the Advancement of Colored People (NAACP) increased nine-fold to more than 450,000 individuals. Black newspapers took up the cry for a "Double V" campaign – victory at home as well as victory abroad. But the growing activism among African Americans, coupled with

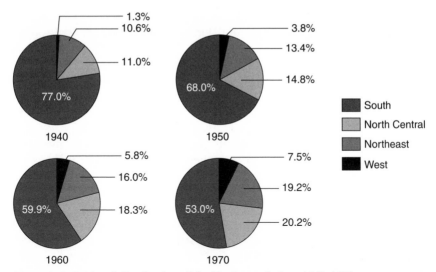

Figure 1–1. Regional distribution of the black population, 1940–1970.

the resurgence of conservatism among the white majority, foreshadowed an era of racial progress amid great conflict.

Truman, Demobilization, and Reconversion

It was one of history's great ironies that Franklin D. Roosevelt did not live to see the end of World War II. Ravaged by the effects of polio, which had left him partially paralyzed since 1921, and by 13 years in the most stressful job in America, he died suddenly at his retreat at Warm Springs, Georgia, on April 12, 1945. "Who the hell is Harry Truman?" Admiral William D. Leahy asked upon hearing that Roosevelt's moderately obscure vice president had taken over. It was an important question, one asked frequently, if less profanely, by many other Americans.

Harry S. Truman was born in Lamar, Missouri, in 1884, the child of a family of farmers that had migrated from Kentucky. A typical son of the middle border, Truman grew up in and around Kansas City. Following his graduation from high school, Truman worked alternately on the family farm and as a bank clerk in town. Upon the outbreak of the Great War, his National Guard unit elected him an officer. The artillery unit in which Truman served saw a good deal of action in France, and through courage and perseverance, Truman worked his way up to the rank of captain. He returned to Kansas City in 1919, and opened a haberdashery with one of his Army friends. Caught up in a postwar depression that crippled the economy, Truman was bankrupt within one year. One business failure followed another, and in desperation he turned to politics in 1922. With the help of the Pendergast political machine, which dominated Kansas City and its environs, Truman was elected a county judge, rising to the post of presiding judge in 1926.

Again with machine support, Truman captured the Democratic nomination for the U.S. Senate in 1934 and won easily in the Democratic landslide of that year. He was, however, received coldly by the nation's political elite. The Washington, D.C., press referred to Harry Truman derisively as "the gentleman from Pendergast." He was, according to one Roosevelt aide, a "small-bore politician of county courthouse caliber." It seemed that Truman's career had come to an end when, in 1939, Big Tom Pendergast was sentenced to federal prison for income tax evasion. Valuing personal loyalty above all else, Truman refused to distance himself from his discredited benefactor. In 1940, the Roosevelt administration threw its support behind one of Truman's rivals in the senatorial primary. Incredibly, without either White House or machine support, Truman won reelection in 1940. Stumping in every city and village in Missouri, he put together a coalition of farmers, blue-collar workers, and ethnic voters, including African Americans. Because of Truman's toughness, his unwavering support for the New Deal, and his work during World War II as chair of a Senate Committee supervising the awarding of government contracts, President Roosevelt selected the Missourian to be his running mate in 1944.

As he readily admitted, Harry Truman came to the highest office in the land ill equipped for his new job. The vice presidency, he declared, had turned him into a "political eunuch." He was somewhat undereducated and had no experience in foreign affairs. Roosevelt had compounded the problem by shutting his vice president out of crucial policy deliberations during the first months of 1945. Uninitiated at the outset, Truman tended toward the view that great power relationships were analogous to Kansas City politics. Dean Acheson complained that the new president favored action over contemplation and wanted to simplify the complex. He sometimes seemed "to think only in primary colors," as Fred Siegel has written. In fact, Truman deliberately cultivated the image of a no-nonsense, toughminded man of action. Aphorisms such as "The Buck Stops Here" and "If You Can't Stand the Heat, Get Out of the Kitchen" adorned his office. That aura of decisiveness masked a deep-seated insecurity. One part of Harry Truman was convinced that in education, experience, and intelligence he was unprepared to be president. Another part believed that if a man of the people could not do the job there was something fundamentally wrong with the system. Unfortunately, the new president's overvaluation of personal loyalty made him prone to cronyism. Indeed, Truman replaced much of Roosevelt's cabinet with personal friends, a practice that infuriated many members of the old administration. After his resignation as secretary of the interior, Harold Ickes retorted, "I am against government by crony."

Finally, he was given to intemperance in public statement. When columnist Drew Pearson dared denigrate his daughter Margaret's singing, he publicly threatened to punch "the son of a bitch" in the nose.

However, Harry Truman did have positive aspects. For example, he was a man of immense personal integrity. He readily accepted responsibility for all aspects of his administration and was absolutely committed to the interests of the United States as he perceived them. He had not sought the presidency, but events having thrust the office upon him, he would not shirk his duty. Truman was a man of great compassion who believed that the government had a responsibility to care for those who were unable to care for themselves. He was a lifelong crusader against legal and social discrimination based on race and religion. Above all, the diminutive midwesterner was tough. Although he sometimes privately broke down in tears under the weight of the office during the early days of his administration, he had no intention of quitting or knuckling under to antireformists at home or would-be aggressors abroad.

The Baby Boomers

The American people wanted to return to normality, variously defined, as quickly as possible following V-J (Victory over Japan) Day. Above all, they wanted to forget about war and things military and return to making love and money. The president and Congress were besieged by demands that they "bring the boys home." In one of the most rapid demobilizations in history, America's military force shrank from 12 million in 1945 to 1.6 million in 1947. Rapid demobilization brought dislocations but not the return of the Great Depression that many feared. The economic impact of the reflux of so many workers on the economy was cushioned by unemployment pay and other Social Security benefits, but particularly by the Servicemen's Readjustment Act of 1944, known as the "GI Bill of Rights." Under its provisions, the federal government spent $13 billion for various veterans' benefits, including unemployment payments, housing subsidies, education both formal and vocational, and small business loans. By 1947, more than 1 million former servicemen were among some 2.5 million Americans attending college. Most importantly, the pent-up demand created by wartime rationing and billions of dollars of forced savings were unleashed on the economy, stimulating the private sector and creating thousands of jobs.

Thus did veterans return to schools, new jobs, wives, and babies. During the postwar years, Americans experienced a population explosion. The birth rate grew from 19.4 per 1,000 in 1940 to 24 in 1946, and did not decline again until the 1960s. The affluence of the postwar period coupled with the cult of the family, which was such a prominent feature of the 1950s, served to make the four-child family rather than the two-child family the norm.

Future social analysts would give the name "baby-boom generation" to this bubble in the demographic curve.

Matured by the war, young Americans in the latter part of the 1940s were serious and focused beyond their years. Veterans returning to college under the GI Bill of Rights were in a hurry; they rushed through the curriculum to begin raising families and making livings. They were more security conscious than the previous generation, a tendency that had as much to do with the Great Depression as World War II. These young men and women shunned risk and preferred to work for large corporations rather than opening their own businesses. "Security had become the big goal," declared *Fortune* magazine. "[They] want to work for somebody else . . . preferably somebody big." The pessimism and quest for security bred by depression and war were partially counterbalanced by optimism spawned by technology. In a brief five-year span from 1945 to 1950, American engineers and scientists gave consumers the automatic car transmission, the long-playing record, the electric clothes dryer, and the automatic garbage-disposal unit. With the lifting of controls, families were able to buy refrigerators, vacuum cleaners, electric ranges, and freezers stocked with frozen foods at unprecedented rates. One of the most important, but least noticed, breakthroughs came in 1945 when the American Gas Association persuaded manufacturers to standardize the size of kitchen cabinets and appliances. The counter workspace would extend 36 inches from the floor and 25 1/4 inches from the wall with a "toe cove" to prevent stubbing. No longer would housewives have to cope with unsightly gaps and bumps, and they could buy new items without having to remodel their entire kitchens.

Crisis in Housing
The preoccupation of returning veterans and the Truman administration was the massive housing shortage. The crisis began in December of 1945, when the first of thousands of returning veterans reached the United States. Because of the depression and the war, there had not been a good year for new housing starts since 1929. Pollster Elmo Roper estimated that almost 19% of all American families were doubled up and 19% were looking for housing. Another 13% would have been in the hunt, he estimated, if prospects had not been so dim. Over the next decade, Americans would require 16 million new homes, *Life* magazine estimated. To deal with the problem, Truman named former Louisville mayor Wilson Wyatt to be federal housing expediter. Wyatt set a production target of 1.2 million units for 1947, but starts fell well below that number. Building materials continued to be in short supply, and the housing industry, burdened by outdated building codes, archaic technology, and lack of capital, could not keep up with demand. For a time, industry leaders even opposed federal subsidies on the grounds that they would lead to "socialized housing." Those units

that were built, even the ghastly prefabricated variety, were too expensive. *Fortune* magazine estimated that veterans would have to earn $58 per week to afford the average new house, but the average weekly wage was only $46 per week.

The problem was eventually solved by a private–public sector partnership. Traditionally, banks and other lenders had followed a very tight mortgage policy, demanding as much as 50% of the total cost of a dwelling as a down payment and allowing no more than 10 years for the note to be paid off. Following the war, however, the Federal Housing Administration (FHA) began insuring housing loans for up to 30 years and requiring only 5% to 10% as a down payment. Reassured by government guarantees of repayment, private lenders eased mortgage terms, bringing them in line with the guidelines set by the FHA. As a result, by 1950, the housing industry had not only revived but had also become one of the primary engines of the flourishing national economy. New home construction jumped from 117,000 in 1944 to 1.7 million in 1950. The keys to recovery were the healthy avarice of the American entrepreneur and 30-year mortgages at 4.5% interest made available through the FHA and the Veterans Administration (VA).

The needs of returning veterans meshed with a consolidation movement among construction firms to produce not only a boom in the housing industry but also a new phenomenon in American residential life – suburbia. In 1946, construction tycoon William Levitt began work on a revolutionary project that would change the way Americans lived. Building on his experience as a maker of prefabricated housing for the Navy during World War II, Levitt purchased a 1,200-acre tract of flat, open land on Long Island, New York. Within just a few months, his workers had built 10,000 inexpensive, separate standing, individual family homes. Levitt transferred the assembly-line techniques pioneered by Henry Ford in the auto industry to the housing business. Teams of semiskilled workers went up one street and down the other laying concrete foundations. They were followed by carpenters, spray painters, and roofers. Levitt purchased appliances en masse and cut costs by using linoleum instead of hardwood floors. To the astonishment of the construction industry, nearly all of the homes in Levittown, as the project came to be known, sold within days. Total cost ranged from $7,000 to $10,000; veterans could get into one of Levitt's inventions and pay as little as $56 per month. The developer moved on to establish even larger communities in New Jersey and Pennsylvania.

Suburbia was based on an irony. Although developments required the felling of trees and pouring of concrete, those who moved out of the city were self-consciously moving to "the country" to enjoy the pleasures of an idyllic pastoral existence. Hence, the names of eastern developments: Stonybrook, Crystal Stream, and Robin Meadows. In fact, suburban housing was dreadfully uniform and monotonous. Floor plans varied little, the lots were small and either square or rectangular, and the neighborhoods generally treeless and flat. One popular song described suburban dwellings as "little boxes made of ticky-tacky." Lewis Mumford, author of *The City in History*, declared the move to suburbia was doing more to destroy the western city than all the strategic bombing of World War II. Instead of the rich, varied culture of ethnic neighborhoods, Americans were opting for a lifestyle in which everybody barbecued, played bridge, mowed their lawns, watched television, and wore the same clothes.

There is no doubt, however, that suburban developments filled a need. the *New York Times* architecture critic Paul Goldberger chided the whole concept as an "urban planning disaster," but admitted that "Levittown houses turned the detached, single-family house from a distant dream to a real possibility for thousands of middle-class American families."

Undoubtedly, suburbia contributed to racial polarization in America and the impoverishment of its inner cities. Major population centers lost inhabitants after the war. As white upwardly mobile families moved to the suburbs, they were replaced by African Americans, Puerto Ricans in the East and Midwest, and immigrants from Mexico and Central America in the West. The outflow of well-to-do whites and businesses that catered to them cut the tax base of the inner city, leading to a decline in housing and public services. Racism prevented middle-class blacks and Hispanics from moving into the white doughnuts that surrounded America's urban centers. "We can solve a housing problem, or we can solve a racial problem," declared William Levitt, "but we cannot combine the two." In fact, Levitt's houses came with closed covenants that limited purchasers to members of "the Caucasian race."

Inflation and Labor Unrest

Housing was only one of Harry Truman's many problems. The administration quickly became caught between its justifiable fear of runaway inflation and demands from business and labor that wartime controls on prices and wages be scrapped. Industrialists, businessmen, and representatives of farm interests pressed Congress to abolish all controls. Manufacturing and agriculture were starved for new equipment and machinery. With billions of dollars in savings, consumers were no longer willing to wait for automobiles, tires, radios, and refrigerators. Nonetheless, determined to hold down inflation, the Truman administration decided to continue the Office of Price Administration (OPA) indefinitely into the postwar period. The National Association of Manufacturers and other business groups responded by insisting that the OPA be dismantled, arguing that controls were delaying full production, perpetuating a flourishing black market, and artificially restricting profits. One Republican partisan denounced the OPA administrators as "the single most important collection of American fascists we've got."

Meanwhile, organized labor, which tended to favor price but not wage controls, set out not only to increase their portion of the economic pie, but also to transform the face of American capitalism. Labor leaders were convinced that workers had not shared equitably in wartime prosperity. Concerned about the return of the 40-hour week, with the accompanying loss of overtime, and by the prospect of an end to the OPA and ensuing runaway inflation, union leaders set about getting everything they could for their members. During the winter of 1945/1946, the nation was racked by strikes in the electrical, automobile, steel, and meat-packing industries. Angry and frustrated by these work stoppages, Truman asked Congress for legislation giving him the authority to declare an emergency and assume direct control over any industry he might deem vital to the national interest, to order all workers back on the job, to subject any resisting labor leader to fine and/or imprisonment, to set wages and prices, and to draft anyone refusing to work into the military. "Let's put transportation and production back to work, hang a few traitors and make our country safe for democracy," he wrote in an unused draft of his speech to Congress. United Autoworker head Walter Reuther proclaimed that the proposal "would make slavery legal" and organized labor pressured Congress into rebuffing the White House. Denied a legislative remedy, the Truman administration intervened and mediated a series of settlements in which labor achieved approximately two thirds of its wage demands and made substantial gains in fringe benefits. Management agreed to these concessions with the tacit understanding that they could pass the costs on to consumers.

No sooner had this crisis been averted than the nation faced in the spring of 1946 another series of potentially paralyzing strikes from the railway brotherhoods and the coal miners. John L. Lewis, the burly, beetle-browed leader of the United Mine Workers, led his men out of the pits on April 1. Genuinely popular with the workers, Lewis told them, "I have pleaded your case not in the quavering tones of a mendicant asking alms, but in the thundering voice of the captain of a mighty host, demanding the rights to which free men are entitled." The strike by the 400,000 mine workers threatened to bring every steam-driven apparatus in America from heaters to locomotives to a halt. The walkout seemed to threaten not only the domestic economy but also European recovery. Citizens began hoarding fuel and food, while the Truman administration warned that hundreds of thousands of Europeans would starve if vital grain and meat shipments were delayed. Management refused to negotiate, whereupon Truman seized the mines. After 59 days, the president brokered an agreement in which the miners received a $1.85-per-day raise and owners agreed to finance a retirement and welfare system. Then, in the midst of the coal strike, the railroad brotherhoods called a nationwide walkout. Under the provisions of the Smith–Connally Labor Disputes Act, the president had the power to seize strikebound plants that were crucial to the war effort. Although his move was of dubious legality, the president invoked this measure and took over the roads, whereupon all the brotherhoods except the Locomotive Engineers and Railroad Trainmen agreed to a compromise settlement. When Truman threatened to go before Congress and seek legislation further restricting the right to strike of workers in occupations vital to the national interest, they too gave in. The strikers remembered that the House and Senate had rebuffed the president in late 1945, but opinion polls showed that Truman's disciplining of Lewis was immensely popular with the public and that antiunion sentiment was building across the United States.

The Conservative Coalition

Truman had managed to restrain organized labor and contain inflation, which rose only 7% during the first 10 months following the war, but his unwillingness to scrap controls offset the credit he received from Congress and the public. Opposition to the OPA mounted until it reached a crescendo in 1946. With the agency's mandate scheduled to expire July 1, Truman appealed to Congress to extend its authority. The House and Senate complied but only after stripping the agency of most of its powers. Truman vetoed the watered-down bill, and in the two-week period that followed inflation increased by 25%. The House and Senate passed a second bill on July 15, continuing price and rent controls for another year. Nevertheless, the Republicans managed to blame the president for the runaway inflation that had momentarily terrified the nation.

The immediate postwar years, then, were ones of stress and frustration. Civilians and veterans alike had comforted themselves during the sacrifices of World War II with expectations of a tranquil, stable postwar America, a land of justice, equality, and expanding opportunity. Instead, they encountered housing shortages, continued rationing, inflation and price controls, crowded classrooms, and an increasingly deadlocked government. The national mood was summed up in the bittersweet 1946 film, *The Best Years of Our Lives*. Naturally, the electorate blamed the party in power. Truman jokes abounded: "He reminds me of an uncle who played the piano in a whorehouse two years before he found out what was goin' on upstairs." As a result, in the 1946 midterm elections, the GOP won control of Congress for the first time since 1928.

During President Truman's first term in office, he and the Republicans in Congress – often joined by southern Democrats – frequently had engaged in bitter battles over aspects of social and economic policy. In September 1945, the president had called on Congress to revive and extend the New Deal. Specifically, he proposed the extension of Social Security benefits to cover millions of new workers, an increase in the minimum wage, the establishment of a national system of health insurance, creation of new regional development projects similar to the Tennessee Valley Authority (TVA), passage of a full employment bill, and reorganization of the executive branch. Congress passed the Employment Act of 1946, but it did not, as its authors orignially intended, commit the federal government to public works projects and control inflation when employment levels fell below a certain level. Rather it provided for the establishment of a three-member Council of Economic Advisers to study economic trends and recommend to the president policies that would prevent or combat recessions and depressions. Congress also approved with some modification the administration's plan for reorganization of the federal government, but the House and Senate would not go beyond these two measures. The Republican victory in the midterm elections of 1946 seemed to guarantee a continuation of congressional recalcitrance.

The leader of the new Republican majority in Congress was Senator Robert A. Taft of Ohio. A states' rights conservative, he was a trenchant foe of the welfare state and preeminent champion of business interests. He spoke for those Republicans who held a pseudoreligious view of America as a largely stateless society of self-regulating individuals. For them, the Great Depression had been a cataclysmic event that had paved the way for the greatest threats to democracy, free enterprise, and individual liberty that the Republic had yet encountered – Franklin D. Roosevelt and the New Deal. Soon after the Eightieth Congress convened in early 1946, Taft and Truman immediately joined battle over the Taft–Hartley bill, the centerpiece of the conservatives' legislative program. According to Republicans, the National Labor Relations, or Wagner Act, which had been passed as part of the New Deal in July 1935, had created an imbalance in the labor–management equation in favor of unions. The American people, angered particularly by the series of wartime strikes staged by John L. Lewis's United Mine Workers, were clearly in an antiunion mood, and the GOP interpreted its victory in the 1946 midterm elections as a mandate to break the back of organized labor.

In June 1947, both houses of Congress passed the Taft–Hartley Act by large margins. Actually, the bill did not go as far as some conservatives wanted. In its final form, the measure outlawed the closed shop (in which union membership was required as a condition of employment) and certain "unfair labor practices" – refusal to bargain in good faith, secondary boycotts (in which members of a nonstriking union boycotted the products of a plant being struck by another union), jurisdictional strikes (in which a union seeking to be recognized by the employer as sole bargaining agent, struck to force that recognition), and exaction of pay for work not performed. It permitted employers to sue unions for breach of contract and to petition the National Labor Relations Board for elections to determine bargaining agents. When the president found that a strike imperiled national health or safety, he was empowered to impose "cooling off" periods and even to seek court injunctions suspending such work stoppages. Finally, the measure required unions to register with and submit annual financial statements to the secretary of labor, forbade union contributions to political parties, and compelled union officials to submit affidavits swearing that they were not members of the communist party. Denouncing Taft–Hartley as nothing less than an act of class warfare that would divide the nation for years to come, President Truman vetoed it in June 1947, only to see his veto promptly overridden by both houses of Congress. With the presidential election looming, he had suddenly become intensely interested in ensuring that organized labor remained within the New Deal coalition. The Taft–Hartley Act stood as the most important achievement of the conservative coalition in the postwar era. Its most severe impact was probably on the CIO's "Operation Dixie," a drive to unionize the traditionally antiunion South. By 1954, 15 states, principally in the South and Southwest, had used the Taft–Hartley Act as authority to pass "right-to-work" laws outlawing the union (or closed) shop. To avoid unions, many labor-intensive industries – textiles, for example – relocated to the right-to-work states. This trend had the effect of ensuring low wages for workers in the states in question and generally retarding the economic development of the South.

In areas free of ideological difference and on subjects not susceptible to political advantage, there was a good deal of bipartisan cooperation during the first Truman administration. An investigation into the circumstances surrounding the surprise Japanese attack on Pearl Harbor and other inquiries had revealed that turf wars and institutional barriers had hampered the war effort, especially during its early stages. In an effort to improve coordination among the armed forces and increase the nation's intelligence capacity, in July 1947, Congress passed the National Security Act. It created a unified military establishment by setting up a cabinet-level Department of Defense, with the Army, Navy, and Air Force becoming subcabinet departments answerable to the secretary of defense. A new body, the National Security Council (NSC), composed of the president; vice president; secretaries of defense, state, and treasury; and the chief of intelligence, met regularly to plan for the nation's strategic well-being. The act made permanent the Joint Chiefs of Staff, which was a creation of World War II, and brought into being a Central Intelligence Agency (CIA) to coordinate intelligence gathering abroad. At the time of its creation, there was no intention to have the CIA engage in covert operations; its mission was simply to gather information. But in future years, the CIA would interpret the provisions in its original charter to authorize it to perform "such other functions and duties related to intelligence" as the NSC might direct, and give it responsibility for "protecting intelligence sources and methods" to allow it to overthrow unfriendly governments, meddle in foreign elections, and even raise secret foreign armies.

At the behest of the Truman administration, Congress also enacted the Presidential Succession Act of 1947, which inserted the speaker of the House and the president pro tempore of the Senate ahead of the secretary of state in the order of succession. This was based on the grounds that elected rather than appointed officials should hold the highest office in the land. In the end, however, the reorganization movement could not escape the blight of partisanship. The Republican Eightieth Congress took it on itself to pass and submit to the states the Twenty-Second Amendment to the Constitution, which limits the president to two terms. It was, as everyone recognized, a belated slap at Franklin D. Roosevelt, although in the future Democrats would have more cause to rejoice at the amendment's existence than Republicans. After three years in office, President Truman was still plagued by lingering doubts concerning his ability to do the job. His approval rating had risen only slightly from the low of 32% he had recorded in 1946. One wag, when asked what Roosevelt would do about the Soviet menace abroad and the deadlock of democracy at home if he were alive, remarked, "I wonder what Truman would do if he were alive." His lack of educational credentials and his sometimes embarrassing deference to successful businessmen alienated liberals within the Democratic Party while his determination to extend the New Deal and his veto of Taft–Hartley aggrieved conservatives. "To err is Truman," was one of America's most popular aphorisms in 1948. The president was not about to back down in the face of his critics, however. Following the example of his predecessors, Truman used the State of the Union address in 1948 to outline the program on which he would run for reelection to office. The theme, he declared, would be social and economic justice for all. He repeated his call for a national health insurance program, extension of Social Security, and an increase in the minimum wage. He also urged Congress to reintroduce rent controls and embrace the notion of federal aid to education.

To Secure These Rights

World War II had created a rising level of expectations among African Americans. During the war, labor shortages coupled with pressure from civil rights activists and certain unions had increased blacks' share of defense jobs from 3% to 8%. A million African American soldiers had fought to preserve democracy in Europe and the Pacific, and in the aftermath of Hiroshima and Nagasaki, they were determined to fight for full citizenship under the law and equality of opportunity at home. "I spent four years in the Army to free a bunch of Frenchmen and Dutchmen, and I'm hanged if I'm going to let the Alabama version of the Germans kick me around when I'm back home," declared one black veteran. Civil rights organizations, such as the NAACP and the Committee on Racial Equality (CORE), the latter formed in 1942 (changed to Congress on Racial Equality in 1944), targeted discrimination in employment; disfranchisement through the poll tax, white primary, and other devices; and terrorism through beatings, burnings, and lynchings. There were some successes.

Employing the nonviolent civil resistance techniques of Indian independence leader Mahatma Ghandi, black activists attacked racial barriers both north and south. In Washington, D.C., Patricia Harris led the first sit-in to protest segregation and exclusion in public facilities. CORE staged a "freedom ride" to contest discrimination in interstate transport. Members traveled by bus south from the nation's capital but were arrested in Durham, North Carolina. CORE members also staged lunch-counter sit-ins in New York, New Jersey, and other northern states. The demonstrators were frequently beaten and arrested, but a growing number of public restaurants stopped segregating blacks and whites. In the South, African American veterans headed straight for their local voter registration offices. Most were threatened, many were beaten, and some were murdered. But there was progress. In Atlanta, 18,000 blacks registered to vote and in Winston-Salem, North Carolina, 3,000. In these two cities and in Greensboro, embryonic black political machines began to emerge. Altogether the number of blacks registered to vote in the South increased from 2% in 1940 to 12% in 1947.

Nonetheless, whites, particularly large land owners in the South and businessmen in northern and midwestern urban areas, were determined that blacks accept their old low-paying, menial jobs and acquiesce in their continued exclusion from the power structure. The Raleigh *News and Observer* was so angered by black veterans collecting government benefits rather than returning to low-wage work that it suggested that the unemployed "ought to be forced to watch themselves starve." In Mississippi, future civil rights leader Medgar Evers and four other African Americans were barred from voting by armed whites. Men in uniform were assaulted just for wearing those uniforms in public. In Georgia, Eugene Talmadge was elected governor by promising to keep blacks away from the polls. For white supremacists that abhorred violence, there were other techniques. The vast majority of blacks in the South worked for whites. Activists, that is, people who sought to exercise their constitutional rights, could simply be fired or thrown off the land they were renting. When veterans rebelled, ugly race riots broke out in cities across the United States, and in the end, African Americans were forced once again to accept discrimination, disfranchisement, and impoverishment.

In 1946, President Truman had appointed the President's Committee on Civil Rights, composed of distinguished Americans of every color and region to look into the state of race relations and make recommendations. Their report, *To Secure These Rights*, published in 1947, described a pervasive pattern of segregation and discrimination, both institutional and informal, that reduced African Americans to second-class citizenship. It called for the "elimination of segregation based on race, color, creed, or national origin, from American life." The president's February 1948 message urged Congress to convert the committee's recommendations into law. In the first special civil rights message by a president, Truman depicted an America where "not all groups are free to live and work where they please or to improve their conditions of life by their own efforts." The president called specifically for a federal law to combat "the crime of lynching, against which I cannot speak too strongly." As he anticipated, it failed to respond. On July 26,1948, through executive order, the president banned racial discrimination in federal hiring and four days later ordered an end to segregation in the armed forces.

Perhaps the most significant development in race relations in the United States during the immediate postwar period was the integration of major league baseball. The wave of racism that swept the United States in the 1890s and that led to the disfranchisement and segregation of African Americans affected the national pastime. Blacks were barred from established professional organizations and relegated to teams in the Negro League, some of which were owned by the proprietors of major league clubs. In spite of the fact that black athletes such as Satchel Paige possessed talents equal or superior to their white counterparts, they were forced to labor in relative obscurity.

During World War II, black activists pushed for the integration of baseball. One who responded was Branch Rickey, owner of the Brooklyn Dodgers. In 1945, he decided that the time had come to break the racial barrier in the nation's national pastime. The man he handpicked to do the job was a remarkable person named Jack Roosevelt Robinson. The child of southern sharecroppers who emigrated to California, Jackie Robinson attended UCLA where he starred in a number of sports. His college credentials helped him land a commission in the military during the war. To break the color barrier in baseball, Rickey wanted a person with the courage to challenge segregation and with the poise to withstand the abuse that would surely accompany that challenge. He was impressed by the fact that Robinson had confronted and overcome efforts to segregate him while he was in the military.

In 1946, Robinson was assigned to the Dodgers' top farm team in Montreal where he proceeded to lead the league in hitting. In April 1947, he made his debut in Brooklyn. He was generally well received in New York, particularly after hometown fans saw what he could do with the bat and glove. On the road, however, he was subjected to verbal and even physical abuse from racist fans. The Saint Louis Cardinals, the major league's southernmost team at that time, even threatened to forfeit rather that take the field with a "Negro." However, the black star persevered. Just after he was picked up by the Dodgers, the press had questioned Robinson on what his future career might prove. He responded, "It proves, or at least it indicates to me, that once the ice is broken and the idea accepted, the thing is entirely possible." Before Robinson's retirement in 1956, several other black athletes had signed major league contracts.

Civil Liberties under Siege

The racism that characterized American life in the years immediately following World War II was part of a larger nativist movement that saw traditional American folkways and institutions, including segregation, being threatened by foreign cultures and ideologies. Conflicts from the Revolutionary War to World War I, featuring relentless appeals to patriotism and paeans to Americanism, had bred intolerance for difference and change. World War II was notable for the relative respect for civil liberties, excepting those of Japanese Americans and German aliens, but wartime tensions coupled with the emerging rivalry with the Soviet Union gave rise to a belated second Red Scare. From 1945 to 1950, nativists sought not only to preserve existing patterns of racial subordination, but also to prevent the emergence of political radicalism in the form of communism. Opportunistic political figures exploited nativist fears for their own purposes. In an effort to discredit New Deal programs and liberalism in general, a group of conservatives declared them to be extensions of Marxism-Leninism, manifestations of an invasion of American political culture by an "alien" ideology. Increasingly, GOP leaders found it profitable to label the Democratic Party as soft on communism. Racists denounced integration as a communist plot to "mongrelize" the United States. Conservative union leaders in the AFL–CIO and other national labor organizations resorted to labeling their enemies as either communists or "fellow travelers" – communist sympathizers.

Despite the fact that the United States was born out of revolution, it had throughout its history proven itself to be one of the most politically conservative societies in history. Anarchism, nihilism, communism, even socialism, which became increasingly mainstream in Europe following World War I, never emerged from the political shadows in the United States. The Communist party gained limited popularity during the Depression as some Americans, disenchanted with capitalism, looked to the Soviet experiment as a hopeful example. Rumors concerning Stalin's massive purges of real and suspected political opponents during the 1930s coupled with the Nazi–Soviet Nonaggression Pact of 1939 did much to discredit the Communist Party of the United States (CPUS). Despite the Soviet–American alliance, party membership continued to decline until it stood at a mere 20,000. Although the Soviet Union did manage to place secret agents within the federal government between 1945 and 1950, and these operatives turned over vital, classified information to the Kremlin, the CPUS never posed a threat to the established order either through the legitimate electoral process or through subversion. The Kremlin rarely used members of the CPUS as spies because they were closely scrutinized by the Federal Bureau of Investigation (FBI), which had thoroughly penetrated the organization. Nevertheless, Americans recoiled from Marxism-Leninism, which they equated with Soviet communism. It was godless, authoritarian, repressive, aggressive, and socialistic. This long-standing ideological aversion, coupled with the military might of the Soviet Union and the superpatriotism spawned by the war, made Americans susceptible to anticommunist hysteria.

The principal instrument available to those who wanted to promote and profit from a campaign against communist subversion was the House Un-American Activities Committee (HUAC). Established originally to combat fascism, the committee was given permanent status and broad powers to investigate domestic subversion in 1945. The legislation converting HUAC to a standing committee was the work of Representative John E. Rankin (D-Mississippi), who had denounced the decision by the Red Cross not to label blood according to race as a communist plot and who had accused "enemies of Christianity" – in particular, Jews – of attempting to take over the national media. Liberals protested. The *Nation* denounced HUAC and pleaded that "the only way to save the country from the indignity of these repeated witch-hunts is to abolish the committee." But nativism, nourished by the burgeoning East–West confrontation, proved too strong.

In 1947, following the Republican victory in the midterm congressional elections, Representative J. Parnell Thomas (R-New Jersey) became chair of HUAC. No sooner had he taken up the gavel than he announced the existence of a conspiracy to overthrow the government, a conspiracy centered in Hollywood. As historian Walter Goodman put it: "[T]o Rankin, Hollywood was Semitic territory. To Thomas it was New Deal Territory. To the entire Committee it was a veritable sun around which the press worshipfully rotated. And it was also a place where real live Communists could readily be found."

Judging from the products that the motion picture industry turned out, it was a hotbed of red-blooded Americanism. It had enthusiastically cooperated with the government in producing wartime propaganda films such as *Thirty Seconds Over Tokyo*. Only three releases, including the absurdly flawed *Mission To Moscow*, could have been interpreted as pro-Soviet. But, as Goodman pointed out, there were communists in Hollywood, principally among members of the Screen Actors Guild. Scriptwriters were mercilessly exploited by ruthless studio heads such as Sam Goldwyn and Jack Warner. They had no control over their scripts, which producers cut and spliced to suit their whim, and they were paid a pittance.

On October 20, 1947, HUAC began hearing testimony from "friendly witnesses" encouraged by Goldwyn and Warner to cooperate with the committee. Actor Gary Cooper denounced communism for "not being on the level." Others, including Adolph Menjou, declared that Hollywood was riddled with reds and fellow travelers. These anticommunists were followed by 10 writers and directors, including Ring Lardner, Jr., and John Howard Lawson, who were or had been members of the CPUS. Upon the advice of their lawyers, they decided to seek refuge in the First Amendment, which guaranteed freedom of speech and political association rather than the Fifth Amendment, which protected citizens from giving self-incriminating evidence. Several were defiant, unrepentant, and abusive in their testimony. The Hollywood Ten were convicted of contempt of Congress and, after the Supreme Court upheld their convictions, sentenced to one year in prison.

HUAC's investigation completely intimidated the motion picture industry. Following the hearings, the heads of all major studios pledged not to hire communists or communist sympathizers. The industry created an unofficial blacklist and dozens of writers, directors, and actors were barred forever from practicing their trade in the United States. Refusing to cooperate in Congress's investigation or being mentioned in another's testimony was frequently enough to earn a writer, actor, or director a place on the blacklist. Soon the witch-hunt spread to New York City, where it contaminated the burgeoning television industry. After refusing to cooperate with HUAC, actor Zero Mostel said, "I am a man of a thousand faces, all of them blacklisted."

While red-baiters in Congress were laboring to rid the entertainment industry of subversive influences, the courts were moving against the CPUS itself. In July 1948, a federal grand jury indicted Gus Hall, Eugene Dennis, and 10 other party officials on charges of violating the Smith Act. Passed in 1940 and then directed primarily against fascists, the Smith Act made it a federal crime to conspire to overthrow the government or to belong to a group advocating its overthrow. The trial, which began in January 1949, quickly degenerated into a shouting match between the defendants and the prosecution. Hall, Dennis, and their lawyers argued that the court had no right to try them because the jury excluded racial minorities and poor people. In the fall, Judge Harold Medina sentenced not only the CPUS officials to prison for violating the Smith Act, but also their lawyers for not curbing their courtroom outbursts.

In a landmark civil liberties decision, in 1951, the Supreme Court upheld the conviction of the Communist party officials. Writing for the majority in *Dennis v. United States*, Chief Justice Fred Vinson ruled that citizens of the United States had no right to advocate violent rebellion when avenues for peaceful change were open to them. Justices Hugo Black and William O. Douglas argued in vain that the CPUS did not advocate forceful overthrow of the federal authority. Determined to leave no room for doubt, Congress in 1950 passed the McCarran or Internal Security Act. That measure proclaimed the existence of an international communist conspiracy, which posed an immediate threat to the United States. Members of communist-affiliated organizations were required to register with the federal government or face a fine of up to $10,000 and imprisonment for up to four years. Registrees could be denied passports and were barred from holding jobs with the federal government or in the defense industry. The McCarran Act authorized the government to deport naturalized citizens and alleged subversives during periods of national emergency. President Truman denounced the McCarran Act as a gross violation of civil liberties and vetoed it. "In a free country we punish men for the crimes they commit," Truman charged, "but never for the opinions they have." Congress promptly overrode his veto in 1951.

In an effort to safeguard the "purity" of American culture and society, nativists attempted to maintain and even strengthen the nation's already rigorous immigration statutes. They were only partially successful, however, because the war had caused tens of thousands of American service people to become intertwined with peoples of other cultures. That intermingling, in turn, had created a refugee problem of horrific proportions. In 1946, Congress passed the War Brides Act, which over the next four years opened America's doors to some 100,000 wives and children of U.S. veterans. Congress was more divided about the 1 million displaced people living in squalid refugee camps in Europe.

World War II had ripped the fabric of European society, uprooting millions of French, Dutch, Belgians, Poles, Czechs, Hungarians, Italians, and Russians from their homes. Many died, many others were able to return home, and others simply had no place to go. As of 1946, Allied occupation authorities in Western Europe operated squalid camps that housed Poles, Lithuanians, Latvians, and Estonians who had fled in the wake of Soviet occupation; Russians who did not want to return home to imprisonment or death; Germans expelled from Eastern Europe; and some 200,000 Jews, many of them survivors of Nazi death camps. In an effort to relieve the suffering of these victims of Nazi and Soviet persecution, Congress in 1948 passed the Displaced Persons Act, which increased immigration quotas by 2,000. Anti-Semites in Congress added restrictive language intended to bar Jewish immigration. A defiant President Truman ordered immigration and naturalization agents to bend the rules as far as possible, but the result was negligible. By the time Congress got around to passing a more liberal displaced persons measure in 1950, a majority of the death camp survivors had immigrated to Israel. Relatively few of the 400,000 people who came to America under the displaced persons legislation were Jewish. In 1952, Congress passed the McCarran–Walter Act, which restored the restrictive provisions of the 1920s immigration legislation, including a quota of 100 for each Pacific and Asian nation.

The Election of 1948

With Harry Truman's popularity plummeting and the Democrats divided, Republicans approached the 1948 presidential election with high expectations. If they could avoid stupid mistakes, the White House seemed to be theirs for the taking. Conservatives favored Robert Taft for the nomination, but many of the rank and file feared that his dour, humorless personality would turn off voters. The eastern wing of the party, moderately progressive in domestic affairs and internationalist in foreign policy, struggled to develop an alternative. They approached the immensely popular Dwight D. Eisenhower, the hero of the Normandy invasion then serving as president of Columbia University, but he had not yet decided whether he was a Republican or a Democrat. Although Thomas E. Dewey had lost to Franklin Roosevelt in 1940, anti-Taftites decided that he deserved another chance. His progressive record as governor of New York and his advocacy of military alliances and foreign aid seemed to put him in the political mainstream, while his attractive appearance and sophistication seemed to make him the perfect alternative to Truman. The Republican convention nominated Dewey on the first ballot and chose California governor Earl Warren as his running mate. The platform endorsed most New Deal reforms as well as the bipartisan foreign policy the Truman administration was then implementing. Like Alfred M. Landon, the Republican presidential candidate in 1936, Dewey just promised to run things more efficiently.

Meanwhile, internecine warfare was wrecking the Democratic Party. The chief rebel in the field was former vice president and secretary of commerce, Henry A. Wallace. During World War II, Wallace had become the preeminent champion of social justice within the Democratic Party. He had declared that the era following the end of hostilities would be "the century of the common man." No longer would government be dominated by political and economic elites. Democracy and equality of opportunity would at long last become realities and, as a result, the good life would come within the reach of everyone. Falling out with the Truman administration over its efforts to discipline organized labor and to resist the spread of communism in Europe, Wallace organized the Progressive Citizens of America in 1947 and worked to rally former New Dealers to his banner.

As the date for the Democratic National Convention approached, liberals struggled to choose between Wallace and Truman. In the end, labor leaders and former New Dealers decided they could not embrace the Progressive Party. Many agreed with Wallace's call for nationalization of basic industries and full and immediate civil rights for African Americans, but they could not tolerate his stand on foreign policy. Wallace's 1946 Madison Square Garden speech, in which he had called for free trade with Eastern Europe and accommodation with the Soviet Union, had convinced many hard-line anticommunists within the Democratic Party that he could not be trusted. Indeed, Cold War liberals had formed their own organization, the Americans for Democratic Action (ADA), to fight for social justice at home and freedom and democracy abroad. This organization included social justice advocates such as Eleanor Roosevelt, intellectuals such as Reinhold Niebuhr and Arthur Schlesinger, Jr., and labor leaders like CIO chief Walter Reuther. After briefly casting about for an alternative to the unpopular

Truman, they approached Eisenhower, but he had still not decided on a party affiliation. Reluctantly, the ADA and CIO decided to cast their lot with the man from Missouri.

In 1948, the Democrats somewhat ironically chose to meet in Philadelphia, the city of brotherly love. By the time the delegates assembled in July, the rebellious left wing of the party had already broken away under Wallace. The task at hand was to keep southerners, up in arms over the president's civil rights program, in the fold. In an effort to avoid an open breach with the sons of Dixie, the administration proposed a plank in the platform that opposed discrimination only in general terms. Civil rights activists, however, wanted to call on Congress for specific action to end lynching, eliminate discrimination in the workplace and housing, and ensure the right to vote to all regardless of color. Speaking for this group, Minneapolis Mayor Hubert H. Humphrey electrified the delegates and set off a 10-minute demonstration when he urged the Democratic Party "to get out of the shadow of states' rights and walk forthrightly into the bright sunshine of human rights." Indignant delegates from Alabama and Mississippi got up and walked out of the convention. Exhausted and dispirited, the remainder of the convention renominated Truman and selected Senator Alben W. Barkley of Kentucky as his running mate.

It was two o'clock in the morning before Truman had a chance to address the convention, but his performance proved worth waiting for. In a rousing acceptance speech, he promised an all-out effort and victory in the end. He was glad to see, he said, that the Republican platform had endorsed many of the programs he had been advocating. To the delight of his audience, Truman announced that he was calling the Republican Eightieth Congress into special session on July 26, the day Missourians planted their turnips. The GOP could make good on their promises, and the American people could then compare its record with his. Taft accused Truman of dirty pool, but the president kept to his course. Congress met for two weeks in late July and early August; as Truman anticipated, it accomplished exactly nothing.

Unbeknownst to the Republicans and most Democrats, Truman had developed a sound strategy for winning the 1948 election. Guided by presidential aide Clark Clifford, the president's advisers recognized that for him to win, he had to capture the midwestern and western farm belts. His strong advocacy of agricultural price supports and his Missouri origins stood him in good stead with this constituency. In metropolitan areas, the Democratic candidate would have to carry labor and African Americans. Truman's veto of Taft–Hartley and his February civil rights recommendations to Congress gave him a leg up with those voters. Finally, the president's inner circle counted on the "Solid South" remaining within the Democratic fold. With the South, Midwest, and West, Truman could afford to lose some traditionally New Deal strongholds in the East which might lean toward

Wallace. The principal problem with this strategy, as it turned out, was the fidelity of the South.

Alienated southerners met in Birmingham, Alabama, "the cradle of the Confederacy," on July 17, waved the stars and bars, consumed immense amounts of bourbon and branch water, paid homage to John C. Calhoun, and formed the States' Rights Democratic Party, subsequently labeled "Dixiecrats" by the press. The new party pledged to do whatever was necessary to preserve the South's "unique" social system and nominated Governor J. Strom Thurmond of South Carolina for the presidency and Governor Fielding L. Wright of Mississippi for the vice presidency. The Dixiecrats hoped to capture enough electoral votes to deny either of the major parties an electoral college victory, thus throwing the election into the House of Representatives where, they hoped, they would be the deciding factor.

Republican confidence mounted as the left and right wings of the Democratic Party pummeled the center. Governor Dewey conducted a mild and dignified campaign, avoiding controversy whenever possible. Disgusted with the GOP candidate's blandness, the Louisville *Courier-Journal* observed that Dewey's four major speeches could be condensed into four "historic" sentences: "Agriculture is important. Our rivers are full of fish. You cannot have freedom without liberty. The future lies ahead." As his campaign began, Harry Truman was one of the few people in the United States in 1948 who believed that he could win. He set out on a 31,000-mile whistle stop campaign, during which he discarded his prepared speeches – he tended to deliver set-pieces in a rather wooden fashion – and employed instead short, fiery, off-the-cuff talks in which he invariably castigated the "do-nothing" Eightieth Congress. "Give 'em hell Harry" became the first presidential candidate to campaign in Harlem. Meanwhile, Clifford, Hubert Humphrey, and various ADA members did their best to link Henry Wallace with communism. He obligingly played into their hands by refusing to criticize Stalin and the Soviet Union, attacking Democrats who had supported the Truman Doctrine and Marshall Plan, and refusing to repudiate the Communist Party of the United States (CPUS) when it offered to aid his candidacy. Late in the campaign, conservative journalists, picking up on the alleged mystical strain in Wallace's personality, asked the independent candidate if he were not the author of the so-called "guru letters," correspondence between Wallace and a Russian theosophist that were filled with references to the occult and referred to Franklin D. Roosevelt as "The Flaming One." When Wallace refused to deny authorship, he became something of a laughingstock.

On election eve, all observers picked Dewey to win; the *Chicago Tribune* went so far as to print extras with a banner headline proclaiming "Dewey Defeats Truman." In one of the most stunning political upsets in American history, Truman captured 303 electoral votes to Dewey's 189. He garnered 24 million popular votes to his Republican challenger's 22 million.

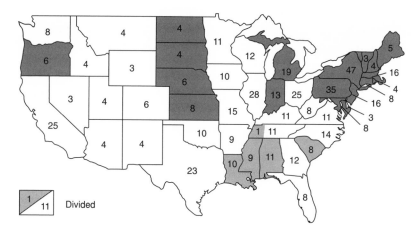

	Electoral Vote	Popular Vote	Percentage of Popular Vote
Democratic Harry S. Truman	303	24,105,812	49.5%
Republican Thomas E. Dewey	189	21,970,065	45.1%
States' Rights Strom Thurmond	39	1,169,063	2.4%
Minor parties –	–	1,442,667	3.0%

Map 1–1. The election of 1948.

Wallace and Thurmond trailed far behind with 1 million each. The Dixiecrats captured the electoral votes of Mississippi, Alabama, South Carolina, and Louisiana, but their total fell far short of the number needed to throw the election into the House. The revolt of right and left had actually worked to Truman's advantage. The Dixiecrat rebellion reassured black voters who had questioned the Democrat's commitment to civil rights, while the existence of the Progressive Party made it difficult to accuse Truman of being "soft on communism." The Republicans were bitter and frustrated; never again, they swore, would they wage a "metoo" campaign.

The Fair Deal

In his annual State of the Union message in 1949, President Truman unveiled the domestic program for his second term. Every American, he told the House and Senate, which had brand-new, although razor-thin, Democratic majorities, was entitled to a "fair deal" from their government.

Truman's Fair Deal included an increase in the minimum wage from $0.40 to $0.75 per hour, an extension of Social Security benefits, repeal of Taft–Hartley, a federal health insurance plan, civil rights legislation, federal funds for the construction of low-cost housing, and a guaranteed income for farmers. Although the president was fresh from a stunning victory and could count on Democratic majorities, a number of factors cast long shadows on the prospects for enactment of his program. Southern Democrats were alienated from the party leadership and were much more likely to cooperate with Taft and the Republicans on domestic legislation than the White House. Harry Truman lacked the political skills of his illustrious predecessor. Perhaps most importantly, despite pockets of poverty, Americans were enjoying an unparalleled period of prosperity. The deprivation and social insecurity that had fueled the New Deal were almost entirely lacking in 1948 and 1949. Finally, Congress and the public were increasingly distracted by Cold War crises abroad and the search for communist subversives at home.

The administration's campaign to repeal Taft–Hartley quickly stalled, primarily because the White House, fearful of losing union support, was unwilling to accept a compromise bill. One of the few areas in which Truman and Taft saw eye to eye was federal aid to education, but even their powerful alliance was not enough to overcome the conflict between Protestants and Catholics over whether aid should be extended to private, parochial schools as well as to public institutions. A $300 million bill that would have made direct grants to the states for the support of public education died in the House. The administration's health insurance plan called for prepaid medical, dental, and hospital care to be funded through payroll deductions, employer contributions, and federal subsidies. As in 1945, the American Medical Association (AMA) chose to view the plan as a conspiracy to limit doctors' incomes and their freedom of action. It denounced Truman's health care scheme as "socialized medicine" and launched a multimillion dollar lobbying campaign. Congress once again succumbed to AMA pressure and, as a result, one of the principal goals of the social justice movement remained unfulfilled.

In April 1949, Secretary of Agriculture Charles F. Brannan presented the administration's farm security plan to Congress. With the goal of maintaining a minimum income for American farm families, the Brannan plan would keep high, fixed subsidies for basic commodities in place. For other perishable products, the Agriculture Department would make up the difference between the market price and what it deemed a fair price. Opponents, including the major farm organizations, criticized the quota provisions of the program, and charged that it would regiment and "socialize" American farming. Even small farmers were concerned because the administration's approach would abandon the concept of "parity," the practice of using the relatively prosperous period from 1909 to 1914 to measure farm supports. Similar to the administration's health care scheme, the Brannan Plan died aborning. The only things that prevented a major farm recession in the late 1940s were huge demands for food and fiber created by the Marshall Plan and the Korean War. The administration's plans for a Fair Employment Practices Committee (FEPC) with the power to penalize job discrimination in both the public and the private sectors foundered on the opposition of former Dixiecrats who referred to the proposed new employment commission as a "Democratic version of Reconstruction." Relying on Senate Rule XXII, which required a two thirds vote to shut off debate, the Upper House filibustered FEPC bills to death in 1949 and 1950.

The second Truman administration achieved some isolated victories. The National Housing Act of 1949, passed in July with the help of Senator Taft, provided funds for slum clearance and for the construction of 810,000 units of low-cost housing. Although it rejected the administration's health care program, Congress approved the Hill–Burton Act, which made federal matching grants available to the states for the construction of nonprofit clinics and hospitals. In August 1950, Congress expanded the Social Security Act, raising benefits and bringing more than 10 million additional people under its umbrella.

Virtually nothing of significance was accomplished on the home front from 1950 to 1952. The conservative coalition continued to hold the balance of power in Congress, and the persistence of prosperity eliminated the economic impetus for social justice. The very poor – blacks, Hispanics, and whites – tended to be disfranchised through law, custom, or apathy. In addition, the outbreak of the Korean War in June 1950 diverted the nation's attention and resources away from domestic reform. Finally, the Truman administration was buffeted by charges of corruption and cronyism throughout the second half of its second term in office. Fueled by Republican partisanship and the disgust of members of Truman's own party, the anticorruption campaign blossomed as congressional committee after congressional committee investigated wrongdoing in high places. Although Truman was never personally implicated in "the mess in Washington," many of his closest associates were. Congressional investigators uncovered a nest of "five percenters" – individuals who sold actual or pretended influence to would-be government contractors. A committee headed by Arkansas Senator J. William Fulbright revealed that officials of the Reconstruction Finance Corporation regularly granted or obtained loans for financially shaky business concerns and then quit and went to work for those same firms at lucrative salaries. Truman, as usual, stuck by his friends. One Gallup poll conducted in the midst of the scandals gave the president a paltry 23% approval rating.

Summary

The years immediately following World War II were ones of recovery, consolidation, prosperity, and limited social progress. Victory over the Axis powers drew the United States together, instilled an unparalleled sense of confidence, and fostered a desire to enjoy the fruits of victory. But a return to normality meant different things to different people. The successful and upwardly mobile wanted to return to the old ways. Because prosperity bred by the war continued throughout the late 1940s and early 1950s, and hundreds of thousands of former working-class Americans were able to move into the middle class, this meant that a majority of Americans were conservative, committed to the status quo. For others – some women, minorities, unorganized industrial workers, and sharecroppers – the good life meant change. African Americans and Hispanics acted individually and collectively to enter the mainstream economically and politically. Although they made some gains, they were largely frustrated by the white power structure. These rising, disappointed expectations created pent-up energy that would burst forth during the 1950s and 1960s. The same was true of those women who sought careers outside the home or for those who simply desired a choice, a choice as to whether to be a mother and housewife, to have a career, or to have both; to have sex on their own terms; or to bear unwanted children.

The GI generation that emerged from World War II was upwardly mobile but generally conservative. Some 2 million Americans were educated under the GI bill, leading to the greater democratization of higher education and of American society in general. Young men and women who entered the professional work force were interested in security, not risk taking – an attitude that dovetailed not coincidentally with unprecedented growth and consolidation in the corporate world. Young people married earlier and at a higher rate. They also had more children. The resulting baby boom laid the basis for the consumerism and youth culture of the 1950s and 1960s. Increasingly affluent, educated whites moved to suburbia leaving much of urban America inhabited by the chronically poor and disadvantaged.

Politically, the post–World War II years were ones of consolidation and modest advance. Republicans and Democrats were committed to the preservation of the basic New Deal structure and, as a result, the federal government continued to play a large role in the economic and social life of the United States. Harry Truman pressed for extension of Social Security and other New Deal programs as well as the establishment of new initiatives in agriculture, housing, education, medical insurance, and civil rights. However, he was generally contained by the conservative coalition, a combination of Republicans and southern Democrats that dominated Congress during these years. Although periodically reviled during his nearly eight years of office, Truman remained president and was able to lead the nation because he represented those qualities most prized by middle Americans: personal integrity, self-reliance, a feeling for the underdog, candor, and courage.

The Truman administration and the nation as a whole were increasingly preoccupied by the search for communist subversives who had allegedly penetrated every nook and cranny of the federal government and who were threatening to take control of the national media. The stresses of World War II, coupled with the anxieties caused by the burgeoning conflict with the Soviet Union, brought America's latent but deep-seated nativism to the fore. Domestic anticommunism became a powerful, even pervasive, force that lay over the land, distorting domestic politics, threatening civil liberties, and severely constraining American foreign policy.

ADDITIONAL READINGS

Berman, William C., *The Politics of Civil Rights in the Truman Administration* (1970).

Bernstein, Barton J., ed., *Politics and Policies of the Truman Administration* (1970).

Blum, John Morton, *V Was for Victory: Politics and American Culture During World War II* (1976).

Donovan, Robert J., *Conflict and Crisis: The Presidency of Harry S. Truman, 1945–1948* (1977).

Donovan, Robert J., *Tumultuous Years: The Presidency of Harry S. Truman, 1949–1953* (1982).

Ferrell, Robert H., *Harry S. Truman and the Modern American Presidency* (1982).

Hamby, Alonzo L., *Beyond the New Deal: Harry S. Truman and American Liberalism* (1973).

Hamby, Alonzo L., *Man of the People: A Life of Harry S. Truman* (1995).

Marcus, Maeva, *Truman and the Steel Seizure* (1977).

Markowitz, Norman D., *The Rise and Fall of the People's Century: Henry A. Wallace and American Liberalism, 1941–1948* (1973).

Olson, Keith W., *The G.I. Bill, the Veterans, and the Colleges* (1974).

2   The Origins of the Cold War

$\mathbf{A}$mericans emerged from the blood, sacrifice, and chaos of World War II hopeful that with the demise of the Axis powers, the world would enjoy a protracted period of peace. In a literal sense it did. John Gaddis and others have referred to the Cold War as the "long peace," emphasizing that during the nearly half century since V-J (Victory over Japan) Day, the great powers have avoided open conflict. Nevertheless, the Grand Alliance that defeated Germany, Italy, and Japan began to disintegrate even before war's end. Furthermore, the Soviet–American confrontation that resulted generated the most horrendous arms race the world has ever seen, created an ever-present threat of nuclear annihilation, and spawned a series of "brush-fire" wars that killed millions.

Roots of Conflict

Ideology

Since 1917, citizens of the Soviet Union and the United States had perceived profound differences between their two societies; after 1945, those differences became magnified and systematized. As a result, the Cold War was profoundly ideological. According to the system of thought that developed in the United States, the Soviet Union – the embodiment of communism and totalitarianism – was the antonym and eternal enemy of the United States, the embodiment of capitalism and democracy. In this mind-set, "Soviet" and "communist" were interchangeable as were "Marxist" and "socialist." Conversely, "free," "democratic," "capitalist," and "American" were synonymous. Cold War ideology ignored the fact that socialism and capitalism were principles for the economic organization of society, whereas democracy and totalitarianism were political precepts.

In the ideology of anticommunism, the United States and its allies boasted political systems characterized by free elections, representative government, and bills of rights guaranteeing fundamental freedoms, especially religion. The Soviet Union and its satellites, which were compelled by force to adopt communism, featured political systems characterized by autocracy, coercion, repression, and the absence of freedom, especially the freedom of worship. In the economic sphere, communist states owned all property and strictly regimented their economies, whereas capitalist states featured free enterprise, a market-oriented system based on competition, opportunity, and human ingenuity. In the geopolitical arena, anticommunist ideology portrayed the Soviet Union as aggressively internationalist, that is, dedicated to unrelenting world revolution until every democratic political system was replaced by Soviet-style communism. Soviet imperialism required the United States to pursue its own internationalist policies – policies essentially defensive in nature designed to protect the free world. Finally, anticommunist ideology reeked of moral superiority: communist totalitarianism was bad, democratic capitalism was good. Proof of this truth can be seen through the atheism of Lenin and his heirs and their outlawing of religion.

An equally rigid ideology pervaded the Soviet approach to the Cold War. Stalin and his associates believed in Karl Marx's materialist interpretation of history. World history had evolved in stages: slavery giving way to feudalism, feudalism to bourgeois capitalism, and capitalism to socialism or communism. In the Soviet mind, capitalism was undemocratic and exploitive. The United States was a plutocracy, that is, a society governed by its economic elite. This avaricious clique – manufacturers, financiers, and property owners – exploited industrial and agricultural laborers in the United States and developing nations abroad. Indeed, the need of capitalist societies for overseas markets and raw materials made them inherently imperialistic. Communism promised to end this exploitation, placing all economic and political power in the hands of the "people" – workers, farmers, soldiers, and bureaucrats. The Soviet leadership tended to view any stable situation as inherently "contradictory," pregnant with the seeds of conflict between communism and capitalism.

In their circularity and tendency to demonize the other, anticommunist and anticapitalist ideology both mirrored and reinforced each other. But ideological conflict was as much a product as a cause of the Cold War. The East–West confrontation grew also out of the conflicting geopolitical goals of the principal members of the Grand Alliance.

The Balance of Power

Throughout the course of wartime diplomacy, one overriding question preoccupied the leaders of the Grand Alliance: what kind of world would emerge from the ruins? Winston Churchill, the British prime minister, was a strong believer in the balance of power. In his opinion, the fate of Europe would continue to determine the fate of the world. Because a basic conflict of interest existed between the Soviet Union and the western democracies, Britain and the United States ought to cooperate in rehabilitating France and Germany as quickly as possible. But because World War II had accelerated Britain's decline into a second-rate power, the United States would have to assume the primary burden for defending Western civilization.

From the outset, Soviet leaders proclaimed that their primary goal for the postwar era was the physical security of the motherland. They were determined to construct a European order in which it would be impossible for another Napoleon or Hitler to ravage the Ukraine and European Russia. Accordingly, in 1942, Soviet Premier Stalin stated his nation's minimum territorial objectives: the full fruits of the Nazi–Soviet Nonaggression Pact – that is, annexation of Latvia, Estonia, and portions of Poland, as well as Lithuania and parts of Rumania and Finland (which the USSR had invaded shortly after the outbreak of war in 1939). The Kremlin further insisted that it would be necessary to establish "friendly" governments along the country's western flank. As it turned out, friendly meant communist. In brief, even as Hitler's soldiers drove relentlessly toward Moscow and Stalingrad, Stalin stood ready to seize any opportunity and use every tactic short of global war to extend Soviet power as far into Europe as possible.

Until 1944, President Roosevelt favored a peace structure built around the concept of the "Four Policemen." Britain, the Soviet Union, the United States, and China would supervise their respective spheres of interest, preventing aggression and fostering democracy and self-determination among the peoples of the region. In 1944, in response to a popular surge of enthusiasm for Wilsonian internationalism, the administration announced with great fanfare that it favored the establishment of a new collective security organization that would keep the peace and promote social justice and economic opportunity around the globe. In reality, Roosevelt never abandoned his affinity for the Four Policemen idea. The United Nations charter, in establishing a Security Council with five permanent members (each of which had veto power) and permitting regional defense arrangements, actually combined the concept of collective security with that of spheres of influence. Above all, Roosevelt was determined to prevent a third world war by holding the Grand Alliance together and promoting the principle of national self-determination.

The postwar objectives of the Big Three were contradictory, if not irreconcilable. The Soviet Union's determination to convert Eastern Europe into a buffer zone and to cripple Germany ran counter to the principle of self-determination so dear to American policymakers and to the balance of power precepts that traditionally guided British diplomats. What Anglo-American diplomats defined as security, the Kremlin viewed as aggression; similarly, the Soviet Union's minimum defense requirements seemed to western officials frankly imperialistic.

The Holocaust

A third factor contributing to the origins of the Cold War, particularly on the American side, was the Holocaust. Since the founding of the republic, the fundamental impulse in American foreign policy had been nonintervention. The United States broke with that tradition infrequently and reluctantly, and then only to protect its perceived strategic and economic interests. For Woodrow Wilson and some progressives, the Great War had been a crusade to make the world safe for democracy. However, for most Americans, it had been a temporary intervention into European affairs to preserve the balance of power and to force the Central Powers to respect American neutrality. Not until the spring of 1945 did most Americans see World War II in Europe as a struggle against genocide. Rather, in the minds of most civilians and soldiers, the United States was fighting to protect its physical and economic security and to maintain its independence. Former isolationists such as Robert Taft and Senate Foreign Relations Committee (SFRC) Chairman Arthur Vandenburg (R-Michigan) supported U.S. participation in World War II following the bombing of Pearl Harbor. But with the defeat of the Axis, they and the conservative majority expected the United States to withdraw its armies from Europe and Asia and let the world go its own way. Revelations concerning the Holocaust, however, converted World War II into a struggle of good against evil in the minds of most Americans, and it subsequently changed the nation's attitude toward the rest of the world.

The invading armies that crossed the Rhine and pushed into Germany discovered to their horror that rumors of a Nazi "final solution" to the "Jewish problem" were true. Anti-Semitism had been a staple of Hitlerian propaganda. As portions of Europe came under German control, SS troops rounded up hundreds of thousands of Jews, Gypsies, and homosexuals and shipped them to concentration camps where they were systematically tortured, starved, shot, and gassed. In total, the Nazis slaughtered some 6 million Jews and 3 million Russians, Poles, and Gypsies at extermination camps at Auschwitz, Treblinka, and other locations. In the wake of the Allied liberation of these camps, U.S. newspapers were filled with pictures of mass graves containing thousands of skeletons and of survivors so emaciated that they were difficult to distinguish from the dead. Reinforcing the wave of revulsion that swept America in the wake of the Holocaust revelations was the growing awareness that during the period when the Nazis had permitted Jews to leave Europe, from 1933 through 1941, the United States had tightened immigration restrictions making it virtually impossible for the millions of future victims of Nazi brutality to find refuge on the other side of the Atlantic. Victory might not be enough, lamented an editorial in the August 30, 1943, issue of the *New Republic*. Calling the inactivity of the western powers "one of the major tragedies in the history of civilization," the article continued, "the moral weakness which has palsied the hands of

our statesmen is nowhere more vividly disclosed than in the now conventional formula ... that only victory will save the Jews of Europe. Will any
of these Jews survive to celebrate victory?"

For Americans, traditionally optimistic and pragmatic, the Holocaust
changed the way they thought about evil. This was not greed, insensitivity,
or brutality but a disembodied evil that threatened the very foundations,
the very notion of civilization. For many people, it awakened a deep-seated
missionary impulse. As the Cold War progressed and propaganda intensified, Americans came to believe that Stalin as an individual and communism as a political system were capable of the horrors committed by Hitler
and national socialism. Similar to Nazi Germany, the Soviet Union was a
totalitarian police state. During the 1920s in his war on Russian kulaks (independent farmers) and during the 1930s in his mass purges of suspected
political enemies, Stalin had proved himself to be as ruthless as Hitler.
As the most powerful and humane nation in the international community,
many Americans concluded, the United States had an obligation to combat
the individuals and institutions capable of such evil.

Seeds of Mistrust

Finally, the East–West confrontation that dominated global politics between 1945 and 1989 was the product of a series of specific events. During
World War II, Churchill had pressed for negotiations on postwar boundaries and political arrangements while the Red Army was still bottled up
within the Soviet Union, but Roosevelt had insisted on postponing such
talks for as long as possible out of a desire to hold the Grand Alliance together. By the end of 1944, however, victory was in sight in both Europe and
the Pacific, and the Americans could no longer stall. The climactic diplomatic conference of the war opened in late February 1945 in the Crimean
resort city of Yalta. As the diplomats opened their discussions, the Red
Army was within 50 miles of Berlin. With much of Eastern Europe within
his grasp, Stalin was in a strong bargaining position. In the Declaration of
Liberated Europe, each of the Big Three promised to hold free elections in
their zones of occupation as soon as possible. Significantly, the statement
did not include enforcement provisions. Germany was divided into zones
of occupation, with the Russians in control of the eastern third, the British
the northwestern third, and the Americans the southwestern third. France
was given authority over a small area in the west. An Allied Control Council
located in Berlin (located deep within the Soviet zone) would make policy
for occupied Germany. Stalin promised to enter the war against Japan 90
days after Germany surrendered. In return, Roosevelt assured the Soviets
that in any peace settlement they would receive the Kuril Islands, Outer
Mongolia, and portions of Manchuria.

With Allied bombs falling all around him, Hitler, together with his mistress, Eva Braun, committed suicide in his Berlin bunker. On May 8, the

German military command surrendered; the war in Europe was over. Following Germany's defeat, the Big Three met again in the Berlin suburb of Potsdam in July. By that time, Truman had succeeded Roosevelt, and in the midst of the meeting, British voters went to the polls in the general election of 1945 and replaced Churchill with the head of the Labor Party, Clement Attlee. Stalin did not have to worry about elections or, apparently, death. At Potsdam, the West reluctantly accepted Polish occupation of German territory as far west as the Oder–Neisse line and acquiesced in the Russian annexation of eastern Poland. In private conversations with his British and American counterparts, Stalin was perfectly candid. "Any freely elected government would be anti-Soviet," he declared, "and that we cannot permit." Truman and his advisers were unhappy about the emerging Soviet spheres in Eastern Europe, but there was little they believed they could do about them short of going to war. The Potsdam conferees also established a Council of Foreign Ministers to sign peace treaties with Italy and the other Axis satellites. The ensuing meetings, which stretched across 1945 and 1946, were characterized by bitter wrangling and deep mistrust. The Italian settlement left Britain and the United States in control of occupation policies; however, in the other treaties, the West was forced to acquiesce in Soviet control of Hungary and the Balkans.

The Dawn of the Atomic Age
In the midst of the discussions at Potsdam over Italy and Eastern Europe, President Truman had to make momentous choices concerning the war in the Pacific. A number of historians believe that Truman's decision to use the atomic bomb against Japan had more to do with a desire to contain communism than with the dynamics of the war against Japan. The new president had three options available to him for ending the war in the Pacific. The first option, and the one considered most likely to be employed, was conventional warfare. As soon as Germany surrendered, plans got underway for the invasion of the Japanese home islands. General Douglas MacArthur, liberator of the Philippines, would move up from the south while an Anglo-American task force would descend from the Aleutian Islands and attack from the north. Truman's advisers told him that the last battle would be ferocious. They estimated a 2-million-person Japanese army in the home islands and another million soldiers in Manchuria, with each fighting to the death. The invasion would require a million soldiers, sailors, and airmen, military planners informed the president, and result in a minimum of 100,000 Allied casualties. D-Day was set for November 1, 1945.

There were those in the administration, however, who urged Truman to end the war through negotiation. Japan was suffering terribly by the summer of 1945. Without effective air defense, Japanese cities were subjected to continuous shelling and bombing. One incendiary raid on Tokyo created a firestorm with winds up to 85 mph and took an estimated 125,000 lives. Assistant Secretary of State Joseph Grew, a former ambassador to Japan, urged the president to offer his former host country a peace that would allow it to retain the institution of emperor. Hirohito had played little or no role in the war, and he was an important cultural and social symbol to the Japanese. At the Potsdam Conference held in Germany in July 1945, Truman discussed the possibility of a negotiated settlement with the newly elected British prime minister, Clement Attlee. In the midst of the conference, the two leaders issued the Potsdam Declaration, an invitation to Japan to surrender unconditionally. They promised not to destroy Japan as a nation or enslave its citizenry; they would not go beyond that, however, and nothing ever came of the Potsdam Declaration.

The third alternative available to the United States for ending the war against Japan was to shock the enemy by dropping one or more atomic bombs on the home islands. Soon after he took the oath of office as president, Truman was informed by Secretary of War Henry Stimson of the existence of the Manhattan Project, the top-secret atomic development program authorized by Roosevelt in 1941. American and émigré scientists had made key breakthroughs at top-secret atomic research facilities at Hanford, Washington, and Oak Ridge, Tennessee. No weapons yet existed, but Truman decided to plan as if they would. He asked Stimson to head a top-secret body, the Interim Committee, which would study the problem and suggest possible ways of using an atomic bomb to end the war against Japan. After due deliberation, the Interim Committee recommended to Truman that if an atomic bomb were developed in time, it be dropped on a "military–industrial target," by which the committee meant an industrial city. Stimson's group briefly considered giving Japan prior warning but decided against it because approximately 10,000 Allied prisoners of war (POWs) remained incarcerated in the home islands. The Japanese would merely herd them into the target area.

Scientists working on the Manhattan Project produced a nuclear fission explosion at the Los Alamos, New Mexico, testing grounds on July 16, 1945. The resulting explosion exceeded their wildest dreams – or fears. J. Robert Openheimer recalled how the words, "I am become Death, the shatterer of worlds," flashed through the mind as he watched the explosion of the first atomic bomb from the control room at Los Alamos. Truman was immediately informed. From Potsdam on July 22, he ordered the Air Force to select one or more targets for bombing and to proceed as the weather allowed. On August 6, 1945 the *Enola Gay* dropped a single atomic device on the city of Hiroshima. The immediate blast completely destroyed a three-square-mile area of the city and incinerated 85,000 human beings. On August 8, the Soviets invaded Manchuria. The next day, the Air Force dropped another bomb on Nagasaki with similar results. On August 14, Japan surrendered unconditionally.

No event in American history has been more controversial than the decision to drop the bomb on Japan (although some 80% of Americans polled approved of the decision at the time). The United States remains the only nation ever to have used an atomic weapon in combat. Critics claimed that the atomic attack was unnecessary, that Truman could have had peace by allowing the Japanese to retain their emperor, which he did anyway. Some of these revisionists argue that the real motive behind the bombing was intimidation of the Soviet Union, with which relations were already deteriorating. Others maintain that the annihilation of the two Japanese cities was revenge for Pearl Harbor and insist that the United States would never have used atomic weapons against nonwhites. Truman argued that the sole reason he ordered the bombing of Hiroshima and Nagasaki was to save American lives. Japan would not surrender, and had the invasion taken place and the American people learned that the president had means to prevent it, he would have been driven from office – and rightly so. Years later, Truman observed that the atom bomb was no "great decision." "It was merely another powerful weapon in the arsenal of righteousness." Intimidation of the Soviet Union was a secondary and not a primary motivation. Nevertheless, the atomic bomb added a new element of tension and anxiety to the burgeoning East–West confrontation.

The Birth of Containment

Truman and other American officials clung to the hope in late 1945 and early 1946 that Soviet authorities would live up to the letter of the Yalta accords and hold free elections in their zones of occupation. They did in fact do so, but only after all political factions except the communists had been eliminated from the country in question. Occupation politics followed a similar pattern in each of the Eastern European countries controlled by the Soviet Union. American newspapers referred to these policies as Stalin's "salami tactics," meaning that he incorporated Eastern Europe into the Soviet sphere slowly, one slice at a time. Moreover, in each case, the Soviet Union was able to "consolidate" power without resorting to the use of overt force. In Hungary, Bulgaria, Rumania, Poland, and finally in Czechoslovakia in February 1948, a similar chain of events occurred. During the first months of occupation, Red Army officials and political commissars would form coalition governments made up of various prewar parties and factions. In each case, however, the all-important ministry of the interior, which controlled the state police, went to a communist. From this vantage point, the communists could "uncover" plots against the state being hatched by rival parties. Inevitably, these organizations were then outlawed and their leaders either liquidated or sent to Siberia until only the communists were left. At that point, the government would hold a plebiscite, carefully controlled, thus fulfilling the letter of the Declaration on

Liberated Europe. A Russian regime was also imposed on Albania while Josep Broz Tito, a Marxist-Leninist who had led the partisan movement against the Nazis and who at that point was a loyal Soviet ally, consolidated his position in Yugoslavia.

During his first year and a half in office, Harry Truman alternated between conciliation and rhetorical confrontation in his dealings with the Soviets. The thrust of his policy, however, was to have the United States live up to the letter and spirit of the Yalta accords and to insist that the Kremlin do likewise. American hesitancy to confront the Soviet Union in deed and in word was due to a number of factors. First, the rapid demobilization of America's armed forces militated against a get-tough stance. Second, Truman was inexperienced in foreign affairs and therefore hesitant to depart from Roosevelt's generally conciliatory policy toward the Soviet Union. To make matters worse, Truman appointed as his first secretary of state James F. Byrnes, a South Carolina politician known more for his ability to manipulate Congress than for his expertise in foreign affairs. Truman's choice grew out of a desire to strengthen his hand with Congress and the Democratic Party, and out of the mistaken belief that Byrnes had been privy to the secret deliberations at Yalta. Truman was swayed by this misperception because as vice president he had been excluded from the foreign policy-making process. In addition, wartime propaganda had generated a groundswell of good feeling toward Stalin personally and the Russian people generally that persisted well into the postwar period. Americans wanted to get back to their families and jobs and stop worrying about the world. Finally – and not coincidentally – they tended to put too much faith in the newly established United Nations.

From April through June 1945, delegates from 50 nations gathered in San Francisco for the United Nations Conference on International Organization (UNCIO). There they hammered out the charter of the new collective security organization that everyone hoped would be able to do what the League of Nations had not been able to do – prevent armed aggression by one state against another and ultimately eliminate the roots of war altogether. The delegates created a three-branch organization, including a general assembly in which all members were represented, a secretariat to carry out the UN's orders, and a security council with permanent and rotating members (permanent members were the United States, the USSR, China, Great Britain, and France). The council had the authority to call on participants to impose economic sanctions on aggressor nations and, if need be, to contribute troops to an international police force. However, the charter contained several loopholes. One provision reserved to member nations "matters which are essentially within the domestic jurisdiction of any state," and another sanctioned regional security arrangements. Most important, the permanent members of the security council possessed an absolute veto, and given the East–West split, that meant that the United

Nations was going to find it very difficult to define "aggression," much less take action against it. Belatedly, the American people began to realize that the new world organization was incapable of containing Soviet imperialism and protecting their overseas interests.

The Iron Curtain Speech

Gradually, the Truman administration's attitude toward Moscow hardened. The first week in March 1946, former British prime minister Winston Churchill journeyed to Fulton, Missouri, where he delivered an address to the students and faculty of Westminster College. The speech, which was billed as a major foreign policy address, had been arranged by President Truman who traveled to Fulton with Churchill and sat on the dais with him. England's most famous citizen warned his audience that an "Iron Curtain" had descended across Europe "from Stettin in the Baltic to Trieste in the Adriatic," and he asserted that there was nothing for which the Russians had "less respect for than weakness, especially military weakness." Continuing, he proclaimed, "What they desire is the fruits of war and the indefinite expansion of their powers and doctrines." The only thing that stood between Western Europe, catastrophically weakened by World War II, and the 500 Soviet divisions present in Eastern Europe was the United States and its atomic bombs. He called for a renewal of the "fraternal association" between English-speaking peoples as the best means of preserving liberty and democracy as alternatives to communist totalitarianism. Many within the United States denounced Churchill as a warmonger, but others could not forget that he almost alone had sounded the alarm in the 1930s, warning the world against Hitler and the Nazis. Perhaps the prophet had spoken again. In the five months following V-J Day, public belief in the possibility of peaceful cooperation with the Soviet Union dropped from 54% to 35%.

It was most significant that Harry Truman had sponsored the Iron Curtain speech. Indeed, he and Secretary of State Byrnes had come to the conclusion that British and American interests in Europe and the Near East were identical and that Soviet expansion must be stopped. Unbeknownst to the American people, the same week that Churchill spoke in Fulton, their president was engaging in his first confrontation with Josef Stalin. During World War II, Iran, rich in petroleum resources and situated at the crossroads between Asia and Europe, had been occupied by the Soviet Union in the north and Britain in the south. At the Teheran conference, the Big Three agreed that the occupying powers would withdraw from Iran no later than six months after the end of the war. Meanwhile, within their zone of occupation, which included the province of Azerbaijan, the Soviets fostered development of the Tudeh party, an indigenous communist movement. Instead of preparing to withdraw as the March 1946 deadline approached, the Soviets massed troops in the north and delivered an ultimatum to the

Shah in Tehran. Moscow demanded the right to keep soldiers in Iran, the formation of a Soviet–Iranian oil company controlled by the Soviets, and the granting of autonomy to Azerbaijan. When the Shah appealed to Britain and America, Truman responded by moving the Sixth Fleet to the eastern Mediterranean and making it clear to Stalin that the United States would use whatever force was necessary to protect Iranian independence. Shortly thereafter, Soviet troops began withdrawing and the crisis faded.

Henry Wallace versus the Hard-Liners
The persistence of neoisolationism, coupled with ongoing liberal sympathy with the Soviet Union, kept Truman from publicly confronting Moscow and pursuing a consistently hard-line policy. In the fall of 1946, however, former vice president Henry Wallace forced his hand. Roosevelt had replaced Wallace with Truman as vice president in 1944, but the Iowan had stayed on in the cabinet as secretary of commerce. An outspoken proponent of Soviet–American friendship, Wallace grew increasingly alarmed as East–West relations deteriorated. "Communists everywhere want eventually a Communist world," Wallace admitted, but "for the moment I believe they are essentially interested . . . in strengthening the Soviet Union as an example of the kind of socialism they have in mind." He became convinced that the president had fallen under the influence of doctrinaire anticommunists. On September 17, 1946, Wallace delivered an address at Madison Square Garden, which was billed as a statement of administration policy. Truman had indeed approved the speech but without reading the text. In his survey of the international situation, Wallace attacked those who would get tough with the Soviet Union and called for Soviet–American friendship to be the cornerstone of postwar American foreign policy. From Germany, where he was promising the inhabitants of the western zones that America would not abandon them to the tender mercies of the Soviets, Jimmy Byrnes screamed in protest. The president would have to choose between him and Wallace, the secretary of state declared. Almost without hesitating, Truman asked for the Iowan's resignation. "I don't understand a dreamer like that," he subsequently wrote in his diary. "The Reds, phonies and the 'parlor pinks' seem to be banded together and are becoming a national danger. I am afraid they are a sabotage front for Uncle Joe Stalin." Truman had made a policy as well as a personnel choice.

In January 1947, Jimmy Byrnes resigned under pressure as secretary of state. His tendency to conduct the foreign policy of the United States without consulting the White House inevitably did him in. The man with whom Truman replaced Byrnes was George C. Marshall, who had served as chairman of the Combined Chiefs of Staff during World War II and who more than any other man was credited with masterminding victory over the Axis. It was most unusual to appoint a military man to the highest diplomatic post in the land, but the former general was absolutely committed to the principle of civilian control of the military. He was, more-over, absolutely loyal to Truman and a strong supporter of the policy of standing up to the Soviets. An excellent administrator, Marshall was de-termined to revitalize the State Department and make it a policy-planning organization as well as a problem-solving body. Specifically, the new secre-tary of state was determined to select able subordinates and then delegate authority.

The nucleus of the new State Department consisted of three men, indi-viduals who more than any other would be responsible for shaping U.S. policy at the dawning of the Cold War. For the position of undersecretary of state in charge of overseeing the entire diplomatic operation, Marshall se-lected Dean Acheson. The Yale-educated Acheson, whose grandfather had been the Episcopal bishop of Connecticut, was a disciple of the Christian philosopher, Reinhold Niebuhr. It was his civic and moral duty, Acheson believed, to stand up to the threat posed by Marxism-Leninism and Soviet imperialism. An Atlanticist and an elitist, the new undersecretary viewed Europe as the flywheel of the global mechanism, and he believed that for-eign policymaking should be left to the experts in the State Department who would periodically inform Congress and the public as to their overall goals, but otherwise operate independently and generally in secret. For assistant secretary for economic affairs, Marshall selected the Houston cotton bro-ker William L. Clayton. A successful international businessman, Clayton was committed to molding the noncommunist world into an interdepen-dent economic unit by lowering trade barriers and establishing stable ex-change rates. To head the newly created policy planning staff in the State Department, Marshall chose George F. Kennan. A career foreign service officer and expert on Russian history and culture, Kennan had served in the Moscow embassy during the 1930s and World War II. A self-described man of the nineteenth century, Kennan hated communism. Lenin, Stalin, and their henchmen were "a swarm of rats" that were seeking to destroy Western civilization, he once observed. The fact that a Sovietologist was selected to oversee long-range planning was most significant.

In the summer of 1947, an anonymous article entitled "The Sources of Soviet Conduct" appeared in the prestigious journal *Foreign Affairs*. It soon became known that the author was none other than George Kennan, and opinion makers came to view the article, correctly, as official government policy. Russian wartime and postwar expansion, Kennan argued, was just another example of the migration westward of barbaric peoples from the recesses of the Asiatic heartland, a process that had been ongoing since the days of Genghis Khan. Because the United States was part of Western civi-lization and had a vested interest in its preservation and because it was the most powerful of the Atlantic democracies, it would have to take the lead in confronting the communist menace. The best policy for the United States in this situation was containment, a policy of less than war itself, but one of opposing force with force, of drawing a line, a defensive perimeter, and daring the Russians, "thus far you shall go and no farther." The communist challenge was a blessing in disguise, Kennan concluded, for it would force the American people to accept "the responsibilities of moral and political leadership that history plainly intended them to bear." An opportunity for the administration to implement the containment policy was not long in coming.

To the Truman Doctrine

In February 1947, Great Britain quietly informed the U.S. government that it was no longer able to fulfill its strategic responsibilities in the eastern Mediterranean. Given the fact that since the construction of the Suez Canal in the nineteenth century, Britain's strategic lifeline to its Far Eastern dependencies had run through that area, it was a most significant statement. At the time of London's notification, there appeared to be two countries in the region seriously threatened by communism. Since 1944, Greece had been torn by civil war as the National Liberation Front (EAM/ELAS) sought to overthrow the prowestern but oppressive monarchy. Because Greek communists played a prominent part in the revolution and because EAM/ELAS received munitions and other supplies from Yugoslavia, the United States and Britain viewed the conflict as one inspired and controlled by the Kremlin. At the same time, the Soviets were massing troops along their common border with Turkey in an attempt to bully Ankara into granting permission for the construction of a Soviet naval base on the Bosporus.

At Acheson and Marshall's urging, Truman decided to step into the breach. Acutely aware that the Republicans had won the midterm elections in 1946, the State Department leadership decided to obtain bipartisan support before the administration approached Congress with a policy statement and funding request for the beleaguered governments of Greece and Turkey. During a late February meeting with the leadership, Acheson described a dire situation in the Near East. The fall of the Greek government and the establishment of a Russian military presence on the straits separating the Black Sea and the Mediterranean "might open three continents to Soviet penetration." The Soviets were "engaging in one of the greatest gambles in history," he told the assembled senators and congressmen, and only the United States was in a position to call its bluff. The new chairman of the SFRC, Arthur Vandenberg of Michigan, was in the process of making the switch from isolationism to activism, primarily because his constituency was full of Polish Americans and others with ties to Eastern Europe. He declared his support for U.S. aid to those nations threatened by "the forces of international communism," but warned that the president would have to "scare hell" out of the American people to gain public support.

On March 12, 1947, Truman asked Congress to approve $400 million in aid to Greece and Turkey. More importantly, he requested approval of a sweeping declaration of Cold War against Soviet imperialism. "It must be the policy of the United States," he declared, "to support free peoples who are resisting subjugation by armed minorities or by outside pressure." The SFRC and House Foreign Affairs Committee quickly scheduled hearings. Critics argued that the Greek government was undemocratic, corrupt, and reactionary, and that Turkey was not a democracy and had remained neutral for most of World War II. Why not let Greece and Turkey pass into the communist orbit as they would simply be exchanging one form of totalitarian government for another? State Department representatives could only answer that things were not always as black and white in foreign affairs as one might desire. With economic aid and encouragement, Greece might move toward democracy, and Turkey was already emerging from the autocratic era of Mustafa Kemal. At any rate, with noncommunist regimes in power, the future was at least hopeful, whereas under communist dictatorships there could be no hope for democracy and individual liberty. Following a brief debate, both houses of Congress approved the aid package and the policy statement justifying it.

Truman's promise to stand by societies threatened by the forces of international communism quickly became known as the Truman Doctrine. Popular and congressional support for the containment policy in general and the Truman Doctrine specifically was based on the melding of New Deal liberals, businessmen, former isolationists, and anticommunist ideologues into a nationalist coalition supporting an activist foreign policy. As one British diplomat put it, the United States was willing to lead the struggle against the Soviet Union because "America could now enter the community of nations while remaining indisputably first."

The Marshall Plan

The Truman Doctrine was designed to prevent a communist takeover through overt aggression or armed subversion; it did not address the social and economic insecurity that threatened to lead to a legitimate takeover by indigenous communist parties. By 1947, Western Europe was in dire economic straits. Hanson Baldwin in the *New York Times* reviewed the "plague and pestilence, suffering and disaster, famine and hardship, the complete political and economic dislocation" that characterized Western Europe following World War II. German and Allied bombing had destroyed most of the continent's industrial base. Drought had killed much of the 1946 wheat crop, and the severe winter of 1946/1947 dimmed the prospects for 1947. Millions of displaced people continued to wander the countryside and glut cities in Germany, France, and Italy. In England, the coal shortage was so great that power had to be shut off for hours each day. Recalling Germany in the 1920s, U.S. officials concluded that political extremism flourished in conditions of economic and social insecurity. By the close of 1946, the French and Italian communist parties were the most powerful political organizations in their respective countries, and it appeared that they would dominate future coalition governments unless something were done to provide food, clothing, and shelter to the suffering masses.

In a Harvard commencement speech delivered in June 1947, Secretary of State Marshall outlined the massive aid program that would take his name. In his speech, Marshall reviewed the devastation, pestilence, and instability that plagued Europe. He called on Britain and the nations of the continent to frame an integrated plan for Europe's recovery. When it had devised a scheme for economic rehabilitation, Europe could count on the United States to supply "friendly aid." Marshall made three things clear in his speech: the United States would not fund a collection of national shopping lists – there would have to be an integrated plan, the scheme would have to provide for the economic reconstruction of Germany, and his invitation extended to the entire continent, including the Soviet satellites and European Russia. Kennan, Acheson, and Clayton believed that for various reasons, they could not exclude the communist powers. Aside from wanting the United States to appear magnanimous, American officials feared that if the Eastern bloc nations were not invited, French and Italian communists would block participation by their countries. The U.S. government hoped that the prospect of integrating their economies with those of the West would ensure that Russia and its client states would never join. As it turned out, they were right.

In late June, British Foreign Minister Ernest Bevin flew to Paris to consult with his French counterpart, Georges Bidault. They, in turn, extended an invitation to Soviet Foreign Minister Vyacheslav Molotov to join them and prepare a response to Secretary Marshall's proposal. When Molotov arrived in Paris on June 28, he immediately proposed that each nation merely survey its reconstruction needs, report them to the United States, and suggest the amount of credit it would require. When Bevin made it clear that such an approach – a "blank check," he termed it – would be unacceptable to the United States, the Soviet foreign minister departed, and the Kremlin subsequently ordered its client governments in Eastern Europe not to participate in the Marshall Plan. As the State Department had anticipated, Russian leaders were not willing to subscribe to a scheme that would revive trade between Eastern and Western Europe and in the process deny the Soviet Union its newly created economic sphere of interest. Moreover, Stalin and his associates were not pleased by the prospect of an international agency determining priorities and quotas for the communist bloc. In September in Polish Silesia, Molotov summoned Russia's satellite foreign ministers, and they disconsolately announced creation of the Molotov Plan, a Russian-led scheme of reconstruction that would allegedly rival and surpass the Marshall Plan.

Throughout the summer and fall of 1947, the Truman administration played on and even fed a mounting anticommunist hysteria in the United

States. The Department of Education sponsored a Freedom Train, which, laden with memorabilia of America's struggle for independence, toured the country gathering support for democracy and "the American way of life." The Truman administration suddenly began cooperating with the notorious House Un-American Activities Committee in its search for communists and fellow travelers who had infiltrated the federal bureaucracy. Spokesmen for Truman and Marshall made the point repeatedly to senators and representatives that the Marshall Plan was above all a weapon in the struggle against world communism. In the spring and summer of 1947, the French and Italians had, at the U.S. government's urging, excluded the communists from their respective ruling coalitions. However, if Europe's economic woes were not addressed, State Department officials told Congress, the communists would force early general elections and most probably dominate the resulting governments.

The U.S. Senate passed the Economic Cooperation Act of 1948 on March 13, by a vote of 69 to 17. On April 3, the House of Representatives followed suit, approving the measure by a 4 to 1 margin. As enacted, the legislation empowered the secretary of state to conclude with each participating country a bilateral agreement signifying its adherence to the purposes of the act. The bill authorized an appropriation of $5.3 billion for the first 12-month period of the program. These funds were to be disbursed and administered by a new agency, the Economic Cooperation Administration (ECA). In an effort to maintain conservative support for the program, the White House named Paul Hoffman, president of Studebaker Corporation, to head the new agency.

Over the next four years, the United States poured $13 billion into Europe and worked with various national governments to establish institutions and processes that would rehabilitate the continent's economies. The stated goals of the Economic Cooperation Act were to increase industrial and agricultural production, establish and maintain internal financial stability, expand foreign trade, and fashion mechanisms of economic cooperation. By 1952, industrial production had increased 30% over prewar levels and agricultural output 11%. The United States forced recipient countries to put up local "counterpart" currencies against Marshall Plan grants. These funds were used in turn to finance national deficits and control inflation. Intra-European trade, virtually destroyed by World War II, was resuscitated in 1952, when, under the auspices of the ECA, a European Payments Union was established. This agency acted as a currency clearinghouse and presided over a general reduction in tariffs, quotas, and other trade barriers. During its eight years of existence, the Union financed $46.6 billion worth of intra-European trade. The goal of European political integration foundered on the rocks of deeply rooted nationalisms, but there was some progress in the economic field. In addition to the European Payments Union, the Marshall Plan nations established the European

Coal and Steel Community. It was during this period that the foundations for the Common Market were established. With the return of prosperity, the appeal of the French and Italian communist parties began to
decline. The Marshall Plan also served U.S. economic interests. With the
revival of its economy, Western Europe became America's largest trading
partner.

The Truman Doctrine and Marshall Plan were America's declaration
of Cold War, that is, its promise to provide economic and military aid to
those nations threatened by international communism. In 1949, the United
States went one step farther and committed American troops to the defense
of Western Europe. Fearful that the Soviet Union would use its superiority in conventional forces in a military assault on Western Europe, Great
Britain, France, and the Benelux (Belgium, the Netherlands, and Luxem-
bourg) countries signed the Brussels Treaty in 1948, providing for collective
self-defense. Then in 1949, in response to a request from Europeans that
the United States demonstrate its willingness to shed blood in the common
defense, President Truman called for the creation of an Atlantic defense
community. On April 4, 1949, in Washington, D.C., the United States joined
with Canada, Iceland, Denmark, Norway, Portugal, Greece, Turkey, and the
Brussels powers to create the North Atlantic Treaty Organization (NATO).
Its key clause stated that "an armed attack against one or more . . . shall be
considered an attack against them all." In 1950, Truman named Dwight D.
Eisenhower to be supreme NATO commander, and he sent four American
divisions to Europe to form the core of a NATO army. It was clear that these
troops were to serve as a tripwire if Soviet troops attacked. In effect, Western Europe had been placed behind an American atomic shield. There was
no evidence of a Russian plan to invade the West, but the Soviets continued
to maintain hundreds of divisions in Eastern Europe and East Germany.
Caught up in the Munich analogy, American officials believed they could
not gamble that the hundreds of thousands of Red Army soldiers were in
Eastern Europe for purely defensive purposes. The creation of NATO led
directly to the formation of the Warsaw Pact, a formal military alliance
between the Soviet Union and the communist states of Eastern Europe,
and heightened tensions throughout the world.

The Berlin Blockade
The first great test of the containment policy in Europe came in the summer
of 1948, when on June 24, Soviet occupation authorities cut off overland
access to Berlin from West Germany. The city was nominally jointly occupied and governed by the four members of the Allied Control Council,
but by 1948, Berlin was becoming increasingly polarized between communist and noncommunist elements. The Kremlin's reasons for making such
a provocative move were fairly clear. Stalin resented the West's refusal to
set up a four-power government for all of Germany as provided for in the

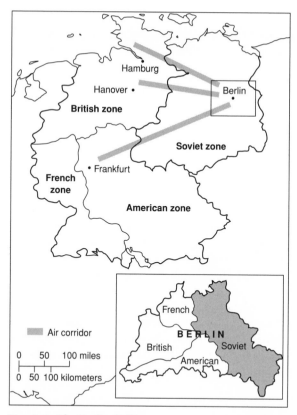

Map 2–1. The Berlin Airlift.

Potsdam accords. He feared that Britain and the United States intended not only to rehabilitate but also to rearm West Germany and unleash it on the Soviet Union. If his former wartime partners could cut off reparation shipments from their zones to East Germany, reasoned Stalin, then the Soviets could prevent access to the 2.4 million inhabitants of Berlin situated some 100 miles inside East Germany. The decision to block access seemed sure either to force the West out of the city and allow Moscow complete control over East Germany or to secure the long-sought four-power governance over all of Germany. In case of the latter eventuality, because of the principal of unanimity, the Soviets would be in a position to block democratic reforms and the creation of a prowestern government. The blockade involved all surface modes of transportation including rail, auto, and water. At the same time, Soviet military authorities, citing "technical difficulties," restricted the flow of electricity into West Berlin. At the outset of the blockade, the inhabitants of the suddenly beleaguered city had about one month's supply of food, coal, and medicine on hand.

The crisis came at a difficult time for President Truman. His party was splitting into factions, his personal popularity was at an all-time low, and the Republicans had nominated a formidable candidate, Governor Thomas E. Dewey of New York, to challenge him in the presidential election of 1948. Some within the administration believed that the 10,000 American and British soldiers in West Berlin were in a strategically untenable position and argued that the city ought to be abandoned. Others, including the U.S. military commander in Berlin, General Lucius Clay, favored breaking the blockade by force regardless of the consequences. Truman did not hesitate. There would be no thought of abandoning the city, he told Secretary of Defense James Forrestal. He and his advisers believed that America's credibility was on the line and that if it did not stick by the West Berliners, noncommunist Europe would lose heart and succumb to communism. General Clay, who equated the fate of West Berlin with the fate of Western civilization, advocated sending an armed convoy over the autobahn and breaking the blockade by force. General Omar Bradley, chairman of the Joint Chiefs of Staff, rejected this foolhardy advice and opted instead for a massive airlift conducted jointly with the British. Construction of an air bridge would force the Soviets to initiate hostilities if that was their intention. At the same time, to remove any doubt from Stalin's mind that the Western powers intended to stick by the West Berliners and proceed with the formation of a West German republic, President Truman ostentatiously announced that Britain had agreed to accept 60 "atomic capable" B-29 bombers.

The B-29 ploy was a bluff. The planes had not yet been adapted to carry a nuclear payload; indeed, the United States had fewer than 50 bombs in 1948, and many of them were not usable. Stalin, through top-level spies he had managed to place in the British and American atomic projects, probably knew that Truman was bluffing, but he chose not to challenge the airlift.

Clay's people estimated that at a minimum West Berlin would require 2,500 tons of food, coal, and medicine a day to survive. A fleet of 52 C-54s and 80 C-47s, as well as elements of the Royal Air Force, began making two flights daily and within one week had reached the minimum level needed to keep the population alive and healthy. New flights were added, and the daily volume reached 4,000 tons. With the Russians standing by in frustration and the morale of the West Berliners soaring, the Truman administration decided that the airlift would constitute the West's permanent response. The air bridge lasted 324 days and at its peak delivered 13,000 tons a day of food, coal, and medical supplies to West Berlin.

After more than ten months, the Soviets agreed to restore overland access to the noncommunist sector of Berlin. The decision not to try to stop the airlift by force had been made at the outset, and the West was reaping massive propaganda benefits from the Berlin Blockade, as the media had

Map 2–2. Cold War Europe, 1950.

termed the incident. On May 12, 1949, citing the opening of a foreign ministers' conference in Paris as justification, the Kremlin ordered its troops
to stand down. The United States had withstood the first major challenge
to the policy of containment, but the Berlin Blockade further polarized

Europe and helped ensure that Germany would remain divided for a generation. While the United States and its West European allies created a West German state – the Federal Republic of Germany – in the fall of 1949, the Russians announced the formation of the German Democratic Republic (GDR), with its capital in East Berlin. As it turned out, the Berlin Blockade was the opening shot in a Cold War that spread from Europe throughout the globe. The second great battleground of the East–West confrontation was Asia.

The Cold War in Asia

Some Americans believed that their country's decision to give Europe first priority during World War II had been a mistake. Beginning in the mid-nineteenth century, U.S. missionaries, businesspeople, and diplomats had spread throughout Asia bringing the blessings of Christianity, industrialism, and smallpox to their "less fortunate" brethren. Americans were particularly enamored of China, a huge nation perceived to be ripe both for economic exploitation and religious conversion. Indeed, although U.S. trade with China comprised less than 2% of the total foreign trade in 1900, the administration of President William McKinley had proclaimed in the open door policy that it would act to defend the territorial integrity and political independence of China. It was the open door policy in turn that led to 50 years of imperial rivalry with Japan, which viewed northern China as its manifest destiny, and helped precipitate the attack on Pearl Harbor. Despite the demise of the open door policy and China's failure to emerge from World War II to be the strong, democratic, regional leader that the United States hoped it would be, a minority of Americans – "Asia Firsters" – continued to believe that their country's primary economic and strategic interests lay in East Asia rather than in Europe.

The war in the Pacific ripped the old colonial order asunder and unleashed the forces of nationalism. From India through Indonesia and Southeast Asia northward to China, Asians struggled to assume control over their own destinies. Inevitably, the Cold War spread from Europe and the Near East to the Pacific basin, as the Soviet Union and its client states on the one hand and the United States and its allies – most of them former colonial powers – on the other hand struggled to control and if possible co-opt the forces of nationalism that were sweeping the region. The first country to experience a nationalist revolution in a Cold War context was China.

Civil War in China

When the war ended in Asia there were actually two political entities in China: the Chinese Nationalist government headquartered in Nanking and a Chinese Communist regime that controlled much of northern China.

The Kuomintang, the revolutionary organization that had succeeded the Manchu dynasty and subdued rival warlords to create a new central government in 1925, had originally included both communists and noncommunists. But within two years, a deep split had developed between the two factions, and after a vicious civil conflict, the Nationalists under Jiang Jieshi drove the communists under Mao Zedong into exile in far northwest China. Following the Japanese invasion, the two factions nominally joined forces, but soon after V-J Day, fighting erupted again. In December 1945, President Truman dispatched General George Marshall to arrange a ceasefire and mediate a permanent settlement. After a year of frustration, Marshall threw up his hands and full-scale civil war erupted.

Despite $2 billion in American aid and superiority in both manpower and material, Jiang and the Nationalists began to lose ground rapidly. In 1949, he and the remnant of his army were forced to take refuge on the island of Taiwan (Formosa). The world's most populous nation was in communist hands. The "fall of China" was a most traumatic experience for Americans. The Republican Party had always been more Asian than Atlantic oriented, and its members were particularly bitter over the turn of events. Led by Senators Robert Taft and Joseph McCarthy and *Time-Life* publisher Henry Luce, the son of missionaries to China, the Republicans blamed the Democratic Party for what they termed one of the greatest foreign policy failures of the twentieth century. McCarthy claimed that Jiang had been betrayed by communists and fellow travelers in the State Department, whereas Taft accused Truman and Dean Acheson, who had become secretary of state in 1949, of pursuing an erroneous Europe-first policy and of appeasing the Soviets. Everyone assumed that Mao Zedong and the Chinese Communists were mere puppets of the Kremlin and that the United States was primarily to blame for the "loss" of China.

Actually, although it was hard for Americans to admit it, U.S. policy was peripheral to the events that occurred from 1947 to 1949. "Nothing that this country did or could have done within the reasonable limits of its capabilities could have changed that result," Dean Acheson later wrote in his memoirs. The most important factor contributing to the communization of China was the corruption and ossification of the Chinese Nationalist Party. In contrast, the Chinese Communists appeared in the eyes of the peasants under their control as paragons of self-sacrifice, if not democracy. Mao and his chief lieutenant, Zhou Enlai, lived abstemiously, and they rigidly disciplined their subordinates. When the sword was drawn in 1947, it was the Communists rather than the Nationalists who were able to count on popular support.

Although the Republicans insisted that the fall of China was well within the Democratic administration's ability to prevent, there was little more that the United States could have done. The U.S. government considered attaching conditions to the $2 billion in aid that it furnished Jiang, but by 1947, it was too late to purge the Nationalist regime of its corrupt and repressive ways. The only alternative was for the United States to have put troops on the ground, but even that would have inflamed nationalist sentiments and played into the hands of the communists. As one historian of the events has noted, the United States insisted on looking at China as a single state with two political parties, whereas in reality what existed was two one-party states. There was absolutely no possibility of reconciliation. In his memoirs, *Fifty Years in China*, Ambassador John Leighton Stuart attributed the outcome of the Chinese civil war to "a gigantic struggle between two political ideologies" and observed sadly that "the great mass of suffering inarticulate victims cared for neither but were powerless to do anything about it."

The Korean War
As if the communization of the world's most populous nation were not enough, in June 1950, Communist North Korea invaded South Korea. For most of the twentieth century the peoples of that peninsula had been victims of foreign exploitation. During the Russo–Japanese War in 1905, Japan had converted the country into a protectorate. Five years later, the informal empire metamorphosized into full-scale colonial status. With Japan's surrender, the United States occupied the area south of the 38th parallel, and the Soviet Union put troops into the territory north of that line. During the next two years, amid bloody fighting that cost nearly 100,000 lives, the Soviets established a peoples' republic under Korean communist Kim Il Sung, while the United States presided over the establishment of a prowestern if autocratic and repressive regime under Syngman Rhee. In September 1947, the United States informed the Soviet Union that it was referring the question of Korean unification and independence to the United Nations. The United Nations duly appointed a commission to visit the peninsula and arrange for countrywide elections, but Soviet occupation authorities announced that the representatives of the world organization were not welcome in their zone. In May 1948, U.S. authorities presided over a carefully controlled election in the south, which Rhee won by an overwhelming margin. Shortly thereafter, the two nations signed an agreement that provided for substantial U.S. military and economic assistance.

Meanwhile in the United States, the emergence of a powerful neoisolationist movement caused the Truman administration to momentarily shrink from the globalism inherent in the Truman Doctrine. Extremists such as Senator McCarthy insisted that America's greatest threat came not from abroad but at home in the form of communist infiltration of the media, the federal government, and educational institutions. More traditional isolationists such as Robert Taft and former President Herbert Hoover insisted that America's resources were limited and that it ought to concentrate on perfecting its own institutions and guaranteeing its own prosperity.

They were particularly adamant about the need to balance the budget. The neoisolationists opposed the stationing of American troops in Europe as part of a NATO armed force and they, somewhat paradoxically, warned about the perils of being drawn into a land war on the Asian mainland. Secretary of State Acheson announced in January 1949 that South Korea was from that point onward outside the American defensive perimeter and would have to rely on the United Nations for protection. Critics later charged that Acheson was trying to appease Hoover, Taft, and like-minded Americans. His supporters disagreed, insisting that he and the administration wanted to emphasize economic and administrative rather than military assistance to South Korea because they believed sound economies and democratic governments were the best insurance against communism. Whatever the secretary's motives, other statements by Acheson and General Douglas MacArthur, head of the American occupation government in Japan, indicated that not only South Korea but also Taiwan could not count on direct U.S. intervention in case of attack.

Of further encouragement to Kim Il Sung and North Korean hard-liners was the deplorable state of the American military. Truman's secretary of defense, Louis Johnson, was dedicated to the proposition that American interests around the globe could be defended on a budget of some $14 billion per year. He was convinced that the atomic bomb would more than compensate for the 10 undermanned and ill-equipped divisions that constituted America's army. The Soviet Union's detonation of an atomic bomb in 1949 seemed not to have shaken that conviction.

According to recently discovered documents in the Russian archives, both the Soviet Union and Communist China gave tacit approval to Kim's plan to forcibly reunify the peninsula. China was already busily supporting anticolonial revolutions in Indonesia and elsewhere. In May 1950, the Truman administration announced plans to negotiate a peace treaty with Japan as quickly as possible. Two things were clear: neither the Soviets nor the Chinese would be part of that process and, under any agreement signed, the United States would have the right to construct military installations in Japan. In both Moscow and Beijing's view, a Korea unified under communist control would serve as a needed counterweight to a rehabilitated and pro-American Japan. Finally, although the conclusion of a Sino–Soviet treaty of friendship and alliance had been signed in February, neither partner trusted the other, and the competition for the allegiance of nations emerging from colonialism had already begun. Although Stalin was determined not to become directly involved in a war for Korean unification, he was not going to stand idly by and allow Mao to receive all the credit.

On June 25, 1950, the well-trained and well-equipped North Korean military crossed the 38th parallel and swept down the peninsula driving Rhee's 65,000-man army before it. Within a week, the communists had overrun the capital city of Seoul. Truman was attending to family business in Independence, Missouri, when news of the attack arrived. He immediately rushed back to Washington, D.C., to confer with Dean Acheson, who had succeeded Marshall as secretary of state in 1949, and his other advisers. From the beginning, they assumed the invasion was part of an extensive Sino–Soviet thrust whose objective was the communization of Asia. Truman did not hesitate. Both Korea and Taiwan were brought back within the American line of defense. On June 26, President Truman directed the Seventh Fleet to begin patrolling the Formosa Strait and authorized the use of the U.S. Army and U.S. Navy in Korea. Following a first-hand report from MacArthur, Truman on June 30 granted permission to use ground troops to ensure that the South Koreans retained control of an enclave around Pusan, a city situated on the southeastern coast. At the same time, he imposed a naval blockade on North Korea. The president regarded the North Korean attack as a simple and direct test of the "free world's" determination to defend democracy and liberty. "Communism," he wrote in his *Memoirs*, "was acting in Korea just as Hitler, Mussolini, and the Japanese had acted ten, fifteen, and twenty years earlier." Korea was "the Greece of the Far East," he explained to reporters.

Taking advantage of the fact that the Soviet representative on the Security Council, Yakov Malik, was boycotting its proceedings in protest of the nonseating of Communist China, on June 25, the United States sought and obtained a resolution condemning the North Koreans as aggressors and calling for their withdrawal from the South. On June 27, with the Soviet representative still absent, the council called on member nations to contribute to a peace-keeping force to defend South Korea, and shortly thereafter designated the United States as head of the UN coalition in Korea. Truman at once named General Douglas MacArthur to command the army of liberation. Although other nations sent troops, the military effort in Korea was American dominated. The United States supplied 50% of the ground forces (most of the remainder came from South Korea), 86% of the naval power, and 93% of the air power.

The situation in Korea initially looked quite hopeless. For six weeks, the communist invaders advanced steadily down the peninsula until elements of the American Eighth Army and what was left of the Army of the Republic of Korea (ROK) were confined to a small enclave around Pusan. With the aid of massive reinforcements and close air support, the embattled UN troops managed to stabilize their perimeter. Then on September 15, MacArthur staged a surprise amphibious landing at Inchon, a port city on the western coast near the 38th parallel. Meeting light resistance, U.S. Marines and Korean troops advanced inland, while their comrades in the south broke out of the Pusan enclave and advanced northward. The North Korean army began to roll up like a window shade. Seoul was recaptured on September 26, and MacArthur's men had soon reached the 38th parallel.

The Truman–MacArthur Controversy

At this point, the Truman administration faced a momentous decision. MacArthur desperately wanted to cross into North Korea, crush the communist forces, and reunify the peninsula. The chances that either the Soviet Union or Communist China would intervene were virtually nonexistent, he insisted. Secretary of State Acheson agreed:

I give the people of Peiping [Peking] credit for being intelligent enough to see what is happening to them. Why they should want to further their own dismemberment and destruction by getting at cross purposes with all the free nations of the world who are inherently their friends and have always been friends of the Chinese against the imperialism coming down from the Soviet Union I cannot see.

Truman was not so sure, but he was persuaded by the argument that if the UN forces merely restored the boundary of the 38th parallel, the North Koreans would invade again at an indeterminate date. On September 27, the president instructed his commander in the field to advance through the north unless he encountered Soviet or Chinese troops. Ten days later, the United Nations decisively approved the decision to reunify.

Truman was determined not to provoke a general war with China and/or the Soviet Union, but Douglas MacArthur, it appeared, saw the Korean campaign as an opportunity to deal communism in Asia a decisive blow. In late September, Zhou Enlai had warned India, which had become China's main link with the West, that it would not "sit back with folded hands and let the Americans come to the border." MacArthur discounted the threat and issued a demand for North Korea's unconditional surrender. On October 9, two American jets strafed a Soviet airfield near Vladivostok, the Kremlin's principal strategic outpost in the Far East. After he apologized to Moscow, Truman interrupted a campaign trip to fly to Wake Island to consult with MacArthur. With great condescension, the American commander assured Truman that the Chinese would not intervene and if they did, their forces would be cut to pieces. "We are no longer fearful of their [Chinese] intervention," the general told Truman. "They have no air force . . . [and] if the Chinese tried to get down to Pyongyang there would be the greatest slaughter." Barely reassured, the president returned to Washington, D.C. On October 16, reports that Chinese "volunteers" had crossed into North Korea to aid their comrades began to filter back to Washington, D.C.

MacArthur continued his advance toward the Yalu, the river boundary separating China and North Korea, in two widely separated columns. By November 21, American troops were within sight of Chinese sentries posted on the other side of the river. On November 21, the UN commander announced with his usual flourish the beginning of his end-the-war campaign and promised that most American soldiers would be home for Christmas. Shortly thereafter, 33 Chinese divisions crossed the Yalu and shattered his columns. Fighting the bitter cold, the mountainous terrain, and the Chinese human-wave charges, American and South Korean soldiers retreated toward the sea. Twenty thousand were captured or killed at Chosin Reservoir. Three weeks later, the front line of battle extended well below the 38th parallel, and it was Zhou Enlai's turn to talk about reunifying Korea.

By the end of January 1951, however, the Eighth Army under the direction of General Matthew Ridgeway had halted the communists' advance, and the allies began to retake the initiative. The counteroffensive, known in military parlance as Operation Killer, featured American firepower. By March, it had succeeded in retaking Seoul and reaching the 38th parallel. The president had learned his lesson, but the general had not. For weeks the "American Caesar," as historian William Manchester would dub him, had been urging a naval blockade of China, air attacks on Chinese military and industrial installations, and the utilization of Chinese Nationalist troops in Korea. Once the north had been reconquered, the allied powers should "sever Korea from Manchuria by laying a field of radioactive wastes – the byproducts of atomic manufacture – across all the major lines of enemy supply." Patiently, the administration explained that because of the Sino–Soviet alliance, such moves would risk a global conflict. To MacArthur's enragement, on March 20, the State Department began to consider a negotiated settlement of the war with the North Koreans and Chinese. Three days later, the general on his own issued a statement demanding that the communist field commanders confer with him, and he threatened to attack China's "coastal areas and interior bases" if they did not. Not content with indirect insubordination, MacArthur addressed a public letter to Representative Joseph Martin, Republican minority leader in the House, in which he called for an all-out war effort in Asia to defeat the communists and criticized "diplomats" for being willing to fight with words only. "It seems strangely difficult for some to realize that here in Asia is where the Communist conspirators have elected to make their play for global conquest ... [I]f we lose the war to communism in Asia the fall of Europe is inevitable," MacArthur observed to Martin and through him to the American people. "The son of a bitch isn't going to resign on me," the president heatedly told General Omar Bradley. "I want him fired." With the concurrence of the Joint Chiefs, Truman on April 11 relieved MacArthur of his command.

Acutely aware of General MacArthur's popularity, especially among conservatives, the Republicans prepared to blast the Democrats once more for being soft on communism and to charge the administration with not supporting its military commanders in the field. MacArthur's firing was a clear indication of the degree of communist infiltration of the federal government, Senator McCarthy declared. "How can we account for our present situation," he asked rhetorically, "unless we believe that men high in this government are concerting to deliver us to disaster?" He began referring to the nattily attired secretary of state as "the Red Dean of Fashion." The conqueror of Manila and Inchon had not been in the United States for 14 years, and the nation welcomed him as a returning hero. He made his way in a triumphal procession from San Francisco to New York, where a ticker tape parade dumped an unprecedented 16 tons of confetti on his motorcade. From there he traveled to Washington, D.C., where he addressed a joint session of Congress. It was from this lofty platform that MacArthur delivered his "old soldiers never die, they just fade away" speech.

Unfortunately for the Truman administration, the general refused to fade away. Former President Herbert Hoover declared MacArthur to be the "reincarnation of St. Paul into a great General of the Army who came out of the East." When MacArthur's greeting had run its course, two senatorial committees held inquiries in May and June of 1951 into "the military situation in the Far East and the facts surrounding the relief of General of the Army Douglas MacArthur." In his testimony, the liberator of the Philippines gave the impression that the pulling and hauling, the moving up and down the peninsula, and the inability to win a clear-cut victory was the work of pusillanimous politicians and political generals in Washington, D.C. He called for an all-out military effort to defeat communism in Asia, even to the point of full-scale war with China, because the course of events in that region would determine the course of world affairs for the "next ten thousand years." Such rhetoric had profound political implications in the prepresidential election atmosphere of 1951/1952.

In what was perhaps its finest hour, the Truman administration fought back. What was at stake, its spokesmen made clear, was not only American security interests, but also the hallowed principle of civilian control of the military. The president made it clear that the supreme commander in Korea had defied him as well as the Joint Chiefs of Staff (JCS), his direct superiors. The administration's chief witness was JCS Chairman General Omar Bradley. MacArthur had been out of the country too long, he said, and had lost sight of global strategy. "Taking on Red China," he declared at the hearings, would have led only "to a larger dead-lock at greater expense." As long as the United States regarded the Soviet Union as the principal adversary and Europe as the principal prize in the Cold War, the all-out conflict in Asia advocated by MacArthur "would involve us in the wrong war at the wrong place at the wrong time and with the wrong enemy." Gradually, the logic of the administration's argument began to take hold, and the furor over MacArthur's firing began to die away. When in June 1951, the Soviet representative to the United Nations suggested an armistice with both sides withdrawing beyond their respective sides of the 38th parallel, the U.S. government welcomed the move. Tense negotiations began at Panmunjom and dragged on through 1952. The stalemated talks became an

The Korean War 1950–1953

→ United States (United Nations) forces
⇐ North Korean forces

CHINA

Chinese intervention Oct. 1950

MANCHURIA

Yalu R.

Dandong

• Sinuiju

• Chosan

• Unsan

Kanggye •

Choshin. Res.

Taedong R.

~ Farthest U.S. advance, Oct.–Nov. 1950

Hyesanjin •
Kitchu •

• Iwon

Chongjin •

NORTH KOREA

Hungnam •

Pyongyang ⊛

Nan R.

Wonsan •

• Sariwon

38°

Haeju •
Kaesong •

Panmunjom •

⊛ Seoul

• Chunchon

Armistice Line July 27, 1953

38th Parallel

SEA OF JAPAN

U.S. landing Sept. 1950

Inchon •

Han R.

Samchok •

SOUTH KOREA

Taejon •

R.

YELLOW
SEA

Kunsan •

Naktong

• Pohang

•: Taegu

Farthest North Korean advance — Sept. 1950

Sunchon •

• Pusan

JAPAN

Tsushima •

Vladivostok

Map 2–3. The Korean War, 1950–1953.

issue in the 1952 election when the Republican candidate, General Dwight
D. Eisenhower, promised to go directly to Korea to end the war. He made
good on his promise, secretly and successfully threatening the communists
with nuclear attack if they did not agree to a compromise settlement.

The Korean War was a "limited war," a unique and frustrating byproduct of the Soviet–American nuclear stalemate as well as a civil war with
deep roots in Korean history. Although the United States possessed atomic

devices that could have been used to devastate North Korea and Communist China, it did not use them for fear of nuclear retaliation by the Soviet Union in the Far East and even Europe. Thus began a generation of covert and limited, conventional conflicts; total mobilization and a complete commitment to victory were unthinkable as long as the world lay under the threat of atomic annihilation. In a sense, however, Korea marked a clear-cut victory for the policy of containment. The United States and its allies had succeeded in "holding the line" against communist aggression. Just as the Berlin Blockade had reassured the noncommunist population of Europe that the Americans would walk the last mile with them, so too did the Korean War demonstrate to the peoples of the Far East that the United States would expend blood and treasure to defend them from the scourge of communism. What it did not solve was the issue of whether the policy of containment was capable of distinguishing between Marxism-Leninism as an economic theory and means to social justice on the one hand and Sino–Soviet imperialism on the other hand. It reinforced the fear among the peoples of developing nations that in its obsessive anticommunism the U.S. government was willing to ally itself with autocratic regimes dedicated to maintaining an unjust status quo.

NSC 68

Perhaps most important, the Korean War virtually destroyed neoisolationism and led to the globalization of containment that had been called for in the Truman Doctrine. Early in 1950, President Truman had commissioned a comprehensive statement of American interests, threats to those interests, and possible responses. The task fell to an ad hoc committee of State and Defense Department officials headed by George Kennan's successor, Paul H. Nitze. The policy statement that they fashioned, NSC 68, argued that any extension of the area under Sino–Soviet control constituted a threat to the United States. Because all points along the boundary of the communist world were of equal importance, the United States would have to implement a perimeter defense. Indeed, Nitze and his colleagues assumed that the U.S. government could not tolerate any change in the balance of power, whether it resulted from military aggression, economic dominance, or loss of credibility. The authors of NSC 68 urged their countrymen to "strike out on a bold and massive program of rebuilding the West's defensive potential to surpass that of the Soviet world" and to meet "each fresh challenge promptly and unequivocally." To deal with the threat posed by international communism, America would have to add to the stockpile of existing nuclear weapons and build the infinitely more powerful "thermonuclear" or hydrogen bomb. Underlying the recommendations of NSC 68 was the assumption that the American economy was infinitely expandable. The government would not have to resort to deficit spending or unpopular taxes to defend the "free world," Nitze and supporters declared; federal expenditures would stimulate the private sector, promoting economic growth and expanding the national tax base. "One of the most significant lessons of our World War II experience," NSC 68 pointed out, "was that the American economy, when it operates at a level approaching full efficiency, can provide enormous resources for purposes other than civilian consumption while simultaneously providing a higher standard of living." The decision in June to fight to save South Korea grew out of NSC 68 and that decision, in turn, was part of a broader diplomatic and strategic offensive that affected virtually every region of the globe.

Vietnam

During the Korean conflict, not only did the Truman administration pledge its faith to Jiang Jieshi by stationing the Seventh Fleet between Taiwan and the mainland, but it also began supplying money and material to the anticommunist government of South Vietnam. From the last quarter of the nineteenth century until the outbreak of World War II, Vietnam had been part of French Indochina, a tightly controlled colonial federation that exported millions of francs worth of rice, rubber, cocoa, opium, and other raw materials. In 1940 and 1941, Japan, an ally of Hitlerian Germany, forced occupied France to cede control of the area; thus, from 1941 to 1945, Vietnam was occupied by the Japanese. In 1941, Ho Chi Minh, a cofounder of both the French and the Vietnamese communist parties, established the Vietminh, a communist-led but broadly based insurgent movement whose goal was to rid Vietnam of foreign control, whether Japanese or French. At first, American operatives in the China–Burma–India theater supported Ho and the Vietminh and opposed French reinfiltration. But with President Roosevelt's death, the onset of the Cold War, and the perceived need to shore up metropolitan France as a bastion against Soviet aggression, the United States tacitly supported France's efforts to regain control of its lost colony. From 1946 to 1954, France and the Vietminh fought a bitter war for control of Vietnam. In an effort to portray itself as something more than a colonial power seeking to reestablish its dominance over a subject people, France in 1950 created the Republic of South Vietnam with former emperor Bao Dai as its head. Meanwhile, Ho and his followers had established the Democratic Republic of Vietnam (DRV) in the north. Although France retained control of Vietnam's treasury, trade, defense, and foreign affairs, the existence of the Bao Dai regime allowed Paris to argue that it was fighting to defend an indigenous, noncommunist republic against the Sino–Soviet puppet regime headed by Ho.

When in 1950 both Moscow and Peking recognized the DRV as the legitimate government of Vietnam, its status as an agent of communist imperialism became fixed in the minds of the Truman administration. The U.S. government extended diplomatic recognition to Bao Dai's regime and provided France with $23 million in overt military aid. All in all, during the next three years, the Truman administration would furnish Saigon and Paris with $775 million in Mutual Defense Funds with which to fight the communists. At the same time, the United States established a small Military Assistance and Advisory Group (MAAG) in Vietnam to screen French requests for aid, assist in the training of Vietnamese soldiers, and advise on strategy.

In throwing its support behind the French-backed Bao Dai regime in Vietnam, the Truman administration was reacting to concerns about the spread of communism not only in Southeast Asia but also in central Europe. Specifically, the U.S. government wanted French cooperation in the construction of a European defense community that included a rearmed Germany. Following the outbreak of the Korean War, Truman, Acheson, and the JCS became convinced of the necessity of rearming West Germany with a view to making it eventually a full-fledged NATO partner. To quiet French and British fears concerning a revival of German fascism and militarism, the United States offered to place anywhere from four to six divisions in Europe as a guarantee against future Soviet – or German – aggression. Millions of dollars of Mutual Aid funds would be available to help Europe beef up their military establishments. Finally, German military units would exist only as part of a NATO multinational military force with an American commander. Reluctantly, the British and French agreed *in principle* to West German participation on the condition that German troops constitute no more than 20% of any NATO force. On the subject of the stationing of American troops and an integrated command, they were enthusiastic. However, Congress was not.

In 1949, during testimony before the House and Senate on the NATO treaty, Secretary of State Acheson had assured legislators that it would be unnecessary to station more than a handful of American troops in Europe. When in 1950 the Truman administration asked for an additional $4 billion in defense funds and a rapid expansion of America's conventional forces, Congress agreed. In September, after Truman announced that it would be necessary to station large numbers of American troops in Europe, Senator Taft, still clinging to neoisolationism despite Korea, accused the administration of deliberate deception. Truman responded by announcing that no more than four divisions would be needed and sent Acheson to the Hill to placate rebellious representatives and senators. Carefully, the secretary of state explained the political and military necessity of sending U.S. troops to Europe. Four divisions would be sufficient, he assured the doubtful, because U.S. and NATO troops were to act as a "tripwire" producing a nuclear response in case of a Soviet thrust into Central Europe. After some debate, the Senate by a vote of 69 to 21 endorsed the administration's proposals for NATO, including the integrated command. In 1950, the administration persuaded Dwight D. Eisenhower to leave his post as president of Columbia University and become the first supreme commander of the North Atlantic alliance.

The Second Red Scare

The Korean War and the debate over European defense policy unfolded in the midst of a burgeoning domestic Red Scare in the United States. Before 1945, communism did not inspire the hysterical fear that it did afterward in large part because it was not linked to Soviet imperialism. With the onset of the Cold War, however, antipathy toward communism mounted. In response to the activities of HUAC and charges from conservatives that the Democratic administration was soft on communism, on March 21, 1947, President Truman issued Executive Order No. 9835, which mandated a loyalty investigation of each federal job applicant and made agency heads "personally responsible" for their employees' loyalty. The review process was to be carried out by the Civil Service and Federal Bureau of Investigation (FBI) but supervised by a central Loyalty Review Board. During the next five years, the Civil Service conducted more than 3,000 investigations and the FBI some 14,000 inquiries. Of 380 employees dismissed under the program, only 221 were subsequently indicted and most of these were never convicted. More significant, 2,500 individuals resigned under suspicion. Most of the cases studied involved charges of "sympathetic association" with alleged subversives or with members of organizations identified by the attorney general as subversive, rather than of sabotage or treason. Nevertheless, in the overheated atmosphere of the early Cold War, such charges were enough to ruin the individuals involved. Moreover, there was absolutely no check on the attorney general's authority to designate groups as "subversive." One constitutional authority of the day denounced the president's decree as "perhaps the most arbitrary and far-reaching power ever exercised by a single public official in the history of the United States." The presidential decree led to a massive increase in the funding and personnel of the FBI and the accumulation of hundreds of thousands of "loyalty files." To make matters worse, in 1951, President Truman modified his original executive order placing the burden of proof on the subject of the investigation rather than the investigating agency.

Still, the second Red Scare might have died aborning if it had not been for the traumatic events that occurred during 1949 and 1950. In addition to the communization of China, the Soviet Union exploded its first atomic device years ahead of when Americans anticipated that they would. Then in February 1950, Great Britain announced the arrest of noted scientist Klaus Fuchs for betraying atomic secrets to the Soviets. Fuchs had worked on the Manhattan project. Shortly after his arrest, Harry Gold, Donald Greenglass, and Julius and Ethel Rosenberg were also arrested as atomic spies. The Rosenbergs would eventually be executed for espionage. But the most celebrated spy case of the century was that of Alger Hiss, a case that drew top administration officials from the president on down into a compromising position. According to his accusers, Hiss had been a member of the Ware group, one of Washington, D.C.'s most important communist cells. Hiss was an Ivy League, establishment figure who had risen through the ranks of the Treasury and State Departments to the highest levels of government. He was considered to be a model young civil servant. In 1939, Whitaker Chambers, a former Soviet agent, had denounced Hiss for betraying his country but had failed to produce any proof. In 1948, Chambers repeated his charges before HUAC. This time the ex-spy produced microfilm of 65 documents he said Hiss had passed to him in 1938. Hiss denied these charges categorically but was indicted by a New York grand jury. Because the statute of limitations for an espionage charge had expired, the crime he was accused of was perjury. President Truman denounced the HUAC investigation as a "red herring," and State Department officials including Dean Acheson testified to Hiss's good character. Nevertheless, in January 1950, Hiss was convicted of perjury and sentenced to five years in prison. "It was the Hiss case that completely changed the public's perception of domestic communism," Richard Nixon, an otherwise obscure member of HUAC who would make a career out of red-baiting, later wrote, "People were now alerted to a serious threat to our liberties." Perhaps, but there were also other factors at work.

GOP strategists remembered that, in the spring of 1948, the Gallup poll found that 65% of the people it questioned believed that foreign policy problems were the most important issue in the campaign and 73% believed that Truman was being too easy on the Russians. Party leaders recalled that Thomas Dewey barely mentioned foreign affairs in his campaign. The lesson was clear. If the Republicans were to regain control of the White House, they would have to pillory the Democrats for being soft on communism at home and abroad. The issue would fuse former isolationists, anti–New Deal conservatives, and hard-line anticommunists into a massive coalition that would sweep the Republicans into the White House. For many, an all-out attack on Truman and Acheson as part of an anti-Red campaign had a visceral appeal. "I look at that fellow [Dean Acheson]," proclaimed a disgusted Senator Hugh Butler of Nebraska, "I watch his smart aleck manner and his British clothes and that New Dealism, everlasting New Dealism in everything he says and does, and I want to shout, Get Out! Get Out! You stand for everything that has been wrong in the United States for years."

Just as had been the case with the Salem witch trials, the American Revolution, and the Second Great Awakening, there was in the anticommunist frenzy of the early 1950s an underlying theme of class resentment or status envy. It was amazingly enough Whitaker Chambers who first identified and described that tension. "No feature of the Hiss case is more obvious or troubling as history," he wrote, "than the jagged fissure, which it did not so much open as reveal, between the plain men and women of the nation, and those who affected to act, think and speak for them. It was, not invariably, but in general, the 'best people' who were for Alger Hiss." Indeed, one prominent red-baiter labeled the movement "Americanism with its sleeves rolled up."

McCarthyism

The Hiss trial and the fears and prejudices it raised set the stage for the rise of Senator Joseph McCarthy and full-scale anticommunist hysteria in the United States. Born on a farm in central Wisconsin, McCarthy entered politics as much out of a lack of vocational alternative as anything else. As county judge, he had endured impeachment proceedings several times. Campaigning on a trumped-up war record, "Tail-Gunner Joe" won election to the Senate in 1946, defeating the eminently respectable Robert LaFollette, Jr. Joe McCarthy presented a dark, heavy-browed, menacing persona, "a truck driver in a blue serge suit," as Richard Rovere would describe him. He was a man with few moral scruples and almost no sense of personal responsibility. Early in 1950, after lunching with two of his political supporters, one of them a staunchly anticommunist Catholic, McCarthy decided that he could use the issue of communist infiltration of American institutions to revive his waning political fortunes. During the next four years, he terrified thousands of Americans through his brutal and indiscriminate attacks.

At a Lincoln's Day address before the Republican Women's Club in Wheeling, West Virginia, McCarthy announced that he had the names of 205 card-carrying communists in the State Department. It could have been 57; no one could tell because of his mumbling. At a subsequent speech, he claimed to know of 81 card carriers. Reporters asked him for proof; instead, he produced new charges. McCarthy asserted that Owen Lattimore, a professor at Johns Hopkins University and an expert on Far Eastern affairs who frequently advised the State Department, was a top espionage agent and implied that he had been responsible for America's numerous foreign policy "disasters" in East Asia. When a subsequent FBI investigation cleared Lattimore, McCarthy turned his fire on Philip Jessup, U.S. representative to the General Assembly of the United Nations.

In the spring of 1950, the Senate established a special subcommittee under Millard Tydings (D-Maryland) to investigate the charges of communist infiltration. That summer, after completing its probe, the Tydings Committee denounced McCarthy's charges as "a fraud and a hoax" that was being perpetrated on the American people. McCarthy declared the committee packed with reds and fellow travelers and continued to campaign against Tydings, who lost his bid for reelection in November 1950. McCarthyites in Maryland circulated a composite photograph (two separate and unrelated pictures cut and spliced together) showing Tydings and Earl Browder, head of the Communist Party of the United States (CPUS) in rapt conversation. The Democratic Party was, McCarthy declared, "the property of men and women... who have bent to the whispered pleas from the lips of traitors... who wear the political label stitched with the idiocy of a Truman, [and] rotted by the deceit of a Dean Acheson."

When the Republicans gained control of Congress in 1952, McCarthy became head of the Committee on Government Operations and subsequently placed himself in charge of its permanent subcommittee on investigations. Soon thereafter, he attacked the Voice of America (VOA), a subsidiary of the U.S. Information Agency, which with administration approval had been ordering the works of leftist writers for its libraries. Ironically, the VOA was a creation of the Cold War, an agency whose primary purpose was to propagandize the people of Europe on the evils of communism and the virtues of capitalism. Even though the State Department began withdrawing books from its overseas libraries that McCarthy deemed subversive, in April 1953, he dispatched committee staffers Roy M. Cohn and G. David Schine to Europe to personally investigate State Department and VOA activities. For six weeks, these two pretentious young red-baiters careened around Europe on a campaign of intimidation.

By 1953, McCarthy's ongoing "investigation" had reached into the media, the entertainment industry, and colleges and universities. Anticommunist directors, producers, and actors vied with each other to come to Washington, D.C., and denounce peers they suspected of communist sympathies. State legislatures swept up by the fervor of the witch-hunt imposed loyalty oaths on the faculties of their state universities. An estimated 500 state and local government employees lost their jobs because they were accused of disloyalty. Some 600 public school teachers and 150 college professors were similarly discharged, most of them for taking the Fifth Amendment, which protects U.S. citizens against self-incrimination. A 1955 study of higher education, entitled *Academic Freedom in Our Times*, charged that "the miasma of thought control that is now spreading over this country is the greatest menace to the United States since Hitler." Its author, Robert M. MacIver, found that no one was willing to discuss controversial issues in the classroom. Students and teachers avoided using words like "liberal," "peace," and "freedom" for fear they could be used to label them as "fellow travelers." In 1951, writing in the *American Scholar*, Professor Laurence Sears warned that "there is a fear that we are losing two of the basic rights we have long cherished – the right of dissent and the right to a fair trail."

Blacklists, usually the products of gossip and innuendo, ruined the careers of dozens of journalists, particularly in the broadcast field, as well as those of actors, writers, and directors. The Motion Picture Association of America ruled that blacklisted Oscar nominees were not eligible for an award, a ban that remained in effect until 1959. Indeed, by 1953, if not before, the search for communists and fellow travelers had become so widespread that McCarthy the man had been transformed into McCarthyism, the movement.

The forces and factors responsible for the second Red Scare are numerous and complex. It was foremost a product of the anxieties of the early Cold War. Even the establishment authors of NSC 68 noted that, as a free society, the United States was operating at a disadvantage in waging the Cold War and that, paradoxically, the federal government might have to curtail freedoms in order to save them. Frustrated by the fall of China and the stalemate in Korea, faced with the possibility of nuclear annihilation, Americans searched for excuses and scapegoats. Convinced of their invincibility and omnipotence, they found an excuse for their inability to win a complete victory over communism in the guise of traitors burrowing from within. Scapegoating became a mass phenomenon.

McCarthyism also emerged as part of a Republican effort to defeat a Democratic administration. Normally intelligent and dignified Republicans such as Robert Taft and Everett Dirksen (R-Illinois), frustrated by the election of 1948 and determined to damage the Democrats in whatever way possible, stood in the wings and cheered on McCarthy. The threat of communist subversion was the perfect political issue, reconciling, as Bertrand Russell once noted, the two principal fears of Americans – taxes and communism. If American reverses abroad were due to betrayal at home, there was no need for huge new expenditures on defense and foreign aid. All that was required was a domestic house cleaning. In this same vein, McCarthyism appealed to former isolationists, particularly German and Irish Americans and to many Catholics who were particularly worried about "godless communism."

Finally, the second Red Scare was a manifestation of the nativist movement that had raised its head throughout America's history. In June 1952, over President Truman's veto, Congress passed the McCarran–Walter Act, which kept in place and tightened the national origins quotas established in 1920 to control and limit immigration. Yet, public opinion polls showed that McCarthyism was not a mass movement, appealing at its height to only a minority of Americans. The majority, however, showed themselves to be markedly unconcerned about the issue of civil liberties and, in the context of the Cold War, were willing to give the inquisitors the benefit of the doubt.

McCarthy's descent occurred even more rapidly than his rise. During the course of his investigation into an alleged spy ring in the Signal Corps at Ft. Monmouth, New Jersey, the junior senator from Wisconsin came across the case of Dr. Irving Peress, a New York dentist drafted during the Korean War. McCarthy charged that the army had promoted Peress to the rank of major and given him an honorable discharge despite the fact that he had taken the Fifth Amendment when being questioned about his allegedly communist activities. He demanded that the names of all people connected with the Peress case be turned over to him. When Secretary of the Army Robert Stevens refused, McCarthy vented his spleen on General Ralph Zwicker, commandant of Camp Kilmer, where Peress had been inducted. Zwicker refused to criticize his superiors or to discuss security procedures in the Army, whereupon McCarthy denounced him as a disgrace to the uniform and observed that he did not have the brains of a five-year-old child. Typically, President Dwight D. Eisenhower denounced McCarthy's bullying tactics while declaring that the Peress case had been mishandled. Eventually, Stevens was forced to turn over Army files and permit military officers and civilian employees to appear before the committee.

At the same time, Stevens and the U.S. Army counterattacked, filing 29 charges against McCarthy; the committee counsel, Roy Cohn; and others. Among other things, the Army charged that the committee had sought a commission and special treatment for Schine, who had been drafted, and had threatened to redouble its investigation if the military did not comply. McCarthy responded with 46 charges of his own, including the allegation that the Army had tried to divert the committee's attention to other branches of the armed services and that it was holding Schine hostage. From April 22 through June 17,1954, hearings were held by the Senate Committee on Government Operations, with Karl Mundt (R-South Dakota) in the chair.

As usual, McCarthy managed to dominate the proceedings, although it was he who was on trial. For 13 days, he browbeat Stevens as a rapt national audience watched on television. McCarthy constantly interrupted witnesses, making insinuating comments or shouting, "Point of order." When the Wisconsin senator implied that a young associate of Army counsel Joseph Welch's was a communist sympathizer, Welch expressed the disgust felt by much of the committee and most of the onlookers by asking rhetorically, "Have you no sense of decency, sir, at long last?" Technically, neither the Army nor McCarthy emerged victorious from the hearings, but the grand inquisitor had clearly lost. A Gallup poll revealed at the close of the hearings that McCarthy's approval rating had dropped to 35%. He had at last become a liability to the Republican Party.

On July 30, 1954, Senator Ralph Flanders, an elderly Republican from Vermont, introduced a resolution calling for McCarthy's removal from the Committee on Government Operations. The Wisconsin senator was as defiant as ever. Acknowledging that he sometimes played hardball, he declared that "as long as I am in the United States Senate ... I don't intend to treat traitors like gentlemen." But the aura of fear and impregnability that for so long surrounded him had began to crumble. Flanders openly ridiculed him: "He dons his war paint ... goes into his war dance ... emits war whoops. He goes forth to battle and proudly returns with the scalp of a pink dentist." The distinguished television journalist Edward R. Murrow ran a series of film clips on his show, "See It Now," showing McCarthy at his worst. As the opposition to McCarthy began to coalesce around Flanders, he and his supporters changed their proposal to a resolution of censure. A select committee of six members headed by the respected Arthur Watkins (R-Utah) heard the charges against McCarthy, all of which centered on the abuse of power. After months of intermittent debate and frantic parliamentary maneuvering by McCarthy and his supporters, the Senate voted on March 2, 1955, in favor of censure. McCarthy's star declined rapidly thereafter. He remained in the Senate, but his power was gone. He died, allegedly of cirrhosis of the liver, in 1955.

The Heritage of Fear

The Cold War and the second Red Scare dominated and distorted intellectual life in America during the late 1940s and 1950s. Most intellectuals were anti-Stalinist, but they were also civil libertarians, deeply committed to the principle of free speech. As East and West fashioned alliance systems and armed to the teeth, and as McCarthy warned against penetration of American institutions by a communist fifth column, activist intellectuals faced a dilemma. How could they defend the right of all Americans, including members of the CPUS, to organize and speak freely without the intelligentsia being labeled soft on communism and forfeiting its political influence? This dilemma was particularly compelling for members of the Americans for Democratic Action (ADA).

An intensely anti-Stalinist organization, the ADA consisted of former New Dealers, labor leaders, civil libertarians, and academics. ADA members had agreed with Henry Wallace and the Progressives about the need to hammer out a full employment policy; ensure comprehensive civil rights for African Americans; provide food, shelter, health care, and education to the disadvantaged; and combat McCarthyism. However, they disagreed with the progressives on the issue of the Soviet Union. Wallace and many of his supporters assumed that communist Russia was evolving toward authentic social democracy; the principal threat to that process, the progressives insisted, was the policy of containment, the brainchild of various reactionary forces in the West. If only the United States and its allies would adopt a strategy of peaceful coexistence, the progressives argued, the United States and the USSR would gradually converge, America moving toward socialism and the Soviet Union toward democracy. The ADA, however, viewed the Soviet leadership as a collection of brutal tyrants who had distorted and manipulated the democratic ideas of Karl Marx. The creation and maintenance of a one-party state through massive coercion was the antithesis of liberalism, they argued.

Under the Smith Act, the conviction of 11 officials of the CPUS for advocating the violent overthrow of the U.S. government deeply divided the membership of the ADA. Some feared that if the organization defended the right of communists and fellow travelers to speak their mind, they would be labeled "soft on communism" and, in the overheated atmosphere of the second Red Scare, marginalized politically. The majority decided, however, that the constitutional principles of freedom of speech and association were too important to abandon. They publicly denounced the Smith Act, Hollywood and media blacklists, and loyalty oaths for college professors as infringements on civil liberties and defended the right of all citizens, even members of the CPUS, to air their views, no matter how "un-American" they might seem. At the same time, the ADA led the way in supporting the Truman Doctrine, Marshall Plan, the Berlin Blockade, and other measures designed to contain communists. Indeed, liberal intellectuals' defense of civil liberties in the midst of the second Red Scare probably made them more militant cold warriors than they otherwise would have been.

Because they were the sparkplugs of reform, the heart and soul of liberalism in America, the choices that activist intellectuals made during the early years of the Cold War were crucial to the history of postwar America. In effect, to maintain their credibility with an intensely anticommunist public and to contain Soviet communism, liberal intellectuals joined the ranks of the cold warriors. As a result, a powerful coalition emerged in the United States – one committed to fighting communism on every front, to use historian Thomas Paterson's phrase. Conservative anticommunists preoccupied with markets and bases backed by a mushrooming military–industrial complex argued that the only way America could be safe in a hostile world was to dominate that world through a network of alliances and overseas bases, and through possession of the largest nuclear arsenal in the world. Joining them were liberal internationalists, many of whom were intellectuals and domestic reformers who saw America's welfare tied to that of the other members of the international community. To a degree, they supported alliances and military aid, but in addition, the liberal internationalists wanted to eliminate the social and economic turmoil that they perceived to be a breeding ground for Marxism and an invitation to Soviet imperialism. They wanted nothing less than to spread the blessings of liberty, democracy, and free enterprise around the world, and to guarantee stability and prosperity to peoples threatened by communist imperialism. The blending of these two strains led to the creation of an empire the likes of which had not been seen since Rome ruled the world.

ADDITIONAL READINGS

Caute, David, *The Great Fear* (1977).
Cumings, Bruce, *The Origins of the Korean War, 1945–1947* (1981).
Cumings, Bruce, *The Roaring of the Cataract, 1947–1952* (1990).

Gaddis, John Lewis, *The United States and the Origins of the Cold War* (1972).

Griffith, Robert, *The Politics of Fear* (1970).

Herken, Gregg, *The Winning Weapon: The Atomic Bomb in the Cold War, 1945–1950* (1980).

Hogan, Michael, *The Marshall Plan: America, Britain, and the Reconstruction of Western Europe, 1947–1952* (1987).

Iriye, Akira, *The Cold War in Asia* (1974).

Kauffman, Burton I., *The Korean War* (1986).

Leffler, Melvyn P., *A Preponderance of Power: The Truman Administration and the Cold War* (1991).

Reeves, Thomas C., *The Life and Times of Joe McCarthy* (1982).

Schaller, Michael, *Douglas MacArthur: The Far Eastern General* (1989).

Sherwin, Martin J., *A World Destroyed: The Atomic Bomb and the Grand Alliance* (1975).

Stueck, William, *The Korean War: An International History* (1995).

Woods, Randall B., and Jones, Howard, *Dawning of the Cold War: The United States' Quest for Order* (1991).

Yergin, Daniel, *Shattered Peace: The Origins of the Cold War and the National Security State* (1977).

3   Staying the Course

Dwight D. Eisenhower and the Politics
of Moderation

In 1952, the American people elected a Republican president, bringing an end to 20 years of democratic rule. The era of Dwight David Eisenhower had begun. Political rhetoric notwithstanding, there was far more continuity than conflict between the programs of the Roosevelt–Truman and Eisenhower administrations. In fact, the goal of Eisenhower's modern Republicanism was to consolidate the economic and social gains of the New Deal and the Fair Deal. Despite differences in emphasis, both the Democratic and the Republican parties, at least their centers, were committed to the "politics of productivity," to use Charles Maier's phrase. Truman and Roosevelt's language and policies emphasized social welfare but depended on the economic activity of the private sector to generate revenues for existing and envisioned programs. Truman, similar to Eisenhower, viewed the successful businessperson as the quintessential American and saw government as the servant rather than the master of the private sector. Also similar to Eisenhower, both Democratic presidents were deeply suspicious of deficit spending and committed to a balanced budget. There were differences in emphasis. For example, Eisenhower recognized that the Depression had accentuated the natural divisions among labor, management, and capital and that the New Deal and the Fair Deal had grown out of these antagonisms. He and the architects of the New Republicanism were convinced that under normal circumstances capitalism would steadily elevate members of the working class into the middle class; that is, a rising tide would lift all boats. Eisenhower and the Republicans were determined to use the power of government to help the private sector flood the United States with prosperity, whereas Truman and the Democrats assumed the vitality of the capitalist system but believed that government ought to help relatively disadvantaged groups – such as laborers, the elderly, and farmers – compete with business for a fair share of the fruits of that system. With the possible exception of agriculture, these "interest groups," to use Eisenhower's terminology, did not enjoy new gains but neither did they suffer setbacks. The phrase coined by historian

Charles Alexander a generation ago to describe the era – "holding the line" – continues to be appropriate.

A Changing of the Guard: The Election of 1952

The political climate in 1952 seemed even more favorable to the Republicans than it was in 1948. The American people were in an ugly mood. While peace negotiations remained deadlocked at Panmunjom, the bloody fighting in Korea continued. Business and labor kicked against the wage and price controls that the war had necessitated, and everyone chafed at wartime taxes. Many Americans had come to view the Truman administration as venal and corrupt, soft on the issue of domestic communist infiltration, and responsible directly or indirectly for the loss of China. The world was in a mess, the country was in a mess, and the man from Missouri was responsible. However, Republican leaders were haunted by the election of 1948. Determined not to underestimate Truman or the Democrats, they searched desperately for a candidate who could recapture 1600 Pennsylvania Avenue for the Republican Party. Senator Robert Taft emerged from his smashing 1950 reelection as the unchallenged Republican leader in Congress, as well as the chief representative of conservatives and neo-isolationists across the United States. The Ohioan spoke for the Midwest and the South, for those who wanted to reduce the size of the federal government, cut taxes, balance the budget, leave social reform to private charities, and promote free enterprise, or at least aggrandizement of the private sector. Given the backlash against "metooism," Taft seemed certain to wrest control of the party from the eastern, liberal wing that had controlled it since 1940. Yet, Thomas Dewey, John Foster Dulles, and Henry Cabot Lodge still represented those Republicans committed to keeping a social safety net in place and combating communism through alliances and foreign aid rather than by means of a domestic witchhunt. The liberal Republicans desperately needed a candidate. Dewey would not suffice because he was a two-time loser. Thus, they turned in desperation to General Dwight David Eisenhower, president of Columbia University on leave and supreme commander of NATO.

Eisenhower was loath to express an interest in politics while in uniform. He believed, as H. W. Brands has written, that it "would smack of Caesarism, or at least MacArthurism." In fact, he was suspicious of democratic politics as practiced at the national level and was repulsed by what he perceived to be the petty selfishness of the masses. An outspoken admirer of Herbert Hoover, he once dismissed the fears of working Americans with the taunt "If all they want is security, they can go to prison." Nevertheless, he followed political events in the United States closely during 1951 and that fall gave his backers significant, although limited, encouragement. Eisenhower won the New Hampshire primary in March and did well in

Minnesota against its favorite son, Harold Stassen, who was on the ballot as a write-in candidate. On April 12, to the relief of his supporters, Eisenhower announced that he would resign his NATO command in June and return to the United States to campaign actively for the nomination. He was particularly concerned that a Taft victory would lead to a dangerous isolationist resurgence. Given the weapons of modern warfare and the dimensions of the Sino–Soviet menace, there would be no time to rearm and recover as there had been prior to American entry into World War II. Naively, Eisenhower continued to believe that the nomination would seek him. The strength and aggressive tactics of the Taft Republicans quickly shattered that illusion. They scoffed at Eisenhower as a superficial candidate who stood for nothing more than "mother, home, and heaven." "Draft Ike," the Taft Republicans cried in a none-too-subtle allusion to the general's support of universal military service, "and he will draft you." In time-honored fashion, they circulated scurrilous stories concerning a wartime affair between Eisenhower and his British driver, Kay Summersby. A delegation from one Midwestern state even visited Abilene, Kansas, Eisenhower's hometown, to ask him if his wife, Mamie, was an alcoholic.

As the Republican National Convention opened, Taft appeared to be slightly ahead of Eisenhower in delegate count, but a number of seats were contested. During the preconvention campaign, Lodge, Eisenhower's campaign manager, complained that state party organizations controlled by Taftites were unfairly excluding individuals from their state delegations who were elected by pro-Eisenhower local and state conventions. Shortly after the gavel came down in Chicago, Eisenhower's forces won a key victory. By a vote of 658 to 548, the convention passed the so-called Fair Play Resolution, according to which no delegate whose seat was contested could vote on the credentials of another delegate. The key votes were provided by the California delegation. Senator Richard M. Nixon had intervened with his fellows in behalf of Eisenhower, thereby ensuring himself of the vice presidential nomination. Lodge used this provision successfully to challenge the Taftite delegations from Texas, Georgia, and Louisiana. The formal vote was anticlimactic, and Eisenhower went over the top on the first ballot.

On March 29, Truman announced that he would not be a candidate. He then attempted to draft Governor Adlai E. Stevenson of Illinois, but the articulate, sophisticated Stevenson demurred. Consequently, when the Democrats convened, also in Chicago, the nomination was still up for grabs. The Truman forces again turned to Stevenson who finally consented to run. Stevenson won on the third ballot, and Senator John J. Sparkman of Alabama, one of the architects of a compromise civil rights plank designed to prevent a Southern bolt, was chosen as his running mate. The Democratic platform demanded a repeal of the Taft–Hartley Act, enactment of a full civil rights program including a Fair Employment Practices

Commission (FEPC), and maintenance of high price supports for farmers. Stevenson initially attracted most groups in the New Deal coalition, but not the crucial Midwestern farm vote. The farmers were sick of the Korean War and refused to support a candidate tainted by association with the administration that had intervened.

On September 12, in an effort to appease the right wing of the Republican Party, General Eisenhower staged a highly publicized meeting with Senator Taft where he signed "articles of cooperation" that had been drawn up by "Mr. Republican." The two men agreed on the need for fiscal responsibility in the running of the federal government, including balancing the budget, and promised to defend liberty and free enterprise against "creeping socialism." By October, Eisenhower had opened up on Democratic policies and the president personally, relying on a formula that Senator Karl Mundt referred to as K_1C_2 – Korea, communism, and corruption. Although Senator McCarthy had repeatedly libeled Eisenhower's hero and mentor, General George Marshall, the general endorsed the Wisconsin demagogue's reelection bid and blasted the Truman administration for its lackluster performance in rooting communist sympathizers out of the federal government. Casting caution to the wind, Eisenhower charged that Truman and Acheson's blunderings had helped cause the Korean War. He promised that, if elected, he would visit the battlefield and bring the war to an "early and honorable" end. He even embraced the conservative, contradictory Republican platform, which simultaneously promised to liberate captive nations behind the Iron Curtain and questioned the need to aid Western Europe. Meanwhile, a united Republican Party was bombarding the Democrats with one of the most well-financed campaigns the country had ever seen.

The Democratic campaign featured a series of articulate, witty television addresses by Governor Stevenson. A man of refined taste, he was intelligent, polished, sophisticated, literate, and self-deprecating. He was also wealthy, divorced, and cosmopolitan – a thoroughly modern man who was filled with self-doubt. As Eisenhower stepped up his attacks, Stevenson's sister, Elizabeth "Buffie" Ives, informed her brother that he "would have to start slugging harder now" and focus on his opponents' shortcomings. "Oh dear, really?" was his reply. Stevenson and other Democratic campaigners tried to portray the general as an unqualified innocent, while somewhat contradictorily attempting to raise the specter of militarization of the civilian sector. Actually, Stevenson was relatively conservative on domestic policy; he disagreed with the president on federal aid for education and he failed to support the administration on repeal of Taft–Hartley, the Brannan Plan, and public housing. Although he paid lip service to civil rights, the Democratic candidate steadfastly maintained that they were the responsibility of the states, the very position traditionally taken by southern segregationists. Stevenson understood that the advent of prosperity and the passage of time had made the class conflict rhetoric of the 1930s anachronistic. His witticisms – "if the Republicans will stop telling lies about us, we will stop telling the truth about them" – nevertheless endeared him to liberals and intellectuals. Unfortunately for Stevenson, the average voter belonged to neither category.

The only major obstacle in the path of the Eisenhower juggernaut involved Republican vice presidential candidate Richard Nixon. On September 18, the *New York Post*, one of the few pro-Stevenson daily newspapers in the United States, reported that for some time Nixon had been the beneficiary of a "secret fund" of more than $18,000 raised by a group of wealthy Californians and that Nixon had regularly drawn on the account for his personal use. Pressure mounted on Eisenhower to dump his running mate; the general's reaction was a combination of self-righteousness and pragmatism. Everyone in his campaign, he told reporters, had to be "clean as a hound's tooth." Then he simply waited; days passed and the "Nixon slush fund" became increasingly more of a cause célèbre. When Eisenhower finally telephoned, Nixon could not contain his anger and resentment. "There comes a time in matters like this," he scolded Eisenhower, "when you've either got to shit or get off the pot." Stifling his anger at what he considered to be Nixon's impertinence, the general told him to explain the situation to the American people. Based on the public's reaction, he would then decide.

On the evening of September 23 with his wife, Pat, on the dais with him, Nixon addressed a national television audience. One wag later noted that the setting, the El Capitan theater in Hollywood, was entirely appropriate. The accused was in turn defensive, aggressive, and deferential. Pat did not own a mink coat, he told his fellow Americans, only a plain "Republican cloth coat." The family had received a present from a charitable Texan, a cocker spaniel named Checkers, but the children had become attached to it and "we're gonna keep it." He was absolutely innocent, he said, but whatever happened, he was going to continue to fight against "the crooks, the communists, and those that defend them." To liberals and Democrats, the Checkers speech seemed a maudlin, disgusting display, but to the typical working man, it portrayed Nixon as an "average Joe" fighting to preserve traditional American values. Eisenhower summoned Nixon to his campaign stop at Wheeling, West Virginia, and publicly embraced him. Nixon would never forget that the general had left him hanging, however, and Eisenhower could never rid himself of the suspicion that Nixon was a political sleazebag.

Ike and Dick fought hard to avert a last-minute swing to Stevenson. The vice presidential candidate was at his red-baiting best, or worst, denouncing Stevenson as "Adlai the appeaser with a Ph.D. from Dean Acheson's College of Cowardly Communist Containment." The swing did not materialize: Eisenhower swamped his opponent 33 to 27 million in the popular vote (55.4% to 44.4%), the heaviest turnout since 1908. Ike won 442

Table 3–1. The election of 1952

Candidates	Parties	Electoral vote	Popular vote	Percentage of popular vote
Dwight D. Eisenhower	Republican	442	33,936,234	55.1
Adlai E. Stevenson	Democratic	89	27,314,992	44.4

electoral votes to Stevenson's 89. In the end, not only Midwestern farmers but also other important elements of the New Deal coalition deserted the Democrats. Catholics alienated by Stevenson's divorce, and Eastern European ethnic groups angered by the Democrats failure to "roll back" the Iron Curtain voted Republican. Eisenhower broke the solid South carrying Virginia, Florida, Tennessee, and Texas. African Americans were the only group that gave Stevenson as high a percentage of its vote as it had given Truman four years earlier. But the most important factor in the election was Eisenhower's personal popularity. The general ran an amazing 19% ahead of other Republican candidates in 1952. The Republicans gained 22 House seats, giving them a majority of 3, but added only 1 Senate seat. Nevertheless, that seat allowed the GOP to organize the upper house as well as the lower.

Eisenhower and Modern Republicanism

Dwight Eisenhower, the third of seven sons, was born on August 14, 1890, in Denison, Texas. Soon after Dwight's birth, his father quit his job in a railroad yard and moved the family to Abilene, Kansas, where he took a job in a local creamery. Abilene was then still something of a frontier community, and young Eisenhower absorbed the small town American values of independence and hard work. Ike proved to be an excellent athlete, excelling in football, and a diligent student. He won appointment to West Point and after graduation decided to make the military his career. Disappointingly, Eisenhower spent World War I stateside as a tank instructor. Indeed, for him the high point of the war was his marriage to Mamie Dowd, the daughter of a well-to-do Denver businessman. In 1926, Eisenhower graduated first in a class of 275 in the army's elite Command and General Staff School. As a result, he was elevated to the War Department during the Hoover administration and then served on Douglas MacArthur's staff in both Washington, D.C., and the Philippines. His knack for planning and coordination caught George Marshall's eye, and after the attack on Pearl Harbor, he brought Brigadier General Eisenhower back to Washington, D.C., to be his chief of operations. The following year, Ike made major general and assumed command of all U.S. forces in Europe. His career climaxed in 1944 when he was named supreme commander of all Allied forces in the European theater and given overall charge of the Normandy invasion. The success of that operation and subsequent campaigns in France and Germany cemented Eisenhower's role as one of the war's true heroes. He returned to the United States in 1945 as a five-star general.

Eisenhower entered the White House with some serious handicaps. No president since Zachary Taylor had had less exposure to civilian life, and Taylor's example was not encouraging. A lifetime in the military had narrowed Eisenhower's intellectual horizons and accustomed him to hierarchy and command rather than the subtleties and compromises of politics. For years political commentators and historians, most of them liberals, would portray Eisenhower as a simple-minded man incapable of fine distinctions and uninterested in the mastery and exercise of power. There was no doubt that Ike was "standard American," almost to the point of caricature. He liked westerns, bourbon, bridge and poker, golf, fishing, gardening, and hunting. His admiration of the successful businessman was so unabashed that it reminded historians uneasily of U. S. Grant.

Yet, it was as a military politician rather than as a blood-and-guts field commander or strategist that Eisenhower had made his mark. The Normandy invasion succeeded because the supreme commander was able to gain the confidence of diverse and contentious personalities and to reconcile their divergent interests. He was a genius at coordination and conciliation, while pursuing a grand objective. When he came to the presidency, he knew how to direct vast projects, was willing to shoulder huge responsibilities, and was familiar with modern bureaucracies. A committed internationalist, he was particularly at home in the realm of foreign affairs. As political scientist Fred Greenstein has observed, Eisenhower was able to combine the frequently contradictory roles of chief of state with party leader better than any other postwar president. In public he strove to avoid partisanship, identifying himself with the "national interest," while behind the scenes he worked skillfully to achieve his objectives through persuasion and compromise. That the goals of this "hidden-hand" presidency were frequently to prevent change made Eisenhower no less of an activist.

In domestic affairs, Eisenhower's views smacked strongly of orthodox Republicanism: devotion to free enterprise and a balanced budget, and a distrust of big government. Yet, unlike many right-wing Republicans, he had no desire to dismantle any and every social program. Eisenhower believed that the New Deal and Fair Deal were deplorable because they were nothing more than the opportunistic accommodation of various interest groups – labor, farmers, the elderly, African Americans – who put selfish interest above the common good. He acknowledged the need for federal programs for the dependent and disadvantaged, but Roosevelt and Truman had gone too far, creating the expectation among all Americans that the government would take care of them if they were unwilling or unable to take care of themselves. He sought instead to keep military spending in check, encourage private initiative as much as possible, and keep federal activities to the bare minimum. Labeling his position "Modern Republicanism," he claimed that he was "conservative when it comes to money and liberal when it comes to human beings." It quickly became apparent that the new president's model was the successful businessman. Similar to Herbert Hoover in the 1920s, Eisenhower extolled the virtues of a corporate economy and declared that the federal government should concentrate on promoting cooperation among private interests for the common good.

Not surprisingly, Eisenhower was a firm believer in good organization and in the delegation of authority to skilled subordinates. He established a White House staff system to act as a policy clearinghouse, naming former New Hampshire governor Sherman Adams "assistant to the president." The members of the Cabinet also assumed large policy-making roles. First among equals was Secretary of State John Foster Dulles. Two prominent corporate executives, George Humphrey and Charles Wilson, headed the Treasury and Defense Departments, respectively. Humphrey was an arch-conservative Cleveland industrialist who was fiercely devoted to the interests of business, large and small. He entered office determined to cut taxes, balance the budget, and free the private sector from federal "red tape." He was also blatantly anti-intellectual; within two years, he had virtually denuded the Treasury Department of economists. As secretary of defense, the new president selected Charles E. Wilson, former chief operating officer of General Motors. An engineer by training, Wilson would make the famous observation that "what was good for the country was good for GM and vice versa." Ezra Taft Benson, a farm marketing specialist and elder in the Mormon Church, became agriculture secretary. Benson's solution to farm problems was simple and straightforward: eliminate government price subsidies and subject farm products to a strict free market mechanism. Eisenhower would privately chafe at Benson's blunt, confrontational style, but he stuck with him through thick and thin. Herbert Brownell, a New York lawyer and close political ally of Governor Dewey, became attorney general. Martin Durkin of the Plumbers and Steamfitters Union was chosen to head the Labor Department. The predominance of wealth on the new cabinet caused one observer to describe Eisenhower's team as "eight millionaires and a plumber."

Farmers, Workers, and the Economy

First on Secretary Humphrey's list of priorities was reduction of taxes and elimination of the federal deficit. Not for nothing had he restored the portrait of Andrew Mellon, the high priest of fiscal conservatism and laissez faire under Presidents Harding and Coolidge, to a place of prominence in the Treasury Department. Eisenhower ordered an immediate end to federal wage, price, and rent controls that had been installed during the Korean

War and, when the Reconstruction Finance Commission's charter expired in 1953, the administration did not seek to renew it. Tax reductions for individuals and corporations went into effect January 1, 1954, and Eisenhower submitted a budget that cut spending for fiscal year 1954 by $6.5 billion over the previous year. Savings were achieved by reducing spending in the areas of foreign aid and defense, among others. In sum, 200,000 civilian employees were removed from federal payrolls during Eisenhower's first term. At the same time, the Federal Reserve Board raised interest rates and reserve requirements.

In response to these deflationary policies, the economy went into a sharp recession. To their dismay, fiscal conservatives in the administration learned that reduced federal expenditures coupled with deflationary policies slowed rather than accelerated economic growth. Moreover, reduced tax collections that accompanied the downturn, coupled with tax cuts, so constricted federal income that balancing the budget became increasingly less possible. With Humphrey complaining and finally resigning in 1957, the Eisenhower administration followed a flexible policy for the rest of the 1950s. In effect, the administration admitted that expenditures for national defense, foreign aid, and social welfare, along with annual outlays such as farm subsidies, could not be reduced below certain levels. This held true not only for social and political reasons, but also for fiscal reasons.

Despite two recessions, one minor and one major, the 1950s were one of the most prosperous decades in American history. The economy grew at an annual rate of 4%, while inflation remained at less than 2%. As of 1960, a record high 66.5 million Americans were employed, and unemployment averaged less that 5% throughout the 1950s. Between 1947 and 1960, real income (adjusted for inflation) increased 29%. A number of factors contributed to this prodigious economic growth. The Eisenhower administration's willingness to learn the lessons of modern budgeting allowed prosperity to take its course. Public spending also played a fundamental role in the boom. A steady increase in defense spending offset cuts in other areas of the national budget. At the same time, state and local expenditures rose steadily from 7% of the gross national product (GNP) to 9.4% by 1960. There was in addition a dramatic increase in private credit during this period. Between 1939 and 1960, mortgage and installment indebtedness grew by a factor of five. Most important, perhaps, was the fundamental health of the American private sector, regulated in the public interest yet free to innovate and expand.

Unfortunately, farmers did not share in the general prosperity of the 1950s. Initially, the administration acted on the premise that what agriculture needed was a good dose of classical economics. Secretary Benson was committed to private enterprise on the farm for ideological reasons, and also because he believed it was the solution to the chronic problems of overproduction and declining prices. To his way of thinking, high, rigid price supports – 90% of parity (a relationship between farm costs and farm income set during an earlier, relatively prosperous period) – had induced farmers to produce more than the nation and the world could consume. In a vicious circle, the more the federal government spent to support prices, the more farmers produced, and the lower prices fell, compelling the government to shoulder an even larger burden. Following a heated battle in Congress, the administration managed to have the principle of flexible price supports incorporated into the Agricultural Act of 1954 – 82.5% to 90% of parity for 1956 and the years following. When farm surpluses and government costs continued to mount in the face of the new program, the administration tried a New Deal approach. In 1956, in an effort to curtail production and drive up prices, the government offered to pay farmers to put a certain percentage of their acreage in a "soil bank" each year. The scheme would serve a double purpose: allow the soil to replenish its nutrients and reduce total farm output. Once again, however, modern technology and the ingenuity of the American farmer combined to defeat the plan. Focusing on their most fertile acreage, farmers used scientific farming techniques and chemical fertilizers to produce more on fewer acres. As a result, by 1958 the federal government was spending more than ever on price supports.

President Eisenhower did not share the Taft Republicans' hostility to organized labor. In fact, unions flourished during the 1950s. Taft–Hartley had restricted the activities of unions but had not interfered with American labor's basic right to organize and bargain collectively for wages and benefits. In early 1955, the Congress of Industrial Organizations (CIO) and American Federation of Labor (AFL) merged, creating a combined membership of 15 million and marking an end to the traditional hostility between industrial and craft unions. Later that year, the United Auto Workers negotiated revolutionary contracts with Ford and General Motors that guaranteed workers a certain percentage of the wages they were then earning even if there were layoffs. In the years that followed, unions built on this model, adding benefits such as profit sharing, extended vacation time, and expanded medical benefits. Wages more than kept pace with inflation during the 1950s and, with the exception of two extended strikes in the steel industry, the American workplace remained tranquil during the Eisenhower era. There were clouds on the horizon – employment and wage levels were increasingly tied to military spending, union bureaucracies were becoming increasingly corrupt and unresponsive to their memberships, and jobs grew fastest in geographical and occupational areas hostile to unionization – but these were distant clouds.

Buoyed by their successes at the bargaining table and by their increasing acceptability to the American public, union leaders became almost as concerned with their public image as corporate executives. The vast majority was made up of cold warriors and ardent supporters of regulated capitalism. When evidence of corruption in the International Longshoreman's Association (ILA) and the International Brotherhood of Teamsters came to light, AFL–CIO leaders actively cooperated with the Eisenhower administration in its campaign to clean up these organizations. In 1953, the New York State Crime Commission revealed that the ILA was dominated by racketeers who regularly terrorized dock workers. The AFL immediately expelled the ILA and moved to establish a separate organization. Four years later, a Senate special committee with young Robert Kennedy as its chief counsel investigated the Teamsters. It found that President Dave Beck and his lieutenants regularly rigged elections and used union pension funds to operate casinos and brothels. The AFL voted to expel the 2.5 million members of the organization and by 1959 Beck was in prison. The Teamsters remained recalcitrant, however, and James R. Hoffa, a Beck protégé, succeeded to the leadership of the union. In a series of bruising encounters with Kennedy, Hoffa made it clear that he and his followers would continue to run the Teamsters as they saw fit.

Partially as a result of these revelations, in 1959 Congress passed the Landrum–Griffin labor bill. The measure, whose chief sponsor was John F. Kennedy (D-Massachusetts), required unions to report publicly on the disposition of funds and to hold secret ballots to determine union representation. The AFL–CIO applauded these provisions but denounced certain sections – added at the insistence of anti-union conservatives – that restricted secondary boycotts and gave states greater control over unions. President Eisenhower endorsed the Landrum–Griffin bill, lauding especially its anticorruption provisions.

Redefining Federal Power

As Republicans had been doing since the very beginning of the New Deal, Eisenhower railed against the encroachment of federal bureaucrats on businesses large and small. He appointed as chairman of the Federal Trade Commission (FTC) a person who had spent his entire career defending corporate clients from the agency. In 1956, when Senator J. William Fulbright (D-Arkansas) and Congressman Fred Harris (D-Oklahoma) introduced a bill in the Senate exempting the price of natural gas from regulation by the Interstate Commerce Commission (ICC), the administration threw its support behind it. The White House and Commerce Department declared that the measure would stimulate the production and facilitate the distribution of this abundant fuel. During the ensuing debate, natural gas consumers – most of them residing in the populous cities of the Midwest and Northeast – began to complain that the deregulation bill was a conspiracy by the giant energy companies to raid their pocketbooks. Eisenhower immediately began to look for an excuse not to sign the measure. During the Senate's deliberations, Republican Francis Case of South Dakota had disclosed that a lawyer for the gas interests had offered him a $2,500 bribe. No one had paid much attention at the time, and the Fulbright–Harris bill had passed both houses by a wide margin. Citing the Case incident, however, Eisenhower declared the natural gas bill to be the product of "arrogant" lobbying methods and sent the measure back to Congress on February 17 with a stinging veto.

If he was unable to lend a helping hand to the giant energy companies and the states that hosted them in the matter of deregulation of natural gas prices, Eisenhower was more successful in the controversial tidelands issue. Since the discovery of huge and immensely rich oil deposits off their coasts, California and the Gulf Coast states had sought to have the federal government recognize their ownership and right to exploit offshore petroleum fields. Washington refused, claiming that the tidelands and their resources belonged to the entire nation and should be used for the benefit of the United States as a whole, not just those parts that geography had blessed. President Truman had twice vetoed measures designed to turn these rights over to the claimant states, and the Supreme Court had twice ruled that the federal government had "paramount rights" in the offshore deposits. During the 1952 campaign, Eisenhower had pledged his support to California, Texas, Louisiana, and other affected states. With his support, Congress passed the Submerged Lands Act of 1953, which granted the states title to coastal lands within their "historic" boundaries.

Not surprisingly, the president was an outspoken opponent of public power projects such as the Tennessee Valley Authority (TVA). Shortly after his election, he is reported to have said, "By God, I'd like to sell the whole thing but I suppose we can't go that far." He and his advisers decided, in fact, that it would be impolitic to stage a frontal assault on the giant agency that had provided cheap power and fertilizer to millions of residents of the Tennessee Valley. Rather, the administration would attempt to combat "creeping socialism" with "creeping privatization." When the TVA discovered that its power production was insufficient to meet the needs of the Atomic Energy Commission (AEC) plant at Paducah, Kentucky, the TVA asked Congress for $100 million to build a new steam plant in Fulton, Tennessee. Administration supporters in Congress managed to defeat the measure, and Eisenhower subsequently threw his weight behind a scheme through which the AEC could obtain power from private sources. According to the plan the White House presented to Congress, a syndicate headed by Edgar H. Dixon of Middle South Utilities, Inc., and Eugene A. Yates of the Southern Company would build and operate a plant in West Memphis, Arkansas. The privately owned plant would contract with the TVA to provide power to the AEC as well as to the people of Memphis. The Dixon–Yates proposal immediately became the major issue in a slashing battle between friends and opponents of public power. The Joint Congressional Committee on Atomic Energy launched a full-fledged investigation and

soon discovered that there had been no competitive bidding in the awarding of the Dixon–Yates contract, that an allegedly better offer by a New
York group had been turned down, and that the TVA had not even been
consulted. Democrats began circling for the kill. Senator Estes Kefauver
(D-Tennessee), who had earned a national reputation investigating organized crime, denounced the Dixon–Yates power company as a "risk-free,
government-granted and government-guaranteed monopoly." In January
1955, Senator Lister Hill of Alabama revealed that the administration had
decided to award the power plant contract to the two utilities' executives largely on the recommendation of Bureau of the Budget consultant
Adolphe H. Wenzell, who also happened to be an officer in a Boston investment firm that Dixon–Yates had retained to finance its project. When
the city of Memphis announced that it was going to build its own power
plant, the Eisenhower administration gratefully announced that there was
no need to proceed with the Dixon–Yates project.

As the administration's approach to the TVA problem demonstrated,
the New Republicanism was committed to the notion of a government–
business partnership to promote economic growth. By 1953 it was clear
that, fiscal conservatism notwithstanding, the Eisenhower administration
was going to have to do something about the nation's transportation infrastructure. Since World War II, the railroads, chronically in debt, had
steadily cut passenger service and abandoned thousands of miles of track.
Meanwhile the nation's road system, built and maintained by state and
local governments, was proving woefully inadequate for the burgeoning
auto and trucking industry that depended on it. It was clear that, like it
or not, the administration was going to have to spend money; the decision would be over which mode of transportation to support. Throughout
1955, interest groups slugged it out as they competed for billions in federal
subsidies. The contest pitted the railroads against the giant auto manufacturers and road construction companies. Highway safety and civil defense
experts weighed in on the side of the road lobby. An interstate highway system, they claimed, would reduce traffic deaths and facilitate the evacuation
of populated areas in case of nuclear attack. The administration decided
to finance America's love affair with the automobile and threw its support
behind the Federal Highway Aid Act of 1956. As passed by Congress, the
measure provided massive federal subsidies for an interstate highway system, some 42,000 miles of controlled-access, four- to eight-lane highways
linking the nation's major population centers. The system was to be completed by 1970 at a cost of $27.5 billion, with the government providing
90% of the money, most of it coming from a tax on gasoline.

The story of the creation of the interstate highway system underscored a
fact of postwar political life. The traditional dichotomy that had identified
government intervention into the economy with liberalism and laissez-faire
with conservatism had disappeared completely. The debate had become

one over which interests government was to serve rather than whether government was to be big or little. Liberals in general wanted to use federal power and tax revenues to extend the welfare state and police the private sector, whereas conservatives were determined to maintain the social status quo while providing subsidies and other stimuli to business and industry.

Black America and the Struggle for Civil Equality

One interest group that had failed to enlist the support of either party (southerners continued to render the Democratic Party impotent in the area of civil rights) was African Americans. Indeed, despite heroic service in the workplace and on the battlefield, in the years immediately following World War II black Americans were as segregated and discriminated against as they had ever been. Yet, currents of change were stirring. The war itself gave African Americans new experiences and skills, and instilled in them a rising level of expectations. The thousands of blacks who moved north to take jobs in the defense industry were able to earn money to finance efforts at race improvement, particularly those of the National Association for the Advancement of Colored People (NAACP), whose membership rose from 50,000 at the beginning of World War II to 450,000 at its end. The spread of the Cold War to developing, nonwhite areas of the world made institutionalized racism a huge handicap for the United States as it competed for the allegiance of the peoples of Asia and Africa. Even though President Truman had been unable to secure passage of his legislative proposals, he had begun desegregation of the armed forces through executive order and succeeded in adding civil rights to the liberal agenda. From the 1948 Democratic convention onward, it would compete for a place on the party's reform program. Finally, the NAACP had won significant victories in the courts. Three upper South states were persuaded to abolish the poll tax: Georgia (1945), South Carolina (1951), and Tennessee (1953). In 1948, in *Shelley v. Kraemer*, the Supreme Court ruled that restrictive housing covenants were unenforceable in the courts.

Although the Republican presidential candidate made substantial gains among black voters in 1956, African Americans actually lost ground in their battle against discrimination during the first Eisenhower administration. For the first time since the Depression, black income began to decline in relation to white. Between 1937 and 1952, black earnings climbed to 57% of that of whites, but during the next five years it dropped back to 53%. The caste system continued to be most pervasive and most firmly institutionalized in the South. In 1944, in *Smith v. Allwright*, the Supreme Court invalidated the white primary, a device that in the largely one-party South had meant disfranchisement for blacks. But neither Roosevelt nor Truman had followed up, and discriminatory application of existing statutes, together with the poll tax, violence, threats of economic reprisals, and other forms of intimidation kept the voting roles overwhelmingly white. In 11 southern states in 1957, only 25% of African Americans were registered and far fewer than that were actually permitted to vote. Although the degree varied from moderate in the upper South to extreme in the lower, African Americans faced segregation or exclusion at lunch counters, on public transportation, in schools, in unions, and in the workplace. Violence continued to mar the region's social life. As late as 1955, a black youth from Chicago, Emmett Till, was killed in Mississippi for "admiring" a white woman. White southerners continued to live in the romanticized, racist world depicted in Margaret Mitchell's book, *Gone With the Wind*. Indeed, class combined with caste to make the black southerner a virtual pariah in his native land.

African Americans who had moved north during and after World War II faced fewer legal and institutional bars, but informal racism was pervasive. Poverty, lack of opportunity, and discrimination compelled blacks to live within rigidly defined ghettos generally situated at the core of deteriorating urban areas. They were forced to take the lowest paying jobs, discriminated against in bank loans and insurance, and systematically snubbed in social settings. Northern black workers earned an estimated $800 per year more than their southern counterparts, not an inconsiderable sum in view of the fact that, in 1954, the average yearly income of nonwhite families was $2,410. Still, black families lagged far behind their white counterparts, whose income for the same period was $4,339 annually. Those who could afford to move to the suburbs were generally prevented from doing so by restrictive housing covenants still pervasive despite *Shelley v. Kraemer*.

The Eisenhower administration was ambivalent about the issue of civil rights. During the 1952 campaign, Eisenhower declared that he hoped for a United States that provided "a true equality of opportunity" for all its citizens, but he cautioned that the president could do little to hasten the creation of such a society. Much as he valued racial justice, he said, the federal government must do nothing in the civil rights area that smacked of "statism" or "paternalism." Thus did Eisenhower oppose the reestablishment of a Fair Employment Practices Commission out of a conviction that compulsory federal intervention ought not to replace state, local, or private responsibility for preventing job discrimination. He told a group of African American leaders in 1958 that he favored "first-class citizenship" for their people, but he cautioned them to be patient and privately denounced as extremist those of their number who were working to overturn racial barriers. His position naturally appealed to white southerners, and he actively sought their votes during both of his campaigns. He was no visceral racist like Senators Richard Russell (D-Georgia) and Strom Thurmond (D-South Carolina), but his attitudes toward African Americans were patronizing and insensitive. The elimination of racial injustice, he repeatedly declared, depended on long-term changes in public opinion.

After his inauguration, Eisenhower, under pressure from New York Congressman Adam Clayton Powell, completed the desegregation of the armed forces. Meanwhile, the White House and the Justice Department pressured operators of hotels, theaters, and restaurants in the District of Columbia to integrate their establishments. This, however, was as far as the administration was willing to go. Even in interstate transportation, a matter clearly within federal jurisdiction, segregationist practices persisted in the lower South.

Brown v. Board of Education

Blocked in Congress and faced with an indifferent executive, African Americans turned increasingly to the courts for redress of their grievances. From its founding in 1911, the NAACP had recognized the potential of a legal strategy that sought to confront white America with the civil rights provisions of the Constitution that they claimed to so revere. In 1938, Charles Houston, the Harvard-educated NAACP lawyer who would train a generation of civil rights lawyers at Howard University, argued successfully before the Supreme Court that the state of Missouri could not logically send black law students out of state to another school to train them to practice law in Missouri. In *Missouri ex. rel. Gaines*, the court required Missouri to either create a fully equal law school or integrate the existing facility. In 1950, one of Houston's protégés, Thurgood Marshall, won a series of landmark decisions. The first of these cases involved George McLaurin, a black student admitted to the University of Oklahoma on "a segregated basis." He was allowed to attend class with whites but had to sit in a separate, roped-off area there as well as in the library and cafeteria. Marshall argued that this physical separation denied McLaurin access to the learned company of his professors and the intellectual stimulation of his fellow students. It was, moreover, a humiliating badge of inferiority. In *McLaurin v. Board of Regents*, the justices ruled that equality could not be measured in terms of physical facilities, library volumes, or dollars alone and that McLaurin's physical isolation ensured that his education would be inferior to that of his white classmates. The decision, it should be noted, affected only graduate education in public institutions. It did not, moreover, mandate integration but rather required that the state of Oklahoma maintain equal facilities for whites and blacks. That same day in 1950, in *Sweatt v. Painter*, the high court issued a decree forcing the University of Texas Law School to admit a black student who refused to attend a state-supported law school for African Americans at Texas State University for Negroes (Texas Southern) in Houston. The majority ruled that the hastily established professional school did not match the University of Texas in faculty, library, or prestige.

Up to this point the NAACP lawyers had concentrated on making local and state authorities live up to the letter of the 1896 *Plessy v. Ferguson* case, which had established the principle of separate but equal. Marshall and his colleagues reasoned that the financial burden of maintaining separate law and medical schools would weaken Jim Crow. Gradually, however, the weight of their arguments and the evidence gathered irrefutably pointed to the fact that separate could never be equal. But to challenge segregation directly would constitute a dramatic strategic shift. After much debate, however, Marshall and his colleagues decided to press ahead. By the spring of 1954, the NAACP Legal Defense Fund was pushing five cases, all of which challenged the principle of educational segregation on its face. The five were combined and docketed under the name of Oliver Brown who was suing on behalf of his daughter Linda, a Topeka, Kansas, schoolgirl who was forced to walk past her neighborhood white school to attend an all-black facility much farther from home. Central to Marshall's argument, made to the Court on December 9, 1952, was that segregation conferred a cumulative stigma on black children. Psychologist Kenneth Clark had demonstrated that young African American girls subjected to Jim Crow inevitably preferred white dolls to black ones, thus demonstrating their self-hatred. Separation implied inferiority, Marshall argued, and the denial of access to any and all educational institutions purely on the basis of race violated the Fourteenth Amendment to the Constitution, which guaranteed to every citizen equal protection of the laws and stipulated that no one could be denied life, liberty, or property without due process. His opponent stood on legal precedent. *Plessy* was the law, and sociological and psychological arguments were irrelevant.

The high court was initially deeply divided. The key figure in the unfolding drama was Chief Justice Earl Warren. As attorney general in California during World War II, Warren had been an active participant in the decision to inter and relocate more than 100,000 Japanese Americans. But he had come to regret deeply his actions, and during the remainder of his life he repeatedly demonstrated his commitment to those who had been denied social justice. In the midst of the controversy over *Brown* in the summer of 1953, Chief Justice Fred Vinson died. President Eisenhower, apparently unaware of Warren's activist tendencies, appointed him to head the court. Vinson had wanted to avoid ruling directly on *Plessy*; his demise was crucial. Reargument took place on December 7, and observers expected a decision to follow quickly. For three months, Warren worked behind the scenes to change the minds of two justices who agreed with Vinson. A majority agreed with him that in the *Brown* case there was a clear-cut societal injustice and a constitutional remedy to the situation, but the chief justice wanted a unanimous decision.

On May 17, 1954, the U.S. Supreme Court ruled unanimously in the case of *Brown v. Board of Education of Topeka* that racial segregation in U.S. public schools violated the Constitution. Education, Warren declared, constituted a central experience in life and was the key to opportunity and advancement in American society. The things that children learned in school remained with them for the rest of their lives. "Does segregation of children in public schools solely on the basis of race ... deprive the children of the minority group of equal educational opportunities?" he asked rhetorically. "We believe that it does." The isolation of black children "from others of similar age and qualifications solely because of their race generates a feeling of inferiority as to their status in the community that may affect their hearts and minds in a way unlikely ever to be undone." The decision concluded, "separate educational facilities are inherently unequal.... Any language in *Plessy v. Ferguson* contrary to these findings is rejected."

The *Brown* decision struck down a historic system of segregation, a symbol of the American caste system legally mandated in 17 states, optional in 4 others. Initial reaction from the South was encouraging. Governor Francis Cherry of Arkansas declared, "Arkansas will obey the law. It always has." Alabama chief executive "Big" Jim Folsom responded to reporters' questions by observing, "When the Supreme Court speaks, that's the law." Several hundred school districts in the border states (Arkansas, Delaware, Kentucky, Maryland, Missouri, Oklahoma, and West Virginia) moved to integrate their schools. Many blacks were jubilant. They took pleasure that an African American had used white men's laws to persuade an all-white Supreme Court to overturn Jim Crow. Yet like a battlefield victory that requires a quick follow-up if it is to have any impact on the overall conflict, the *Brown* decision was no more than that. To be effective, it would have to be enforced. Attorney General Herbert Brownell had overcome Eisenhower's misgivings and filed an *amicus curiae* brief on behalf of the plaintiff in the *Brown* decision, but the president was not pleased at the outcome. Indeed, he declined to render a public endorsement of the Supreme Court's decision.

Most important, the Justice Department urged the Supreme Court to take a "go slow" approach to implementation, and the justices complied. The high court's "implementation decree," the so-called *Brown II* decision, handed down on May 3, 1955, rejected the NAACP's request to order instant and total school desegregation. It assigned responsibility for planning to local school boards and delegated responsibility for supervising the pace of desegregation to local federal judges, requiring only that a "prompt and reasonable start toward full compliance" be made and that the integration of classrooms proceed "with all deliberate speed." Warren and his colleagues refused to set a deadline. In fairness to the chief justice, it should be noted that he accepted gradualism as the cost of unanimity. Without this concession, he could never have won over the two hesitant justices on the court. Moreover, gradualism was entirely consistent with the legal culture and the whole philosophy of post–World War II liberalism. It was not clear in 1955 that "with all deliberate speed" would be interpreted as a justification for deliberate foot dragging.

White Backlash

The Eisenhower administration took no action early in 1956 when University of Alabama officials expelled Autherine Lucy, the first black person admitted to the institution, on the grounds that her presence threatened public order. He remained similarly passive when racial disturbances broke out at the opening of school that year in Mansfield, Texas; Hoxie, Arkansas; and Clinton, Tennessee. Indeed, Eisenhower would later confide to an aide that "the Supreme [C]ourt decisions set back progress in the South at least fifteen years.... Feelings are deep on this.... And the fellow who tries to tell me that you can do these things by force is just plain nuts." Following the civil liberties decisions of the 1960s, he termed Warren's appointment "the biggest damnfool mistake I ever made."

Encouraged by the Eisenhower administration's attitude and the "all deliberate speed" ruling, white supremacists in the South began organizing to fight the *Brown* decision. Their first and perhaps most effective tactics were delay and obstruction. Local districts refused to act, forcing the NAACP to file more than 2,000 separate suits seeking relief through injunction. With plaintiffs and NAACP representatives being harassed by white supremacists, school authorities filed countersuits and various motions. When several years later, the federal court forced action, local school authorities came up with plans providing for only the most limited and gradual integration. Those black students admitted to class were threatened with bodily harm, cursed, spat upon, and psychologically abused in a multitude of ways.

By the end of 1955, no fewer than 568 separate segregationist organizations, including a revived Ku Klux Klan with a membership estimated at 200,000, were operating in the United States. Local white Citizens' Councils resorted to everything from ostracism to economic boycott to violence in an effort to, as Eisenhower put it, "see that their sweet little girls are not required to sit in schools alongside those big sexually advanced black boys." Senator Harry Flood Byrd (D-Virginia) called for a policy of "massive resistance." Invoking the memory of John C. Calhoun, Georgia, Mississippi, and Virginia passed resolutions of interposition. "The Deep South Says Never" read the title of a series of articles by John Bartlow Martin on the segregationist movement. "If we submit to this unconstitutional, judge-made integration law," declared a Council leader, "the malignant powers of atheism, Communism and mongrelization will surely follow." In March 1956, 101 members of Congress signed the Southern Manifesto, which condemned the *Brown* decision as a usurpation of the constitutional power of the states and called on the sons and daughters of Dixie to use "every lawful means" to block implementation.

Throughout late 1955 and early 1956, state legislatures passed laws designed to frustrate *Brown*. Hundreds of different measures were enacted, some revoking the licenses of school employees teaching mixed-race classes, others appropriating state funds to subsidize tuition to all-white private academies, and still others completely shutting down school systems that had been ordered to desegregate. A favorite measure was the "pupil placement law," a measure that theoretically guaranteed each pupil "freedom of choice" in selecting a school. Assignment could not be based on race, but local school boards could use "psychological fitness" and "morality" as criteria. Inevitably, black and white children were assigned to separate schools. These laws also attacked the NAACP. In some states, it became a crime for a state employee to belong; in others, the organization was forced to publish the names of its members, thus exposing them to harassment; and in still others, the NAACP was branded a subversive organization. In the wake of massive resistance, 246 branches of the NAACP went out of existence.

Perhaps the toughest task facing black civil rights leaders in the twentieth century was convincing their brethren that they controlled their own fate and that, if they were ever to defeat oppression by the white majority, they would have to take matters into their own hands. In the mid-1950s, this message began to register, and as a result, civil rights became an authentic mass movement. On December 1, 1955, in Montgomery, Alabama, "the cradle of the Confederacy," a black seamstress and former NAACP official, Rosa Parks, refused to give up her seat to a white and move to the back of the bus. She was duly arrested. Three nights later black community leaders gathered at the Dexter Avenue Baptist Church; formed the Montgomery Improvement Association; chose as its head the young, charismatic minister, Martin Luther King, Jr.; and launched a bus boycott among local blacks.

Martin Luther King and the Montgomery Bus Boycott

King would seem to have been an unlikely candidate to lead a mass movement to overturn Jim Crow. As the son of a prominent black cleric in Atlanta, one of the few southern cities with a thriving, independent black middle class, King was spared the grosser aspects of white racism. An excellent student, he jumped two grades in high school and, at age 15, entered Morehouse College, a first-rate, all-black institution in Atlanta. "Mike" King dreamed of being a teacher or lawyer, but at his father's insistence, he opted for the ministry. He subsequently went on to graduate from Crozer Seminary in Pennsylvania and earn a Ph.D. in systematic theology from Boston University. King's student essays reflected the influences of social gospel writers, Reinhold Niebuhr's speculations on the fallen state of man, and the nonviolent civil disobedience philosophies of Henry David Thoreau and Mahatma Ghandi. As pastor of the Holt Street Baptist Church in Montgomery – his first assignment out of seminary – the young intellectual learned to trim sermons in order to cater to the emotional as well as the intellectual needs of his congregation. By the end of his first year of service when he moved to the Dexter Street congregation, King had become a charismatic preacher as well as an intellectual and committed racial leader. "In our protest there will be no cross burnings," he told his audience that night in Montgomery. "No white person will be taken from his home by a hooded Negro mob and brutally murdered. . . . We will be guided by the highest principles of law and order." He quoted Christ, "Love your enemies, bless them that curse you, and pray for them that despitefully use you."

The original goal of the boycott was simply to force the bus authority to make seating available on a first-come, first-served basis, but after Mrs. Parks decided to appeal her conviction, its goal became the judicial invalidation of Alabama's segregated seating law. An effective car pooling system enabled the protesters to bring the municipal transport authority to the verge of bankruptcy. King was arrested for orchestrating the boycott, and black leaders were subjected to threats and isolated instances of violence. However, even after a year of harassment by Montgomery police and intense economic and psychological pressure from the white politicians and segregationists, the boycott remained in place. In 1956, the Supreme Court ruled the state's segregated coach law unconstitutional. The boycott enjoyed coverage by the national and international media, making King a minor celebrity and, in the process, affording the boycotters a certain amount of protection. The ultimate goal for King was to reunite a broken community through the power of Christian love. "We will soon wear you down by our capacity to suffer," he told his antagonists, "and in winning our freedom we will so appeal to your heart and conscience that we will win you in the process."

Little Rock

The first major test of the *Brown* decision came in Arkansas in the fall of 1957. Little Rock seemed an unlikely scene for a dramatic confrontation between state and federal power over the issue of school integration. This upper South capital city had desegregated its bus system without violence and had been among the first communities below the Potomac actually to make preparations for compliance with the *Brown* decision. On the day following the Supreme Court's historic pronouncement, the Little Rock school board instructed Superintendent Virgil T. Blossom to draw up a plan for compliance. Neither Blossom nor the board was enthusiastic about integration, but they had no intention of defying the high court ruling. The Little Rock Phase Program that Blossom announced in May 1955 provided for token desegregation, starting in September 1957 at one senior high school and ending in 1963 with small numbers of blacks attending class in the city's elementary schools.

While the Little Rock school board was quietly preparing to integrate, Arkansas segregationists were marshalling their forces, determined to provoke a confrontation. In the summer of 1955, when white supremacists in the small east Arkansas community of Hoxie attempted to force the school board to reverse its decision to bring 25 black children into the previously all-white school, the federal district court ruled in favor of the board and black children. With the air thick with threats of violence, the Federal Bureau of Investigation (FBI) was called in, and segregationists in eastern Arkansas recoiled in horror at the specter of federal intervention. Following the Hoxie decision, segregationists demanded a special session of the legislature to enact various measures of resistance.

Governor Orval Faubus, who had been labeled a communist by his opponents for attending the radical Commonwealth College and who had opened a number of state jobs to blacks, seemed determined to remain above the fray. But the "segs," as moderates referred to opponents of school integration, put forward a fire-breathing, implacable white supremacist named Jim Johnson to run against him in the 1956 gubernatorial primary. The previous year, Johnson, who was an associate justice of the Arkansas Supreme Court, had urged a Pine Bluff audience to "do what needs to be done" to stop integration. Johnson lost, but Faubus responded to the segregationist challenge by throwing his support behind a campaign to get an interposition amendment (an amendment to the state constitution asserting the state's right to "interpose" its authority between the federal government and the people of the state) on the November ballot. From that point onward, the governor was tarnished in the eyes of the moderates, and he gravitated silently but surely toward Arkansas' white supremacists.

With nine black children scheduled to enter Central High on September 3, 1957, Faubus appeared on television on the evening of September 2 and reminded Arkansans that a majority of voters had approved an interposition amendment to the Constitution in 1956. As governor, he was bound to enforce this legislation until it was declared unconstitutional. For this reason and to avoid violence, the state's National Guard would be stationed around Central High to prevent any black children from entering. That same evening, Blossom and the school board released a public statement asking the "Little Rock Nine," as they came to be called, to remain at home until the legal issues involved had been settled. When, however, federal district judge Ronald Davies ordered the board to carry out its desegregation plan, the nine would-be pupils braved the mob surrounding Central High on September 4, only to be refused admittance by armed guardsmen.

On September 21, Judge Davies ordered Faubus to cease his obstructionist tactics. The governor promptly removed the National Guard, departed for a southern governors' conference, and predicted violence if blacks again attempted to enter Central High. On Monday morning, September 23, desegregation began under the protection of city police and a limited number of state troopers. The nine black children, carefully trained by Daisy Bates and other local civil rights leaders, braved a gauntlet of abuse. A shrieking crowd surrounded them shouting, "two, four, six, eight, we ain't going to integrate," and "niggers, keep away from our school. Go back to the jungle." The students entered Central High, but by lunchtime the mob outside had become so large and belligerent that they were removed. "They might go in there," one Little Rock man who lived in the neighborhood remarked on national television, "but I bet they don't come out." That afternoon the mayor asked the Eisenhower administration for federal troops to restore order. The president immediately federalized the National Guard. That evening units of the 101st Airborne Division arrived in Little Rock. The following morning federal troops escorted African American students to Central High School and cleared the mobs from the school area.

Eisenhower had acted reluctantly but decisively. Not to have done so, he told a southern senator, would have been "tantamount to acquiescence in anarchy and the dissolution of the union." More specifically, the president had dispatched troops to Little Rock to uphold the authority of the federal government; the executive branch had acted to enforce the rulings of the judicial branch. Eisenhower became the first chief executive since Reconstruction to use federal troops to protect black Americans in the exercise of their constitutional rights. The segregationists' hope of a divided federal authority was dashed. They were hardly reconciled, however.

Indeed, by this point, Little Rock had become the focus of southern resistance to court-ordered integration. "I must vigorously protest the highhanded and illegal methods being employed by the armed forces of the United States...who are carrying out your orders to mix the races in the public schools of Little Rock, Arkansas," Richard Russell cabled Eisenhower. "These troopers are disregarding and overriding the elementary rights of American citizens by applying tactics which must have been copied from the manual issued the officers of Hitler's storm troopers." Segregationist speakers poured into the city from throughout the South. Race relations deteriorated, and the Capital City Citizens' Council suddenly became a major player in city politics. Central High School assumed the appearance of an armed camp, and the nine black students were subjected to a daily ordeal of spit, obscene gestures, and physical threats. All the while, Governor Faubus displayed a growing talent for demagoguery, denouncing the federal presence as foreign occupation, and accusing the soldiers of entering the girls' physical education dressing rooms.

Little Rock was important in no small part because it was the first civil rights drama to be covered extensively by television. Although 39 million households in America boasted television sets by 1957, radio was still the dominant news medium. In those days before videotape and satellite feeds, news film had to be developed and projected at a handful of regional stations. Because such procedures were time consuming, today's news usually became yesterday's news. The major networks carried no more than 2.5 hours of news and public affairs programming each week. Nightly television news broadcasts ran a mere 15 minutes. Only NBC boasted field reporters, a grand total of two. One of these was John Chancellor who covered the Midwest and South. Because the Little Rock story dragged out over several weeks, television was able to cover it. The crisis seemed of such monumental proportions that NBC was moved to extraordinary steps. Each afternoon Chancellor flew to Oklahoma City to appear on the "Huntley–Brinkley Report." News footage of white racists hurling obscene ephitets and spitting at neatly dressed, stoic black youths shocked the nation and marked the beginning of a revolution of consciousness.

Eisenhower's continuing preference was to do nothing, but as Chester Pach has observed, the president was attempting "impartiality on an issue in which neutrality was impossible." The vast majority of white southerners were determined to take advantage of the passivity of the federal government to resist implementation of the *Brown* decision and other laws mandating equal treatment for African Americans. White citizens councils spread like wildfire across the region in the mid-1950s. At their height, these councils counted 250,000 members. The councils were, however, respectable only in comparison to the Klan. They succeeded in pushing interposition resolutions through several state legislatures, open invitations to state authorities to defy federal edicts. In addition, they organized economic and social boycotts of those that crossed the color line or condoned such action.

The Civil Rights Act of 1957

With northern liberals increasingly up in arms and critics of all political persuasions reminding the administration that the Republican Party was the party of Lincoln, President Eisenhower presented a civil rights bill to Congress in 1956. At the heart of the measure was a voting rights provision. In some southern states, poll taxes, literacy tests, and fear kept black registration at less than 20%. In areas of Mississippi, no blacks voted. The bill, introduced late in the year, carried over into the 1957 session. During the intervening presidential campaign, Eisenhower went out of his way to reassure recalcitrants in the South. "We are not going to settle this thing," he warned, "by a great show of force and arbitrary action." Congress wrangled over the bill through the summer, finally approving a watered-down version in September 1957. The Civil Rights Act of 1957 provided fine and imprisonment for those found guilty of interfering with a citizen in his or her effort to vote. But, in a major concession to the South, the bill provided for jury trials for those accused. Because blacks were systematically barred from serving on juries, convictions were sure to be few and far between. Senator Richard Russell (D-Georgia), the leader of the Dixie contingent in the Senate, declared the jury trial provision to be "the sweetest victory in my twenty-five years as a Senator."

The civil rights movement that began in Montgomery and continued in Little Rock and other cities was significant for its inclusion of working-class blacks. The institutional anchor of the movement had for years been the NAACP, but King decided to add to that. In January 1957, a month after the end of the successful Montgomery boycott, he founded the Southern Christian Leadership Conference (SCLC) in an effort to bring black churches to the forefront of the struggle for racial justice and equal rights. Then on February 1, 1960, a spontaneous event added momentum and yet a third important constituency to the civil rights movement. Four students from North Carolina Agricultural and Technical College in Greensboro, North Carolina, sat down at a Woolworth's lunch counter and refused to leave after being denied service. The "sit-in" movement spread to other cities – Raleigh, Charlotte, Little Rock, Nashville, and Birmingham – and to other types of facilities – "wade-ins" at public swimming pools and "kneel-ins" at churches. One of the participants in the Charlotte sit-in told reporters that he and his fellows were just seeking their "God-given" rights. "All I want is to come in and place my order and be served and leave a tip if I feel like it," he said. In April 1960, the mostly student participants, black and white, in the sit-in movement formed the Student Nonviolent Coordinating Committee (SNCC). From this point onward, the SCLC and SNCC spearheaded the direct action phase of the civil rights movement. Demonstrators pledged to nonviolence were subjected to water hoses, beatings, repeated arrest, police dogs and, in some cases, murder by white vigilante groups. But their activities dominated the national media and stirred the conscience of a nation. All the while, the NAACP continued to whittle away in the courts at legalized racism.

Summary

As the end of the Truman administration approached, the American people longed for unity, tranquility, and security. In the 1952 presidential election, they selected Dwight David Eisenhower, a man whom they correctly perceived to be dedicated to these goals. The new president and his team were committed to implementing modern Republicanism at home and containing Sino–Soviet expansion abroad. In its domestic policies, the administration left New Deal reform structures in place while pushing for a government–business alliance to advance prosperity on all fronts. It became obvious during the 1950s that in the postwar period the overriding question was not whether the federal government would act but whom it would act in behalf of. Under Eisenhower, its tendency was to favor the private sector, to nurture corporations, agribusiness, and entrepreneurs rather than labor unions, small farmers, and consumers. But the new Republican Party differed from the Democrats more in emphasis than in kind. Twice the Eisenhower administration increased federal spending to pull the United States out of economic recessions, a tactic usually associated with

Keynesian liberals, and it made no attempt to hamper unionization. Indeed, membership in labor unions soared in the 1950s, reaching an all-time high. Democrats meanwhile struggled to redefine the meaning of liberalism in the midst of a period of unprecedented economic growth.

Not all Americans sought to maintain the status quo. A rising level of expectations fueled by the rhetoric associated with the struggle against the Axis and by increasing economic opportunity prompted African Americans to embark on what one historian has labeled the second reconstruction. While, in the courts, the NAACP moved from demanding that separate facilities really be equal to insisting that true equality could only be achieved through integration, a charismatic black preacher named Martin Luther King employed the techniques of nonviolent civil disobedience to mobilize the black masses and attack Jim Crow in the streets. Sensing federal indifference, the white South attempted to resist school integration and voter registration, but King and the SCLC would not relent. Indeed, new, more confrontational organizations like SNCC sprang up. By the end of the decade, much remained to be achieved on the civil rights front, but the nation's conscience had been aroused.

ADDITIONAL READINGS

Alexander, Charles C., *Holding the Line: The Eisenhower Era, 1951–1962* (1975).

Ambrose, Stephen E., *Eisenhower: Vol. II, The President* (1984).

Bartley, Numan V., *The Rise of Massive Resistance: Race and Politics in the South During the 1950s* (1969).

Branch, Taylor, *Parting the Waters: America in the King Years, 1954–63* (1988).

Burk, Robert F., *Dwight D. Eisenhower: Hero and Politician* (1986).

Burk, Robert F., *The Eisenhower Administration and Black Civil Rights* (1984).

Carter, Dan T., *The Politics of Rage: George Wallace, the Origins of the New Conservatism, and the Transformation of American Politics* (1995).

Garrow, David J., *Bearing the Cross: Martin Luther King, Jr., and the Southern Christian Leadership Conference* (1986).

Greenstein, Fred I., *The Hidden-Hand Presidency: Eisenhower As Leader* (1982).

Pach, Chester J., Jr., and Elmo Richardson, rev. ed., *The Presidency of Dwight D. Eisenhower* (1991).

Rose, Mark H., *Interstate: Express Highway Politics, 1941–1956* (1979).

Sitkoff, Harvard, *The Struggle for Black Equality, 1954–1980* (1981).

4 Containing Communism and Managing the Military–Industrial Complex

The Eisenhower Administration and the Cold War

Shortly before he left office after serving two full terms as president of the United States, Dwight Eisenhower delivered one of the most notable farewell addresses in American history. On the eve of his departure, the general turned president looked back over the first 15 years of the Cold War with mixed feelings. Communism had been contained without a war between the world's nuclear superpowers. But there had been a price – the gradual conversion of the United States into a garrison state. The joining of a huge military establishment with a mushrooming arms industry was unique in the American experience, he observed to his countrymen. "The total influence – economic, political, even spiritual – is felt in every city, every State house, every office of the Federal government." Eisenhower then issued a dire warning: "In the councils of government, we must guard against the acquisition of unwarranted influence, whether sought or un-sought, by the military–industrial complex. The potential for the disastrous rise of misplaced power exists and will persist." The story of the Eisenhower administration's foreign and defense policies was the struggle, on the one hand, to contain communist aggression and subversion, and on the other hand, to limit the power of the business–labor–academic coalition that had become dependent on that very struggle.

In foreign affairs, Dwight Eisenhower was not fundamentally unhappy with the course of American policy since 1945. As NATO's first commander-in-chief, he had been a loyal advocate of Truman's containment policy. Similar to Acheson, Taft, and McCarthy, he believed in the existence of a monolithic communist threat directed from the Kremlin, which, if the United States and its allies were not ever-vigilant, would spread commu-nism across the globe through a combination of intimidation, subversion, and, if circumstances were right, armed aggression. However, Eisenhower disagreed with both Taft and McCarthy in other areas. He did not believe that the principal threat was communist burrowing from within or that the United States could entrust its security to chains of island bases in the Atlantic and the Pacific Oceans. Rather, the principal menace was from abroad, and the battle fronts were economic and political, as well as strategic. The problem posed by international communism was best dealt with by U.S.-led alliance systems and American-financed programs of overseas economic and military aid. As was true in the domestic sphere, continuity rather than change was the watchword in foreign affairs during the Eisenhower administration. The task ahead, all agreed, was to contain communism within its current boundaries until the Sino–Soviet empire inevitably rotted from within.

John Foster Dulles and "Rollback"

The man whom Eisenhower selected to advise him on foreign affairs was an obvious choice. Sixty-four when he became secretary of state, John Foster Dulles could boast of a diplomatic career that stretched back to 1907, when he had been part of the American delegation to the Hague Peace Conference. He was the nephew of Robert Lansing, secretary of state during World War I, and his grandfather, John Foster, had served as secretary of state under President Benjamin Harrison. A member of the prestigious Wall Street law firm of Sullivan and Cromwell, Dulles was typical of those members of the eastern financial and cultural establishment who repaid their debt to society and enhanced their prestige by going into public service.

Dulles was an articulate, bright, intense man; he had written a number of treatises and pamphlets on international affairs. During the 1952 campaign, he had taken the lead in criticizing Truman, Acheson, and the Democrats for opening up Eastern Europe to communist domination, allowing China to fall, and becoming involved in an indecisive quagmire in Korea. A prominent Presbyterian layman, Dulles appeared in public to be a dogmatic, uncompromising anticommunist. His rhetoric was laced with value-laden epithets, such as "immoral," "enslavement," and "banditry." In a *Life* magazine article published in 1952, Dulles insisted that the United States must adopt "a policy of boldness," which would enable the country "to retaliate instantly against open aggression by Red armies, so that if it occurred anywhere, we could and would strike back where it hurts, by means of our own choosing." His critics would charge that he insisted on seeing every international crisis through the prism of the Cold War, forcing nations to choose between the "free world" and international communism, and that he relied too heavily on military alliances and arms aid to achieve his foreign policy objectives. In reality, Dulles was generally patient and flexible in the behind-the-scenes negotiations that constituted the bulk of modern diplomacy. His hard-line rhetoric was intended as much to appease the conservatives within his own party as anything else. Moreover, Dulles did not dominate foreign policymaking or President Eisenhower, as was commonly assumed at the time. He did enjoy an extremely close relationship with the president, and strengthened by the presence of his younger brother, Allen, as director of the Central Intelligence Agency (CIA), Dulles was undoubtedly one of the twentieth century's strongest secretaries of state. But he acted as Eisenhower's partner, and the president was influenced by others in his entourage, particularly Humphrey and Wilson. Indeed, it was the president who took direct responsibility for various covert activities conducted by the CIA, the development of both the B-52 intercontinental nuclear bomber and the Polaris missile-launching submarine, and the integration of atomic weapons into the U.S. arsenal. Eisenhower publicly adopted the posture of a passive president because he and his advisers believed that is what the American people, exhausted by a generation of war and depression, wanted.

The Bricker Amendment

Perhaps the most important consideration impelling Dwight Eisenhower to enter the political arena was his fear that a resurgent isolationism would force America to retreat from the international arena, thus exposing the world to yet another cycle of aggression and war. It seemed a very real possibility that the United States would once again "retreat from responsibility" during Eisenhower's first term. In September 1951, Senator John W. Bricker (R-Ohio) had introduced a constitutional amendment designed, he claimed, to protect the American people from executive tyranny and, more important, from the nefarious influence of foreign ideologies and cultures. A staunch conservative on domestic matters and an authentic isolationist in foreign affairs, Bricker was a favorite butt of liberal jokes. "Intellectually he is like interstellar space," declared John Gunther in *Inside U.S.A.*, "a vast vacuum occasionally crossed by homeless, wandering cliches." The Bricker amendment stipulated that executive agreements would become effective only after congressional action; no treaty of any kind, moreover, would become law until accepted by both houses of Congress. Any treaty provision that contravened the Constitution was to become automatically null and void.

The Ohioan's proposal to restrict the executive branch's freedom of action in foreign affairs stemmed from a number of specific but related concerns. In the early days of the amendment, the driving force behind it was the American Bar Association, the bulk of whose membership was afraid that liberals at home, in league with socialists and communists abroad, intended to use international conventions to force anti-lynching, anti-poll tax, and antidiscrimination legislation on the South. They were joined by Bricker and anti–New Deal Republicans concerned about "creeping socialism." The conservative coalition had become convinced that the United Nations, through vehicles such as the Human Rights Declaration of 1948 and the Genocide Convention, was attempting to force America to become a racially integrated welfare state. In addition, a number of Republican senators, moderate as well as conservative, backed the amendment because of their anger over what they viewed as Franklin Roosevelt's secret, personal, and deceitful diplomacy at Yalta and over Harry Truman's "cowardly" policy of containment. In declaring his support for the Bricker amendment, for example, Senator H. Alexander Smith (R-New Jersey) cited the "outrageous Yalta accords, entered into by President Roosevelt individually with Stalin and Churchill without even the knowledge of [the] Secretary of State."

Eisenhower believed these fears and prejudices to be grossly exaggerated, and he set about defeating the Bricker amendment. Because he did not want to alienate the Taft wing of the Republican Party, the president had to rely on ingenuity and intrigue. He never took a public stand against the amendment while he labored behind the scenes to strangle it. For two years between 1951 and 1953, the White House obstructed and delayed. When an exasperated Bricker finally succeeded in introducing the measure, Secretary Dulles testified before Congress, lavishly praising the Ohio conservative, while informing members of the Senate Judiciary Committee that his proposal went too far in restricting executive action in the field of foreign affairs. In succeeding interviews with Bricker, who absolutely refused to compromise, the president managed to focus the ire of conservatives on Dulles rather than himself. At a press conference on July 1, 1953, Eisenhower announced his support for an amendment declaring any international agreement that conflicted with the Constitution to be null and void. At the same time, he gave encouragement to the Committee for the Defense of the Constitution by Preserving the Treaty Power, a public interest group devoted to defeating the Bricker amendment. Then in early 1954, he enlisted the support of Senate Democrats. To the frustration of the Brickerites, one compromise version of the amendment after another was defeated. The original proposal, complex and confusing, was modified, simplified, and reintroduced as Senate Joint Resolution 1 on January 7, 1953. It was subsequently defeated. "If it's true that when you die the things that bothered you most are engraved on your skull," the president told an aide, "I'm sure I'll have there the mud and dirt of France during invasion and the name of Senator Bricker."

The White House found Senator Joe McCarthy's brand of isolationism – for so it deemed McCarthyism – no less repugnant than Bricker's. Although he personally detested McCarthy and genuinely opposed extremism and witch hunts, Eisenhower contributed to the atmosphere of hysteria that both fed and was fed by McCarthy. In April 1953, the president signed an executive order authorizing the heads of federal departments to dismiss any employee about whom there was reasonable doubt concerning not only their loyalty but their "good conduct and character" as well. Similar to McCarthy, Eisenhower tended to confuse "New Dealism" with socialism if not communism. Shortly after he took the oath of office, pressure mounted on the president to commute the death sentences of Julius and Ethel

Rosenberg, convicted of transmitting atomic secrets to communist agents. After due deliberation, Eisenhower refused and denounced the Rosenbergs for "immeasurably increasing the chances of atomic war." (Materials from the Soviet archives have since revealed that Julius was guilty, but that the information he passed on was worthless.) Finally, Eisenhower and Dulles vied with both the Brickerites and McCarthyites in denouncing the Yalta accords as a traitorous compromise with the forces of international communism.

Indeed, during the 1952 campaign, Dulles and other foreign policy spokesmen had castigated the Democrats for "selling out" Eastern Europe to the communists and implied that, rather than containing communism, it would "roll back" the Iron Curtain whenever the opportunity presented itself. The first real test of the administration's intent in regard to pushing back communism in Europe came in June 1953, when workers in East Berlin and other parts of Soviet-occupied East Germany rioted to protest factory speedups and food shortages. As Russian tanks put down the uprising, all the U.S. government could do was "deplore" its suppression and praise the heroism of the rioters. In 1956, the Eisenhower administration was presented with a second chance to prove its mettle in regard to "captive peoples." Encouraged by an apparent liberalization process in the Soviet Union, in the fall of that year, Hungarian dissidents attempted to institute democratic reforms and withdraw from the Soviet satellite system. Stalin had died in 1953, and for two years his would-be successors had struggled for ascendancy. In 1955, Nikita Khrushchev emerged from the pack to become first secretary of the Communist Party of the Soviet Union (CPSU). In 1956, at the Twentieth Congress of the Russian Communist Party, the new Soviet leader had attacked the crimes of the Stalin era and hinted at a relaxation of internal restrictions. Nationalist and democratic elements in Poland and Hungary subsequently began pressuring Soviet authorities for more autonomy and multiparty elections. Khrushchev managed to placate the Poles, but events in Hungary soon got out of hand. Roving bands of militant students and workers attacked government buildings, defaced symbols of Soviet power, and retaliated against members of the communist secret police. Despite the fact that the United States never had any intention of intervening, the CIA-controlled Radio Free Europe broadcast militant calls to arms within Hungary and implied that help from the western democracies would be forthcoming. Emboldened by this apparent support, Hungarian nationalist leader Imre Nagy, whom the Soviets had released from jail in an effort to appease the militants, announced not only the formation of a coalition government, but also Hungary's intention to withdraw from the Warsaw Pact. Faced with the collapse of their Eastern European empire, Khrushchev and his generals acted. On November 4, Soviet tanks rolled into Budapest and during the fighting that followed 30,000 Hungarians and 7,000 Russians died. Newsreels showed freedom fighters in Budapest launching futile attacks against Soviet tanks with Molotov cocktails and small arms, and then being cut down in the streets. To the end, the revolutionaries sent out urgent pleas for help as they fought vainly. All they could elicit was an embarrassed silence.

Containment in Asia: The Formosa Crisis

A corollary to the Eisenhower administration's pledge to liberate Eastern Europe was its promise to "unleash" Jiang Jieshi to reconquer mainland China. Truman's decision to station the Seventh Fleet in the Straits of Formosa at the outbreak of the Korean War and his refusal to employ Chinese Nationalist troops in that conflict had been criticized by a group of Asia-first Republicans as too weak. Despite campaign promises to abandon the pusillanimous policy of the Democratic administration, Eisenhower and Dulles soon recognized through their policies that the problem was not to contain Jiang but rather to protect him. Angry over the UN's refusal to seat Communist China's representative to the Security Council, Premier Zhou Enlai declared in early August 1954 that his government would "liberate" Formosa (Taiwan) at the first opportunity. Shortly thereafter, communist artillery batteries began intensive bombardment of Quemoy and Matsu, two islands that were part of a 350-mile chain stretching along and just adjacent to the mainland but controlled by the Nationalists. Fearful that the shelling was a prelude to a full-scale invasion, Secretary Dulles stopped off in Taipei on his way home from the Manila Conference and signed a Mutual Defense Treaty with Jiang. Under its terms, both parties agreed to view an attack on the other's territory in the Pacific as a threat to its interests. The United States reserved the right to decide if and when it would act to protect the offshore islands. The crisis persisted, however.

In January 1955, after the Communists invaded Yikiang Island, Eisenhower asked Congress specifically for authorization to use troops to defend Formosa. There was some grumbling about the administration's refusal to indicate whether "related islands in friendly hands" were covered, but both houses passed the Formosa Resolution by large margins. In March, Dulles asserted in a speech that to contain the "aggressive fanaticism" of the Chinese, the United States was willing to employ "new and powerful weapons of precision which can utterly destroy military targets without endangering unrelated civilian centers." Despite the fact that America possessed no such weapon, Beijing apparently believed the secretary of state was referring to a new version of the atomic bomb. In April, the shelling ceased.

For reasons that are still unclear, the Communists began bombarding Quemoy and Matsu again in August 1958. By this point, Jiang had stationed fully one third of his army on the two islands. At the same time that Eisenhower announced that the United States would fight to defend the two islands, Dulles declared that Jiang had been "rather foolish" in so distributing his troops. Using Indian intermediaries, he suggested to Beijing that if it would agree to a de facto cease fire, he would persuade Jiang to reduce his garrison. The United States, he added, had "no commitment of any kind" to aid the Nationalists in regaining the mainland. In response, the Chinese Communists eased pressure on Taiwan but reserved the right to shell Quemoy and Matsu on alternate days of the week.

Brinkmanship and "The New Look"

During the Eisenhower era, the United States refused to become involved in "brush-fire" wars in part because it had learned the "lessons" of Korea and in part because the nation's conventional forces were deteriorating dramatically. The neglect was intentional, a byproduct of the administration's defense policy. Almost as soon as they took office, Eisenhower, Dulles, Humphrey, and Wilson had to come to grips with the problem of how to reconcile a reduced budget with a militantly anticommunist posture. The chief lesson Ike and his associates drew from Korea was that limited wars fought with conventional weaponry on the periphery of the communist world only drained the nation's resources and weakened its allies' resolve. Secretary Humphrey continually preached that big, expensive government, including bloated defense budgets, would corrupt the currency, drain capital away from the private sector, and do what the Soviet Union could never do – destroy the Republic from within. Yet the communist threat was ever-present.

The administration's synthesis of the seemingly antithetical objectives of military economy and global defense was the doctrine of strategic deterrence that Dulles dubbed massive retaliation. To get "more bang for the buck," the administration would concentrate its funds on the Air Force, specifically the Strategic Air Command (SAC), deliverer of the atomic bomb. Instead of becoming bogged down in a land war in Asia, Latin America, or the Middle East, the United States would brandish its nuclear arsenal in any direct confrontation with the forces of international communism. When it or its allies were faced with aggression from the Soviet Union or its proxies, Dulles argued, the United States must be prepared to go to the brink of nuclear war. "The ability to get to the verge without getting into the war is the necessary art," he told a *Life* reporter in 1956. Under the plan worked out by Humphrey and Wilson, total military expenditures would drop from about $50 billion in 1954 to $35 billion by 1957. In 1955, President Eisenhower asserted America's willingness to use nuclear weapons if necessary. Massive retaliation was based on a kind of clear internal logic. If in fact all communist roads led to Moscow and every Marxist revolution threatened to expand the area of Soviet influence, it was absurd to battle the symptoms of the disease. The most efficient response was to destroy the source. This logic applied, however, only as long as the United States maintained clear superiority over the Soviet Union in both nuclear weaponry and means of delivery.

If Dulles and Eisenhower rejected the economic implications of NSC 68 (the Truman-era policy statement committing the United States to battle the forces of international communism everywhere it threatened to expand), they nevertheless embraced the notion that America's response to communism must be global. Indeed, the Republicans seemed as determined as the Democrats to fight communism on every front. Confronted by the exigencies of his Republican budget and by the limitations of massive retaliation as an instrument of foreign policy, Eisenhower turned to the CIA as an inexpensive and relatively safe method for projecting American power abroad. Originally designed as an intelligence-gathering agency, the CIA expanded under Allen Dulles to include covert operations. During the Eisenhower era, agents not only gathered information but also intervened in the political processes of other nations, distributing aid, organizing coups, and even carrying out assassinations. In addition to massive retaliation and covert operations, Eisenhower and Dulles proposed to contain communism through a series of military alliances; indeed, it appeared during the 1950s that the secretary of state was intent on building a military fence around the Sino–Soviet sphere of influence. In 1954, Dulles traveled to Manila to preside over the creation of the Southeast Asia Treaty Organization (SEATO). Britain, France, Australia, New Zealand, the Philippines, Thailand, and Pakistan promised to view an attack on any one of them as a threat to their own peace and safety. That same year the United States engineered the creation of, but did not join, the Middle East Treaty Organization (METO; subsequently renamed CENTO), which included Turkey, Iraq, Britain, Pakistan, and Iran.

Brinkmanship and alliance building proved to be ineffective strategies. The Soviets sought to project their power not by means of military aggression but rather through forging ideological links with anticolonial revolutionary movements in developing areas and providing nonwestern governments with economic and military aid. During the first Eisenhower administration, Dulles refused to recognize the crucial role of foreign economic aid, stressing arms support almost exclusively. Covert operations seemed somewhat more successful, but the victories were short term and very costly. The U.S. government seemed oblivious to the fact that indigenous nationalism and local rivalries were far more important in most third world crises than the East–West confrontation. In its obsession with the Cold War, the Eisenhower administration tended always to align the United States with entrenched, prowestern oligarchies and to see revolutionary nationalism as part of the international communist conspiracy. As a result, American policy frequently drove local nationalist movements into the arms of Communist China and the Soviet Union.

Vietnam and the Demise of French Colonialism

Competing with Formosa for the Eisenhower administration's attention in the Pacific was Vietnam. Despite massive economic aid by the Truman administration, the French were staring defeat in the face by 1954. Led by General Vo Nguyen Giap, Vietminh troops had surrounded a French garrison near Dienbienphu on the Chinese–Laotian border. In an ill-advised gamble, the French commander had positioned several thousand troops in an effort to cut off supplies coming from Communist China to the Vietminh and to draw Giap's troops into a pitched battle in which supposedly superior French firepower would prevail. In the midst of a horrific siege, the French chief of staff arrived in Washington, D.C., and informed the Eisenhower administration that only direct U.S. military intervention could save the day. Admiral Arthur Radford, chair of the Joint Chiefs of Staff, supported him and urged that 60 B-29s pound the communist positions around Dienbienphu. General Matthew Ridgway, Army chief of staff and a seasoned infantryman, argued against U.S. intervention. Once American lives were lost, he insisted, Congress and the public would demand total victory. That would require 7 divisions, 12 if the Chinese intervened. A Pentagon study concluded ominously that three tactical nuclear weapons "properly employed" could lift the siege.

Dulles and Nixon favored intervention, but Eisenhower made it clear that both Congress and Great Britain would have to go along before he would agree. When Senate Majority Leader Lyndon Johnson refused to back an intervention resolution and British Prime Minister Winston Churchill declined to participate, Eisenhower sent the French emissary home empty-handed. Little public sentiment existed for armed intervention in the First Indochinese War. The United States had just extricated itself from the Korean conflict. Years later, in a television interview with CBS news commentator Walter Cronkite, he explained, "I couldn't think of anything probably less effective [than an air strike]... unless you were willing to use weapons that could have destroyed the jungles all around the area for miles and that would have probably destroyed Dienbienphu itself." It should be noted, however, that the president was fully prepared at the time to employ atomic weapons against China had it intervened. On May 7, 1954, the Vietminh's red battle flag went up over the French command bunker at Dienbienphu. The next morning at Geneva, delegates from nine countries assembled around a horseshoe-shaped table to decide the fate of Indochina.

By the time the Geneva Conference opened, the Vietminh controlled most of northern Vietnam, the communist-led Pathet Lao was struggling against French colonial rule in Laos, and the war-weary French people were ready to abandon Southeast Asia. Though the United States was not an official participant in the Geneva deliberations, Dulles worked behind the scenes to ensure that at least part of Vietnam remained noncommunist. Because both the Soviet Union and Communist China preferred to see Indochina "balkanized" rather than united in a confederation headed by Ho Chi Minh, American diplomacy was successful. Under the terms of the Geneva accords signed in June, Cambodia and Laos obtained their independence. Vietnam was to be divided at the seventeenth parallel, the north to be ruled by Ho and the Vietminh, and the south by former emperor Bao Dai. All foreign troops were to be withdrawn from Vietnam within a year, and an international commission was to supervise nationwide elections to be held no later than July 1956.

As had been the case in Korea, what was to have been a temporary dividing line hardened into one of the most impermeable boundaries in the world. Bao Dai formed the south into the Republic of Vietnam and persuaded the staunchly anticommunist Catholic politician, Ngo Dinh Diem, to become prime minister. Within a year, Diem had ousted Bao Dai and created a presidential system with him as its head. With full American support, Diem rejected unification elections in 1956 because he knew that Ho and the Vietminh would win. Bitter but determined, the communists waited, biding their time and building their strength.

Offending the Good Neighbor: Eisenhower and Latin America

As was true of most American presidents, Eisenhower displayed a greater propensity to intervene more directly in the Western Hemisphere than in other parts of the world when U.S. interests appeared to be threatened. Also, similar to his predecessors, Eisenhower permitted U.S. companies with holdings in Latin America to persuade him that their interests were identical to the national interest. Finally, he and Dulles fell into the trap of attempting to quash nationalist revolutions in the name of protecting the Americas from an extrahemispheric threat – in this case, international communism. To avoid a series of Koreas, however, the Eisenhower administration attempted to achieve its objectives in Latin America and other parts of the developing world by means of covert CIA operations rather than direct military intervention.

At the end of World War II, the foreign policy goals of the United States diverged from those of Latin America. The Truman administration was determined to perfect the hemispheric collective security system that had been started during World War II. The governments of the American republics, their economies first bloated by U.S. and Allied spending during the war and then deflated by the sudden end of these massive purchases, wanted economic and technical assistance to industrialize and diversify their economies. The primary threat to stability in Catholic Latin America, they insisted, was poverty and social insecurity, not Sino–Soviet imperialism. In hopes of ultimately persuading the United States to launch "a Marshall Plan for the Americas," the Latin American states cooperated with Washington's plans for a regional security system. In 1947, at Rio de Janeiro, the nations of the hemisphere agreed to view an attack on one as an attack on all. The following year, the signatories to the Pact of Rio created the Organization of American States (OAS). This UN-like body was entrusted with settling disputes between member nations. Each state had one vote, and most issues were to be decided by a two-thirds vote. At Rio and subsequently at Bogata where the OAS came into being, Latino diplomats pressed the Truman administration for commodity agreements, tariff reductions, and direct financial aid. The U.S. government responded by urging its neighbors to rely on their own private sectors and private investment from the United States. Gradually, Washington's preference for Western Europe and Japan, evidenced by the billions of dollars spent in those areas for reconstruction, coupled with its apparent insensitivity to the hemisphere's needs, created a rising tide of anti-Americanism south of the Rio Grande.

Warned of this trend, in June 1953, Eisenhower dispatched his brother, Dr. Milton Eisenhower, to discover the causes of the deteriorating U.S.–Latin American relationship. In his report, the president's brother pointed out that everything, at least in the absence of war, had to take a back seat to economic cooperation and development. At the same time, the National Security Council, while recognizing the need to raise living standards, recommended that the United States rely on trade and private investment and warned that the number one problem was the drift toward "radical and nationalistic regimes." Such governments were especially susceptible to communist subversion. As the president and Secretary Dulles pondered this conflicting advice, the administration was confronted with what it viewed as a Soviet effort to establish a beachhead in the New World.

Guatemala

In 1951, Colonel Jacobo Arbenz Guzman assumed the presidency of Guatemala. He and his supporters were convinced that confiscation and redistribution of large landed estates, together with heavier taxation if not expropriation, were necessary to achieve economic progress and social justice. Communist participation in his government was minimal, consisting of only 4 of his 51-vote majority in the Guatemalan parliament. Washington paid little attention to developments in Guatemala until August 1953, when the government seized lands belonging to the United Fruit Company. Although the land was not in use and the Arbenz government offered compensation, United Fruit executives were offended and alarmed. Shortly thereafter, the assistant secretary of state for Latin American affairs charged Guatemala with "openly playing the communist game." In February 1954, when Arbenz refused to restore the confiscated acreage or to allow the issue to be submitted to the Court of Arbitration at the Hague, the State Department concluded that he was a thoroughgoing Marxist-Leninist and, as such, a tool of Moscow. More than a few Guatemalans suspected that the charges of communism were a smoke screen to camouflage a program of coercion against Arbenz on behalf of the United Fruit Company.

At the tenth annual meeting of the Inter-American Conference, which convened in Bogata in March, the U.S. delegation sponsored a general anticommunist resolution that did not mention Guatemala by name but that was clearly aimed at that country. The "Declaration of Solidarity . . . Against International Communist Intervention" labeled international communism as a threat to the peace and safety of the hemisphere and committed the republics to cooperate in combating it. Although few delegates believed that their intensely Catholic populations were vulnerable to Marxism-Leninism, most went along in the knowledge that the United States would never provide economic aid to any nation that refused to stand up and be counted against communism. Indeed, only Guatemala voted against the resolution, although Argentina and Mexico abstained.

Within weeks of the close of the Bogata meeting, U.S. relations with Guatemala reached a crisis stage. On May 17, the State Department announced that a shipment of 1,900 tons of Czech arms had arrived in Guatemala, dangerously tipping the military balance of power in Central America. Hurriedly, the U.S. government concluded bilateral security pacts with Nicaragua and Honduras and began rushing arms to those countries. Throughout the spring, a Guatemalan exile force under the command of Colonel Carlos Castillo Armas had been training in the jungles of Honduras with CIA help. Broadcasting from Honduran territory, the CIA-run radio station, Voice of Liberty, helped convince Guatemalans that Castillo's force was large and well equipped. Air raids on Guatemala City carried out by U.S. pilots helped spread panic. Early in the morning hours of June 18, Castillo's makeshift army of 150 men invaded their homeland. When the army refused to fight for Arbenz, his regime collapsed. Washington immediately recognized the new Castillo government and extended substantial economic aid.

The White House and State Department were convinced that the United States had helped an indigenous anticommunist movement thwart a communist takeover in the strategically important Caribbean. In fact, it had thrown its support behind an authoritarian figure who ruled through intimidation. Before he was assassinated in 1957, Castillo Armas would suspend the right of habeas corpus, end land reform, abolish collective bargaining, and narrow the franchise. To many Latinos, it seemed that the United States had once again invoked the threat of extrahemispheric intervention in an effort to protect one of its powerful vested interests.

The Suez Crisis

Nowhere were the limitations of the Eisenhower–Dulles approach to foreign policy more apparent, however, than in the Middle East. A number of factors contributed to instability in that strategically vital area during the 1950s and to converting it into a Cold War battleground. The first was the breadth and depth of Arab nationalism. For centuries, the Ottoman Empire had exploited the area stretching from Egypt to Iraq. With the demise of the empire in the aftermath of World War I, Britain and France took control of the newly created nations of Iraq, Lebanon, Syria, Jordan, and Palestine as protectorates under the League of Nations. World War II loosened formal ties between the Arab states and their "protectors," but economic domination and informal political control remained. By the 1950s, the region seethed with discontent and mistrust of the West.

A second factor that contributed to instability in the region and added impetus to Arab nationalism was Zionism, the movement to establish a Jewish homeland in Palestine. In 1917, the British government, under pressure from the World Zionist Organization and its own Jewish population, issued the Balfour Declaration, which promised to help create a separate Jewish state in Palestine. In the late 1930s and 1940s, Nazi persecution drove tens of thousands of Jews to seek refuge in Palestine. In response to Arab pressure, the British attempted to limit immigration during and immediately after World War II. From 1946 through 1948, British authorities were subject to attacks both from Jewish terrorists seeking to have immigration restrictions lifted and from Arab terrorists determined to keep out Jewish refugees. In 1947, Britain threw up its hands, announced that it was turning Palestine over to the United Nations, and withdrew the following May. Immediately, war erupted between a Jewish army and military forces consisting of Palestinians and members of the Arab League. As their soldiers drove Arab units out of Palestine, Jewish leaders proclaimed the new state of Israel. Within hours the Truman administration had extended diplomatic recognition. Half the Arab population, nearly 1 million people, fled their homes. Beginning in 1948, the humiliated Arab states refused to recognize Israel, tried to strangle the new state economically, and continually threatened to annihilate Israel in a second war.

Further contributing to unrest in the Middle East was the maldistribution of wealth in the form of petroleum deposits. By the 1950s, Arab rulers with oil resources had worked out arrangements with the Arabian-American Oil Company, Dutch Shell, and various British concerns in which the huge profits earned from the extraction and refining of petroleum were divided evenly between the country in question and the extracting company. But the nations of the Middle East with the largest and most deprived populations, notably Egypt, Jordan, and Syria, possessed almost no oil. These nations, aware that their boundaries were the creations of western diplo-mats at the 1919 Versailles Peace Conference, had to stand by and watch their populations live in mud huts and struggle to eke out a living from the arid land while the royal families of Qatar and Kuwait grew obscenely rich.

In the Middle East, as in other developing areas, the Eisenhower ad-ministration found itself pitted against revolutionary nationalists who fre-quently called for nationalization of western-owned property. At times Washington acted to protect vested American interests and strategic petroleum reserves and at times to prevent communist penetration of the region. Because the Eisenhower administration tended to equate revo-lutionary nationalism with Sino–Soviet imperialism, those goals became intertwined.

The first Middle East testing ground for the Eisenhower–Dulles foreign policy was the strategically important country of Iran. World War II had severely depleted America's petroleum resources. It seemed possible by the early 1950s that the United States and its allies would become increas-ingly dependent on Middle Eastern oil. In 1951, the tough-minded, anti-British prime minister of Iran, Mohammad Mosaddeq, had nationalized the Anglo-Iranian Oil Company. Two years later, Mosaddeq, supported by the communist-dominated Tudeh party, seized control of the government, sending the youthful Muhammad Reza Shah (King) Pahlavi into exile. That fall, Britain and the United States cut off economic and technical aid to the Mosaddeq regime, which, threatened with bankruptcy and civil strife, turned to the Soviet Union for aid.

The Iranian government's approaches to Moscow, together with the left-ist leanings of the ruling Tudeh party, convinced the U.S. government that the Mosaddeq regime was controlled by the forces of international com-munism. Eisenhower decided on covert action to check Teheran's "down-hill course toward Communist-supported dictatorship." Forces loyal to the Peacock throne, armed with British and American weapons, engineered a military coup, drove Mosaddeq from power, and restored the Shah to his throne. In August 1953, the Shah signed an agreement that divided the country's oil production rights between a British concern (40%), an American consortium (40%), and two other foreign firms, one French and one Dutch. In 1957, the CIA began helping the Shah's government build a secret police apparatus, SAVAK, which would use torture, imprisonment, and execution in an attempt to suppress all opposition to the throne.

Nowhere was Arab nationalism and anti-Zionism stronger than in Egypt – populous, potentially powerful, but chronically poor. In July 1952, the Egyptian government's inability to gain control of the Suez from Britain, together with domestic problems, led to a bloodless revolution. Out of the group of junior officers who overthrew the corrupt regime of King Farouk emerged Colonel Gamal Abdel Nasser. The charismatic

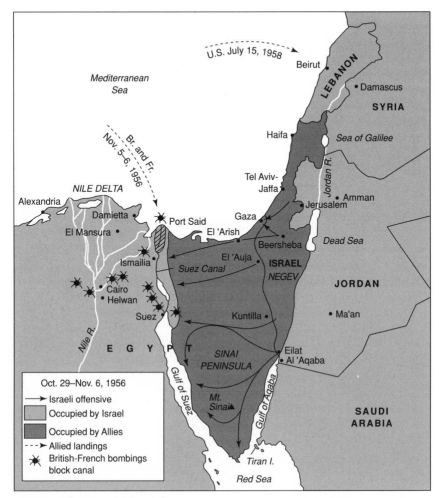

Map 4–1. The Suez Crisis, 1956.

officer-politician transformed Egypt into a republic, launched a program of economic reform, including land redistribution, and adopted an ultra-nationalist stance in foreign policy. The centerpiece of Nasser's economic development plan was the High Aswan Dam, which would increase Egypt's arable land by one third and protect the thousands of farmers who lived in the Nile Valley from floods. In December 1955, the United States offered an initial grant of $56 million, with Britain adding another $14 million. Nasser then delayed acceptance, dickering with the Soviets for better terms. That fall, he mortgaged Egypt's entire 1956 cotton crop in a huge arms deal with the Czechoslovakian government. In May 1956, he defiantly severed diplomatic ties with Nationalist China and recognized the government in

Beijing. Infuriated by Nasser's flirtation with the forces of international communism, in July 1956, Dulles withdrew the American offer of aid in the construction of the High Aswan Dam. The secretary of state put the matter simply, "Do nations which play both sides get better treatment than nations which are stalwart and work with us?" Humiliated and angry, Nasser announced a week later the nationalization of the Universal Suez Canal Company, which was owned mainly by British and French stockholders. Egyptians would run the canal, and the revenues earned would be used to finance the Aswan project.

Dulles's rash action threatened the interests of America's two principal allies, Britain and France. Not only did their citizens own the canal company, but the two Western European nations received massive amounts of petroleum and other raw materials through the canal. Finally, their prestige was on the line. Israel also felt threatened by the takeover and even more by the military buildup in Egypt. For more than a year, Palestinian fedayeen (guerrillas) operating out of the Sinai peninsula had been carrying out hit-and-run attacks far into Israel. On October 29 the Israelis invaded the Sinai and drove toward the Suez Canal. Ignoring Dulles's pleas for calm, Britain and France issued an ultimatum to both combatants to keep their troops 10 miles on either side of the Suez. When Nasser refused, British and French paratroopers seized the canal. It became clear in retrospect that Tel Aviv, London, and Paris had acted in collusion. On October 30, the United States placed a resolution before the Security Council calling on Israel and Egypt to stop fighting and on Israel to withdraw its troops. Britain and France vetoed this and a similar Russian resolution. Making the most of the situation, Moscow threatened to send volunteers into the area and rain missiles on London and Paris. Eisenhower responded by announcing that the United States would use force to prevent Soviet intervention. The United Nations subsequently negotiated a cease-fire, British and French troops withdrew, and the Egyptians began administering the canal fairly and efficiently.

The U.S. government's efforts to restrain Britain and France won some plaudits in third world capitals, but overall, American interests suffered as a result of the Suez crisis. Dulles's diplomacy had driven Nasser into the hands of the Russians, split NATO, and heightened Arab nationalism. In a largely irrelevant gesture, President Eisenhower announced on January 5, 1957, that the United States would defend the nations of the Middle East against Soviet attack. With some difficulty, the administration persuaded Congress to pass a joint resolution called the Eisenhower Doctrine, which approved this gesture. The Suez Crisis probably came too late to have much impact on the 1956 election and, to the extent that it did, helped the incumbent. The American people have always been loath to change leaders in the midst of an international crisis.

The Election of 1956

Despite the Dixon–Yates controversy, the failure to roll back the Iron Curtain, and the recession, Eisenhower's popularity continued to grow. Republicans looked forward to retaining the White House for another four years, but in September 1955, disaster struck. The president suffered a major heart attack while vacationing in Denver. As the nation held its breath and Press Secretary James Haggerty issued hourly reports, famed Boston heart specialist Paul Dudley White rushed to the scene. Within a month, White certified Eisenhower fit enough to be transferred to his Gettysburg farm. With Vice President Nixon presiding over Cabinet meetings in his absence and the White House staff under Sherman Adams functioning smoothly, the nation's first citizen made a rapid recovery. By January, GOP leaders were pressing Eisenhower to declare for a second term. He demurred, expressing his desire to retire to a quieter life on the farm. Yet, Eisenhower once again felt the call of duty. After delivering a vigorous State of the Union address in January, he announced his candidacy to a national television audience.

The 1956 presidential election lacked the tension and excitement of the 1952 campaign. The country was prosperous, at peace, and with the demise of McCarthy, relatively united. The Republican carapace, observed one political pundit, was as smooth and undentable as an "I Like Ike" button. Nonetheless, Adlai Stevenson, once again nominated by the Democrats, labored gamely to put forward an alternative to "the politics of complacency." Eisenhower easily countered Stevenson's pledge to end the draft and institute an all-volunteer army. After all, GOP campaigners asked, "Who was it best to trust on this subject?" Democrats tried to raise the health issue, warning voters that if they elected Eisenhower, they would have a "part-time President." Ike responded by having his doctors publicly certify his fitness for office. Stevenson infuriated his opponent by criticizing the administration for not taking up Khrushchev on his proposal for a nuclear test ban treaty. Nixon publicly labeled Stevenson a naive appeaser, and Eisenhower wrote to a friend that "the Stevenson–Kefauver [Estes Kefauver of Tennessee was the Democratic vice presidential nominee] combination is, in some ways, about the sorriest and weakest we have ever run for the two top offices in the land."

There was no last-minute switch to Stevenson, no miracle repeat of 1948. Eisenhower won in a landslide capturing 457 electoral votes to his opponent's 73. His margin in the popular vote was a whopping 9 million out of 62 million cast. Ike's personal popularity and his absolute domination of the political center had defeated the New Deal coalition. He made gains in every area over his 1952 totals. The Democrats retained control of both houses of Congress – 49 to 47 in the Senate and 234 to 201 in the House – making

Eisenhower the first president since Zachary Taylor in 1849 to begin his term with both the Senate and House in opposing hands.

Soviet–American Relations and the Nuclear Arms Race

As they struggled to reconcile the principles of equal protection, the law, and equality of opportunity with the facts of interracial life and to strike a balance between fiscal conservatism and the welfare state, Americans lived continually under the threat of nuclear annihilation. In response to the brilliant technological arguments of émigré scientist Dr. Edward Teller, and pressure from professional anticommunists, in 1949, the nuclear scientists and the U.S. military had reluctantly endorsed a research project to develop a hydrogen bomb, nicknamed the "super" by scientists. On November 1, 1952, on Eniwetok Atoll, the first American thermonuclear explosion took place. At Bikini Atoll on March 1, 1954, American technicians successfully tested a hydrogen bomb. The H-bomb's most outstanding and horrifying feature was its almost unlimited potential. Simply by adding deuterium fuel, the explosiveness of the super could be increased many times over. The first H-bomb was not only twice as powerful as expected but extremely "dirty" as well, generating a great deal more radioactive fallout than the atom bomb.

In August 1959, the Joint Congressional Committee on Atomic Energy reported that an attack on the United States might kill 50 million people and seriously injure an additional 20 million, while destroying or making uninhabitable half the United States' dwellings. In an effort to ease the tension created by the advent of nuclear weapons, in July 1955 in Geneva, Switzerland, Eisenhower met with the leaders of Britain, France, and Russia. Nothing concrete came out of the discussions on disarmament, reunification of Germany, and East–West cultural and commercial contacts. Nevertheless, the atmosphere was so congenial that reporters began referring in their dispatches to the "Spirit of Geneva." Khrushchev and Soviet Premier Nikolai A. Bulganin continually invoked the need for "peaceful coexistence" and "the relaxation of world tensions." Eisenhower was at his most amiable. When he declared at one point that "the United States will never take part in an aggressive war," Bulganin replied simply, "We believe that statement."

Sputnik

However, the spirit of Geneva was short lived. Russia's invasion of Hungary and its efforts to project its power into the Middle East during the Suez Crisis convinced many Americans that the thaw was over. To make matters worse, advances in Soviet rocketry seemed to render "massive retaliation" and "brinkmanship" irrelevant. On October 4, 1957, the Soviet Union shocked the West by sending the world's first man-made satellite, Sputnik (traveling companion), into orbit. That accomplishment, realized before the United States had perfected its own missile system, upset the scientific and potentially the military balance between the two countries. On November 2, the Russians launched Sputnik II, with a payload six times heavier than that carried by the first Russian space vehicle, again proving their apparent superiority in missile technology. This demonstration of engineering skill devastated most Americans. *Newsweek* lamented the deplorable state of American science and education. Democratic Senator Stuart Symington of Missouri, a former secretary of the Air Force, warned that "unless our defense policies are promptly changed, the Soviets will move from superiority to supremacy. If that ever happens our position will become impossible." The Soviet Union also possessed the largest army in the world and was developing a navy second only to that of the United States. Secretary Dulles warned that Russia had overcome the "preponderance of power" that the United States had enjoyed since 1945.

Indeed, in the wake of Sputnik, Americans became well-nigh obsessed with Soviet science and technology. Ignoring the fact that Russia had concentrated its resources on the military sector and, in so doing, doomed the rest of the economy to obsolescence and inefficiency, Americans were overcome by a sense of inferiority. Conservative Senator Styles Bridges of New Hampshire sounded the alarm, declaring that the "time has clearly come to be less concerned with the depth of pile of the new broadloom rug or the height of the tail fin of the new car and to be more prepared to shed blood, sweat and tears." Sputnik seemed to confirm Democratic charges that the GOP was the party of hedonism and materialism and that Eisenhower was more interested in playing golf than in defending the free world.

Pressure on the White House to embark on a crash missile development program and attend to the neglected conventional forces of the United States was tremendous. In November 1957, Senate Majority Leader Lyndon B. Johnson of Texas opened his Inquiry into the Satellite and Missile Programs. Later that year, the report of the Gaither Committee, a panel of prominent citizens named by the president to study the nation's strategic defenses, was leaked to the press. It was an alarmist document, arguing that Strategic Air Command bases would be virtually defenseless in the face of an enemy attack. The president and other fiscally conservative Republicans recoiled at the budgetary implications of the Gaither report.

In his 1958 State of the Union address, Eisenhower admitted that he had underestimated the psychological impact of Sputnik. He assured the American people that research and development in intercontinental ballistic missiles (ICBMs) and long-range bombers were continuing, and he announced the reorganization of the Pentagon. However, the Cold War, the president insisted, had to do with more than guns, missiles, and bombs. He asked Congress not to reduce funding for foreign trade and aid, and he introduced legislation designed to improve basic education and scientific research. Shortly afterward, Congress passed the National Defense Education Act authorizing the expenditure of $1 billion over seven years to enable the states to improve secondary and college education in science, mathematics, engineering, and foreign languages. At the same time, the president rejected a tax cut, an overall increase in federal spending, and deficit spending. Military expenditures for missiles and other weapons increased but not to the extent that the suddenly hawkish Democrats wanted. The president knew, but could not say for security reasons, that the top-secret U-2 surveillance plane would give the United States plenty of warning in the event of a Soviet nuclear attack. Defense spending was $42.7 billion in fiscal 1957, rising in 1959 to only $46.6 billion, and then declining to $45.9 billion in fiscal 1960.

In fact, popular anxiety over the "missile gap," a term coined by Democratic political strategists, could not have been more ill founded. Indeed, according to historian Walter McDougal "more new starts and technical leaps occurred in the years before 1960 than in any comparable span" in American history. During Eisenhower's watch, Atlas, the first U.S. intercontinental ballistic missile (ICBM), became operational, while plans for Titan, a liquid-fuel rocket, got underway in 1955. The U.S. Navy began development of the Polaris submarine and the Air Force Minuteman, a solid-fuel ICBM that could be launched in 60 seconds. These programs came to fruition in the early 1960s, giving the United States a powerful triad of deterrence consisting of the B-52, the Polaris, and the Minuteman. But once established, popular perceptions were hard to change. The Eisenhower administration continued to suffer from the alleged missile gap for the remainder of its term in office.

Sputnik created a grudging respect for the USSR in the minds of some Americans, ironically making the prospect of peaceful coexistence more attractive than it might formerly have been. In the spring of 1958, advocates of Soviet–American rapprochement had been heartened when a 23-year-old Texan named Van Cliburn won the Tchaikovsky International Piano and Violin Festival held in Moscow. His rendition of the Third Piano Concerto by Sergei Rachmaninoff set off a frenzy of applause in the packed auditorium. His victory and reception were widely and appreciatively reported in the American press.

The Second Berlin Crisis
But Soviet–American relations took a nosedive when suddenly on November 27, 1958, Khrushchev demanded that the United States, Britain, and France withdraw their 10,000 soldiers from West Berlin, declare it a demilitarized free city, and negotiate directly with the East German government for terms of access. He set a six-month deadline and subsequently announced that the Soviet Union was going to sign a separate peace treaty with the German Democratic Republic (GDR) and withdraw its occupation

forces. The Russians had urged German reunification under various guises but had adamantly opposed free elections while linking the settlement of the German question to a general European security arrangement, including the withdrawal of American forces from the continent. Soviet leaders were especially concerned about West Berlin, a monumental propaganda thorn in their side. Not only had some 3 million East Germans, generally the most educated and enterprising, escaped through this portal since 1945, but the thriving, brightly lit western zone stood in sharp contrast to the drab, poverty-stricken eastern zone, a continual reminder of the promise of capitalism and failures of communism. But the West did not recognize the GDR, and the threat of a Soviet pullout implied a new Berlin blockade.

Soviet and Western foreign ministers met in May 1959 to discuss the Berlin and German situation; the British, French, and Americans held firm, with the result that the Soviets extended their ultimatum for another 18 months. Secretary of State Christian Herter (Dulles had died of cancer earlier in the year) returned from Geneva and warned that western officials were convinced that the Soviet Union intended to incorporate West Berlin and eventually all of Germany into the communist camp. Against his better judgment, in an effort to avoid a showdown over Berlin, Eisenhower authorized the American delegation at Geneva to extend an invitation to Khrushchev to visit America. What ensued was a 10-day highly publicized tour from which the Soviet leader extracted every ounce of propaganda value. He toured urban factories and an Iowa farm, finishing his cross-country trek in Hollywood, where after witnessing the filming of "Can-Can," he delivered a fiery speech against pornography. Later in the year, Eisenhower and other western leaders invited Khrushchev to attend a summit meeting in Paris in May 1960, to discuss Germany and related European questions.

Some two weeks before Khrushchev and Eisenhower were to meet, on May 1, Soviet authorities announced that they had shot down an American plane some 13,000 miles inside Russian air space over Sverdlovsk. Washington responded by declaring that an American weather plane had drifted off course and was missing. There was absolutely no intention of violating Soviet air space, the State Department declared. At that point, Moscow sprung its trap. The downed aircraft was no weather plane; it was a U-2 spy plane operating out of Turkey under CIA supervision, the Kremlin declared. The U-2, its cameras filled with photos of top-secret Soviet military installations, and its pilot, Francis Gary Powers, had been captured intact. Powers had confessed. Secretary of State Christian Herter admitted that American reconnaissance had been flying secret missions over communist territory for years and implied that they would continue to do so. Khrushchev responded by threatening to rain down rockets on European bases used by the United States for espionage. Eisenhower grudgingly assumed public responsibility for the flights and left for the Paris summit. Only hours into the meeting, Khrushchev demanded that Eisenhower apologize for the invasion of Soviet air space and punish those who were responsible. When the grim-faced president refused to back down, Khrushchev walked out. He subsequently cancelled Eisenhower's planned visit to Russia and made it clear that there could be no serious negotiations on Berlin or any other issue until a new president had taken office.

Summary

East–West relations were no better at the close of the Eisenhower administration than they had been at its dawning, but they were no worse either. Dwight Eisenhower and his foreign policy team were determined to contain communism, and they hoped to do it without plunging the globe into nuclear war and without bankrupting the United States. The administration was successful on all three points. Neither the United States, the Soviet Union, nor Communist China went to war with one another or became directly involved in the regional and local conflicts that dotted the geopolitical landscape during the 1950s. Through nuclear threat, alliance building, and covert operations, the Eisenhower administration successfully projected its power throughout the world. But it frequently did so in an indiscriminate and counterproductive manner. Washington insisted on viewing every local and regional conflict through the prism of the Cold War, ignoring purely indigenous factors such as nationalism, tribalism, and socioeconomic deprivation and insisting that a faction or government declare itself for or against the "free world." In the process, Eisenhower and Dulles frequently arrayed the United States against the forces of revolutionary nationalism and on behalf of autocratic, repressive regimes who were representing the entrenched economic interests of their country. Ironically then, in the name of freedom, democracy, and social progress, the United States during the 1950s often sided with those who were committed to autocracy, repression, and reaction.

ADDITIONAL READINGS

Anderson, David L., *Trapped By Success* (1991).

Ball, Howard, *Justice Downwind: America's Nuclear Testing Program in the 1950s* (1986).

Divine, Robert A., *Blowing in the Wind: The Nuclear Testing Program in the 1950s* (1986).

Divine, Robert A., *Eisenhower and the Cold War* (1981).

Hahn, Peter L., *The U.S., Great Britain, and Egypt, 1945–1956* (1991).

Kahin, George McT., *Intervention: How America Became Involved in Vietnam* (1986).

Rabe, Stephen G., *Eisenhower and Latin America* (1988).

5 Capitalism and Conformity

American Society, 1945–1960

Postwar Economic Boom

The 15 years following the end of World War II comprised a period of remarkable economic growth for the United States. Despite widespread fears among economists and public officials, a recurrence of the Great Depression did not materialize. The postwar boom in America was fueled by a number of factors. First, long-unsatisfied demand for consumer products coupled with massive savings created a huge market, a market that was sustained by unparalleled population growth. Second, World War II had expanded and modernized American industry. At war's end, plants converted from military to civilian production and began producing increasingly cheap, high-quality products. Third, technical innovations enabled old industries to produce new, improved products and led to the establishment of new enterprises in electronics and plastics. Fourth, worker productivity increased dramatically and steadily during these years. Fifth, after an initial downturn, government spending on a burgeoning foreign aid program and the Korean War stimulated the private sector.

From 1945 to 1947, pent-up consumer demand and savings more than compensated for reductions in government spending, which dropped from an annual rate of $100.5 billion for 1944 to $44.8 billion by the end of the 1940s. The economy lost steam in 1948, as Americans at last satiated their demand for items such as automobiles and refrigerators that were denied them during World War II. As manufacturing stockpiles grew, so did unemployment. Inflation, slowed but not controlled by Truman's policies, added to the nation's economic woes. But the downturn was only a modest setback, and recovery was on its way when the Korean War intervened. Fueled by new government expenditures and an aggressive private sector, the economy grew steadily until 1953. The end of the Korean War, together with the Eisenhower administration's determination to balance the budget and control inflation, led to another downturn in 1954. However, the recession was, like the 1948 slump, brief and mild. Fueled by a

121

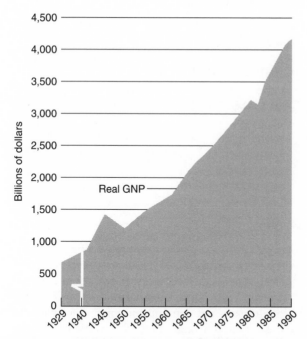

Figure 5–1. Gross national product, 1929–1990.

tax cut and increased investment by business, economic indices reached all-time highs. From 1957 to 1958, the United States suffered through the worst recession it had experienced since World War II Cutbacks in private investment, coupled with drops in defense spending and exports, sent the economy into a tailspin. However, economic stabilizers such as Social Security and unemployment relief cushioned the impact, and by the end of the Kennedy administration, the United States once again embarked on a period of unparalleled economic growth.

With the exception of three mild recessions, the U.S. economy boomed during the 1950s. By the close of the decade, personal income had reached an annual rate of $227.5 billion, up from a record $171.1 billion in 1945. Productivity increased dramatically. From 1947 to 1956, the growth was 200% per capita. The average unemployment rate during the 1950s was 4.5% and the total number of people employed exceeded 60 million by the end of the 1950s. Inflation averaged between 1% and 2% during these years. Per capita income, in constant dollars, rose from $2,150 in 1947 to $2,699 in 1960. The median income for a family of four was $5,620. As of 1956, U.S. corporations were paying some $12 billion per year in dividends. The gross national product (GNP) grew from $309.9 billion in 1947 to more than $500 billion by the end of the 1950s. It was estimated that the net worth of all Americans by 1960 was $875 billion.

Perhaps most notably, by 1960, the American economy had completed its transformation from a simple production economy, in which the primary task was to meet basic human needs, to a consumer economy, in which it was assumed that food, shelter, and clothing were being attended to and that the task ahead was to stimulate and expand consumption in a never-ending drive to increase production and raise profits. The postwar economy was also characterized by a decline in some traditional industries, such as coal, textiles, and public transportation; the continued growth of certain "mature" manufacturing industries, such as automobiles and housing; and the emergence of new businesses. Construction of all varieties boomed during the postwar years, but one-family residences and apartments, retarded by a decade of depression and war, displayed especially marked growth. Factory sales of cars and trucks averaged almost 7 million per year during the 1950s, and in the peak year of 1955, more than 9 million vehicles were sold. General Motors, Chrysler, and Ford pioneered the concept of "planned obsolescence," in which each new model eclipsed old models by being equipped with bigger engines and featuring radically altered styles. Led by Dow, Monsanto, DuPont, and other conglomerates, the chemical industry boomed during the postwar era, growing at an annual rate of 10% between 1947 and 1960. Aircraft manufacturing and electronics fared almost as well. The first globe-circling passenger airline was inaugurated by Pan American Airways on June 17, 1947, when the America, a Lockheed Constellation, took off from New York for Gander, New Foundland. The roundtrip fare from New York was $1,700. Commercial and military aviation reinforced each other, and companies such as Boeing, McDonald-Douglas, and General Dynamics became multibillion dollar enterprises.

A number of factors were responsible for America's midcentury economic bonanza. A most obvious contributor was public spending. The period did not witness a significant rise in expenditures for federal entitlement programs – Social Security, veterans benefits, or unemployment – however, under the Eisenhower administration, the momentum toward creation of a welfare state did slacken somewhat. Yet, outlays for military purposes more than compensated for this, as Defense Department allocations accounted for more than 50% of the total national budget each year of the Eisenhower presidency. Moreover, state and local expenditures for public services rose steadily during this period – from 7% of the GNP in 1950 to 9.4% in 1960. Those who had jobs were more likely than ever to be working for someone other than a business employer. Whereas in 1929, only 15% of the labor force had worked outside the private sector, by the early 1960s, about one third of all employed people were paid by government, educational institutions, or nonprofit organizations. During the 1950s, the private economy was able to create only one tenth of all new jobs.

Technology and Credit

In the postwar period, there was an explosion of theoretical and practical knowledge. In 1946, the first electronic digital computer went into operation at the Moore School of Electrical Engineering in Philadelphia. It contained 18,000 vacuum tubes, occupied a 30-foot by 60-foot room, and weighed some 30 tons. During the next generation, computers would shrink in size, increase in speed, and proliferate to the point where they would be as common as televisions. Dozens of new inventions in other areas led not only to greater production but also to state-of-the-art products that made the United States easily the world's leader in electronics, aviation, mass communication equipment, and pharmaceuticals.

If manufacturing production was revolutionized during the 1920s by the concept of scientific management, it was further transformed during the 1945 to 1960 period by the idea of automation. Quite simply, automation meant the substitution of machines for humans in the operation of other machines. Gradually, automation crept up the production and managerial ladder until individual workers or managers operated a network of labor-saving devices that vastly increased manpower production. "Automation," *Business Week* observed in the 1950s, "[is] the art and science of going through as many stages of production as possible with as little human help as possible."

The technology revolution along with automation had a profound effect on the American workforce. The number of factory operators during the 1950s actually decreased by 4%, although the average factory wage increased dramatically. The employment slack was more than taken up, however, by new clerical positions, which increased 23% during this period, and by an explosion in the service industry. In 1956, the United States crossed the line from being an industrial to a postindustrial state; that is, more workers were involved in white-collar jobs than blue-collar positions. The new service industries – government bureaucracy, sales, advertising, telecommunications, dry cleaning, banking – were designed to help consumers do what they did best: accumulate money and acquire goods.

Not surprisingly, organized labor waned in the postindustrial environment. Already weakened by anticommunism, by the rise of the conservative coalition, and by its wartime and postwar strikes, union membership stubbornly refused to rise. By 1960, the unionized portion of the country's nonagricultural workers stood at 31.4% compared with 31.5% for 1950. In the new service industries, labor succeeded in organizing less than 5% of the nation's technicians, engineers, and draftsmen, and less than 3% of its 8.5 million office workers. In their conservative, wage–benefit approach, as well as in their compensation packages, union executives came to resemble the corporate executives with whom they negotiated.

Agriculture, at least its largest operators, benefited from automation and the technology revolution. Stimulated by mechanization of farm operations, agricultural production soared following the war. New and better tractors, harvesters, and planters, combined with potent fertilizers, herbicides, and pesticides, enabled American farmers to vastly increase their yield and their lead over their international rivals. At the same time, new technologies and scientific management contributed to overproduction and increased costs, in the process driving thousands of small farmers out of business. America featured 1.7 million fewer agricultural owners in 1959 than in 1950, and the number of farms declined from 5.4 million in 1950 to 3.7 million in 1959. For those who stayed on the farm, the quality of life improved dramatically during the postwar years. Only 25% of farm households were electrified before World War II. By 1960, this number had risen to 80%, and a majority of homes also featured refrigerators, televisions, and telephones.

Almost as important in stimulating the postwar economic boom as government spending and technological innovation was the explosion in consumer credit. In 1950, the Diner's Club issued plastic credit cards to select members in New York to enable them to eat at fine restaurants without having to demean themselves with cash transactions. The credit card subsequently took America by storm. Sears, Roebuck alone could boast 10 million accounts by the end of the Eisenhower administration. Banks, automobile companies, and savings and loan institutions literally pled with customers to buy products on time. By 1960, 60% of all cars were bought on credit, some on terms as easy as $100 down and three years to pay. In 1955, 40% of all VHA-financed homes were purchased without a down payment. As a result of this credit expansion, by the end of the first postwar decade, 81% of American families had managed to purchase television sets, 96% had acquired refrigerators, and almost 89% possessed washing machines. By the mid-1950s, installment indebtedness in the United States had reached $27 billion, 10 times what it had been in the 1920s. There were many prices to pay for buying on time, but one of the most important was the loss of personal freedom. The growth of private debt was accompanied by the emergence of a sizable new industry whose function it was to investigate, report, and maintain files on the purchasing habits and repayment records of millions of individual Americans. Based on information gathered without a person's consent, and frequently knowledge, the credit rating became the average American's most important asset.

Toward Oligopoly
The trend toward consolidation of commercial, financial, and manufacturing enterprises that had begun during the latter part of the nineteenth century accelerated in the post–World War II years. Six hundred corporations

constituted only 0.6% of the whole, but they earned 53% of America's corporate income. Oligopoly, the domination of a business or industry by a few firms, became the rule. Aluminum production and distribution were in the hands of three concerns, while Ford, General Motors, and Chrysler dominated auto-making. Three giant networks controlled television programming through production facilities and distribution affiliates. Between 1940 and 1960, bank deposits increased 400%, but the number of banks declined by 1,000. In petroleum, 15 firms employed 86% of all workers, while in steel, 13 concerns employed 85% of the industry workforce. Many of these giants were "multinational"; that is, corporations such as International Business Machines, Eastman Kodak, and Texaco maintained operations in dozens of countries. International Telephone and Telegraph, for example, owned more than 300 subsidiaries around the world that employed 500,000 people.

Somewhat ironically in a nation that worshipped free enterprise, American business continued to lead the way in devising means for eliminating competition. During the industrial revolution, business consolidation had taken place around two principles: horizontal and vertical integration. The first involved acquiring enterprises that manufactured the same products; the second, gaining control of supporting operations. Thus did U.S. Steel attempt to acquire or drive out of business directly competing firms, while also gaining control over the ore fields that supplied its smelters and the railroads that carried its product. The favored means to monopoly in the post–World War II economy, however, was the conglomerate in which vastly different enterprises – food processing and motion pictures, for example – were brought under the same roof by a team of powerful financial managers. The objects of the exercise were to concentrate capital to facilitate research and development and to diversify, thus ensuring survival and prosperity to the whole in case one member should be hit by recession. The emergence of the conglomerate made it even tougher for small enterprises to compete because they could not match the giants' ability to develop and market new and better products. During the 1950s, America's top 500 concerns absorbed more than 3,000 smaller businesses.

Conformity and Materialism

In the midst of this plenty, a new type of society emerged characterized by a drive for conformity in dress, architecture, and gender roles; an obsession with consumption; and an insensitivity to the American underclass. As America moved into the postindustrial era, consumption became a virtual obsession. The proportion of homeowners in the population increased by 50% during the period from 1945 to 1960, and almost everyone owned an automobile. There were all sorts of new gadgets to purchase; in 1947, the Polaroid Land camera, developed by Edwin H. Land, went on sale. The first camera with its own dark room, the Polaroid could turn out a picture in seconds and was an instant success. Spending on advertising increased 400% and almost tripled the amount the nation spent on education. Producers of consumer products spent millions of dollars glorifying consumption and then reaped huge profits satisfying the need they had created. Analysts realized that Americans had unprecedented amounts of real income to spend by the 1950s, but lingering memories of the Depression had an inhibiting effect. Unconsciously harking back to the early colonial period when Puritan burghers insisted that material success was a badge of divine favor, advertisers preached that possession of the latest model car and the newest type of refrigerator was not only fun but also positively moral.

Throughout most of U.S. history, but especially during the Depression and World War II, waste had been considered uncivil and even immoral. The consumer culture changed this. Planned obsolescence caused Americans to junk almost as many automobiles as Detroit produced. Everything seemed designed to be quickly used and then discarded. Everyone rushed to purchase the newest novelty – for the working class, televisons, hoolahoops, disposable lipsticks, and electric carving knifes; for the wealthy, Corvettes, Christian Dior gowns, and larger houses. European tours, previously considered the domain of the very rich, became commonplace for millions of middle-class Americans.

In the new consumer culture, shopping became a major recreational activity. The shopping center replaced the town square as community focal point. In 1945, the nation could boast but eight of these modern marketplaces, but by 1960, 4,000 retail complexes dotted the land. *Homo consumptus* assuaged his or her anxiety, defeated boredom, and satisfied status cravings by submerging in a sea of products. Leading the charge to the malls were adolescents. The baby-boom generation enjoyed more disposable income than any of its predecessors and generated a special market that included transistor radios, teen fashions, and 45 rpm vinyl records. However, the shopping center was more than just a place for the young to satisfy their material cravings; it became one of the prime loci of socialization.

Television
A new medium made it possible for Old Gold cigarettes, Chevrolet automobiles, and General Electric washing machines to render themselves irresistible to the American public – television. In fact, acquiring a television set in itself became a badge of consumerism fulfilled. At the outbreak of World War II, 9 out of 10 households featured radios; Americans spent almost as much time listening to the radio as they did working. In 1946, there were only 8,000 primitive black-and-white televisions; by 1960, 45.8 million high-quality sets adorned 90% of the nation's living rooms. As of that date, the average set owner spent more time viewing than they did

working. *TV Guide* became the fastest growing periodical of the 1950s, and the "electronic hearth" transformed the way Americans lived. Instead of reading, exercising, conversing, or congregating, the nuclear family gathered faithfully before "the tube" to watch their weekly mystery or variety show.

Initial telecasts featured minor sports such as wrestling and cheap documentaries. There were only two networks – NBC and DuMont – and they broadcast only a few hours a night. In 1948, television gave the public its first dramatic fare. Because the industry was centered in New York City, initial productions were remakes of Broadway plays. "The Philco Television Playhouse" and "Studio One" began in this fashion. In these days before coaxial cable, performances were filmed and then shipped to affiliates for rebroadcasting. As telecasts increased from once per month to once per week, Broadway could not keep up, and the networks began commissioning original teleplays, Reggie Rose's "Twelve Angry Men" and Paddy Chayefsky's "Marty" being among the most notable early efforts. As the television audience increased, hour-long theatrical productions multiplied to include "Playhouse 90," "Robert Montgomery Presents," and the "Hallmark Hall of Fame." In addition, comedy extravangazas, such as Sid Caesar's "Your Show of Shows," and straight variety productions, such as "The Ed Sullivan Show," attracted legions of devoted followers. Situation comedies were also popular from the start: "Mr. Peepers" with Wally Cox was set in an everyman high school, while "The Life of Riley" starring William Bendix featured a protagonist with a working-class background. Nothing could match the popularity of "The Honeymooners" headlined by Jackie Gleason and "I Love Lucy" starring Lucille Ball, however.

These "sitcoms" were 30-minute domestic serials that reaffirmed American culture's notions about itself. Both "Lucy" and "The Honeymooners" were affirmations of the strength and sanctity of the family. Lucy was a zany former actress married to an ebullient Cuban band leader; the protagonist was continually being seduced by the possibility of reviving her career, but in the end opted to stay with her tolerant, forgiving husband. Ball, a slapstick genius, became a national institution. When the actress became pregnant, so did her character; CBS issued weekly bulletins on her condition and filmed a special program entitled "Lucy Goes to the Hospital," which attracted 44 million viewers.

While American viewing families devoted Monday evenings to Lucy, they reserved Saturdays for Jackie Gleason, who starred with Audrey Meadows as a working-class bus driver eking out an existence in Brooklyn. "The Honeymooners" was set in the couple's two-room flat and centered around Ralph Kramden's get-rich quick schemes. Kramden was undereducated, intensely ambitious, and prone to blame outside forces for his plight in life. He was proud, pompous, and at times insensitive to the emotional needs of his wife. Basically a decent sort, however, Kramden ultimately did the right thing and admitted the error of his ways to his stoic, I-told-you-so wife, Alice. The program inevitably ended with the rotund, chagrined Gleason telling his stage wife, "Alice, you're the greatest."

Throughout the first decade after World War II, television could boast a core of serious dramatic programs with a small but devoted coterie of viewers. By the mid-1950s, however, high-quality dramas were increasingly replaced by westerns, police thrillers, and the ubiquitous quiz show, most notably "The $64,000 Question" and "Twenty-One." These latter programs became an overnight smash, attracting both middle- and working-class Americans. Watching the Italian shoemaker Teddy Nadler answering obscure questions on opera seemed to affirm the democratization of the intellect in America. Then came the tragedy of Charles Van Doren, a bright, personable young Columbia professor. The son of noted literary critic Mark Van Doren, Charles answered his way to hundreds of thousands of dollars of prize money and national celebrityhood. Then a disgruntled loser revealed that the program was rigged; Van Doren had been coached. The co-conspirator subsequently admitted as much to a congressional investigating committee. What astounded many concerned observers was America's apparent lack of concern over the scandal. Van Doren only wanted money and fame; how could anyone fault him for aspiring to the American Dream?

In the early 1960s, Newton Minnow, Chairman of the Federal Communications Commission, declared television to be "a vast wasteland" and challenged television producers to actually sit through a day's programming. The reasons for the deterioration of television as an art form were several. At one level, it was a matter of class. Initially, sets were expensive, costing $500 to $600. Consumers of television fare were affluent and educated, perfect customers for the dramatic playhouse. Between 1949 and 1959, the number of privately owned sets increased from the hundreds of thousands to the millions, while the number of commercial televison stations rose from 69 to 566. Expenditures on advertising went from $58 million to more than $1.5 billion. In such a market; every rating point meant big money. Serious dramatic productions could never hope to command a mass audience, and so they declined.

The "electronic hearth" changed the way Americans thought, dressed, and acted. The new medium made its adherents at once more cosmopolitan and more provincial, more active and more passive. Americans were more aware of what Marshall McLuhan would call "the global village," but they also substituted vicarious for real experience. Sitcoms, westerns, and variety shows became placebos that insulated the common man from the hurts and anxieties of human existence. McLuhan, initially an enthusiast about television, came to deplore it, predicting that addiction to "the tube" would cause Americans to forget what the written word looked like. He was wrong, of course, just as were those monks of the Middle Ages who had bemoaned the coming of the printing press because it would render memory obsolete. Humans had and would continue to find means of escape from the drudgery, danger, frustration, and anxieties of everyday life. Education, spirituality, friendship, community, and experience remained just as important to meaningful human existence as ever.

The Movies

Threatened with extinction by television, the motion picture industry at first fought the new medium and then accommodated. Prior to 1939, Hollywood took 67.4 cents of every American entertainment dollar. As of that year, the population stood at 130 million; surveys indicated that between 52 and 55 million of this number attended an average of one movie per week. The industry was dominated by the "big five": Loew's, Inc., which owned Metro-Goldwyn-Mayer; Twentieth Century-Fox; Radio-Keith-Orpheum; Warner Brothers; and Paramount. Universal, United Artists, and Columbia were much smaller. The big five dominated because they owned chains of theaters; independents had to rent all of a studio's films to show one of them. These studios also signed actors and actresses to long-term contracts, enabling them to stockpile and monopolize talent. Movie attendance, encouraged by the federal government to take America's mind off the ominous international situation, increased during World War II. Then the bottom fell out.

To its dismay, the movie industry quickly learned that Americans were willing to exchange a huge screen and expensive productions for the convenience of home viewing. Lawyers for Hollywood initially succeeded in keeping television from using movies or Broadway plays sold to motion picture studios, but the pertinent court order was later overturned. To make matters worse, in 1948, the Justice Department sued Paramount and the seven other majors for conspiring to restrain trade. A federal court ordered the studios to separate production from exhibition. Hollywood staggered as attendance dropped, and the number of films produced annually decreased to a fraction of the wartime average.

The studios fought back by renting out their facilities to independent producers who assumed most of the risk. United Artists led the way, charging not only for use of its facilities but also up to 30% of the profits for distributing a film. Only RKO, bled dry by Howard Hughes, went under. To better compete with television, the movie industry concentrated on doing things that the home entertainment medium could not. Cinemascope provided Technicolor, three-speaker moving pictures whose impact on the senses could never be matched by television. Another way to compete was to screen things that television dared not show. Actually, Hollywood during its early years had shown a bent for prudery. To preempt the Catholic-formed League of Decency, in 1933, the Motion Picture Producers and Distributors Association established a Production Code Administration to censor movies. The rules were quite specific: female breasts, buttocks, pelvic areas, and navels had to be covered, and couples, even if married, could not share the same bed. Censorship, however, proved no match for the twin pressures of public demand for titillating material and competition from television. In 1956, Elia Kazan's "Baby Doll" and "The Man with the Golden Arm," starring Frank Sinatra as a drug addict, failed to receive the seal of approval but made money anyway. In 1957, the French film "And God Created Woman" featured a nude Brigette Bardot and opened the floodgates. In general during the 1950s, the quantity of films decreased, but quality did not. "From Here to Eternity," "On the Waterfront," "Bridge on the River Kwai," and "A Streetcar Named Desire" became classics.

The Youth Culture

Perhaps the most remarkable film phenomenon of the 1950s was the advent of a new type of hero – young, sensitive, tough, misunderstood, and noncomformist. In "Rebel Without a Cause," "The Wild One," "East Of Eden," and "From Here To Eternity," Marlon Brando, Montgomery Clift, and James Dean thrilled young audiences with their raw but "cool" sexual power, their controlled rebelliousness, and their wounded vulnerability. Dean, a high school athlete and drama enthusiast from Indiana, dropped out of college in California and enrolled in acting school in New York. An instant success, he starred in a series of successful movies that included "East of Eden," "Rebel Without a Cause," and "Giant." Destined to be destroyed by the system that he could neither understand nor tolerate, Dean's character was a thrilling antidote to what many considered the mindless conformism of the 1950s. In 1955, at age 24, James Dean was killed when his speeding Porsche collided with another automobile.

Dean, Clift, and Brando became icons in a distinctive youth culture that emerged in the 1950s. Repelled by the insecurity and need for conformity of their parents and anxious at the prospect of nuclear annihilation, American young people rebelled either actually or vicariously. In inner cities, juvenile delinquency and gang fights became commonplace. According to FBI records, one half of arrests for robbery, assault, burglary, and murder were of people 18 and younger. In suburbia and small towns, teenagers cruised in their hotrods, drinking beer and experimenting with sex. The black-jacketed, duck-tailed, switch blade–wielding hood became a youth hero. To the amazement of author Irving Schulman, his novel *Amboy Dukes*, intended to be an expose of delinquency and gang violence, became something of a bible to young American males impressed by the characters' macho courage.

A more sophisticated tale of alienation and rebellion was J. D. Salinger's *The Catcher in the Rye*, read by hundreds of thousands of middle- and upper-class youth. The protagonist, Holden Caulfield, is repelled by polite societies' expectations and conventions. In view of the greed, corruption, and materialism that seemed to pervade the adult world, pressures to conform to a conventional morality seemed the height of hypocrisy. Yet in rejecting society, Caulfield did not encounter satisfaction and fulfillment, but loneliness. Poses of virtuous innocence, he discovers, were no substitute for human contact. Yet, Salinger's call was for young people to question authority and convention; if one conformed, he or she should be fully aware of the consequences.

Holden Caulfield and many of his generation were confused and anxious because traditional truths did not seem to provide answers to the problems of modern society. The blinding pace of change in the postwar world seemed to have rigidified their patents, who sought reassurance in material accumulation and conformity. Repelled and frustrated, young people indulged themselves in shopping sprees at the mall, sex in the backseats of their automobiles, and groupie adulation of entertainment personalities. This divergent search for reassurance in a world haunted by Hiroshima and the Holocaust bore the seeds of a deep general alienation.

From Folk to Rock

On the musical scene, folk music attained a degree of prominence as Joan Baez, Pete Seeger, and Woody Guthrie sang of traditional American and Anglo-Saxon culture, while composing and performing tunes that protested oppression and exploitation at home and abroad. Meanwhile, The Kingston Trio and Harry Belafonte were popularizing traditional folk and calypso music among the children of the conservative middle and upper classes. But the most striking phenomenon of the American musical scene was the dramatic rise of rock and roll.

Prior to the advent of the new genre, mainstream popular music in the 1950s had featured such insipid tunes as "How Much Is That Doggy in the Window" and "The Ballad of Davy Crockett." Unbeknownst to most whites, African Americans had developed music that resonated with African rhythms and southern melodies. Known to those few disc jockeys who paid attention as "race music" in the 1930s and 1940s and rhythm and blues in the 1950s, this genre, which grew out of the black cultural experience, paved the way for rock and roll. In 1952, a Cleveland disc jockey featured rhythm and blues (R&B) on a new program entitled "Moondog's Rock 'n' Roll Party." Originally, the term rockin' and rollin', like jazz, had referred to sexual intercourse. Moondog, whose real name was Alan Freed, employed the term to refer to the type of dancing associated with the music and, in 1954, moved his operation to New York. That same year, Bill Haley came out with the revolutionary "Rock Around the Clock," the theme song for the popular movie "Blackboard Jungle," and the rock-and-roll movement was underway. The music stirred white middle-class youth, and as a result, barriers separating white and black music began to fall.

Corresponding with and stimulating the growth of rock and roll was the development of a huge record market among young people. Teenagers were a relatively new but potent consumer group in a country made up of individuals who increasingly enjoyed a prolonged adolescence before entering the workforce. By 1959, the money spent by and on teenagers topped $10 billion per year. In an effort to tap this huge market, record producers developed new high-fidelity techniques and introduced the 45 and 33 1/3 rpm records. What they really needed, however, was a white performer that could present black music forms to white teenagers. The answer to their dreams appeared in the guise of Elvis Presley, a poor, white truck driver from Tupelo, Mississippi. He taught himself the guitar, learned the R&B style and, by 1954, was performing on regional radio shows across the South. His personal appearances featured a bump-and-grind routine that American parents equated with the sexual act, but that he attributed to the revivalist preachers of his youth. In 1956, Presley's "Don't Be Cruel," "Love Me Tender," "Heartbreak Hotel," and "I'm All Shook Up" sold more than 15 million records. To the horror of conservatives, Ed Sullivan booked Presley for his Sunday night television show, although the variety show impresario compromised by having his cameras focus on Presley only from the waist up.

Presley's detractors denounced him as a sex maniac. Priests and ministers declared him to be immorality personified. The frenzied shrieks by thousands of adolescent girls that accompanied his performances seemed to conservatives to confirm what Dr. Kinsey was saying about the sexual appetite of the female species. These condemnations only served to fuel Presley's career. "The King," as he later came to be known, spent two years in the U.S. Army in the late 1950s, before emerging to make 25 undistinguished movies. However, his stage performances remained the gyrating, sensual productions that had first brought him to national attention.

Elvis Presley constituted a watershed in the history of popular culture. Previously, youths had largely adopted adult tastes – Glen Miller and Frank Sinatra, for example – but Presley was their own. "Elvis was to pop culture what Jack Kerouac was to art," William O'Neill wrote. Presley was working class, sexy, rebellious, and in a sense countercultural. He built on and reinforced the young rebel, biker image established by Marlon Brando in "The Wild One" in 1953 and James Dean in "East of Eden." Elvis Presley gave teenage Americans the sense of identity and separateness they so desperately longed for in the conforming 1950s.

The New Car Culture

Proliferation of automobiles had almost as great a cultural impact on the nation as the spread of television. In 1947, Congress authorized the construction of 37,000 miles of additional highways and, by the end of the 1950s, work on the interstate highway system was well underway. As a result, Americans began traveling in unprecedented numbers. Car production skyrocketed from 2 million in 1946 to 8 million in 1955. As they struck out for a national park, the seashore, or the mountains, mobile Americans transformed the tourist industry into a phenomenon of the masses. Thousands of "service stations" sprang up across the United States to provide fuel and basic creature comforts. Walt Disney started the first major theme park – Disneyland – in California. Motel and hotel receipts increased 2,300% during the 15 years following World War II. The automobile also changed America's eating habits. In 1954, a high school dropout named Ray Kroc came up with a revolutionary concept; a fast-food stand that would make cheap food quickly available to auto travelers. His compact stands began turning out meals consisting of french fries, colas, and 15-cent hamburgers by the millions. The McDonald's empire was born.

The dramatic increase in car ownership accelerated white, middle-class America's move to the suburbs. Between 1950 and 1960, 13 million new homes were constructed in America, 11 million of them in suburbia. At the height of the great European exodus of the late nineteenth century, 1.2 million people came to the United States each year. During the 1950s, the same number moved to suburbia annually. By 1960, 18 million Americans had carved out a niche on the "crabgrass frontier." Many of these suburban enclaves grew up outside the nation's major urban areas – New York, Philadelphia, and Chicago – but others were built adjacent to Miami, Memphis, Dallas, and Albuquerque – the capital centers of the burgeoning "Sun Belt." Most of the early inhabitants of suburbia were young, white, lower middle class, and upwardly mobile. As suburbia matured and these people climbed the economic ladder, however, they could improve their status by moving further out into richer developments featuring larger houses and more spacious lots. Indeed, cities came to be surrounded by concentric circles of developments – the further out the ring, the higher the socioeconomic status. As a number of historians and sociologists have noted, there was an anti-urban, anti-modern undertone to the suburbia craze, what Bennett Berger called "complex pastoralism: the use of modern techniques to re-create the Jeffersonian idyll of homeowning freeholders."

The "Crabgrass Frontier"
Suburbia both symbolized and reinforced one of the dominant characteristics of postwar American society – the demand for conformity. America's shift from an industrial to a postindustrial state was marked by the emergence of a powerful new managerial class. These specialists in management, marketing, and finance were linked to the vast corporations and conglomerates for which they worked not only by rising salaries and benefits, but also by a culture that emphasized loyalty and conformity. IBM and other companies expected their employees to dress conservatively, live conservatively, and vote conservatively. The traditional "inner-directed,"

self-made American was replaced by salaried managers who were "other-directed," to use David Reisman's terms. To move from group to group in an increasingly differentiated bureaucracy, the organization man suppressed his individuality, spurned conflict, and sought guidance and approval from the environment around him. The object of the exercise was to conform rather than to mold. What emerged in America in the 1950s, wrote C. Wright Mills, was "the picture of society as a great salesroom, an enormous file, an incorporated brain, a new universe of management and manipulation."

Critics of postwar American life, such as sociologist William Whyte, argued that the corporate environment of the organization man extended to and suffused all aspects of American life. While new schools of industrial relations taught that workers should seek their identities and sense of fulfillment as parts of the workforce, progressive education emphasized curricula that encouraged socialization rather than curiosity, and corporations used personality tests to screen out employees that might be too eccentric or independent. Whyte, a former editor of *Fortune* magazine, lamented the passing of the old Protestant work ethic and entrepreneurial risk-taking and their replacement by a social ethic that placed a premium on cooperation, security, and the well-being of the group.

Nowhere was the drive to socialize more apparent than in suburbia, however. In Irving, Texas, and Levittown, Pennsylvania, one had to go along to get along. To be different was to risk painful ostracism. Suburbanites had the right number of children, automobiles, and spouses. Privacy and individuality were viewed as nothing less than subversive. Tract houses in suburbia almost always shared a common backyard or faced each other on a treeless street, or both. Newcomers were greeted by a neighborhood "welcome wagon" and could establish themselves by joining the evening promenade where neighbors freely interacted trading gossip and family histories. Impromptu cookouts, morning coffees, and Friday bridge games involved suburbanites in a constant flow of social activity. Those who kept to themselves or repeatedly rebuffed overtures were regarded with suspicion if not hostility. This highly socialized atmosphere encouraged volunteerism and cooperation, which took on various forms from babysitting pools to parent–teacher association (PTA) projects. It also encouraged conformity. People wore the same clothes, watched the same television programs, and observed the same social mores.

Perhaps the dominant social more among white middle-class families in the postwar era was to get married early and have more children. Indeed, no institution in American life enjoyed such unprecedented growth as the family. By 1950, nearly 60% of all 18- to 24-year-old women were married, and they had three and four instead of the traditional two children. The birth rate for third children between 1950 and 1960 increased from 18.4 live deliveries per 1,000 women to 22.8 and that for fourth went from 9.2 to

14.6. During the first decade of the new half century, the nation's population grew by 30%; America's birthrate approached that of India!

The "Feminine Mystique"

The skyrocketing birthrate reinforced a veritable cult of feminine domesticity that emerged during the 1950s. Women who had entered the workforce in droves during World War II and functioned as factory workers, traffic cops, and managers were told to go back to the home, make room in the workforce, and prepare to be the perfect helpmate to their returning veteran-husbands. Weddings in the 1950s were often preceded by a bachelor party and a shower for the bride replete with gifts that defined her future role in life: Mixmasters, Osterizers, and Sunbeam irons. An article entitled "Home Should Be More Wonderful Than He Remembers It" lectured women on their postwar roles. Forget your own preferences, they were told; find out what sort of home your man wants and build it for him. Magazines, motion pictures, popular literature, and advertisements depicted the "ideal woman" of the 1950s. According to *Life* and *Reader's Digest* she was "pretty and popular," a mother of four who had married in her late teens, well dressed, well groomed, an emotional and sexual helpmate to her husband, den-mother, PTA activist, efficient homemaker, and pal to her fellow housewives. In advertisements, child-rearing was invariably depicted as an exciting challenge, never as an anxiety-producing rollercoaster. On television and billboards, babies never cried. Women who wanted independent careers or who expected their husbands to share domestic chores had succumbed to "feminism," which the dominant culture derided as creeping masculinity. In *Modern Women: The Lost Sex*, Ferdinand Lundberg and Marynia Farnham attributed nearly every social ill – from alcoholism to crime to war – to "neurotic" career women who abandoned their children to the care of others, neglected their husbands, and competed with men in a man's world, thereby increasing aggression at every level. If women lacked a sense of fulfillment, they could turn to sewing, canning, or flower arranging. Sociologists later discovered that girls during the 1950s had been trained to select dolls to play with rather than trucks or guns, and that adolescent females frequently responded to pressure to suppress their intellectual instincts so as not to jeopardize chances for marriage and family.

At the heart of what Betty Friedan later called "the feminine mystique" was the notion of the indispensable female. The flywheel of modern society, so the argument ran, was the housewife and mother. Her unconditional, nurturing love was a haven from the competitive, dog-eat-dog world of factory and office. The ideal suburban wife – efficient, beautiful, loving – existed to help the organization man reach new levels of success and fulfillment. Educators, politicians, ministers, and, indirectly, popular television shows broadcast the message that the modern woman should limit her horizons to hearth and husband. In short, the high priests of American culture proclaimed simultaneously that women were inferior to men and that they existed solely to enhance and enrich the existence of men.

June Cleaver, the dutiful housewife and mother on television's "Leave It to Beaver," may have been the ideal of the dominant culture and a model aspired to by some American women, but even she suffered confusion and conflict. American women during the 1950s went to high school and college; they had intellectual interests and ambition. Many a college co-ed played dumb to get a husband and then suffered through a life of frustration with a mate her intellectual and educational inferior. In 1946, a *Fortune* poll asked American women whether they would prefer to be born again as women or men. A startling 25% answered men as compared with only 3% of men who answered women. Cut off from the world of mental stimulation and experience that were available to their husbands, others resorted to tranquilizers and alcohol. Indeed, consumption of tranquilizers skyrocketed from 462,000 pounds in 1958 to 1.15 million pounds in 1959. Even *Life* magazine, which in 1956 had touted the "ideal" middle-class woman, observed in 1959 that once her children were raised, the suburban housewife was left only with a mind-numbing round of club meetings and card parties.

In reality, life was far more complex and confusing for middle-class suburban families than advertising, the media, and popular literature would lead one to believe. Some women challenged the prevailing cultural wisdom. By 1960, twice as many women were employed as in 1940, and 35% of all women older than 16 held a job. The proportion of working wives doubled from 16.7% in 1940 to 31.7% in 1960. In fact, by the end of the decade, working wives made possible the continuation of middle-class existence for a majority of suburban families. Statistics indicate that, prior to 1945, the female labor force had been made up primarily of single women and married women from lower-income families. During the postwar period, the bulk came from married women who either had ascended to middle-class status or entered it by going to work. In households where the husband earned from $7,000 to $10,000 per year, the percentage of women who worked outside the home increased from 7% to 25% during the 1950s. This rush to employment of middle-class married women may have represented a challenge to the cult of domesticity, but it did not constitute a threat to family values. Indeed, the bulk of married women who entered the work force did so after the age of 35 when their children had been reared. Two thirds of married women who worked outside the home declared that the reason they did so was because it made them feel "important" and "useful," but they could also comfort themselves with the knowledge that their incomes made possible the very middle-class existence that the culture held up as ideal.

A Child-Centered Society

Middle-class attitudes toward child rearing changed dramatically during the 1950s. Families became much more democratic and child centered. Deeply influenced by Dr. Benjamin Spock's *The Pocket Book of Baby and Child Care* and Dr. Arnold Gesell's *The Child from Five to Ten*, parents ceased to view their offspring as lumps of clay to be molded or animal instincts to be restrained. Rather, children were perceived to be innately marvelous beings far more in need of freedom and nurture than boundaries and discipline. According to experts fun, play, love, and sympathetic understanding were the key ingredients in child rearing. An offspring's wants and needs were said to be the same. It was understandable, Spock wrote, for parents to want to punish children with isolation and spankings for rudeness, violent behavior, disobedience, thumb-sucking, bed-wetting, and, later, masturbation. But he encouraged parents to show tolerant understanding rather than judgment. In some cases, this approach yielded happy, well-adjusted young people; in others, it bred household tyrants who could manipulate otherwise hardheaded and rational adults with a tear or a simple complaint. Spock's approach was particularly seductive and damaging for parents who did not want to bear the stress of setting and enforcing boundaries, preferring instead to be just another child among children.

Dr. Spock was widely blamed by traditionalists for the wave of "permissiveness" that seemed to be sweeping the public school system during the 1950s, but he was just part of a larger trend. Since the turn of the century, the ideas of philosopher and educator John Dewey had been percolating down through the education hierarchy. Dewey argued that traditional forms of education featuring rote memorization and teaching to a text went against human nature and impeded rather than facilitated learning. Determined to save American school children from being bored to death, Dewey urged adoption of practices in which the child initiated activity. Students would learn by "doing," by engaging in problem-solving activities in cooperation with others. A pragmatist, Dewey argued that knowledge like values was relative. That is, what was true or good for one generation or even individual might not be true for another. By the 1950s, progressive education was achieving popularity at all levels. Teachers shunned authoritarian ways and rigid curricula; classrooms and classes became less and less structured.

Progressive education had its critics. Anti-Deweyites pointed out that a child's immediate interests might not prepare him or her for the long run. That is, that the child rather than the teacher, trained and experienced, knew better what was intellectually authentic and of lasting value seemed to be illogical and absurd to some. In *Educational Wastelands*, the historian Arthur Bestor lamented the prevalence of assemblies, field trips, and individual projects. Rudolph Flesch's *Why Johnny Can't Read* raised a great hue and cry, and caused many to pronounce American education moribund.

In truth, tests subsequently demonstrated that students raised on progressive education did as well on standardized tests measuring achievement, curiosity, and responsibility as those exposed to traditional methods.

The Sexual Revolution

Sex had always been a fundamental preoccupation of American culture, but the subject had generally been dealt with implicitly, indirectly, and subtly. This began to change in the 1950s. In 1955, Hugh Heffner began publishing *Playboy*, an immensely popular magazine featuring an endless array of gorgeously seductive women in an equally endless variety of nude poses. The magazine's "Playboy philosophy" legitimized sex outside the marriage bond, arguing that between consenting adults any sexual activity was not only permissible but also beneficial. Sex was a normal, healthy part of life, with or without commitment or emotional involvement. One of the decade's most popular books was Vladimir Nabokov's *Lolita*, the story of a middle-age academic's sexual obsession with a bubble-blowing teenager, and her sexual domination of him. The sex symbol of the 1950s was the buxom, sensuous, platinum blonde movie star, Marilyn Monroe. She and other starlets such as Jane Russell and Shirley Booth discovered, as Booth later told Johnny Carson, that the future lay in "tits and ass, tits and ass." Monroe's sexuality was at once seductive and innocent. The public message she conveyed was that it was she who was to be satisfied and that it was she who was in control. Monroe's private life was a shambles, however, and after marriages to playwright Arthur Miller and baseball star Joe DiMaggio and numerous affairs, one with President John F. Kennedy, she took her own life.

The 1950s were an unlikely setting for a sexual revolution, but they served as the stage for one of modern history's greatest sexual revolutionaries – Alfred C. Kinsey. An established biologist at the University of Indiana, in the late 1930s, Kinsey turned to the study of human sexuality. In 1938, he organized a course on marriage and family life and began compiling sexual histories of his students. Local moralists were offended and demanded that Kinsey give up either his course or his research. He chose to stick with the latter and in 1948 published *Sexual Behavior in the Human Male*. Five years later, *Sexual Behavior in the Human Female* followed. These books were based on thousands of interviews, many of them conducted by Kinsey himself. The so-called Kinsey reports demolished many myths surrounding sexuality, the primary one being that women were incapable of enjoying sex and submitted to it only for purposes of procreation. According to his sample, admittedly skewed toward white, middle-class college graduates, 50% had had intercourse before marriage, and one out of four girls had experienced orgasm by age 15. More than one wife in four questioned had had an extramarital affair, and the vast majority did not regret it. Perhaps most importantly, Kinsey demonstrated that women could and did enjoy sex as much as men, that activities such as masturbation, previously considered "perversions," were normal and even healthy, and that hetero-sexuality and homosexuality were not alternatives but poles at each end of a continuum along which all human beings fell. According to his findings (later shown to be almost double the actual figure), 10% of men were pri-marily homosexual for at least three years of their life and 4% were exclu-sively homosexual throughout their lives. Not only the religious right, but also respected theologians such as Reinhold Niebuhr and prominent scien-tists such as anthropologist Margaret Mead, condemned Kinsey's work for threatening public health and morals. In 1954, the Rockefeller Foundation cut off funding for his research. Undeterred, Kinsey continued his work until his death in 1956. No American did more to demystify sexuality than Alfred Kinsey, and women gained particularly from his demolition of the double standard traditionally applied to them.

Neither the *Playboy* philosophy, Marilyn Monroe, nor the infidelity recorded in Kinsey's studies posed the threat to the American family that moralists claimed they did. Amid sexual fantasies and extramarital affairs, that institution stood like a rock. The divorce rate increased immediately after World War II, but then declined steadily to 2.5% at the end of the 1950s. The prospect of extramarital sex continued to arouse as much fear as pleasure. For the vast majority during the 1950s, marriage continued to be very much the norm.

A Homogeneous Religion

The forces of conformity that were so strong during the early postwar period, coupled with the anxieties of the Cold War, led to a religious re-vival that was simultaneously intense, pervasive, and amorphous. Overall, church membership increased from 64.5 million (49% of the total popula-tion) in 1940 to 125 million (64%) in 1965. All religions and denominations gained, but leading the way were Roman Catholics, Baptists, and southern Pentecostalists. Noting that Marx had dismissed religion as the opiate of the masses, FBI Director J. Edgar Hoover seemed to equate religious belief with patriotic duty. President Eisenhower was a conspicuous participant in White House prayer breakfasts. Indeed, following his election in 1952, he proclaimed that government must be based on "a deeply felt religious faith – and I don't care what it is." In 1954, Congress added the phrase "one nation under God" to the Pledge of Allegiance. The following year, "In God We Trust" was emblazoned on the nation's currency.

In fact, observers, some with alarm and some with satisfaction, noted a blending of the secular culture and institutionalized religion. Led by Norman Vincent Peale, whose *Power of Positive Thinking* sold millions of copies, many contemporary religious figures concentrated on quiet-ing the American middle class's anxieties in the nuclear age. Confronted simultaneously with the omnipresent threat of "the bomb," the implacable competition with international communism, and the corrosive effects of an overweening materialism, the American people were in dire need of re-assurance as they confronted the second half of the twentieth century. The Protestant Council of New York instructed its television and radio speak-ers to abjure condemnation, controversy, and guilt. Their task was to "sell" religion, and to that end their messages "should project love, joy, courage, hope, faith, trust in God, good will." Peale offered a simple "how-to" course in personal happiness. Shun negative thoughts, trust in God, and be joyful and enthusiastic, he preached. The fruits of such an approach would be not only spiritual but also secular. Indeed, his Dale Carnegie approach to religion promised to make the practitioner "a more popular, esteemed, and well-liked individual." One chapter in Peale's *A Guide to Confident Living* was entitled "How to Think Your Way to Success." Another promised to show the reader "How to Get Rid of Your Inferiority Complex." In an earlier era, Protestantism had demanded constant, agonized soul-searching, but by the 1950s it had become for many, according to Russell Kirk, a religion amounting to "little more than a vague spirit of friendliness, a willingness to support churches – providing these churches demand no real sacrifices and preach no exacting doctrines."

Noting a pervasive search for identity among third-generation Ameri-cans in a rapidly changing social milieu, Will Herberg insisted that one's religion had become the American way of life and vice versa. According to a Gallup poll, 53% of Americans questioned could not name a single book of the New Testament; thus, Herberg observed that Americans believed in ethical behavior and living the good life, rather than in any particular creed. Much of the new religious growth took place in suburbia and was part of that distinctly homogenized culture. The ecumenical movement that grew in strength during the 1950s was partly a reflection of the blurring of dis-tinctions between denominations and religions and partly a cause of it. The World Council of Churches held its Second Assembly in Evanston, Illinois, in 1954, and received the backing of the Vatican as well as American Jewish and Protestant leaders.

There were, of course, serious alternatives to this syrupy, sin-free ap-proach to religion. The 1950s witnessed a new interest in revivalism and fundamentalism. One of the most striking preachers of the period was a young, well-dressed Baptist evangelist named Billy Graham. In sincere ha-rangues that stressed the sovereignty of God and the absolute wisdom of the Bible, the charismatic Graham drew hundreds of thousands of Americans to huge amphitheaters, such as Yankee Stadium and Madison Square Gar-den. Graham and other fundamentalists offered clear moral and spiritual guidelines for middle-class Americans who craved substance and focus in their religion and for working-class Americans threatened by alcoholism, unemployment, and family disorganization.

Meanwhile, the intelligentsia were drawn by the preachments of Reinhold Niebuhr and Will Herberg, theologians who attacked the "feel-good" religion propounded by the dominant culture. Niebuhr, who taught and preached at the Union Theological Seminary in New York, was the towering theological and philosophical figure in the movement known as Christian neo-orthodoxy. He attacked the materialism, complacency, and conformity that seemed to permeate postwar America. World War II and the atomic age had proved that sin and evil were real and permanent, and that man could not perfect the universe through his own efforts. Humans were called on not to ensconce themselves in a cocoon but to love the world and assume some responsibility for its problems. True peace involved the endurance of pain; the root of sin, he reminded Christians, was self-love. Herberg, a former communist theoretician who had converted to Judaism, insisted that professions of religious belief without a defining theological content were barren. He argued that many third-generation Americans turned to Protestantism, Catholicism, or Judaism out of a need to belong rather than from spiritual longing and conviction. Another critic of the feel-good, pray-for-success movement in American Christianity observed that "the best and truest experiences of religion come when a person has given up asking 'What do I require of God?' and learned to ask humbly 'What does God require of me?'" Responding in part to these appeals to confront the social evils that plagued contemporary America, the Presbyterians admitted women to the ministry in 1955, and the following year the General Conference of the Methodist Church banned racial segregation among its congregations. In 1959, the General Synod of the United Church of Christ publicly urged an end to segregation, and stressed the role of the church in ameliorating social problems and advancing the cause of peace.

Religion was not without its defenders in the intellectual community. In 1951, the young, conservative, Catholic social commentator, William F. Buckley, caused a stir with the publication of *God and Man at Yale*. Buckley ridiculed existentialism, modernism, pragmatism, and amoral artifices created by ivory tower intellectuals seeking to escape the wages of sin and evil. He charged academia in general and Yale in particular with a pervasive antireligious bias. Secular humanists professed tolerance but then hypocritically refused to allow committed Christians to teach on their faculties. Life, including intellectual life, should like Christianity be rooted in authority and obedience, Buckley insisted. Without universal truths, everything would become relative, and existence would be ruled by the law of the jungle. Somewhat paradoxically, Buckley also lauded the free market economics espoused by the Austrian school. His *National Review* attempted to combine laissez-faire capitalism, rooted in Protestant individualism and resistance to authority, with religious conservatism, based in reverence for authority and revealed truth. Buckley enjoyed the stretch, but it proved too much for some of his followers.

Poverty in America

Despite the affluence of the postwar period, substantial segments of the population were cut off from the American Dream. Various studies showed that 20% of all Americans lived below what was considered the poverty line – $3,000 for a family of four in 1960 and $4,000 for a family of six. An objective analysis of the economy revealed a number of worrisome trouble spots. Among the rapidly growing elderly population – those persons 60 years of age and older – 60% tried to exist on $1,000 per year or less. Social Security payments averaged a mere $70 per month, and many senior citizens had no health care. Blue-collar workers without a high school education generally made less than $3,000 per year. Plagued by inflation and mounting installment debt, even the tens of thousands of new members of the middle class were insecure, faced as they were with the ever-present possibility of falling back down the socioeconomic ladder.

Poverty in America, however, was deepest and widest among four groups: African Americans increasingly isolated in inner-city ghettos, mill and factory workers in New England and the Carolinas, Appalachians who lived in the coal region that stretched from western Pennsylvania to northern Georgia, and residents of the rural South, both black and white. In 1962, Michael Harrington published an influential book entitled *The Other America* in which he revealed in cold statistics and passionate prose that there existed in the nation a "culture of poverty." During the 1950s, approximately 1.8 million African Americans were driven off the farms of the rural South by mechanization and enclosure. Most chose to migrate to the cities of the Northeast and Midwest, hoping to find employment in industry or service. The vast majority were disappointed. Increasingly, blacks found themselves living in inner-city ghettos recently abandoned by whites, particularly ethnics, who headed with their skills and tax monies for the suburbs. Only education, employment opportunity, and minimum levels of social and economic security would allow the poor to improve their lot, but there was no way for them to gain access to these essentials. Those living in slums and depressed areas such as Appalachia were cut off from educational opportunity, medical facilities, and meaningful employment. Poor, ignorant, helpless, and ignored, they were locked in a vicious circle in which poverty denied opportunity and lack of opportunity perpetuated poverty. To make matters worse, television and advertising constantly reminded the disadvantaged of the world that lay forever beyond their reach.

By the end of the 1950s, the complacency that seemed to pervade American culture and society had spawned a series of powerful critics, some sophisticated, some savage, and some inane. In 1956, John Keats published a searing attack on American suburbia entitled *The Crack in the Picture Window*. He ridiculed the crabgrass frontier as a vast cultural and intellectual desert, its landscape marred by thousands of identical, non-descript dwellings, its inhabitants obsessed with mass consumption and conformity. Commuter fathers, he wrote, were always at work, and "mothers were always delivering children; obstetrically once and by car ever after." Two years later, liberal economist John Kenneth Galbraith reminded Americans that affluence was not an automatic cure for social ills; it was what the nation did with its money that mattered. If America was to create and sustain a valid and vibrant democracy, it would have to spend more on the public sector to clear slums and erect low-cost housing, enhance public education both qualitatively and quantitatively, and provide affordable health care for all. The new focus of American liberalism should be the quality of life and not merely the quantity of wealth. David Reisman, whose *The Lonely Crowd* first appeared in 1950, continued to bewail the predominance of the other-directed individual and the disappearance of core values that acted like a gyroscope and that, in the nineteenth century, had allegedly produced the self-assured, achieving citizens that realized their potential and made America great.

During the 1950s, both conservative traditionalists and liberals criticized the consumerism of the Eisenhower era. Both groups agreed that the masses had proved sadly incapable of resisting the siren's songs of advertising agencies and became only too plainly mired in a bog of bad taste and superficiality. *Humanus Americanus* had abandoned architecture, classical music, and art, both serious and popular, for the hamburger stand, tail-finned automobile, and amusement park. The credulous, untutored masses seemed to be making George Santayana's aphorism come true: in a democracy, he once observed, "people do what they wish but do not get what they want." American conservatives, of course, wanted rejection of the welfare state, mass culture, and the giant corporation and a return to the halcyon days of self-reliance, private conscience, and self-actualization. Liberals such as John Kenneth Galbraith hoped that the state could be used to recreate the vigorous, virtuous public culture that supposedly reigned during the New Deal and World War II.

The Beat Generation

Toward the close of the decade, a small group of alienated intellectuals, led by Jack Kerouac and Allen Ginsberg, attempted an existential and artistic rebellion against the conforming culture. Kerouac's novel *On the Road* and Ginsberg's poem *Howl* invited those turned off by "I Love Lucy" and Levittown to drop out and experiment. Kerouac was a handsome, working-class youth who went to Columbia on a football scholarship but who soon immersed himself in alcohol, sex, and "rebellious behavior." Advised by a dean to seek psychotherapy, Kerouac chose William Burroughs, a drug addict who had killed his wife accidentally while trying to shoot an apple off her head with an arrow. Kerouac migrated to the West Coast where he teamed up with Neal Cassady, a frenetic hedonist who sought the salvation of the soul through satisfaction of the body's appetites. The two subsequently made a cross-country jaunt by automobile. High on drugs and alcohol, Kerouac chronicled their three-week odyssey on a continuous roll of paper. Following several rejections, *On the Road* was published in 1957. A reviewer in *The New York Times* declared that the book would do for the "Beat Generation" what Hemingway's *The Sun Also Rises* had done for the Lost Generation.

A year earlier Kerouac had met Allen Ginsberg in San Francisco. Ginsberg, a Columbia student of Lionel Trilling's who had been expelled for writing obscenities on a dormitory wall, had come west in pursuit of a homosexual relationship with Cassady. In 1956, Lawrence Ferlinghetti, another Beat poet, published Ginsberg's *Howl and Other Poems* in San Francisco under his City Lights Books imprint. City Lights was both a store and a press. The 118-line lead poem had been written while Ginsberg was under the influence of drugs, and it featured a dizzying kaleidoscope of words and subjects, including travel, insanity, art, atheism, homo- and heterosexual intercourse, dope, and alcohol. The San Francisco police seized the book, declaring it to be obscene. In the trial that followed, a host of literary authorities testified to the artistic and literary merit of Ginsberg's work. The court agreed and lifted the ban. The trial was not only a landmark in the free speech movement, but it also brought the Beat Generation to the nation's attention.

Beat was both a literary and social movement. Before Ginsberg and Kerouac happened on the scene, serious literary scholarship was based on the New Criticism, which was devoted to a close textual reading of the great works, and contemporary authors such as Ernest Hemingway, William Faulkner, and their younger protégés, Saul Bellow and Norman Mailer, concentrated on traditional themes and values. Beat writers denounced mainstream literature and rationalistic criticism. The roots of authentic literature, they argued, were spontaneity, emotional release, Eastern religion, and intuition. The beats sought personal rather than social or political solutions to their problems and society's problems. They despised technology and derided both professionalism and specialization. Through esoteric art forms, drug experimentation, relentless sex, Eastern religion, and vagabondage, the beats sought to escape what they perceived to be the horror of American middle-class existence.

Intellectual and Artistic Life

The social critics and beats were overreacting, however. American cultural life was not nearly as barren and banal as they would have the world believe. If popular culture was exemplified by the organization man, the

suburbanite, and the conspicuous consumer during the 15 years following World War II, high culture and intellectual life were characterized by
the experimenter and the iconoclast. Leading the way in the minor cultural renaissance that took place in the late 1940s and 1950s were dozens
of émigré intellectuals and artists who fled European totalitarianism. During the 1930s, the Rockefeller and Carnegie Foundations, the New School
for Social Research in New York, and the Emergency Committee in Aid
of Displaced Foreign Scholars helped scientists, historians, social scientists, musicians, and philosophers escape from the stultifying, repressive,
and violent societies emerging in Italy, Germany, and the Soviet Union.
This massive brain drain stands as a great and ironic gift to America from
Mussolini, Hitler, and Stalin.

    In music, Otto Klemperer took over the Los Angeles Philharmonic,
George Szell the Cleveland Symphony, and Bruno Walter the New York
Philharmonic-Symphony. These composers improved on performances of
the classic works of Mozart, Bach, Beethoven, and Handel and introduced
American audiences to the avant-garde works of Igor Stravinsky and Gus-
tav Mahler. In ballet, George Ballanchine brought the traditions of Tsarist
Russia to the New York Ballet and combined them with features of American music and dance, including jazz and folk dance. Ballanchine's choreography emphasized action and tempo over plot and music. Out of the
tradition he established came other choreographers and troupes, including the Dance Company of Harlem. In architecture, Ludwig Mies van der
Rohe, Walter Gropius, and Charles Le Corbusier grafted onto the American
skyscraper elements of the Bauhaus School of the 1920s, an approach that
emphasized geometrical forms, functional efficiency, and glass and steel
construction materials. The new perfectly proportioned office buildings,
museums, and hotels created in this genre were designed to fit in unob-
trusively with older structures. Some critics found the new buildings sleek,
exciting, and provocative, others believed them to be sterile, alienating, and
incredibly elitist.

    The psychoanalytical theories of Sigmund Freud had already dramati-
cally shaped and misshaped the way Americans thought about the sources
of human conduct and the disorders of the mind. The rise of European
totalitarianism and World War II brought to the United States a group
of psychologists and analysts who sought to modify or even refute the
Freudian tradition. During the war, Surgeon General Dr. William C. Men-
ninger used a number of Jewish émigré analysts to train Army and Navy
doctors. After the war, these physicians, who had been taught and who
taught that man is more than an automaton determined by his or her subconscious, spread out across the United States and the medical community.
In *Childhood and Society*, the German-born Erik Erikson showed how the
human personality goes through stages as it progresses through the life
cycle and how it is not fixed by unchanging psychosexual drives or discrete

traumatic events. Anticipating Karl Jung, Bruno Bettleheim explained in *Symbolic Wounds* that all humans are both male and female. Challenging if not refuting Freud's notion that women suffer from penis envy, Bettleheim argued that men appreciate and even envy women's capacity for giving birth and nurturing. Another German émigré, Eric Fromm, blended Marxist theory with Freudian theory in arguing that aggressive, selfish behavior originates not in a frustrated libido – that is, in the suppression of basic biological drives – but in the dynamics of social class and economic inequity. His *Escape From Freedom* described Germany as an authoritarian culture in which individuals were willing to turn themselves and their nation over to an all-powerful father figure rather than endure the travail of choice and responsibility.

In political and social thought, the European émigrés inspired both the radical and conservative tradition in America. A number of refugee economists and political scientists were profoundly skeptical of liberalism as it existed in America during the 1930s, 1940s, and 1950s. Frederick von Hayek led a coterie of Austrian intellectuals who warned that in its emphasis on planning, regulation of the private sector, and commitment to social and economic justice for all, the emerging welfare state was threatening to obliterate individual freedom. In *The Road To Serfdom* and other books, von Hayek argued that all collectivist systems, whether the program espoused by the socialists in Britain's Labor party or proposals to expand the New Deal in America, would lead to state-controlled societies and to dictators such as Hitler and Stalin. They condemned liberals in the United States for abandoning the principles of nineteenth-century "authentic" liberalism: small government, free market economics, and laissez faire. American conservatives embraced the Austrian school and used its arguments throughout the postwar era to warn their countrymen and women against the dangers of "creeping socialism."

Another group of German thinkers, Marxists such as Herbert Marcuse and Theodore Adorno, bemoaned the loss of individualism and freedom in America, but they blamed capitalism rather than the welfare state. Marcuse and his fellows studied mass culture – advertising, marketing, popular music, and fashion trends – and portrayed a society that found its identity in products, and thus was susceptible to manipulation and domination by those who manufactured their possessions. In America, the most bourgeois of societies, the possibility of self-realization had been swallowed up in a massive web of advertising-driven illusions and creature comforts. While the Austrians argued that only capitalism could save America, the Germans insisted that capitalism had already destroyed the country.

A number of émigrés who fled Europe during the 1930s and 1940s were disillusioned with both religion and modern science for failing to anticipate, prevent, or even relate to the evils of totalitarianism. To them, pragmatism seemed nothing more or less than a means for acquiescing in evil.

They were well aware that John Dewey had no answer for Nazi Germany's aggressions and had opposed U.S. entry into the war. The response of refugee intellectuals such as Hannah Arendt and Walter Kaufmann to this perceived philosophical and moral void was existentialism. In a world full of evil and perhaps purposelessness, individuals had to rely on their own experience, conscience, and will to make crucial choices concerning good and evil, guilt and innocence. Existentialism was an ultimate crisis philosophy. Science purported to predict what humankind would do, religion what it ought to do. Neither was as satisfactory a guide as the individual him- or herself. One thing was clear to the existentialists; humans had to choose. The very process made them free; indeed, it defined their humanity.

Modernism and Expressionism

Modernism – a movement involving the self-conscious effort to break with the past and develop new forms of expression – affected psychology, the social sciences, and philosophy during the postwar decades, but it dominated the arts. Clearly, high-culture devotees continued to worship classical music. The dynamic composer and music personality Leonard Bernstein, who was traditionally trained, hosted a popular Sunday afternoon program, "The Joy of Music," in which he explained the intricacies of classical music. But he felt no compunction about branching out and composing music for the Broadway musical "West Side Story," a Romeo and Juliet plot set in the cultures of contemporary street gangs.

The 1940s and 1950s witnessed the flowering of a uniquely American art form – jazz. Some classical musicians such as Bernstein not only defended, but also experimented with, jazz. Modern jazz featured spectacular improvisation, but within a context of discipline and restraint. The medium ranged from the soft, aesthetic intricacies of the Modern Jazz Quartet to the sophisticated but mood-inspiring variations of Dave Brubeck to the accessible, more traditional renditions of Duke Ellington. The jazz artists' jazz player, however, was John Coltrane. His complex, moody compositions and renditions awed a generation of listeners and artists, as well as inspired the next generation of jazz musicians.

In the visual arts, a new generation of painters rejected hierarchy and structure to a degree unknown in the world of painting. America continued to produce realists and impressionists such as Andrew Wyeth, whose work featured mood-struck human subjects in an austere rural Pennsylvania setting, and Georgia O'Keefe, who combined sexual representation, desert landscapes, and vivid color. But the talk of the art world was the abstract expressionists, a tradition that grew out of cubism and surrealism, but one that was, similar to jazz, uniquely American. The "New York School" of painting began during the early 1940s and flowered after the war. Influenced by existentialism, these painters and art critics thought of painting more as action than as form or function. For centuries, art had been based on the assumption that it should represent or at least approximate objective reality. The impressionists stressed the transitional and individual nature of that reality, but were representational nonetheless. Abstract expressionists such as Willem de Kooning, Robert Motherwell, and especially Jackson Pollock rejected that notion. The New York painters applied paint in seemingly random blobs, streaks, and strokes. Their renditions evoked images and moods, but they were as spontaneous and unpredictable as the painting process itself. Pollock came to personify abstract expressionism. He trained under Thomas Hart Benton to paint traditional western landscapes, but by the 1940s, all recognizable forms and structures began to disappear from his work. By the 1950s, Pollock was producing paintings made by laying huge expanses of canvass flat on the floor while he whirled over it, applying globs, dabs, and streaks of various colored paints at a frantic pace. Art critic Harold Rosenberg described the process and object of abstract expressionism: "At a certain moment the canvas began to appear . . . as an arena in which to act rather than as a space in which to reproduce, redesign, analyze, or 'express' an object, actual or imagined. What was to go on the canvas was not a picture but an event."

Abstract expressionism was wildly controversial. Traditional artists and some art critics denounced the genre as pure fraud, devoid of intellectual, emotional, and visual content. During the second Red Scare, anticommunists decried abstract expressionism as a communist conspiracy to corrupt American culture. Ironically, communist and radical critics denounced the New York School as decadent and antisocial. They found it narcissistic in its total lack of socially redeeming content. For Marxists as for Marx, the object of art should be the rendering of social injustices, the glorification of the socialist state, and the evocation of self-sacrifice. McCarthyites wanted pictures of the founding fathers at work on the Constitution, whereas communists demanded representations of heroic workers in industrial settings. Abstract expressionists thought both agendas, all agendas, absurd, and they went about their art-as-action splashing and dripping with renewed gusto.

Drama

The dramatic stage produced works during this period that were the antithesis of complacency and conformity. Strongly influenced by Henry James and Nathaniel Hawthorne, Eugene O'Neill and Tennessee Williams produced plays that ripped away at individual and societal illusions. Both O'Neill, a fallen away Irish Catholic, and Williams quarreled with God for producing a creation in which cruelty, madness, want, and disease were so appallingly apparent. O'Neill's characters in plays like *The Iceman Cometh* and *A Long Day's Journey into Night* were too vulnerable and flawed to live without illusions, which allowed them to cope with reality, but too honest to believe in and retain those illusions. Frequently, they destroyed themselves and those around them. Many sought solace in the bottle or random sexual activity. Similar to Hawthorne, O'Neill rejected America's Calvinist heritage of hard work and sacrifice as loveless and lifeless. The Protestant work ethic was at its root materialism run wild. Despite its victory over fascism and its wealth, America, O'Neill declared, was the world's greatest failure. Although they donned the garb of comfortable conformity, O'Neill's characters felt betrayed and bereft.

Tennessee (Thomas Lanier) Williams wrote a series of classic dramatic plays that were subsequently turned into movies. Similar to O'Neill in *Long Day's Journey into Night*, Williams portrayed troubled families where illusion, convention, vulnerability, and mortality clashed. In his first play, *The Glass Menagerie* (1945), Laura, a young girl of delicate health, is rejected by the suitor her mother has so painstakingly courted for her. In desperation, she turns to her collection of fragile glass animals for comfort and companionship. *A Streetcar Named Desire* featured Blanche DuBois a middle-age, neurotic woman who employs colored lamp shades to soften the lines on her face and who hides her sexual desires under a mask of refined manners. Stanley Kowalsky, the working-class character that served as a vehicle to stardom for Marlon Brando, is both attracted and abused, and rapes her. The incident strips Blanche of her illusions of gentility and innocence. "I've always depended on the kindness of strangers," she declares as she is carted off to a mental institution. Similar to O'Neill, Williams values sensitivity, intelligence, and honesty, but was angered and frustrated that these traits seemed to destroy as often as they nurtured.

Perhaps the most satirical play of the late 1940s and 1950s was Arthur Miller's *Death of a Salesman*. The protagonist, Willy Loman, is a successful traveling salesman, a believer in and liver of the Horatio Alger myth of hard work, self-reliance, and success at any price. Loman is the hail-fellow-well-met who can sell anything. Meeting his quotas and manipulating buyers is his be-all and end-all, and he has raised his sons, Biff and Happy, to share that ethos. As he nears the end of his career, however, he finds himself devoid of authentic human relationships, alienated from his family, and rejected by his boss as a failure. Devastated, Loman commits suicide. *All My Sons*, a play about a successful businessman's error that led to the death of 21 airmen during World War II, and other Miller plays excoriate individuals who allowed society to define their identity and give meaning to their existence.

Literature
Art, like life, consumes, and this was at no time and in no place truer than in postwar America. One of the English language's most promising poets of the period was Sylvia Plath. She published her first poem at age nine and went on to a brilliant academic career at Smith and Cambridge where she met her future husband, Ted Hughes. She bore two children, and

simultaneously lived and rejected the life of the 1950s housewife. After the breakup of her marriage, her poems, many of which were collected and published as *Ariel*, brooded on the death of her father, miscarriages, the Holocaust and Hiroshima, the anti-intellectualism and tyranny of McCarthyism, and the joy and pain of love. On a winter evening in 1963, she set out a snack for her children and then gassed herself to death.

Another who proved unable to bear the cruelties and paradoxes of life was Ernest Hemingway, although one suspects he chose to die as much out of fear of boredom as despair over the human condition. One of America's literary giants during the interwar period, Hemingway appeared to have become artistically impotent during the 1940s. He then surprised and gratified his followers with *The Old Man and the Sea* in 1952, an allegory about an elderly fisherman whose marlin is consumed by ravening sharks. As is true of Hemingway's other works, there was no chance of triumph or success. Life was a losing proposition whose only consolation was courage and dignity in the face of evil and violence. In 1961, "Papa" Hemingway took his favorite shotgun off the rack and blew his head off.

Some American novelists were understandably preoccupied with the issues of war, society, and personal experience. Norman Mailer made his first of many splashes on the literary scene with the publication of *The Naked and the Dead* (1948), which described the excruciating experiences of a combat outfit laboring in the Pacific theater. Two of the best examples of this genre were James Jones' *From Here To Eternity* (1951) and the *Thin Red Line* (1962), works that explored the ability of war and of the threat of death to strip life down to its bare essentials.

Social Criticism

Among academic disciplines, perhaps the most active and fruitful during the 15 years following World War II was sociology. Intellectuals were understandably obsessed with discovering the roots of totalitarianism, dissecting evolving notions of democracy and republicanism, and either challenging or, less often, defending Marxism. Two sociologists, Daniel Bell and Seymour Lipset, declared that the immediate postwar period marked the "end of ideology." The war had discredited millenarian, deterministic social theories from Marxism to fascism. Liberal democracy as it was developing in the West was producing a mass society, but a society that was open, pragmatic, and nondogmatic. Individuals were driven more by status than class. They looked forward to a society that tested every theory, social construct, institution, and political process to see if it produced the greatest good for the greatest number. There were no absolutes, and the world was better for it. Slavish attachment to abstractions had produced the Holocaust and the Soviet police state. Harvard University's Talcott Parsons extended these notions. He and his students became convinced that, in the modern world, society had taken the place of religion rewarding normal or socially constructive behavior with status, money, and influence, and deviant or antisocial behavior with ostracism, powerlessness, and loss of freedom.

C. Wright Mills, an intense Texan who rode to his classes at Columbia University on a motorcycle, saw a much less benign America, however. In *The Power Elite* and other books, he argued that power in modern society was exercised by a series of "establishments": the military, big business, the federal bureaucracy, labor unions, and agribusiness. However, he rejected the Marxist notion of a revolutionary working class determined by the Hegelian dialectic to overthrow capitalism. America was and would continue to be ruled by power elites who were shrewd enough to appease the masses and maintain social and political stability. Although academics and political theorists acknowledged Wright's ideas and scholarship, few gave them credence until in 1961 in his farewell address, President Dwight D. Eisenhower warned of the dangers posed by "the military–industrial complex."

Harvard economist John Kenneth Galbraith acknowledged in *American Capitalism: The Concept of Countervailing Power* that society in the United States consisted of various power centers and interest groups, but existing political processes and institutions ensured that no one would become dominant and be in a position to force its will on others. For example, big labor would join with the federal government to restrain big business. Through interest groups, consumers would organize to protect themselves. Thus constrained, large corporations were a positive good, producing higher-quality products at ever lower prices. Bell and Parsons agreed, arguing to Mills that power in America was based more often on consent than coercion and that modern bureaucracies characteristically dispersed power so that various units acted as a check on each other.

Historians of the 1950s, many of them former Marxists who during the Depression had predicted that class conflict would either destroy America or change it beyond recognition, were faced with the task of explaining continuing prosperity and stability. In *People of Plenty*, David Potter argued convincingly that the key to understanding the conservative nature of American society was its material abundance. The availability of cheap land and plentiful power and mineral resources had meant opportunity and the continuing prospect for upward mobility by the masses. American democracy had evolved with relatively little class conflict because wealth was not created by one group taking from another; rather it simply expanded. Potter recognized the psychological and spiritual dangers of abundance, but he continued to regard it as the key to understanding America's historical success. Richard Hoffstadter was a little less triumphal, but nonetheless saw American society as consensus based. There was, he argued, a great deal of consistency in the programs put forward by the major political figures and parties in America from Thomas Jefferson to Herbert Hoover. Equality of opportunity set within a context of the rule of law was the defining characteristic of American democracy. Movements such as populism and progressivism, which seemed so radical and threatening to conservatives of the times, were to Hoffstadter conservative movements aimed at preserving traditional social and political values from powerful groups who wanted to regiment and dominate the economy and political system.

Summary

The period from 1945 to 1960 was one of unparalleled, sustained material prosperity. The pent-up demand released by World War II, coupled with new technologies and high, continuing levels of government spending, drove the GNP ever upward, enriching the superrich and pulling large segments of blue-collar Americans up into the middle class. At the same time, large, residual pockets of urban and rural poverty persisted with its victims caught in a web of ignorance, crime, deprivation, and powerlessness. While American business during these years continued to consolidate, the economy made the transition from an industrial to a postindustrial condition characterized by increased employment in white-collar enterprises, especially government-related jobs.

Above all else, the World War II generation hoped to rid themselves of the ghosts of war and depression. Prosperity gave them the means to do so, and the result was a rampant consumer culture fueled by a mushrooming advertising industry and installment buying. Americans went into debt for all sorts of things, but the most pervasive commodities of the 1950s were television and automobiles. Both of these devices bred the conformity for which the decade is so famous. Television was both stimulating and stultifying. It introduced Americans to a national and global culture, but also created uniformity particularly as sets became increasingly more affordable and programming reflected the lowest common denominator. The automobile facilitated white middle-class America's continuing flight to the suburbs, where physical proximity and architectural uniformity produced immense pressures on its denizens to dress, act, and think alike. Participation in organized religion increased during the late 1940s and 1950s, but that religion seemed increasingly creedless, a civil religion based on conventional morality, patriotism, and community rather than sin, suffering, and redemption.

An emerging youth culture simultaneously wallowed in the consumerism of the period and rebelled against its conformity. Their heroes were rebel-without-a-cause James Dean and rock-and-roll star Elvis Presley. In magazines and newspapers, on television, in movies, and from the pulpit, American women read and heard that they must fill the role of homemakers and shun careerism, but they continued to demand the right to choose and increasingly worked outside the home. The families of the baby-boom generation were relatively child centered, with the emphasis on nurturing and creativity rather than discipline and boundaries. This philosophy pervaded public education, which increasingly disparaged rote memory and core curriculum, and emphasized student-initiated programming and goal setting.

Despite laments by social and cultural critics over the barrenness of American life, the United States experienced a mild renaissance in the arts and literature during the 1950s. In art, architecture, music, and dance, European émigrés brought new ideas and energy to the nation's high culture. Playwrights, novelists, and poets continued to examine the human condition in all its cruelty, joy, and paradox with skill and insight.

ADDITIONAL READINGS

Barnouw, Erik, *Tube of Plenty* (1982).
Feldstein, Martin, ed., *The American Economy in Transition* (1980).
Fite, Gilbert C., *American Farmers: The New Minority* (1981).
Green, James R., *The World of the Worker: Labor in Twentieth-Century America* (1980).
Hodgson, Godfrey, *America in Our Time* (1976).
Jackson, Kenneth, *Crabgrass Frontier: The Suburbanization of the United States* (1985).
Kazin, Alfred, *Bright Book of Life: American Novelists and Storytellers From Hemingway To Mailer* (1973).
Marty, Martin E., *Pilgrims in Their Own Land* (1984).
Marty, Martin E., *Protestantism in the United States: Righteous Empire*, 2nd ed. (1986).
May, Elaine T., *Homeward Bound: American Families in the Cold War Era* (1988).
Polenberg, Richard, *One Nation Divisible: Class, Race, and Ethnicity in the United States Since 1938* (1980).
Ravitch, Diane, *The Troubled Crusade: American Education, 1945–1980* (1983).
Rosenberg, Harold, *Discovering the Present: Three Decades in Art, Culture, and Politics* (1985).
Rothschild, Emma, *Paradise Lost: The Decline of the Auto-Industrial Age* (1973).
Stein, Herbert, *Presidential Economics: The Making of Economic Policy From Roosevelt To Reagan and Beyond* (1984).

6 Liberalism Reborn

John F. Kennedy, Lyndon B. Johnson, and the Politics of Activism

As the 1950s drew to a close, a profound malaise seemed to settle over the United States. Dwight Eisenhower had been the ideal president for a nation exhausted by first the Depression, then World War II, and finally the anxieties associated with the Cold War. Toward the close of the 1950s, however, Americans seemed to have decided that eight years of holding the line and clinging to the status quo was enough. A renewed longing for direction and purpose emerged. The launching of Sputnik and the Soviet Union's challenge to American science and technology acted as a catalyst causing politically active Americans to question not only the adequacy of American education, but also the ordering of national priorities.

Liberalism Transformed

The pervasiveness of conservatism and complacency in the immediate post-war era had been due in part to a crisis in American liberalism. Throughout the 1950s liberals – those committed to peaceful change, to social justice at home and abroad – had struggled to reconcile their idealism with the realities of World War II and its aftermath. The evil that lay behind Hitler's death camps and the Armageddon-like implications of Hiroshima left liberals shaken and confused. Many of these same idealists were subsequently disillusioned by the persistence of totalitarianism and aggression in the form of Sino–Soviet communism. Indeed, for many liberals, the corruption of Marxism seemed to threaten idealism itself. Finally, they decried the second Red Scare and the emergence of the national security state as proof that America, in the name of fighting totalitarianism, was adopting many of its trappings. Among Christian and Jewish liberals, and even agnostics and atheists, Reinhold Niebuhr's neo-orthodox theology became symptomatically voguish. In view of the Holocaust and communist totalitarianism, he argued, a belief in the perfectibility of man was absurd. Niebuhr, who served as a spiritual and intellectual guide for a whole generation of cold warriors, had as early as 1932 rehabilitated the notion of original sin. There lurked in the human psyche a capacity for evil so immense and hidden that no intellect could fully comprehend it nor could any institution control it. Neibuhr was no nihilist but rather a profoundly cautious pragmatist.

Gradually but inevitably, however, liberals shook off their lethargy and set forth once again on their perennial search for economic and social justice. In 1960, CBS correspondent Edward R. Murrow aired "Harvest of Shame," and during the years that followed television began to expose pockets of poverty as cameras followed civil rights activists into the Deep South and social workers into Appalachia. Michael Harrington's *The Other America*, published in 1962, was read by tens of thousands of liberals across the country. His revelations concerning the prevalence of poverty in the United States among children, the elderly, minorities, migrant workers, the uneducated, and the inhabitants of chronically depressed areas such as Appalachia galvanized the compassionate and socially conscious into action. The debate on national purpose that followed in the wake of Sputnik, in particular, encouraged advocates of change to think that the United States was ready for a new agenda. The putative complacency and conservatism of the Eisenhower administration provided the perfect foil for the activism of the 1960s.

The cutting edge of the newly revived liberalism was the nation's liberal intelligentsia. Concentrated on the East Coast, chiefly in New York City and Cambridge, Massachusetts, but with active elements in every city and town in the country, it constituted an energetic and influential subculture situated at the very heart of the nation's communication system. One sector of liberal opinion, anesthetized by the prosperity of the postwar years and repelled by Soviet-style communism, gave higher priority to cultural than economic issues. The Americans for Democratic Action's (ADA) original manifesto had called for the extension of the New Deal "to insure decent levels of health, nutrition, shelter, and education," and at the same time for constant vigilance to protect the individual "from concentrated wealth and overcentralized government." In 1956, however, Arthur Schlesinger, Jr., a Pulitzer prize–winning historian and a moving force in the ADA, wrote an article for the *Reporter* in which he argued that liberals must move beyond the "quantitative liberalism" of the New Deal. Poverty still existed, of course, but "the central problems of our time are no longer problems of want and privation." The times called for a "qualitative liberalism" dedicated to bettering the quality of people's lives and opportunities. In 1958, economist and social critic John Kenneth Galbraith published the soon-to-be widely read *The Affluent Society.* In this book, he lambasted the private waste of American consumer culture with its indifference to the public welfare. In the spirit of Thorstein Veblen, he prescribed less advertising, less acquisitiveness, and more public spending for schools, slum clearance, and social security. There was nothing fundamentally wrong with capitalism, Galbraith wrote. Big business was just another interest group in his countervailing society.

Others within the liberal community rejected the Schlesinger–Galbraith approach as too elitist. They argued that an economic and social underclass consisting of inner-city blacks and Puerto Ricans and the rural poor in Appalachia and sharecropping South were slipping through the cracks. Leon Keyserling, the Truman administration's chief economist, penned a scathing indictment of *The Affluent Society*. He called for countercyclical deficit spending to combat recession and increase production, and for redistribution of income. More instead of less money needed to be earmarked for mothers with dependent children, the unemployed, and the disabled. Moreover, the government ought to launch educational and job programs that attacked the culture of poverty. Meanwhile, on the left, socialists such as Norman Thomas continued to call for the nationalization of basic industries and the perfection of the welfare state.

By the last years of the Eisenhower administration, a consensus emerged among liberals that blended the New Deal agenda with that of the cultural critics. Schlesinger, Keyserling, and journals such as *The New Republic* called for massive public expenditure to promote economic growth and higher taxes to fund welfare, educational, and environmental programs. Liberals joined together in support of a vigorous space program and federal action to secure civil rights for minorities, and they managed to elect a group of Democratic activists to the Senate in 1958: Philip Hart of Michigan, Frank Church of Idaho, and William Proxmire of Wisconsin. All looked forward to the 1960 presidential election as an opportunity to reinvigorate the public sector and put an end to the national orgy of consumption.

It should be noted that there was as much elitism in the liberal community as there was in the conservative community. Although they bled for the common man, Schlesinger and company were profoundly distrustful of him. Many agreed with Columbia University's Robert Nisbet who argued in *Quest for Identity* that the intelligent, self-reliant individualist of Jefferson's dreams had been ground up by historical forces that destroyed associations of family, village, church, and craft union. These homogenizing forces had created "mass man," a new breed susceptible to organization and manipulation by unscrupulous demagogues and totalitarian institutions. Here was the key to understanding such phenomena as Nazism and communism and the appeal of such individuals as Stalin and Hitler. They promised to the lonely, rootless masses an "absolute, redemptive state." In many respects, liberals believed that democracy had to be saved from the people. Indeed, the principal question facing America in the 1960s was which elite to trust: the liberal intellectuals and academics and the politicians who appropriated and ultimately shared their views, or the representatives of business and industry and the politicians who shared their perspective.

It should also be noted that the reviving liberal impulse coincided with and was reinforced by an awakening among college students. Inspired by John F. Kennedy's candidacy for the presidency, appalled by the specter of nuclear annihilation, aroused by the revealed mistreatment of blacks in the South, college students began organizing, questioning, and debating. The most pervasive student organization, the National Student Association (NSA), continued to attract members, while conservatives organized a new body, the Young Americans for Freedom (YAF), and liberals the Students for a Democratic Society (SDS). Dissident journals sprang up on campuses across the United States: *New Freedom* at Cornell, *Studies on the Left* at Wisconsin, and *Alternatives* at Illinois. Students participated in the civil rights movement in ever-increasing numbers. At Harvard, in the spring of 1960, 1,000 students held a walk for nuclear disarmament and a similar number demonstrated in San Francisco against House Un-American Activities Committee (HUAC) hearings being held in the Bay area. The student movement would act as a powerful force for change during the remainder of the 1960s.

The Election of 1960

Sensing Eisenhower's vulnerability, four United States senators entered the lists for the Democratic presidential nomination in 1960: Hubert H. Humphrey of Minnesota, Lyndon B. Johnson of Texas, Stuart Symington of Missouri, and John F. Kennedy of Massachusetts. Humphrey was the darling of civil rights groups and labor unions, while Johnson could claim the support of the South as his native region as well as the loyalty of the party leadership for his years of effective service as majority leader. A former secretary of the U.S. Air Force, Symington could rely on the increasingly powerful military–industrial complex to be his political base. Kennedy could capitalize on his run for the vice presidential nomination in 1956 and, after his loss, his dogged work on behalf of the doomed Stevenson–Kefauver ticket. Meanwhile, Adlai Stevenson waited in the wings, prepared to step in if no clear winner emerged.

As the campaign opened, polls showed that next to Stevenson, Kennedy was the most popular Democratic aspirant. His political advisers – including his brother, Robert, and Theodore Sorensen – had done a good job of keeping Kennedy's image before the public. Handsome and charming, Kennedy managed to appear both self-effacing and intelligent. He also managed to project the image of a World War II hero. Political commentator William V. Shannon, noting Kennedy's celebrity status, wondered "what has all this to do with statesmanship," but there it was. At the same time, the junior senator from Massachusetts labored under a number of handicaps: his youth, his support of Joe McCarthy, and his religion. The latter, his Catholicism, was the weightiest of his albatrosses. Indeed, Kennedy and his strategists decided early on that he would have to enter virtually all the primaries to demonstrate to party leaders that he would not be crippled as Al Smith had been in 1924 and 1928 by his Catholicism. Kennedy came out firing. "Nobody asked me if I was a Catholic when I joined the United States Navy," he declared during the primary in West Virginia, an overwhelmingly Protestant state. "Nobody asked my brother if he was a Catholic or Protestant before he climbed into an American bomber to fly his last mission." With the aid of his father's money, Kennedy won an impressive victory in West Virginia. None of his rivals had been able to match his ability to put together an organization, dominate the all-important medium of television, or master the details of local political situations.

It was obvious to Kennedy, however, that even though he had enough delegate votes to win the nomination, he would have to have the enthusiastic support of the party's liberal intellectuals if he were going to win the general election. These guardians of Democratic ideals were distinctly wary of the glamorous junior senator from Massachusetts. They remembered that the candidate's father, Joseph P. Kennedy, had as ambassador to Great Britain repeatedly advocated appeasement of Nazi Germany. As a member of the House, Jack Kennedy had joined Joe McCarthy in charging that fellow travelers were exerting undue influence on the nation's East Asian policy. Indeed, the candidate's brother, Robert, had served as minority counsel on McCarthy's investigating subcommittee. In 1959, Kennedy made the first of what was to be many trips to Cambridge, during which he courted Schlesinger, Galbraith, McGeorge Bundy, and other liberal academics. In 1960 he flooded the intellectual community with copies of his campaign tract, *Strategies for Peace*. Harris Wofford, a campaign aide who helped prepare the pamphlet, later recalled that it deliberately put Kennedy's left foot forward. During the primaries, he went out of his way to flatter Midwestern intellectuals, and his speeches began to reflect the liberal agenda. Kennedy called for more public spending for education, public works, and care for the elderly and disabled. He declared his allegiance to the principles of equality under the law and equal opportunity for all, without endorsing the specific objectives of the civil rights movement. From coast to coast, he blasted the Eisenhower administration for its apathy, its materialism, its devotion to business interests, and its failure to combat communism – intellectually, strategically, and economically. Above all he promised the nation energy and vision. Reluctantly, Democratic liberals abandoned their favorites, Stevenson and Humphrey, and placated themselves with the thought that, although Kennedy might be a "Johnny come lately," he was a glamorous one who had a realistic chance to win.

When the Democrats gathered in Los Angeles in July, Kennedy swept to victory on the first ballot, swamping Johnson and Symington. In a move that shocked and angered liberals but that undoubtedly strengthened the ticket, Kennedy asked Johnson to serve as his running mate. The Texan was favored by white southerners and, amazingly, by the head of the National Association for the Advancement of Colored People (NAACP). It was an agonizing decision, and the Kennedy camp was split. Indeed, Robert Kennedy returned to the Texan's hotel suite three times suggesting that he decline. Acting on Sam Rayburn's advice, Johnson stuck to his acceptance. The Texan would never forgive the younger Kennedy for his doubts, and theirs was a feud that would affect national affairs in a dramatic fashion during the next eight years.

The race for the Republican nomination was a comparatively closed affair. The only serious rival to Vice President Richard M. Nixon was Nelson Rockefeller, who had defeated Averell Harriman for the governorship of New York in 1958. The GOP was still the minority party, and its leaders knew it. They had enjoyed control of the White House for the past eight years because of Dwight Eisenhower's popularity and not because of any major organizational or ideological victories. Consequently, the president's endorsement of the GOP nominee was crucial. He did not like Richard Nixon, preferring the secretary of the treasury, John Anderson, a quiet Texan who had no chance at the nomination. The vice president seemed to him to be a tin man, incapable of conviction and even genuine feelings. Rockefeller was handsome, hard driving, and the epitome of the eastern, liberal wing of the party, but Eisenhower regarded him as a wealthy spendthrift who would permanently unbalance the budget. Reluctantly, the president endorsed the author of the Checkers speech.

In 1959, Rockefeller withdrew from a race he never really entered and focused his efforts instead on liberalizing the GOP platform for 1960. It just so happened that his efforts coincided with and complemented Nixon's attempts to moderate his own image as a red-baiting, partisan political opportunist. In an effort to unify the party and stake out a claim to America's all-important political center, Nixon flew to New York for a secret meeting with Rockefeller. In the "Compact of Fifth Avenue," Nixon agreed to support a platform that called for preservation of New Deal/Fair Deal reforms and an ongoing effort to secure equal rights for African Americans and other minorities. Although the old Taft wing of the party denounced the compact as a betrayal of the hallowed principles of Republicanism, Nixon was easily nominated on the first ballot. He subsequently named Henry Cabot Lodge, Jr., a prominent member of the eastern, liberal wing of the party, as his running mate.

Embracing the role of challenger, Kennedy took the initiative. He gave top priority to the Cold War and how to stop losing it. The Democratic candidate made much of the alleged missile gap and the Eisenhower administration's apathy in the face of communist inroads in Africa, the Middle East, and Asia. The newly developed Soviet missile system would be, he warned, "the shield from behind which they will slowly but surely advance – through Sputnik diplomacy, limited brush-fire wars, . . . internal revolution...and blackmail. The periphery of the Free World will slowly be nibbled away." Kennedy promised increased funding for the missile program so that America could regain the "lead" from the Russians and prevent a surprise attack. To deal with Khrushchev's wars of liberation, he announced that he would rebuild the nation's neglected conventional forces. In another variation on the theme of getting the country moving again, Kennedy promised to divert resources to the neglected infrastructure and extend the blessings of American civilization to the disadvantaged. Borrowing from John Kenneth Galbraith, he insisted that the task ahead was to improve the quality of life, and he blasted the Republicans for their lack of community spirit. Kennedy promised to rid the nation's urban areas of their slums, provide quality education to every school child, guarantee adequate health care to the elderly, and bring prosperity to chronically depressed areas. "[I]f you are tired, then stay with the Republicans," the Democratic nominee declared. "America cannot stand still...this is a time of burdens and sacrifice; we must move." If his vision matched that of Franklin D. Roosevelt, so did his vagueness.

Many pundits predicted that the civil rights issue was a landmine that could destroy the Kennedy candidacy. By 1960, it was the most highly charged domestic issue facing the nation. Kennedy needed the South desperately, but Democratic liberals expected him to come out forcefully for equal rights and nondiscrimination and to promise to employ the power of the federal government to achieve those goals. Some were ideologically committed, whereas others, joined by big city bosses, were worried about the GOP's historic identification with civil rights and feared losing northern states where the vote looked close and black voters might decide the election. By the time the campaign opened, Kennedy had decided to run as the civil rights candidate and leave the South to Johnson. He promised to introduce a bill as soon as he was inaugurated to eliminate discrimination in federal housing. He even obliquely endorsed the civil disobedience tactics then being employed by the movement. The president, he said, had to exert moral leadership "to help bring equal access to facilities from churches to lunch counters, and to support the right of every American to stand up for his rights, even if on occasion he must sit down for them." Then as the campaign got into full swing, the Democratic candidate was presented with an opportunity to show his true colors.

In October, Martin Luther King, Jr., was arrested in Georgia on trumped up traffic charges and sentenced to two months at hard labor. His family, who endured days without even knowing where he was, feared that he would not emerge from the infamous Georgia prison system alive. Kennedy telephoned Coretta Scott King, pregnant and distraught, to offer his condolences. At the same time, unbeknownst to Kennedy, his brother Robert called the judge in charge and pled with him to set bail. Whether his act of sympathy won Kennedy more support in the nation at large than it lost him among segregationists is unclear. It did help soften his image as a hard-edged, opportunistic young politician, swung the black community in his favor, and attracted the avid support of former President Truman. On the stump for the Democratic candidate, Truman declared that Nixon had "never told the truth in his life." In San Antonio, he told members of a large gathering that "you ought to go to hell" if they voted for the GOP nominee.

When Nixon discussed civil rights, he also avoided specifics. The GOP candidate emphasized instead his experience and his role as inheritor of the Eisenhower mantle. Similar to Republican candidates since Wendell Willkie, he implicitly promised not to tamper with the basic structure of the welfare state. Given his eight years as vice president, he rather than Kennedy would be in a position to stand up to Khrushchev and the Soviets. The issue, Nixon declared, was who could "best continue the leadership of Dwight D. Eisenhower and keep the peace without surrender for America and extend freedom throughout the world." A Gallup poll taken immediately after the two conventions gave Nixon a 50% to 44% lead over Kennedy. An unusually small number of voters indicated that they were still undecided.

In an effort to eat into the Republican lead, the Kennedy camp challenged Nixon to a series of four debates. Only in this way, Democratic strategists believed, could their candidate answer the charges of inexperience and force Nixon into the position of defending a passive administration. The Republican candidate's advisers warned him to refuse, but he was proud of his forensic skill and psychologically incapable of dodging a challenge. Both candidates understood that the impressions they made in their first confrontation would be hard to alter. Kennedy prepared like a skilled trial lawyer, mastering position papers until the points were second nature to him. On September 26, the curtain rose on one of contemporary history's most memorable dramas. Speaking first, Kennedy invoked the image of a revived, activist, successful America. He appeared sun-tanned, self-assured, and competent. For some reason, Nixon suppressed his natural pugnacity and declared that the only difference between him and his opponent was "not about the goals for Americans, but only about the means to reach those goals." His me-tooism did not serve him well. Whether because of studio lighting or an inept makeup person, Nixon appeared unshaven and drawn. Worse, he perspired, causing his makeup to run. A poll of radio listeners showed the debaters had tied. A postelection survey indicated, however, that, of the 4 million Americans who indicated they had been decisively influenced by the debate, 3 million had voted for Kennedy. Most rated the three remaining debates a draw, but the damage had been done.

Nevertheless, Kennedy's margin of victory was razor thin. He garnered just 118,574 more votes than Nixon out of a total of 68.3 million cast. His margin in the electoral college was considerably larger, 303 to Nixon's 219 (with 15 for segregationist Harry F. Byrd of Virginia). The Democratic

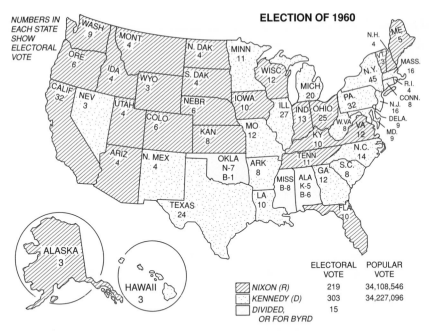

Map 6–1. Election of 1960: Kennedy–Nixon election results.

candidate trailed behind his party, which retained control of both houses of Congress. The continuing strength of the conservative coalition boded ill for Kennedy's legislative program, however. The new president recognized that his election had been far from a sweeping mandate and, despite his inspiring rhetoric about new directions and vigorous action on all fronts, his administration would be marked by caution and moderation.

Kennedy's inaugural address, delivered beneath a brilliant winter sun, focused on foreign policy. Indeed, it appeared to be a call to arms. "Let the word go forth to friend and foe alike," he intoned, "that the torch has been passed to a new generation of Americans, born in this century, tempered by war, disciplined by a hard and bitter peace, proud of our ancient heritage." Under his leadership the nation would "pay any price, bear any burden" to preserve liberty and advance the cause of freedom. He urged peoples in the developing nations to resist totalitarianism, and he promised American aid in their struggle to eliminate poverty and achieve social justice. "Eisenhower embodied half the needs of the nation," Norman Mailer wrote at the time, "the needs of the timid, the petrified, the sanctimonious and the sluggish." Kennedy saw himself as the man who represented the other half of America, someone who would in Mailer's words insist "that the country and its people must become more extraordinary and more adventurous or else perish."

The New Frontier

JFK

John F. Kennedy came into the world on May 29, 1917, the first president to be born in the twentieth century. He was the second of Joseph P. and Rose Fitzgerald Kennedy's nine children. Joe Kennedy was a self-made millionaire. A Boston Irishman, he had attended the city's prestigious Latin School and Harvard College, and then made a large fortune playing the stock market, producing movies, and importing liquor. His courtly, attractive wife was the daughter of John F. ("Honey Fitz") Fitzgerald, mayor of Boston. Joe Kennedy's wealth and power were to play a major role in the lives of his children, particularly that of his second son.

A victim of scarlet fever, diphtheria, allergies, asthma, and a chronic back problem as a child, Jack managed in spite of these infirmities to participate in the intellectual and physical contests that were part of the Kennedy milieu. He attended the Choate School, where he excelled socially, achieved academically, and participated athletically. Not surprisingly, he and his family chose Harvard College where he devoted more time to athletics and extracurricular activities than his studies. Jack's senior thesis, based in part on interviews in Europe arranged by his father, focused on Britain and the coming of World War II in 1940. The theme of Kennedy's work was that democracies are ill equipped to defend themselves against aggressive totalitarian states. "The efforts of democracies are disjointed," he wrote. "They don't have the intensity or long-range view that dictators do." Joe Kennedy subsequently persuaded journalist Arthur Krock to rewrite the wooden text and, with the help of Krock's literary agent, the study was published under the title, *While England Slept*. It should be noted that Jack Kennedy was not active in political organizations, and he showed no signs of a social conscience. The New Deal had come and gone apparently without affecting him.

Joe Kennedy took a keen interest in public affairs and, in fact, served as U.S. ambassador to Great Britain during the late 1930s. He dreamed of directing national affairs from behind the scenes, primarily by elevating his offspring to high office. His political ambitions focused on Joe Jr., who was scheduled first for the United States Senate and then, if things went well, for the presidency. Joe's death in a bombing mission over France in 1944 ended that plan and, from then on, it was Jack who was groomed for political office.

Jack had followed Joe into the service, enlisting in the U.S. Navy soon after the war erupted. Despite his bad back and in part because of his father's influence, he won a commission and became a PT boat commander in the South Pacific. In an incident that Joe Sr. took care to publicize, Jack's boat was sliced in two by a Japanese destroyer on August 2, 1943. Showing the courage and coolness under fire that were to mark his presidency,

Kennedy guided his surviving crew to a nearby island and then swam to a neighboring atoll to radio for help.

Although somewhat reluctant, Jack agreed to run for the House of Representatives from Massachusetts' eleventh district, which spanned Boston and its northern suburbs. Kennedy was inexperienced and somewhat shy, but his good looks, quiet charm, and war record made him a legitimate contender from the outset. "We're going to sell Jack like soap flakes," Joe told newspaper columnist Arthur Krock. That attitude, his extended family, which served as a ready-made political organization, and his father's money paved the way for victory. Kennedy served three terms in the lower house, distinguishing himself primarily by the conservatism of his views. Then, in 1952, Kennedy took Henry Cabot Lodge, Jr.'s Senate seat away from him.

Within a year of his senatorial victory, America's "most eligible" bachelor had married Jacqueline Bouvier in Newport, Rhode Island. The bride was smart, beautiful, and socially prominent; the wedding was high society's event of the year. Kennedy's philandering continued to be a well-kept secret, and the nation viewed Jack and Jackie as the ideal young couple. In the U.S. Senate, however, the junior senator from Massachusetts was viewed as an inattentive playboy. His name was not attached to any significant legislation, and he rarely attended meetings of the Senate Foreign Relations Committee, his major committee assignment. His attention and ambition were focused elsewhere.

In 1956, with the help of Theodore Sorensen, his administrative assistant, and Jules Davids, a Georgetown University professor, Kennedy published *Profiles in Courage*. The book, helped along by Joe Kennedy and Arthur Krock, won the Pulitzer Prize. That same year Kennedy ran unsuccessfully for the Democratic vice presidential nomination. Given the thumping that Eisenhower delivered to Stevenson, his defeat was a blessing in disguise. The effort sharpened Kennedy's skills as a practical politician and, working assiduously to burnish his image with the party's intellectuals, he won the Democratic nomination for the presidency in 1960.

Beyond the White House staff, Kennedy and his talent scouts identified gifted intellectuals from the academic and business world to replace the conservative, unimaginative men of the Eisenhower era. The best and brightest of them all was McGeorge Bundy – summa cum laude at Groton, the first Yale student to earn three perfect scores on his college entrance exams, and dean of Harvard College at 34 – who became national security adviser. Systems analyst par excellence Robert McNamara, former head of Ford Motor Company, became secretary of defense. To run the State Department, Kennedy chose Dean Rusk, former Rhodes Scholar and president of the Ford Foundation. Arthur Schlesinger, Jr., who would serve as court historian in the Kennedy administration, was positively euphoric: "One's life seemed almost to pass in review as one encountered Harvard classmates, wartime associates, faces seen after the war in ADA conventions, workers in Stevenson campaigns, academic colleagues, all united in a surge of hope and possibility."

The new administration was determined to convey an image of vigor and style, and it succeeded. The White House launched a physical fitness program, and soon children across the United States were performing calisthenics, hiking, and playing softball as part of the regular school curricula. Famous artists, musicians, actors, and dancers flocked to Washington, D.C., to entertain the first couple. The nation's capital was, according to Schlesinger, "brighter, gayer, more intellectual, more resolute."

Kennedy enjoyed excellent relations with the media. His press secretary, Pierre "Plucky" Salinger, persuaded him to conduct regular, live press conferences. Kennedy's easy mastery of detail, his self-effacing humor, and celebrity good looks charmed the press corps and the public to whom they reported. Like many introverts, Kennedy did better with large crowds than he did with individuals and small groups. In these latter settings, he frequently came across as formal and distant. This, coupled with the facts that he was considered an outsider by his colleagues in the House and Senate, did not use Lyndon Johnson in the legislative process (Johnson's area of greatest expertise), and seemed unwilling to fight for even those legislative projects most important to him, boded ill for the New Frontier.

Domestic Affairs: A Mixed Record

Kennedy began his presidency by focusing on what he termed five "must" bills: an increase in the minimum wage, health insurance for senior citizens, federal aid to education, housing legislation, and aid to depressed areas. In February, the administration introduced an education bill that would provide $2.3 billion to the states for the construction and maintenance of school facilities and for teacher salary supplements. The bill was based on the assumption, widely held in the 1940s and 1950s, that inferior education stemmed from state and local governments simply not being able to bear the financial burden required by America's free, compulsory school system. As of 1960, local governments provided 56% of school funding, state governments 40%, and the federal government only 4%. The administration measure immediately foundered on the shoals of race and religion. Determined to reassure the country concerning his commitment to separation of church and state, the president made it clear that federal money would go to public schools only. Catholics and their congressional spokesmen responded by announcing their implacable opposition to the bill. They were joined by southern legislators who saw the measure as the opening wedge of a federal effort to integrate public schools by gaining financial leverage over them. The measure never became law.

The administration's minimum wage bill proposed to raise the basic national wage to $1.25 and extend coverage to 4.3 million new workers.

Southern representatives, speaking for large, nonunion laundry operators, forced Kennedy to compromise by excluding their workers. That concession in turn offended liberals. The House rejected the measure by 186 to 185. Kennedy eventually won acceptance of the $1.25 mark but at the expense of 350,000 laundry workers.

Medical insurance for the elderly also encountered rough sledding in 1961. The American Medical Association declared that Kennedy's proposal would introduce "compulsion, regulation and control into a system of freely practiced medicine." The organization and its spokesmen were wrong, of course. The bill, also introduced in February, would have levied a 0.25% increase in Social Security payroll taxes to pay hospital and nursing costs incurred by individuals eligible for Social Security old-age benefits. The White House mounted a public relations campaign that featured a televised address by Kennedy to a throng of senior citizens in Madison Square Garden. Despite opinion polls that showed a majority of Americans favored the concept of Medicare, the Senate defeated the administration's proposal by a vote of 52 to 48. The vote revealed an emerging pattern that would characterize congressional action throughout the New Frontier period: only 5 Republicans voted for the measure and 27 Democrats, mostly from the South, cast their ballots in opposition.

On the plus side, Congress passed Kennedy's "depressed areas" bill in April, providing for a four-year, $394 million redevelopment program for areas plagued by chronic unemployment. Unfortunately, in 1965, Congress refused to continue funding for the program. Congress also approved the administration's housing legislation in June 1961, although it refused to create a Department of Urban Affairs, largely because Kennedy had tagged Robert Weaver, an African American, to be its first head. Overall, Congress appropriated $4.88 billion to fund slum clearance; build housing for the poor, elderly, and college students; and provide low-interest loans for middle-income families.

The New Frontier fared much better in its second year than its first. In 1962, Congress passed the Trade Expansion Act. In this, the first significant trade revision measure enacted since Franklin Roosevelt's time, the president was given authority to cut tariff duties by 50%, to eliminate tariffs altogether on certain goods, and to retaliate against "unfair" trade practices. The bill led to increased commerce with the European Common Market. Because it allowed Americans to trade with Europeans on more equal terms, the measure helped correct the imbalance of payments. The Manpower Development and Training Act established programs to retrain workers who suffered because of inadequate or obsolete skills. Many such workers, it was anticipated, would be relegated to the unemployment rolls by newly admitted, cheaply produced foreign goods.

Congress proved to be positively enthusiastic about the New Frontier's space program, however. Kennedy had chided the Eisenhower administration for permitting the missile gap with the Russians to develop. Shortly after cosmonaut Yuri Gagarin and astronaut Alan B. Shepard made their historic flights into outer space, Kennedy urged Congress to commit the United States "to achieving the goal, before this decade is out, of landing a man on the moon and returning him safely to the earth." President Kennedy was intimidated by the estimated cost – $30 to $40 billion over 10 years – but he was convinced that the project was justifiable on scientific and defense grounds. Congress doubled NASA's budget in 1962 and again in 1963. Talk of a missile gap began to subside when on February 20, 1962, Lieutenant Colonel John H. Glenn flew around the earth three times in his Mercury space capsule, *Friendship 7*, and splashed down safely in the Caribbean that same afternoon. At last the Americans had beaten the Russians in a leg of the space race; people were much more impressed with Glenn than with Shepard, although Shepard's achievement was probably greater. America remained ahead in the missile/space race from that point to the present. Glenn and his fellow astronauts became instant celebrities. Millions of Americans held their collective breath during blastoffs and then watched entranced on television as the capsules and their human cargoes circled the earth.

Perhaps more significant in the long run than the manned space flights was the launching of Telstar on June 10. Telstar was the experimental communications satellite developed by AT&T and Bell Laboratories. Soon it was relaying live television pictures from Andover, Maine, to France and Great Britain. A year later a secret military satellite released some 400 million tiny copper hairs into polar orbit, providing a cloud of reflective material for relaying radio signals from coast to coast within the United States.

Another issue over which Kennedy had chastised the Eisenhower administration was agriculture. Kennedy had little experience with farm problems and expressed even less interest. "I don't want to hear about agricultural policy from anyone except you, and I don't want to hear about it from you," he had told John Kenneth Galbraith. Under Eisenhower's secretary of agriculture, Ezra Taft Benson, price supports had declined, which in the face of continuing overproduction meant declining income for farmers. Republican vulnerability over the issue was such that candidate Kennedy could not resist. Indeed, during the 1960 campaign, he declared it to be his number one domestic priority. Under the direction of U.S. Department of Agriculture head Orville Freeman, a bright, industrious, and skillful administrator, new subsidies helped raise net farm income $1 billion in 1962 alone when farm income reached an eight-year high. One of those whose income rose most dramatically was Texas agribusinessman Billie Sol Estes, who bilked the federal government and small farmers of hundreds of thousands of dollars, primarily by selling equipment bought with federal subsidies. Graft by Estes and other large farmers helped give federal subsidies a bad name and crippled future efforts at farm relief.

When Kennedy entered the White House, the United States was mired in its fourth postwar recession. More people were out of work in 1960 than in any year since 1945. Indeed, in January the unemployment rate hovered near 7%. During the previous three and a half years, the annual growth rate had averaged 2.5% rather than the historic 3.5%. The president had criticized his predecessor for neglecting the economy and pursuing outmoded laissez-faire policies. But if the truth be known, Jack Kennedy entered the presidency as a fiscal conservative. His father had never liked the New Deal, and, although wealthy, the Kennedys were notoriously tight fisted. The president's principal economic adviser was not John Kenneth Galbraith but Secretary of the Treasury Douglas Dillon, a wealthy Republican. The former Wall Street financier favored reductions in federal expenditures and an investment tax credit to induce business to expand the private sector. By midyear, the economy began to improve, stimulated ironically by increases in federal spending, primarily for military purposes. At the outset of his administration, Kennedy persuaded Congress to appropriate $3.7 billion for "urgent" national security needs and an additional $3.5 billion for defense during the Berlin crisis. The Cold War, it seemed, had made the president an inadvertent Keynesian.

Fearing inflation, the Kennedy administration worked to hold down wage and price increases. In April 1962, Secretary of Labor Arthur Goldberg pressured the United Steel Workers to accept a modest 2.5% increase in benefits in their contract negotiations with owners in return for a tacit commitment from the steel companies not to raise prices. When shortly thereafter, U.S. Steel President Roger Blough announced a $6 per ton increase, and his seven closest competitors followed suit, Kennedy exploded. "My father always told me that all businessmen were sons-of-bitches," he raged to staffers, "but I never believed him till now." The president ordered the FBI to begin investigating a possible conspiracy among the executives, and the Defense Department announced that it was henceforth awarding contracts only to those concerns that had not raised prices. The crisis ended 72 hours after it had begun. On April 12, Bethlehem Steel announced that it was rescinding the price increase; U.S. Steel soon followed suit.

Sometime in 1962, President Kennedy accepted the Keynesian notion that temporary deficits were acceptable to revive economic growth. But he did not embrace Keynes' emphasis on public works and welfare expenditures by the federal government to create jobs and stimulate demand, an approach that had been urged on him by Galbraith since the beginning of the administration. Rather, the president listened to Walter Heller, chairman of the Council of Economic Advisers, and opted for a general tax cut. Heller argued that an across-the-board reduction in federal taxes would prompt business to expand and consumers to consume. In the fall of 1963, the administration introduced a measure providing for a tax reduction of $13.6 billion – $11 billion for individuals and $2.6 billion for corporations – spread over three years. Kennedy did not live to see passage of the Revenue Act of 1964, but it would have a significant impact on the economy. By the end of 1965, the unemployment rate had plummeted to 4.5% and the annual growth rate had increased to 6.3%. The GNP increased by $100 billion during that same period.

The Second Reconstruction

The phase of the civil rights movement that began with the Brown decision and the Montgomery bus boycott crested during the Kennedy–Johnson administrations. The massive migration of southern blacks into northern cities had finally tipped the balance in northern states to the point that Democrats had to start competing for black votes. In addition, blacks in the South had finally organized themselves to an extent that they could threaten public order.

In a 1956 speech, Martin Luther King, Jr., outlined the gains he believed had been made as a result of the Montgomery experience:

"(1) We have discovered that we can stick together for a common cause; (2) our leaders do not have to sell out; (3) threats and violence do not necessarily intimidate those who are sufficiently aroused and non-violent; (4) our church is becoming militant, stressing a social gospel as well as a gospel of personal salvation; (5) we have gained a new sense of dignity and destiny; (6) we have discovered a new and powerful weapon – non-violent resistance."

During the boycott, King and his associates had been advised by two pioneering northern pacifists, Bayard Rustin of the War Resister's League and Glenn Smiley of the Fellowship of Reconciliation. In 1957, King had decided to institutionalize the nonviolent civil disobedience techniques he had learned from Mahatma Gandhi, Rustin, and Smiley. Together with the Reverend Ralph Abernathy, he brought together more than 100 black ministers to found the Southern Christian Leadership Conference (SCLC). The establishment of the SCLC marked the addition of a new militant, nonviolent, direct action component of the civil rights movement, a compliment to the traditional legal action approach taken by the NAACP. Membership in the SCLC grew rapidly at first, but then quickly tapered off. Indeed, in the absence of a dramatic, media-arousing confrontation, the civil rights movement itself began to lose momentum.

The decision on February 1, 1960, by four North Carolina A&T students to stage a sit-in at the Woolworth's lunch counter in Greensboro provided the spark for which King and his colleagues had been waiting. The Greensboro incidents proved to be only the first of a wave of sit-ins that swept though the South during 1960 and 1961. In Philadelphia, 400 ministers asked their congregations not to shop at businesses that did not hire blacks. Altogether some 70,000 people, most of them black but some white, participated in sit-ins against a variety of segregated public facilities.

In Nashville, the Reverend James Lawson trained would-be activists in non-violence seminars. He and his coworkers developed rules of conduct that would become the standard for the movement: "Don't strike back or curse if abused.... Show yourself courteous and friendly at all times.... Report all serious incidents to your leader in a polite manner. Remember love and nonviolence." Such discipline frequently required great courage. In Atlanta, a white threw acid into a demonstrator's face and, during sit-ins in Houston, segregationists pulled out a protester, flogged him, and carved "KKK" in his chest. When African Americans attempted to integrate public beaches in Biloxi, Mississippi, a white mob brandishing guns and clubs chased them, eventually shooting eight. But efforts at intimidation failed; the number of demonstrations mounted. The picket line "now extends from the dime store to the United States Supreme Court and beyond that to national and world opinion," observed a Greensboro, North Carolina, paper.

The heart of the New South was Atlanta, the region's leading metropolitan area and home to the South's largest and most influential black bourgeoisie. The city's black middle class might have been well-to-do and educated, but they were still segregated or denied access to public facilities. In March 1960, 200 black students from Morehouse, Spelman, and other local black colleges staged sit-ins at the State Capitol, City Hall, and commercial facilities. After the police arrested 76 demonstrators, Julian Bond and his fellow students formed the Appeal for Human Rights and demanded an end to segregation as well as equal access to jobs, education, and housing. In October, Martin Luther King, Jr., and 36 students were arrested in the all-white Magnolia Room restaurant in Rich's Department store. After a prolonged boycott of white merchants by black Atlantans, the segregationists relented in September 1961, and integration of Atlanta's public facilities began. These acts of individual and group assertiveness served a dual purpose – they desegregated the facilities in question and generated a new sense of empowerment and self-esteem in the participants. "I possibly felt better on that day than I've ever felt in my life," remembered Franklin McCain, one of the Greensboro students. The sit-ins, one demonstrator wrote, were a "mass vomit against the hypocrisy of segregation.

Although most African Americans seemed to support the sit-in and boycott movements, not all did. Many members of the traditional black elite – teachers, politicians, barbers, dry cleaners, and lawyers – had made their money and gained their influence by cooperating with the white power structure and by acquiescing in institutionalized segregation. A substantial number felt threatened by student protests and boycotts that they perceived would upset business relationships and political patronage arrangements. There were also a substantial number of African Americans of all classes who in the name of survival did not want the racial boat rocked. The president of Southern University in Baton Rouge, Louisiana, for example, forced the entire entering class of 1960 to reenroll so that "agitators" could be weeded out. During the first year of the sit-ins, black college administrators expelled more than 140 students and fired almost 60 faculty members. It was in part this generational and philosophical gap that had led to the formation in April 1960 of the Student Nonviolent Coordinating Committee (SNCC) in Raleigh, North Carolina. The organizers of SNCC recognized the importance of student protestors retaining control over their own movement. They stressed democracy and the stimulation of grass-roots leadership as well as Ghandian techniques of nonviolent civil disobedience. Beginning in the fall of 1960, SNCC field workers spread out across the South, initiating and supporting local, community-based activities. Three quarters of the first field workers were younger than 22 years old. Bob Moses, a former Harvard graduate student, summed up SNCC's philosophy: "Go where the spirit say go and do what the spirit say do."

Robert Kennedy was increasingly sympathetic to the crusade for nondiscrimination and equality under the law for African Americans; the president's attitude toward the civil rights movement was much more equivocal. During the 1960 presidential campaign, Kennedy had praised the sit-in movement as part of the general reform spirit he was trying to arouse. But the president and his advisers also wanted to retain as much political support among white southerners as possible. Segregationist sentiment remained very strong in the South, and Kennedy's margin of victory over Nixon had been razor thin. The region's representatives in Congress had managed to water down the Civil Rights Act of 1960 to the point where it was virtually meaningless. Indeed, in the wake of its passage, Democratic Senator Joseph Clark of Pennsylvania, a civil rights advocate, had declared that his side had "suffered a crushing defeat," calling the bill "only a ghost of our hopes." In fact, the Kennedy administration's most significant action in the field of civil rights was to reinvigorate the Civil Rights Division of the Justice Department. Under Eisenhower, the new branch of Justice, authorized by the 1957 Civil Rights Act, had lain fallow. Attorney General Robert Kennedy assembled a group of bright, activist lawyers under the leadership of Burke Marshall and urged his team members to go out into the field and confront racial animosity first hand. The Civil Rights Division had some success in speeding school desegregation, but confronted with a new outburst of racial violence in 1961, Kennedy's lawyers and marshals became temporarily paralyzed.

The Freedom Rides
In the spring of 1961, the Congress of Racial Equality (CORE), headed by civil rights veteran James Farmer, planned a series of "freedom rides" to test southern compliance with recent court orders banning segregation on buses and in terminals engaged in interstate travel. The SCLC and several branches of the NAACP decided to lend financial aid. Farmer and the other organizers anticipated confrontation; indeed, that was the purpose of the

operation. "Our intention," he later declared, "was to provoke the southern authorities into arresting us and thereby prod the Justice Department into enforcing the law of the land." The organizers of the freedom rides notified the FBI and the Justice Department of their plans but never received any reply. The first week in May, 13 riders, both black and white, split into two groups and departed Washington, D.C., for Alabama and Mississippi. The first group encountered only sporadic harassment until it reached Anniston, Alabama, where a white mob smashed windows and slashed tires. Outside of town en route to Birmingham, the bus was firebombed. The mob reassembled, surrounded the bus, and beat the freedom riders with clubs and pipes as they fled the burning vehicle. As SCLC workers from Birmingham rescued the bruised and bleeding riders, the second bus was pulling into Anniston.

In Birmingham, the two groups were reunited but only after yet another attack by white extremists in the bus station. According to a CBS reporter who covered the incident, rampaging segregationists dragged the riders into alleys, "pounding them with pipes, with key rings, and with fists." Though the police station was only two blocks from the terminal, no officers appeared. It was Mother's Day, the chief subsequently explained, and most of his men were home "visiting their mothers." A contingent of FBI agents did witness the assault, but they stood by passively and took notes. Those activists left standing decided to press on to Montgomery, but they were not able to persuade a bus to take them. Exhausted and battered, these first riders agreed to be flown to New Orleans where they disbanded. On May 20, however, a fresh group of 21 riders, having assembled and trained in Nashville, boarded a bus in Birmingham destined for Montgomery. The state police provided protection until the riders reached Montgomery's city limits. All was quiet when the vehicle pulled into the capital city's terminal, but as the passengers disembarked, they were surprised and attacked by a white mob; this assault left one white rider paralyzed from the neck down. Another passenger suffered a broken leg, and another severe burns after he was doused with gasoline and set on fire. Montgomery police stood by as the brutality unfolded.

Television footage and news photos of the carnage at Montgomery shocked the nation and the world, including southern white businessmen and journalists. The freedom rides were at last front-page news. Gradually, the Kennedy administration succumbed to pressure, much of it from the southern white press, to intervene. When a collection of enraged whites surrounded Montgomery's First Baptist Church in an attempt to break up a rally on behalf of the freedom riders, Attorney General Kennedy sent in 400 federal marshals to prevent bloodshed. On behalf of his brother, who was about to attend his first summit meeting with Nikita Khrushchev, Robert pleaded with civil rights leaders to suspend further demonstrations lest the president be embarrassed. "Doesn't the Attorney General know that we've been embarrassed all our lives?" Ralph Abernathy replied. The Justice Department eventually petitioned the Interstate Commerce Commission to issue clear rules prohibiting segregation on interstate carriers. CORE proclaimed victory in its battle against Jim Crow on the highways, but Farmer and other civil rights leaders continued to be dismayed by the reluctance with which the Kennedy administration supported the constitutional rights of African Americans. Events at the University of Mississippi in the fall of 1962 did not serve to allay those misgivings.

The Politics of Confrontation
In September, at the urging of Governor Ross Barnett, the university rejected the application of James H. Meredith, an African American, for admission. Meredith had obtained a federal court order requiring "Ole Miss" to register him; consequently, the Justice Department was forced to intervene. On September 28, a U.S. Court of Appeals found Barnett guilty of civil contempt. Two days later, Meredith was escorted onto the University of Mississippi campus by U.S. marshals. Over the radio, Barnett encouraged resistance to the "oppressive power of the United States," and an angry mob of several thousand whites, many of them armed, laid siege to the campus on September 30. In the violence that ensued, three people were killed; the marshals, several of them severely wounded, were able to hold off the rioters only with the help of 300 federalized national guardsmen. Some locals began referring to the incident as the "Last Battle of the Civil War." After the attorney general appealed for a "hundred day cooling-off period," President Kennedy reluctantly dispatched 23,000 troops. On October 1, Meredith began attending class, but the Oxford campus continued to be the scene of segregationist protests and disruptions. At his graduation, there were still 500 federal troops and marshals on guard.

By the end of 1962, civil rights leaders were once again in search of a crisis that would keep the nation's attention focused on their movement. The conscience of the white majority needed to be outraged. In addition, Martin Luther King, Jr., James Forman of SNCC, and James Farmer of CORE were convinced that President Kennedy needed to be forced to lend substantive rather than just rhetorical support for the drive to end discrimination and segregation. The president's habit of expressing concern while avoiding action lest he alienate white southerners had brought scant results. At the end of 1962, 2,000 southern school districts remained strictly segregated; only 8% of black children in the South attended school with whites. At that rate, civil rights leaders estimated, it would take 50 years for blacks to gain access to public facilities and 100 years to achieve equality in job training and employment. Adding to King's sense of urgency was his vulnerability to attack by Malcolm X, leader of the Nation of Islam, and other black nationalists who charged that the SCLC's approach was not only too soft and gradualist but also wrong headed. Malcolm ridiculed nonviolence and rejected the virtues of integration. Confrontation in all of its forms, militant self-defense, and black chauvinism were necessary to preserve both the physical and psychological well-being of African Americans, he argued.

The staging ground that King and his advisers selected for the next act in the civil rights drama was Birmingham, Alabama, the most pervasively and rigidly segregated big city in America. City authorities had closed down parks and other public facilities rather than integrate them. Fewer than 10,000 of the city's 80,000 registered voters were black, although African Americans constituted 40% of the population. Between 1957 and 1967 Birmingham – local blacks nicknamed it "Bombingham" and their neighborhood "Dynamite Hill" – would be the scene of 18 racial bombings and 50 cross burnings, all of which had been tacitly or expressly condoned by city authorities, including police commissioner Eugene T. "Bull" Conner. Stout, jowly, and bigoted, Conner had devoted himself to "keeping the niggers in their place." The very defensiveness and rashness of its leaders made Birmingham a vulnerable target, however. Acknowledging the danger involved, King believed that an assault on segregation in Birmingham would reveal southern "brutality openly – in the light of day – with the rest of the world looking on." Thus, Kennedy would be forced to act.

King and his staff arrived in Birmingham in early April and immediately put into operation their secret Plan "C" – "C" for confrontation. They issued a public call for an immediate end to discriminatory employment practices and segregation of public facilities. In the days that followed, small groups of mainly black protesters staged lunch counter sit-ins and marched on city hall. During one of these latter activities, King was arrested and imprisoned. During his incarceration, he penned his famous *Letter From the Birmingham Jail*. Written on a newspaper smuggled into him, the 19-page missive was subsequently reprinted in scores of newspapers across the United States. The letter was an eloquent defense of civil disobedience; it argued persuasively that the protesters rather than the forces of law and order in Birmingham represented the Judeo-Christian ethic and the spirit of the Constitution. Hitler's laws were legal but manifestly unjust. It was in fact immoral to continue to acquiesce in the oppression of black Americans.

Once out of jail, King embarked on the greatest gamble of his career. On May 2, 1,000 black children, some only six years old, set out from the Sixteenth Street Baptist Church in Birmingham headed for city hall. Conner arrested them. When another thousand gathered in the church for a second march, he attempted to seal the building exits. As some escaped, he loosed police dogs and turned fire hoses on the children. Panicked black parents hurled rocks and bricks at the police who in turn assaulted everyone in their path. A national television audience was horrified by the water hoses, which spewed streams of water strong enough to take bark off of trees, by the snarling canines, and by the truncheon-wielding police. *Time* magazine painted a vivid picture: "There was the Negro youth, sprawled on his back and spinning across the pavement, while firemen battered him with streams of water.... There was the Negro woman, pinned to the ground by cops, one of them with his knee dug into her throat.... The blaze of bombs, the flash of blades, the eerie glow of fire, the keening cries of hatred, the wild dance of terror in the night – all this was Birmingham, Ala." The demonstrations continued throughout the first week in May, peaking on May 7. With their city portrayed daily as a hotbed of racial violence, fearing even wider bloodshed, and under pressure from federal authorities, the Senior Citizen's Committee, a group of whites secretly selected by the Chamber of Commerce to negotiate with the black protesters, came to terms with King and his cohorts. The SCLC won its demand for desegregation of lunch counters and other public facilities and for "the upgrading and hiring of Negroes on a non-discriminatory basis," albeit in planned stages.

Birmingham galvanized even the poorest and most disorganized southern blacks, swelling the ranks of the SCLC, CORE, SNCC, and NAACP. If Birmingham, a bastion of extreme racism, could be forced to accept integration, African Americans came to realize, so could any and every other community in America. The example of the black children was particularly compelling. The descendents of those freed by the Civil War agreed with King who in his Birmingham manifesto had equated "wait" with "never." The major civil rights organizations became more militant, competing with each other in sponsoring protests, demonstrations, sit-ins, and lawsuits. More important, perhaps, the wanton brutality of Bull Conner's police had sickened much of white America, contributing to the political energy for executive and legislative action on behalf of civil rights. "The whole country was trapped in a lie," declared activist Casey Hayden. "We were told [in school] about equality but we discovered it didn't exist."

Frustrated, angry, and paranoid, southern segregationists struck back. Cross burnings, night ridings, and bombings multiplied at a frightening rate during 1963. In June, Medgar Evers, NAACP field representative in Mississippi, was shot dead by a sniper outside his home in Jackson. Three months later, after black youths attempted to desegregate several previously all-white schools, a huge dynamite bomb shattered the Sixteenth Street Baptist Church in Birmingham. In the rubble lay the dead bodies of four girls, ages 11 to 14, who had been changing for choir practice.

Proclaiming that "events in Birmingham ... have so increased the cries for equality that no city or state or legislative body can ... ignore them," President Kennedy asked Congress to pass a civil rights law that barred segregation in public facilities, authorized the federal government to withhold funds from programs that discriminated, and empowered the Justice Department to initiate school desegregation suits. On August 28, 1963, 200,000 Americans, both black and white, descended on Washington, D.C., to express their support for the measure. The March on Washington marked the culmination of a long-held dream of A. Philip Randolph, the legendary head of the Brotherhood of Sleeping Car Porters, the first all-black union. Not until after Birmingham was he able to persuade the SCLC, NAACP, and National Urban League to support his "radical" idea. The participants, who included hundreds of nationally prominent church and civic leaders, marched peacefully from the Washington Monument to the Lincoln Memorial. There they heard pledges of support from politicians; the folk music of Peter, Paul, and Mary; and the gospel songs of Mahalia Jackson. The culmination of the March on Washington was Martin Luther King, Jr.'s incomparable "I Have a Dream" speech:

I have a dream that one day on the red hills of Georgia the sons of former slaves and the sons of former slaveowners will be able to sit down together at the table of brotherhood.

I have a dream that one day even the State of Mississippi, a state sweltering with the heat of injustice, sweltering with the heat of oppression, will be transformed into an oasis of freedom and justice.

I have a dream that one day down in Alabama with its vicious racists . . . little black boys and black girls will be able to join hands with little white boys and white girls as sisters and brothers.

I have a dream today.

The Death of a President

During the fall of 1963, President Kennedy and his advisers seemed to be devoting more attention than usual to politics. In September, the president toured 11 western states and then followed up with a series of major speaking engagements on the East Coast. Given the fallout from the administration's efforts in the field of civil rights, Ted Sorensen and Bobby Kennedy were particularly worried about Democratic prospects in the South. In the 1964 presidential election, Texas would be crucial, and Lyndon B. Johnson's presence on the ticket was no guarantee that the Lone Star state would remain loyal. In 1963, the state party machinery was paralyzed by a bitter feud between a liberal faction headed by Senator Ralph Yarborough and the conservative wing dominated by Governor John Connally. Following a visit to Florida in mid-November, Kennedy flew to Texas for speaking engagements in several cities, an inspection of the space facilities in Houston, and mediatory talks with party leaders.

The tour got off to a great start as Kennedy and his entourage, which included Johnson and Connally, were greeted by enthusiastic crowds in Houston, San Antonio, and Ft. Worth. The tour was to end in Dallas, a thriving hub of commerce but also a seat of virulent right-wing radicalism. As the presidential motorcade proceeded from Love Field to the Dallas Trade Mart where Kennedy was to deliver a luncheon address, nothing seemed amiss. The weather was clear and cold, and the crowd that lined the route was large and positive. As the president's car passed the Texas School Book Depository, several shots rang out, fired from its upper floor. Two bullets struck Kennedy in the head and neck. The president's wife, holding a fragment of her husband's skull in her hand, went into shock. Governor Connally was also wounded but not fatally. The fallen president was rushed to Parkland Hospital, but doctors could not revive him. He died at 1:00 PM.

Only an hour after the assassination, Dallas police arrested Lee Harvey Oswald for the murder. A deeply disturbed former Marine, Oswald had lived in the Soviet Union for a time, married a Russian woman, and once had been a member of the Fair Play for Cuba Committee. Although a self-professed Marxist, Kennedy's assassin had also belonged to right-wing organizations, making it difficult subsequently for investigators to identify his motives. In a bizarre twist, Oswald was himself shot and killed while being moved to another jail. His assassin was Dallas night club owner Jack Ruby.

Struck down in his prime and at a time when his presidency seemed on the verge of realizing its promise, Kennedy was transformed almost overnight into a transcendent figure, his every action encased in an aura of romance. "What was killed in Dallas," journalist James Reston wrote, "was not only the President but the promise. The death of youth and the hope of youth, of the beauty and grace and the touch of magic." In the first month after Kennedy's assassination, more than 700,000 mourners paid their respects at his grave in Arlington National Cemetery. Americans found it difficult to comprehend such tragedy; they were driven to sentimentality. Out of the nation's grief was born the legend of Camelot, whose gallant young prince gave America a moment of glory before dying for its sins, but who also opened the way for change and growth. "Don't let it be forgot," historian Samuel Eliot Morrison concluded his massive history of the American people (citing a Broadway musical), "that once there was a spot for one brief shining moment that was known as Cam-e-lot."

Taking the Stage

Lyndon B. Johnson took the oath of office as president of the United States aboard Air Force One as it prepared to take John F. Kennedy's body back to Washington, D.C. Johnson's detractors, who included most of the people in the fallen president's entourage, noted that he was careful to have his picture snapped with Jacqueline, her husband's blood still spattered over her suit. Other, more fair-minded observers noted that he readily gave over the presidential cabin to the grief-stricken family and took his seat among the throng of reporters in the front of the plane. As John Morton Blum has noted, Johnson reacted to the assassination of his predecessor much as Theodore Roosevelt had to McKinley's death. He was shocked and saddened, yet he looked forward to his duties with anticipation and expectation. He was shrewd enough to remain in the background until after the funeral, and he went to great lengths to assure the United States that he intended to follow through on Kennedy's program. Back in the Capitol, one of his first acts was to address a subdued Congress. Noting that Kennedy had begun his inaugural address with "Let us begin . . . ," the new president declared, "Let us continue . . ." That is, the nation's leaders should focus their energies on passing pending legislation: the education, tax cut, foreign aid, and civil rights bills. But Johnson also let the solons know that he had a vision of his own, a sweeping liberal agenda that included an end to racial discrimination, employment for all wanting to work, peaceful coexistence with the communist powers, and real social security for the elderly. In the first days of his administration, Johnson repeatedly reminded dubious liberals, many of whom were more attracted by Ivy League slickness than demonstrated commitment to redistribution of wealth and equality under the law, that the inspiration and model for his public life had been Franklin Delano Roosevelt.

LBJ

Lyndon Baines Johnson was born on August 27, 1908, in a farmhouse near the central Texas town of Stonewall. He was the eldest of the five children of Samuel Ealy Johnson, a farmer and schoolteacher who served five terms in the lower house of the Texas legislature representing the Hill Country district, which included Johnson City and Marble Falls. His mother, Rebekah Baines Johnson, was also a schoolteacher and, compared with her rough-hewn husband, a person of refinement. An active, healthy child, Lyndon learned the alphabet by age two, and by age four his mother had taught him to read. When he was five, the family moved to the town that bore his family's name. In high school, the eldest Johnson child proved to be an unwilling but rather successful student. He graduated in 1924 at age fifteen, president of his class of seven. After three years of travel and odd jobs, Lyndon enrolled at Southwest Texas State Teacher's College where he was an excellent student and star debater. Johnson graduated in 1930 and immediately went to work for the Houston Independent School District teaching at the secondary level. Bored with his new job, Johnson left Texas for Washington in 1931, where he became secretary to newly elected Congressman Richard Kleberg, owner of the famed King Ranch. Within months he had mastered the system and ingratiated himself with veteran Capitol Hill operatives. In 1934, he married Claudia Alta (Lady Bird) Taylor, whose dignified loyalty and family wealth would serve Johnson well during the remainder of his life. In August, 1935, Franklin Roosevelt appointed the 26-year-old Johnson head of the National Youth Administration (NYA) in Texas. In the process of running this New Deal agency, he found work for thousands of unemployed young people and helped thousands more get through high school and college.

In 1937, Johnson quit the NYA to run for Congress. He won and, as a Roosevelt loyalist and devoted New Dealer, quickly became one of the White House's favorites. A hyperactive and successful legislator, he brought the Rural Electrification Administration and cheap electricity to central Texas. He also availed his constituents of low-cost farm loans, public housing, and lower freight rates. When World War II erupted, Johnson, a naval reservist, was the first member of Congress to go on active duty. Commissioned a lieutenant colonel, the Texan spent most of the war as Roosevelt's political emissary to the Pacific theater. He was awarded a silver star for gallantry by General Douglas MacArthur.

In the spring of 1948, Johnson decided to run for the Senate against the powerful, ultraconservative former governor of Texas, Coke Stevenson. In a bitterly contested campaign in which both sides engaged in voter fraud, Johnson won by 87 votes. Among his enemies in Texas, he would be known thereafter as "Landslide Lyndon."

For the next 12 years, the U.S. Senate would be Lyndon B. Johnson's oyster. He quickly rose to the post of Democratic whip where he dispensed favors and mobilized the members for crucial votes. In 1952, he was elected Democratic minority leader at age 44, the youngest man ever to be chosen for a Senate leadership post, and in 1955 after his party regained control of Congress he was elected majority leader. From this lofty position, Johnson acted as power broker, guiding through key pieces of legislation for the Eisenhower administration and seeing that he and the Democrats received a fair share of the credit. "Ike couldn't pass the Lord's Prayer in Congress without me," he boasted. In fact, the Texan proved to be a genius at the arts of persuasion and favor trading. He refused to sign the Southern Manifesto and helped guide the civil rights bills of 1957 and 1960 through Congress, thus building a reputation as a politician with a national rather than a regional perspective. Nevertheless, liberals mistrusted him because they were prejudiced against southerners. Liberals preferred the ineffectual and illiberal but smooth-talking, good-looking Kennedy for president in 1960. Furthermore, they resented what may have been Kennedy's shrewdest – and most liberal – political decision: choosing Johnson as his running mate.

Lyndon B. Johnson was a gigantic figure – physically, mentally, and emo-tionally. Six-foot four and simultaneously as beautiful and ugly as a hound dog, Johnson was a dynamo forever laboring to cajole or coerce legislators, interest groups, and the press into supporting his programs. Following a stint covering the Texan when he was majority leader, one reporter wrote, "He comes into a room slowly and warily, as if he means to smell out the al-legiances of everyone in it." A man of immense accomplishment and intense insecurity, Johnson was determined to prove to the eastern establishment that he was greater than any figure that it had produced. His personality was a study in paradox. He could be kind and cruel, thoughtful and insensitive, crude and sophisticated, candid and disingenuous, or cunning and naive. He worked his staff unmercifully; indeed, few lasted more than a year. Constantly struggling to accommodate his lofty ideals to political reality, he exuded cool confidence and iron determination one minute and exhibited fits of doubt and self-pity the next. As Hubert Humphrey, the vice president he both admired and abused, put it, Johnson was a reflection of the nation: "He was an All-American president. He was really the history of this country, with all of the turmoil, the bombast, the sentiments, the passions."

Johnson's record in the Senate was neither liberal nor conservative; he was not at core an ideological man. Similar to his hero, Franklin D. Roosevelt, Johnson was a professional politician first and foremost. Nonetheless, his fundamental outlook had been enduringly shaped by his background and formative experiences. Most obviously, he was a white southerner who had grown up in a depressed, underprivileged region, influenced by southern populism. He was imbued with real concern for the poor and the deprived, and he accepted the populist prescription of positive governmental action as a means of restoring opportunity. His vision of the ideal community reflected the Galbraith–Schlesinger call for the state to take responsibility not only for the material survival of its citizens, but also for the quality of their lives. The Great Society, said Johnson, was to be "a place where the city of man serves not only the needs of the body and the demands of commerce but the desire for beauty and the hunger for community."

Fulfilling the Promise

The new president moved quickly to satisfy the national curiosity and anxiety about Kennedy's assassination. The question on virtually everyone's mind was, had Lee Harvey Oswald acted alone or had he been part of a larger conspiracy involving Russia, Cuban exiles, the radical right, organized crime, or even some agency of the U.S. government? Various self-proclaimed witnesses came forward to claim that they had seen a second shooter on a grassy knoll in front of the book depository and that they had heard more than three shots. It later came to light that Oswald had family ties to a "mafia" member who had expressed the determination to kill Kennedy for his continuing pressure on organized crime. As evidence of the Kennedy administration's clandestine efforts to assassinate Castro came to light, some Americans concluded that the Cuban leader was behind the president's death. Others were convinced that the CIA and/or right-wing Cuban émigrés, angry over Kennedy's insufficient support for the Bay of Pigs invasion in 1961, were involved.

Johnson asked the chief justice, Earl Warren, to head a commission to investigate the killing. The panel that included Georgia Democratic Senator Richard Russell, Republican Congressman Gerald Ford of

Michigan, former CIA Director Allen Dulles, and former Secretary of Defense John J. McCloy collected hundreds of thousands of pages of materials from government agencies and interviewed 94 witnesses. The report of the Warren Commission, which appeared on September 27, 1964, ran to 296,000 words. To the enragement of conspiracy buffs, Warren observed that "the facts of the assassination itself are simple, so simple that many people believe it must be more complicated and conspiratorial to be true." The report declared that the commission did not uncover "any evidence sufficient to justify a conclusion that there was a conspiracy to assassinate President Kennedy." However outlandish some of the anti–Warren commission theories were, Warren's official story was remarkably hasty and often careless. In the long run, Warren and Johnson's effort to reassure an increasingly skeptical public backfired, leaving room for critics to poke holes in it even when – as was usually, although not always, the case – their own alternative theories were even weaker than Warren's.

The two legislative projects that Johnson inherited from Kennedy were the tax cut measure and the civil rights bill. The new president embraced them both because they coincided with his philosophy and they would, he perceived, burnish his image for the forthcoming election in 1964. By the time Johnson took the oath of office, the tax bill that Walter Heller had persuaded Kennedy to sponsor had passed the House. Heller had persuaded the powerful chairman of the Ways and Means Committee, Wilbur Mills (D-Arkansas), that the multibillion measure was needed to stimulate investment, increase employment, and eventually cut the budget through increasing the nation's tax base. Mills and Heller were willing to accept a federal budget of $102 to $103 billion; Johnson was not. Determined to placate businessmen and financial leaders who had considered Kennedy hostile and fiscally irresponsible, Johnson forced his departments and agencies to cut spending requests and submit a budget of $98 billion. With Senate conservatives such as Harry Byrd (D-Virginia) satisfied, the tax cut measure sailed through the Senate. Coming as it did during a period of almost no inflation, the tax cut was followed by a $52 billion increase in the gross national product during the year following its passage, and unemployment fell to 4.5%.

The Civil Rights Act of 1964

At the time Lyndon Johnson became president, a national consensus on behalf of a comprehensive civil rights bill had begun to take shape. Shortly before his assassination, President Kennedy had abandoned three years of caution and come out unequivocally for equal opportunity and equality under the law for African Americans. In June 1963, he had used federal troops to face down Governor George Wallace and desegregate the

University of Alabama. In July, he had gone on national television and declared that America could not call itself a free country until all of its citizens were free: "We face . . . a moral crisis as a country and a people. It cannot be met by repressive police action. It cannot be left to increased demonstrations in the streets. It cannot be quieted by token moves or talk. It is a time to act in the Congress, in your state and local legislative body, and, above all, in all our daily lives." The following week the administration introduced into Congress a sweeping measure that would outlaw segregation in public facilities, cut off federal funds to programs that discriminated, and ensure full voting rights for all Americans regardless of race. Kennedy's assassination in November put the bill on hold.

Lyndon Johnson's commitment to end discrimination and ensure equal opportunity for African Americans was both moral and political. He understood that the violent outbursts in Little Rock, Selma, and Oxford marked the death throes of an unjust and undemocratic system. The South, he believed, would have to rid itself of institutionalized racism and the brutality and demagoguery of the extreme segregationists if the national consensus that he so craved was to occur. "I knew that if I didn't get out in front on this issue," he later wrote, "they [the liberals] would get me. They'd throw up my background against me, they'd use it to prove that I was incapable of bringing unity to the land I loved so much. . . . I had to produce a civil rights bill that was even stronger than the one they'd have gotten if Kennedy had lived." This is exactly what he did. The Civil Rights Act of 1964 prohibited discrimination in places of public accommodation; mandated a cutoff in funds to federal programs that discriminated; outlawed discrimination in employment on the basis of race, color, religion, sex, or national origin; authorized the Justice Department to institute suits to facilitate school desegregation; created the Equal Employment Opportunity Commission; and provided technical and financial aid to communities desegregating their schools. The word "sex" had been added by conservative Congressman Howard W. Smith to the list of categories protected from discrimination as part of a plausible but vain attempt to block passage; he assumed that northerners would not grant equality to their daughters and ex-wives in exchange for black votes. Although the amendment attracted little attention at the time and passed, it would serve ironically as an opening wedge for women's rights advocates who would mount a major assault on sexual discrimination later in the 1960s.

Skillfully, Johnson and his congressional liaison staff put together a congressional coalition of liberal Democrats and moderate Republicans. As usual, the field of battle would be the Senate, where a group of Dixie senators led by Richard Russell prepared to filibuster the measure to death. Acting in close support were conservative Republicans like Barry Goldwater, who warned that the proposed legislation would create a "federal police force of mammoth proportions" and lead to the "destruction of a free society." The key to victory, the president told Hubert Humphrey, the leader of pro–civil rights liberals, would be Senator Everett Dirksen, the Republican minority leader from Illinois. "You and I are going to get Ev," he declared. "It's going to take time.... You've got to let him have a piece of the action. He's got to look good.... You drink with Dirksen. You talk to Dirksen. You listen to Dirksen!" The strategy worked. After securing revisions in the bill making it clear that it was directed at the de jure segregation of the South and not the de facto segregation that existed in most northern cities, Dirksen produced enough votes to enable the administration to impose cloture on the Russell-led filibuster in June. (In all previous civil rights debates, a minority had exercised an effective veto because Senate Rule 22 required a two-thirds vote to end debate [cloture]. Southerners would threaten to keep discussion going forever, forcing civil rights advocates to back down and let the Senate attend to other business.) The Senate passed the Civil Rights Act of 1964 by a vote of 73 to 27.

In his moving tribute in 1973, black novelist and intellectual Ralph Ellison claimed that Johnson was, in the view of African Americans, the first president wholly committed to civil rights; he was *their* president. Perhaps Ellison and his brethren sensed that Johnson embodied the philosophical, moral, and political core of white America that blacks as a minority had to have. He was that core in its pure, concentrated, and politically active form. Those who converted civil rights into a mass movement among blacks recognized Johnson as the person who could make it acceptable to the white masses. Johnson's commitment had to do with more than his need to be loved and his determination to prove himself to Kennedy liberals. There was a variety of southern moderation advocated by Clayton Fritchey, Harry Ashmore, and others that got underway in the late 1940s. It proposed sacrificing the demand for integration to the more easily attained and valuable right to vote and equal protection under the law. Johnson came out of that tradition; the civil rights acts of the 1960s marked a compromise between the uncompromising demand for integration made by W. E. B. DuBois and Martin Luther King, Jr., and the gradualist, tokenistic concessions offered by southern moderates.

It was true that Johnson embraced civil rights in the late 1950s out of a desire to become a national leader and perhaps capture the White House, but it should be noted that his ardent support of the 1964 Civil Rights Bill put him at great risk. If he alienated the South, he would strengthen the conservative coalition that he had worked so hard to disband. He might win the 1964 presidential election, but he would be legislatively hamstrung. The Great Society would lay stillborn. Passing civil rights and keeping southern congressmen and senators on board was a brilliant achievement and a risky gamble. It could not last, which is why Johnson, perhaps tragically, rushed through so many of his legislative victories.

The Crusade for Economic Opportunity

The day following his predecessor's assassination, Johnson had told an aide: "I am a Roosevelt New Dealer. As a matter of fact...Kennedy was a little too conservative to suit my taste." In response to a genuine commitment to help the poor of all colors and ages as well as with an eye to the 1964 election, Johnson declared "unconditional war on poverty" and embraced a program that had its roots in the last days of the Kennedy administration. Influenced by Harrington's work on the culture of poverty and by the fact that the tax cut bill raised upper- and middle-class incomes but provided no help to the poor who paid no income tax, Kennedy had asked the Council of Economic Advisers (CEA) to make recommendations. Those proposals were presented to Johnson the day after he became president. He endorsed them enthusiastically.

The CEA report kept the Aid to Dependent Mothers and Children as the centerpiece of the welfare system, but it suggested a new device, the Community Action Program (CAP), for breaking the cycle of poverty. In it, local welfare recipients and public officials would participate in planning for programs to stimulate local business, reduce unemployment, and provide for the basic needs of the community. In his antipoverty message delivered to Congress on January 8, 1964, Johnson made community action the centerpiece of his antipoverty program and recommended that it be funded initially with $500 million. In addition, the president created the Office of Economic Opportunity, an independent executive agency that was authorized to coordinate the War on Poverty and direct programs not already supervised by existing cabinet departments. He named Sargent Shriver – John and Robert Kennedy's brother-in-law, who as first director of the Peace Corps had established a reputation as an able and imaginative administrator – as the first head of the OEA. The Economic Opportunity Act created 10 separate programs, including the Job Corps, to provide vocational training to young men and women; Head Start, to help preschoolers from disadvantaged backgrounds succeed in public school; Upward Bound, to ready impoverished teenagers for college; and Volunteers in Service to America (VISTA), to place teachers, engineers, and agricultural experts to help the poor. "The war on poverty is not a struggle to support people," declared the president, "It is a struggle to give people a chance."

Congress passed the Economic Opportunity Act by overwhelming margins in 1964. Johnson called the act the beginning of the end of poverty in America. He exaggerated. Community action programs remained amorphous, and in some areas – Chicago, for example – community leaders used the local CAP to enrich themselves financially or politically. With the meager resources at their command, the CAPs were unable to cope with the grinding poverty, the deteriorating infrastructure, and the shrinking tax base that plagued inner-city America. The Economic Opportunity Act became weighed down with distorting provisions such as that requiring 40% of Job Corps participants to be assigned to civilian conservation camps – relics of the New Deal that taught skills irrelevant to the complex American economy of the 1960s.

The Election of 1964

In 1964, these flaws were not yet apparent, and President Johnson used the antipoverty program to launch his bid for election in his own right. At a commencement address at the University of Michigan, Johnson outlined his vision of the future. He and Congress would legislate a "Great Society" in which poverty, ignorance, and discrimination would disappear from the land. In the tradition of the New Deal and the Fair Deal there was something, or at least the promise of something, for everyone: investment incentives for business, full employment for industrial workers, price supports for farmers, civil rights for blacks and other minorities, social security for the elderly, and expansion of antipoverty programs for social workers and bureaucrats. Similar to Franklin Roosevelt, who used the Works Progress Administration and other programs to construct the New Deal voting coalition, Johnson envisioned the Great Society promises and programs as devices that would simultaneously raise living standards, achieve social security and justice, and bring into being a voting coalition that would ensure his triumph as well as that of the Democratic Party. As luck would have it, the Republicans were busily abandoning the center the president was assiduously plotting to capture.

Contorted by internal bickering and frustrated by the Democratic resurgence of the late 1950s and early 1960s, the GOP abandoned the moderate course it had been following since 1940 and succumbed to the siren song of militant conservatism. John F. Kennedy's presidency corresponded with the emergence of a new radical right movement whose members *Time* magazine labeled the Ultras. Drawn from all classes and walks of life, but particularly numerous in the Southwest and California, the new right was ultrapatriotic and xenophobic. There were at times overtones of racism and religious fundamentalism to the movement. Its adherents called for a return to basic values, but paradoxically distrusted democracy, convinced as they were that it had become corrupted by traditional politicians and "liberals." Intensely anticommunist, they argued that it was a natural progression for liberalism to degenerate into socialism and socialism into communism. The Ultras were represented by a variety of far right organizations that had sprung up in the late 1950s and early 1960s. In 1959, Robert Welch founded the John Birch Society and, shortly thereafter, Tulsa evangelist Billy James Hargis established the Christian Anti-Communist Crusade. Wealthy oilman H. L. Hunt sponsored the radio programs and columns of retired FBI agent Dan Smoot, while Clarence Manion, a former law school dean at Notre

Dame, warned the country about the dangers of communist subversion. For these activists, Fred Siegel has written, politics "was not so much a matter of pursuing material interests as a national screen on which to project their deepest cultural fears." In a wittier and more civilized tone, William F. Buckley attempted to appeal to conservative intellectuals in the *National Review*. All were convinced that liberal Republicans, such as Governor Nelson Rockefeller of New York and William Scranton of Pennsylvania, had rejected true conservative principles and sold out the Republican Party to liberalism or worse.

The darling of the new right was Senator Barry M. Goldwater of Arizona, the heir to a department store fortune and a reserve Air Force general who had first been elected to Congress in 1952. There seemed to be two Goldwaters, columnist Richard Rovere noted; one was the easy-going, affable southwesterner whom most senators knew personally and the other was the humorless, ideologically rigid author of *The Conscience of a Conservative*. That book, ghost written by Goldwater's handlers as a campaign tract, called for reduced government expenditures, elimination of government bureaucracies, an end to "forced" integration, reassertion of states' rights, an end to farm subsidies and welfare payments, and additional curbs on labor unions. Above all, Goldwater called for "total victory" over communism both at home and abroad. Negative in domestic policy and aggressive in foreign, Goldwater, who had never authored a bill, declared, "My aim is not to pass laws but to repeal them." Containment was too defensive, "like a boxer who refuses to throw a punch."

Early in the 1960s, conservative party operatives, such as Peter O'Donnell of Texas, Clifton White of New York, and John Grenier of Alabama, set about capturing the party for Goldwater and the doctrines of the new right. They were the intellectual and political heirs of Robert Taft, convinced that the "metooism" of Thomas Dewey and the eastern, liberal wing of the party, which had controlled the presidential nominating process since the Roosevelt era, had bankrupted the GOP politically and failed to offer the voters a clear choice. As these true believers gained control of grass roots organizations within the party, and as Goldwater assumed an ever-higher profile, the moderate wing of the party wallowed in disarray. Conservative activists held a rally at Madison Square Garden and thousands applauded as Brent Bozell, editor of the *National Review*, called on the United States to tear down the Berlin Wall and immediately invade Cuba. Eisenhower, barred from seeking a third term by the Twenty-Second Amendment, balked at throwing his support to another moderate. Richard Nixon had temporarily retired from politics after losing his bid for the governorship of California in 1962. The chief challenger to Goldwater was the attractive, liberal governor of New York, Nelson Rockefeller, but a recent divorce and remarriage to a divorcée hurt him, particularly with Protestant fundamentalists who were an important faction within the new right. Rockefeller managed to eliminate another moderate, Henry Cabot Lodge, Jr., in the Oregon presidential primary, but then lost to Goldwater in the crucial California contest. Governor William Scranton of Pennsylvania made a gallant last-minute effort to overtake Goldwater, but O'Donnell and company had already gained control of too many state delegations. At the Republican convention in San Francisco, held during the second week in July, the delegates chose Goldwater and William E. Miller, New York congressman, chairman of the GOP National Committee, and accomplished political polemicist. The right-wing majority indulged itself by openly ridiculing Rockefeller and the moderate wing of the party at the convention. They could ill afford the luxury. Goldwater, who declared in his acceptance speech that "extremism in the defense of liberty is no vice!" and that "moderation in the pursuit of justice is no virtue!", would need every vote that he could get.

There was no revolution in the Democratic Party comparable to that which swept the GOP in 1964. Lyndon B. Johnson's nomination was a foregone conclusion. The segregationist governor of Alabama, George Wallace, challenged the president in several early primaries. Running on a states' rights, anti-integrationist platform, Wallace appealed not only to many white southerners but also to working-class whites in northern urban areas who were frustrated by their marginal economic position and angered by the rioting in black ghettoes that swept cities in New York, Pennsylvania, and New Jersey in the summer of 1964. He blamed rioting and black power not on poverty or racism but on a "conference of world guerrilla warfare chieftains in Havana, Cuba" who were giving orders to federal "bearded beatnick bureaucrats." Blasting the federal government for favoring blacks over whites and for standing by in the face of a breakdown in law and order, he captured one third of the vote in the three northern states in which he campaigned. But Wallace's candidacy was more a shot fired across the bow of the Democratic center than a serious threat to take control of the party and, as soon as Johnson began to assert himself, the Alabama segregationist withdrew.

The controversy that existed in Democratic Party ranks centered on the Texan's choice for vice president. The Kennedy entourage, many of whom remained in government, believed that Johnson owed Robert Kennedy the position. Convinced that Johnson would never have been president had John F. Kennedy not chosen him as his running mate in 1960, McGeorge Bundy, Larry O'Brien, and Robert McNamara, among others, privately pushed the attorney general. They insisted that the United States wanted a continuing Kennedy presence in the highest councils of government. But Johnson was a sensitive man. He knew that the Kennedyites, Robert included, viewed him with a combination of resentment and contempt. The Texan put an end to speculation by announcing in July that he deemed it inadvisable for any member of the cabinet to be considered for the second place on the ticket. After dangling the job before a number of other aspirants, he chose Hubert Humphrey. Johnson selected the Minnesotan because he was the darling of the party's liberal wing and was effusive in his promises of personal loyalty to the president, and his selection would block Bobby Kennedy's path to the presidency. Meanwhile, Kennedy resigned his cabinet post and ran successfully for the Senate from New York.

At the Democratic convention held in Atlantic City August 24–27, Johnson was nominated by acclamation, and the delegates adopted a platform calling for enactment of the Great Society program and a foreign policy based on containment and competitive coexistence. The most notable event of the 1964 Democratic gathering was the effort by the Mississippi Freedom Democratic Party (MFDP) to challenge the all-white regular Mississippi delegation for its seats at the convention.

MFDP

In the spring of 1964, the focus of the "second reconstruction" had shifted to Mississippi, perhaps the most racially divided and economically backward state in the union. Although African Americans constituted 42% of the state's population, only 5% were registered to vote. The median income for black families was less than $1,500 per year, less than one third of that for white families. Similar to its economy, Mississippi's politics were dominated by a tiny white elite that had manipulated white working-class prejudices to keep blacks "in their place" for more than a century. Early in 1964, Bob Moses and David Dennis of CORE created the concept of Freedom Summer. Black and white college students, carefully trained in the techniques of nonviolent resistance and political activism, would not only spread across rural Mississippi encouraging African Americans to register to vote, but also teach in "freedom schools" and organize a "freedom party" to challenge the all-white Mississippi Democratic party. That spring flyers appeared on college campuses across the North; they read, "A Domestic Freedom Corps will be working in Mississippi this summer. Its only weapons will be youth and courage." In June, students from more than 200 universities and colleges met with representatives of the Council of Federated Organizations in Oxford, Ohio. Most were from affluent families and the best universities. They came for different reasons, but most held the view that segregation was morally wrong. "There is a moral wave building among today's youth," one declared, "and I intend to catch it!"

The organizers of Freedom Summer anticipated violence, and they were right. On June 21, reports reached Moses and Dennis that three young project workers – Andrew Goodman, Michael Schwerner, and James Chaney – had disappeared near Philadelphia, Mississippi. Goodman and Schwerner were white, Chaney black. Six weeks later, the three were discovered buried in an earthen dam. Goodman and Schwerner had been shot in the heart and Chaney beaten to death. "In my twenty-five years

Table 6–1. The election of 1964

Candidates	Parties	Electoral vote	Popular vote	Percentage of popular vote
Lyndon B. Johnson	Democratic	486	43,126,506	61.1
Barry M. Goldwater	Republican	52	27,176,799	38.5

as a pathologist and medical examiner," declared the attending physician, "I have never seen bones so severely shattered." An FBI investigation subsequently uncovered a conspiracy involving local law enforcement officers and members of the Ku Klux Klan to murder them. Before the summer was out, three more civil rights workers died violently. A volunteer from the Mississippi Summer Freedom Project wrote home in July 1964 about the violence: "Yesterday while the Mississippi River was being dragged looking for the three missing civil rights workers, two bodies of Negroes were found. Mississippi is the only state where you can drag a river any time and find bodies you were not expecting." In McComb, there were 17 bombings in three months, and white extremists burned down 37 black churches.

Undeterred, black and white youths traveled the state talking to black sharecroppers and building "freedom schools" to educate poor, sometimes illiterate, blacks in the practices of democracy. Activists also attempted to register blacks in Mississippi's Democratic Party, but to no avail. Indeed, after a summer of arduous, dangerous labor by 1,000 activists, only 1,600 African Americans had been registered. Volunteers responded by enrolling nearly 60,000 disenfranchised blacks into the MFDP, and they in turn elected 44 "freedom delegates" to attend the 1964 Democratic Convention.

The Philadelphia murders came to light only two weeks before the opening of the Democratic Convention. When the MFDP sent its own delegation to Atlantic City, the Johnson-controlled credentials committee offered a compromise whereby the black organization would receive two of Mississippi's seats. "We didn't come all this way for no two seats!," declared MFDP member Fannie Lou Hamer. Her subsequent pleas for justice on national television were so powerful that Johnson called a press conference in an effort to bump her off the air. The regular Mississippi delegation subsequently walked out over the liberal civil rights plank in the platform, but those in charge of the convention refused to allow the MFDP to take its place. "I question America," proclaimed an embittered Hamer, the granddaughter of slaves, "[I]s this America, the land of the free and the home of the brave?" The Johnson forces did promise that the seating of an all-white Mississippi delegation would not be allowed in 1968.

An exuberant Johnson announced to the assembled delegates that all was well and that a huge consensus would sweep the Democrats into office in November. He was aware that he occupied the great political center and that most Americans saw him as the only alternative to the extremes of both right and left. Barry Goldwater played nicely into the Texan's hands. In foreign policy, the Republican candidate charged the Democrats with being soft on communism and pursuing a "no win" policy. But he went further. When asked about the simmering war in Southeast Asia, he told reporters, "I'd drop a low-yield atomic bomb on the Chinese supply lines in North Vietnam or maybe shell 'em with the Seventh Fleet." The GOP candidate was equally inept when it came to domestic policies. In Tennessee, in the heart of the area refurbished by the TVA, he condemned public power. He opposed Medicare for the elderly, and Democratic campaigners recalled for voters that Goldwater had once proposed making Social Security "voluntary." The president presented himself as a prudent guardian of American interests abroad and condemned the Republicans as trigger-happy jingoes. "They call upon us to supply American boys to do the job that Asian boys should do," he declared, and late in the campaign the Democrats briefly ran a controversial 30-second television ad showing a young girl picking daisy petals followed by an atomic blast. Johnson's postscript suggested that the first image symbolized the world the Democrats would make and the second the one the Republicans would produce.

November did indeed bring a Democratic landslide of staggering proportions. Johnson and Humphrey garnered 43.1 million votes to 27.1 million for Goldwater and Miller. The Democrats carried 44 states and the District of Columbia, which represented 486 electoral votes, whereas Goldwater was able to claim only the Deep South and his native state of Arizona. Johnson's coattails proved relatively long. The Democrats, who already enjoyed large majorities in both houses, gained 38 seats in the House and 2 in the Senate. In state races, the Republicans lost more than 500 seats in state legislatures. More important, because state assemblies were going to have to redraw voting districts in accordance with the Supreme Court rulings in *Baker v. Carr* (1962) and *Wesberry v. Sanders* (1964), which ordered reapportionment based strictly on the basis of population, the Democrats were in a position to guarantee their long-term future.

The Great Society

The Youth Movement
Johnson was the embodiment of traditional courthouse politics – a patriarchal figure committed to socioeconomic justice but thoroughly conventional in cultural matters. It was somewhat ironic that he was elected president in the midst of a youth movement of unprecedented proportions. Because of World War II and the Depression, birth rates had declined during the 1930s and early 1940s; in 1960, the average age was 34. Then the baby boom hit. The number of young people (ages 18 through 24) increased

from 16 to 45 million between 1960 and 1972, and the average age dropped to 17. The very mass of youth created problems – for example, increased juvenile delinquency and teenage pregnancies. It also caused a crisis in higher education. California alone was forced to build 49 new campuses to deal with the influx. *Time* named their 1966 "Man of the Year" the "man – and woman – of 25 and under."

In 1964, the year Johnson won his landslide victory, American youth seemed to have discovered hedonism all over again. During spring break, Ft. Lauderdale, Florida, was deluged with students in search of "sex, sand, suds, and sun." The police arrested 2,000 young people for public promiscuity and drinking. By summer, the miniskirt had made its appearance; by Labor Day, the party had moved to Hampton Beach, New Hampshire, where 10,000 girls and boys indulged themselves in the new fad of "bundling," that is, sleeping together on the beach. The older generation was not quite ready for the new morality. More than one third of all high school graduates went away to college. There they found the hidden hand of their parents in the form of *in loco parentis*, a term meaning "in place of the parents." On most campuses, women had to be 21 years old before they could live off campus, dorms were strictly segregated by sex, and students were subjected to strict curfew. Most colleges prohibited smoking, "parking," and imposed dress codes that barred males from wearing T-shirts and jeans and females from wearing pants or shorts. University of Houston co-eds had to cover their legs while walking to the athletic field. More important, perhaps, students had virtually no say in the rules and regulations of the institutions where they paid tuition. Administrators dictated course offerings, degree curriculums, and extracurricular activities. Unlike regular citizens, collegiates could be tried by civil and university officials. An underage student who drank beer could be found guilty of violating state law and university regulations – jailed and expelled. Inevitably, students revolted.

A banner headline appeared on the front page of an underground student newspaper at the University of Florida: "NO RESTRICTION MAY BE PLACED ON STUDENT DRINKING, GAMBLING, SEXUAL ACTIVITY, OR ANY SUCH PRIVATE MORAL DECISION." Shortly thereafter in October 1964, students at the University of California, Berkeley, who ranged from liberal supporters of the civil rights movement to conservative champions of individual liberties, banned together to launch the Free Speech Movement (FSM). The organization materialized when Chancellor Clark Kerr issued a decree banning sidewalk solicitations by student political groups. Thereupon, several hundred protesters staged a sit-in. Within days more than 2,000 students, including the conservative Youth for Goldwater, had brought the university to a virtual standstill. Kerr eventually relented, but the FSM developed into what philosophy major and student firebrand Mario Savio described as an onslaught on the modern university and the "depersonalized, unresponsive bureaucracy" that allegedly afflicted all of American life.

The Berkeley free speech demonstration marked the first major student revolt of the 1960s. Student newspapers followed developments closely, and students at Brandeis, Harvard, Indiana, and Texas organized to demand their constitutional rights. Many of their elders were not impressed. The "UC rebels" were "intolerable and insufferable," proclaimed *The San Francisco Examiner*. They should be expelled. Obey the rules or leave, declared an Oakland paper. Ominously, the new president of the United States could not have agreed more.

The Civil Rights Act of 1965
Overjoyed at being elected in his own right, Lyndon B. Johnson moved to capitalize on his mandate. He was a man in a hurry. "Every day while I am in office," he told an aide, "I'm going to lose votes. I'm going to alienate somebody.... We've got to get this legislation fast. We've got to get it during my honeymoon." As 1964 gave way to 1965, President Johnson assembled a collection of task forces made up of White House staffers, cabinet officials, and university professors to make recommendations as to how best to implement the goals of the Great Society. Johnson's commitment to racial equality for African Americans earned him the support of Roy Wilkins, head of the NAACP, and other black leaders, and one of the task forces was assigned to the still unsolved problem of equal rights. But events rather than government reports pushed the civil rights movement to the next level.

The Freedom Summer project of 1964 had drawn national attention to the deplorable racism in Mississippi and to the fundamental importance of votes to the civil rights movement. The 900 volunteers established 40 schools that taught reading, writing, arithmetic, civics, and African American history to blacks living in rural Mississippi. Nearly 60,000 black voters enrolled in the Mississippi Freedom Democratic Party.

Nevertheless, white resistance to black enfranchisement remained strong and, consequently, Martin Luther King, Jr., decided in early 1965 to provoke Johnson and Congress into taking dramatic action on voting rights. Unbeknownst to the leader of the SCLC, the president, who was somewhat jealous of King, had allowed the FBI to continue the wiretapping of his phones that had begun under Robert Kennedy. If there was any pushing to be done, Lyndon Johnson liked to do it.

Undeterred by White House reservations concerning his plans, King organized a series of demonstrations in Alabama to protest the continuing refusal of white authorities to grant black citizens the right to vote. Dallas County, in which Selma was located and in which African Americans comprised a majority of the citizenry, boasted only 325 black voters compared with 9,800 white voters. Throughout January 1965, King led marchers to the courthouse to demonstrate on an almost daily basis. Sheriff James

G. Clark carefully avoided violence and, as the national media's attention began to wane, King decided to escalate the drama. He announced a march from Selma to Montgomery, a distance of 54 miles, to present a petition to Governor George Wallace. Wallace issued an order prohibiting the march and King, at President Johnson's request, withdrew to Georgia. Led by SNCC, the rank and file of the voting rights movement decided to march anyway. At the Pettus Bridge outside of Selma, with television cameras rolling, 100 of Clark's deputies and 100 state police set upon the demonstrators with tear gas, clubs, and cattle prods. The nation was aghast at the sight of Alabama's finest beating defenseless men, women, and children. The president finally stepped in, federalizing the Alabama National Guard, and the march was completed between March 21 and March 25.

Initially angered by the demonstrations in Alabama, the pragmatic Johnson leaped to take advantage of the backlash against the segregationists. In a nationally televised address to Congress on March 15, he was at his moralizing best. "There is no constitutional issue here," he declared. "There is no moral issue. . . . There is only the struggle for human rights. . . . And should we defeat every enemy, and should we double our wealth and conquer the stars, and still be unequal on this issue, then we will have failed as a people and a nation." Senators and representatives rose and gave him a standing ovation. Two days later, the Johnson administration submitted a carefully crafted voting rights bill to Congress. With Everett Dirksen leading the coalition of liberal Democrats and moderate Republicans who supported the Civil Rights Act of 1964, the Senate shut off debate with a two-thirds cloture vote, the second in two years. By the end of July, both houses had passed their versions of the Voting Rights Act, and a conference committee resolved the differences. The president signed the measure on August 6. This, one of the most important civil rights bill enacted to that date, authorized the attorney general to appoint federal election supervisors for states or districts that had literacy tests or other restrictive devices and in which fewer than 50% of eligible voters cast their ballots in 1964. Those interfering with legitimate voters in their efforts to cast their ballots were to be subject to fine or imprisonment or both. The results were dramatic. Federal intervention forestalled violence in most cases and, by the following summer, one half of southern adult blacks had registered to vote.

Just as important to the establishment of full political equality for African Americans as the Civil Rights Act of 1965 was the Supreme Court ruling that congressional districts within each state had to be roughly equal in population and its subsequent decision that both houses of state legislatures had to be apportioned on the basis of population. Previously, many states had apportioned on the basis of geography or tradition. The Voting Rights Act of 1965, together with the "one man, one vote" principle handed down by the Supreme Court in *Baker* (1962) and *Reynolds vs. Sims*

(1964), and the Twenty-Fourth Amendment (1964), which outlawed poll taxes, did much to democratize the political process in the South and throughout the United States. Black participation in local, state, and federal elections increased dramatically and steadily as segregationists withdrew from the field and organizations such as the Southern Regional Council mobilized and registered African Americans.

In an effort to increase employment opportunity for minorities, in 1966 Johnson issued an executive order requiring employers to take "affirmative action to ensure that applicants are employed . . . without regard to their race, color, religion, or national origin." Tax dollars employed millions of Americans; the new order seemed to require that all races be proportionally represented in that workforce. As Johnson observed, "You do not take a person who for years has been hobbled by chains and liberate him, bring him up to the starting line of a race and then say, you're free to compete with all the others." In 1967, the word "sex" was added to the executive order and the next year the government required government contractors to develop "specific goals and timetables" to achieve equal employment.

The War on Poverty

Next to civil rights, the War on Poverty was Johnson's top legislative priority. The Economic Opportunity Act of 1964 had been a beginning, but it was only a beginning in the president's eyes. As historian Mark Gelfand and others have pointed out, the Johnson administration had three courses open to it in its campaign to solve the problem of poverty in America.

The first approach could view poverty's persistence as a matter of mal-distribution of power. America was an oligopoly in which the corporations and banks indirectly controlled the political process and economic institutions. The solution was a further democratization of the political process through elimination of campaign contributions from big business and wealthy individuals, through direct government financing, and through a cap on donations. Such an approach also called for an across-the-board redistribution of the nation's wealth by means of a sharply progressive tax or other mechanism. Although the community action programs were a step in this direction, they were a minor step, and the War on Poverty attempted no mass redistribution of resources. Indeed, this first approach involved pitting social classes against each other to a certain extent, and Johnson was above all a consensus president. "This government will not set one group against another," he declared some six months after becoming president. "We will build a creative partnership between business and labor, between farm areas and urban centers, between consumers and producers."

A second approach to the problem of institutionalized poverty involved income guarantees. According to proponents of this philosophy, the cycle of poverty could be eliminated simply by providing the poor with the necessities of life through mechanisms such as food stamps, rent supplements, and free health care. The problem, in other words, was quantitative. The well-to-do majority could simply tax poverty out of existence. But this approach flew in the face of the deep-seated, long-standing conviction in America that the individual was responsible for his or her success or failure. Individual striving and enterprise had made the nation great and would continue to do so. Since the founding of Massachusetts Bay Colony, Americans had feared the dole, viewing it as a mechanism that would lead to moral as well as material stagnation.

The third approach, which had its contemporary roots in progressivism and the civil rights movement, assumed that every American craved middle-class status and had the drive and ability to achieve it. Each in fact would do so, but some were held back by artificial restraints. The cycle of poverty in which the ignorant and unskilled lacked the means to obtain training to cure their ignorance and so remained poor and increasingly alienated was the primary obstacle. This assumption underlay the philosophies and programs of East Coast liberal foundations manned by upper-class intellectuals. Everyone wanted to conform and ascend – the task was to make available the social and economic resources to enable them to do so. By providing incentives to the poor, these foundations – and by extension the federal government – could break the cycle of downward mobility by instilling confidence and creating a reinforcing pattern of achievement.

Not surprisingly, the Johnson administration's poverty programs attempted to combine all three philosophies. The community action programs begun in 1964 continued to proliferate after the president's election. In 1966 at the White House's behest, Congress passed the Model Cities Act, which funneled development funds directly to city governments. The measure was ostensibly designed to supplement community action, but in truth Johnson was increasingly disillusioned with Community Action Programs, complaining that Shriver was recruiting too many "crooks, communists," and "kooks" into the program. In fact, city officials were offended by many CAP programs, and those who ran municipal government could deliver far more votes than CAP activists could. In 1965, Congress passed amendments to the Economic Opportunity Act that more than doubled the first-year authorization for VISTA, the Job Corps, and other youth and community action programs. In 1966, the administration pushed through Congress the Appalachian Regional Development Act, the long-awaited "TVA for Appalachia," which provided $1.1 billion for highway construction, regional health centers, and resource development. The measure was based on the assumption that improvement of these basic services would stimulate the economy of the region and create jobs. Appalled by the existence of widespread hunger in the midst of massive farm surpluses, the Truman and Eisenhower administrations had given away food to the poor. The Kennedy administration attempted to systematize the practice by giving the poor "food stamps," which could be redeemed at grocery stores. In 1964, at President Johnson's behest, Congress passed the Food Stamp Act. The measure would, Johnson predicted, "help achieve a fuller and more effective use of food abundances" and "provide improved levels of nutrition among low-income households."

By late 1966, the War on Poverty was grinding to a halt, the victim in part of structural and philosophical flaws and in part of the Vietnam War. Opponents of the conflict in Southeast Asia, who also tended to be liberals on domestic matters, deserted the president en masse, joining conservatives who were angered by mounting budget deficits. The CAPs polarized and paralyzed communities that they were supposed to revivify. The social workers and community activists who ramrodded the original CAPs organized the poor, led rent strikes, picketed city halls, and attempted to take over local school boards. Entrenched political operatives responded with outrage. Critics on the right, such as Chicago's Mayor Richard Daley, a power within the national Democratic Party, implied that the federal government was subsidizing communism, while on the left, community activists decried efforts by the government to restrain the CAPs as "manipulative and paternalistic."

Most importantly, the entire amount spent by the federal government on poverty programs between 1964 and 1967 was $6.2 billion. These sums were proverbial drops in the bucket. The president's programs reflected the belief that individual Americans should be given access to opportunity and thus be motivated to rise above the poverty cycle. Moreover, much of the money spent on the War on Poverty went to landlords, construction companies, social workers, doctors, and lawyers. Local politicians and businessmen co-opted programs for their own purposes. There was, in addition, excessive bureaucracy and corruption. Hastily conceived, many of the vocational programs trained young people for jobs that did not exist.

Yet, the War on Poverty was a beginning. Not taking into account inflation, the number of families living on $4,999 a year had shrunk from 42% at the beginning of the 1960s to 19.2% at the end of the decade. (Although the overheated economy, stimulated by massive government spending for the war in Vietnam, had something to do with the decline.) Sociological studies indicated that Head Start had "a powerful, immediate impact on children." The training offered by the Job Corps resulted in small reductions in unemployment for teenagers and young adults. Even the controverted CAPs gave a sense of empowerment to some impoverished inner-city dwellers and demonstrated that most poor people wanted to work and desperately wanted to improve their socioeconomic status. In short, Johnson's War on Poverty constituted a short but significant step down the road to solving one of the United States' most intractable and important problems.

The Education President

Although the War on Poverty was the centerpiece of the Great Society, there were other facets as well, several of them more soundly conceived and implemented. Johnson wanted to be known as "the education president," and he more than any other man who occupied the Oval Office deserved that sobriquet. For Johnson, poverty, discrimination, and ignorance were a part of the same cloth. Indeed, as a young high school teacher in south Texas, Johnson had witnessed the interrelationship first hand. The president was committed to the notion that every child ought to have as much education as he or she could absorb and that the federal government was obligated to help him or her do so. However, several historic obstacles stood in his path. Parochial school advocates argued that Catholics, Jews, and Protestant fundamentalists who sent their children to private, religious institutions should not be taxed to support public schools, whereas advocates of secular, public education insisted that tax money not be spent to encourage any religion, much less a specific religion. Conservatives were opposed to governmental intrusion into yet another field; southerners among their number were particularly afraid that Washington would use federal aid to education to force integration on unwilling school districts. At the same time, black activists such as Congressman Adam Clayton Powell were urging that federal aid in fact be used to end discrimination in education.

The education issue revealed Johnson at his consensus-building best. Assistant Secretary Wilbur J. Cohen and other Health, Education, and Welfare (HEW) staff members had been working on Catholic leaders since the Kennedy administration. White House staffer Douglas Cater, a native southerner, Harvard graduate, and Johnson loyalist, tackled Dixie congressmen and senators. Meanwhile, the president coerced and cajoled. By 1965, the administration had won support from both the National Educational Association and the National Catholic Welfare Conference for a new approach based on the needs of individual students rather than schools per se. Much of the segregationist venom had been drawn during the debate over the 1964 Civil Rights Act, which had assured (in name, if not in fact) African Americans equal access to southern schools.

Standing in the one-room schoolhouse near Stonewall, Texas, where he had begun his own education, Johnson signed the Elementary and Secondary Education Act in April 1965. It was the first federal aid to K–12 education bill passed in U.S. history. The measure carried an authorization of just more than $1 billion to be granted to local school districts to pay for new facilities or new staff to equalize educational opportunity for poor children. It made funds available for textbooks, library facilities, adult education, special education for the disabled, and educational administration. Private schools were able to benefit from the program, particularly in the areas of library materials and educational television.

The Johnson administration followed up its victory by persuading Congress to enact the Higher Education Act of 1965. The president recalled teaching at a "little Welhausen Mexican school [in Cotulla, Texas]," and remembered "the pain of . . . knowing then that college was closed to practically every one of those children because they were too poor." The median income in 1960 was $6,000. Almost 80% of high school graduates with a family income of twice that amount attended college, but only one third attended college if their family income was half the median. In addition, the primary reason that students dropped out of college was financial difficulty. The Higher Education Act expanded basic aid to U.S. colleges and universities, established a program of low-interest student loans, and extended special aid to small institutions struggling with low enrollment, disadvantaged student populations, and shrinking budgets. More than 140,000 able but needy students became eligible for aid under the measure. By the end of 1965, the federal government was pouring more than $4 billion per year into the national educational system. Aside from Head Start, the administration's educational programs did little for those children who suffered from motivation deprivation and lack of family support; however, for the ambitious and focused but needy student, the education acts were an unmixed blessing.

Medicare and Medicaid

Johnson's commitment to the social justice movement and, more important, his ability to deliver on its promises, was nowhere better demonstrated than in the story of Medicare. The effort by liberals to provide affordable health care to the elderly stretched back to the Roosevelt administration. For years, lobbying by the AMA and private health insurers had stalled various bills. The president had made what was for him a half-hearted effort to get a health care measure through Congress in 1964, but he had failed. However, virtually the entire "class of 1964," the 65 Democrats newly elected to Congress, were committed to Medicare. In 1965, Johnson turned up the heat on conservatives. Sensing that the nation was determined to have a comprehensive plan for the elderly, representatives of the medical profession and insurance companies in Congress introduced their own plan, but it would be voluntary and privately financed through insurance companies. Congress struggled to resist the intense lobbying effort staged by Medicare opponents, but in the end well-financed lobbyists forced the House and Senate to include vast subsidies and protection for "private" doctors and insurers.

The Medical Care Act of 1965 extended to Americans 65 years of age and older immediate relief from the massive burden of health care costs in the United States. The $6.5 billion measure established a basic plan, generally referred to as Medicare, which was compulsory and financed by a payroll tax. This system, administered by the Social Security

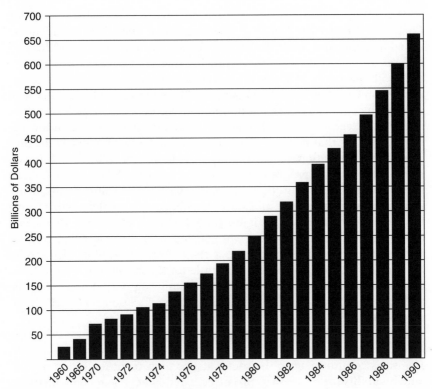

Figure 6–2. Total spending on health care, 1960–1990.
Source: Department of Health and Human Services.

Administration, covered most hospital and some nursing home stays, diagnostic costs, and home health care visits. A second supplementary system was voluntary. It would be funded by premiums paid by participants and revenue generated by the general Medicare fund. This system was designed to cover approximately 80% of other medical costs, including doctors' bills. Ironically, conservatives paid little attention to a proviso in the Medical Care Act of 1965 that provided federal funds to the states to help cover the medical expenses of the indigent. In future years, however, this provision, dubbed Medicaid, would be under intense criticism.

Although popular, Medicare was costly and inefficient. Doctors were allowed to set fees, and some abused the privilege. In effect, lobbyists for the AMA, hospitals, and other components of the health industry had succeeded in limiting the federal government's role to that of bill payer. Between 1970 and 1990, the annual price tag for Medicare rose from $7.6 to $111 billion, and Medicaid from $6.3 to $79 billion. Nevertheless, the program provided a degree of public protection for the elderly and indigent where none had previously existed.

As was true of the New Deal, there was supposed to be something for everyone in the Great Society. Contradicting Johnson's image as an uncouth Texan who cared only about beer, barbecue, and crude jokes, the president turned out to be a most effective patron of the arts and humanities. During his term in office and at his urging, Congress established the National Endowment for the Humanities and the National Endowment for the Arts. The two agencies were empowered to make grants to scholars, artists, and performers who were innovators in their fields. In time, the national endowments became two of the most important cultural arbiters in the United States.

From Conservationism to Environmentalism

There was in the Johnson program protection for the environment, consumers, and workers as well. "The water we drink, the food we eat, the very air we breathe are threatened with pollution," Johnson told Congress in February 1965. "We must act . . . for . . . once our natural splendor is destroyed, it can never be recaptured." As was true of much of the Johnson program, environmental protection had its roots in the Kennedy administration. In 1961, Kennedy had named Arizona Senator Stewart Udall secretary of the interior. Udall and Kennedy had become friends in the 1950s, and the Arizonan had played a key role in delivering his state to the Democrats in the 1960 presidential election. Udall and the environmentalists of the 1960s went beyond the narrowly gauged conservation movement that had characterized environmentalism since the Progressive era. In line with the liberal philosophy being espoused by Schlesinger and Galbraith, they insisted that the goal was not simply to conserve pockets of beauty, wildlife, and natural resources but to preserve and enhance the "quality of life" in cities and towns as well as mountains, forests, lakes, and deserts. Udall declared,

No longer is peripheral action – the "saving" of a forest, a park, a refuge for wildlife – isolated from the mainstream. The total environment is now the concern, and the new conservation makes man, himself, its subject. The quality of life is now the perspective and repose of the new conservation.

The Kennedy administration had sponsored a White House conference on the environment in 1962 and pushed through Congress legislation creating the Cape Cod National Seashore, but it was not until publication of Rachel Carson's *Silent Spring* (1962) that nationwide support began to build on behalf of the new environmentalism. A marine biologist with the U.S. Fish and Wildlife Service, Carson had written a celebrated series of nature essays collected and published in 1951 as *The Sea Around Us*. As the economy exploded in the years after World War II, Carson had become increasingly disturbed by the pollution of the nation's rivers, lakes, and underground aquifers by DDT and other pesticides. Because it was used to eliminate malaria-carrying mosquitoes and insects that destroyed food and fiber crops, DDT had been hailed as a wonder chemical and used indiscriminately. In *Silent Spring*, Carson demonstrated through massive research that indiscriminate use of toxic chemicals was poisoning the nation's water supply and food sources, thus threatening the health of human beings and animals alike. A number of magazines, pressured by their food advertisers, refused to serialize *Silent Spring*. Finally, the *New Yorker* agreed to publish her findings. Although pesticide manufacturers mounted a massive campaign to discredit Carson as a hysteric, *Silent Spring* became the text of the burgeoning environmental movement.

Nature, Carson argued, did not exist to be exploited by man; rather humankind was part of nature and had an obligation to live in harmony with it, enhancing the quality of the natural habitat as humans were enhanced by it. She and her disciples did not call for the elimination of pesticides, merely their regulation. She claimed that private companies and public agencies did not have the right indiscriminately to contaminate the environment with toxic substances without the knowledge of the public. Similar to Upton Sinclair's *The Jungle*, a turn-of-the-century exposé of the brutal exploitation of labor and grossly unsanitary conditions in the meatpacking industry, Carson's *Silent Spring* sparked a public demand for regulatory legislation. The Johnson administration was more than ready to respond. Under the Water Quality Act of 1965, all states were required to enforce water quality standards for interstate waters within their borders. The following year, Maine Senator Edmund Muskie pushed the Clean Waters Restoration Act through Congress. The measure authorized more than $3.5 billion to finance a cleanup of the nation's rivers, streams, and lakes and to block further pollution through the dumping of sewage or toxic industrial waste.

It was a natural step for environmentalists to move from concern about water purity to a focus on clean air. President Johnson's Task Force on Environmental Pollution, established in 1964, documented the damage being done to the environment by toxic emissions from coal-burning factories and auto exhaust systems. The nation was shocked to learn that air pollutants created "acid rain," which fell back to earth tainting food crops and further corrupting the water supply. On Thanksgiving Day in 1965, New York City experienced an ecological catastrophe, an air inversion that concentrated almost two pounds of soot per person in the atmosphere. Eighty died and hundreds were hospitalized. In the wake of the Third National Conference on Air Pollution in 1966, Congress passed the Air Quality Act of 1967, which set progressively stricter standards for industrial and automobile emissions. The polluting industries invested billions of dollars in lobbying for amendments. As a result standards were to be set jointly by industry and government. In 1969, Congress passed the National Environmental Policy Act, requiring, among other things, that federal agencies file environmental impact statements for all federally funded projects. The following year, the House and Senate established the Environmental Protection Agency. These were but the first shots in the ongoing battle to protect the public and nature from air and waterborne pollutants.

On another environmental front, Udall joined with Lady Bird Johnson to launch a preservation and beautification movement that would protect wilderness areas and make inhabited areas as visually attractive as possible. In 1889, John Muir had formed the Sierra Club in an effort to save the giant redwoods of California's Yosemite Valley. During the years that followed, the Sierra Club and other wilderness preservation groups made some headway, but they were no match for the lumber companies and mining interests that insisted on the unrestricted right of private enterprise to exploit the public domain. From the time Johnson had been director of the National Youth Administration in Texas, Lady Bird Johnson had taken an intense interest in preserving portions of the environment in their natural state and cleaning up the American landscape. During the 1930s, she had cofounded a movement to establish a system of roadside parks. She, along with her husband and Stewart Udall, helped persuade Congress to pass the Wilderness Act of 1964, a legislative initiative the Sierra Club and Wilderness Society had been touting for 10 years. The measure set aside 9 million acres of national forest as wilderness areas, protecting them from timber cuttings and strictly regulating public access. The following year, the Wild and Scenic Rivers Act extended federal protection over portions of eight of America's most spectacular waterways. Mrs. Johnson was gratified by these successes but was determined to do something about inhabited areas as well.

At the first lady's behest, the president convened in 1964 the Task Force on the Preservation of Natural Beauty. The national beautification movement focused first on Washington, D.C. Determined to convert the nation's capital into a model community, Mrs. Johnson worked through the National Park Service and private donors to beautify Pennsylvania Avenue and create a system of parks throughout the city. She subsequently championed the Highway Beautification Act of 1965 in the face of stiff opposition from the Outdoor Advertising Association. As finally passed, the compromised law banned or restricted outdoor billboards outside commercial and industrial sectors and required the fencing of unsightly junkyards adjacent to highways.

Critics of the administration dismissed leaders of the beautification movement as dilettante elitists, "the daffodil and dogwood" set. Rats, open sewage, and unsafe buildings were more of a problem than green space, advocates for inner-city dwellers argued. Mrs. Johnson responded by persuading Walter Johnson to head the Neighborhoods and Special Projects Committee, a body whose goal was to clean up and beautify the mostly black, poorer neighborhoods of Washington, D.C. Compared with racism, war, poverty, and social injustice, the beautification movement paled, but it was an authentic aspect of the larger environmental movement and important in part because it involved members of the American aristocracy in that movement.

That portion of the environmental movement that sought to protect human beings and the national habitat from polluting industries reinforced, and was reinforced by, the consumer protection movement. Congress's enactment of a bill imposing the first federal standards on automobile emissions marked a victory for both groups. In 1965, Ralph Nader, a muckraking young lawyer who would become the guru of consumer advocacy, published *Unsafe at Any Speed*, an attack on giant automobile companies like General Motors, which allegedly placed design and cost considerations above safety. He played a key role in securing passage of the Fair Packaging and Labeling Act and the Automobile Safety Act, both passed in 1966. Near the close of Johnson's term, Congress enacted the landmark Occupational Health and Safety Act, which imposed new federal safety standards on the American workplace.

Shooting for the Stars

Similar to his predecessor, Lyndon Johnson was an enthusiastic supporter of the space program. The civilian-controlled National Aeronautics and Space Administration (NASA) had been established in 1958, but the Eisenhower administration gave higher priority to the development of new, sophisticated defense systems rather than space technology. During the Kennedy administration, Congress had twice doubled NASA's appropriation, and the president had announced the goal of putting a man on the moon by the end of the 1960s. It was Johnson who was largely responsible for achieving that objective. He relentlessly pushed Congress to appropriate additional millions of dollars for the space program. Construction on the massive Johnson Space Center in Houston began during his tenure. In June 1966, *Surveyor 1* made the first U.S. soft landing on the moon after a flight of 231,483 miles in a little more than 63 hours. It immediately began transmitting television pictures of the moon's surface and whetted the nation's appetite for a manned mission. Then on July 16, 1969, *Apollo 11*, manned by Neil A. Armstrong, Edwin E. Aldrin, Jr., and Michael Collins blasted off for the moon. On July 20, Armstrong and Aldrin entered the Lunar Excursion Module *Eagle* and began the descent to a landing site near the Sea of Tranquility. At 4:17 PM, Armstrong radioed: "Houston, Tranquillity Base here. The *Eagle* has landed." Several hours later, Armstrong became the first person to walk on the moon. His exclamation, "That's one small step for man, one giant leap for mankind," became one of the most famous quotations of the twentieth century.

Summary

By the end of 1966, the Great Society was winding down. It did so in part because the president had accomplished much. At the height of the administration's legislative onslaught, columnist James Reston quipped that LBJ was "getting everything through the Congress but the abolition of the Republican party, and he hasn't tried that yet." In less than two years, Johnson had signed bills that touched virtually all aspects of American life – health care, civil rights, taxes, poverty, air and water quality, education, recreation, and technology.

Johnson's personality and his success in pushing his reform program through Congress puzzled liberals and intellectuals, many of whom could trace their advocacy of social justice measures back to the New Deal. He simply did not fit their image of the consummate liberal – sophisticated, subtle, refined, quietly confident, and eastern educated. When in June 1965 a Festival of the Arts and Humanities was held at the White House featuring exhibitions of paintings, sculpture, and photography; prose and poetry readings; music recitals; and a ballet, academics and art critics scoffed. Poet Robert Lowell refused to attend. The Texan seemed to glory in telling crude jokes and was sometimes given to sexist and paternalistic images in conversation. He was prone to fits of rage, vendettas, and paroxyms of insecurity and self-pity. In short, declared Johnson's detractors, he had style, but no class.

Johnson's critics and admirers – it was difficult to delineate with the passage of time – gave him his due, but they did so grudgingly. "If the Great Society was a failure in many respects," writes Dewey Grantham, "it was an audacious failure." William Chafe noted that Kennedy was drawn to the poor and oppressed intellectually and philosophically. He had studied the problem and realized the importance to the nation of solving it. Johnson's sympathy was just that, a "gut" feeling based on experience rather than analysis. Historians such as William Leuchtenburg attributed Johnson's success, and his failures, to an overabundance of ego. According to him, the Texan dedicated his life to outdoing his political "daddy," Franklin D. Roosevelt. Radical historians ridiculed his obsession with consensus and wrote off many of his Great Society programs as self-indulgent mechanisms that intentionally or accidentally served the status quo. "We made mistakes, plenty of them," recalled Johnson's domestic adviser, Joseph Califano. "But our excesses were based on high hopes and great expectations and were fueled by the frustration of seeing so much poverty, ignorance, and illness amidst such wealth."

Johnson's determination to be all things to all people and his sense of urgency produced programs that were sometimes ill conceived and contradictory. Many of his initiatives were starts without finishes. The philosophy that underlay the poverty program was no different from that which underpinned the progressive movement. Yet he accomplished much more than any of his predecessors in certain fields – civil rights, for example. Nevertheless, by the 1980s, he was seen at best as a tragic figure and, at worst, a Machiavellian demagogue that manipulated and distorted American society for his own psychic gratification.

By trying to steer a middle course in his quest for equality and social justice, Johnson exposed himself to attacks from both the right and left. He did not, moreover, kowtow to ambitious editors and reporters. Overly sensitive to criticism, jealous of his reputation, he never seemed to understand that the media would exercise its judgment regardless of what he did. He played favorites, tried to rig the news, scolded reporters and columnists in public, and eventually alienated those he was trying to woo. Johnson appointed capable subordinates to advise him on domestic matters. He kept on Kennedy's foreign policy team. Domestic affairs specialist Joseph Califano and speech writer Harry McPherson were bright and not afraid to challenge their boss. But Johnson treated many of his subordinates, especially cabinet members, with contempt and they did not love him for it. The Texan was generally a poor administrator, incapable at times of delegating authority. It was also true that his older, more individualistic style of leadership no longer commanded respect in a corporate–bureaucratic culture. He was egomaniacal in the sense that he was a control freak and wanted everyone to love him; when they did not, he became frustrated and angry. But all these flaws to a greater or lesser extent appeared in Johnson's predecessors, especially in his beloved Franklin D. Roosevelt. But he alone had to bear the onus of Vietnam.

ADDITIONAL READINGS

Blum, John Morton, *Years of Discord: American Politics and Society, 1960–1974* (1991).
Brauer, Carl, *John F. Kennedy and the Second Reconstruction* (1977).
Caro, Robert, *The Path To Power* (1983).
Caro, Robert, *Means of Ascent* (1989).
Dallek, Robert, *Lone Star Rising: Lyndon Johnson, 1908–1960* (1991).
Dallek, Robert, *Flawed Giant: Lyndon Johnson and His Times, 1961–1973* (1998).
Giglio, James N., *The Presidency of John F. Kennedy* (1991).
Lemann, Nicholas, *The Promised Land: The Great Black Migration and How It Changed America* (1991).
Matusow, Allen, *The Unraveling of America: A History of Liberalism in the 1960s* (1984).
McDougall, Walter A., *The Heavens and the Earth: A Political History of the Space Age* (1985).
Murray, Charles, *Losing Ground: American Social Policy, 1950–1980* (1986).
Parmet, Herbert, *JFK: The Presidency of John F. Kennedy* (1983).

Polk, Kenneth, *Scouting the War on Poverty: Social Reform Politics in the Kennedy Administration* (1971).

Reeves, Thomas C., *A Question of Character: A Life of John F. Kennedy* (1983).

Schlesinger, Arthur M., Jr., *A Thousand Days* (1966).

Schwartz, John E., *America's Hidden Success: A Reassessment of Public Policy From Kennedy To Reagan* (1988).

Urofsky, Melvin, *The Continuity of Change: The Supreme Court and Individual Liberties, 1953–1986* (1991).

7 The Wages of Globalism

Foreign Affairs During the Kennedy–Johnson Era

$\mathbf{T}$ he activist foreign policies of the post-1945 era that helped produce the war in Southeast Asia were a melding of the philosophies of conservative anticommunists, who defined national security in terms of bases and alliances and were basically xenophobic, and of liberal reformers, who were determined to safeguard the national interest by exporting democracy and facilitating overseas social and economic progress. Spearheading the first group were former isolationists such as Henry Luce who believed that if the United States could not hide from the world it must control it, rabid anticommunists who saw any expansion of Marxism-Leninism as a mortal threat to the United States, and elements of the American military and corporate establishments with a vested interest in the Cold War. Joining these realpolitikers, true believers, and political opportunists were the leading lights of the liberal community – Arthur Schlesinger, Dean Acheson, Joseph Rauh (head of the Americans for Democratic Action), and Hubert Humphrey. Products of World War II, these internationalists saw America's interests as being tied up with those of the other countries. They opposed communism because it constituted a totalitarian threat to cultural diversity, individual liberty, and self-determination. Amid the anxieties generated by the Cold War, anticommunism was a political necessity for liberals whose views on domestic issues made them ideologically suspect. Conservatives and their liberal adversaries may have differed as to their notions of the ideal America but not over whether America was ideal or whether it was duty bound to lead the "free world" into a new era of prosperity and stability.

A Call to Arms: JFK and the Cold War

John F. Kennedy's overriding interest had always been foreign policy. Most of his inaugural address was devoted to it, and he frequently justified his domestic policies in terms of America's ongoing competition with the Soviet

Union. Kennedy's foreign policy suffered from a basic contradiction, however. He and his advisers insisted that they were out to make the world safe for diversity and that under their leadership the United States would abandon the status quo policies of the past and support change, especially in the developing world. The Kennedy people did not object to Eisenhower's intervention into the internal affairs of other nations, but rather to the ineptness with which he intervened. In a special address to Congress in May 1961, the president declared that "the great battleground for the defense and expansion of freedom today is ... Asia, Latin America, Africa and the Middle East, the lands of the rising peoples." According to Arthur Schlesinger, Jr., Kennedy fully understood that in Latin America "the militantly anti-revolutionary line" of the past was the policy most likely to strengthen the communists and lose the hemisphere. He and his advisers planned openings to the left to facilitate "democratic development." Specifically, the administration projected an ambitious foreign aid program that would promote social justice and economic progress in the developing nations and in the process funnel nationalist energy into prodemocracy, anticommunist channels. Modernization through American aid would ensure that the newly emerging nations would achieve change through evolution rather than revolution.

At the same time, the administration saw any significant change in the balance of world power as a threat to American security. Kennedy, Bundy, Rusk, and McNamara took very seriously Khrushchev's January 1961 speech offering support for "wars of national liberation"; it was, they believed, evidence of a new communist campaign to seize control of anticolonial and other revolutionary movements in economically underdeveloped regions. If the "third world" were not to succumb to the siren's song of Marxism-Leninism, then the United States and other "developed" countries would have to demonstrate that economic progress could take place within a democratic, capitalist framework. But the logic of this position, as John Gaddis pointed out, was that the United States really would need a world resembling itself in order to be secure. Thus, the United States found itself supporting only those revolutionary movements that were democratic, favorable toward or at least tolerant of free enterprise, and staunchly anticommunist. "Our first great obstacle," Kennedy said, "is still our relations with the Soviet Union and China. We must never be lulled into believing that either power has yielded its ambitions for world domination."

One of the great restraints on Dwight D. Eisenhower's foreign policy had been the fiscal philosophy that underlay it, namely, that America's resources were limited and that global activism and higher defense spending would bankrupt the nation. Kennedy's election marked the return of the Keynesians under the leadership of John Kenneth Galbraith. It would be better to err on the side of boldness, the famed economist advised his new chief. "Ike avoided criticism on nearly every single step and now stands condemned on his aggregate performance," he told Kennedy. "Every single thing that Roosevelt did was attacked, and he was brilliantly vindicated on the overall result." The American economy had not reached maturity; rather it was in the midst of an indefinite expansion. Judicious government spending would only enhance the process. As far as defense was concerned, domestic and foreign interests were assumed to be complementary: the economy could withstand and even benefit from spending for national defense. It was no accident that the architects of NSC 68 – notably Dean Acheson, Dean Rusk, and Paul Nitze – were influential advisers in the Kennedy circle.

As noted, Kennedy's definition of presidential leadership called for the chief executive to be more than just a moral and legislative leader. To him, the presidency had become overinstitutionalized under Eisenhower, and he was determined to free the office from its bureaucratic prison. This was particularly true in foreign affairs. Under Eisenhower, the National Security Council (NSC) had become a dominant force with a planning board, an Operations Coordinating Board, and a special assistant for National Security Affairs. Kennedy named McGeorge Bundy, former dean of the faculty at Harvard, to be his national security adviser but then cut him loose from the NSC proper. While Bundy and his 10- to 15-person staff drafted policy options for the president, the NSC remained in limbo. Even though Kennedy continued to listen to Secretary of Defense Robert McNamara and Secretary of State Dean Rusk, the president relied primarily on Bundy. Further contributing to this reliance was Rusk's approach to his job. A former Rhodes Scholar and director of the Rockefeller Foundation, Rusk recalled in his memoirs that Kennedy expected him to outline problems and pose alternatives without being an advocate of any one of them. Consequently, he refused to provide independent advice to the president in the presence of others. Indeed, one Washington wag observed that even when Rusk was whispering in Kennedy's ear, he believed that there was one too many participants in the conversation.

Determined to deal with the Kremlin from a position of strength, Kennedy and McNamara announced that America's nuclear arsenal would increase until it contained 1,000 intercontinental ballistic missiles. "We dare not tempt [the Soviets] with weakness," the president declared. The nuclear buildup frightened Nikita Khrushchev, the Soviet premier; as he well knew, the Soviet Union already lagged far behind the United States in delivery vehicles. Instead of stability, the Kennedy–McNamara buildup touched off an arms race that brought the world to the brink of nuclear war in 1962, and saddled the United States with a massive $50 billion annual military budget by 1963. But for Kennedy, McNamara, and Rusk, the nuclear arms race was just one of many contests with the communist powers.

During the 1960 presidential campaign, Kennedy had been sharply critical of the Eisenhower policy of massive retaliation. His impression that conventional forces had been woefully neglected was reinforced by reading retired General Maxwell Taylor's *Uncertain Trumpet* (1960) and by McNamara's alarmist report that the U.S. Army consisted of a mere 14 divisions, only 11 of which were combat ready. During his first year, the president increased the regular military budget by 15%, doubled the number of Army divisions in ready reserve, and increased the number of combat units in both the Navy and the Marines. In response to the counterinsurgency theories then being espoused by Taylor and others, Kennedy instructed the Special Warfare Center at Ft. Bragg, North Carolina, to train a new type of soldier capable of meeting communist guerrillas on their own terms. In the 1950s, anticommunist forces in Malaya, the Philippines, and Greece had successfully employed guerrilla tactics to defeat insurgents, and the administration was convinced that these techniques were suitable for dealing with Khrushchev's wars of national liberation. The Special Forces at Ft. Bragg – the green berets – increased from fewer than 1,000 to 12,000 during the Kennedy administration. In January 1962, the White House created a special group (counterinsurgency) chaired by General Taylor and including Attorney General Robert Kennedy. Indeed, counterinsurgency along with civil rights, poverty, and labor racketeering had captured the younger Kennedy's imagination. The Taylor group saw the Special Forces not only as a paramilitary unit capable of sabotage and counterterrorism, but also as a progressive political and social force that would assist local governments in winning the hearts and minds of indigenous peoples.

Indeed, the Special Forces were the military aspect of a larger effort to identify the United States with the themes of anticolonialism and nationalism. Another Kennedy initiative designed to demonstrate America's commitment to economic progress and social change was the Peace Corps. During a campaign rally at the University of Michigan in October 1960, Kennedy asked 10,000 students if any of them would be willing to give two years of their lives working in Asia, Africa, or Latin America. Their enthusiastic response impressed him. Under its first director, Sargent Shriver, the Peace Corps sent 7,000 youthful volunteers to 44 countries to teach English, train native peoples in the techniques of scientific farming and modern home economics, build hospitals, and combat disease. The stated objectives of the program were to provide a skill to an interested country, to teach other cultures about America, and to increase young America's understanding of other peoples. "The whole idea," declared one teenage volunteer, "was that you can make a difference.... I really believed that I was going to be able to change the world." But for Kennedy the Peace Corps was more than an exercise in altruism. He spoke of halting communist expansion by helping to develop the resources of the Third World.

The Cuban Revolution and the Bay of Pigs

Indeed, by the time President Kennedy took the Oath of Office, U.S. officials were deeply concerned about communist inroads in Cuba, an impoverished island only 90 miles off the coast of Florida. Since the Spanish–American War, Cuba had been an informal dependency of the United States dominated politically by Washington and exploited economically by North American corporations and investors. From 1934 until 1959, Cuba was governed by Fulgencio Batista, a military dictator whose rule typically catered to Cuba's wealthy upper classes and U.S. business interests. Inevitably, revolutionary nationalism took root among the island's impoverished masses and, in 1959, Batista was overthrown by Fidel Castro, an idealistic, appealing young revolutionary who, clad in fatigues and smoking a cigar, rode into Havana in a jeep. The Eisenhower administration recognized the new government six days after its formation, and American businessmen rushed to pay their taxes. The U.S. government was certain that the U.S.-trained military would not allow the revolution to get out of hand. It was wrong.

Castro declared 1959 to be the Year of the Revolution and announced that he was a Marxist-Leninist. A roundup of former Batista supporters turned into a state-sponsored effort to crush dissent. The next year was designated the Year of Agrarian Reform and, before 1960 had ended, Castro had seized approximately $1 billion of American-owned property in Cuba. The Cuban leader began referring to Eisenhower as a "gangster" and a "senile White House golfer." In the fall of 1960, Castro ventured to New York, delivered a four-and-a-half-hour harangue to the UN general assembly, and publicly embraced Nikita Khrushchev. Frightened by the apparent penetration of the Western Hemisphere by the forces of international communism, the Eisenhower administration authorized the training and arming of a Cuban exile army of liberation under direction of the Central Intelligence Agency (CIA). On January 20, 1961, John F. Kennedy inherited this scheme.

During the presidential campaign in speech after speech, Kennedy focused on Cuba, blasting Eisenhower and Nixon for letting the Ever Faithful Isle (so dubbed by the Spanish during their 300-year reign there) fall under the sway of a communist. Kennedy probably believed, in fact, that the revolution had been subverted. Almost as soon as he took the Oath of Office, the new president was briefed on the American-sponsored effort by anti-communist Cubans determined to retake control of their island. The CIA authors of the operation naturally advocated it, asking none too subtly if the president was as willing as his Republican predecessor to permit and assist these exiles to free their homeland from dictatorship. They reminded him that the invasion army, some 1,450 strong, was well along in its training at secret bases in Guatemala. What was to be done with them if the operation was cancelled? They would in all likelihood return to Miami and spend their time making trouble for the administration. Finally, the CIA representatives argued that time was of the essence; the Soviet Union was daily supplying Castro with MIG fighters and other equipment.

There were dissenting voices – Schlesinger, Galbraith, and J. William Fulbright, chairman of the Senate Foreign Relations Committee – who argued that Castro did not really pose a significant threat to U.S. security and that America's all-too-apparent hand in the affair would destroy its standing with the multitude of developing and semi-independent countries struggling to escape the blight of colonialism. Cuba, Fulbright asserted, was "a thorn in the side, not a dagger in the heart." Philip Bonsal, America's ambassador to Cuba, advised the government that the Cuban revolution was exclusively nationalistic, and only U.S. hostility was pushing Castro into the arms of the Soviets. Nevertheless, after obtaining the written endorsement of the Joint Chiefs of Staff (JCS), Kennedy gave the go-ahead with only one condition attached – no overt participation in the operation by U.S. armed forces. The president reasoned that if U.S. personnel participated, the American people would not tolerate failure, and the landings could quite possibly escalate into war with the Soviet Union.

Early in the morning of April 17, 1961, the Cuban Exile Brigade landed at the Bay of Pigs on the southern coast of Cuba. The soldiers achieved tactical surprise, fought well, and inflicted heavy casualties on Castro's forces, which soon numbered more than 20,000. But the exiles soon ran out of ammunition. The tiny rebel air force, flying outdated B-26s, failed to destroy Castro's planes in an April 15 attack and, as a result, Cuba's defenders enjoyed air superiority and sank an exile freighter loaded with ammunition and communications equipment. On the second day of the operation, with ammunition running out and casualties mounting, the exiles surrendered.

The administration learned of the collapse of the Bay of Pigs operation on the evening of April 18. Huddling with his advisers, Kennedy rejected a request by members of the JCS and the CIA for U.S. intervention to rescue the exiles and topple Castro. Such blatant aggression, he declared, would only weaken the nation's hand in the global struggle against communism. The president accepted full responsibility for the Bay of Pigs fiasco, and a fiasco it had been. American sponsorship of the invasion violated the charters of the United Nations and the Organization of American States. It revived fears of Yankee imperialism in Latin America and undercut the United States' position throughout the developing world. "We looked like fools to our friends, rascals to our enemies, and incompetents to the rest," *The New York Times* declared. Politically, the Kennedy administration seemed to have alienated both the Democratic left and the Republican right. Liberals were convinced that the president had turned over American foreign policy to the military and CIA, whereas conservatives accused Kennedy of weakness in being willing to tolerate the existence of a communist "beachhead" only 90 miles away. "How could I have been so stupid, to let them go ahead?" Kennedy lamented. "All my life I've known better than to depend on the experts."

Humiliation continued to fester in the president's breast, as well as in his brother, Robert. In late April, when Castro offered to negotiate differences between the two countries, Secretary of State Rusk declared self-righteously that "communism in this hemisphere is not negotiable." The government responded to this perceived threat in two very different ways. Professing fears that Castro would be able to make good on his promise to spread his revolution throughout Latin America, the administration worked to alleviate poverty and promote social justice throughout the hemisphere. In the spring of 1961, the president held a reception for Latin American diplomats and announced what he called an "alliance for progress," a vast aid program designed to speed the modernization process. The great task that lay before them, Kennedy declared, "is to demonstrate to the entire world that man's unsatisfied aspiration for economic progress and social justice can best be achieved by free men working within a framework of democratic institutions." In August 1961, economic and finance ministers from all American republics except Cuba met at the Uruguayan resort of Punta del Este and signed the charter of the Alliance for Progress. It promised Latin America $20 billion for economic development, spread over the rest of the 1960s, half to come from the United States and half from international lending institutions. At the same time, President Kennedy approved Operation Mongoose, a CIA-supervised effort to overthrow Castro by means of covert operations. By 1962, 400 Americans and 2,000 Cubans were spending $50 million a year in this "secret war." Saboteurs tried every imaginable scheme to disrupt the Cuban economy, and the CIA contracted with organized crime figures to assassinate Castro. Both the Alliance for Progress and Operation Mongoose turned out to be exercises in frustration.

The Cuban problem was, in part, an offshoot of the larger Soviet–American rivalry that had been raging since the end of World War II. Scholars speculated that Kennedy's failure in the Bay of Pigs incident made him more bellicose in dealing with Khrushchev and the Soviets than he otherwise would have been. Whether this was true, Soviet–American relations deteriorated sharply during the summer of 1961, as the two nations became embroiled once again over the Berlin issue. The first week in June, Kennedy and Khrushchev held a summit meeting in Vienna where the Soviet leader attempted to browbeat and intimidate his much younger counterpart. The main topic was Berlin. It was absurd, Khrushchev declared, that 16 years had passed without a peace treaty with Germany. If the West did not agree to terms by the end of the year, the Soviet Union would sign a separate treaty with East Germany. In that event, as both men knew, West Berlin would be at the mercy of the hard-line communist government of East Germany. If the Americans wanted war, Khrushchev declared, there was nothing that he could do about it. "It will be a cold winter," Kennedy responded ominously. Later to an aide he declared angrily that "if Khrushchev wants to rub my nose in the dirt, it's all over. . . . All Europe is at stake in Berlin."

Strongly influenced by former Secretary of State Dean Acheson, who still smarted from Republican charges of being "soft on communism," Kennedy took a tough line on Berlin. In a July 25 address to the nation, the president declared that the United States would stand by the people of West Berlin: "We cannot and will not permit the Communists to drive us out of Berlin, either gradually or by force." Americans, he said, "do not want to fight, but we have fought before." He requested and obtained from Congress $3.5 billion more for the armed forces, doubled and then tripled the monthly draft call and, most ominously, announced a civil defense program that included subsidies for establishment of nuclear fallout shelters in existing structures.

Khrushchev's renewal of the Berlin ultimatum stemmed from his fears of a West Germany armed with nuclear weapons and his desire to force the West to accept a reunified, neutralized Germany; but it also grew out of a shorter range concern. Drawn by the freedom and prosperity of West Berlin, 4,000 East Germans, most of them students, technocrats, and professionals, were crossing into the noncommunist sector of the city each week. The outflow not only gravely weakened East Germany but also was a propaganda disaster for international communism. On August 13, 1961, the Soviets began construction on a barbed wire and concrete wall that would eventually divide the city and serve as a symbol of the separation of East Germany from West Germany. Although the noncommunist world expressed shock and outrage, Kennedy privately welcomed the development. He did not want to go to war over Berlin, and he recognized the wall as a face-saving device for Khrushchev. In fact, on October 17, in a speech before the 22nd Congress of the Communist Party of the Soviet Union (CPSU), Khrushchev terminated the deadline for the German peace treaty. Soviet–American tensions eased during the next several months, but it was just the calm before the storm.

The Cuban Missile Crisis

Following complaints by Castro that the United States was plotting to overthrow his government by force, the Soviet Union began sending weapons and military personnel to Cuba. The buildup included medium range ballistic missiles (MRBMs) capable of raining down nuclear warheads on American cities, ILB-28 bombers, and Soviet troops. Khrushchev's provocative decision to place offensive nuclear weapons [as opposed to surface-to-air missiles (SAMs)] grew out of a desire to protect communist Cuba, but it was also a response to hard-liners within the Politburo who were worried about the massive imbalance in nuclear delivery systems that then existed. As of 1962, the Soviets possessed somewhere between 20 and 44 intercontinental ballistic missiles (ICBMs) and no submarine-launched missiles. The United States, by comparison, could boast 161 ICBMs and 144 Polaris sea-launched ballistic missiles (SLBMs).

Eager to make points against a Democratic administration prior to the midterm congressional elections in 1962, Republican Senator Kenneth Keating of New York rose in the Upper House to charge that there were 1,200 Russian troops in Cuba as well as "concave metal structures" that could very well be the beginnings of a "rocket installation." To that point, U-2 flights had revealed the existence of only SAMs in Cuba. The first week in September, Soviet Ambassador Anatoly Dobrinin informed the administration that his country would do nothing to upset the international status quo before the U.S. midterm elections and stated specifically that no offensive weapons would be placed in Cuba. Immediately thereafter, the White House, responding to Republican charges, announced that there were no Soviet offensive weapons in Cuba and that none would be tolerated. However, Keating, fed information to the contrary by Cuban exiles, refused to relent.

Dobrynin was in fact deceiving the Kennedy administration. U-2 photographs analyzed on October 15 revealed that Soviet technicians were building sites from which both 1,000-mile MRBMs and 2,200-mile intermediate range ballistic missiles (IRBMs) could be launched against the United States. The president was frightened and angry. It seemed to him that Khrushchev was deliberately and deceitfully upsetting the balance of power. The challenge could not go unanswered. "The 1930s," he observed, "taught us a clear lesson: aggressive conduct, if allowed to go unchecked and unchallenged, ultimately leads to war." To monitor the situation and suggest options, Kennedy created the Executive Committee of the National Security Council (ExComm), which included the principal cabinet officers, the national security adviser, the chairman of the JCS, Maxwell Taylor, and former Ambassador to the Soviet Union Llewellyn Thompson. During the following week, ExComm mulled over a number of responses but focused increasingly on two: an air strike to destroy the missile sites or a naval blockade to prevent Russia from landing nuclear warheads in Cuba. Although most favored an air strike initially, the consensus gradually began to shift in favor of a blockade. An air strike would kill Soviet personnel, and Khrushchev might very well respond by blasting American Jupiter missile sites in Turkey. Moreover, Kennedy's military advisers indicated that such an attack would only take out approximately 90% of the missile sites. The president feared that the Kremlin might order the surviving warheads launched against American cities. The blockade, which Americans called a "quarantine" because technically a "blockade" was an act of war, had the virtue of allowing Khrushchev a face-saving way out and permitting a more controlled escalation on the U.S. government's part. "My brother is not going to be the Tojo of the 1960s," Robert Kennedy declared, clinching the argument in behalf of a blockade.

By the end of the first week of the Cuban missile crisis, U-2 photos indicated that the Russians were building six medium range and three intermediate range sites. Potentially, these sites could launch 36 nuclear warheads capable of killing 80 million people in the United States. There was, however, no direct evidence that there were actual nuclear warheads in Cuba or plans to put them there.

In fact, the Ever Faithful Isle was bristling with nuclear weapons. The Soviet freighter *Indigirka*, carrying 45 SS4 and SS5 warheads, 12 Luna ground-to-ground rockets armed with 2-kiloton warheads, and six 12-kiloton bombs for IL-28 bombers, arrived in Cuba some three weeks before the crisis began. The Luna weapons had a range of 30 miles and were attached to Soviet motorized infantry regiments around Havana and Guantanamo. The IL-28 had a range of 750 miles.

On October 22, Kennedy went on national television to announce the presence of the missiles and the imposition of a naval quarantine. He called on the Kremlin to "halt and eliminate this clandestine, reckless and provocative threat to world peace and to stabilize relations between our two nations." Khrushchev denounced the move as American piracy and informed the world that he was ordering Soviet ships on the high seas to ignore the blockade and proceed to Cuba. Two days later, as the world held its breath, the Soviet flotilla stopped just short of the naval picket line set up some 500 miles east of Cuba. Nevertheless, aerial photographs of the island showed that Soviet technicians were continuing work on the sites. Unbeknownst to the United States, the *Aleksandrovsk*, carrying 24 more strategic warheads and 44 FKR cruise missiles armed with 12-kiloton warheads, had arrived in Cuba the day before the blockade went into effect. The FKR was a scaled-down, pilotless version of the MIG jet, with a target guidance system effective up to 100 miles.

As the missile crisis deepened, intense anxiety gripped the United States. Many Americans had read Nevil Shute's novel, *On the Beach*, subsequently made into a movie, about an American submarine crew that had survived a nuclear Armageddon. Parents suddenly had to confront the possibility that their children would have no future. Shelves emptied in grocery stores across the country, as owners of bomb shelters, built in the 1950s, stocked up in hopes of surviving the initial blast and the subsequent period of radiation fallout. Public schools hastily devised emergency evacuation plans and staged atomic bomb drills. Visions of the apocalypse haunted the collective imagination.

With sentiment mounting within administration councils for an air strike, Khrushchev sent the president two remarkable and contradictory letters. The first, an absolutely confidential communication, offered to dismantle the Soviet missile sites in return for an American promise not to invade Cuba. "If you have not lost your self-control," he wrote Kennedy, "we and you ought now to pull on the ends of the rope in which you have tied the knot of war." A subsequent letter, apparently written under pressure from hard-liners in the Kremlin, offered to remove the Soviet MRBMs and IRBMs in return for withdrawal of the Jupiter missiles in Turkey as well as the promise not to invade Cuba. After much discussion, several members of ExComm suggested that the president ignore the second letter and respond to the first. He did just that. In a telegram, the White House proposed that in return for removal of the offensive missiles from Cuba under UN supervision, the United States would lift its quarantine and give assurances against an invasion. Determined to allow Khrushchev as much maneuvering room as possible, Kennedy, referring to the missiles in Turkey, indicated that the United States would be willing to discuss other weapons installations at a later date. On October 28, Moscow radio broadcasted Khrushchev's reply. He agreed fully with the president's proposal, thus ignoring the second letter. Horrified that Castro had urged him to launch strategic nuclear missiles against the United States at the height of the crisis, Khrushchev removed all nuclear warheads, tactical and strategic, by December 1962.

A Thaw in Soviet–American Relations

The Cuban missile crisis had brought the world to the brink of war and for no good reason, most scholars subsequently agreed. Operation Mongoose had driven Castro to distraction. He and others in the Kremlin believed that the Kennedy administration was planning another Bay of Pigs or even a direct invasion. For its part, the Soviet leadership had treated the situation purely as a problem in international relations, ignoring the political situation in the United States. Robert Kennedy told his brother that he would have been impeached had he allowed the missiles to remain in Cuba. Yet in his obsession with Castro and Cuba, Jack Kennedy had been more than partially responsible for their stationing there. Indeed, the Cuban missile crisis had as much to do with Kennedy's humiliation over the Bay of Pigs, his humbling by Khrushchev at Vienna, his inexperience, and his unwillingness to appear weak before the 1962 midterm elections as with any rational calculation of national self-interest. It is true, however, that once the crisis began, both leaders acted with restraint. Kennedy's rejection of the air strike option probably saved the world. Participants at a recent conference on the crisis learned that there were tactical as well as strategic warheads in Cuba. Soviet field commanders had permission to use those weapons against an American attacking force without permission from Moscow. Robert McNamara admitted that had the Soviets used such weapons against an American force, the demand for a nuclear response against the Soviet Union would have been overwhelming. But Kennedy had been lucky. As historian Thomas Patterson has observed, the Kennedy administration "bequeathed to successors an impressive fixation both resistant to diplomatic opportunity and attractive to political demagoguery."

In the wake of the Cuban missile crisis, Kennedy and his advisers sensed a slight thaw in Soviet–American relations. "We were in luck," Ambassador to India John Kenneth Galbraith wrote afterward, "but success in a lottery is no argument for lotteries." The Russians had made good on their promise to allow the U.S. Navy to inspect ships carrying dismantled missiles out of the Ever Faithful Isle. In 1963, as a result of the Cuban confrontation, Kennedy and Khrushchev agreed to an emergency phone and teletype, or "hotline," connection between Washington, D.C., and Moscow. It provided instant communication between the heads of the two superpowers when one or the other feared miscalculation in a crisis. NSC Deputy Director Walt Rostow and Kennedy's science advisor, Jerome Weisner, both of whom had been American delegates to the 1960 Pugwash Conference, a privately funded international meeting designed to reduce the chances of nuclear war, urged the president to make a test-ban treaty part of détente. In March 1963, Kennedy authorized his arms control representatives in Geneva to begin discussions in earnest on a treaty. In June, he announced that the United States would no longer test nuclear arms in the atmosphere "so long as other states do not do so." Khrushchev was interested. He wanted to relieve the pressure the military budget was exerting on the Soviet Union's slumping economy. A diplomatic coup might restore his position with his countrymen and aid in the propaganda struggle the Soviets were waging with Communist China in the developing world. Both France and China wanted desperately to develop their own nuclear capability; neither Khrushchev nor Kennedy wanted "proliferation" of nuclear weapons. Finally, concern was mounting in both countries about the amount of radioactive material the frequent atomic tests were spewing into the atmosphere. On June 10, 1963, Kennedy announced that representatives from Russia, Britain, and the United States would meet in Moscow to discuss a nuclear test-ban treaty.

In an effort to assure America's European allies that they were not about to be sold out, Kennedy made a highly publicized trip to Berlin. More than one million people lined the path of the president's motorcade, waving American flags and pelting the passing cars with flowers. Addressing a crowd of 150,000 West Berliners in front of City Hall, Kennedy hailed the city as the front line of the global struggle against communism. "Today, in the world of freedom," he declared, "the proudest boast is 'Ich bin ein Berliner.'"

The American delegation was led by Averell Harriman, a seasoned diplomat who had gained valuable experience during World War II as Franklin D. Roosevelt's special representative to the Soviet Union. Within days, the three delegations had reached agreement and signed a pact that outlawed all nuclear tests in the atmosphere, in outer space, on land, and under water, but allowed them to continue underground. During the following months, nearly 100 nations signed the test-ban treaty, although the signatories included neither Communist China nor France. Under heavy administration pressure, the U.S. Senate approved the treaty by a vote of 80 to 19.

Critics of the treaty in the United States, headed by Dr. Edward Teller, father of the hydrogen bomb, and certain members of the military, had argued during the debate over ratification that the test-ban treaty would jeopardize America's nuclear superiority. They were mistaken. The measure, which did not provide for on-site inspection or ban underground explosions, did little to slow down the nuclear arms race. The measure's importance was as a symbol of détente. Coming as it did in the wake of the Cuban missile crisis, it de-escalated the Soviet–American confrontation and gave hope to a world that had lived in constant fear of nuclear annihilation. Shortly after signing the test-ban treaty, Kennedy proposed a joint Soviet–American expedition to the moon. In addition, he approved the sale of $250 million worth of surplus wheat to Russia, which was beginning experience a chronic grain shortage.

The Congo

In Cuba, John F. Kennedy had had to confront the classic dilemma that faced all Cold War presidents: what was to be done when anticolonial, nationalist revolutions embraced Marxism-Leninism. Despite his oft-repeated sympathy for anticolonial movements and socioeconomic justice in the developing world, Kennedy placed anticommunism at the top of his priorities and waged undeclared, mostly secret war on the Cuban revolution. He made similar choices in regard to two other Third World, Cold War hot spots – the Congo and Vietnam. In fact, Kennedy mentioned Africa nearly 500 times in his campaign addresses, and the team he assembled in the State Department, including Chester Bowles as undersecretary and G. Mennen Williams as assistant secretary for African affairs, believed that the United States ought to help the 17 newly independent nations on that continent establish viable, self-reliant democracies. The Food for Peace program and the Peace Corps were active in Africa, and loans from the Agency for International Development (AID) nearly doubled during the next two years. "Africa for the Africans" was the administration's initial cry.

When Kennedy took the Oath of Office, the Congo was teetering on the brink of chaos. In 1960, Belgium reluctantly agreed to independence for its central African colony, but it did so without laying any groundwork for economic and political stability. The Belgians simply pulled up stakes and departed, except from Katanga province, rich in mineral ores. There, Belgian businessmen and technicians protected by government troops remained in control. Shortly after Brussels proclaimed independence in June, the Congolese army rebelled against its white officers and widespread looting of the Belgian community ensued. Belgium sent paratroops to protect its citizens, and the infant republic split into three parts: Katanga, governed by the pro-Belgian Moise Tshombe; the Congolese government proper headed by President Joseph Kasavubu; and a splinter faction headed by Kasavubu's Prime Minister Patrice Lumumba and Antoine Gizenga. As prime minister, Lumumba had approached the Soviet Union about possible arms aid, causing him to be labeled a communist by the West. On January 17, 1961, the world learned that Lumumba had been assassinated by Katanga thugs. When later that year a coalition government acceptable to the Gizenga–Lumumba faction came to power, and its head, Cyrille Adoula, asked for U.S. aid in crushing the Katanga rebellion, Kennedy refused. To American conservatives such as Senator Barry Goldwater (R-Arizona), Katanga had become a symbol of capitalism and anticommunism. Moreover, the president did not want to anger Belgium, a reliable member of the North American Treaty Organization (NATO). In 1962, an Indian-led UN force helped Adoula crush the rebellion, but the Kennedy administration got no credit with African nationalists. The White House was not going to make itself vulnerable to the "soft on communism" charge. That inclination promoted a policy of nonintervention in the Congo but just its reverse in Southeast Asia.

Vietnam: Staying the Course

The war in the Pacific, it will be remembered, gave a strong filip to anticolonial movements throughout the area, and Indochina was no exception. Shortly after Japan's surrender in August 1945, Ho Chi Minh, leader of the Vietminh, a broad-based but communist-led resistance movement, proclaimed from Hanoi the existence of a new nation, the Democratic Republic of Vietnam (DRV). During the next year and a half, the French, with the help of the British in the south and the Chinese Nationalists in the north, managed to partially reestablish themselves. In November 1946, a bitter colonial war erupted between the French and the Vietminh, culminating in 1954 with France's defeat at the battle of Dienbienphu. A subsequent peace conference at Geneva provided for the temporary division of the country at the 17th parallel. The French withdrew from the peninsula but left an anticommunist regime in place in the south under Emperor Bao Dai and his prime minister, Ngo Dinh Diem. Within a year, Diem had ousted Bao Dai and instituted a presidential system with himself as chief executive. Meanwhile, in the north Ho consolidated his power as head of the DRV.

There was no doubt that Ho, one of the cofounders of the French Communist Party, was a Marxist-Leninist or that the DRV was a totalitarian regime. After both Moscow and Beijing recognized Ho as the legitimate ruler of all Vietnam in 1950, the United States concluded that the DRV was a Sino–Soviet satellite and that Ho was a puppet of Stalin and Mao Zedong. Throughout the 1950s, the Eisenhower administration poured economic and military aid into Vietnam. Diem, a principled, patriotic man, briefly attempted land and constitutional reform, but he proved unsuited to the task of building a social democracy. A devout Catholic and traditional mandarin by temperament and philosophy, he distrusted the masses and had contempt for the give-and-take of democratic politics. Increasingly, he relied on his family and loyal Catholics in the military and civil service to rule a country in which 90% of the population was Buddhist. His brother Nhu used the government-sponsored Can Lao Party, a thoroughly intimidated press, and the state police to persecute and suppress opponents of the regime. As corruption increased and democracy all but disappeared, a rebellion broke out in the south against the Diem government. In 1960, the DRV decided to give formal aid to the newly formed National Liberation Front (NLF), the name assumed by the anti-Diemist revolutionaries.

America's decision to intervene in Vietnam was first and foremost a product of the mindset that developed during the period from 1945 to 1950. The United States emerged from World War II strong and confident, basking in the knowledge that it had led a mighty coalition of powers to victory against the forces of international fascism. With the onslaught of the Cold War, realpolitikers preoccupied with markets and bases joined with liberal idealists who wanted to spread the blessings of freedom, democracy, and a mixed economy to the rest of the world. In turn, they joined together to call for an all-out effort to defeat the forces of international communism. They had self-consciously learned only one simple lesson from Munich (the 1938 European conference during which the western democracies surrendered portions of Czechoslovakia to Nazi Germany in return for Hitler's promise not to seize another foot of European territory); that is, appeasement of an aggressor only breeds further aggression. They had "learned" during the Greek crisis of 1944–1948 that if one nation in a particular region fell to the forces of international communism, its neighbors were likely to follow suit like dominos. Finally, during this period, most Americans bought into the notion of the existence of a monolithic communist threat. That is, despite differences over approach, all communists were committed to world revolution and all were subject to direction from Moscow and/or Beijing. These assumptions and perceptions became so deeply rooted in the collective American consciousness that the nation was blinded to other issues threatening the international status quo, such as anticolonialism, nationalism, peonage, and political repression. As Ho Chi Minh's Marxist philosophy and his ties to the communist superpowers became apparent, all these assumptions rose to the surface of America's collective consciousness.

But, NSC 68 notwithstanding, the United States did not intervene in every brushfire war where communists or Marxists were involved. A variety of factors prompted President Kennedy to view South Vietnam as the place where the leader of the free world would make its stand. He classified the conflict in South Vietnam as one of Khrushchev's wars of national liberation, a test of his administration's resolve just as much as Berlin or Cuba. Kennedy and his advisers fully accepted the "domino theory." Following the administration's agreement in 1961 to the neutralization of Laos, a landlocked nation wracked by communist insurgency, Kennedy and his advisers believed that they had to hold the line in South Vietnam. "At this point we are like the Harlem Globetrotters," McGeorge Bundy remarked, "passing forward, behind, sidewise, and underneath. But nobody has made a basket yet." Experts in the state and defense departments and in the intelligence agencies were aware of the burgeoning Sino–Soviet split, but they believed that the communist superpowers would present a common front in any international crisis and that they were committed to promoting Marxism-Leninism in the developing world. In the fall of 1961, as the guerrilla war intensified, Assistant Secretary of State Walt Rostow and the president's military aide, General Maxwell Taylor, returned from a fact-finding trip to South Vietnam to recommend the dispatch of 8,000 combat troops. Kennedy decided against direct military intervention, but he ordered an increase in aid to Diem and the introduction of additional military advisers. The number of American uniformed personnel grew from several hundred when Kennedy assumed office to 16,000 by 1963.

Despite American aid, the Diem regime became increasingly isolated from the masses. Bribes and intimidation by civil servants and military officials alienated peasant and urban dweller alike. Law 10/59, which the government pushed through the rubber stamp national assembly, gave Nhu's police and special forces the power to arrest and execute South Vietnamese citizens for a variety of crimes, including black marketeering and spreading seditious rumors about the government. By 1963, the nation teetered on the brink of chaos with the Peoples Revolutionary Army (the military branch of the NLF), or Vietcong (VC) as the Americans referred to it, in control of the countryside, students and intellectuals demonstrating in Saigon and Hue, Buddhist monks burning themselves in protest, and high-ranking military officers hatching a variety of coup plots. Madame Nhu, Diem's imperious and vitriolic sister-in-law, dismissed the self-immolations as "Buddhist barbecues," while her husband remarked that if more wanted to seek immortality, he would gladly furnish the gasoline and matches.

Shortly before his own assassination in November, 1963, Kennedy tacitly approved a military coup in Saigon, which led to the deaths of both

Diem and Nhu. The president sensed that the United States was on the verge of plunging into a morass from which it could not extricate itself. He frequently observed that only the South Vietnamese themselves could establish a broad-based, noncommunist government and make the sacrifices necessary to sustain it. "In the final analysis, it is their war," the Kennedy told CBS newsman Walter Cronkite. "They are the ones who have to win or lose it. We can help them, give them equipment, send our men out there as advisers, but they have to win it." Without that commitment, all the American aid in the world would be for naught. Yet, he was unwilling for both political and strategic reasons to stand by and watch Vietnam fall to the communists. Not only would America's credibility with its allies be damaged, but there also would be a Republican-led, anticommunist backlash at home that could possibly produce a new wave of McCarthyism.

The Domino Theory Ascendent: LBJ and Vietnam

Allen J. Matusow wrote that Lyndon B. Johnson was a "complex man notorious for his ideological insincerity." If by that Matusow meant that Johnson wielded ideological justifications for pragmatically based policies already decided upon, he was right. Johnson also shared that trait with most other successful presidents, notably the two Roosevelts. Johnson was in basic agreement with the foreign policies of the Kennedy administration: military preparedness and realistic diplomacy, he believed, would contain communism within its existing bounds. To keep up morale among America's allies and satisfy hard-line anticommunists at home, the United States must continue to hold fast in Berlin, oppose the admission of Communist China to the United Nations, and continue to confront and blockade Cuba. He was aware of the growing split between the Soviet Union and Communist China, and the possibilities inherent in it for dividing the communist world. He also took a flexible, even hopeful, view of the Soviet Union and Nikita Khrushchev. It was just possible, he believed, that Russia was becoming a status quo power and as such would be a force for stability rather than chaos in the world. The United States must continue its "flexible response" of military aid, economic assistance, and technical/political advice in response to the threat of communism in the developing world. However, there was nothing wrong with negotiating with the Soviets at the same time in an effort to reduce tensions. Insofar as Latin America was concerned, Johnson was an enthusiastic supporter of the Alliance for Progress. As a progressive Democrat, he was drawn to the Schlesinger–Goodwin philosophy of seeking openings to the Democratic left. At the outset of his administration, it appeared that the new president did not buy into the myth of a monolithic communist threat. He was a staunch supporter of trade with Yugoslavia and Poland. To all appearances then, Johnson was a cold warrior, but a flexible, pragmatic one.

Nevertheless, Johnson was no more ready than his predecessor to unilaterally withdraw from South Vietnam or seek a negotiated settlement
that would lead to neutralization of the area south of the 17th parallel. In
the first place, he was, as McGeorge Bundy has noted, "a hawk." He had
not been contaminated by the cynicism that affected youths after World
War I, claiming as he wrote in his college newspaper in 1927 that it had
been necessary "to make the world safe for democracy." Like so many other
Americans of his generation, Johnson had learned the "lessons" of Munich.
He would not reward "aggression" with "appeasement" in Southeast Asia
or anywhere else. In a typically vulgar analogy, he declared: "If you let
a bully come into your yard one day, the next day he'll be up on your
porch, and the day after that he'll rape your wife in your own bed." In
addition, he seemed genuinely smitten with Diem and with the determination of the "brave people of Vietnam" to resist a communist takeover.
As the nation and the world would learn, Lyndon Johnson was that variety of southerner for whom compassion could become an all-consuming
obsession.

In addition, the Texan felt compelled, for practical as well as political
reasons, to carry out the policies of his predecessor. After all, he had not
been elected in his own right, and he was acutely sensitive to the dangers
of appearing disloyal to Kennedy. Moreover, Johnson felt constrained to
demonstrate to the world, allies and antagonists alike, that America's period
of grief and self-searching would not diminish its strength or weaken its
commitment to its allies. Thus it was that in his first message to Congress
and the nation on November 27, 1963, Johnson assured his audience that
he would uphold American commitments "from South Vietnam to West
Berlin."

Above all, Johnson feared that right-wing adversaries would hound him
should South Vietnam fall to communism, just as Harry Truman had been
hounded and his policies circumscribed by Joe McCarthy after the fall of
China. Even though, as he indicated in his conversations with Senator Fulbright, he may have wanted to question the assumptions that underlay the
original containment policy, including the monolithic communist threat
and the domino theory, he dare not lest the debate fracture the domestic
consensus he so desperately desired. Johnson had no intention of allowing
the charge that he was soft on communism to be used to destroy the Great
Society programs.

Finally, there was bureaucratic momentum. Lyndon Johnson was well
aware of his inexperience in foreign affairs. As a consequence, he retained Kennedy's top advisers and relied heavily on them. Rusk in State,
McNamara in Defense, and National Security Adviser McGeorge Bundy
had all played prominent roles in shaping Kennedy's Vietnam policy. As
George Kahin and other historians have pointed out, they had a deep personal stake in upholding that policy.

On November 24, 1963, President Johnson instructed Ambassador Henry Cabot Lodge, Jr., to assure the generals who had overthrown Ngo Dinh Diem that they had the full support of the U.S. government. Two days later, the NSC incorporated his pledge into policy, affirming that it was "the central objective of the United States" to assist the "people and Government of South Vietnam to win their contest against the externally directed and supported communist conspiracy."

The post-Diem regime, as corrupt and unpopular as the one it replaced, was soon overthrown by another regime under General Nguyen Khanh. It was not much of an improvement. The countryside became increasingly insecure as peasants, alienated by the strategic hamlet program, either joined the Vietcong or acquiesced in their activities. Meanwhile, in the nation's cities, students and Buddhist activists demonstrated against the war and against a government that not only permitted but also engaged in widespread corruption. Saigon took on the appearance of an armed camp, with concrete sentry stations and barbed wire at nearly every intersection. General Khanh responded to this situation by gradually isolating himself both from the populace and from his own government.

Despite his promise to hold the line in Southeast Asia, Lyndon Johnson and his civilian advisers were absolutely opposed to a massive commitment of land forces on the Asian mainland at the outset. An infusion of U.S. troops, they reasoned, would undercut South Vietnam's prospects for self-reliance, provoke hostile propaganda throughout the developing world, and generate domestic dissent that would threaten both the Great Society programs and Johnson's chances for reelection. Thus, in mid-March the president rejected a recommendation by the Joint Chiefs of Staff for a drastic escalation of the war.

The Gulf of Tonkin Incident

Despite Johnson's rejection of the JCS's proposal, escalation did occur. In the spring of 1964, Johnson replaced the ineffectual Paul Harkins with General William Westmoreland as commander of U.S. forces in Vietnam. A decorated veteran of both World War II and Korea, Westmoreland was intelligent and loyal. He was an expert manager, an executive in uniform, who was confident that he could do the job with whatever tools the president gave him. During the next nine months, the United States increased the number of its advisers from 16,300 to 23,300 and poured an additional $50 million into Vietnam. By the summer of 1964, American soldiers were working with South Vietnamese officers at virtually every level, while civilian technicians spread out across the country to teach Vietnamese peasants scientific farming, doctors and nurses established rural health clinics, and public administration experts counseled village elders on modern methods of governance. Imports of American milk, fertilizer, and gasoline were sold for local currency, which was then used to pay South Vietnamese military and civilian officials.

Despite these efforts, South Vietnam grew increasingly less secure. According to American figures, by the late spring of 1964, 50% of the land area and 40% of the population were in NLF hands. In part, those figures were the result of military rule. Khanh and the Military Revolutionary Council (MRC) proved unable to create a democratic political structure or a social system that the average Vietnamese was willing to fight and die for. Indeed, led by the Buddhists, many inhabitants of the South viewed the government in Saigon as a ruthless dictatorship supported by a foreign power – the United States. Also contributing to the physical insecurity of the South was the decision by the government of North Vietnam in 1964 to take a more active role in the war. In that year, engineering battalions began widening and modernizing the Ho Chi Minh trail, a web of jungle paths extending south through Laos and Cambodia, entering South Vietnam at various points from just below the 17th parallel to just above Saigon. In 1964, 10,000 North Vietnamese Army (NVA) regulars made their way south along this network; three years later the number had risen to 20,000 a month.

In response to the deteriorating security situation in South Vietnam, some of Johnson's advisers devised a plan that called for the president, after first obtaining permission from Congress, to authorize a gradually escalating bombing campaign against North Vietnam. The administration, they realized, would require a specific provocation to justify such a move. Advocates of a bombing campaign did not have long to wait. On August 1, 1964, an American destroyer, the USS *Maddox*, was on patrol off the coast of North Vietnam in the Tonkin Gulf. Unbeknownst to Congress and the American people, the destroyer was acting in support of South Vietnamese seaborne commandos who were raiding north of the 17th parallel. North Vietnamese patrol boats attacked the *Maddox* and were fought off. Briefed on the incident, Johnson ordered the destroyer to continue its patrol and had the USS *Turner Joy* join it. In close support was the aircraft carrier *Ticonderoga*. On the night of August 4, in the midst of heavy seas, the *Maddox* reported contact with the enemy, and the American ships fired at what they believed were communist gunboats. Ignoring subsequent warnings from American naval personnel involved in the incident that the second attack might not have even occurred, the president ordered retaliatory attacks on North Vietnamese torpedo boat bases. The national press applauded the president's action. The attack on the *Maddox* was the "beginning of a mad adventure by the North Vietnamese Communists," declared the *New York Times*. The *Washington Post* hailed Johnson's "careful and effective handling of the Vietnam crisis." The president's approval rate shot up to 70%.

Immediately, Johnson went to Congress and asked for permission to take "all necessary measures to repel any armed attacks against the forces of the United States and to prevent further aggression." Senator J. William Fulbright, chairman of the Senate Foreign Relations Committee, other

Democrats, and moderate Republicans supported the resulting Gulf of Tonkin resolution because they believed that the president was really trying to control the war and that he was working to prevent a communist takeover while keeping America's role to a minimum. Fulbright and the Democrats, moreover, were convinced that Johnson needed greater freedom of action to fend off Barry Goldwater and the radical right in the 1964 presidential election. Following a brief debate, the Senate approved the Gulf of Tonkin resolution by a vote of 88 to 2. The discussion in the House lasted only 40 minutes, and the vote was unanimous. Johnson's easy victory increased his already large sense of mastery over Congress and led him to believe that he could proceed in Southeast Asia without further consultations. "It's like Grandmother's shirt," Press Secretary George Reedy said, referring to the resolution, "It covers everything." When doubts surrounding the authenticity of the second attack later became public, many senators and representatives would conclude that the White House had deliberately deceived them.

The Decision to Bomb

In February 1965, with coup and countercoup plots cropping up all around him, General Khanh resigned. The Joint Chiefs of Staff and General Maxwell Taylor, then ambassador to Vietnam, once again pressed the president to implement the "carefully orchestrated bombing attack" against North Vietnam that they had been advocating. Johnson continued to resist. He did not, he said, "wish to enter the patient in a ten-round bout when he was in no shape to hold out for one round." Influenced by the more hawkish of his advisers, however, the president soon concluded that the political situation in the South would never improve until there was security from communist attacks, and he blamed those attacks primarily on North Vietnam rather than the National Liberation Front and the Vietcong. On February 6, Vietcong units attacked a U.S. Army barracks in Pleiku and a nearby helicopter base. A month later, communist guerrillas destroyed an enlisted men's barracks at Quinhon. Apparently in response to these provocations, the president ordered a bombing campaign against North Vietnam. But Rolling Thunder was a gradually intensified campaign that was to continue regardless of provocations. Its goal was to force North Vietnam to stop sending troops and supplies into the South. Clearly, Pleiku and Quinhon were the pretext rather than the cause of the aerial assault on North Vietnam.

Anticipating retaliatory attacks by NVA and Vietcong troops, General Westmoreland asked for combat troops to protect the giant American air base at Danang. On March 8, 1965, two Marine battalions splashed ashore, the first regular combat units to be sent to Vietnam. But Westmoreland and the JCS wanted to do no less than change basic American strategy. By mid-March they had concluded that if the war in Vietnam were to be won, the

United States would have to assume a direct role. Consequently, he asked for two Army divisions, one to be stationed in the Central Highlands and the other in and around Saigon. At a high-level conference in Honolulu in April, McNamara, Taylor, and the JCS decided to put 40,000 troops in Vietnam and continue the bombing campaign against North Vietnam for six months to a year. They instructed Westmoreland to pursue an enclave strategy, that is, to restrict his troops to protecting a 50-mile area around major strategic positions leaving the countryside to the Army of the Republic of Vietnam and its auxiliaries.

To say that the Johnson administration escalated the war in Vietnam in secrecy would be to exaggerate. Nevertheless, the president continued to lead the American people to believe that the bombing of North Vietnam and the introduction of combat troops were in response to specific communist provocations rather than long-range strategic moves designed to provide security to a nation suffering from acute political instability. There was no call to arms, no mobilization. The first week in May, Johnson asked Congress for a $700-million supplementary appropriation for Vietnam and made it clear that passage would constitute approval of his policies. Ever ready to support troops in the field, Congress ignored the objections of Senators Frank Church (D-Idaho), George McGovern (D-South Dakota), and Wayne Morse (D-Oregon) and voted for the package by overwhelming margins. The *New York Times* proclaimed that "no one except a few pacifists here and the North Vietnamese and the Chinese Communists are asking for a precipitate withdrawal. Virtually all Americans understand we must stay in Vietnam at least for the near future."

Antiwar Stirrings
Nevertheless, the bombing of North Vietnam stimulated the infant anti-war movement in the United States. Faculty at Michigan, Syracuse, and Harvard held "teach-ins" against the war, and students staged small protest meetings. In April, 20,000 people assembled in Washington, D.C., to demonstrate against the escalation. They sang along with folksingers Joan Baez and Judy Collins and listened to Students for a Democratic Society (SDS) President Paul Potter call for a massive social movement to change America. Members of the crowd waved placards that read, "Get out of Saigon and into Selma. Freedom Now in Vietnam. War on Poverty not on People." Meanwhile, UN Secretary General U Thant joined a handful of antiwar senators in calling for a negotiated settlement to the war leading to the neutralization of Vietnam. Johnson responded to this criticism by sending the best and the brightest in his administration across the United States to explain his policies and gain support for the war. On April 7, the president delivered a major policy speech on Vietnam at Johns Hopkins University. He offered "unconditional negotiations" with the Democratic Republic of Vietnam (DRV) and outlined his plans for a billion-dollar

"Tennessee Valley Authority" for the Mekong Delta if the communists should cease their aggression. The speech was designed to mollify critics of the war rather than produce a negotiated settlement. The administration had no negotiating strategy. As long as the United States was committed to maintaining an independent, anticommunist state south of the 17th parallel, there would be no basis for negotiation. Ho Chi Minh was determined to reunify the country, expel foreign troops, and establish his version of a socialist system. The communist-led NLF viewed the military government in Saigon as a foreign-controlled, puppet regime dominated by northern Catholics intent on exploiting and oppressing the predominantly Buddhist South.

For five months following General Khanh's departure, South Vietnam was ruled ineffectively by a coalition of civilians headed by Phan Huy Quat. The Catholics felt he was too close to the Buddhist hierarchy, and the military unjustifiably accused him of plotting to negotiate with the NLF. In June, a military junta of ten senior officers took over in Saigon and selected Air Force General Nguyen Cao Ky to be prime minister. A flamboyant figure clad in a purple flying scarf and armed with twin revolvers, Ky seemed more qualified to be a playboy or a gangster than a political leader. His publicly stated admiration for Adolf Hitler did not reassure policymakers in Washington, D.C.

Americanizing the War

With the countryside no more secure than it had been in late 1964, and despite South Vietnam's demonstrated inability to establish a viable political system, the U.S. government decided on yet another escalation. Assistant NSC Adviser Walt W. Rostow argued that the United States and South Vietnam would never win the war unless they destroyed North Vietnam's industrial base. Meanwhile, Westmoreland and the military chiefs were pushing Johnson to abandon the enclave strategy and authorize a "search-and-destroy" approach, whereby a vastly expanded American force would be free to move about Vietnam seeking out and attacking the enemy wherever it was found. Although he had deep misgivings, Lyndon B. Johnson approved a course of action in late July that would result in a massive expenditure of lives and money in Vietnam in pursuit of goals that were at best ill defined. He directed the Air Force and Navy to intensify bombing of North Vietnam, although he limited activity to the area south of the 20th parallel, and he authorized saturation bombing by B-52s in areas of South Vietnam where the guerillas were particularly active. Most significant was his approval of Westmoreland's request for an additional 100,000 troops and a search-and-destroy strategy.

In late 1965, the first major battle of the war occurred. When the VC and NVA launched an offensive to capture control of the Central Highlands and cut South Vietnam in half, Westmoreland sent an airborne division to the Ia

Drang Valley, a densely forested area near Plieku, to stop them. For three days the Americans battled three North Vietnamese regiments. One U.S. battalion, outnumbered seven to one, withstood a dozen enemy human-wave attacks. American spotters called in massive air strikes, and artillery-men fired so fast that at times the barrels of their guns glowed red-hot. Brief but violent engagements continued for five days. In one of the last engagements near landing zone Albany, American units suffered a 60% casualty rate. A survivor recalled dead enemy snipers hanging from trees, tangled piles of bodies, and the ground sticky with blood. He labeled the scene "the devil's butcher shop." Between 2,000 and 3,000 NVA and VC were killed, while U.S. dead amounted to 240. For nearly two years after Ia Drang, the NVA avoided engaging U.S. troops in conventional warfare. Devastated by American firepower and combat training, the enemy shifted back to the guerrilla warfare tactics of ambush and hit and run. The battle momentarily whetted the U.S. public's appetite for the war. Columnist Joseph Alsop declared Ia Drang to be a series of "remarkable victories," and *U.S. News* trumpeted America's soldiers who had beat the "best the Communists could throw at them." "We'll lick them," declared Secretary of State Dean Rusk. The administration overestimated the public's stomach for a war of attrition, however.

As fighting intensified in Vietnam in 1965, the administration justified America's growing involvement on a number of grounds. The insurgency in the south was not indigenous, Johnson and his advisers insisted: the NLF and VC were creatures of North Vietnam whose aggression was comparable to North Korea's invasion of South Korea in 1950. The Gulf of Tonkin resolution was a natural extension of the Southeast Asia Treaty Organization (SEATO) treaty in which signatory nations agreed to come to each other's aid as well as designated nations in Southeast Asia if their "peace and safety" were endangered. The war in Vietnam constituted a violation of the UN Charter, which called on members to act jointly to combat aggression and authorized regional collective security organizations for that purpose. Finally, but most important, a failure to defend South Vietnam would indicate a lack of resolve to the communist world and undermine U.S. prestige among allied and uncommitted nations.

A War Without Fronts
Although he had taken a crucial step in Southeast Asia, the president continued to resist pressure to mobilize the United States for an all-out effort. He did address the country and told it that he was sending more troops, but he refused to call up the reserves or declare a state of national emergency. He was determined to do enough to satisfy "the Goldwater crowd" without inflaming public passions to the point where he could not control them. Missing from this analysis was the answer to the question of "how much was enough?" Even as the Johnson administration dramatically

escalated the war in Vietnam, it failed to face the possibility that politically and economically, South Vietnam did not exist. Nor did it succeed in
defining precisely U.S. strategic goals in the region or in calculating the
cost of achieving those objectives. Underestimating North Vietnam's will,
American policymakers assumed that they could simply apply more and
more firepower and continue to introduce troops until the communists
gave up.

American bombing of North Vietnam increased in both intensity and
scope during the period from 1965 through 1967. Johnson authorized
American pilots to attack not only troop concentrations and transportation networks, but also supply dumps, steel mills, and petroleum storage
tanks. Gradually, American operations moved up the peninsula until Navy
and Air Force planes were attacking targets around Hanoi and Haiphong.
The tonnage of American bombs dropped on the north increased from
63,000 in 1965 to 226,000 in 1967, and inflicted an estimated $600 mil-
lion in damage on a country whose entire population hovered at or below
what the census bureau defined as the poverty line for American incomes.
According to American estimates, 52,000 civilians were killed during the
course of Rolling Thunder between 1965 and 1968, and by 1967 there were
reports of significant malnutrition in the nation's cities. Nevertheless, the
North continued to pour troops into the South. Teams of engineers supervising peasant conscripts repaired damage almost as soon as the sound
of attacking bombers had faded. Entire munitions plants were disassem-
bled and rebuilt underground. The Soviet Union and Communist China
vied with each other to replace destroyed tanks, trucks, and munitions. By
1967, major population centers were surrounded by anti-aircraft systems,
and U.S. aircraft losses amounted to 500 by the end of that year. Finally,
captured American airmen gave Hanoi great leverage when peace negotiations would at last get underway.

Meanwhile, on the ground, Westmoreland's aggressive strategy required
more and more men. By the end of 1966, 431,000 American military personnel were either directly or indirectly involved in the war in Vietnam.
Sophisticated computers were put to work predicting the enemy's movements. The U.S. command declared areas where the VC and NVA were
particularly active to be free fire zones, and from 1965 through 1967 American B-52s dropped more than 1 million tons of bombs on South Vietnam.
To strip the enemy of cover, C-123 Ranch Hand crews sprayed more than
100 million tons of defoliants, including Agent Orange, over the jungles and
forests. Yet the countryside became less, rather than more, secure. Hanoi
recognized that its opponents were vulnerable in three areas: the South
Vietnamese government, the South Vietnamese military, and U.S. public
opinion. After the NVA fought several division-level engagements early in
the war, it concentrated on small-unit, hit-and-run operations.

As had happened with occupying powers from time immemorial, the
United States found the enemy's guerrilla tactics difficult to deal with. The

VC refused to wear uniforms for the most part, and it was very difficult to tell friend from foe. "You always had to watch your back," one soldier observed. In the village "you had women and kids as warriors and you really didn't know who was trustworthy and who wasn't. It was all a battlefield." With no fixed battle lines, body count became the measure of failure or success. By late 1967, even allowing for inflation, U.S. and allied forces had inflicted 250,000 casualties on their opponents. Unfortunately, 200,000 Vietnamese reached draft age each year.

To many people's surprise, the Ky government managed to endure, although the Air Force ace failed to generate any broad-based popular support. Increasingly, the Army of the Republic of Vietnam (ARVN) was shunted aside by the American military, thus suffering still another blow to its already shaky morale and prestige. In February 1966, President Johnson traveled to Honolulu to hold an ostentatious meeting with General Ky at which he publicly embraced his diminutive ally and reaffirmed America's commitment to South Vietnam.

In part, the Honolulu summit was designed to draw attention away from televised hearings on the war then being conducted by the Senate Foreign Relations Committee. The powerful chairman of that body, J. William Fulbright, had supported the Gulf of Tonkin resolution. He was assured at the time that the resolution would not involve the United States in a wider war in Southeast Asia. The ensuing escalation left the Arkansan feeling deceived and betrayed. In January 1966, after the administration ended a month-long bombing halt, Fulbright decided to challenge the administration publicly over the war, beginning with an official investigation into the origins and justification of American involvement in Vietnam. With CBS television covering the hearings live, a host of distinguished Americans, including General James Gavin and George Kennan, State Department planner and architect of the containment policy, urged the administration to proceed with extreme caution in Vietnam. The committee grilled Maxwell Taylor and Secretary of State Dean Rusk for hours, and Fulbright read a letter from an anonymous soldier who declared that the United States was losing the war. America, argued the disillusioned GI, had simply replaced France in the role of the hated westerner in the eyes of both the North and the South Vietnamese. Fulbright's disgust with the administration, especially Rusk, was palpable.

Despite the Honolulu Conference, Ky's troubles mounted. In April, he had to dispatch 2,000 troops to Danang, ferried in on U.S. helicopters, to put down an uprising headed by a disaffected corp commander and a Buddhist monk. Undeterred, the Buddhist hierarchy, normally apolitical, continued to lead demonstrations and protests, organize boycotts, and mobilize other dissident elements in response to official oppression and corruption. In response to pressure from the Buddhists and their student allies, the government in Saigon convened a constituent assembly in September. Delegates voted in favor of an American-style constitution complete with

Map 7–1. The Vietnam War, to 1968. Wishing to guarantee an independent, noncommunist government in South Vietnam, Lyndon Johnson remarked in 1965, "We fight because we must fight if we are to live in a world where every country can shape its own destiny. To withdraw from one battlefield means only to prepare for the next."

bicameral legislature and strong president. In the ensuing election, the military ticket with General Nguyen Van Thieu running as president and Ky as vice president won, but it did so with only a 35% plurality of the vote.

Meanwhile, the huge American presence in South Vietnam and the billions of dollars that accompanied it was shredding the fabric of Vietnamese society. Funds generated by the war went for consumer goods and not infrastructure and manufacturing. Virtually all Vietnamese were dependent directly or indirectly on the United States for their livelihood. Prices increased by as much as 170% during the first two years of the buildup. Corruption was always present in Vietnam, but during the second Indo-Chinese war, no transaction was possible without a payoff, and life consisted more and more of the strong preying on the weak.

Revolt at Home

By 1967, the war had spawned a bitter, divisive debate within the United States. On the right were those who insisted that the administration was not doing enough. Goldwater Republicans and conservative Democrats, most of them southern, were "hawks." Communism was an unmitigated evil, the regime in Hanoi was an extension of Sino–Soviet imperialism, and Vietnam was the keystone in a regional arch that they believed would collapse if America lost its nerve. Led by Richard Russell of Georgia and John Stennis of Mississippi in the Senate and Mendell Rivers in the House, these superpatriots enjoyed close ties to the JCS and the entire military–industrial complex. They chafed under the restrictions imposed on the war by Lyndon Johnson; he would not allow American troops to invade North Vietnam nor the Air Force to bomb communist sanctuaries in Cambodia, and he demanded that the United States do whatever was necessary to win a military victory.

Acting as a counterpoint to the hawks were a diverse collection of individuals and groups who opposed the war, viewing it variously as immoral, illogical, or counterproductive. The antiwar coalition included establishment figures such as Senators William Fulbright (D-Arkansas), George McGovern (D-South Dakota), and Wayne Morse (D-Oregon), but gradually drew in figures who were not professional politicians or policymakers, such as civil rights leader Martin Luther King, Jr., actress Jane Fonda, pediatrician and author Dr. Benjamin Spock, and heavyweight champion Muhammad Ali. As historians George Herring and Charles DiBenedetti pointed out, the doves were responding to essentially three frames of reference. For lifelong pacifists such as A. J. Muste and the Catholic priests Daniel and Philip Berrigan, all wars were immoral, but Vietnam was especially evil because the nature of the enemy and the threat posed to U.S. interests were both debatable. Next there were disillusioned Cold War liberals such as Fulbright and former Undersecretary of State George Ball. They had initially supported the Cold War believing that in combating communism, the United States was fighting for freedom and peaceful coexistence and against totalitarianism and imperialism. Over time they had come to view the Soviet Union as a traditional power that must be contained but that could be negotiated with. In its obsessive anticommunism, the United States was siding with military dictators and building an empire that had the potential to become as repressive as the one established under Sino–Soviet auspices. Indeed, they argued, the war in Vietnam was undermining America's credibility with the very people in the Third World whose allegiance the West was struggling to gain. Finally, the antiwar movement included left-wing students and intellectuals, many of whom had been active in the civil rights movement and who saw the war as an expression of an essentially corrupt political and economic system. Because this third strain, which became known as the New Left, grew out of established radical organizations, was related to the civil rights movement, and sometimes seemed to overlap with the burgeoning counterculture of the 1960s, it was initially the most visible component of the antiwar coalition.

As American television displayed the horrors of Vietnam on a daily basis and escalating American involvement produced a dramatic expansion of the draft, the increasingly student-driven antiwar movement gained momentum. Until 1965, the mass of young people in the United States paid little attention to the war in Vietnam. The sixties generation was having too much fun testing its new moral limits. *Newsweek* surveyed students on a number of college campuses and found that more than 90% expressed confidence in higher education, big corporations, and the federal government, and more than 80% were satisfied with college and held positive views about organized religion and the armed forces. That would change. In November 1965, some 30,000 people convened in Washington, D.C., to stage the largest demonstration against the war to that time. As the bombing and troop levels increased, the protests and demonstrations grew correspondingly. Opposition to the conflict in Southeast Asia took many forms. Students against the war burned their draft cards, fled to Canada, or even mutilated themselves as part of a dual effort to protest the war and avoid serving in Vietnam. By war's end, the draft resistance movement had produced 570,000 draft offenders and 563,000 less-than-honorable discharges from the military. Folk singer Joan Baez refused to pay that part of her income tax that went to support the war. Muhammad Ali filed for conscientious objector status, a move that produced some derision given his career as a professional pugilist. Three enlisted men – the Ft. Hood Three – challenged the constitutionality of the war from their encampment in Texas and refused to fight in what they termed an "unjust, immoral, and illegal war." But it was the mass demonstrations, carried inevitably by the major networks live or on the nightly news, that had the greatest impact on the public and the White House. In the spring of 1967, 500,000 marchers of all ages converged on New York City's Central Park, some of them chanting "Hey, hey, LBJ, how many kids did you kill today?" That October 100,000 antiwar activists gathered in Washington, D.C. For a time, one third of their number managed to block the entrance to the Pentagon, which protest leaders termed the "nerve center of American militarism." Returning veterans were sometimes subject to harassment and ostracism. On returning home from Vietnam in 1968, one soldier recalled how "there was a lot of antiwar movement going on. It hadn't been like that when I left, so I wasn't expecting it." Because he had no money, he decided to hitchhike home, but soon found that in a uniform "you were the kiss of death. No one would touch me."

Many Americans were offended by antiwar protests and demonstrations. They tended to lump participants together with those who staged the urban riots of the mid-1960s and with counterculture extremists who, for example, attempted to glorify multiple-rapist Caryl Chessman as a revolutionary hero. Indeed, polls showed that a majority of the American people found the antiwar movement, especially its counterculture, "hippie" component, more repugnant than the war itself. But the countless demonstrations and acts of defiance kept popular attention focused on the war and created a sense of disunity that helped sap the will to fight that war. As demonstrators became more unruly and police less tolerant and more repressive in their handling of the protests, it seemed to many people that the conflict in Vietnam was spreading to the United States and threatening its fundamental processes and institutions.

Popular support for the war, particularly Johnson's handling of it, dropped off sharply during 1967. In early August, the president was forced to go to Congress and ask for a 10% surtax on incomes to help cover the skyrocketing deficit. Suddenly, business leaders began to voice doubts about the war and formerly hawkish publications, such as *Time* magazine, began to insist on a basic reconsideration of policy. As draft calls climbed to 30,000 a month and the total American death toll reached 13,000, hawks as well as doves began to view the war as a mistake. Johnson's approval rating began to plummet.

By 1967, the administration itself was deeply divided over the war. On the one hand, the JCS continued to press for an all-out commitment, and Westmoreland requested 200,000 additional troops. On the other hand, White House staffer Bill Moyers and Undersecretary of State George Ball resigned in 1966, in part out of opposition to the war. Indeed, by late 1966, Robert McNamara, who had played such a prominent role in the decisions to escalate, was coming to the conclusion that the costly conflict in Southeast Asia was impairing America's ability to resist communist aggression and subversion in other, more important areas of the globe. The former Ford executive was concerned, moreover, that the cost of the war was promoting runaway inflation and undermining the economic health of the nation. The bombing of North Vietnam, he confessed to Johnson in 1967, was doing no good. Virtually all major military targets had been destroyed, and still the NVA kept coming. He advised the president to limit strikes to staging areas just north of the 17th parallel and to place a ceiling on troop levels. McNamara would leave the administration at the end of the year to take a position as head of the World Bank.

While Johnson was struggling with the complex issues of Southeast Asia, he had to deal with a host of other areas and problems: rioting in Panama, chaos in the Dominican Republic, a major outbreak of fighting in the Middle East, the ongoing campaign to achieve détente with the Soviet Union, and the dual effort to either oust or co-opt Fidel Castro. Inevitably, these issues and events became intertwined with Vietnam and demonstrated the dangers of overcommitment.

Managing the Cold War: The Rest of the World

The Dominican Crisis

The conditions in Latin America that had prompted the Kennedy administration to launch the Alliance for Progress and search for "openings to the left" continued to persist. Although some republics had taken tentative steps down the road to democracy, most were still ruled by military strong men who represented the army, the large landowners, and foreign capitalists, particularly U.S. companies. Huge economic gaps separated tiny elites from an impoverished peasantry and proletariat. Despite the Good Neighbor Policy, Point Four, and the Alliance for Progress, many Latinos remembered and resented years of Yankee intervention. Moreover, despite its rhetoric, Washington, D.C., in its insistence on funneling aid through private channels, seemed as intent as ever in supporting its corporations with vested interests in Latin America.

Lyndon Johnson was sensitive to the plight of the Latin masses, but he was more sensitive to the continuing threat Fidel Castro posed to his administration – in a political if not a strategic sense. Johnson could not forget how much public support the GOP had attracted by accusing Kennedy and the Democrats of failing to liberate Cuba. The direction that his Latin American policy would take became apparent when he appointed Thomas Mann, a Texas lawyer and former ambassador to Mexico, assistant secretary of state for Latin American affairs. A strident anticommunist, Mann was committed to maintaining political stability in the republics to the south, ensuring that they would continue to be lucrative investment fields for U.S. capitalists. When revolution erupted in the Dominican Republic, toppling the existing government and producing chaos in the capital city, it was the Mann philosophy that prevailed.

The causes of the Dominican Republic's many troubles were varied, but most were rooted in the 30-year dictatorship of Rafael Leonidas Trujillo

Molina. Trujillo had brutally suppressed all opposition, turned the army into his personal palace guard, and ravaged his country's fragile economy. Then, in the summer of 1961, assassins shot him in the head. His family tried to perpetuate his tyranny without him, but failed and then fled into exile. In December 1962, the Dominicans elected the liberal intellectual, Juan Bosch, to the presidency. Seven months later, a military coup overthrew him, its leaders charging that he was too tolerant of communists and Marxism. Despite support from the Johnson administration for the new government of Donald Reid Cabral and the presence of some 2,500 Americans on the island, stability eluded the Dominicans. Drought, widespread unemployment, strikes, sabotage, and continuing opposition from dissidents kept the country in constant turmoil. From exile in Puerto Rico where he was employed as a college professor, Juan Bosch directed the disruptive activities of the Dominican Revolutionary Party (PRD).

The spring of 1965 found the Dominican military deeply divided. A minority was devoted to Bosch's return, but the majority regarded him as a dangerous revolutionary who would "open the door to the communists" and, more to the point, do away with the military's privileges. When officers loyal to Reid Cabral attempted to arrest some of their fellows for plotting against the government on behalf of Juan Bosch, the PRD declared a general uprising and surrounded the presidential palace. At this point, the anti-Bosch military, led by the pious and reactionary General Elias Wessin y Wessin, issued an ultimatum to the PRD demanding that it cease its insurrection and turn over power to the army. Wessin had become convinced that Bosch and the PRD were encouraging the Castroite 14th of June Movement. When the rebels ignored his demand, air force planes began bombing and strafing the palace, as well as the slums of Santo Domingo, which were Bosch strongholds and, in the minds of the military, seedbeds of communist agitation. The brutal attacks inflamed the population, which flooded into the streets in response to calls from the PRD. At this point, Santo Domingo teetered on the edge of chaos. Under the auspices of Ambassador W. Tapley Bennett, who decided that the embassy could no longer remain aloof, the anti-Bosch military put together a junta headed by Col. Pedro Bartolome Benoit. The primary purpose of this government was to request armed intervention by the United States.

On the afternoon of April 28, while President Johnson met with his advisers on Vietnam, Undersecretary Mann and Bennett exchanged a flurry of telegrams. Bennett managed to convince the State Department that given General Wessin and Colonel Benoit's inability to control the situation in Santo Domingo, there was a very real danger of a communist, Castro-controlled takeover in the Dominican Republic. All "responsible" elements agreed that U.S. Marines should be dispatched at once, and he agreed with them, Bennett declared. Mann then advised the ambassador that he must compel Benoit to base his request for American intervention on the need to protect American lives. "We did instruct our Ambassador to go back to Benoit...and in order to improve our juridical base asked him to specifically say that he could not protect the lives of American citizens," Mann subsequently admitted to the Senate Foreign Relations Committee (SFRC). In his later cables, as a result, Bennett insisted that the large number of Americans residing at the Hotel Embajador were in danger of being killed or wounded.

The first week in May reporters flooded into the Dominican Republic determined to check out the administration's version of events. They quickly discovered that no American civilian had been killed or even wounded at the Hotel Embajador or anywhere else on the island. Pressed, anonymous sources in the American embassy declared that they had in their possession the names of 58 communists who had led the uprising against Reid Cabral. Editorials in the *New York Times*, New York *Herald Tribune*, and *Washington Post* began to question the administration's reasoning and veracity. The notion that 58 communists posed a massive threat in any Latin American country, even one as small as the Dominican Republic, seemed ludicrous.

The ever-sensitive Johnson overreacted. He began exaggerating. He described scenes that never took place, misquoted cables for dramatic effect, and ridiculed his detractors. More troops were going into Santo Domingo; the issue was now greater even than the loss of American lives, he proclaimed. The Dominican Republic must be saved from "other evil forces." On television he told the American people that another Cuba seemed likely in the Dominican Republic. "We don't intend to sit here in our rocking chair with our hands folded and let the Communists set up any governments in the Western Hemisphere," he declared. Soon 20,000 American troops were in place in and around Santo Domingo.

Senator Fulbright led a chorus of critics inside and outside the United States. There was no communist menace in the Dominican Republic, the chairman of the SFRC declared. Professional anticommunists in the State Department had formed a tacit alliance with "Latin American oligarchs who are engaged in a vain attempt to preserve the status quo – reactionaries who habitually use the term communist very loosely." Various Latin nations pointed out that the interjection of troops violated the charter of the Organization of American States (OAS), which stipulated that "no State or group of States had the right to intervene, directly or indirectly, for any reason whatever, in the internal or external affairs of any other State." Predictably, the U.S. force became bogged down in the struggle between the faction of the military loyal to bankers, businessmen, and large landowners and the faction loyal to Bosch, which was committed to social change and economic justice.

Although Johnson loudly continued to defend his actions in the Dominican Republic, the State Department arranged for an OAS meeting in Washington, D.C., in May 1965, where the members' deputy foreign ministers narrowly voted to send an inter-American peace force to the unsettled island. Under cover of this multinational army, U.S. forces withdrew. In June 1966, Joaquin Balaguer, a moderate rightist, defeated Bosch in the presidential election. Balaguer quieted the island by taking a few of Bosch's followers into the cabinet, but his opponent remained bitter. "A democratic revolution had been smashed by the leading democracy of the world," he proclaimed. But Johnson remained convinced that he had prevented the establishment of yet another communist beachhead in the Western Hemisphere. "What can we do in Vietnam if we can't clean up the Dominican Republic?" he remarked to an adviser.

In 1967, in an effort to revive flagging interest in the Alliance for Progress, Johnson convened leaders from some 20 Latin American nations at the Uruguayan resort of Punta del Este. His stated goal was to create a mini-Marshall Plan for the hemisphere, but disgruntled senators led by former foreign aid supporters, such as Fulbright and Senator Wayne Morse (D-Oregon), passed a resolution indicating that the Upper House would not go along with the massive aid program that Johnson envisioned. By the end of the 1960s, the Alliance had made little impact on Latin America. Aid had not been tied to land reform, rent controls, or the economic diversification necessary to produce new jobs. By 1969, the United States had spent $9.2 billion on hemispheric development, but so great was the population growth that gross productivity per capita increased by only 1.5%.

Much recent scholarship has argued that Johnson's anticommunism was political rather than philosophical and emotional. The Dominican intervention stemmed from his fear that the GOP would accuse him of presiding over the creation of another Cuba. Similarly, he remembered Joe McCarthy's vicious and profitable attacks on Truman and Acheson for "losing" China to the communists. In support of their interpretation, these historians cite the fact that while pursuing bellicose policies in Southeast Asia and Central America, Johnson worked quietly to further the policy of détente that had begun during the last days of the Kennedy administration. Nikita Khrushchev was suddenly deposed in October 1964, but his successors, Leonid Brezhnev and Alexei N. Kosygin, indicated their willingness to work on improved relations with the West. Advocates of détente such as Fulbright argued that the Soviet Union was a satiated, status quo power that wanted peaceful coexistence just as much as the United States did. In 1964, Russian and American diplomats worked out an agreement providing for the exchange of scholars, artists, and scientists. They inaugurated direct air service between Washington, D.C., and Moscow. President Johnson took up the cause of nuclear nonproliferation. Following three years of difficult negotiations, the Soviet Union, the United States, Great Britain, and 58 other nations signed the historic document. It constrained

Map 7–2. Retreat of colonialism after 1945.

UNITED
KINGDOM

TUNISIA
1956

MALTA
1964

CYPRUS
1960

SYRIA
1944
1961

Egypt & Syria

JORDAN
1946

ISRAEL
1948

KUWAIT
1961

PAKISTAN 1947

MOROCCO
1956

ALGERIA
1962

LIBYA
1951

QATAR
1971

OMAN 1951

INDIA
1947

WESTERN
SAHARA

MAURITANIA
1960

MALI
1960

NIGER
1960

CHAD
1960

SUDAN
1956

YEMEN
1967

DJIBOUTI
1977

CAPE VERDE
1975

SENEGAL
1960

GAMBIA
1965

GUINEA-BISSAU 1974

GUINEA 1958

SIERRA
LEONE
1961

IVORY
COAST
1960

BURKINA
FASO
1960

GHANA
1957

TOGO
1960

BENIN
1960

NIGERIA
1960

CAMEROON
1960

CENTRAL
AFRICAN REP.
1960

SOMALIA
1960

MALDIVES
1965

SRI LANKA
(CEYLON)
1948

SÃO TOME AND
PRÍNCIPE 1975

EQUAT
GUINEA
1968

CONGO 1960

GABON
1960

UGANDA
1962

RWANDA
1962

BURUNDI
1962

KENYA
1963

Kikuyu

Nairobi

SEYCHELLES
1976

ZAIRE
1960

TANZANIA
1961

ANGOLA
1975

MALAWI
1964

GOMOROS
1975

ZAMBIA
1964

ZIMBABWE
1965

MOZAMBIQUE
1975

MADAGASCAR
1960

NAMIBIA
1990

BOTS-
WANA
1966

SWAZILAND
1968

LESOTHO
1966

the nuclear powers from transferring atomic weapons technology to third parties and committed the nonnuclear powers to refrain from manufacturing or receiving nuclear weapons.

Cracks in the Alliance

America's North Atlantic allies generally welcomed the Johnson administration's efforts to achieve détente, but a number of allies believed that they did not go far enough. In fact, most were increasingly concerned about the drain on U.S. (and, therefore, Western) power and prestige caused by Vietnam. For these and other reasons, NATO began to lose cohesiveness. The principal advocate of an independent course for Europe was France's Charles De Gaulle, who not only called for the neutralization of Southeast Asia but also extended formal diplomatic recognition to the People's Republic of China in 1964 and made overtures to the communist governments of Eastern Europe. Announcing that his country no longer wanted to be tied to an alliance dominated by the United States and Great Britain, whom he labeled non-European powers, de Gaulle withdrew France militarily from NATO in 1966 and compelled the alliance to remove its headquarters from French soil. The Atlantic alliance was further weakened by a bitter dispute between Greece and Cyprus, a Mediterranean island whose Greek and Turkish populations had lived in a state of mutual hostility for decades.

The Johnson administration shared Kennedy's vision of a vast free trade area stretching from the Atlantic community to Japan within which goods and services could move without hindrance. That vision if not wrecked became temporarily snagged on the rocks of French nationalism. De Gaulle not only blocked Britain's entry into the Common Market, but worked assiduously to prevent the melding of Europe's economies with those of Asia and the Western Hemisphere. Nevertheless, the so-called Kennedy Round of negotiations conducted under the auspices of the General Agreement on Trade and Tariffs started in due course and was completed by 1967. Despite intense differences over issues such as access to the continent for U.S. agricultural products, the negotiators managed a series of agreements that cut tariffs on goods traded among the United States and the Common Market countries by an average of 35%.

The Middle East Cauldron: The 1967 War

In the aftermath of World War II, the United States took on the role of protector of the noncommunist world from Soviet and subsequently Chinese imperialism and from the "scourge" of Marxism-Leninism. Indeed, some policymakers and most Americans came to equate Marxism-Leninism with Sino–Soviet imperialism. The enormous task the United States defined for itself, then, was to protect the entire world from direct and indirect communist aggression. With the development of other global power centers and the growing importance of such non–Cold War issues as anticolonialism and the socioeconomic gap between the northern and southern hemispheres, America's ability to act as arbiter of world affairs diminished sharply. The United States would have to pick and choose, intervening in those areas that bore directly on its national interest strategically and economically defined. Vietnam prevented such a rational course. Indeed, America's inability to prevent the outbreak of the Six-Day War in the Middle East in 1967 and the polarization that followed indicated just how out of balance United States foreign policy was in the 1960s. Given America's increasing dependence on the Middle East for oil and its special relationship with the new state of Israel, its interests were far more compelling in that area of the world than in Southeast Asia.

Relations between pan-Arab nationalists, led by Egypt's Gamal Abdel Nasser, and Israel had grown increasingly tense in the years following the 1956 Suez crisis. The United States insisted that it was following a "balanced" policy in the region supplying both sides with arms, but in reality the aid that it rendered to Israel, direct and indirect, far outstripped that given to Israel's enemies. In fact, most aid given to the Islamic states went not to the so-called front-line nations bordering Israel, such as Egypt, Jordan, and Syria, but to Saudi Arabia and the conservative (that is, religious, socially and politically hierarchical, and diplomatically cautious) Gulf emirates. Meanwhile, Nasser continued to receive planes, tanks, and artillery from the Soviet Union. In 1964, he joined with other Arab leaders in sponsoring creation of the Palestinian Liberation Organization (PLO) whose objective was to destroy the state of Israel and secure the return of the hundreds of thousands of Palestinians who had been driven from their homes in 1948.

In May 1967, Nasser persuaded the United Nations to withdraw the peacekeeping force that had been inserted between Egyptian and Israeli forces following the Suez imbroglio. The two adversaries faced each other directly across a huge demilitarized zone for the first time since 1956. Nasser moved quickly to fill the void. He ordered his army and air force to occupy the Sinai Peninsula, which it did, in the process seizing the strategically crucial town of Sharm el-Sheikh, which overlooked the Gulf of Aqaba. This waterway, separating Egypt from the Arabian Peninsula, was Israel's only outlet to the Indian Ocean. At the same time, PLO fedayeen guerrillas launched attacks against Jewish settlements from their bases in the Sinai as well as from Jordan and Syria.

Convinced that the front-line states and the PLO intended to attack, the Israelis decided to stage a preemptive strike. On June 6, the Israeli air force flew across the Mediterranean to avoid Egyptian radar and then attacked from the north. Catching Egypt's planes on the ground, the Israelis virtually destroyed Nasser's air force. This scene was repeated in Jordan and Syria. For the next six days, the Israeli army followed up on this initial success invading and occupying the Sinai, the old city of Jerusalem, the West Bank of the Jordan, and the strategic Golan Heights just inside Syria's border. With the capture of Sharm el-Sheikh, the Israelis once again controlled an outlet to the Arabian Gulf and through it the Indian Ocean.

Moscow and Washington, D.C., stayed in close touch throughout the crisis using the "hotline" telephone, lessening the chance that the Six-Day War would escalate into a great power confrontation. Indeed, it was the Soviet Union that introduced and ushered a cease-fire resolution on June 11 through the UN Security Council. When that measure passed and the combatants signed off on it, the fighting came to an end. In November, the Security Council approved Resolution 242, which was designed to bring about a negotiated settlement to the ongoing Middle East crisis. It called for a multilateral guarantee of Israel's borders in exchange for a return of the territory seized in the Six-Day War. In addition, Israel would enjoy free access to "regional waterways" (Nasser had ordered the Suez Canal blocked with sunken ships shortly after Israel attacked) in the area, whereas the Palestinians could look forward to "a just settlement of the refugee problem," a provision they interpreted to mean the conversion of what used to be called Palestine (Israel and parts of the current state of Jordan) into a multinational state, including both Jews and Palestinians.

The United States supported Resolution 242 but was at the same time extremely sympathetic to Israel's fears concerning its security. The Jewish state insisted that the Arab nations would have to extend formal recognition and give guarantees before the land seized in the Six-Day War was returned. As the United States continued to replace Israeli military equipment and to subsidize the Israeli economy, an angry Nasser severed diplomatic ties with Washington, D.C. When Israel refused to evacuate the Sinai and return the Gaza Strip, the West Bank, and the Golan Heights, Moscow severed relations with Tel Aviv. The U.S. government and various third parties attempted mediation but with no success. Fedayeen border raids and terrorist attacks mounted in number, while Israel ruled the territories under its control with an iron hand. The region remained ripe for another explosion.

Summary
Both the Kennedy and Johnson administrations were committed to peaceful coexistence with the communist superpowers and desirous of promoting social justice and democracy in the developing world. Indeed, the presidents and their foreign policy advisers recognized that the United States would have to dissociate itself from the vestiges of western imperialism if it and the free world were to win the battle for hearts and minds. Unfortunately, the American people and many of their political representatives were unwilling or unable to distinguish between Marxism-Leninism as a

social and economic theory and Sino–Soviet imperialism. Thus, it was that when revolutions in Cuba and Vietnam, revolutions that were primarily indigenous and aimed at overthrowing entrenched oligarchies and their foreign sponsors, endorsed Marxism-Leninism and accepted aid from the communist superpowers, the U.S. government threw caution to the winds, going to war with the DRV and seeking the overthrow of Castro.

America's obsession with Cuba and Vietnam distorted its relationship with the rest of the world. Its opposition to revolutions in those countries destroyed its credibility with revolutionary nationalists from all nations and of every ideological persuasion. It stretched the nation's military and economic resources to the breaking point and polarized American society. The United States was not able to overthrow Castro, but it made allegiance to the anti-Castro crusade a litmus test for every government in the hemisphere. Neither was it able to defeat revolutionary nationalism in Vietnam. The ongoing war strained the North Atlantic alliance, creating fears among America's allies that the United States had lost both the will and the ability to help defend Western Europe. In its determination to combat communism on every front, it seemed America had rendered itself incapable of defeating it on any front. Many policymakers and sophisticated observers in the United States understood the imbalance and distortion Vietnam and Cuba had introduced into American foreign policy, but the strength of domestic anticommunism barred them from pursuing a more pragmatic course.

ADDITIONAL READINGS

Beschloss, Michael, *The Crisis Years: Kennedy and Khrushchev, 1960–1963* (1991).

Brands, H. W., *The Wages of Globalism: Lyndon Johnson and the Limits of American Power* (1995).

DeBenedetti, Charles, and Charles Chatfield, *An American Ordeal: The Antiwar Movement of the Vietnam Era* (1990).

Higgins, Trumbull, *The Perfect Failure: Kennedy, Eisenhower and the Bay of Pigs* (1987).

Kahin, George McT., *Intervention: How America Became Involved in Vietnam* (1986).

Kuniholm, Bruce R., *The Origins of the Cold War in the Near East: Great Power Conflict in Iran, Turkey and Greece* (1980).

Paterson, Thomas, Ed., *Kennedy's Quest for Victory: American Foreign Policy, 1961–1963* (1989).

Schulzinger, Robert D., *A Time for War: The United States and Vietnam, 1941–1975* (1998).

Young, Marilyn B., *The Vietnam Wars, 1945–1990* (1991).

8   The Dividing of America

Vietnam, Black Power, the Counterculture, and the Election of 1968

Fundamental divisions in American society and basic flaws in the nation's approach to international affairs came to the surface during the 1960s and roiled the political and social waters. The decade had begun on a hopeful note with the election of a young, seemingly idealistic president by a populace ready for change. But John F. Kennedy's victory was by the barest of margins. A substantial portion of the American people were fundamentally conservative, determined to cling to the mores and folkways that had so long prevailed. The illusion of consensus that Kennedy's triumph and the enactment of Lyndon B. Johnson's Great Society programs created was just that, an illusion. The great "silent majority," a term Richard Nixon would coin in 1970, was white, lower middle class, and determined to protect its hard-won social and economic gains. They distrusted government, seeing it as an agency of unwanted racial integration and taxation, and they believed that minority groups ought not to disturb social tranquility in their various quests. Indeed, many viewed women, blacks, and Hispanics as having selfish special interests. They believed that the only good communist was a dead one, that all Americans ought to be Christians, and that government existed to help them to do what they wanted to do. This conservatism was deepened and broadened by the increasingly strident posture taken by the disadvantaged and by opponents of the war in Southeast Asia.

Black Power: The Radicalization of the Civil Rights Movement

The civil rights movement had created a rising level of expectations among African Americans, and released anger and resentment that had been suppressed for decades. When traditional forms of protest and nonviolent civil disobedience failed to end discrimination and create equal opportunity, young blacks rejected the gradualist approach espoused by the National Association for the Advancement of Colored People (NAACP) and the

Southern Christian Leadership Conference (SCLC). Revolutionary activists such as Stokely Carmichael, H. Rap Brown, and Bobby Seale took over existing organizations or formed new ones that called for whatever means necessary, including violence, to achieve equality and opportunity for African Americans. They were aided and abetted by black writers and intellectuals such as Eldridge Cleaver (*Soul on Ice*, 1967) and James Baldwin (*The Fire Next Time*, 1963) who moved beyond Richard Wright and Ralph Ellison in their anger and their vision of an apocalyptic end to the struggle of African Americans against oppression and exploitation.

At the same time the civil rights movement provided an example and stimulus to thousands of white, affluent college students, those baby boomers who had reached college age in the 1960s and who despite the comfort of their existence felt powerless and unfulfilled. During the 1960s, these rebels without a cause found what they were looking for. Some went South to participate directly in civil rights activities. Others joined the free speech movement and devoted themselves to democratizing the nation's colleges and universities. Still others worked to change the fundamental philosophy on which America's political and economic institutions were based. By 1968, virtually all had united in opposition to the war in Vietnam, a conflict they believed epitomized all that was wrong with American society: its racism, its ignorance of and prejudice against other cultures and lifestyles, its seduction by the military–industrial complex, its white male elitism, and its imperial arrogance. In 1968, they clashed with those Americans who believed that their country with all its flaws was still the land of the brave and the home of the free, that despite inequities in society, the Constitution and the free enterprise system were the best means available for creating opportunity and equality, and that the war in Vietnam, if mishandled, had been entered into with the highest of motives. The result was a year of violence and strife that brought the United States to the edge of a national nervous breakdown.

The Ghettos Explode

The Black Power movement had its roots in slavery and reconstruction, but more immediately in the sharp disillusionment of African Americans with the gains of the contemporary civil rights movement. Long smoldering resentment burst forth in a series of ghetto riots that pockmarked the national landscape during the last half of the 1960s. Less than a week after President Johnson signed the 1965 Civil Rights Act, young, unemployed African Americans had begun looting, firebombing, and otherwise wrecking businesses in the Watts area of Los Angeles. Their objective, they announced to the media, was "to drive white 'exploiters' out of the ghetto." Firemen answering the alarm were attacked with rocks and bottles. Police and the National Guard moved in, arresting looters and shooting those who resisted. Devastated by the outbreak of racial violence, Martin Luther King,

Jr., flew to Watts only to be heckled by the militants. When at long last the rioters had exhausted themselves, the ghetto lay in smoldering ruins. The militants had destroyed $34 million worth of property, and in response the authorities had killed 34 rioters and wounded nine. "If a single event can be picked to mark the dividing line" of the 1960s, *Life* editorialized, "it was Watts." The outburst of violence "ripped the fabric of democratic society and set the tone of confrontation and open revolt."

The Watts uprising and subsequent outbreaks of violence in America's inner cities were the products of a number of forces. The civil rights movement created a rising level of expectations among African Americans, but the legislation enacted by Congress did little to improve the conditions of blacks living in the North, Midwest, and West. In Philadelphia, Chicago, and Detroit, African Americans dwelt in ghettos created not by law but by political and economic institutions controlled by whites and rooted in prejudice. Big city political machines provided only token representation to blacks and, as a result, ghetto dwellers received inadequate and unequal funding for sewers, streets, and schools. As manufacturing moved to the suburbs or to smaller towns, African Americans were left stranded without transportation to reach fleeing jobs or the means to relocate. Their facilities jammed with blacks who were excluded from white housing by unwritten covenants; slumlords charged exorbitant rates for crumbling, rat-infested apartments. Unable to reach suburban shopping malls and discount houses, inner-city dwellers had to shop at neighborhood businesses which frequently engaged in merciless price gouging. Families disintegrated, school dropout became epidemic, and those who did not succumb to crime and drugs were terrorized by those who did. "You've got it made," a resident of Watts told a white from Los Angeles. "Some nights on the roof of our rotten, falling down buildings we can actually see your lights shining in the distance. So near and yet so far. We want to reach out and grab it and punch it on the nose."

As one ghetto after another followed Watts's example in the searing summers of 1965 and 1966, Black Power advocates began to eclipse King, the SCLC, the NAACP, and the black churches in the struggle for the hearts and minds of the African American masses. The leading prophet of regeneration through violence was Malcolm Little, the former convict who had renamed himself Malcolm X and risen to the top of the black Muslims. The Muslims, or Nation of Islam (NOI), was a puritanical association of African Americans that practiced a variation of the Islamic creed and that drew its converts primarily from the pimps, drug pushers, and generally down-and-out of the big city ghettos. Similar to other black Muslims, Malcolm X (he had rejected his surname because it had been bestowed during slavery) preached black pride and self-reliance. Black, not white, was beautiful. He also argued that blacks had for so long been abused and reviled that the only way they could liberate themselves spiritually, as well as politically and economically, was through violent struggle. "If someone puts a hand on you," he told his followers, "send him to the cemetery." In his best-selling *Autobiography of Malcolm X* (1965), he admitted that his position was extremist. "The black race here in North America is in extremely bad condition. You show me a black man who isn't an extremist," he declared, "and I'll show you one who needs psychiatric attention." *Newsweek* called him a "spiritual desperado ... a demagogue who titillated slum Negroes and frightened whites."

Malcolm X broke with Elijah Muhammed, the head of the Nation of Islam who became intensely jealous of his charismatic disciple, and made a pilgrimage to Mecca, the holiest city of Islam, where he encountered the ethnic and national diversity of the Islamic world. It changed his entire outlook toward race and "the white man." Upon his return, he embraced integration and socialism, founding the Organization of Afro-American Unity in June 1964. On February 21, 1965, Malcolm X was assassinated during a speech at Harlem's Audubon Ballroom, allegedly by members of an NOI chapter enraged at his "betrayal." Although he had turned toward integration before his assassination in 1965, Malcolm's message of black nationalism and black pride had an enduring impact on African American youth. "I never knew I was black," stated Denise Nicholas, "until I read Malcolm."

Outbreaks of violence occurred in Chicago, Tampa, Atlanta, and Cleveland, but none of these incidents could match the Detroit race riot of 1967 for destructiveness. In the Twelfth Street district, the heart of the ghetto, the population density was twice what it was for the rest of the city. Detroit's African Americans suffered from the same systemic problems that plagued other inner-city blacks, but in addition, there was a long history of hostility between the residents and the police who were continually accused of brutality. One hot Saturday night following a police raid on a black night club, the ghetto blew up. A spirit of nihilism reigned as residents gave themselves over to random acts of theft and destruction. The governor declared the city in open rebellion and called up the National Guard whose young, inexperienced, and frightened members continually opened fire (150,000 rounds), sometimes on those who were assaulting them, the firemen who were battling the flaming ghetto, and innocent bystanders. The violence ended only after the 101st Airborne was called in. Thirty-three black and 10 white Americans lay dead. One returning Vietnam veteran surveyed the smoldering ruins and proclaimed the scene worse than anything he had experienced in Vietnam.

The administration had been aware of the deep-seated problems that plagued America's inner cities. Daniel Patrick Monynihan wrote a controversial report for the president that detailed the disintegration of the black family and probed the causative factors. Former Illinois governor Otto Kerner headed a team that compiled the comprehensive *Report of the National Advisory Committee on Civil Disorders* (1968). In his State of the Union message of January 1966, the president had attempted to keep the momentum generated by the march to Montgomery and passage of the Voting Rights Act alive. He asked Congress to pass legislation eliminating discrimination in housing and jury selection and to make racially motivated assault against a person a civil rights violation. The House of Representatives passed this package, albeit by narrow margins, but as Minority Leader Everett Dirksen (R-Illinois), Johnson's erstwhile ally in the struggle over civil rights legislation, stood passively by, the Senate twice refused to vote cloture in the face of an ongoing southern filibuster. Johnson introduced blacks into the federal government at the highest levels, elevating famed NAACP lawyer Thurgood Marshall to the Supreme Court from the federal circuit court and naming Robert C. Weaver to head the new Department of Housing and Urban Development, but these moves were small compensation for defeat of the 1966 bill.

It was no coincidence that the militancy embodied in the black Muslim philosophy began to spread through the African American community in 1966. Members of Student Nonviolent Coordinating Committee (SNCC) elected the radical firebrand Stokely Carmichael president over John Lewis, a pacifist. Similarly, the Congress of Racial Equality (CORE) replaced James Farmer, an advocate of nonviolence, with the militant, confrontational Floyd McKissick. In the opinion of the new leadership, both black and white liberals were dangerously misguided. "We have to make integration irrelevant," Carmichael declared. During a protest march in Greenwood, Mississippi, in the summer of 1966, Carmichael began the rhythmical chant of "Black Power! Black Power!"; it immediately caught the attention of the media and captured the imagination of black militants.

Young African Americans were becoming increasingly angry by the mid-1960s over the unfairness of the draft. Blacks were the poorest and least educated sector of society and, like poor whites, few were attending college during the draft-age years, 19 to 26. Across the United States, local draft boards were made up overwhelmingly of local business and professional people, meaning that they were 99% white. In the South, boards not only drafted black youths en masse but singled out civil rights activists. After Bennie Tucker and Hubert Davis, both black, filed to run for city offices in Mississippi, they were inducted. Another activist, Willie Jordan, was sentenced to five years in prison when he showed up a few minutes late for his draft physical.

Observers of the civil rights movement began noticing a change in the movement during James Meridith's "walk against fear" in June 1966. Following his graduation from the University of Mississippi, Meredith began a 225-mile walk from Memphis to Jackson to demonstrate that a black man could walk on a southern highway without fear of harm. Accompanied only by a minister and journalist, he set out. On the second day, a white man stepped out of the undergrowth and fired three shotgun blasts into Meredith. Doctors at a Memphis hospital subsequently removed more than 100 pellets from his legs, back, and head. The heads of the major civil rights organizations, King of SCLC, Young of the Urban League, McKissick of CORE, and Carmichael of SNCC, rushed to Memphis to plan a continuation of the march. It was clear from the outset that the Meredith March would be different from Selma. In 1966, SNCC and CORE had expelled all white members. In Memphis, the older moderates wanted to issue a call to white liberals to join them not only in the march but in a drive for voter registration, but the militants advocated a march of blacks only, condemnation of Lyndon B. Johnson and white liberals, and the employment of a black Louisiana group, Deacons for Defense, for protection. Roy Wilkins and Whitney Young departed, leaving an uneasy King to march with the hard-liners. Each night the marchers, which included only a handful of whites, pitched camp and held a rally. King preached brotherhood and nonviolence, while Carmichael and McKissick urged armed resistance. In Greenwood, Carmichael was arrested for pitching his tent on the grounds of a black high school. Released on bond, he addressed a huge rally. "The only way we gonna stop them white men from whuppin' us is to take over," he declared. "We been saying freedom for six years and we ain't got nothin'. What we gonna start saying now is Black Power!" The crowd roared back, "Black Power!"

Later that year, Bobby Seale and Huey Newton, two young black college students in Oakland, California, founded the Black Panther party. The Panthers donned black berets and black leather jackets, and began carrying loaded weapons. In 1967, as the California legislature debated a measure that would prohibit the carrying of loaded firearms, armed Panthers walked the halls of the state capitol. Seale, Newton, and Eldridge Cleaver, the ex-convict who the Panthers named their first "Minister of Education," issued a manifesto calling for the traditional civil rights objectives of full employment, equality of opportunity in education, an end to police brutality, and decent housing. Added to those, however, were more radical goals such as exemption of black males from military service, all-black juries for African American defendants, and an "end to the robbery by the capitalists of our Black Community." Cleaver subsequently published his autobiographical *Soul on Ice* (1967), hailed as the 1960s sequel to Ralph Ellison's *Invisible Man*. In essence, Cleaver issued a call to arms to America's 20 million blacks to "harness their number and hone it into a sword with a sharp cutting edge." H. Rap Brown, who succeeded Carmichael as chairman of the SNCC, told a group of stunned reporters that "violence is as American as cherry pie."

The militants of the 1960s were also profoundly influenced by Frantz Fanon's *The Wretched of the Earth*. A black West Indian psychiatrist and political radical who participated in the Algerian uprising against the French,

Fanon depicted a world in which all whites were engaged in a conspiracy to colonize and exploit all nonwhites. Fanon called upon the oppressed to rise en masse against their white exploiters and their colored collaborators. He extolled the "therapeutic value" of violence that would simultaneously break the back of organized colonialism and heal the psychic wounds of centuries of oppression. Universalist in his outlook, Fanon also called upon the Third World to rise up and right the injustices committed by the First. In his scheme of things, blacks were not a humble minority petitioning whites for their rights but an aroused majority determined to seize their birthright.

The significance of the Black Power movement lay more in its psychological aspects than its specific objectives. A 1967 survey of Detroit African Americans found that 86% favored integration, whereas only 1% favored separatism; in Chicago, 57% believed that Martin Luther King, Jr., best represented their position, whereas only 3% chose Carmichael. Cultural autonomy and ethnic self-determination were political impossibilities in the United States, a nation built on the presumption that cultural diversity cannot and must not devolve into political separatism. Similar to Marcus Garvey, a black nationalist that headed a back-to-Africa movement during the 1920s, Black Power advocates saw the need for African Americans to embrace their own history, to take pride in their unique experience, and to realize that their historic powerlessness was a product of white oppression, not an innate genetic flaw. Like Martin Luther King, Jr., Carmichael, McKissick, and Seale saw the need to convince the black masses that they and not whites were ultimately responsible for their own destiny, but they rejected the church-based, nonviolent approach because it involved cooperation with patronizing white liberals and perpetuated blacks' sense of dependence. They, like Nat Turner, the slave preacher who had led a bloody uprising in antebellum Virginia, reveled in apocalyptic visions of violent revolution against a satanic white power structure, and they publicized those visions in the belief that they would rid the black community of 300 years of shame and guilt. The Black Power movement was then primarily one of racial assertiveness and cultural empowerment.

Sociologist Harry Edwards, a Black Power advocate who taught at San Jose State University, understood America's love affair with sports. He argued that the growing presence and influence of black athletes in amateur and professional athletics offered a unique opportunity to make a statement. Specifically, Edwards called upon black athletes to boycott the 1968 Olympic games to be held in Mexico City. Some did participate in the boycott, while others who attended demonstrated in behalf of black power. During the playing of the U.S. national anthem, sprinters Tommie Smith and John Carlos, who had won gold and bronze medals, raised their gloved fists in the Black Power salute. Not all of the American athletes were supportive. A day later, in the Olympic village, the U.S. rifle team hung a banner out their dorm window that read, "Win the War in Vietnam: Wallace for President."

In the wake of the founding of the Black Power movement, young African Americans stopped straightening their hair, adopting the more natural "Afro" look, and began wearing traditional African dashikis. Black authors published books, short stories, and poems exploring and extolling the African and African American heritage. Black history and black studies courses began appearing in college curricula across the United States. Cultural activists even went so far as to reject traditional English as exploitive and oppressive, and to argue that the street patois spoken by working-class blacks was a legitimate language with its own perceptible and definable rules. "Soul" became the defining term for those who sought the essence of blackness. Soul singers such as Aretha Franklin and James Brown captured the proud, defiant, at times melancholy and at times joyous mood of black America in the 1960s. In Detroit, the Reverend Albert Cleage established the Shrine of the Black Madonna complete with a 30-foot statue of a black madonna and child.

Congressional inaction on the 1966 civil rights bill was a reflection of a mounting white backlash against the Black Power philosophy of militants such as Carmichael, Cleaver, and McKissick, and the rioting and civil disorder that wracked U.S. cities. White-collar workers living in ethnic neighborhoods in the North organized to keep blacks out of their residential enclaves, schools, and labor unions. In Chicago, King and the Reverend Jesse Jackson led an open housing march through a white neighborhood. Local whites responded by hurling bottles and rocks, waving Confederate flags, and shouting "Martin Luther Coon." Frightened white suburbanites huddled in their tract houses and increasingly voted for conservative legislators determined to slow, if not block, the pace of integration. Members of the House voted to make rioting a federal crime, and Congress actually passed legislation denying antipoverty funds to people who incited or participated in riots. "Are we going to abdicate law and order... in favor of a social theory that the man who heaves a brick through a window or tosses a firebomb into your car is simply the misunderstood and underprivileged product of a broken home?" Michigan Representative Gerald Ford asked. The 1966 midterm elections were a disaster for the Democrats, who lost 47 seats in the House and 3 in the Senate. Civil rights advocate Paul Douglas of Illinois was defeated by a coalition of racists opposed to "open occupancy housing." The United States, to Lyndon B. Johnson's dismay, had become thoroughly polarized over the issue of nondiscrimination and equal opportunity for African Americans. He, like other moderates and liberals, was deeply frustrated. "What do they want?" Johnson asked, referring to the urban rioters and Black Power advocates. "I'm giving them boom times and more good legislation than anybody else did, and what do they do – attack and sneer. Could FDR do better? Could anybody do better? What do they want?"

The New Left

The civil rights movement of the 1950s and early 1960s served as a catalyst for a student movement dedicated to nothing less than the reformation of America's political and economic life. The individual affluence of the 1950s, coupled with unprecedented governmental spending on education – between 1945 and 1965 expenditures increased annually from $742.1 to $6.9 billion – swelled the ranks of college students. To the children of the 1950s, other than the Cold War, which most viewed as simply anxiety producing rather than challenging, there seemed to be no battles worth fighting and no walls worth scaling. The consensus culture, particularly pervasive among their middle-class parents, coupled with widespread prosperity, left college students no outlet for their idealism. Civil rights changed all that; the Montgomery boycott and the march on Selma awakened college youth to the fact of racism and caused them to embark upon a sweeping examination of American society as a whole. Out of that quest came a systematic critique and a new sociopolitical philosophy known as the New Left.

As an explicitly political protest movement, the New Left traced its origins to 1960 when Al Haber and Tom Hayden, two University of Michigan students who had been profoundly influenced by Jack Kerouac and other members of the Beat Generation, the civil rights movement (especially SNCC's voter registration campaign), and the working-class radicals of the 1930s, founded the Students for a Democratic Society (SDS). Two years later, Hayden penned the Port Huron statement, which was a call to arms to university and college students to rise up against and change a political and social system that oppressed the poor and nonwhite and that swallowed up individual freedom in a sea of conformity. Hayden and his fellow activists soon adopted the name New Left to distinguish the movement from the more explicitly Marxist Old Left of the 1930s. The Free Speech Movement (FSM), born in 1964 on the campus of the University of California, Berkeley, was distinct from the New Left, but in its demand for student rights and freedom of expression, it was complementary.

Over time, members of the SDS and sectors of the FSM became increasingly preoccupied with national politics and foreign affairs. Appalled by the ongoing war in Vietnam, by the persistence of racism, by the pervasiveness of the military–industrial complex, and by the perceived hypocrisy of middle-class morality, students, and academics turned out first a comprehensive critique of American politics and society and then a devastating indictment of American foreign policy.

The New Left was mostly a revolt among American intellectuals and college students against liberal politics. In its early days when the New Left focused on the twin evils of discrimination and imperialism, the movement began to define itself in terms of its differences from traditional New Deal liberalism. The founders of the New Left argued that liberals saw politics as a means to resolve conflicts whereas New Leftists perceived it to be a means to achieve a moral society. Liberals had unlimited faith in the electoral process, whereas New Leftists were moving beyond elections to direct action, both as a tactic to achieve justice and as an empowering process sufficient unto itself. Whereas most liberals were committed to America's anticommunist world mission, the new left struggled to detach itself from the Cold War and increasingly tended to blame both sides for having caused the conflict. Beyond the issues, New Leftists tended to distrust all established institutions as roadblocks both to social justice and to authentic personal relationships.

By the mid-1960s, the great enemy of the New Left had become "corporate liberalism," a term coined by Carl Oglesby, a 35-year-old writer who became president of the SDS in 1965. The term was not new to the movement, but Oglesby's linking of it to American foreign policy was. The men who engineered the war in Vietnam "are not moral monsters," he said. "They are all honorable men. They are all liberals." The American corporate machine they oversaw was the "colossus of history," taking the riches of other nations and consuming half of the world's goods. Being decent men, corporate liberals rationalized their rapacity and their policy of counter-revolution with the ideology of anticommunism, defining all revolutions as communist and communism as evil.

Oglesby's critique of American foreign policy paralleled and no doubt borrowed from the burgeoning revisionist school among historians of American foreign relations. In 1959, William Appleman Williams had published *The Tragedy of American Diplomacy*, an interpretive survey of twentieth-century American foreign policy. Its thesis was simple. In America, the most capitalistic of all nations, industrialists, manufacturers, and financiers comprised the ruling elite, dominating every aspect of the nation's life. At the turn of the century, as manufacturing outstripped agriculture as the nation's leading enterprise, the captains of industry felt the need for overseas markets to absorb their surplus production. Flexing their political muscles, they persuaded the executive and its foreign policy apparatus to search out markets and investment opportunities and in general to make the world safe for American business. Every major crisis and trend in twentieth-century foreign affairs, according to Williams, was a response to or part of this "open door" diplomacy. In New Left terminology, open door became a synonym for a foreign policy that had as its objective American economic domination of overseas areas. Vietnam was but the latest and most glaring example of the new American imperialism.

Student Protest and Vietnam

Increasingly, the Vietnam War became the focus of the New Left and the student movement generally. Frustrations encountered in the unsuccessful effort to bring the war to a close spilled over into other areas of student concern, however, and eventually radicalized the movement to the point of political irrelevancy. When the SDS endorsed draft resistance, its membership swelled. Some draft-eligible activists showed their disapproval of the war by burning their draft cards; others fled to Canada where they continued to criticize U.S. involvement in Vietnam. Students demanded the removal of Reserve Officer Training Corps (ROTC) units from their campuses or demonstrated against industries with large defense contracts. Dow Chemical, which manufactured napalm, became a favorite target. "I didn't go to college in 1965 expecting to become a radical," recalled Judy Smith, "but I didn't expect the Vietnam War to develop the way it did either. . . . It would have been immoral to just go on with college and career plans when the war was still going on." The year 1967 bore witness to two large national antiwar demonstrations. Employing the civil rights movement's Mississippi Freedom Summer as a model, the SDS, together with pacifists and disillusioned liberals, persuaded 20,000 people to participate in Vietnam Summer. Then, in the fall of 1967, 50,000 antiwar protesters gathered in Washington, D.C., for Stop the Draft Week. They prayed, picketed, protested, and eventually packed the Arlington bridge and surrounded the Pentagon in an effort to bring the alleged center of the military–industrial complex to a halt. Hundreds sat down in the Pentagon parking lot. "Soon diggers started bringing in food and joints," wrote Thorne Dreyer. "A real festival atmosphere was in the air." Many talked to the troops stationed to guard the military's nerve center, chanting "join us" and singing "we'd love to turn you on." A few put flowers in the troop's rifle barrels. Some smoked dope into the evening; others sipped wine and built campfires. "Near midnight," reported Martin Jezer, "paratroopers of the 82nd Division replaced the MPs on the line. With the marshals at the rear they began massing at the center of the sit-in preparing to attack. . . . The brutality was horrible. Nonresisting girls were kicked and clubbed by U.S. marshals old enough to be their fathers . . . cracking heads, bashing skulls." Conservatives were appalled, not at the carnage but at the protests themselves. Republican gubernatorial candidate Ronald Reagan observed to reporters, "If you ask me, the activities of those Vietnam Day teach-in people can be summed up in three words: Sex, Drugs, and Treason." House Democratic leader Carl Albert declared that the march on the Pentagon was "basically organized by International Communism."

It should be noted that the anti–Vietnam war protests, demonstrations, and teach-ins transcended the objective they were designed to accomplish. These "political prayer meetings," to use Frederick Siegel's phrase, generated a sense of community among students and gave a sense of purpose to students "bred in at least modest comfort." There was a pervasive feeling among young people and intellectuals of loss of identity and isolation. Vance Packard's hugely popular *The Hidden Persuaders* (1957), which featured a picture of George Orwell's Big Brother on the cover, argued that the advertising industry was in fact creating a creeping cultural totalitarianism from which there was no escape. Herbert Marcuse's 1965 book, *One-Dimensional Man*, was an indictment of western capitalist societies that skillfully stimulated and manipulated material wants in ways that caused humans to settle for the illusion of happiness. Through creation and nourishment of a rampant consumerism, these "benign" plutocracies destroyed the masses' capacity for political dissent, critical thought, and even authentic sensual pleasure. Denied hardship and hard choice, America's rebellious youth read Packard, Marcuse, and C. Wright Mills; denounced bureaucracy, whether governmental or academic; and insisted on their right to individual expression and spontaneity. This demand, somewhat paradoxically, served as a common bond and generated a sense of community. Belonging without the compulsion of conformity seemed suddenly attainable.

The Counterculture

Indeed, many – although not all – participants in the student protest movement of the 1960s embraced alternative lifestyles known collectively as the counterculture. In July 1967, *Time* published a cover story that introduced "the hippies." The magazine traced the phenomenon back to 1965, and termed it "a wholly new subculture, a bizarre permutation of the middle-class American ethos." In the mid-1960s, a few of the young and alienated had moved into the Haight–Ashbury neighborhood of San Francisco near Golden Gate Park. Dressed in anything unusual – granny gowns, pirate or old west costumes, Victorian suits, British mod fashions – they attended happenings, smoked and sold marijuana, and chalked colorful designs on the sidewalks. Some adopted new names such as Apache, Coyote, Superspade, White Rabbit, and Blue Flash. In New York City, they gathered in the East Village. Long-haired women, bearded men, and interracial couples went to poetry readings, attended experimental theater at Cafe la Mama, browsed at boutiques such as the Queen of Diamonds, or read underground publications such as *Fuck You/A Magazine of the Arts*. In the spring of 1967, hippies in San Francisco announced a "Summer of Love." "If you go to San Francisco," sang Scott McKenzie in a popular song, "wear a flower in your hair." Altogether, 75,000 visited "the Haight" that summer before returning to their college campuses. *Time* reported in the fall, "Today hippie enclaves are blooming in every major U.S. city from Boston to Seattle, from Detroit to New Orleans; there is a 50-member cabal in, of all places, Austin, Texas." The magazine noted that there might be 300,000 hippies, and "by all estimates the cult is a growing phenomenon that has not yet reached its peak."

The Beatles, Janis Joplin, Jimi Hendrix, and other rock stars of the 1960s sported long hair; bell-bottom trousers; colorful, flowery shirts; and beads, thus declaring their "hipness." Members of the counterculture attempted to use dress as a means of social protest and as an expression of their individuality. The hippies shunned makeup, burned candles and incense, decorated their living quarters with eastern religious symbols, and rode around the United States in garishly painted buses. They shopped at army surplus and Salvation Army stores for fatigues, which they coupled incongruously with sandals and peace symbols. Female hippies wore flowers in their hair and perfected a new sartorial art form – the tie-dyed T-shirt. Splashing brightly colored dye randomly on knotted white T-shirts, they achieved a Jackson Pollock-like effect that could only be described as psychedelic. In 1968, author Tom Wolfe penned *The Electric Kool-Aid Acid Test*, in which he described the counterculture's typical hippie. "His hair has the long jesuschrist look. He is wearing the costume clothes. But most of all, he now has a very tolerant and therefore withering attitude toward all those who are still struggling in the old activist political ways... while he, with the help of psychedelic chemicals, is exploring the infinite regions of human consciousness."

Conservatives derided the counterculture with being obsessed with sex and drugs, and they were partially correct. Hippies engaged in premarital and extramarital sex more frequently and more openly than any previous generation. This sexual revolution was made possible in part by the development of two new contraceptives: an oral contraceptive, nicknamed "the Pill," and the intrauterine device (IUD). Many members of the counterculture participated in random sex with multiple partners because they enjoyed it and because they viewed it as a political statement. To reject the dominant culture's sexual mores was to reject its political institutions, repressive values, and even the war in Southeast Asia. In fact, the sexual revolution transcended the counterculture. William Masters's and Virginia Johnson's *Human Sexual Response* (1966) built on the Kinsey Reports in demythologizing sex and demonstrating that sex was as desired and enjoyed as much by women as men. By the end of the 1960s, unmarried undergraduates with no particular political agenda were "shacking up" on a regular basis.

Todd Gitlin, an early president of the SDS and a historian of the 1960s, noted that as the decade wore on, "to get access to youth culture, you had to get high." The Beatles frequently "dropped acid"; that is, they ingested lysergic acid diethylamide (LSD), a synthetic substance that produced vividly colored, psychedelic hallucinations. One of their most famous albums, "Sergeant Pepper's Lonely Hearts Club Band," could not have been made without it. However, the favored drug of the counterculture was marijuana, which when smoked produced a mild, mellow high. Much more addictive and debilitating was heroin, a drug favored by many musicians. Others combined these drugs with addiction to alcohol, barbiturates, and cocaine. The symbol and spokesperson for the drug culture was Dr. Timothy Leary, a Harvard professor who had discovered hallucinogenic mushrooms during a trip to Mexico. He openly advocated the use of drugs and was fired from Harvard in 1963. In his *Psychedelic Review* and International Foundation for Internal Freedom, he advocated the legalization and widespread use of drugs. "Tune in, turn on, and drop out," he advised America's youth. Ken Kesey, author of *One Flew Over the Cuckoo's Nest*, founded a mobile commune called the Merry Pranksters. The Pranksters traveled up and down the West Coast organizing "acid tests" – rock and roll concerts enhanced by the free distribution of LSD. These parties, chronicled in unconventional prose by Wolfe in *The Electric Kool-Aid Acid Test*, spawned a new musical term – "acid rock." Even after it became clear that LSD and other drugs were not the relatively harmless escapes from reality that they were first believed to be – "bad trips" led to perpetual nightmares, and the craving for heroin and other hard drugs drove some into theft and prostitution – counterculture members clung to drugs as a sign of solidarity and resistance to the repressive dominant culture.

So alienated became some members of the counterculture that they decided to withdraw from society and form communes. Similar to the nineteenth-century communitarian experiments, such as that featured in Nathaniel Hawthorne's *Blithedale Romance*, the 1960s efforts at cooperative existence were plagued by the tension between the human longing for belonging and connectedness, on the one hand, and a maximum of individual freedom, on the other hand. Some communitarians were college students who rented a house or apartment complex; others were back-to-the-landers, members of the middle class alienated by the dog-eat-dog ethos of corporate life or the shallowness of the consumer culture. They purchased farmhouses, agreed to divide all work and share all costs equally, and began raising organic gardens. These efforts by the hippies to live in harmony with each other and nature frequently fell afoul of human nature. Conflicts over funding and work as well as tensions arising from fluid sexual relationships often caused the break up of communes. Those governed by a rigid hierarchy or devoted to an eastern religion seemed to last the longest.

An individual who typified the hope and despair, the charm and the destructive narcissism, of the counterculture was singer Janis Joplin. A native of Port Arthur, Texas, Joplin was a smart, talented young woman, but devoid of the looks it took to be a popular high school student. She rebelled against her parents and teachers, dressed in outrageous hippie clothing, and began running with classmates who lived on the edge of the drug-crime culture.

She experienced the hedonism of Venice, California, for a brief period after graduation but then returned to enroll at the University of Texas. There she gained local fame singing blues and folk tunes in local honky-tonks and cabarets. Her outrageous, aggressive behavior and appearance, and obscenity-studded performances, earned her the sobriquet "Ugliest Man on Campus." She finally found her place in the San Francisco counterculture scene. Singing for Big Brother and the Holding Company and other bands, she took the psychedelic rock scene by storm. In her abused, husky but electrifying voice, she exuded anger, passion, love, and despair. Her personal life was chaotic. A promiscuous bisexual, Joplin found satisfaction, both physical and emotional, elusive. A manic-depressive, she combined Southern Comfort with a variety of drugs. She died of a drug–alcohol overdose in a Los Angeles fleabag hotel in 1970.

For some, rejection of traditional sexual mores and family structures were part of an intellectual protest against capitalism and elitist politics. For others, intellectual descendents of Jack Kerouac and the Beat Generation, politics and all forms of organized civic activity were corrupt; for them, an alternative lifestyle was not an accoutrement but the essence. "The sixties generation was not narrowly political," Tom Hayden later observed. Most students were more concerned with the climate of opinion than specific programs and policies. There was in New Left and related writing, in fact, a call to cultural anarchism. A genre of writing sought to point out the irrationality and perversity of conventional mores by portraying the societally defined insane as more humanly authentic than those defined as sane. In *The Divided Self: An Existential Study in Sanity and Madness* (1965), British psychiatrist C. D. Laing suggested that psychosis could constitute a liberating pathway to deeper awareness. Novelist Ken Kesey developed in *One Flew Over the Cuckoo's Nest* (1963) a protagonist whose resistance to established societal norms caused him to be incarcerated in an insane asylum, but whose free spirit served as a liberating, therapeutic force on his fellow inmates. Significantly, conservative, middle-class Americans who generally made no distinction between reformers and anarchists increasingly saw free love, drug experimentation, and disrespect for authority as the objects of the protest movement.

In more tranquil times, American society might have easily tolerated the Black Power movement, the New Left, and the counterculture. The 1960s were not tranquil times. By 1967, *Life* was referring to the 1960s as the "Decade of Tumult and Change." Conservative, conventional Americans already felt threatened by the forces of international communism. They were supportive of the war in Vietnam, but increasingly frustrated at the inability of the United States to win a victory. The rhetoric of Black Power, ghetto riots, the constant indictment of capitalist America by the New Left, and the perceived undermining of traditional values by the hippies proved unbearable. By the spring of 1968, the United States was profoundly disunited.

Increasingly, the focus of that disunity and disquiet was the seemingly end-less war in Vietnam.

Vietnam: A Bloody Stalemate

The U.S. military units that fought in Vietnam were the best-trained, best-equipped, best-fed in the nation's history. Americans relied heavily on tech-nology in their struggle to defeat the NVA and the Vietcong (VC). In an effort to deprive the enemy of cover, C-123 Ranchhand crews, operating under the slogan "Only You Can Prevent Forests," dropped thousands of tons of herbicides on the lush green countryside. These chemicals, includ-ing Agent Orange, destroyed an estimated 50% of Vietnam's timberlands and unintentionally caused long-term health problems for thousands of GIs who came in contact with them. Huge computers processed millions of pieces of data in an effort to predict when and where the enemy would strike. Needle bombs, smart bombs, and ever more sophisticated targeting devices guided U.S. ordinance to its targets. C-47 gunships called Puff the Magic Dragons bristled with automatic weapons that were capable of firing 18,000 rounds a minute. Above all, however, the helicopter gunships, which could move troops quickly around the countryside and spot and destroy enemy troops from the air, were the technological symbol of the American presence in Vietnam.

Somewhat ironically, the U.S. Air Force and the U.S. Navy dropped twice as many bombs on the South as the North, more than 1 million tons be-tween 1965 and 1967. Fighter-bombers flew close support for Army and Marine infantry. According to the "pile on" concept, spotters would call in an air strike on a suspected enemy position. After a devastating pounding, ground troops would move in and kill or capture the survivors. "Blow the hell out of them and police up," was how one officer described the approach. As the war progressed and frustration over inability to come to grips with an elusive enemy mounted, entire areas of South Vietnam were declared "free-fire zones" in which the military was allowed to blast indiscriminately.

In 1965, Ho Chi Minh mobilized North Vietnam for an all-out effort to "foil the war of aggression of the U.S. imperialists" in the south. Hanoi recognized that the prime targets of opportunity in the war were American public opinion and the shaky political/military regime in Saigon. Through guerrilla and conventional warfare, the NVA and Vietcong would harass, maim, and kill as many American and South Vietnam personnel as pos-sible in an effort to destabilize the government in Saigon and destroy the American people's will to fight. Tactically, NVA and VC forces relied on am-bushes and hit-and-run operations; the idea was to "cling to the enemy's belt" to avoid a knock-out punch from superior American firepower.

Vietnam was a war without front lines and frequently one without territorial objectives. Consequently, "body count" became the means of measuring victory. Because the VC and sometimes the NVA refused to wear uniforms and frequently sprang from or hid among South Vietnamese villagers, it was difficult to tell friend from foe. This led not only to the slaughter of innocents, but inflated body counts. "'If it's dead and Vietnamese, it's VC,' was a rule of thumb in the bush," recalled Phillip Caputo. Great pressure developed throughout the military hierarchy to keep the count high. As a result of padding at every level, enemy casualty figures were inflated by as much as 30%. Still, it is estimated that American and South Vietnamese forces had wounded or killed 220,000 VC and NVA soldiers by the end of 1967. The problem was that more than 200,000 young men reached draft age in North Vietnam each year. During peak periods in the 1960s, Hanoi was able to move as many as 400 tons of supplies per week and as many as 5,000 soldiers down the 600-mile-long Ho Chi Minh Trail, which stretched from the North through Laos and Cambodia and into South Vietnam.

Only 10% of the U.S. personnel sent to Vietnam were combat soldiers, but because of the unconventional nature of the war, virtually no area was completely safe. VC cadre regularly bombed, grenaded, or strafed cafes and barracks. For those wearing the combat infantry badge, the 13-month tour of duty could be hellish. Most recruits were from working-class families and boasted a high school education if that. The war plucked them from their familiar towns and neighborhoods and sent them half-way around the world to fight a war in which it was frequently impossible to distinguish friend from foe and over which their countrymen and women were increasingly divided. There were occasional division-level battles, in the A Shau Valley or along the demilitarization zone (DMZ), for example, but most action was at the squad level. Westmoreland's search-and-destroy approach called for constant patrolling in the bush. American GIs either ambushed or were ambushed. The natural environment was hostile. One could stay wet for days and even weeks during the monsoon seasons. Soldiers had to deal with leeches, poisonous snakes, and insects, while constantly confronting the possibility of instant death from both communist soldiers or their civilian sympathizers, many of whom were women and children. More than one soldier received a bullet in the back from an 11- or 12-year-old.

The fact that the military attempted to make fire bases and rear areas as much like home as possible did not necessarily help alleviate the stress of fighting in Vietnam. Indeed, the huge PXs with all the latest consumer goods, bowling alleys, movie houses, and westernized Vietnamese bars made it difficult for American personnel to leave home behind, to acquire the psychological toughness that combat requires, and simply to return to the bush from base camp. For most, existence consisted of long periods of overwhelming boredom and loneliness punctuated by brief bursts of intense terror.

As the war dragged on, the fighting became increasingly savage. Ho and his chief commander, General Vo Nguyen Giap, prosecuted the war with the insensitivity of ideologues. They were willing to trade the lives of their soldiers for strategic or psychological advantage, that is, to sacrifice their country for victory. The VC and North Vietnamese cadre reflected that chilling obsession. Communist operatives in the South did not hesitate to brutally assassinate or maim innocent villagers to intimidate the civilian population into cooperating with them. They delighted in ambushing and booby trapping American soldiers, frequently with the objective of maiming rather than killing. Confronted with a war without front lines and a savage foe, American soldiers struck back blindly. Stories of atrocities committed by U.S. soldiers began to appear in the U.S. press by the late 1960s. In areas where the Vietcong was active, GIs tended to blame the civilian population for harboring them. During a Marine search-and-destroy mission in Cam Ne in August 1965, American troops rousted the villagers whom they suspected of collaborating with the enemy from their huts and set the dwellings on fire with cigarette lighters. CBS newsman Morley Safer and his camera crew taped the scene, which included anguished, pleading villagers. Vietnamese became "gooks" whose ears were considered legitimate war trophies. Increasingly in the field, GIs considered any Vietnamese they encountered fair game: "If it moves, it's VC," became the watchword. The most appalling atrocity of the war occurred in March 1968, when Charlie Company under the command of Lieutenant William Calley massacred more than 200 innocent men, women, and children at the village of My Lai. Calley's superiors managed to cover up the incident for a year, but it eventually became public. Revelations concerning My Lai and publicity surrounding Calley's trial in 1970 would create widespread disgust with the war.

The Six-Day War in the Middle East and the threat it posed to American economic and strategic interests increased pressure on President Johnson to end the war in Vietnam. There was no dearth of peace initiatives; officials counted some 2,000 official and unofficial attempts between 1964 and 1968 to bring about a negotiated settlement. In June 1967, Johnson held a summit meeting with Soviet Premier Kosygin at Glassboro, New Jersey. The two leaders failed to reach concrete agreement on either the Middle East or Vietnam, but the meeting seemed to point to the possibility of a peace in Southeast Asia brokered by the great powers. Opinion polls taken later that year indicated that a majority of Americans considered U.S. intervention in Vietnam to be a mistake.

In September during a speech in San Antonio, Texas, President Johnson outlined a new negotiating position – the "San Antonio formula." The United States would halt all aerial bombardment of North Vietnam if the administration was assured that the move "will lead promptly to productive discussions." The president dropped his demand that the NVA withdraw from South Vietnam, asking that the communists neither attempt additional infiltration nor launch new attacks during the pause. Two months

later, the U.S. government agreed to negotiate with the National Liberation Front (NLF) as a separate entity. For its part, Hanoi made some concessions. The North Vietnamese dropped their demand that all American
troops be removed from the South before the start of negotiations. But
despite these compromises, neither side had really departed from its fundamental position. The Johnson administration was determined to settle
for nothing less than an independent, noncommunist nation south of the
17th parallel, whereas the government in North Vietnam was determined
to see a unified country established under its control and free of foreign
influence.

In 1967, the Johnson administration tacitly admitted that the "nation"
it had been defending was little more than a hollow shell. That year it
embarked on a massive new pacification effort in Vietnam. The Civil Operations and Revolutionary Development Support under Robert Komer
organized 57-man teams of Vietnamese who would go and live in a village,
providing physical security and helping with agricultural development and
various civil projects. Under the Chieu Hoi program, VC deserters were offered not only amnesty but employment. Simultaneously, the Central Intelligence Agency (CIA) station chief in Saigon, William Colby, presided over
creation of the Phoenix Program, a counterinsurgency strategy in which
Vietnamese trained by the CIA would penetrate VC cadre and "neutralize"
communist operatives and their sympathizers. Through mass arrests and
assassinations, the Phoenix Program dramatically reduced the influence of
the Vietcong, but it also identified the government in Saigon as well as the
United States with arbitrary justice and indiscriminate violence.

In response to this "Accelerated Pacification Program" and a higher
body count, General Westmoreland made a series of optimistic public announcements in the fall of 1967. According to U.S. statistics, American
and Army of the Republic of Vietnam (ARVN) forces were close to reaching the "crossover point," whereby more enemy soldiers were being killed
than were being drafted in North Vietnam. The American commander informed Johnson that it would be possible for the United States to begin a
gradual withdrawal within two years, during which the South Vietnamese
would be able to assume responsibility for their own defense. The president brought Westmoreland back to the United States to reassure Congress
and the American people. The president told the congressmen that "Westmoreland has turned defeat into what we believe will be a victory. It's only
a matter now of will." However, the light at the end of the tunnel turned
out to be a mirage.

Tet

Ho and General Giap well understood the Clauswitzian maxim that war is
the extension of politics. Sensing mounting war weariness in the United

States, the North Vietnamese leadership in conjunction with the NLF decided on a major offensive designed to demonstrate that no part of South
Vietnam was secure. Regular units of the NVA would lure American forces
into outlying areas where they would be engaged in diversionary battles,
while VC units would smuggle themselves into the cities and towns of
South Vietnam. At a given signal, they would attack military and police
facilities and government buildings. They hoped the populace would rally
to the VC banner, but even if they did not, America's hopes for a victory in
the near future would be shattered. Its morale destroyed, the United States
would agree to the establishment of a temporary coalition government in
the South and then withdraw.

The communists' strategy worked to perfection. In October and November 1967, units of the NVA attacked the U.S. Marine base at Con Thien
near the Laotian Border, Dak To in the Central Highlands, and the towns
of Loc Ninh and Song Be near Saigon. Most significant, two divisions of
North Vietnamese troops laid siege to the Marine garrison at Khe Sahn in
the mountains near the Laotian border. As Westmoreland shifted forces to
meet these threats, Vietcong operatives smuggled arms and supplies into
Saigon, Hue, and other cities. Early in the morning of January 30, 1968,
in the midst of Tet, the Vietnamese lunar new year and the most festive of
national holidays, the Vietcong struck. In all, the communist sappers and
small arms teams hit five of the South's six major cities, 36 of 64 provincial capitals, and more than 60 district governments. Americans turned on
the six o'clock news to see a Vietcong team occupying the courtyard of the
American embassy in Saigon. Seventy-five hundred Vietcong and North
Vietnamese troops overran and occupied Hue.

American and ARVN forces quickly rallied. Within days, U.S. and South
Vietnamese soldiers had cleared Saigon. In the weeks that followed, they
drove the communists from virtually every other city and town they had
occupied, forcing them deep into the countryside and inflicting huge casualties. In Hue, the occupying forces held out for three weeks. Allied forces
pounded the ancient city into rubble and then cleared what remained in
house-to-house fighting. Estimates of VC and NVA killed in action ran to
5,000. The liberators uncovered the graves of 2,800 government officials,
police, and soldiers massacred by the communists. In fact, Tet constituted
the worst single defeat suffered by the fighting forces of the DRV and NLF.
More than 40,000 communist soldiers were killed or wounded. The infrastructure of the Vietcong lay shattered, never fully to recover.

If the communists suffered a tactical setback as a result of Tet, they
gained a major strategic victory. American casualties were high – 1,100
killed in battle – and the ARVN lost 2,300 men. The fighting killed 12,500
civilians and created as many as 1 million new refugees. But the real casualty was morale on the homefront. The images from the Tet Offensive that
flashed across America's television screens were horrific and haunting: U.S.

diplomats in shirtsleeves firing out of the windows of the American embassy; Air Force and Navy planes dropping canisters of exploding napalm on South Vietnamese villages; house-to-house fighting amid the rubble of Hue, once one of Southeast Asia's cultural treasures; the haggard faces of the besieged Marines at Khe Sanh; and the image of Saigon's police chief casually firing his revolver into the head of a captured VC. "We had to destroy it in order to save it," declared an American officer standing on the outskirts of what once was a Mekong Delta village.

Americans had been led to believe by Westmoreland's optimistic accounts that victory was just around the corner. How could that be when the VC could penetrate the very symbol of U.S. power in Southeast Asia, the American embassy compound in Saigon? "What the hell is going on?" demanded the respected CBS television anchor Walter Cronkite. "I thought we were winning the war." The credibility gap "had become a canyon," as historian Terry Anderson put it. In the weeks that followed, Cronkite and other former administration supporters advised the president to negotiate a withdrawal. The United States had acted honorably and done everything in its power to ensure the survival of freedom and democracy in Southeast Asia. Now it was up to the Vietnamese. "If I've lost Cronkite," President Johnson lamented, "I've lost America." All across the United States, the Tet Offensive caused Americans to verbalize doubts that had been lurking in their subconscious. Was there really a viable nation south of the 17th parallel? If so, why were the Vietnamese not willing to fight and die to defend it? How could the U.S. military command have been caught so off guard? Did Tet indicate that American strategic thinking was either fatally flawed or totally unrealistic? As opinion analyst Samuel Lubell noted, Americans shared a "fervent drive to shake free of an unwanted burden." Citizens were confused, frustrated, and impatient. As one housewife commented, "I want to get out but I don't want to give in."

Westmoreland and Chairman of the Joint Chiefs of Staff (JCS) Earl Wheeler sensed that Tet had had a jarring effect on U.S. public opinion, but they were soldiers. From their perspective, the enemy was on the run; the time had come to deliver a knockout blow. After conferring together in Saigon in February, the two military leaders proposed an aggressive plan for ending the war. U.S. and ARVN units would stage an amphibious landing north of the 17th parallel and simultaneously attack NVA sanctuaries in Laos and Cambodia. These strikes would be accompanied by intensified bombing of the north. To implement this "two-fisted" strategy Westmoreland requested an additional 205,000 soldiers.

Johnson informed the commander that he would do whatever was necessary to lift the siege of Khe Sanh, which had continued through the Tet offensive, and he authorized the dispatch of 10,500 additional troops. But implementation of the wider plan, the president sensed, would outrage the international community and cause a major backlash in the United States.

"I feel like a hitchhiker caught in a hailstorm on a Texas highway," he remarked to an aide. "I can't run. I can't hide. And I can't make it stop." The new secretary of defense, Clark Clifford, advised Johnson to go slow while he, Clifford, conducted a major reassessment of the war. Clifford, a long-time political activist and adviser to Democratic presidents, discovered that the Pentagon was really just feeling its way in Vietnam and that the military chiefs could not say with any accuracy how many men and how much force it would require to finally subdue the Vietcong and NVA. Westmoreland's "two-fisted" strategy would require calling up the reserves and further burdening the American people, and all this in an election year. To the enragement of Westmoreland and the JCS, Clifford recommended the deployment of only 22,000 additional men and a "highly forceful" approach to Thieu and Ky to get their house in order so that South Vietnam could assume greater responsibility for the war. The White House endorsed the Clifford approach almost without comment.

In essence, however, Johnson had decided not to decide. He was as determined as ever not to "surrender" in Vietnam, that is, not to unilaterally withdraw unless and until the continued existence of an independent, noncommunist Vietnam was assured. But he had at the same time denied his field commander's request to follow up on what was clearly a smashing victory. Not surprisingly, domestic support for the war continued to erode. Approval of Johnson's handling of the conflict in Southeast Asia, which had been driven up to 40% by the 1967 public relations campaign, plummeted to 26% during Tet. Seventy-eight percent of those people queried indicated that they were certain that the United States was making no progress in the war. Disillusionment spread among American troops in Vietnam, a number of whom chalked "UUUU" on their helmets standing for "The Unwilling, led by the Unqualified, doing the Unnecessary for the Ungrateful." Meanwhile, a group of veteran diplomats and policy analysts, the Senior Informal Advisory Group on Vietnam (dubbed "the Wise Men" by the press), which included former Secretary of State Dean Acheson and former Secretary of Defense Robert Lovett, called for the "gradual disengagement" of Americans from the war.

The Pueblo Incident

No matter how hard they might try, presidents find it impossible to focus on a single crisis or set of issues for very long. Their agendas inevitably become packed with meetings, lobbying sessions, and crises, all of which compete for the attention of the chief executive and most of which affect each other. Lyndon B. Johnson was not immune to this problem. In the midst of the Tet Offensive and its aftermath, the president had to deal with the Pueblo crisis, an incident that brought the United States and North Korea to the brink of war. On January 23, 1968, a week before the beginning of the communist offensive in South Vietnam, the North Korean navy and air force surrounded and seized an American intelligence ship, the *USS Pueblo*. The belligerent government of Kim II Sung insisted that the ship and its 83-man crew had violated North Korean waters and committed an act of war. In the United States, nationalists pressured the Johnson administration to go in with all guns blazing, bomb strategic North Korean port facilities, and rescue the U.S. sailors. Instead, the president chose to show restraint. The U.S. government condemned the seizure, noting that the *Pueblo* had been cruising 15 miles off the coast in international waters, well outside both the 3- and 12-mile limits. (North Korea claimed a 50-mile limit.) Following 11 months of negotiation and a confession and apology from Captain Lloyd M. Bucher, Pyongyang released the crew but not the ship. Bucher subsequently renounced his confession, declaring that it had been extracted under duress. Nevertheless, he was court-martialed for surrendering without a fight and for cooperating with the enemy. Most importantly, however, the president had refused to escalate a crisis, the outcome of which would not affect vital American interests one way or another.

Turning Point: The Election of 1968

By 1968, the American political milieu was as fragmented as it perhaps had ever been in the history of the republic. Despite the Great Society programs and Johnson's emphasis on social justice, liberals constituted only a portion of the consensus that the president had molded in 1964 and 1965. The coalition that had swept the Democrats to victory in 1964 encompassed the center of the political spectrum, including moderate Republicans and businesspeople who were frightened by Goldwater extremists, as well as traditionally Democratic southerners, urban machine politicians, blue-collar union members, and almost all African Americans. By 1968, that coalition was splintering. Some Cold War liberals plus the hard-hat contingent, machine Democrats, and southerners continued to view the war in Vietnam as a struggle of good against evil and a conflict the United States had to win to preserve its power and prestige in the world. These were the same people who were increasingly concerned about urban riots, who viewed integration as something intended only for the Deep South, if at all, and who were dubious about welfare and antipoverty programs. Lyndon Johnson found himself driven increasingly into the embrace of this faction because of his own commitment to win in Vietnam. In so doing, he found himself ironically at odds with those who had been most ardent in their support of the Great Society programs.

As of 1968, the antiwar movement included traditional conservatives such as Fulbright, who were concerned about the threat posed to republican institutions and processes – representative democracy, a free press, an economy rooted in equality of opportunity – by the war. It also encompassed New Deal/Fair Deal liberals who favored integration of all schools and public facilities, redistributive taxation, and increased government spending for welfare and education. Although they agreed with much of the socioeconomic agenda espoused by the SDS, the FSM, and the New Left in general, these antiwar liberals found it difficult to work with individuals who rejected "the system." They certainly did not want to be identified with counterculture radicals, some of whom by 1968 were expressing open admiration for Ho, the NVA, and the VC.

Even before Tet, antiwar liberals within the Democratic Party had become convinced that it was necessary to prevent Johnson's renomination in 1968. John Kenneth Galbraith, then national chairman of the Americans for Democratic Action (ADA), addressed antiwar rallies throughout 1967, while another ADA member, Allard Lowenstein, launched a "dump Johnson" movement on college campuses and among Democratic politicians. The favorite of the antiwar liberals was Robert Kennedy, but he refused to throw his hat in the ring, in part because he knew how hard it was to defeat a sitting president and in part because he knew he would be accused of putting personal ambition and revenge ahead of his country's interests. Those committed to ousting Johnson turned finally to Eugene J. McCarthy, the quiet, thoughtful, quixotic liberal from Minnesota. He announced his candidacy on November 30, 1967 and proceeded to win 42.4% of the vote in the New Hampshire primary to President Johnson's 49.5%. "Dove bites Hawk," a journalist quipped. Exit polls indicated that most of McCarthy's support came from those disenchanted with the war – both hawks and doves. With the exception of speechwriter Richard Goodwin, the entire effort was directed by students. Harvard graduate student Sam Brown managed the campaign; the candidate's daughter, Mary, left Radcliffe to help; and returning Peace Corps volunteer John Barbieri operated the mass mailings.

Johnson Abdicates

On March 22, Johnson officially rejected Westmoreland's proposals for expanding the war. His position compromised, the general returned to the United States to become Army chief of staff. Privately, Johnson railed against "the establishment bastards," the wise men and antiwar liberals, who were calling for irrevocable deescalation. McCarthy's showing in the New Hampshire primary had been a bitter blow. On the evening of March 31, a somber, haggard president went on nationwide television to announce that henceforward bombing would be limited to the area just north of the DMZ. The United States, he declared, was ready for comprehensive peace talks anywhere, anytime. He announced that Averell Harriman would represent the administration if such talks materialized. The Texan then dropped a bombshell. "I shall not seek, and I will not accept, the nomination of my party for another term as president," he told a stunned nation.

Johnson's motives have been the subject of much subsequent debate. Politics was his whole life and had been since his college days. Yet, a second term with the country bitterly divided would not really be worth having. He had suffered a major heart attack while majority leader, and his wife desperately wanted him to guard his health by stepping down. It was clear, moreover, that further domestic reform would be impossible. Given the bitter personal animosity displayed toward him by Republicans and liberal Democrats alike, there was even some doubt that he could win. Finally and most importantly, abdication might reunify the United States and convince the North Vietnamese and NLF of the sincerity of his offer to negotiate.

Ho responded positively to President Johnson's initiative and, after some maneuvering, peace talks opened in Paris on May 13, 1968. They immediately deadlocked. The North Vietnamese demanded an unconditional halt to the bombing, but Harriman and Johnson would agree only on condition that the communists reciprocate with a deescalation of their own. The NVA negotiators refused to abandon the war in the South, leaving the Americans and ARVN with a free hand to deal with the insurgency. As days turned into weeks, General Creighton Abrams, the new U.S. commander in Vietnam, sought to keep maximum pressure on the VC and NVA and assisted the ARVN in its frantic efforts to expand the areas in South Vietnam under government control.

Meanwhile, Robert Kennedy had changed his mind and decided to compete for the Democratic presidential nomination. Following McCarthy's strong showing in New Hampshire, Kennedy's wife, other family members, and friends had urged him to run. Johnson was not going to end the war in Vietnam or solve the nation's urban problems, the New York senator believed. He would make a stronger candidate than McCarthy, and if he did not run, he would be missing perhaps his only chance to be president. On March 16, Kennedy announced his candidacy in the same Senate caucus room in which his brother had declared eight years earlier. He admitted he had made a mistake in supporting the war in 1962 and 1963. "I run to seek new policies," he declared, "policies to end the bloodshed in Viet Nam and in our cities, policies to close the gap that now exists between black and white, between rich and poor, between young and old in this country and around the rest of the world." Bobby Kennedy was youthful, ambitious, charismatic, and ruthless. While John F. Kennedy promised to spread the blessings of liberty and democracy to the less fortunate of the world, his brother set his goal as saving America from itself. He immediately plunged into the campaign, attracting large crowds as he pointed toward the Wisconsin primary. Kennedy had the advantage of being able to appeal to antiwar liberals, blacks, the poor, working-class Catholics, urban ethnic groups, and other components of the lower middle class who had formerly been supporters of the war and who were moderate to conservative in their political views.

Johnson's withdrawal opened the way for a third candidacy, that of Vice President Hubert Humphrey. Running as Johnson's heir apparent, the Minnesota liberal could count on the support of party regulars across the United States. An unenthusiastic supporter of the president's Vietnam policies, Humphrey was closely identified with the civil rights acts of the 1960s and had been a champion of organized labor throughout his public life. Despite the fact that he had been a devoted servant of liberal causes since he was first elected mayor of Minneapolis, Humphrey conceded the left to his opponents. Given the popular obsession with Vietnam and his sometimes obsequious support of Johnson, he had little choice. When Humphrey was asked, "Whatever happened to the liberal program you stood for?" he answered, "It passed. Does that upset you?" While McCarthy and Kennedy waged high-profile campaigns, Humphrey concentrated on lining up convention delegates.

The Assassinations

In the midst of the 1968 presidential primary campaign, Martin Luther King, Jr., launched his Poor People's Campaign. He wanted to simultaneously highlight the plight of the nation's poor regardless of color, alert middle-class America's conscience, and form poor blacks, Chicanos, and whites into a formidable political coalition. Although he had not made any public announcement, King intended to "get behind Bobby." On April 4, America's most renowned civil rights leader traveled to Memphis to lead a demonstration on behalf of striking garbage workers. Earlier in the day, a white petty crook, James Earl Ray, had told his brother that he was going to "get the big nigger." That evening, while standing on the balcony of the Lorraine Motel, King was shot and killed by the white racist and ex-convict. As rumors of a conspiracy involving White Citizens' Councils, the Federal Bureau of Investigation (FBI), and a host of other organizations swirled, riots broke out in a dozen cities, the worst being in Washington, D.C., and Chicago. Ironically, African Americans burned down their own ghettos in rage over the killing of the nation's most famous advocate of nonviolence.

As news of King's death went out over radio and television, new waves of rioting wracked the United States. "When white America killed Dr. King," declared Stokley Carmichael, "she declared war on us." In Washington, D.C., more than 700 fires turned night into day and completely obscured the Capitol. Although some whites rejoiced at King's murder – a delighted FBI agent in Atlanta was overheard to say, "They finally got the s.o.b.!" – most were shocked and saddened. President Johnson declared a national day of mourning. On that Sunday, hundreds of thousands of Americans, black and white, marched arm in arm singing freedom songs. After stalling for more than two years on Johnson's proposed Fair Housing Act, Congress passed it. The measure prohibited real estate agents from discriminating when they sold or rented property.

In the wake of the assassination, Kennedy met with King's closest associates. The Reverend Ralph Abernathy, who succeeded King as head of the SCLC, subsequently declared that "white America does have someone in it who cares." In fact, Robert Kennedy seemed to identify far more than his brother with Americans of color who had for so long been victims of discrimination and exploitation. He actively supported Cesar Chavez in his uphill battle to organize migrant farm workers in California. The Puerto Rican community in New York had been an essential part of his constituency since his election to the Senate. By May, Kennedy's well-financed campaign was in high gear; he defeated a favorite-son candidate who was running as a Humphrey stand-in in the Indiana primary. When McCarthy triumphed in Oregon, the two prepared for a showdown in California, a state whose large electoral vote made it crucial to any presidential campaign. McCarthy's young supporters stuck by him, but he was no match for the handsome, charismatic Kennedy. A bland speaker who seemed to lecture his audiences, the Wisconsin senator sounded like "the dean of the finest English department in the land," as Norman Mailer put it. The grinning Bobby, hair flopping, hand perpetually extended, blitzed the state and called in all his family's political debts. Shrieking young women vied with large contingents of Mexican Americans, mobilized by Caesar Chavez, for a glimpse of the candidate. On June 4, Kennedy won with 46% of the vote to McCarthy's 42% and seemed well on his way to the nomination. With only 12% of the vote, Humphrey appeared doomed. But then as Kennedy was leaving a victory celebration in Los Angeles, he was shot and killed by a Jordanian immigrant named Sirhan Bishara Sirhan. Although his exact motives remained unclear, Sirhan was an Arab zealot who probably killed Kennedy because of his long-standing support for Israel. His body was placed aboard a plane with his widow and two others – Jacqueline Kennedy and Coretta Scott King. The United States staggered under this new blow. There were no riots, only a stunned silence and thousands gathered at St. Patrick's Cathedral in New York City to pay their respects. With the assassination of America's two most charismatic political reformers and with riots sweeping the nation's urban centers, it seemed as if America was coming apart at the seams.

Reinforcing that conviction was widespread student unrest in the spring of 1968 – unrest that more and more frequently turned violent. In late 1967, a faction of the SDS leadership led by Tom Hayden rejected participatory democracy and nonviolent civil disobedience. He could "shoot to kill" if necessary, Hayden declared. The organization also became more authoritarian and dictatorial. V. I. Lenin replaced Jean Jacques Rousseau as the SDS's philosophical guru and icon. In April 1968, Mark Rudd, head of the SDS chapter at Columbia University, led a demonstration to protest the university's decision to build a gymnasium in a long-established black neighborhood. A confrontation ensued between administration officials and student protesters as Rudd and his followers occupied university buildings, ransacked administrative offices, and forced the cancellation of classes. The institution was headed by Grayson Kirk, who sat on the board of the university's Institute for Defense Analysis, partially funded by the Department of Defense and the CIA, and who believed that the current student population was dominated by those who "reject authority, [and] take refuge in turbulent, inchoate nihilism." Columbia officials called in the police, who attacked the students with clubs and fists. After dozens of bleeding protesters were driven to jail in waiting paddy wagons, the campus paper denounced the whole affair as a "brutal, bloody show." The violence created sympathy among previously neutral components of the student body, and a strike shut down the university for the rest of the semester. Similar clashes, most of which centered around or began with antiwar demonstrations, broke out at Harvard, Cornell, and San Francisco State. To some students Columbia seemed to prove that the establishment was repressive, insensitive, and corrupt. The only alternative, declared an activist, was "revolutionary social change.... We, the youth, have no place but a revolutionary one in the present-day decaying America." Richard Nixon declared that Columbia was the "first major skirmish in a revolutionary struggle to seize the universities," and Congressman Robert H. Michel warned that the radicals' next target would be "City Hall, the State Capitol, or even the White House."

The Democrats Unravel

It was in this overheated atmosphere that the Democratic National Convention assembled in Chicago in August. The meeting itself was an angry, bitter affair in which the delegates quickly polarized into anti- and prowar factions. The hawks who spoke in effect for Lyndon B. Johnson voted down a "peace" plank advocated by McCarthy and Senator George McGovern of South Dakota, which called for "an unconditional end to all bombing in North Vietnam" and adopted instead a plank endorsing the administration's quest for "an honorable and lasting peace" in Vietnam. The doves' plank, declared Ohio Congressman Wayne Hays, would play into the hands of radicals who want "pot instead of patriotism, sideburns instead of solutions. They would substitute riots for reason." Although McCarthy managed to attract some of Kennedy's delegates and he consistently led the vice president in the polls, Humphrey easily captured the nomination on the first ballot. "Clean Gene" was a mercurial, enigmatic personality, arrogant with his staff, and alternately inspiring and stultifying on the stump. Most professional politicians distrusted him and had heaped ridicule on his "children's crusade." Without winning one state primary, Humphrey had worked behind the scenes to line up almost 1,500 delegates. He also supported "Johnson's war." "Nothing would bring the real peaceniks back to our side," confided an aide to a reporter, "unless Hubert urinated on a portrait of Johnson in Times Square before television – and then they'd say to him, why didn't you do it before." To be his running mate, Humphrey chose the environmentalist and moderate liberal Edmund Muskie of Maine. In domestic affairs, the Democratic platform was generally liberal. The convention refused to seat the segregated and segregationist Mississippi delegation, and it democratized the process by which convention delegates would be selected for 1972. No one seemed satisfied, however. Black northern delegates sneered at white southerners, calling them racists, while antiwar delegates and administration supporters traded insults.

As the Democratic delegates jousted within Chicago's cavernous amphitheater, a wrenching spectacle was unfolding on the streets outside. An army of antiwar protestors, anti-establishment crusaders, and counterculture figures had descended on the city. From the earnest and well-scrubbed supporters of Eugene McCarthy, to the SDS, to the nihilistic Yippies (the Youth International Party), the crowds spanned the antiwar spectrum. Most were bent on peaceful demonstration, but a faction led by Abbie Hoffman, who told reporters that his "conception of revolution is that it's fun," were determined to provoke violence. In fact, it was counterculture extremists who managed to seize the spotlight. A former SNCC organizer and would-be standup comic, Hoffman represented all that respectable, middle-class America detested. Ridiculing the notion of "character" and conventional morality, he declared marijuana and LSD to be the only sure paths to higher consciousness and enlightenment. The Yippies spread rumors that they were going to put LSD in Chicago's water supply and use female members to seduce Humphrey candidates. Mayor Daley ordered an army of 12,000 policemen to cordon off and control the demonstrators. He persuaded the governor to station some 6,000 Illinois National Guardsmen armed with rifles, flame throwers, grenade launchers, and bazookas outside the city as backup. He also ordered his plainclothes police to infiltrate protest organizations, and the federal government sent 1,000 agents to Chicago. For every six demonstrators during the convention, there was one undercover agent. The governor ordered his troops to protect the water supply and the *Chicago Tribune* published a series of revelations concerning "plans by Communists and left-wing agitators to disrupt the city." When some of the Yippies and SDS members began hurling bags of urine and screaming obscenities, the police went berserk. For three days, a national television audience watched as Daley's men beat not only the demonstrators but some innocent bystanders as well. As journalist Nicholas Von Hoffman noted, the police had "taken off their badges, their name plates, even the unit patches on their shoulders to become a mob of identical, unidentifiable club swingers." Middle-class America was repelled and, in Miami, Richard

Nixon and the rest of the Republican Party prepared to take advantage of that revulsion.

Nixon Returns

Following his defeat by John F. Kennedy in 1960, Nixon had run for governor of California and lost. His second defeat in two years embittered him. "You won't have Nixon to kick around any more," he told reporters. But the former House Un-American Activities Committee (HUAC) member was as resilient as he was mercurial. Nixon moved to New York, joined a prestigious law firm, made a great deal of money, and worked on reestablishing his ties with the national Republican establishment. He dutifully campaigned for Goldwater in 1964 and then began lining up delegates for 1968. The liberal wing of the party led by Nelson Rockefeller initially threw its support behind Michigan Governor George Romney, a dynamic businessman who had revived the failing American Motors Company. However, a series of political blunders, including ill-advised statements on Vietnam, immediately crippled his candidacy. Rockefeller, with his money and panel of intellectuals, made a move but quickly faded. On Nixon's right was Governor Ronald Reagan of California who had defeated Edmund G. "Pat" Brown by more than 1 million votes in 1966.

Rockefeller was never a threat to the Nixon candidacy. Republicans from the traditional conservative to the ultra rightist detested him either on ideological grounds or because they perceived him to be nothing more than a rich opportunist. Reagan was more of a problem. Nixon protected his right flank, however, when he met with southern Republicans led by Senator J. Strom Thurmond (who had switched parties after the Democrats embraced civil rights) in Atlanta on May 31, assuring them that he shared their views on busing and law and order. Consequently, when the GOP gathered in Miami Beach in early August, Nixon was nominated on the first ballot. To be his running mate, he selected Spiro T. Agnew, the Maryland governor who had attracted national attention by his explicit, public denunciation of urban rioting. In his acceptance speech, Nixon proclaimed that a "new voice" was being heard across America, not "the voices of hatred, the voices of dissension, the voices of riot and revolution." He represented, he said, "those who did not break the law, people who pay their taxes and go to work, people who send their children to school, who go to their churches, people who are not haters, people who love this country." The platform was less of a surprise. It called for a national war against crime, reform of the welfare system to encourage a maximum number of poor to work, and a stronger national defense. Indeed, the Cold War, punctuated by hot spots such as Korea and Vietnam, had led to the establishment of a huge military–industrial complex; by 1968, it had become an important part of the GOP constituency. On Vietnam, the platform promised simultaneously to "de-Americanize the war" and not to accept a "camouflaged surrender."

George Wallace and the Politics of Hate

Meanwhile, George C. Wallace, who had made a brief run at the Democratic nomination before withdrawing, had established the American Independent Party. Appealing to the worst in the American people, he blamed urban rioting on Black Power advocates and their "socialist" white allies. He none too subtly hinted that integration ought to remain a personal choice. He blamed the federal government and especially the Supreme Court for encouraging racial unrest as well as for coddling criminals and tolerating welfare cheats. His campaign would not be limited to the South, he predicted to supporters: "the people of Cleveland and Chicago and Gary and St. Louis will be so goddamned sick and tired of Federal interference in their local schools, they'll be ready to vote for Wallace." To the delight of large, raucous crowds, he blamed the nation's problems on "briefcase totin' bureaucrats, ivory-tower guideline writers . . . and pointy-headed professors" who did not know how to "park a bicycle straight." Selecting Air Force General Curtis E. LeMay to be his running mate, the Alabama governor promised total victory in Vietnam.

To an extent Wallace was right about his ability to capture the public imagination. Political prognosticators watched in amazement as his rating in the polls climbed from 9% in May 1968 to 16% in June, and in September, just after the Democratic Convention, to 21%. Wallace's primary appeal was to southern farmers, small businesspeople, and blue-collar workers, and to northern so-called white ethnics – urban-dwelling, working-class descendents of Polish, Irish, Italian, and Baltic immigrants. Ridiculed by black revolutionaries and white liberals alike, they turned on the establishment with a vengeance. Indeed, for them the establishment was the liberal establishment. Playing the politics of alienation, Wallace affirmed his supporters' belief in the existence of a conspiracy by the media, the federal government, blacks, and communists to take what was theirs, especially their sense of worth and patriotism.

In the ensuing campaign, Nixon managed to seize the political middle with Wallace on his right and antiwar liberals on his left while subtly appealing to the same fears that Wallace was exploiting. The "new Nixon" appeared relaxed and self-confident, posing successfully as a harmonizer, an antidote to the angry and divided Democrats and a conservative alternative to the race-baiting Wallace. Nevertheless, Humphrey was a skilled, experienced campaigner. On September 30, the "Happy Warrior" established some distance between himself and President Johnson. "I would stop the bombing of North Vietnam as an acceptable risk for peace," he told a Salt Lake City audience (transmitted from a television studio because the candidate did not dare risk heckling from antiwar protesters),

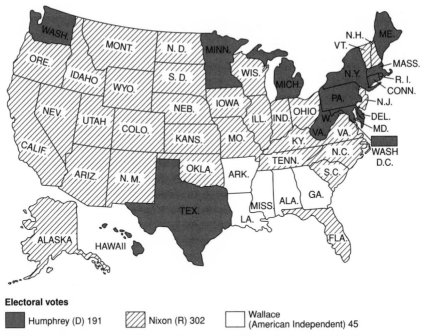

Electoral votes

■ Humphrey (D) 191   ▨ Nixon (R) 302   □ Wallace (American Independent) 45

Map 8–1. Map shows Nixon, Humphrey, and Wallace election results of 1968.

"because I believe it could lead to success in the negotiations and thereby shorten the war." As October progressed, some of Wallace's labor supporters began to return to the Democratic fold as did antiwar liberals who were more afraid of Nixon and "the bombsy twins," as Humphrey called Wallace and LeMay, than they were repelled by the Johnson foreign policy. When on November 1, Johnson announced a total halt in the bombing of North Vietnam, Humphrey drew virtually abreast of Nixon in the polls. Going on the attack, the Democratic nominee challenged his opponent to a debate. When the Republicans refused, Humphrey dubbed Nixon "Richard the Chickenhearted." A week before the election, McCarthy endorsed his party's selection: "I'm voting for Humphrey, and I think you should suffer with me," he told the American people.

When the final tallies were counted on Election Tuesday, however, Richard Nixon had won a narrow victory. The Republican ticket polled 31.7 million votes, 43.4% of the total, while Humphrey and Muskie rolled up 31.2 million, 42.7% of the whole. Wallace trailed far behind with 9.9 million, which amounted to 13.5% of the electorate. The Independent Party candidate carried 5 southern states, while Humphrey ran ahead in 13 and Nixon carried 32. In a sense, the election was close, but in another sense it amounted, as Theodore White observed, to a "negative landslide" of gigantic proportions. Since 1965, the Democrats had squandered a plurality of more than 16 million votes. The fragile consensus that Johnson had stitched together had been ripped apart by Vietnam, inflation, urban rioting, and the white backlash against the second reconstruction. The Democrats saw defections from nearly every component of the New Deal coalition – labor, the South, urban ethnics, liberal intellectuals, and farmers. Humphrey won a mere 38% of the white vote; only massive majorities among blacks and Jews kept him in contention. Even the reliable black vote fell 11% from 1964. "What a year," declared *Time* in one of its patented essays, "one tragic, surprising and perplexing thing after another." To Americans besieged by war, civil strife, and self-doubt, Richard Nixon represented the familiar, tried and true way, the comforting middle ground. Little did they know that his personal flaws would produce a constitutional and political crisis of monumental proportions.

ADDITIONAL READINGS

Berman, Larry, *Planning a Tragedy* (1983).

Brands, H. W., *The Wages of Globalism: Lyndon Johnson and the Limits of American Power* (1995).

Caute, David, *The Year of the Barricades: A Journey Through 1968* (1988).

Chalmers, David, *And the Crooked Places Made Straight: The Struggle for Social Change in the 1960s* (1991).

De Benedetti, Charles, and Charles Chatfield, *An American Ordeal: The Antiwar Movement of the Vietnam Era* (1990).

Gaddis, John Lewis, *Strategies of Containment: A Critical Appraisal of Postwar American National Security Policy* (1982).

Herring, George C., *America's Longest War*, 2nd ed. (1986).

Karnow, Stanley, *Vietnam: A History* (1983).

Small, Melvin, *Johnson, Nixon and the Doves* (1988).

Spector, Ronald, *After Tet* (1992).

Summers, Harry, Jr., *On Strategy: A Critical Analysis of the Vietnam War* (1981).

Turner, Kathleen J., *Lyndon Johnson's Dual War: Vietnam and the Press* (1985).

White, Theodore H., *The Making of the President, 1968* (1969).

Young, Marilyn B., *The Vietnam Wars* (1990).

9   Realpolitik or Imperialism?

Nixon, Kissinger, and American Foreign Policy

Richard Nixon entered the White House determined to create a new international order that would simultaneously contain communism and restore America's freedom of action. The author of this vision was Henry Kissinger, a German-born academic known for his admiration of Austrian Chancellor Klemens von Metternich, a nineteenth-century states-man whose approach to international relations had been distinctly non-ideological and counterrevolutionary. Specifically, Nixon and Kissinger, appointed by the president to be national security adviser, wanted to se-cure "peace with honor in Vietnam" by weakening the Vietcong (VC) and North Vietnamese and strengthening South Vietnam so that the armies of Nguyen Van Thieu could win a battlefield victory on their own. Thus freed from the Vietnam quagmire, with its prestige restored and its military undistracted, the United States could assume the role of arbiter of world affairs. The new Republican administration accepted the implications of NSC 68 – that it was necessary to battle communism on every front – but be-lieved that global containment could be achieved through diplomacy rather than force of arms. In Kissinger's view, the Soviet Union and to a lesser ex-tent Communist China were on their way to becoming satiated, status quo powers. If the United States could disarm their fears and appeal to their economic interests, the two communist superpowers might be persuaded to take their places as responsible members of the international commu-nity. Then, as had been true in the days of Metternich, who presided over the Concert of Europe following the defeat of Napoleon Bonaparte, the great powers could act to control revolutions that threatened international sta-bility. While maintaining an intimidating nuclear and conventional force, the United States would project its power through diplomacy, coercing or cajoling regional rivals into signing peace agreements rather than fighting prolonged and bloody wars. Such a policy was profoundly insensitive to the social and economic injustice and intense nationalism that characterized most Third World societies and that fueled the revolutions that the U.S. government hoped to contain. As had been true during Metternich's time, realpolitik during the Nixon–Kissinger era would provide only a temporary respite from an apparently endless cycle of great power rivalry, revolution, and war.

Inauguration day 1969 dawned gray and ugly. The mood in Washington, D.C., was as nasty as the weather. The only happy person in the entire city, columnist Russell Baker wrote, was Lady Bird Johnson. Baker overheard a black man and a white man exchange racial epithets as the crowd pressed them together. Antiwar demonstrators were pervasive and belligerent. All along Pennsylvania Avenue, they burned the small American flags distributed by the Boy Scouts and shouted, "Ho, Ho, Ho Chi Minh, the NLF is going to win." As Stephen Ambrose noted, this was the first disruption of an inaugural parade or ceremony in the 180 years of the American presidency. Not even in 1861, as the United States prepared to descend into the Civil War, had anything like it occurred. When the Nixons' limousine reached 13th Street, demonstrators cursed the couple and deluged their car with sticks, stones, beer cans, and bottles. By 15th Street, the motorcade had left the protestors behind and the inauguration proceeded peacefully. Nevertheless, the outbursts and the mood that underlay them augured ill for the future.

The New Realism

President Nixon

Richard Nixon was born in Yorba Linda, California, of Quaker parents, the second of five sons. He grew up in nearby Whittier, graduating in due course from Whittier College, where he spent most of his time studying and riding the bench as a second stringer on the football team. After a successful stint at Duke University Law School, he returned to Whittier to practice law and marry a local school teacher, Thelma "Pat" Ryan. During World War II, Nixon served as a naval supply officer in the South Pacific. Similar to another famous veteran who would defeat him for the presidency in 1960, Nixon entered politics in 1946, defeating Congressman Jerry Voorhis. He displayed in that first campaign the single-mindedness, combativeness, and demagoguery for which he would become famous. In Washington, D.C., he naturally gravitated to the House Committee on Un-American Activities. Four years later, Nixon moved up to the Senate after defeating Helen Gahagan Douglas. His tactics were outrageously McCarthyite, featuring red baiting and guilt by association. He led the Republican attack on the Truman administration for "losing" China to the communists and was selected to be Ike's running mate in 1952.

Nixon was simultaneously crude and shrewd, complex and simple. He saw himself as the purveyor and protector of the simple American virtues, fidelity to family, God, and country; the guardian of liberty and free enterprise; the symbol of order and respect for authority. Inspired by his austere, demanding mother, Nixon was driven to succeed and to make a difference, but he was profoundly insecure. He trusted no one, whether a member of Congress, the average person on the street, or a member of his own entourage. His days were frequently consumed with the search for enemies and traitors; that is, those who were opposed to him and his policies. At times, this quintessential middle American showed signs of paranoia and schizophrenia. He bombarded his chief aides with memos in which he referred to himself in the third person. At the same time, Nixon was intelligent and empathetic with those he believed had been victimized by circumstance. He could be shy and appealing at one moment and ruthless and self-righteous at another. His capacity for self-pity was famous. He was also obsessed with image, both his and the nation's. In a directive to White House Chief of Staff H. R. Haldeman, at the end of his first year in office, Nixon outlined the presidential persona he wanted to project:

RN [he habitually referred to himself by his own initials] being the first President, since Wilson, who does some of his own speech writing, the fact that after all the talking about weakness on television that he has made effective use of the medium, the fact that no President in this century has had more opposition in the press and among the TV commentators and that in spite of that opposition has been able to maintain majority support.

Nixon's view of the press was, to use Stephen Ambrose's word, "incredible." He greatly exaggerated its importance and then declared war on it. For Nixon, his presidency was in part a struggle with the "liberal establishment press" to project his idealized self and place his views before the public.

At the end of November 1968, Nixon summoned Henry Kissinger to his transition headquarters in the Pierre Hotel in New York. Kissinger recalled that the president-elect was painfully shy and alternately boastful and deferential. "Rather touchingly," he gave Kissinger the names of several Duke University law professors who could vouch for his intellectual acumen. Nixon made it clear that he did not trust the State Department; its bureaucracy was not loyal to him. It was staffed by "Ivy League liberals who . . . had always opposed him politically." Nixon told his guest that he wanted to be his own secretary of state and that he intended to revitalize the National Security Council (NSC). Two days later, he asked Kissinger to be his national security adviser and the Harvard professor eagerly accepted.

The Adviser
Henry Kissinger seemed an unlikely choice to be Richard Nixon's foreign policy guru. A Bavarian-born Jew, he had escaped from the Nazis when he was 15. As soon as World War II broke out, he went to his Bronx recruitment office and enlisted. His language skills landed him in Army counterintelligence. Following a stint in civil government in occupied Germany, he

earned his doctorate and secured a position at Harvard's school of government and public affairs. There he gained control of the Harvard International Seminar, through which many of the world's future movers and shakers would pass. Denied tenure at Harvard, he went to work for the Council on Foreign Relations and subsequently published *Nuclear Weapons and Foreign Policy*, which attempted to make limited nuclear war respectable. He returned to Harvard, served briefly as Nelson Rockefeller's foreign policy adviser in 1964, and during the 1968 presidential campaign ingratiated himself with both the Republican and Democratic candidates. Although he was feeding the Nixon people inside information on the Paris peace talks when Humphrey began to surge in October 1968, Kissinger wrote the Democratic candidate denouncing Nixon and offering his services.

Kissinger was a garrulous, sociable man who enjoyed the company of women, good food, opera, and parties. Nixon was painfully shy, frequently self-conscious, single minded, and hobbyless. His idea of a good time was to take a walk on the beach in his brogans and talk politics. The new national security adviser felt strong contempt for the middle-American politician and made no secret of it. (There were, however, few men for whom Kissinger did not feel contempt.) Yet, there were similarities between the two men. Despite Kissinger's dates and books, he was in many ways as insecure socially and intellectually as his new boss. The two men were loners in their respective professions. They trusted no one and consequently went through life virtually devoid of friends. Both men loved intrigue for intrigue's sake and both were insatiably ambitious. Using Nixon's office and his political power base, Kissinger intended to create a new world order, with the United States at the center and himself at the controls. Nixon perceived Kissinger to be egotistical and deceitful, but eminently useful. The wizard of Cambridge would simultaneously provide the philosophical rationale for the openings to Russia and China and tell him how to end the war in Vietnam, without splitting the country down the middle. The national security adviser would, moreover, subdue the vast foreign policy bureaucracy in Washington, D.C., and bend it to Nixon's will.

To Senate Foreign Relations Committee Chairman J. W. Fulbright's delight, Kissinger endorsed the asymmetrical approach to containment that Fulbright and George Kennan had been pushing since the 1950s. "I believe that we do have interests in every part of the world," Kissinger declared, "but I do not believe that we can be the principal protectors of all these interests everywhere simultaneously." Such indiscriminate globalism, he and Fulbright agreed, were beyond the nation's physical and psychological resources. The former Harvard academic defined the national interest in economic and strategic terms. Indeed, his anticommunism stemmed not from ideological considerations, as his critics charged, but from a belief that Russia and China were totalitarian, expansionist powers that posed a threat to America's physical security. He was not a missionary determined to reproduce the American way in every corner of the globe. Other governments and cultures should be judged on a de facto basis, he argued, and dealt with according to the threat they posed to American security and trade. Despite his commitment to peace and stability, Kissinger recognized that the world the Cold War had made was a dangerous place. America, he argued, must be prepared to defend its interests with everything from diplomacy to nuclear weapons.

Vietnam: "The Will to Win"

Prior to taking office, Nixon and Kissinger had stoutly defended America's commitment to South Vietnam. During the 1968 campaign, the Republican candidate had consistently blasted Lyndon B. Johnson for not doing more on the battlefield to pressure the North Vietnamese; he seemed particularly enthralled with bombing. To Nixon, victory depended on "the will to win," and he boasted to Kissinger that unlike Johnson, "I have the will in spades." He told voters that America's stand in Vietnam was necessary to contain Chinese communist expansion and allow "free" Asian nations the time to grow strong enough to defend themselves. Kissinger's position more closely resembled that of Richard Russell. Early policymakers had exaggerated the importance of Vietnam to the national interest, but once committed, the United States could not afford to back down. The dispatch of hundreds of thousands of American troops had settled the matter, he argued, "for what is involved now is confidence in American promises."

By inauguration day on January 20, 1969, however, both Richard Nixon and Henry Kissinger were convinced that the war in Vietnam had to be ended. Indeed, during the campaign, Nixon had let it be known that he had a "secret plan" to end the conflict in Southeast Asia. Some students of the Nixon administration argue that extrication from Vietnam topped its list of diplomatic priorities and that the president and his NSC adviser used the Soviet Union's desire for trade and arms reductions and China's desire to end its international isolation to persuade those two nations to abandon Hanoi. Others insist that the two wanted to end the war to clear the way for the openings to Moscow and Beijing and the creation of a new world order with themselves as arbiters. Whatever the case, both men believed that their political future and their place in history depended on their ability to extricate America from Vietnam. After reading a British Institute of Strategic Studies paper declaring that the United States, exhausted by its "recent experiences at home and abroad" had lost "the desire and ability" to be the dominant power in the world, Nixon sent Kissinger a copy. "Very important and accurate," the latter commented.

But any peace achieved would have to be "peace with honor" and that meant no unilateral withdrawal and no abandonment of the Thieu regime. Nixon had led the attacks on Truman for the loss of China and, similar to

Johnson, feared the political backlash and the deep divisions that would result if it appeared he had "lost" Vietnam. More importantly, both he and Kissinger believed that it was imperative to deal with China and the Soviet Union from a position of strength rather than weakness. The opening of communications with Moscow and Beijing and subsequent negotiations would be dangerous and counterproductive if it appeared the United States was being forced out of Southeast Asia by a tiny, underdeveloped nation such as North Vietnam.

Richard Nixon wanted to end the war in Vietnam, but prompted by the Joint Chiefs of Staff (JCS); his new military adviser, General Andrew Goodpaster; and Kissinger, the president initially believed that he could do so by winning rather than losing. "I refuse to believe," Kissinger declared, "that a little fourth-rate power like North Vietnam doesn't have a breaking point." The North Vietnamese were on the run, Nixon's advisers reported. In 1967, having fought an unsuccessful guerrilla war, the communists had decided to change tactics. The result had been Tet, a disaster for the VC. This had been followed by North Vietnamese Army (NVA) offensives in May and August 1968. Both had been turned back and, in the process, B-52s had pulverized enemy troop concentrations. The North Vietnamese had withdrawn 40,000 troops from the south and were in Paris because they had reached a dead end militarily. If Goodpaster and the JCS were correct, the war was virtually won on the battlefield. America could afford to be tough and drive a hard bargain at the negotiating table, the president decided.

Nixon and Kissinger's strategy was to couple great power diplomacy with force in an effort to win an "honorable" peace at the Paris negotiations. As part of this plan, the president was prepared to threaten the very survival of North Vietnam to break the enemy's will. Analogizing between his situation and that faced by Eisenhower in Korea in 1953, Nixon believed that the threat of annihilation could be used just as effectively against Hanoi as it had against Pyongyang. His image as a hard-line anticommunist would make his warnings credible. "They'll believe any threat of force Nixon makes because it's Nixon," he told White House Chief of Staff H. R. Haldeman. "We'll just slip the word to them that, 'for God's sake, you know Nixon's obsessed about Communism . . . and he has his hand on the nuclear button.'"

In March, the president sent a personal message to Ho Chi Minh expressing his firm desire for peace and proposing as a first step the mutual withdrawal of American and North Vietnamese troops from South Vietnam and the restoration of the demilitarized zone as a temporary political boundary.

Cambodia
He did not even wait for an answer. For years the JCS had urged Johnson to bomb communist supply routes and staging areas in Cambodia, but to no

avail. Nixon gave the go-ahead, but insisted that the bombing be kept secret. In the ensuing operation, code-named MENU, 3,360 B-52 raids were flown over Cambodia during which American planes dropped more than 100,000 tons of bombs. The stated military objective of the aerial assault was to limit North Vietnam's capacity to launch an offensive against the South, but Nixon's primary motive was to indicate he was prepared to take measures that Johnson had avoided, thus frightening Hanoi into negotiating on his terms. The raids killed an untold number of civilians and accelerated the tragic destabilization of Cambodia. The North Vietnamese simply moved deeper into the Cambodian jungles.

On February 3, Senator Fulbright announced that the Senate Foreign Relations Committee (SFRC) was creating an Ad Hoc Subcommittee on U.S. Security Agreements and Commitments Abroad. Stuart Symington would chair the panel, which would include Fulbright (D-Arkansas), John Sparkman (D-Alabama), George Aiken (R-Vermont), John Sherman Cooper (R-Kentucky), Mike Mansfield (D-Montana), and Jacob Javits (R-New York). Fulbright noted that, under existing treaties, the United States could possibly be committed to using its armed forces in 42 countries. The U.S. government was then providing military aid to 48 countries. Furthermore, 32% of all Americans under arms were stationed outside the continental United States, most of them in an elaborate network of overseas bases. Fulbright and the staff of the SFRC were vaguely aware of the presence of American troops in Laos, Thailand, and perhaps Cambodia in connection with the Vietnam War. They also knew that the military had signed hundreds of agreements with governments in Latin America, Europe, Asia, and the Near East to cooperate in resisting communism. But the exact number and scope of those agreements were carefully guarded state secrets. The tendency of the military to fill a void and create a mission for itself, coupled with congressional delegation of authority to the executive, had created a system in which the United States was pledged to defend other nations without the public's knowledge or permission. Following lengthy and thorough investigations, Fulbright told reporters that the Symington Committee would identify these commitments. The unspoken goal of the panel was to get the military out of the foreign policy-making business and to compel the executive to once again seek congressional approval for the diplomatic commitments that it made.

The day following creation of the Symington Committee, Fulbright reintroduced the national commitments resolution, a measure originally proposed in the summer of 1967 at the height of his bitter feud with Lyndon B. Johnson. Similar to Fulbright's 1967 resolution, the 1969 version sought a nonbinding Senate endorsement for the proposition that a "commitment" made by the executive to a foreign power would not be viewed as a commitment unless it had received congressional approval. Promising his colleagues that the congressional statement of purpose that he proposed would not affect current military involvement in Vietnam, the chairman insisted that the resolution would redress a constitutional imbalance that was the product more of natural forces than a conspiracy by would-be dictators. Napoleon long ago observed that "the tools belong to the man that can use them," Fulbright told the Senate. No executive could be expected to voluntarily limit its freedom of action. Congress would have to assert itself.

On June 26, 1969, with strong support from both liberals and conservatives, the U.S. Senate passed the national commitments resolution by a vote of 70 to 16. As amended by John Sherman Cooper (R-Kentucky), the measure defined national commitment to mean "use of the armed forces on foreign territory or a promise to assist a foreign country, government or people by the use of the armed forces or financial resources of the United States, either immediately or upon the happening of certain events." Although Vietnam was specifically excluded, the *Washington Post* declared that "throughout the debate, it was apparent it [the resolution] was the Senate's answer to the U.S. involvement in Vietnam."

"Balance of Terror": The U.S., USSR, and the Arms Race

Nixon and Kissinger's new world order called for a stable relationship with the Soviet Union. The two were committed to containment but were not adverse to the idea of dialog, a position that had been partially responsible for the honeymoon with Fulbright and other advocates of détente. But the national security adviser believed that America's strategic position vis-á-vis the Soviet Union had steadily deteriorated under Jack Kennedy and Lyndon B. Johnson. Implicit in Kissinger's version of détente was "linkage," an updated version of the old balance of power approach to international affairs. Instead of negotiating military, economic, and political issues piecemeal with the Soviets, Nixon and Kissinger would demand general settlements, linking problems such as Vietnam and the Middle East with concessions on trade and disarmament. In the area of arms control, the president and his national security adviser saw negotiations with the Soviets as a means to extract concessions across a broad range of issues, including Vietnam. As far as the "balance of terror" was concerned, Kissinger, Nixon, and Secretary of Defense Melvin Laird were committed to establishing American supremacy, which they saw as the key to maintaining international stability. None of these men seemed to see any contradiction between détente and the drive for U.S. strategic dominance.

At the outset, Nixon and Kissinger faced a pending arms control matter left over from the Johnson administration. The Nuclear Non-Proliferation Treaty had been signed in June of 1968, but despite Johnson's proddings, the Senate had refused to move on the measure. Indeed, the treaty remained bottled up in the SFRC throughout the summer and fall of 1968. The Soviet invasion of Czechoslovakia that fall made Congress more unwilling than ever to take action. Following Nixon's election, the Senate heeded his request not to act until the new administration could take over. The Senate did not ratify the Nuclear Non-Proliferation Treaty until November 24, 1969, one week after the strategic arms limitations talks opened in Geneva.

In 1966, U.S. intelligence had discovered that the Soviet Union was in the research and development stage of a rudimentary antiballistic missile (ABM) system. The ultimate goal of that program was to ring Moscow and other cities with missiles that could destroy incoming enemy missiles and bombers in case of a nuclear attack. Possession of such a system by one of the superpowers and not the other would open up the possibility of a first strike (the possessor being invulnerable to retaliation) and thus upset the nuclear balance of power. It seemed clear that an ABM race would constitute a dangerous escalation of the arms race, one that could very possibly bankrupt the participants. Several times Johnson and Soviet Premier Aleksei Kosygin discussed conducting negotiations on limiting both offensive and defensive weapons, but nothing ever came of their conversations. Consequently, in 1968, the president persuaded a reluctant Congress to pass legislation appropriating $1.195 billion for the construction of an American ABM system. When the Nixon administration took over the project, renamed it Safeguard, and announced that it was going to approach Congress for several billion more dollars, Fulbright and his anti-imperialist colleagues decided that the time was propitious to make a stand against this particular weapons system and the military–industrial complex in general.

As the battle lines formed, the national press predicted a major political confrontation, a "dramatic struggle" between "those who support the military budget and those who want to redirect resources toward solving hard social problems." Cost estimates for the completed ABM system ran as high as $40 billion. Leading the revolt were Democrats Fulbright, McGovern, Symington, and Mansfield, and Republicans Cooper, Javits, and Charles Percy (R-Illinois). Even Everett Dirksen, responding to the cries of Chicagoans who were outraged at the scheduled construction of an ABM facility only 30 miles away from their city, expressed reservations. But the insurgents, as Laurence Stern pointed out, would be fighting an uphill battle. "The Defense Department has the biggest larder of benefits – money, real estate and plants – with which to foster friendliness and fealty. It maintains a congressional liaison establishment on Capitol Hill that is courteous, ever-willing, and second to none among the executive agencies." Taking point for the Pentagon were such proven cold warriors as John Stennis, John Tower, Robert Dole (R-Kansas), Robert Byrd, and Strom Thurmond. But the heart and soul of the ABM team was Senator Henry M. "Scoop" Jackson (D-Washington) who, although a liberal Democrat on most domestic matters, was a tiger on defense issues. Jackson was a committed cold warrior both philosophically and politically. Without the aerospace industry, he believed, the economy of his home state, Washington, would collapse.

The climactic debate over ABM began the first week in July. The real issue, Jackson told the Senate, was the nature of the threat facing the United States. Make no mistake about it, the Washingtonian proclaimed, "we face a very rough adversary, a very dangerous adversary, and an unpredictable one." That was not the issue at all, Fulbright responded. The issue was whether the Senate would be able "to reassert some control over the military department." If it did not, the United States would indeed become a national security state in which democracy, individual liberty, economic viability – everything – would be subsumed to the well-being of the military–industrial complex.

After four weeks of debate, polls showed the Senate evenly divided. The first and key vote would be on an insurgent amendment to continue research and development but to postpone actual construction of the first two Safeguard sites for a year. It was defeated on August 6 by a vote of 51 to 49. The closeness of the vote was a triumph, Charles Percy told fellow opponents. "In winning the support of half of all Senators, we established the principle that the Senate is no longer willing to accept without question the judgment of the military that a particular weapons system is vital to national survival."

Nixon and Kissinger did not support arms control per se. They were unenthusiastic about the Nuclear Non-Proliferation Treaty, and refused to push France and West Germany to ratify it. Kissinger's aides recalled that he worked frantically throughout the early months of the administration to master the technicalities of arms control negotiations. But he did so to dominate the bureaucracy and control the process. In fact, the administration's policy was to pay lip service to the notion of ending the arms race while seeking strategic superiority over the Soviets. While Kissinger emphasized to reporters that "an attempt to gain a unilateral advantage in the strategic field" was "self-defeating," foreign affairs observers remembered that Nixon had campaigned in 1968 on a promise to deal with the Soviets only "from a position of superiority."

As Soviet and American diplomats negotiated furiously in Geneva on an arms limitation treaty, the Nixon administration went to Congress in February 1970 and asked for $1.5 billion to fund the second phase of Safeguard. The administration insisted that the ABM program was a crucial bargaining chip that chief negotiator Gerard Smith needed to work out a meaningful strategic arms limitation agreement with the Soviets. Privately, the White House admitted that the GALOSH ABM system the Soviets had recently constructed around Moscow had been built to protect it from "an irresponsible terroristic attack from China, or from France, or even Israel," and that it was not sophisticated enough to shield the capital from a U.S. attack, but that in constructing a new weapons network the Kremlin had, nevertheless, destroyed the balance of power. The United States would either have to escalate offensively or continue to work on its defensive ABM system. Anti-imperialists in the Senate took up the cudgels they had dropped in the wake of the heart-breaking 51-to-49 tally on the first phase of the ABM the previous year. But the vote, held in August, was not as close as the 1969 barn burner. By a vote of 52 to 47, the Senate approved the administration's request for $1.5 billion.

Vietnamization

Despite mounting congressional and public impatience with the Nixon administration's policies in Southeast Asia, the president was no more willing to make the hard choices than had Kennedy or Johnson. On May 14, 1969, Nixon addressed a national television audience on Vietnam. "I know that some believe I should have ended the war immediately after my inauguration by simply withdrawing our forces from Vietnam," he said. "That would have been the easy thing to do and it might have been a popular move." But he could not do it, the president declared somberly. To simply withdraw would have been to have "betrayed my solemn responsibility as President." He intended to end the war permanently, Nixon declared, "so that the younger brothers of our soldiers in Vietnam will not have to fight in the future in another Vietnam some place in the world." The United States had given up on winning a purely military victory, Nixon told the American people, but neither would his government accept a settlement in Paris that amounted to a "disguised defeat." The United States would agree to withdraw its troops from Vietnam according to a specified timetable if Hanoi would agree to withdraw its forces from South Vietnam, Cambodia, and Laos according to a specified timetable.

Nixon's secret diplomacy and implied military threats had absolutely no impact on North Vietnam. To have accepted the notion of mutual calibrated withdrawal that left the Thieu government in place and the National Liberation Front (NLF) outside the power structure would have been to have relinquished goals for which Ho and his colleagues had been fighting for a quarter of a century. The North Vietnamese delegation publicly dismissed the proposal made in Nixon's May television address. They would, if necessary, sit in Paris "until the chairs rot," they said.

Meanwhile, Nixon was proceeding with the "go for broke" strategy that had begun with the secret bombing of Cambodia. He was determined, he said, to "end the war one way or the other – either by negotiated agreement or by force." Nixon had Kissinger convene a special subgroup of the NSC to draw up plans for "a savage, decisive blow against North Vietnam." The operation that Kissinger's group came up with, code-named "Duck Hook," called for massive bombing attacks on the major cities, a blockade of North Vietnamese ports, and even the possible use of tactical nuclear weapons to keep the Chinese out of the conflict. Nixon had his aides leak word to selected newspeople that a major escalation of the war was under consideration.

Ho Chi Minh refused to be bluffed. Hanoi did agree, however, to secret peace talks outside the Paris framework. On August 4, in the first of a long series of contacts, Kissinger met privately with North Vietnamese diplomat Xuan Thuy. Kissinger repeated Nixon's peace proposals and ultimatum, but Xuan Thuy responded with the standard North Vietnamese line that the United States would have to withdraw all its troops and abandon Thieu to secure an agreement. To Nixon's enragement, Ho delivered a public rebuff. Hanoi Radio declared that it was Nixon and not North Vietnam that was prolonging the war and expressed the hope that the fall peace offensive in the United States would "succeed splendidly."

Nixon and the Antiwar Movement

Nixon had campaigned in 1968 as a peace candidate. Frustrated expectations inevitably produced a revival of the antiwar movement, which had become disorganized, demoralized, and largely dormant since the disastrous Chicago convention. As it became apparent that Nixon's "secret plan" to end the war was either unworkable or a sham, a wave of protest and demonstrations disturbed nearly 400 of America's 2,500 college campuses. The 1969 disorders were more confrontational and violent than previous eruptions. Nerves on both sides of the picket line were raw. Patience was at a premium. Occupation of administration buildings seemed almost always to end with beatings and arrests. Authorities hauled away more than 4,000 students on campuses from San Francisco State to Swarthmore, while 7% of U.S. schools reported violent protests involving property damage or personal injury.

In 1969, despite this violence, or perhaps because of it, the main burden of regenerating the antiwar movement fell on its more conservative elements, primarily liberals who wanted to work within the system. The activities and makeup of the participants reflected this shift. The resurgence of springtime activism culminated in the organization of the Moratorium and the New Mobilization, which, according to Charles De Benedetti and Charles Chatfield, "combined . . . to rally the most potent and widespread antiwar protests ever mounted in a western democracy." On June 30, the Vietnam Moratorium Committee issued its call for a nationwide work stoppage to demonstrate opposition to the war in Southeast Asia. The New Mobilization Committee to End the War in Vietnam was determined to organize the broadest possible spectrum of antiwar citizens in "a legal and traditional protest action." In pursuance of that goal, the New Mobilization Committee called for a national demonstration in Washington, D.C., to begin on November 13. Participants would demand America's immediate withdrawal from Vietnam.

For a time, the administration had refrained from attacking the antiwar movement and Kissinger actually appealed to student protesters. "Give us a year," he told seven student leaders. "No, I mean it. Come back here in a year. . . . If you come back in a year and nothing has happened," he said, "then I can't argue for more patience." But in fact, Nixon, Agnew, speechwriters Pat Buchanan and Ray Price, and White House staffers H. R. Haldeman and John Ehrlichman divided antiwar protesters into two groups: communists and cowards. Much opposition to the war, they insisted, stemmed from opposition to the draft and mounting U.S. casualties. Most student dissidents simply wanted, as Nixon later put it, "to keep from getting their asses shot off." The rest were fellow travelers or card-carrying communists. The CIA was pressed to document links between overseas communists and the domestic antiwar movement. Late in the spring, after the CIA reported for the third time in three years that it had no evidence of significant communist involvement in the antiwar movement, White House aide Tom Huston told its officials to expand their investigation with a most "liberally construed" interpretation of communist. Meanwhile, the president had authorized the creation of COINTELPRO, a program eventually employing 2,000 agents, that infiltrated antiwar organizations, provoked disturbances, and initiated a massive program of "disinformation," that is, lies.

The first week in June, frustrated by the stalemate in Vietnam and angered at the opposition to his ABM program, Nixon went after his critics. In a graduation speech at the Air Force Academy, he decried the "new isolationists" who would have the United States "turn its back on the world." Leaving Colorado Springs, Nixon flew to Midway for a meeting with President Thieu. Having blasted the anti-imperialists, Nixon then pandered to them. Following his meeting with Thieu, he announced the immediate withdrawal of 25,000 troops from Vietnam. He took the occasion to proclaim a new departure in American foreign policy – the Nixon Doctrine. The United States would continue to defend its allies and strategic interests around the globe but would "look to the nation directly threatened to assume the primary responsibility of providing the manpower for its defense." Shortly thereafter, the administration cancelled the November and December draft calls. The action was the result of "progress in Vietnamization," the president announced. But opponents of the war were not appeased.

The second phase of the fall peace moratorium was scheduled to take place in mid-November. Specifically, the New MOBE and the Vietnam Moratorium Committee planned separate but complementary actions for November 13 through 15 with the Moratorium concentrating on local activities and the New MOBE focusing on mass actions in Washington, D.C., and San Francisco. When the appointed day arrived, hundreds of volunteers gathered near Arlington National Cemetery for the March Against

Death. Eventually 45,000 individuals, each carrying a lighted candle and a placard inscribed with the name of a dead GI, marched solemnly and silently across the Arlington Memorial Bridge. The process took 36 hours. Perhaps 500,000 Americans gathered on Saturday morning, crowding onto the Mall from the west side of the Capitol to the Washington Monument. For five hours they listened to Coretta Scott King, Senators McGovern and McCarthy, and antiwar performers such as Peter, Paul, and Mary. "Bells Toll and Crosses Are Planted Around U.S. as Students Say 'Enough!' to War," reported the *New York Times*. Both the mass gatherings in Washington, D.C., and the moratoriums that occurred all across the United States stood in sharp contrast to the bedlam and violence of Chicago. They were peaceful and dignified, many with religious overtones. Overwhelmingly white and mostly young, the demonstrators were disciplined and good spirited. This, the largest mass demonstration in American history, gave the lie to predictions by the Nixon administration that the Moratorium would be dominated by communists and "hippies," and would turn violent.

Nixon had justified the fall draft cancellations as part of his "new" policy of Vietnamization. Actually, it was an approach he had inherited from Dwight D. Eisenhower and Lyndon B. Johnson. This approach, Melvin Laird explained, involved reliance "on indigenous manpower organized into properly equipped and well-trained armed forces with the help of material, training, technology and specialized military skills furnished by the United States." In a major television address on November 3, the president spelled out his Vietnamization policy in some detail. It seemed to offer the alluring prospect of reducing U.S. casualties and of terminating American involvement in an honorable fashion, regardless of what North Vietnam did. He also announced a schedule for further troop withdrawals. Having apparently placated critics of the war, Nixon then went out of his way to antagonize them. He dismissed the protesters as an irrational and irresponsible rabble, and accused them of sabotaging his diplomacy. He openly appealed for the support of the people he labeled the "great silent majority," and finished his speech with a dramatic flourish: "North Vietnam cannot humiliate the United States. Only Americans can do that."

Appealing to the New Forgotten American
In fact, Vietnamization was designed to appeal not to doves but to hawks and former supporters of the war who had become alienated. In the spring of 1969, Pat Buchanan and his conservative coworkers had identified the core of Nixon's constituency and advised him on how best to enlarge it. Aside from the well-to-do industrialists, financiers, and professional people who traditionally voted Republican, Nixon's broadest potential appeal was to the lower middle class, which ironically had been converted into "haves" from "have nots" by the New Deal. Above all, they were preoccupied with preserving their newly won wealth (modest though it was) and social status.

The new "forgotten American," to use *Time* and *Harper's* label (the term was first used in American politics by Raymond Moley), had little or no college education, but possessed a steady job, a home mortgage, and two vehicles. He watched Ed Sullivan on Sunday night, read *Reader's Digest*, and frequented the horse races or the betting parlor. A number of common views bound these Americans together. This was, as *Harper's* put it, "the man under whose hat lies the great American desert, who watches the tube, plays the horses, and keeps the niggers out of his union and his neighborhood, who might vote for Wallace (but didn't), who cheers when the cops beat up on demonstrators, who is free, white, and twenty-one." They still admired the military and respected the police. They were shocked to see respected clergymen, sometimes their clergymen, leading open housing demonstrations. They were appalled when they read of millionaires getting away with paying no taxes. They had saved to send their kids to a college they could never have attended and then became enraged when their institution or one like it disintegrated into protest and disorder. They were appalled at the drug use, bizarre dress, and the impudence of young people. Most blamed "Marxism" specifically and college professors in general for alienating their children from them. They believed they were being forced to pay the real price of integration, while assorted social planners and liberal moralists sent their children to private schools. There existed among the forgotten Americans a vague but deep-seated contempt and hostility toward the so-called establishment centered in the Northeast and perceived to be predominantly liberal.

Tactically, the "silent majority" speech was a brilliant stroke. As the Democratic National Committee put it, "the national mood on Viet Nam is at the same time glum and tired, but unwilling to accept outright defeat." Having announced a plan for ending the war, Nixon denounced those who had been demanding its end. In so doing, he made it possible for the Americans who had at one time supported the war in Vietnam, but who had turned against it, to support a scheme for American withdrawal without seeming to oppose the war. A Gallup poll indicated that 77% of Americans backed the president's plan, with only 6% in opposition. By a six-to-one margin, people agreed that antiwar protests actually harmed the prospects for peace.

Although shaken by the size of the fall demonstrations, Nixon publicly feigned indifference. His confidence, it seemed, was well placed. In the weeks that followed, it became increasingly clear that the president's silent majority speech had temporarily neutralized the effects of the protest. A November 29 Gallup Poll indicated that 57% of those questioned approved of Nixon's handling of his job; only 30% disapproved. The polls continued to show solid support for the administration; in late November, pro-Nixon rallies were held in numerous cities. In the immediate aftermath of the moratoriums, the antiwar movement grew quiescent again. "We've got those liberal bastards on the run now," the president told his advisers, and he intended to keep them on the run.

Richard Nixon had selected Spiro Agnew for several reasons, but he could not have anticipated that his vice president would become the conservative gadfly that he did. For the first 11 months of the administration, Agnew was virtually invisible. But beginning in late 1969, he hit the Republican banquet circuit with a vengeance. Sometime during the previous year, Agnew had found time to read Irving Kristol's right-wing polemic, *On the Democratic Idea in America*. His staff boiled down the essays in that work into a series of hard-hitting speeches. America was in danger of being overwhelmed by "a spirit of national masochism." The war in Vietnam was just, the crusade to contain crime and protect property was laudable, and the patriotic businessmen and working people who elected and supported Richard Nixon were the heroes of the American Republic. Agnew blamed the nation's woes on liberal academics, "an effete corps of impudent snobs," as well as on print and broadcast news executives, "a small and unelected elite." Agnew, it should be noted, was attacking not only the liberal establishment but also the upper-class Brahmins of the Republican Party, such as Rockefeller, William Scranton, and George Romney.

By the spring of 1970, the flaws in Nixon's policy of Vietnamization were becoming apparent. In an effort to build on the tranquility that followed in the wake of the silent majority speech, he announced on April 20, 1970, the withdrawal of 150,000 additional troops during the next year. But no matter how useful Vietnamization was in terms of quelling domestic dissent in the United States, it was counterproductive of the goal of forcing North Vietnam to negotiate a settlement that would leave the Thieu government intact. The logic of the situation was that Hanoi only had to wait and refuse to make concessions; eventually the Americans would be gone and the pitifully weak Thieu regime could be summarily dispatched. Indeed, General Creighton Abrams had bitterly protested the new troop withdrawals, warning that they would leave South Vietnam dangerously vulnerable to enemy military pressure. Increasingly impatient with the stalemate in Southeast Asia, Nixon began once again looking around for an opportunity to demonstrate to the North Vietnamese that "we were still serious about our commitment in Vietnam." His chance was not long in coming.

Cambodia

Throughout the Vietnam War, Prince Norodom Sihanouk had worked desperately to insulate Cambodia from the fighting. As part of an earlier understanding with Hanoi, Sihanouk agreed to ignore sanctuaries established by the VC on the Vietnamese–Cambodian border. In exchange, Hanoi promised not to aid the small Cambodian communist movement, the Khmer Rouge. The decision by the Nixon administration in 1969 to embark on its top-secret bombing campaign inside Cambodia helped upset the delicate balance Sihanouk had established. In March 1970, while he was in Europe, the prince was overthrown by Prime Minister Lon Nol who had the support of Cambodia's intensely anticommunist military commanders. Although the United States played no direct role in the coup, according to George Herring and William Shawcross, Lon Nol was well aware of the U.S. government's disapproval of Sihanouk's neutralism. He therefore believed that the United States would not only tolerate but also reward a pro-western coup. Following Sihanouk's overthrow, the United States quickly recognized the new government and began providing it with covert military aid.

For years the American military had wanted to do more than just bomb North Vietnamese and VC sanctuaries in Cambodia. The JCS longed to invade and destroy the communist enclaves on the ground. With a friendly government now in power, they could act. On April 29, South Vietnamese units with American air support attacked an enemy sanctuary on the Parrot's Beak, a strip of Cambodian territory 23 miles from Saigon. On April 30, American forces assaulted Fishook, a North Vietnamese base area 55 miles northwest of Saigon. That night Nixon went on national television and justified the invasion as a response to North Vietnamese "aggression." The real target of the operation, he explained, was the Central Office for South Vietnam (COSVN), the "nerve center" of North Vietnamese operations, although the Department of Defense (DOD) had made clear to him that it was uncertain as to where COSVN was located or whether it even existed. At a subsequent press conference on May 8, Nixon promised that all American units would be out of Cambodia by the second week of June and all Americans, including advisers, would be out by the end of the month.

Nixon's Cambodian incursion had in fact produced only limited tactical results. According to the U.S. command, American troops killed some 2,000 enemy troops, cleared more than 1,600 acres of jungle, destroyed 8,000 bunkers, and captured large stocks of weapons. The invasion no doubt helped relieve pressure on the Army of the Republic of Vietnam (ARVN) and the Thieu Government, thereby buying some time for Vietnamization. But COSVN turned out to be little more than a handful of thatched huts sitting atop a network of tunnels; the NVA moved back into the area as soon as the Americans and South Vietnamese left. Coming as it did in the wake of Sihanouk's overthrow, the invasion shattered Cambodian neutrality.

Within minutes of the president's televised address, antiwar activists took to the streets in New York and Philadelphia and, in the days that followed, protests erupted across the country. The scores of marches and rallies that engulfed campuses from Maryland to Oregon were characterized by a sense of betrayal; the war was being expanded under the pretense of ending it. On April 28, Senator George McGovern, one of Congress' most outspoken doves, had introduced a resolution calling on the president to end all U.S. military activity in Southeast Asia by December 31, 1971.

"Every senator in this chamber is partly responsible for sending 50,000 young Americans to an early grave," he told his colleagues. "This chamber reeks of blood.... And if we do not end this damnable war, those young men will someday curse us for our pitiful willingness to let the executive carry the burden that the Constitution places on us." His resolution was defeated by a vote of 55 to 39.

Meanwhile, the previously dormant antiwar movement continued to gain momentum. In Cambridge, Massachusetts, students occupied Harvard buildings to protest the university's refusal to take a stand against the Vietnam War or to withdraw its investments in racist South Africa. At Berkeley, Governor Ronald Reagan mobilized a battalion of police to confront more than 5,000 students and community residents who had seized a vacant lot and turned it into a "people's park." Armed helicopters sprayed tear gas on the demonstrators from above, while police shotgun fire blinded one student and killed another. Then the first week in May, Kent State students protested the Cambodian invasion by staging violent demonstrations and firebombing the ROTC building. Upon hearing the news, Nixon called the student demonstrators a bunch of "bums" at an informal briefing session at the Pentagon. Meanwhile, Ohio Governor James Rhodes called out the National Guard and declared martial law. When he ordered guardsmen onto the campus of Kent State, students held a peaceful demonstration to protest. Suddenly, the troops turned and opened fire. Their fusillade left 4 students dead and 11 wounded. Two of the young women killed were simply walking to class. In 10 terrifying seconds, *Time* reported, the Kent State campus was converted "into a bloodstained symbol of the rising student rebellion against the Nixon Administration and the war in Southeast Asia." Within days, 1.5 million students were participating in a boycott of classes, shutting down about one fifth of the nation's campuses for periods ranging from one day to the rest of the school year. Violent demonstrations prompted the governors of Ohio, Michigan, Kentucky, and South Carolina to declare their universities in a state of emergency, and governors of 16 states activated the National Guard to curb rioting at 20 universities. These events caused one college president to bemoan "the most disastrous May in the history of American higher education."

Congress and the "End the War" Movement

Most people who demonstrated against the war were peaceful, law-abiding citizens and, as the burgeoning anti-imperialist movement in Congress revealed, the antiwar movement had expanded to include political moderates and the culturally conventional. Nevertheless, "the movement" was decentralized, undisciplined, and fluid. There was no common leadership or accepted strategy. In 1970, the antiwar community became simultaneously more moderate and more radical. The Students for a Democratic

Society (SDS) had succumbed to bitter factional feuding. At its 1969 convention, the SDS split into the Progressive Labor Party, a group of self-proclaimed Maoists, and the Weathermen (from Bob Dylan's lyric, "You don't need a weatherman to know which way the wind blows"), headed by Bernadine Dohrn, a Marxist and avowed revolutionary. Several hundred Weathermen, pledging to "bring the war home to America," subsequently went underground. The Weathermen Underground looked forward to a communist victory in Vietnam – an eventuality they believed would mark the beginning of the end of U.S. imperialism. At the same time, they declared virtual war on the state. Between September 1969 and May 1970, radicals carried out some 250 bombings, including draft board meeting sites, ROTC buildings, and a Bank of America branch near Santa Barbara, California. In August 1970, a group of student terrorists on the University of Wisconsin campus, calling themselves the "New Year's Gang" detonated a large car bomb on campus, leveling the building housing the Army Mathematics Research Center and killing one student. These activities received a disproportionate amount of coverage from the media, and many Americans perceived that the movement was becoming more rather than less radical.

There were in fact those Americans who believed that the protesters killed at Kent State got what they deserved. Indeed, opinion polls showed that a majority of Americans supported the invasion and now believed that campus demonstrations were America's primary domestic problem. Incensed by Mayor John Lindsay's order to fly American flags at half staff in honor of the dead, a group of New York construction workers attacked antiwar protesters on May 8 with fists and clubs, wounding 70. Several days later, President Nixon accepted a "hard hat" from a group of working-class patriots and, on May 20, 100,000 construction workers and longshoremen staged a prowar rally in New York City, waving American flags and singing, "God Bless America." Many prowar Americans, even some of those who had originally supported the war and subsequently become disenchanted, believed that the protests trivialized the sacrifices that patriotic Americans had made and were making. Veterans were particularly galled. "The peaceniks might not be attacking the integrity of the American soldiers directly," veteran Michael Clodfelter wrote in his 1976 Vietnam memoir, "but they were proselytizing against the war as dishonorable and contemptible and we who were the participants in this conflict felt that, by implication, we too were being made contemptible."

In the summer of 1970, in the wake of the Cambodian demonstrations, an embittered president declared virtual warfare on people he considered his enemies: the "madmen" on the Hill, the "liberal" press, and those who marched in protest. "Within the iron gates of the White House," Charles Colson later wrote, "a siege mentality was setting in. It was 'us' against 'them'. Gradually, as we drew the circle closer around us, the ranks of 'them' began to swell." According to H. R. Haldeman, "Kent State marked a turning point for Nixon, a beginning of his downhill slide toward Watergate."

Five days after Nixon announced the incursion into Cambodia, members of the SFRC accused him of usurping the legislature's war-making power and denounced the "constitutionally unauthorized, presidential war in Indochina." The charge quickly became a rallying cry inside and outside of Congress. The president of the Amalgamated Clothing Workers Union demanded that congressional constraints be imposed on the president. The American Civil Liberties Union campaigned for an immediate end to the war on the grounds that it was not constitutionally declared and therefore deprived Americans of their civil liberties. Even the hawkish House was up in arms. Representative George E. Brown (D-California) introduced a resolution of impeachment, and Richard D. McCarthy (D-New York) proposed a declaration of war on North Vietnam in the expectation that it would be overwhelmingly defeated.

On April 10, 1970, the SFRC voted unanimously to repeal the Gulf of Tonkin resolution and approved the Cooper–Church amendment to the 1971 Military Sales Bill. Authored by John Sherman Cooper and Frank Church, the amendment would cut off funds for U.S. military operations in Cambodia after June 30, 1970, the date Nixon had set for withdrawal in the midst of the postinvasion brouhaha.

Confronted with a reactivated antiwar movement and an incipient rebellion in Congress, the administration embarked on a campaign of calculated divisiveness during the spring and summer of 1970. Nixon and his henchmen attempted to make Vietnam a symbol of the integrity of the presidency and of America's core values. Administration figures brandished the symbols of American nationalism at every opportunity. The White House sponsored a lavish "Honor America Day" in the Capitol on the Fourth of July. The president and his supporters began wearing flag jewelry. Throughout the summer, the American Legion, the John Birch Society, the Christian Crusade, and other right-wing organizations charged that the peace symbol was a Marxist emblem, an anti-Christian insignia, or a sorcerer's symbol. During the 1970 mid-term election campaign, Agnew urged blue-collar Democrats to prove their patriotism by voting Republican. As for protesters, he declared, it was "time to sweep that kind of garbage out of our society." Despite this hawkish onslaught, the first week in July after six weeks of tumultuous debate the U.S. Senate approved the Cooper–Church amendment to the military sales bill by a vote of 75 to 25. It was a momentous occasion, the first time the Upper House had passed a clear-cut anti–Vietnam War resolution.

In truth, however, Cooper–Church was a flank attack on the war in Southeast Asia. Emboldened by their success in the Senate, the doves decided to stage a frontal assault. George McGovern and Senator Mark Hatfield proposed attaching an amendment to a pending arm sales bill, cutting off funds for all U.S. military operations in Southeast Asia after December 31, 1970. It was the ultimate end-the-war measure.

By the summer of 1970, Richard Nixon was losing the battle for the political middle ground on Vietnam. No longer was the antiwar movement in Congress a protest of the liberal left. A majority of Democrats and a sizable minority of Republicans were now actively opposed. Not for 100 years had Congress mounted such a challenge to a commander-in-chief with troops fighting in the field as that mounted against Richard Nixon in the summer of 1970. In fact, by late June, polls showed that nearly 50% of all Americans advocated getting out of Vietnam immediately and only 15% favored staying. Contributing to this alienation was the plight of those American servicemen being held by communist North Vietnam.

The Unravelling of the Vietnam Consensus

By 1970, the number of American prisoners of war (POWs) held by the communists or listed as missing in Southeast Asia ran into the thousands, and the issue of their treatment and return had become one of the most sensitive of the war. Two weeks after the midterm elections in November, Nixon made a bold move to take away the POW issue from opponents of the conflict in Southeast Asia. Early one Saturday, 250 American fighter-bombers struck targets across the demilitarization zone (DMZ) and within the Hanoi–Haiphong "do-nut," the first resumption of bombing since the Johnson-initiated pause in the fall of 1968. The attacks were, however, a diversionary tactic designed to cover a daring raid by U.S. Air Force and U.S. Army Special Forces units on the Son Tay prison camp 23 miles west of Hanoi. American fighters swooped in and blasted guard towers and concertina-wire fences, but when the U.S. helicopters nestled in and disgorged their commandos, there was no sign of life. The communists had cleared out days before and taken their prisoners with them. Writing in the *Washington Star*, Clayton Fritchey observed that even if the Son Tay raid had been successful, it would have subjected other Americans in captivity to torture and death. "There is a smell of desperation about this adventure," he mused. "It is not the considered action of a great power."

Meanwhile, the administration was stepping up its war against its critics. In January, the *New York Times* reported that 1,000 U.S. Army agents were employing computers to collect the names of civilians in an operation code-named Continental U.S. Intelligence or Conus Intel. In subsequent congressional investigations, Pentagon officials revealed that the military had compiled dossiers on 25 million Americans. FBI documents revealed that J. Edgar Hoover had ordered surveillance of student and peace groups, and had gathered information on thousands of citizens, many with no criminal records. On numerous occasions, the agency had bugged the phones of movement organizations without court authorization. Thus did America's leading crime prevention agency engage in illegal activity. House of Representatives Majority Leader Hale Boggs demanded the resignation of FBI Director Hoover, then age 76, accusing him of using "tactics of the Soviet Union and Hitler's Gestapo," but to no avail.

For two years, Richard Nixon had attempted to bully and negotiate his way out of the Vietnam quagmire. Strategically and politically, America's position in Southeast Asia was worse than when he took the Oath of Office. Nevertheless, in early 1971, the president decided to continue his policy of lashing out at the enemy while backing out of the ring. To appease critics at home, the timetable for American troop withdrawals was accelerated. Over the protests of General Abrams, Nixon ordered the removal of 100,000 troops by the end of the year, leaving 175,000 men in Vietnam of whom only 75,000 were combat forces. At the same time, in February, the White House authorized a major ground operation, code-named Lam Son, against communist sanctuaries in Laos. The president's justification was the same as that for Cambodia – to buy time for Vietnamization by disrupting enemy supply lines.

The Laotian invasion was met with stiff resistance from the NVA. Spies in Saigon had ferreted out the ARVN's scheme, and the enemy was waiting. In an effort to discredit Vietnamization, General Giap threw 36,000 troops into the fight. ARVN units supported by American planes and helicopters inflicted heavy losses on the enemy but suffered a 50% casualty rate themselves. The evacuation itself resulted in the loss of 140 helicopters and their crews. Television images of South Vietnamese soldiers clinging to the skids of American evacuation helicopters reinforced the popular notion in the United States that the war was being lost. The Laotian incursion fueled the movement in the Senate to impose both specific and general limitations on the president's war-making powers. Hatfield and McGovern asked Fulbright to join them in cosponsoring a reworked version of their 1970 "End the War" amendment. It would "propose" that the White House set a timetable for the withdrawal of all U.S. armed forces from Vietnam by December 31, 1971. After that date, funds would remain available only for release of POWs, protection of South Vietnamese "who might be endangered," and continued assistance to the government of South Vietnam.

Then, on March 29, 1971, after a sensational trial, Lt. William Calley was convicted by a military tribunal of killing "at least 22" unarmed civilians in the Vietnamese village of My Lai in March 1968. In fact, Calley and other members of Charlie Company had murdered an estimated 200 villagers whom they suspected of harboring VC cadre. Twenty-five officers were charged as accomplices in the atrocity or with participation in the subsequent cover-up, but only Calley was convicted. In February 1971, the Vietnam Veterans Against the War conducted their own "Winter Soldier Investigation." More than 130 veterans stepped forward and horrified the nation with tales of beatings, maiming, and rape. "I personally used clubs, rifle butts, pistols, knives" in torturing prisoners, one confessed. Another remembered pushing manacled prisoners out of helicopters. Hard on the heels of the traumatic Calley trial and Winter Soldier revelations came publication by the *New York Times* of the Pentagon Papers, a top-secret history of the war commissioned by Robert McNamara. The papers, purloined by former DOD civilian official Daniel Ellsberg, demonstrated not only that officials in the Kennedy and Johnson administrations involved the United States in the war without clear objectives or a comprehensive strategy, but also that they misled the American people while doing so. Contrary to popular belief and official accounts, John F. Kennedy had known of and approved the plot to overthrow Diem, the CIA reported in 1964 that it did not believe the domino theory was relevant to Asia, and intelligence experts had informed Lyndon B. Johnson that the insurrection against the regime in Saigon was primarily indigenous instead of being directed from Hanoi. Not surprisingly, disenchantment with the war reached an all-time high in mid-1971 with a stunning 71% of Americans expressing the opinion that it had been a mistake to become involved in the conflict in Southeast Asia. Of those polled, 58% declared the war to be immoral, whereas only 31% of Americans approved of the way President Nixon was handling the war. "I don't give a damn any more who wins the war," declared columnist Arthur Hoppe. "But because I hate what my country is doing in Vietnam. I emotionally and often irrationally hope that it fails."

By 1970/1971, the war was taking a terrible toll on the armed services. The antiwar movement was burgeoning within the enlisted ranks in Vietnam and at home. The Vietnam Veterans Against the War had become one of the most active and visible of the antiwar organizations. Unlike their fathers who returned home after World War II, Vietnam veterans rarely talked of heroism, duty, and honor. "From Vietnam," wrote veteran Raymond Mungo, "I learned to despise my countrymen, my government, and the entire English-speaking world, with its history of genocide and international conquest. I was a normal kid." The average age of an enlisted man in Vietnam was 19 (compared to 26 in World War II), and these teenagers were increasingly frustrated living and fighting in an alien culture in which it was difficult if not impossible to tell friend from foe. Moreover, the Army's policy of a one-year tour of duty meant that most soldiers spent at least their last three months just trying to survive. Vietnamization killed what remained of American troop morale. Estimates of drug use by uniformed personnel in Vietnam ran as high as 40%. Racial incidents increased geometrically. "Commanders of every unit I visited are extremely concerned about the increasing antagonism of the young black soldiers," former astronaut Frank Borman reported to Nixon after a fact-finding trip to Vietnam. They felt singled out and victimized by a draft system that discriminated against the poor and less educated. Indeed, the average GI felt singled out and discriminated against. Draft boards had always granted deferments to young people affluent enough to attend college. Until the summer of 1968, student deferments could be extended for graduate or professional school, and educational deferments were awarded to graduate teaching assistants and public school teachers. With degree in hand, the graduates gained employment with defense contractors, engineering firms, and other corporations that could guarantee an employment deferment. Young men from wealthy families were particularly immune to military service. In three upscale New Jersey suburban towns, not one of their high school graduates died in Vietnam (while ghettoized Newark lost 111) and, of the 30,000 male graduates from Harvard, Princeton, and MIT in the decade following 1962, only 20 died in the war. Furthermore, because most blacks and poor whites did not have a skill or could not get the right type of union induction, they were prime candidates for infantry training and then for Vietnam.

"Fragging" incidents, in which enlisted personnel tossed grenades into bunkers occupied by officers who were suspected of exposing their men to needless danger, amounted to 2,000 in 1970 alone. "It didn't happen every day," one soldier recalled, "but after a while it got to be an unwritten rule. You get these guys that want to come over with schoolbook tactics, and they might want to do something that's detrimental to the company. Then you're talking about people's lives. The first firefight you get in, somebody takes him out. 'Killed in action.'" Increasingly, noncommissioned officers had to negotiate patrol duty with their squads. While in previous wars refusing to obey orders was treated as a most serious offense, "punishable by death," this was not the case in Vietnam. Faced with demoralized troops who wanted to go home, generals did not even give reprimands to most soldiers who refused orders. For every 100 soldiers serving in Vietnam that year, 17 went AWOL and 7 deserted. In fact, more than 500,000 soldiers deserted during the war, a record number. "If Nixon doesn't hurry up and bring the GIs home, they are going to come home by themselves," one veteran predicted. Despite the hard line taken by the JCS and Goodpaster, numerous career officers both active and retired were pleading with Secretary of Defense Melvin Laird to end the war before their beloved Army, Navy, and Air Force were destroyed.

Just as had been the case in the latter stages of the Johnson administration, the violence in Vietnam seemed to have infected American society. In September 1971, prison inmates at the Attica State Prison in New York rioted. The inmates took several guards and prison workers hostage. A tense standoff followed as 1,500 state troopers and other law enforcement officers surrounded the facility. When word leaked that inmates were killing and torturing each other and that at least one hostage had died, the police staged a land and air assault on the facility. Nine prison guards and 28 inmates died in the carnage. Black activists pointed out that just as a disproportionate number of black Americans were being drafted and dying in

Vietnam, a disproportionate number of blacks were inmates at Attica and thus killed and wounded in the assault.

The Politics of Diplomacy

Tasting Peace

Professional politician that he was, Richard Nixon never let his eye stray very far from the next election. The Twenty-Sixth Amendment to the Constitution lowering the voting age to 18 went into effect in 1971, and Republicans feared the worst. Given the expanded electorate, the continuing stalemate in Southeast Asia, and mounting public opposition to the war, the president perceived that he would have to have a peace settlement to be reelected in 1972. To this end, he directed Henry Kissinger to make a dramatic new proposal in his secret talks with North Vietnamese negotiator Le Duc Tho in Paris. The United States would withdraw from the South within seven months of the signing of an agreement. In return, Hanoi would merely have to turn over American POWs and refrain from any major operations in South Vietnam.

The Nixon administration's offer touched off the most intensive peace negotiations of the war. In response to the U.S. government's new proposal, Le Duc Tho agreed to release the POWs as American forces departed, provided the United States withdrew its support from Thieu prior to any political settlement. Although Kissinger told friends that he could "almost taste peace," it was not to be. "If there is one issue where I have drawn the line," Nixon told Haldeman, "it is on Vietnam where I have insisted that our goal must be a South Vietnam capable of defending itself." Translated, that meant that the president believed that it would be more politically damaging for him at that point to abandon Thieu than to fail to reach agreement with the North Vietnamese. Thus, this new, most promising round of talks was broken off in November, both sides having decided that they could achieve their objectives outside the negotiating process.

The China Thaw

Contributing to the U.S. government's decision to hold the line in Southeast Asia was Nixon's conviction that his achievements in other areas would compensate for the failure to reach a peace accord with North Vietnam. In July 1971, Richard Nixon stunned the world by announcing that he intended to accept an invitation from the communist government in Beijing to visit China. Up to that point, it had been political poison for a public figure to even suggest establishing diplomatic relations with Communist China. Taiwan, which still held China's seat on the UN Security Council, had many influential friends in the United States, not the least of whom was Richard Nixon. Indeed, as a California congressman, Nixon had lashed the Democrats unmercifully for "losing" China to the communists. But as commentators pointed out, it was Nixon's credentials as a conservative that made it politically possible for him to make such a daring move.

Early in 1969, Nixon had directed Kissinger to reassess America's relationship with mainland China to see if a reestablishment of relations was both necessary and possible. Kissinger was more than happy to oblige. The ultimate practitioner of realpolitik, he told reporters in December 1969, "we will judge other countries, including Communist countries . . . on the basis of their actions and not on the basis of their domestic ideology." That same year, the U.S. government eased travel and trade restrictions with what it significantly referred to as the People's Republic of China. In addition, the president terminated patrols of the Taiwan Strait by the Seventh Fleet. When war broke out in 1971 between India (supported by the Soviet Union) and Pakistan (which received help from China), the Nixon administration tilted toward Pakistan. That same year in April, a team of American table tennis players were invited to China where they were badly beaten by the world champions. Nevertheless, even at the time, "ping-pong diplomacy" was seen as an important step toward rapprochement. During one of his top-secret shuttles to Paris, Kissinger detoured to Pakistan and subsequently Beijing to elicit the invitation and finalize details for the presidential trip. During his exhilarating 49-hour visit, Kissinger met with and was captivated by Zhou Enlai. "Cosmopolitan" and "infinitely intelligent" were some of the superlatives the national security adviser subsequently lavished on the Chinese premier. The two men agreed that their respective ties to North Vietnam and Taiwan should not keep their nations from working out a modus vivendi. Both agreed that it was in the interests of the United States and China to prevent the growth of Soviet power. Former critics of the administration, such as Fulbright and Senator Edward Kennedy, who had been particularly active in pushing for a rapprochement with Beijing, lined up to hail Kissinger upon his return, whereas anticommunists shrank in horror from the proposed opening.

For a week in February, Nixon – accompanied by his wife, Pat, Kissinger, and a huge entourage of officials and reporters – basked in the glow of unremitting international press attention. His handshake with Premier Zhou Enlai seemed to wipe away 20 years of hostility and isolation. The president visited the Great Wall and the Forbidden City where he and Kissinger toasted their hosts. There were extended talks with the powerful, mysterious Mao Zedong. In the short run, the visit produced only a series of innocuous communications, but in the long run it proved to be the first step in a reversal of policy. Following his meeting with Chinese leaders, Nixon announced that the "ultimate relationship between Taiwan and the Mainland is not a matter for the United States to decide." In August, the State Department announced that it supported admission of the Peoples' Republic to the UN, where its representatives would sit simultaneously with

Taiwan's delegates. This "two Chinas" policy lasted until October, when the UN General Assembly approved the admission of Communist China and expelled representatives of the Nationalist government.

As previously noted, in 1971 and 1972, the U.S. government's desire for rapprochement with Beijing led it to support Pakistan in its war with India. In December 1971, East Pakistan, the most populous and poorest section of that country, rebelled against the government of Ayub Khan, which had for years persecuted and discriminated against them. The Bengalis, as the residents of East Pakistan were known, were aided by Indian troops who fought Pakistani troops in both the east and the west. China sided with Ayub Khan, who had helped arrange Kissinger's initial trip to Beijing, and so did the United States. Turning a blind eye to human rights abuses committed by the Pakistanis against the Bengalis, the Nixon administration allowed the Pakistani government to purchase arms in the United States, and it provided diplomatic support in various forums. The rebels eventually succeeded in establishing the state of Bangladesh, but Indian–American relations were severely damaged.

The opening to China was part of Nixon and Kissinger's larger scheme of establishing an international balance of power. Beijing cooperated because it craved trade with the West, as well as the recognition and respectability that admission to the United Nations would bring. Between 1966 and 1971, China had been convulsed by the "Great Cultural Revolution." At the urging of Chairman Mao and his wife, thousands of fanatical Red Guards, youthful communist zealots, had roamed the countryside terrorizing the populace into ideological orthodoxy. The rampage had done much to destroy the bureaucracy, technocracy, and local party structures in China. After five years of internal chaos and international condemnation, Mao and especially Zhou Enlai craved a return to normality. Rapprochement with the United States would both signal and accelerate such a trend. For its part, the Nixon administration feared falling behind its North American Treaty Organization (NATO) partners, most of whom had opened both trade and diplomatic relations with Beijing. Both nations were increasingly apprehensive concerning Japan – the United States for economic reasons and China for political and military reasons. Détente would open Chinese markets to American goods and give Beijing an effective mediator in its efforts to reestablish relations with Tokyo. There was also the Soviet Union. Tensions between the Peoples' Republic and Nationalist China had mounted steadily, with actual border clashes in 1970 and 1971. Détente with the United States just might give Moscow pause, Mao and Zhou believed. Finally, the Nixon administration hoped that normalization of relations with Beijing would further isolate Hanoi and lead to a peace agreement that would leave the Thieu government intact. This latter scheme necessitated an opening not only to Communist China but also to the Soviet Union.

Détente, Linkage, and Soviet–American Relations

Kissinger anticipated that the opening to China would add impetus to the movement toward détente with the Soviet Union; he was right. As he hoped would be the case with China, the national security adviser believed that Russia could be enmeshed in a network of economic and security agreements that would make conflict with the United States out of the question. "The Soviets want a predictable administration. And in a curious way, I think they want one that puts limits on them," Kissinger announced smugly. "Their system is not capable of operating under the principle of self-restraint." Aside from avoiding a nuclear Armageddon, détente with the Soviet Union might sever the economic, strategic, and psychological cords connecting Moscow with Hanoi. Brezhnev might even be persuaded to pressure the North Vietnamese into making peace. In addition, the U.S. government felt the need to approach the Soviets lest its European allies proceed without them. Various socialist parties in Western Europe had long been calling for a reduction of tensions with the communist bloc. Joining them in ironic union were businesses that saw lucrative trade and investment opportunities with the Eastern bloc. Indeed, in 1969, after the Social Democrats came to power in West Germany, a consortium of companies and banks signed a $1 billion trade deal with Moscow. French, Italian, Dutch, and British firms rushed to sign similar deals. Soon their representatives were joining with Soviet technocrats in joint ventures for constructing refining facilities, auto factories, and machine tool plants. By 1970, American businesses were pressuring the Nixon administration to create an economic open door for them as well.

Shortly after Nixon announced that he was going to Beijing, the Kremlin issued an invitation for him to attend a summit in Moscow. He agreed, and the meeting was scheduled for May 1972, barely three months after his triumph in Beijing. Nixon and Kissinger arrived in Moscow and immediately entered into a series of intensive discussions with Leonid Brezhnev and other Soviet leaders. The event dominated American newspapers and television, leaving little room for the Democrats and their election year attacks on the administration. The talks ranged across arms control, space and scientific cooperation, and trade. No concrete agreement was reached on the latter topic, although Brezhnev agreed to establish a joint commission to discuss ways to facilitate exchange of nonstrategic items. Later in the year, a crop failure in the Soviet Union would lead to a massive, unprecedented purchase of American cereals. Yet, what concerned Moscow more than any other issue was the nuclear arms race. It had become clear during the internal debate in the United States in 1969/1970 over the creation of an antiballistic missile system that the Nixon administration equated security with superiority. The Soviets enjoyed an edge in land-based ICBMs, but the United States, relying on its triad of submarine-launched missiles,

ICBMs, and strategic bombers, boasted more warheads and strategic flexibility. Brezhnev and his associates, not surprisingly, found such a strategic approach unacceptable and pressed hard during the Americans' visit for an authentic arms limitation agreement. Their efforts resulted in the inking of the Strategic Arms Limitation Treaty (SALT).

SALT I included three basic agreements. The first, in the form of an official treaty requiring a two-thirds vote of the Senate, would limit each side to 200 ABMs to be divided between two sites: one in the capital and the other at an offensive missile site at least 800 miles away. The theory underlying the ABM pact was that with such severe restrictions on its defense, each country would be deterred from launching a missile attack against the other lest their own population be wiped out. The second was a five-year executive agreement that put limits on land-based and submarine-launched missiles. This Interim Agreement on Limitations of Strategic Armaments restricted new land-based ICBMs to the number contemplated by U.S. planners, a number one third less than that scheduled for production by the Soviet Union. Included in the "Basic Principles," signed by the two leaders, was a statement that called on the Soviet Union and the United States to "do their utmost to avoid military confrontations" and to "recognize that efforts to obtain unilateral advantage at the expense of the other" would be inconsistent with the agreement.

In the wake of the openings to Moscow and Beijing, *Time* magazine declared Nixon and Kissinger to be their co–men of the year. Détente with the communist powers, declared the magazine, constituted "the most profound rearrangement of the earth's political powers since the beginning of the cold war." Anti-imperialists in the Senate, such as Fulbright and Church, vied with each other to voice their support. Cold warriors were deeply distressed at the whole idea of détente and with the SALT treaty specifically. Henry "Scoop" Jackson, who was then running for the Democratic nomination for the presidency, charged that the treaty, which allowed the Soviets 300 more land-based missiles than the United States, was a sell-out. In public forums and in testimony before Congress, Kissinger insisted that America retained technical superiority and that the United States was leading the way in developing new weapons systems not covered by the Soviet–American treaty. Jackson was not impressed. Congress approved both the ABM treaty and SALT, but the Washington senator managed to add an amendment to the latter requiring that the United States be allowed to build as many land-based missiles as the Soviet Union, an amendment that sent Soviet and American negotiators back to the bargaining table. For the next two years, liberal cold warriors joined by conservative nationalists hammered away at détente. In 1974, to the great irritation of the Soviets, Congress passed the Jackson–Vanik Amendment, which denied most-favored nation trading privileges to the Soviets until they allowed all citizens within their borders to immigrate as they wished. Moscow was particularly angry because communist authorities had allowed 30,000 Russian Jews, a historically persecuted minority, to leave for Israel and the West that same year. Brezhnev and his countrymen viewed Jackson–Vanik as a blatant attack on Soviet sovereignty. Despite two subsequent summit meetings with Brezhnev in 1973 and 1974, Soviet–American relations were chilled by the time Nixon left office.

Denouement in Vietnam

Vietnam had been the subject of extended debate at both the Beijing and Moscow summits. The communist superpowers both expressed a desire to see the war in Southeast Asia end, but neither Mao nor Brezhnev had any intention of pressuring North Vietnam into accepting "peace with honor." Indeed, in late March between the two summits, the NVA launched a division-level, three-pronged attack against South Vietnam. Supported by Soviet tanks, 120,000 troops crossed the DMZ, invaded the Central Highlands from Laos, and struck the area northwest of Saigon from Cambodia. At the time, there were 95,000 American troops left in Vietnam.

As Nixon and Kissinger well understood, the objective of the NVA offensive was to discredit Vietnamization and further arouse antiwar sentiment in the United States. The president decided to retaliate with air power and economic pressure. "The bastards have never been bombed like they're going to be bombed this time," he told an adviser. From March to October in an operation named "Linebacker I," thousands of B-52 sorties dropped 112,000 tons of bombs on the North. American planes hit targets in and around Hanoi and Haiphong for the first time since 1968, and computer-guided "smart bombs" destroyed railway lines running into China. In addition, the U.S. Navy mined Haiphong harbor and imposed a naval blockade on the entire North. The president instructed Kissinger, "You tell those sons of bitches that the President is a madman and you don't know how to deal with him. Once re-elected I'll be a mad bomber."

The 1972 offensive and the American response left both sides bloodied, but did not significantly alter the geopolitical situation in Southeast Asia. With the help of American air power, ARVN managed to repulse the NVA attack, inflicting 100,000 casualties on the enemy and suffering 25,000 itself. The savage bombing of the North rekindled the antiwar movement and, with demonstrations erupting all across the United States and Congress up in arms, Nixon directed Kissinger to initiate a new round of secret talks with Hanoi's representatives in Paris.

From late summer on, the two nations began inching toward a compromise. During three weeks of intensive negotiations, Kissinger and Le Duc Tho hammered out the fundamentals of an agreement. Within 60 days after a cease-fire, the United States would withdraw its remaining troops from Vietnam and North Vietnam would return the American POWs. A political settlement would then be arranged by a tripartite National Council of Reconciliation and Concord, made up of the Saigon government, the VC, and neutralists. The council would administer elections and assume responsibility for implementing the agreement.

In his haste to get an agreement, Kissinger had badly miscalculated Thieu's willingness to accommodate the United States as well as the depth of Nixon's commitment to Thieu. Of all the parties concerned, the Saigon government had the least interest in an agreement providing for an American withdrawal, and it found the terms Kissinger and his counterpart had fashioned to be totally unacceptable. Thieu protested bitterly to Kissinger that he had not been consulted in advance of the negotiations and hinted to Nixon that he was prepared to tell the world on the eve of the election that the administration had sold South Vietnam down the river.

In addition, with the 1972 presidential election imminent, the White House came to see the war as an asset rather than a liability, at least in the short run. "Our great fear," Charles Colson recalled, was that a settlement "would let people say, 'Well, thank goodness the war is over. Now we can go on and worry about peace and we will elect a Democrat because Democrats always do more in peacetime.'" Nixon immediately backed away from a peace accord, and negotiations remained stalled throughout the remainder of the fall. Whether the electorate's reluctance to change leadership in the midst of an international crisis determined the outcome of the 1972 election is unclear. The Democrats did in fact nominate an explicitly antiwar candidate, Senator George McGovern of South Dakota, however, and the incumbent subsequently swamped him. Assured of a second term, the Nixon administration once again turned its attention to the crisis in Southeast Asia.

With the secret talks in Paris still deadlocked, Kissinger advised breaking off negotiations. This should be followed, he told Nixon, by a massive bombing campaign against the North. These attacks, he made it clear, would not lead to a military victory or to a communist withdrawal from the South, but rather would convince Thieu that the United States had "gone the extra mile" on South Vietnam's behalf. "I believe we could [then] obtain a prisoner for military disengagement deal by next summer," he told the president. The whole point of the bombing campaign would be to convince the American and South Vietnamese people that the Nixon administration had acted on "principle," that is, refused to simply abandon an ally. Having made a "good faith" effort, the administration would then abandon its ally, that is, "disengage with honor," as Kissinger put it.

As Americans celebrated Christmas in 1972, U.S. Air Force B-52s dropped 36,000 tons of bombs on the North, more than the total amount for 1969–1971. Despite desperate attempts by the North Vietnamese authorities to evacuate the civilian population, 1,600 civilians were killed. North Vietnamese gunners shot down 15 B-52s and 11 other aircraft, adding to the number of American POWs. The Christmas bombings produced a firestorm of outrage in the United States. Critics accused the president of waging war by tantrum, and congressional doves promised a definitive end-the-war resolution upon their return to Washington, D.C., from the Christmas recess.

Peace negotiations between Henry Kissinger and Le Duc Tho resumed in Paris on January 8. The atmosphere was tense but businesslike. In a matter of days, the diplomats worked out an agreement essentially similar to the one discussed prior to the 1972 elections. The United States agreed to withdraw its troops from Vietnam in a specified time period in return for repatriation of the POWs. The Nixon administration was not required to withdraw support from the Thieu government, but NVA troops were free to remain in the South, and the accords granted recognition to the Provisional Revolutionary Government, the political apparatus established by the NLF. President Thieu protested, but to no avail. Nixon quietly let the South Vietnamese leader know that if he did not endorse the accords, the United States would cut off aid. Thieu held out for a time, but then acquiesced. It was just a matter of time until direct American participation in "America's longest war" came to an end.

Nixon had captured the presidency in 1968 by promising "peace with honor." The administration's prolonged disentanglement resulted in an additional 20,553 American battle deaths, bringing the total to more than 58,000. The fighting from 1969 through 1973 took more than 100,000 ARVN and 500,000 NVA and VC lives. The conflict fueled an already alarming inflationary trend in the United States and shook the nation's confidence to its core. America had taken up the burden of world leadership in the wake of World War II, believing that it was fighting to save freedom, democracy, and indigenous cultures from the scourge of totalitarianism. It had been confident of its ability to cope with any crisis and make any sacrifice. In Vietnam, however, the United States threatened to destroy what it would save. In its obsession with the Cold War, it ignored the truth that for many people, regional rivalries, socioeconomic grievances, and religious differences outweighed strategic and ideological considerations.

The internal struggle in Vietnam reached a denouement more quickly and suddenly than most had anticipated. The peace agreements simply made possible a continuation of the war without direct American participation. The North attacked, the South counterattacked, and the Nixon administration bombed NVA sanctuaries in Laos and Cambodia.

The movement to undermine the imperial presidency's war-making powers culminated with congressional passage of the War Powers Act in the fall of 1973. The measure, originally introduced by Senator Jacob Javits of New York, required the president to inform Congress within 48 hours of the deployment of American military forces abroad and obligated him to withdraw them in 60 days in the absence of explicit congressional endorsement. As he had promised, Nixon vetoed the War Powers Act, but

Congress voted to override on November 7, 1973. The following week the House and Senate endorsed an amendment to the Military Procurement Authorization Act, banning the funding of any U.S. military action in any part of Indochina. In the spring of 1975, the North Vietnamese mounted a major offensive, and the ARVN collapsed within a matter of weeks. With South Vietnamese military and civilian officials struggling to be part of the departing American diplomatic contingent, Saigon fell to the NVA and VC on April 30, 1975.

Nixon later claimed that if Congress had not imposed restraints on him as commander-in-chief, he could have prevented the ignominious defeat of the Thieu regime. In fact, if the president had not been embroiled in the Watergate scandal by 1973, Congress may never have had the courage to pass the War Powers Act or cut off funds for further military activity in Indochina. In turn, however, the stresses associated with the war and the antiwar movement gave rise to the siege mentality in the White House that had made Watergate possible. Whatever the case, that scandal, breaking as it did simultaneous with the denouement in Vietnam, destroyed Richard Nixon's presidency and further contributed to the national malaise.

Containing Latin America: Nixon and Chile

Like almost all U.S. presidents before him, Richard Nixon viewed the world in terms of regions in which American interests were more or less vitally involved, with Latin America topping the list of priorities. Like most of his predecessors, Nixon refused to address the socioeconomic roots of political instability in the Latin republics while ensuring that no foreign power or ideology obtained a foothold in the hemisphere and that the area remained open to American investment. In some cases, the president and his foreign policy advisers were able to distinguish between Marxism-Leninism and Sino–Soviet imperialism, but not in Latin America. Indeed, the administration's pragmatism, its willingness to tolerate other ideologies, seemed to stop at America's shores. Nowhere were these tendencies more apparent than in U.S.–Chilean relations.

The president of Chile in 1970 was the successful, popular democrat, Eduardo Frei. He would easily have been reelected in the presidential contest scheduled for the fall of that year, but under the constitution he could not succeed himself. In September, socialist candidate Salvador Allende won a plurality but not a majority of the popular vote. Under the Chilean constitution, Congress was empowered to choose a president and was scheduled to do so in October. Although it had the legal right, Congress had never ignored the popular will.

Allende's first-place finish in the popular poll frightened the Nixon administration. At a press conference in Chicago, Kissinger told reporters that he feared that the political coalition supporting Allende, Popular Unity, was the opening wedge for a communist onslaught against Chilean liberties, an offensive that could spread quickly to Argentina and Peru. Although the International Telephone and Telegraph Company, fearing nationalization of its properties in Chile, spent $1 million to defeat Allende, the socialist won the congressional poll. As ITT had feared, Allende began nationalizing foreign-owned companies in Chile soon after he was inaugurated. In response, Nixon and his advisers decided to "make the economy scream." They slapped an informal embargo on trade with Chile, terminated most economic assistance, caused the International Monetary Fund (IMF) and other international agencies to deny loans to the new government, and fomented discontent within the Chilean military establishment. The stratagem worked. Housewives demonstrated against the ensuing scarcity and high cost of food, a general strike in October virtually paralyzed the Andean republic's economy, and inflation that year boosted the cost of living by more than 130%.

Inevitably, on September 11, 1973, the uprising came; a group of military officers, dissatisfied with Allende's socialist program and with the political gridlock they attributed to democracy, overthrew the Popular Unity regime. Allende died fighting in the presidential palace, either by suicide or murder. American agents were in touch with the coup plotters throughout and knew beforehand that the officers would strike. Latinos remembered the Big Stick and dollar diplomacy; critics insisted that U.S. interference in Chilean affairs had far more to do with the desire to protect vested American interest – ITT had contributed heavily to the Nixon war chest – than with ideology. U.S. intervention into Chilean affairs sent a chill through Latin America. It seemed that North American policy had returned to the days of Theodore Roosevelt, when intervention was justified on the grounds of keeping the European imperial powers out of the Western Hemisphere. Only the perceived external threat had changed. What remained constant were U.S. economic interests in Latin America and their continuing influence on the foreign affairs establishment.

The Yom Kippur War

Although Henry Kissinger was Jewish, he shared with the president a conviction that American Zionists (those favoring all-out U.S. aid to the state of Israel in its continuing battle with the Arab world) exerted excessive influence on U.S. foreign policy. Because they perceived good relations with the Arabs to be crucial to containing Soviet expansion and because much of the world's untapped oil reserves lay beneath the sands of the Arabian Peninsula, both favored a more "balanced" approach to the Arab–Israeli conflict. In cooperation with Senator Fulbright, Kissinger and Secretary of State William Rogers worked quietly for a lasting settlement, one that included an Israeli willingness to trade peace for land and an Arab willingness to recognize the legitimacy of the Jewish state and to sign peace treaties with it.

Most of the Arab world had severed formal ties with the United States in the aftermath of the Six-Day War in 1967, in which the Israelis, using American arms and supplies, had crushed the Soviet-supplied Egyptian and Syrian forces. During the fighting, the Israelis had seized and occupied portions of Egypt, Syria, and Jordan. Despite UN Security Council Resolution 242, which called on Israel to return conquered lands to the Arabs in return for secure, recognized boundaries, peace continued to elude the Middle East. As of 1969, Israel controlled all the Sinai Desert up to the western bank of the Suez Canal; the Gaza Strip, a narrow coastal area jutting toward Tel Aviv from the Sinai seized from Egypt; the Golan Heights, a strategic hill area from which, before the war, Syrian and Palestinian gunners had lobbed artillery shells into Jewish settlements taken from Syria; and East Jerusalem and the West Bank, both of which had been seized from Jordan.

The dilemma facing the Nixon administration in 1969 was stark. The Arabs had insisted that Israel surrender its conquered lands before serious negotiations leading to normalization of relations could start, whereas the Israelis had demanded recognition of Israel's right to exist as a state as the price for talks on disengagement. Yasir Arafat, head of the Palestine Liberation Organization (PLO), had insisted that much of Israel belonged to his people by right of 2,000 years of continued occupancy. The goal of the Arafat-led radical fedayeen movement was the creation of a "democratic secular state" in which "Jews, Arabs, and Christians would live together with equal rights."

As 1970 came to a close, the level of conflict between the Palestinians and Egypt, on the one hand, and Israel, on the other, increased to the point where the Nixon administration decided it would have to take a gamble to break the diplomatic impasse and avert a general war. During an address to an audience of Foreign Service officers, Secretary of State William Rogers suggested that Israel withdraw to its pre-1967 boundaries in return for recognition from Egypt. He also called for a broadly based settlement in the Middle East, involving negotiations between Israel and Jordan over the West Bank, the future of United Jerusalem, and the Palestinian refugee problem. Israel and American Zionists immediately denounced the "Rogers Plan," as it was called, as a sell-out of Israeli interests.

In 1970, Nasser died, elevating his little known vice president, Anwar Sadat, to the Egyptian presidency. By 1973, Sadat had become completely frustrated with his inability to move the Arab–Israeli conflict off dead center. With the Syrian government of Hafez al-Asad, which advocated a policy of implacable hostility to Israel, threatening Cairo's leadership of the Arab world and with both the United States and the United Nations apparently unwilling to pressure Israel any further, Sadat decided on war. On

October 6, with Israelis distracted by Yom Kippur, a Jewish high holy day, Egyptian troops crossed the Sinai Peninsula, driving the surprised Israeli army before it while Syrian forces advanced up the Golan Heights.

Despite its determination to pursue a more balanced policy toward the Middle East, the Nixon administration did not resist when the government of Israeli Prime Minister Golda Meir requested a massive emergency airlift of planes, tanks, and ammunition. Pro-Zionists such as Senator Jacob Javits (R-New York) joined with Scoop Jackson and other ardent cold warriors to demand all-out aid to the Israelis. Public opinion polls showed that 46% of Americans supported Israel in the Yom Kippur War, whereas only 6% favored the Arabs. The U.S. response was also prompted by news that on October 10 the Soviets had begun replacing destroyed Arab armaments through an airlift and by means of accelerated surface shipments. American intelligence operatives reported to the White House that the new Soviet equipment sent to Egypt included Scud surface-to-surface missiles, some of which were armed with tactical nuclear warheads. Assured of American support, the Israelis took the offensive. Israeli troops drove into Syria, and a tank force crossed the Suez Canal and encircled an entire Egyptian army. By October 17, Israel appeared poised for another sweeping triumph.

On that same day in Kuwait, the Persian Gulf members of the Organization of Petroleum Exporting Countries (OPEC) met. They voted to raise the price for their petroleum by 400%. Arab delegates also voted to suspend oil shipments until the United Nations carried out Resolution 242. On October 19, in response to the arms airlift and a request from Nixon to Congress for a $2.2-billion appropriation to pay for more jets for Israel, Saudi Arabia embargoed oil exports to the United States. Nevertheless, following a 36-hour lobby phone blitz by the American Israel Public Affairs Committee, Congress passed the aid package. Over the next few weeks, gas prices rose dramatically throughout the Western world and Japan.

The effectiveness of the Arab oil boycott, together with mounting Egyptian and Syrian losses, forced the United States and Soviet Union into uneasy and temporary alliance. Moscow and Washington, D.C., agreed to a cease-fire proposal, rushed it through the Security Council, and then pressured their respective client states into accepting it – or so they thought. After agreeing to a cease-fire on October 22, the Israelis fought on, widening their bridgehead in Egypt and improving their bargaining position for the forthcoming negotiations. On the 24th, Brezhnev wrote Nixon proposing U.S.–Soviet intervention to impose a cease-fire. He warned that if the Israelis did not stop fighting at once and the U.S. government procrastinated, the Soviet Union might have to act unilaterally. Nixon and Kissinger responded by slowing arms shipments to Israel, while placing American forces worldwide on nuclear alert. America, they hoped to indicate, was not going to tolerate Soviet intervention.

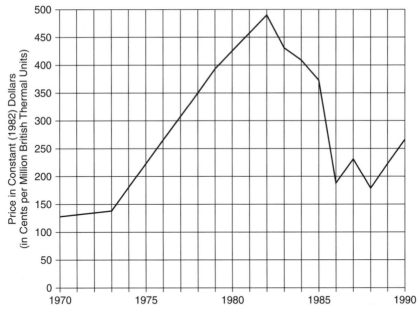

Figure 9–1. Crude oil prices, 1970–1990.

Source: U.S. Energy Information Administration, *Annual Energy Review.*

Long-time Nixon observers in Congress and the press were skeptical about the strategic need for the nuclear alert. Brezhnev ignored it and agreed to Nixon's proposal for a settlement, as did Sadat. In another resolution, the Security Council demanded that the belligerents return to the line of battle of October 22. On October 26, the United States canceled the nuclear alert and the Soviet Union reduced its degree of readiness. Nixon went on television to describe the crisis surrounding the nuclear alert as the worst crisis the nation had faced since the Cuban missile crisis of 1962. The consensus among skeptics, however, was that the president wanted to draw attention away from the burgeoning Watergate scandal.

The Arab oil boycott, which lasted from October 1973 to March 1974, created both diplomatic and political problems for the United States. At that point, America was dependent on the Middle East for only 12% of its petroleum, but Western Europe and Japan imported up to 80% of their oil from the Arab states. The boycott was threatening the existence of NATO. Meanwhile, in the United States, unemployment rose two percentage points to 7% while long lines of frustrated consumers formed at gasoline stations. The price of gas soared from $0.40 to $0.50 per gallon. In response to the crisis created by the Arab boycott, in November 1973, Kissinger began 18 months of "shuttle diplomacy," during which the national security adviser (soon to replace Rogers as secretary of state in 1974) flew back and forth between Arab capitals and Tel Aviv, cultivating Sadat and Hafez Assad of Syria and arranging troop disengagements from the Sinai and Golan Heights and the reopening of the Suez Canal. In return, OPEC ended its embargo, and the energy crisis temporarily eased in the United States. In the summer of 1974, Nixon made a highly publicized tour of the Middle East, during which he received a tumultuous reception in Cairo and a more reserved welcome in Israel. Kissinger was hailed as a conquering hero by the U.S. media and, in 1974, when the secretary of state was hauled up before the SFRC on charges that he had approved illegal wire taps of his aides' phones, Congress voted its "complete confidence" in him. Shuttle diplomacy was laudable as a study in crisis management, but did nothing to get at the fundamentals of the Arab–Israeli conflict.

Summary
Evaluations of the Nixon–Kissinger foreign policy vary. By 1974, when the president was forced to resign because of the Watergate scandal, there were no remaining combat troops left in Vietnam. Yet, peace with honor had cost tens of thousands of lives; in the opinion of many Americans, this had brought neither peace nor honor. The Republic of South Vietnam was still under siege from the VC and the NVA; a communist takeover seemed inevitable. Americans were confused and angry, some believing that the entire war had been a mistake, a product of the imperial presidency and the military–industrial complex, whereas others viewed the aborted war as a righteous struggle against the forces of godless communism – a struggle that could have been won had it not been for cowards and political radicals at home. The Nixon administration's effort to win votes with the former by pulling out of Vietnam and with the latter by blaming the withdrawal on the former only deepened the national wounds inflicted by Vietnam. Some observers viewed Vietnam as primarily a manifestation of the larger struggle between the democratic West and the communist East. Nixon and Kissinger's opening to China and the Soviet Union clearly changed the international climate, making, in the opinion of many, another Vietnam impossible. Nixon's courage in defying one of his key constituencies, the anticommunist right, was remarkable. Yet the administration's reluctance to grant parity in nuclear weapons to the Soviet Union together with Henry Jackson's campaign to subvert the SALT I agreement and force Moscow to accept America's definition of human rights brought Soviet–American relations to a new post–missile crisis low. Finally, Nixon and Kissinger's insensitivity to socioeconomic injustice in the developing world, and especially its anticommunist, probusiness policies in Latin America, boded ill for the future. As critics of American foreign policy pointed out, the Cold War was only marginally important and sometimes irrelevant to the struggles of submerged peoples to achieve national self-determination, social justice, and economic prosperity.

ADDITIONAL READINGS

Ambrose, Stephen, *Nixon: Vol. I, The Education of a Politician, 1913–1962* (1986).
Ambrose, Stephen, *Nixon: Vol. II, The Triumph of a Politician, 1962–1972* (1989).
Brodie, Fawn M., *Richard Nixon: The Shaping of His Character* (1981).
Ehrlichman, John, *Witness To Power: The Nixon Years* (1982).
Haldeman, H. R., *The Haldeman Diaries: Inside the Nixon White House* (1994).
Hoff, Joan, *Nixon Reconsidered* (1994).
Isaacson, Walter, *Kissinger: A Biography* (1992).
Kissinger, Henry, *The White House Years* (1979).
Nixon, Richard M., *In the Arena* (1990).
Nixon, Richard M., *RN: The Memoirs of Richard Nixon* (1978).
Parmet, Herbert, *Richard Nixon and His America* (1990).
Reichley, A. James, *Conservatives in an Age of Change* (1981).
Safire, William, *Before the Fall: An Inside Look at the Pre-Watergate White House* (1975).

10 The Limits of Expediency

Richard M. Nixon and the American Presidency

Despite Richard M. Nixon's reputation as a conservative ideologue in domestic affairs, earned over the years for his unceasing partisan attacks on the New Deal, Fair Deal, and Great Society, he proved as pragmatic and opportunistic in social and economic policy as he had in foreign affairs. Indeed, in its commitment to equality of opportunity, a social safety net for the chronically disadvantaged, a balanced budget, and minimal support for civil rights initiatives, the Nixon approach seemed to be a continuation of Dwight D. Eisenhower's modern Republicanism. The president did not cut Great Society programs, and he continued the Model Cities program, increased funding for food stamps, Medicare, and Medicaid. He also signed a measure that reduced the voting age to 18, a bill that subsequently became the Twenty-Sixth Amendment to the Constitution. When classical economic remedies did not suffice to pull the United States out of the economic doldrums that gripped it, the president shocked his conservative supporters by turning to Keynesian remedies. An astute political animal, the president understood that with only 43% of the popular vote in 1968 and facing hostile Democratic majorities in both houses of Congress, he would have to pursue centrist policies if he wanted to win a second term.

Personally, the new president felt sympathy and compassion for the downtrodden; his Quaker upbringing and the deaths of two brothers had affected him profoundly. At the same time, he had absorbed the bootstrap, self-made man mentality from his father, and he despised those who had made their political fortunes catering to the nation's have-nots. However, Nixon was much more hostile to existing government bureaucracies than even Eisenhower. The White House was unremitting in its efforts to sidestep or scale back governmental agencies, especially those concerned with economic and social issues. Nixon declared war on the federal bureaucracy, both because it was good politics in a nation grown suspicious of and discontented with the federal government and because the president truly believed that such agencies were filled with New Deal/Fair Deal liberals bent on thwarting his will.

Encouraged by conservative intellectuals such as William F. Buckley, William Safire, and Kevin Phillips, Nixon believed that he was presiding over and guiding a major political realignment in American politics. In *The Emerging Republican Majority* published in 1969, Phillips identified a new political alliance consisting of suburbanites, blue-collar workers, businesspeople, Catholic ethnic groups, and philosophical conservatives that was emerging to replace the New Deal coalition. Republican leaders believed they could appeal to the fears of these constituencies, flanking the Democrats on the right, while reassuring them of the GOP's commitment to equality of opportunity and its aversion to racism and class warfare, thus flanking Wallace on the left. Nixon and the GOP believed that they could create and maintain a political majority by portraying themselves as responsible, patriotic defenders of the public order, while labeling the Democrats as the permissive representatives of minorities, welfare cheats, spoiled brat radicals, and uncompetitive businessmen and farmers.

Playing to the Silent Majority: Nixon's Domestic Policies

The Southern Strategy

Nixon realized instinctively in 1968 and explicitly in 1969 that one of the principal strongholds of the forgotten man was the American South, and that if he were going to sustain his presidency and preserve his Vietnam consensus, he would have to control that region. Although Nixon had a long-established record as a supporter of the civil rights movement, he made significant inroads in the 1968 election into the old Confederacy, historically a Democratic stronghold. He had done so in part by assuring such leaders as J. Strom Thurmond of South Carolina of his sympathy for their position on questions such as school busing and law and order. Southern conservatives had been delighted with his choice of Spiro Agnew as his running mate. The GOP platform had promised an all-out war against crime and reform of the welfare laws, as well as a stronger national defense. In 1969, Nixon told Haldeman and Ehrlichman that the major weakness with administration programs was that they did not speak to working-class whites. "We keep talking of the minorities ... and overlook our greatest potential."

The president's southern strategy called for him to repopulate the Warren Court with conservatives, and he wasted no time. In May 1969, under intense fire for having taken expensive gifts from financier Louis Wolfson, Abe Fortas resigned from the Supreme Court. Nixon had scored points with the legal community and pleased both liberals and conservatives by appointing the able and moderate Warren Burger to be chief justice. The replacement for Fortas was another matter. "With this one," Ehrlichman remembered Nixon telling him, "we'd stick it to the liberal, Ivy League clique who thought the Court was their own private playground." The president

ordered Attorney General John Mitchell to come up with a strict constructionist from the South. Similar to Haldeman and Ehrlichman, Mitchell,
who was sometimes referred to within the administration as "El Supremo,"
was a man of no political experience. He had made his mark by helping
Governor Nelson Rockefeller devise a scheme to circumvent New York's
constitutional limit on bonded indebtedness. In opposing renewal of the
1965 Voting Rights Act, Mitchell had dismissed it as "essentially regional
legislation." The attorney general's choice, Judge Clement F. Haynsworth
of South Carolina, chief judge of the Fourth Circuit Court of Appeals, was
less than eminent. He was a wealthy segregationist with an undistinguished
legal record who belonged to several exclusive clubs. In *School Board of the
City of Charlottesville v. Dillard*, he had insisted that children in schools under desegregation orders be allowed to transfer. Contrary to the contentions
of the Supreme Court in the *Brown* decision, he argued that integration
increased rather than decreased the sense of inferiority among black students. Southerners of all political inclinations were initially gratified that
Nixon had named one of their own and northerners assumed that the new
nominee would be as qualified as Berger, but as details of Haynsworth's
background came to light, liberals took up sword and buckler to fight the
nomination. In November 1969, following a furious debate, the Senate
voted 55 to 45 against his confirmation.

The Senate's rejection of Clement Haynsworth had humiliated and therefore incensed Nixon. In the aftermath of that debacle, he ordered Attorney
General Mitchell to come up with another name. He wanted a southerner,
a strict constructionist, and a man free of any possible conflict-of-interest
charge, he said. Mitchell's choice was Judge G. Harold Carswell, a Floridian
who had recently been appointed to the Fifth Circuit Court of Appeals.
Carswell met Nixon's requirements, but he was also an ignoramus and a
racist. As a candidate for the Georgia legislature in 1948, he had declared
that "segregation of the races is proper and the only practical and correct way of life." Furthermore, his qualifications for the high court were
simply nonexistent. As a district and later circuit judge, Carswell was reversed on appeal 40% of the time. He had, moreover, been abusive to civil
rights lawyers in his court and often dismissed their suits without a hearing. Bryce Harlow, the Eisenhower assistant whom Nixon had brought in
to handle congressional liaison, informed the president that the senators
"think Carswell's a boob, a dummy. And what counter is there to that?
He is."

By the time the Senate began formal debate on the Carswell nomination in late March, the Floridian was taking hits from all directions. The
American Bar Association (ABA) repudiated its earlier endorsement as evidence came to light that Nixon's choice for associate justice had belonged
to an all-white Florida State booster club in the early 1950s and that he was
cofounder of a segregated private golf club. Even his supporters damned

him with faint praise. Senator Roman Hruska (R-Nebraska) took to the floor of the Senate to defend the administration's nominee. "The President appoints these people," he declared, "and even if he were mediocre, there are a lot of mediocre judges and people and lawyers. Aren't they entitled to a little representation?" Russell Long agreed that "[b]rilliant...upside down thinkers" on the Supreme Court were destroying the United States. What the country needed, he declared, was a "B student or C student."

As the Senate prepared to take up the controversial nomination, a large crowd gathered on the steps of the Capitol. Inside, Senators and staff aides filled the well of the chamber. A number of distinguished guests, including 83-year-old Ernest Gruening, a veteran of liberal causes, filled rows of chairs five deep behind the senators' desks. The galleries were packed. Tension filled the chamber as the clerk began to call the roll. There was scarcely a sound as the names were read. It soon became apparent that a small band of southerners led by Senator Fulbright, together with a dozen liberal Republicans, were voting with northern Democrats. When the final vote tally was read, Carswell and Nixon had lost. The vote was 51 to 45. The packed gallery cheered and applauded.

As rejection of the Haynsworth and Carswell nominations demonstrated, presidents operate under very real constraints when nominating justices to the Supreme Court. The need to appeal to the political center and the Senate's prerogative to confirm compels a degree of moderation and quality. A perfect example was Nixon's early 1969 appointment of Warren Burger to be chief justice. The tall, white-haired midwesterner was intelligent, dignified, and a political middle-of-the-roader. Following Carswell's rejection, the president selected Harry Blackmun, Minnesotan and 16-year veteran of the Eighth Circuit Court of Appeals. Blackmun's positions turned out to be to more liberal than those of his old friend, Burger. When Justice Hugo Black retired in 1970, Nixon finally had his chance to select a southerner. His somewhat surprising choice was Lewis Powell, Jr., of Virginia, a highly respected former president of the ABA. As president of the Richmond Board of Education, Powell had outraged segregationists by advocating conscientious compliance with the *Brown* decision. Powell reassured conservatives somewhat, however, when during his nomination hearings, he declared himself to be a believer in judicial restraint, the principle that held that federal jurists should render decisions only when absolutely compelled to do so by conflict with the law. Nixon's final nominee, Arizonan William Rehnquist, was a thoroughgoing conservative. An avid supporter of Barry Goldwater in 1964, Rehnquist had, as one of John Mitchell's assistant attorney generals, urged the Justice Department to challenge the *Miranda* decision and other decisions designed to protect criminal defendants from arbitrary questioning and search. Somewhat surprisingly, however, Rehnquist found himself perpetually in the minority during the next decade.

Law and Order Versus Civil Liberties

In proposing "strict constructionists" for the Supreme Court, Nixon was attempting not only to implement his southern strategy but to fulfill his campaign promise to restore "law and order" to a nation allegedly teetering on the brink of anarchy. The GOP and the Nixon administration labored frantically to keep alive memories of the 1968 Democratic National Convention in Chicago. Federal Bureau of Investigation (FBI) Director J. Edgar Hoover ordered his field agents to do everything in their power to alert the public to the "depraved nature and moral looseness of the New Left" and to "destroy this insidious movement." The federal courts did their part by conducting several highly publicized trials of prominent radicals. The most famous of these courtroom dramas was the trial of the "Chicago Eight," a group of dissidents charged by the Justice Department with conspiracy to cross state lines to incite a riot. The trial, which unfolded in Chicago from October 1969 through March 1970, confirmed leftists' worse fears about a justice system thoroughly corrupted by "the establishment" and conservatives' worst nightmares about a society and culture teetering on the brink of anarchy. The Chicago Eight included such movement celebrities as the Yippies' Abbie Hoffman and Jerry Rubin, Black Panthers leader Bobby Seale, and Students for a Democratic Society (SDS) luminaries Tom Hayden and Rennie Davis. Presiding over the trial was 73-year-old Julius Hoffman, a traditionalist determined to enforce respect for the court. However, Rubin and company refused to cooperate. Wearing outlandish garb, they laughed and sneered at the proceedings, shouting "bullshit" over the testimony of paid police informants and referring to Judge Hoffman as "Julie." When Seale accused the judge of being a "blatant racist" and cursed the prosecutor, Hoffman ordered him bound and gagged. Activists and some moderates were appalled at the sight of a black defendant sitting manacled before a white judge and prosecutor. While respect for authority plummeted on major college campuses and respect for dissent and alternative lifestyles among conservatives, never high in any case, evaporated, Nixon enthusiastically assumed the pose of a strong leader who could defend the United States against the forces of anarchy. The convictions of the Chicago Eight were overturned on appeal in May 1972.

The administration authorized widespread use of wiretapping and other electronic surveillance devices in the war against organized crime and persuaded Congress to provide increased support for the Law Enforcement Assistance Administration. The Organized Crime Act of 1970 limited immunities granted under the Fifth Amendment and permitted judges to lengthen sentences of criminals found to be particularly dangerous. In the opinion of conservative America, which certainly included the president, the court's decisions on criminal rights, school prayer, and obscenity had been far too permissive. Particularly galling were the Warren Court's rulings in *Gideon v. Wainwright* (1963) in which the majority had held that all defendants in criminal cases, regardless of their ability to pay, were entitled to legal counsel. Clarence Gideon had been charged with theft; too poor to hire an attorney, he was found guilty and sentenced to prison. In *Gideon*, the court ruled that if defendants could not afford an attorney, then the state must provide one (thus did the system of public defenders expand dramatically). In *Miranda v. Arizona* (1966), the justices held in a five-to-four decision that before police questioned persons suspected of a crime, they were required to inform them of their right to remain silent and to legal counsel, and that anything they said might be used against them. Many observers expected that with the Blackmun, Powell, and Rehnquist nominations, a new conservative majority would begin to chip away at the Warren Court's rulings, especially in the area of criminal law. The Burger Court's record during the Nixon administration was clearly mixed, however. In 1972, for example, in *Furman v. Georgia*, the justices declared the death penalty to be "cruel and unusual" punishment, except when decreed in specific circumstances by state or federal law. In *Mapp v. Ohio*, the court ruled that police must obtain evidence legally, upholding the Fourth Amendment's protection against "unreasonable searches and seizures."

Deliberate Speed: Implementing Civil Rights

The president was a master of taking away with one hand what he seemingly was offering with the other. This was as true in the area of civil rights as it was in Vietnam. "We are opposed to segregation in any form, legal and moral, and we will take action where we find it, and where it amounts to a violation of an individual's rights," Spiro Agnew told an audience at Williamsburg, Virginia. "But our opposition to segregation does not mean we favor compulsory or forced integration; and we remain opposed to the use of federal funds to bring about some arbitrary racial balance in the public schools." In 1968, the Supreme Court had ruled in *Green v. Board of Education* that "freedom of choice" laws – that is, state legislation that allowed parents to select any school within a district for their child to attend – were unconstitutional because they obstructed the drive to achieve racial balance. The court was "right on Brown and wrong on Green," candidate Nixon declared. In short, the administration declared war on segregation and discrimination, and then proclaimed itself powerless to do anything about them – local option instead of forced busing, states' rights instead of federal intervention.

To implement his southern strategy, Nixon selected as attorney general the dour, pipe-smoking lawyer and Republican partisan John Mitchell. The new attorney general was a long-time Nixon adviser and loyalist, and a prophet of the emerging Republican majority. At the same time that the White House was assuring Americans of the president's commitment to equal rights for all, Mitchell was opposing an extension of the Voting Rights Act of 1965. He and conservatives in the Justice Department subsequently obstructed enforcement of the 1968 Fair Housing Act. The pace of desegregation slowed noticeably in the South as the Justice Department and Health Education and Welfare Department (HEW) became suddenly passive in dealing with recalcitrant districts. In the summer of 1969, the administration announced that the September 1969 school desegregation deadline would be enforced for all southern school districts except those with "bona fide educational and administrative problems." So extreme did Mitchell become that attorneys in his own civil rights division in the Justice Department rebelled.

The key issue as far as civil rights during the Nixon administration was concerned, however, was busing. It was one of those visceral issues, cutting across racial attitudes, educational philosophies, and parental fears, that the president was so adept at exploiting. Busing was also an issue that cut across regions. Many northern, urban centers were characterized by de facto segregation. That is, the races were physically separated by choice and economic circumstance rather than by law. As early as 1961, federal courts ruled that busing across school districts was an acceptable way to end de facto as well as de jure segregation. In March 1970, President Nixon asked Congress to approve $1.5 billion in aid for school districts under court order to desegregate. In his message recommending passage, however, the president drew a distinction between residential patterns resulting from choice and those produced by discriminatory laws or practices. To the dismay of civil rights activists, he promised that "transportation beyond normal geographical school zones for the purpose of achieving a racial balance will not be required." In the months that followed, the administration tacitly encouraged a white backlash against the forced transfer of students. A "new evil," Nixon called it, "disrupting communities and imposing hardship on children – both black and white." Outraged whites burned school buses in Denver, Colorado, and Pontiac, Michigan, while in Boston, School Committeewoman Louise Day Hicks endeared herself to her white, working-class Irish constituents by leading a drive to disallow busing as a means to achieve racial balance. Having contributed to the public outcry against busing, in 1974, the Nixon administration sponsored a congressional measure insisting that federal and state authorities resort to busing only as a last resort.

Surprisingly, the Burger Court served as a counterbalance to the executive in the area of civil rights, consolidating and even extending the rulings of its predecessor. In 1969, the Nixon White House pressured HEW to petition the Fifth District Court asking for a delay in the desegregation of 23 Mississippi school districts. Never before had the federal government intervened to slow the pace of integration. The National Association for the Advancement of Colored People (NAACP) filed suit and the high court decreed in *Alexander v. Holmes County* that desegregation must proceed "at once." In *Griggs v. Duke Power and Light Co.* (1971), the court ruled that the

1964 Civil Rights Act outlawed discriminatory effects as well as intentions. In this case, a united court ruled that a high school diploma and intelligence test had no bearing on the job to be performed and that if they barred blacks from employment, they were discriminating. In 1971, Burger and his colleagues handed down a long-awaited busing decision in *Swann v. Charlotte-Mecklenburg Board of Education*. The high court upheld a lower court ruling that had ordered mandatory busing of some 13,300 children in the Charlotte area to achieve integration. "Desegregation plans," the decision held, "cannot be limited to the walk-in school." Bus transportation was an "integral part of the school system" and, as such, a legitimate tool to achieve racial balance. The parents of white children affected were not placated by subsequent clauses that prohibited busing over distances that threatened the integrity of the education process or the health of the children, although they did provide openings for Mitchell and his underlings to delay and obstruct.

It should be noted that in upholding busing as a means to facilitate integration, the Supreme Court inadvertently undermined the public school system in certain areas and contributed to the decline of the nation's inner cities. Offended by forced busing, white middle-class parents frequently switched their children to private, often religious schools, moved to the suburbs, or both. Whites who stayed were likely to vote against millage issues designed to raise funds to support public schools. Those who left eroded the tax base. White flight, encouraged in part by busing, left the cores of the nation's urban areas primarily African American and Hispanic and overwhelmingly poor.

Welfare Reform: The Family Assistance Plan

The conservative majority that had elected Richard Nixon in 1968 was worried not only about crime in the streets and forced integration but also about the burgeoning welfare state. Indeed, many suburbanites, blue-collar urban dwellers, and farmers large and small had become convinced that the social welfare system had degenerated into a dodge for those unwilling to work and that a number of its programs, particularly Aid to Families with Dependent Children (AFDC), were having a corrosive effect on the nuclear family. In effect, they charged, this latter program was paying women to bear children out of wedlock and to remain unmarried. At a more fundamental level, conservatives believed AFDC, Medicare, Medicaid, and various War on Poverty programs were undermining the American work ethic. Finally, they argued, expenditures for so-called entitlement programs were unbalancing the national budget and undermining the economy. Even liberals were dissatisfied with the existing system. AFDC was woefully underfunded; in 18 states, the average welfare check was $31 per month, and every dollar earned by a working welfare parent was deducted from the benefit.

Richard Nixon shared the insecurities and prejudices of the "silent majority" to an extent, but he was conflicted by feelings of compassion and empathy for the downtrodden. For the president, a classic American underdog, such feelings were natural. As was the case with Vietnam and civil rights, the president attempted to satisfy both sides in the debate, thus salving his psyche and serving the cause of political expediency. He was determined to do away with Great Society programs that did not work, he told his advisers, and to reform the welfare system without abandoning the poor, a move that he correctly perceived would be politically disastrous. The first months of the Nixon administration saw increases in Social Security payments and presidential support for more funds for low-income public housing. When in a 1971 television interview, Nixon vowed to change the national preoccupation from war to "clean air, clean water, open spaces, and a welfare reform program that will provide a floor under the income of every family with children," right-wingers in the White House threatened to rebel. Nixon was undaunted.

The centerpiece of the administration's domestic program was a welfare reform plan that the president and his political advisers believed would satisfy liberals by continuing a federal helping hand to the poor and conservatives by doing away with the multitude of programs and bureaucracies created by the Johnson administration. "I like the idea of working off welfare checks," he wrote John Ehrlichman. The man who Nixon selected to head up welfare reform was Daniel Patrick Moynihan, a New York Democrat who served as assistant secretary of labor in both the Kennedy and the Johnson administrations. A trained and able social scientist and an ambitious politician, Moynihan came from a long line of progressive Catholic social thinkers who combined compassion for the poor with a determination to maintain the nuclear family. As an official in the Labor Department, he had written a controversial history and analysis of the African American family, describing the growth of one-parent households among black families and the deteriorating social status of black males. Broken homes, Moynihan argued, were both responsible for and the inevitable product of the culture of poverty. Nixon found convincing the New York Democrat's arguments that the current welfare system had to be totally reformed and named him to head the Urban Affairs Council, a body intended to be to domestic policy what the National Security Council (NSC) was to foreign policy.

What Moynihan had in mind was a guaranteed annual income – a "negative income tax" to use economist Milton Friedman's phrase. Under the Family Assistance Plan (FAP) introduced into Congress in late 1969, the federal government would make direct cash payments to ensure an income of $1,600 a year to families whose earnings fell below the poverty level. Such a family unit would be eligible, in addition, for up to $820 a year in food stamps. The head of household would have to work for the family to receive such a subsidy. FAP would replace all federal welfare grants to the states. "The problem of poor people is they don't have enough money," Moynihan observed during a television interview. "Cold cash! It's a surprisingly good cure for a lot of social ills."

The administration anticipated that FAP would please liberals and the poor themselves. No longer would the wages of working parents be deducted from welfare benefits. FAP would eliminate a cumbersome and intrusive federal bureaucracy that probed and analyzed welfare families. At the same time, the White House anticipated that conservatives would line up behind the FAP because it rewarded work and targeted the poor generally rather than minorities, women, and broken families. In fact, FAP satisfied neither liberals nor conservatives. On the right, the Chamber of Commerce denounced the plan as a first step toward a guaranteed national income – creeping socialism. On the left, the National Welfare Rights Organization condemned FAP as "anti-poor and anti-black" and called for a guaranteed annual income of $5,500 a year, a plan that would have affected one half of the families in America and cost $71 billion in 1970. Indeed, outraged at the February 1970 publication of a private memo from Moynihan to the president declaring that "the time may have come when the issue of race could benefit from a period of benign neglect," liberals were convinced that the assistance plan was part of a pattern of "institutionalized racism." Senator McCarthy labeled it the "Family Annihilation Plan." Although FAP, supported by House Ways and Means Committee Chairman Wilbur Mills, passed the House of Representatives, a coalition of conservatives and liberals defeated the proposal in the Senate in 1970 and again in 1971.

In 1972, Democrats in Congress proposed modifications in the FAP that would increase benefits to $2,600 per year for a family of four living below the poverty line (more than $11,000 in 1992 dollars) and provide for cost-of-living raises. At this point, Nixon decided to appeal to conservatives, and he came out in opposition to this liberal, "big spending" proposal. Senator George McGovern, the 1972 Democratic presidential candidate, subsequently made himself and welfare reform the object of public ridicule by proposing a "$1,000 a year taxable payment for every American." Congress finally passed a welfare reform bill shortly before the 1972 election, but it did nothing for the working poor. It established the Supplementary Security Income, a guaranteed income for senior citizens, many of whom were not poor, and for the blind and otherwise disabled.

The New Federalism
During the 1968 presidential campaign, Nixon had promised to return control of public affairs to the people. A central tenet of the conservative faith was that, since the New Deal, a huge, self-serving federal bureaucracy had grown up that was answerable to no one and that acted as a insulating

layer between the people and their elected officials. In his 1971 State of the Union address, the president asked Congress to join him in fashioning a "new American Revolution" or "new federalism." What Nixon had in mind was a system of "revenue sharing" whereby the federal government would gradually eliminate specific programs and instead refund tax monies to the states and localities for them to use for community development as they saw fit. No more intrusive federal bureaucracy, Nixon promised. Using no-strings-attached "block grants" from the federal government, localities could devote their turn-back tax dollars to urban or rural development, mass transit, job training, and law enforcement. Congress expressed reservations about revenue sharing. Local control might mean that the monies would not reach the targets for which they were intended. Without effective oversight, the possibilities for corruption were greatly enhanced. In the past, local control had meant discrimination against minorities and women. Nevertheless, in 1972, Congress passed the State and Local Fiscal Assistance Act. Over a 5-year period, the federal government would distribute $30.2 billion with $5.2 billion allocated in 1972, two thirds going to local governments and one third to the states. Within months, however, mayors and governors were complaining that because existing programs were being eliminated or cut, the federal government was just taking away with one hand what it was giving with the other. In reality, during hard times towns and cities used block grant monies to pay for operating expenses; rarely did funds go directly to the poor. In response, Congress passed the Comprehensive Employment and Training Act (CETA) in 1973, setting aside block grant funds for the vocational training of the poor. Over the next 10 years, 600,000 people made their way through the program.

Containing Environmentalism

It appeared at the outset that the Nixon administration was going to take up where the Great Society had left off on environmental problems. Nixon regarded Senator Edmund Muskie as perhaps the greatest threat to his re-election prospects in no small part because the Maine legislator had identified himself with clean air, clean water, and consumer safety. He paid homage to the burgeoning environmental movement in moving words, declaring that "we must learn not how to master nature but how to master ourselves, our institutions and our technology." To head the Interior Department, Nixon appointed Walter J. Hickel of Alaska, who proceeded to prosecute the Chevron Oil Company for polluting the Gulf of Mexico, halt oil well drillings in the Santa Barbara channel after a disastrous spill, and hold up construction on the Alaska pipeline for fear it would cause irreparable damage to the tundra. At the same time, the president was clearly enamoured of big business, a traditional Republican constituency, and it was that relationship that eventually triumphed. In November 1970, Nixon fired Hickel. In 1971, after Henry Ford II told John Ehrlichman that installation of air bags in American automobiles was "impracticable," Nixon overrode his own Department of Transportation and blocked regulations requiring their installation. In a memo complaining about the high cost of antipollution measures, John Ehrlichman declared, "Conservation is not the Republican ethic." Ignoring the fact that Theodore Roosevelt had been one of the founders of the conservation movement, Nixon replied, "I completely agree – We have gone overboard on the environment." The White House threw its full support behind the development of a supersonic transport (SST), which environmentalists argued would cause both noise and air pollution.

Environmentalism was an issue whose time had come, however, and its opponents were at long last on the defensive. Under the leadership of Senator William Proxmire of Wisconsin, the Senate blocked further appropriations for the SST in December 1970. The Democratic-controlled Congress then went on to enact the Occupational Safety and Health Act of 1970 and the National Air Quality Control Act of 1970. The latter measure tightened air pollution standards and penalties and called for a 90% reduction in pollution from automobile exhausts by 1975.

"Nixonomics"

Richard Nixon had worked as a young lawyer for the Office of Price Administration and there had acquired a distaste for government intervention into and regulation of the economy. Throughout his political career, he had echoed Robert Taft's paens to laissez-faire economics. Ever the political pragmatist, however, Nixon as president came to recognize that the Depression and New Deal had forever changed America. Conservatives might bridle at the thought of government-engineered income redistribution, but they along with liberals expected the U.S. government to foster prosperity. As the 1960s came to an end, the nation suffered from mounting inflation and increasing unemployment. Inflation was the result of Lyndon B. Johnson's efforts to pay for the war in Vietnam and the Great Society programs without raising taxes. Vietnamization and the winding down of the war in Vietnam also contributed to unemployment. Returning veterans flooded the job market just as the defense industry began cutting back. Boeing Aircraft, the huge Seattle-based aircraft producer, reduced its workforce from 101,000 to 44,000. Economists referred to this unusual combination of recession and inflation as "stagflation." The inflation rate in 1967 amounted to a manageable 3%; by 1973, it had reached 9% and by 1974, 12%. It would remain in double digits for the rest of the 1970s. At the same time, unemployment, at a low of 3.3% when Nixon took office, climbed to 6% by 1973 and showed no signs of abating.

Similar to his former boss, Dwight D. Eisenhower, Nixon initially took a conservative approach to solving the problems of inflation and unemployment. Traditional Republican philosophy called for inflation to receive first priority. According to classical economic theory, with inflation and deficits under control, business would acquire the capital and confidence to invest in new plants thus creating additional jobs and reducing unemployment. In 1969, when asked about the possibility of imposing wage and price controls to suppress inflation, Nixon replied, "Controls. Oh, my God, no!... We'll never go to controls." In an effort to cool off the economy and thus reduce inflation, the president successfully urged the Federal Reserve Board to raise interest rates sharply in 1969. At the same time, the administration cut expenditures for health, education, and welfare, but outlays for the war in Vietnam, Safeguard, and the space program more than offset those meager savings. The result was recession.

By the spring of 1970, the economy was in the doldrums. The average stock price as recorded by the Dow-Jones index dropped from 1,000 to near 700. All the major economic indices showed alarming declines; industrial production, new home construction, and automobile sales fell off precipitously. Fueled by continued spending on the war in Vietnam, the space program, and entitlement programs (guaranteed, cost-of-living indexed social programs), the federal deficit mushroomed to $23 billion in 1971. Spending on the food stamp program alone grew from $250 million in 1969 to $2.2 billion in 1971. Meanwhile, certain European and Asian economies were growing stronger and more efficient, crowding American goods out of international markets and making deep inroads into the U.S. domestic economy. The year 1971 saw the first U.S. trade deficit since the 1890s, and the value of the dollar on international money markets dropped precipitously as investors lost confidence in the soundness of the world's leading economy. As the nation's trade imbalance climbed ever upward, gold flowed out of the country. Indeed, America's gold reserves had dwindled from a 1946 high of $21 billion to around $12 billion by the end of 1971. The Democrats named the phenomenon of lagging production and surging inflation "Nixonomics." Everything that should be going up – employment, productivity, corporate profits – was going down, declared Lawrence O'Brien, chair of the Democratic National Committee, and everything that should be going down – inflation, the deficit, prices – was going up.

Stung by criticism from the business and banking community, if not from the Democratic opposition, Nixon reversed himself, much as Eisenhower had during his second term. In August 1971, the president announced a new economic policy. Under authority previously granted him by Congress, and which he had vowed never to use, he was imposing a freeze on wages and prices for 90 days. To deal with the trade deficit, the United States was severing the ties between the dollar and gold, allowing American currency to float freely against other currencies in international markets, finding its true value. The Nixon administration believed that the value of the dollar established during the 1944 Bretton Woods Conference was artificially high; as the dollar became cheaper in relation to other currencies – its value fell by approximately 10% after the president's announcement – American exports would, it was hoped, become more attractive and the trade deficit would decline. In effect, devaluation suspended the international monetary system established by the 1944 Bretton Woods Conference in which the dollar, linked by a fixed ratio to gold, had served as the world's economic anchor. In addition, the United States was imposing an immediate 10% surtax on imported goods. There was also to be a 10% tax credit for investment in new plants and equipment. Finally, the president announced the establishment of a Cost of Living Council under newly named Secretary of the Treasury John B. Connally to monitor the program. In fact, it was Connally, the pragmatic, tough-minded, and ambitious three-term governor of Texas, who had largely been responsible for the new economic policy.

Handsome, supremely self-confident Connally "was everything Nixon wasn't but wanted to be," Fred Siegel states. Faced with the decline of U.S. competitiveness, Connally and Nixon chose not to break up monopolies through antitrust suits or expose American manufacturers to the hard realities of international competition. They chose instead to try to redefine the role of the dollar, even if that meant risking the collapse of the international economy. Indeed, Connally proved to be an old-fashioned economic nationalist. It was doubly unfair for the Europeans and Japanese to shield themselves under the American military umbrella and simultaneously raise trade barriers against U.S. goods, he argued. Unburdened by any cultural affinity for Western Europe, he divided foreigners, according to Richard Whalen, into two groups: "cooperative and uncooperative."

The departure from gold and the imposition of a surtax were largely bluffs. Like most other modern Republicans, Nixon believed fervently in the benefits of international trade. It was certain that if the U.S. government continued to resist a new monetary agreement, its competitors would devalue their currencies and discriminate against American exports. In December 1971 at an international economic meeting in Washington, D.C., the United States agreed to reduce the exchange rate of the dollar by about 12% and to abolish the surcharge in return for a commitment by the other major trading nations to increase the value of their currencies. Nixon, it seemed, was reliving the early days of the New Deal when Franklin D. Roosevelt first torpedoed the London Economic Conference, and then moved toward international currency and trade agreements. The trade deficit increased at a somewhat decelerated rate in 1972, but continued to be a major problem. After the 90-day mandatory period, observance of wage and price guidelines became voluntary and inflation continued at a double-digit pace.

At the same time the administration experimented with nationalist economic policies on the international front, Nixon announced his conversion to Keynesianism. Over the protests of conservatives, he declared that when the economy encountered widespread unemployment and declining profits, the federal government had an obligation to "prime the pump." Accordingly, the White House was submitting to Congress a "full employment" budget for 1972, one that envisioned an $11.6 billion deficit. With federal funds stimulating the private sector, the DOW average topped 1,000. But the upswing was temporary and illusory. Inflationary pressures remained and then increased dramatically in the wake of the Arab boycott. Inflation hit 11% in 1974, and the following year unemployment reached 8.5%. Americans began to sense, correctly, that the nation's economic woes were due to long-term, systemic problems and were beyond the ability of any one presidential administration or government agency to remedy.

Nixon and the Women's Movement

Not surprisingly, the Nixon administration took pains to distance itself from the burgeoning feminist movement. The broad-based women's movement that entered the political arena in full force in the 1960s and 1970s was made up of individuals from all age groups, social strata, and lifestyles. Politically, the feminist movement focused on the Equal Rights Amendment (ERA), an addition to the Constitution affirming women's rights to equal treatment and nondiscrimination in all walks of life. In 1971, 200 women gathered in Washington, D.C., to establish the National Women's Political Caucus, dedicated to placing women in office at all levels of government. ERA aroused the ire of many working-class and suburban families, especially those caught up in evangelical and pentecostal movements inside and outside the mainstream denominations. Traditionalists insisted that passage of the ERA would lead to legalized abortion, conscription of women, unisex toilets, and destruction of the nuclear family.

Nixon made it clear that he sided with opponents of the ERA, and he announced that it would be madness to require colleges and universities receiving federal funding to provide equal athletic facilities for men and women. The president openly sided with "right-to-life" opponents of abortion, declaring that he would do everything in his power to protect "the sanctity of human life – including the life of the yet unborn." Perhaps most significantly, Nixon vetoed a bill passed by the Democratic majority providing for a national system of day care centers. Feminists and labor activists had long clamored for such a system. In their view, the modern family featured spouses that shared work and child rearing more or less equally. While middle- and upper-class women viewed the right to work and have their children cared for as a right, many poor women viewed it as a necessity. But Catholics and conservative Protestants perceived the day care center bill to be a threat to the family, taking the time-honored view that a woman's rightful place was in the kitchen and nursery. Nixon agreed. In his veto message, he declared that he opposed legislation that would pledge "the vast moral authority of the national government to communal approaches to child rearing, over against the family centered approach." This so-called family approach, of course, ignored the increasing prevalence of two-income households.

As was true of the modern civil rights movement in its early stages, the women's liberation movement that became visible in the 1960s scored its biggest gains in the courts. Indeed, the Burger Court went far beyond its predecessor in addressing questions of gender discrimination. Radicals and centrists hoped that the court would find a constitutional basis for declaring categorically that the sexes must be treated equally under the law. Instead, in *Reed v. Reed* (1971), a case invalidating an Idaho practice of giving preference to men over women as executors of estates, Burger and his associates held that laws differentiating between the sexes had to be "reasonable, not arbitrary." The high court cited provision of the 1964 Civil Rights Act and the Equal Pay Act of 1973 in outlawing corporate hiring practices that discriminated against mothers with small children [*Phillips v. Martin Marietta* (1971)] and requiring the armed forces to provide the same pay scale and benefits for female as male soldiers [*Frontiero v. Richardson* (1973)].

For many in the women's movement, the single most important issue in public life was the right of a female to abort an unwanted pregnancy. Many states had had statutes on their books for years making abortion a felony. As a result, women from upper- and middle-class to desperately poor, women from middle-aged to college or high school age, women from all walks of life risked their lives by having "back alley" abortions performed. In doing so, they submitted their bodies to strangers who used crude instruments and harsh chemicals that could kill and maim. Because abortion was illegal, these unscrupulous individuals were answerable to no one. By the 1960s, college co-eds had available to them "abortion undergrounds," which guided them to safe practitioners, many of them physicians practicing abortion secretly, out of conscience. These networks did little, however, to help poor women with their unwanted pregnancies. More important, participants in the women's movement saw the issue as key; if the state did not recognize the right of women to exercise control over their own bodies, there could never be equality in other areas.

In 1973, the Supreme Court agreed to rule on a case involving a destitute Texas woman who wanted to abort her pregnancy because she did not want her child to grow up in poverty. Texas was one of those states in which abortion, regardless of the circumstance, was punishable by fine and imprisonment. Lawyers representing feminists and the American Civil Liberties Union argued that the right of privacy established in *Griswold v. Connecticut* should be extended to a woman's right to abort her pregnancy. Justice Harry Blackmun and six of his colleagues agreed, but issued a compromise ruling designed to appease opponents of abortion. *Roe v. Wade* stipulated that women had an absolute right to abortion during the first 13 weeks of pregnancy, when it was agreed that a fetus could not sustain life on its own. During the middle third of the pregnancy (second trimester), states could regulate but not outlaw abortions. Abortion was prohibitable under state law during the last 13 weeks.

The Election of 1972

With unemployment and inflation rates still high and the Vietnam peace negotiations in Paris apparently going nowhere, the Democrats looked forward to the 1972 presidential election with some hope. The early leading contender for the Democratic nomination was Senator Edward M. Kennedy of Massachusetts. "Teddy" Kennedy was fourth in the line of succession Joseph and Rose Kennedy had established, and many political commentators had initially viewed him as no more than that. But the younger Kennedy proved himself to be a hard-working friend of organized labor, the poor, and Catholics, a figure less flamboyant and abrasive than Robert and hence more effective. He was a strong campaigner popular with both party regulars and reformers. Unfortunately for Kennedy and perhaps for the Democrats, a personal scandal intervened and ruined his candidacy. One July evening in 1969, while driving back from a party on Chappaquidick Island off Martha's Vineyard, the intoxicated Kennedy drove his car off a bridge into the sea. A young woman who was a passenger in the car drowned despite Kennedy's repeated efforts to save her. Incredibly, Kennedy did not report the accident until the next morning. Subsequent revelations concerning his efforts to cover up his wrongdoing cast doubt on his leadership qualities, to say the least. Chappaquidick effectively ended his chance to be president. Nixon's personal lawyer, Herbert Kalmbach, spent a considerable amount of money left over from the 1968 campaign to keep the story in front of the public.

With Kennedy out of the picture, the front runner for the Democratic nomination became Senator Edmund Muskie of Maine. Muskie was opposed to the war in Vietnam and a dedicated environmentalist, but he was temperate in speech and conventional in dress, a dignified, moderate candidate that had the potential to appeal to both liberals and the political center. Muskie was forced, however, to share center stage with Hubert Humphrey, who had been reelected to the Senate in 1970. On the left, first-term Senator George S. McGovern announced his intention to enter the primaries and to make ending the war the number one issue in the election. On the right, George Wallace had returned to the fold, determined, as he put it, to turn the Democratic Party upside down. Finally, Muskie had to contend with several minor candidates: Senator Henry M. Jackson of Washington, champion of the military–industrial complex, Israel, and organized labor; black Congresswoman Shirley Chisholm of New York; and New York Mayor John V. Lindsay, a liberal Republican recently turned Democrat.

Nixon and the Committee to Re-elect the President (CREEP) were apprehensive concerning Muskie's candidacy. They feared that the New Englander was perceived to be a moderate on both race and foreign policy and thus attractive to the political center, particularly in the South. To deal with this threat, the White House hired Donald Segretti and a number of other political operatives to sabotage Muskie in the primaries. They were amazingly successful. Segretti and his team planted stories during the New Hampshire primary in the arch-conservative *Manchester Union-Leader* to the effect that, at the same time Muskie supported blacks, he was prejudiced against French Canadians, an important constituency in New England. Indeed, charged a *Union-Leader* editorial, Muskie had referred to them as "canucks," a disparaging term. After the paper reprinted a magazine story charging that Muskie's wife drank too much and cursed frequently, the Maine senator called a press conference. In anger and frustration, he broke down in tears before television cameras and in the process did irreparable damage to his image as a calm rationalist, a person always in control.

While Humphrey, still contaminated by his association with Lyndon B. Johnson, maintained a low profile, McGovern and Wallace, the candidates of the left and right, battled it out in the primaries that remained. Insisting that the United States ought to win or withdraw from Vietnam, and preaching the states' rights, law-and-order doctrines that had made him a force in 1968, Wallace captured several southern primaries and ran well in Michigan and Maryland. "What did these so-called lib'rals bring us?" Wallace asked his admiring supporters. "Drugs. Riots. Bureaucrats. Contempt for the average citizen, taxes that crush him and leave no freedom. Wars that can't be won.... That's what they brung us." While campaigning in Maryland, however, he was shot and critically wounded on May 15 by Arthur Bremer, a 21-year-old janitor/bus boy and social misfit. Wallace lived but was paralyzed from the waist down and had to withdraw from the race. Meanwhile, McGovern, who called Vietnam "a moral and political disaster – a terrible cancer eating away the soul of the nation," had defeated Humphrey in the California primary. That state's 45 electoral votes gave the South Dakotan an excellent base as the Democratic convention opened in Miami Beach on July 10.

The 1972 gathering in Florida was far different in composition from the 1968 Democratic National Convention. The delegates had been elected under rules established by a committee formed following the 1968 Chicago debacle. That body, chaired by Senator McGovern, ruled that state delegations had to reflect the proportion of women, minorities, and young people in that state's population. The results were astounding. African American Fannie Lou Hamer, who because of her color had been kept off the official delegation of Mississippi in 1964, now represented that state. Instead of Chicago Mayor Richard Daley, black activist Jesse Jackson represented

Illinois. The New York contingent included Congresswoman Bella Abzug, *Ms.* editor Gloria Steinem, NOW leader Betty Friedan, and members of the Gay Liberation Front. Surveying the California delegation, actress Shirley MacLaine remarked delightedly that it "looked like a couple of high schools, a grape boycott, a Black Panther rally, and four or five politicians who walked in the wrong door." Columnist Ben Wattenburg predicted that "there won't be any riots in Miami because the people who rioted in Chicago are on the Platform Committee." McGovern happened to be strong with each of the three groups that his reform committee had targeted, and as a result he was easily nominated on the first ballot. The convention picked Senator Thomas F. Eagleton, a Catholic, a liberal, and a long-time friend of organized labor for second place on the ticket. McGovern's managers failed, however, to manage the Miami convention in a way that would reconcile the party's various factions. Feminists, African Americans, and students openly ridiculed Hubert Humphrey and jeered Mayor Richard Daley. Many party regulars went home determined to sit on their hands. "There is too much hair and not enough cigars at this convention," declared one veteran politico. Hunter Thompson's unintended parody on the Vietnam War – "the only way to save the Democratic Party is to destroy it" – seemed about to come true. In his acceptance speech, McGovern appealed to Americans to "come home," to abandon the effort to remake the world in their image, to reconcile social and generational differences, and to concentrate on achieving equal rights and social justice in the United States.

The Republican convention was nothing more than a political rally conducted by an incumbent and his supporters who were sure of victory. The delegates were professional politicians; indeed, more than 80% had been office holders. Journalist Theodore White depicted the California delegation thusly: "they came from paintings by Norman Rockwell – stately, big-bosomed clubwomen; silver-haired men with pince-nez eyeglasses . . . and the young men all looking as if they had showered and come in fresh, with neckties, from a workout with the track team." Nixon had easily fended off challenges from Representative Paul N. "Pete" McCloskey, a liberal Californian and opponent of the war, and Representative John Ashbrook of Ohio, a conservative who was upset with the administration's economic policies and its openings to China and Russia. Amid the pageantry, flowery rhetoric, and a plethora of Hollywood political groupies, Nixon called for "a new America bound together by common ideals." The protests of Ron Kovic, the wheelchair-bound veteran and author of *Born on the Fourth of July*, and the handful of other Vietnam Veterans Against the War (VVAW) activists who had been admitted to the convention were drowned out.

Nixon and CREEP were delighted with McGovern's nomination. They perceived that he was easily the most beatable of the Democratic aspirants; they were right. The son of a Methodist minister, McGovern had earned a doctorate in history from Northwestern University. His dissertation was an exposé of the Rockefeller family's brutal handling of a miner's strike in the West. He was, as John Blum has said, "an idealist in a cynical calling." Like so many political novices, he believed that he could realize all of his policy agenda without compromising. And that agenda was sweeping. McGovern favored legalizing both abortion and marijuana. He endorsed a plan that would establish a system of redistributive taxation and grant every American $1,000 annually. At a time of mounting distrust of government, McGovern was proposing to have the government do more. To the horror of the military and defense workers, McGovern proposed a cut in the Pentagon budget of $30 billion. The United States, he declared, should abandon the Thieu government in South Vietnam and withdraw all its troops in return for repatriation of prisoners of war (POWs). Vietnamization amounted to simply "changing the color of the corpses." Most galling to hawks, however, was the South Dakotan's proposal of sweeping amnesty for draft dodgers and deserters. Nixon's supporters dismissed the Democrat as the "candidate of the 3 As: acid, abortion, and amnesty."

During the campaign, McGovern came across as not only idealistic and absolutist, but indecisive. Soon after the Democratic convention, journalists with the covert help of CREEP operatives uncovered the fact that three times during the 1960s Senator Eagleton had been hospitalized for "nervous exhaustion and fatigue" and had undergone psychiatric care for "depression." McGovern, who had not been told of his running mate's medical history, at first stuck by the Missourian. But within days he caved in to pressure from his political advisers and asked Eagleton to withdraw. To replace him, McGovern selected Sargent Shriver, the former Peace Corps director and the Kennedy brothers' brother-in-law.

Despite this setback, McGovern waged a strenuous campaign. He not only reiterated his stand on the issues but hit at alleged corruption in the Nixon administration. His camp implied that the president had received millions of dollars from special interest groups in return for favors – ITT in return for a favorable settlement of an antitrust suit and the dairy industry in return for a sharp rise in milk price supports, for example. The Democrats sensed a real opening when the news broke that on June 17 five men had been caught burglarizing the headquarters of the Democratic National Committee in the Watergate apartment complex in Washington, D.C. Among the intruders were two former White House aides and a member of CREEP. The public, however, proved unresponsive. The mood of the nation had turned upbeat; Kissinger announced during the campaign that "peace is at hand." The White House dismissed Watergate as a "third-rate burglary attempt," and the American people believed it.

Even as election night television coverage got underway, it was apparent that Nixon was headed for a landslide victory. The incumbent's 47.1 million popular votes and 520 electoral tallies made him the most successful GOP candidate in history. With 29.1 million votes, McGovern managed to carry only Massachusetts and the District of Columbia. The New Deal coalition was in shambles. Of all its elements, McGovern managed to carry only African Americans. Nixon later recalled that "McGovern's perverse treatment of the traditional Democratic power blocs . . . made possible the creation of a New Republican Majority as an electoral force in American politics," and he was right. Sixty-five percent of middle-class voters – half of the electorate – voted for Nixon.

Richard Nixon's overwhelming reelection and the apparent demise of the Democratic Party devastated liberals. They could not believe that he was anything other than the manipulative, exploitive "Tricky Dick" of the McCarthy era and Checkers speech. On inauguration night, a so-called antiwar counterconcert was held in Washington, D.C. It featured Leonard Bernstein conducting Joseph Haydn's *Mass in the Time of War.*

Watergate: The Constitution under Siege

During the 1972 presidential campaign, George McGovern had complained bitterly about Republican "dirty tricks" – fake letters identifying Democratic candidates with unpopular or unsavory causes, planted hostile questioners or hecklers, and particularly the attempted break-in into Democratic National Committee headquarters in the Watergate building. He asked voters to reject a candidate and party that were doing nothing less than trying to subvert the democratic process. Most dismissed his complaints as the whinings of a sore loser.

In fact, McGovern's charges were true, although the conspiracy was deeper and the wrongdoing more widespread than he suspected. Richard Nixon had fostered an atmosphere within the White House that encouraged political and ideological zealots to take the law into their own hands. There had always been a streak of paranoia in his personality. He had long believed that the national press, the Ivy League intelligentsia, and the cultural elite believed him to be a poorly educated boor. Had he not offered to provide Harvard academic Kissinger with references from the Duke Law School faculty when he was hiring Kissinger to be national security adviser? His defeat in 1960 by the ultimate establishment symbol, John F. Kennedy, only deepened Nixon's sense of inferiority. Even election to the highest office in the land did not make a dent. He saw enemies everywhere: in the press, in academia, in the NAACP and other civil rights organizations, in the Sierra Club and various environmental groups, and even in Hollywood. The president, together with Haldeman and Ehrlichman, compiled an enemies list that included such diverse figures as actress Jane Fonda, New York Jets quarterback Joe Namath, actors Steve McQueen and Tony Randall, and Senate Foreign Relations Committee Chairman J. William Fulbright. The White House pressured the Internal Revenue Service to harass the president's enemies. Over a two-year period, that agency launched investigations of 4,300 individuals and 1,025 groups that the chief executive considered his enemy. When Secretary of the Treasury George Schultz complained, the president wrote him off as a "candy ass." In the summer of 1970, in the wake of the Cambodian demonstrations, an embittered president declared virtual warfare on those he considered his enemies: the "madmen" on the Hill, the "liberal" press, and those who marched in protest.

The Nixon administration's panicked reaction to criticism following Cambodia and Kent State sowed the seeds of its downfall. Shortly before the invasion of Cambodia, the Weathermen faction of the SDS had bombed the New York headquarters of three major U.S. corporations, including the Bank of America. White House aide Tom Huston subsequently told H. R. Haldeman that not only was the SDS determined to overthrow the government by force, but it was also fully capable of doing so. In response to his aide's hysteria, the president authorized Huston to assemble a team of "countersubversives" who would ferret out and neutralize enemies of the Republic (and of Nixon – to him the two were interchangeable). In addition, under the Huston Plan, intelligence agencies were directed to install wire taps, open mail, and even break and enter to gather information that could be used to thwart opponents of the administration. According to recently released White House tapes, Nixon, angered by publication of the Pentagon Papers, ordered Haldeman on June 30, 1971, to burglarize the Brookings Institution, for whom Daniel Ellsberg had worked, and remove any damaging material related to Vietnam. "But who do we have to do it?" Haldeman asked. Nixon merely repeated, "You're to break into the place." There was in fact a group in existence that had been set up for just such a job. In March 1971, Nixon, with Kissinger's compliance, approved a plan by Haldeman and Ehrlichman to assemble a team of former FBI and CIA agents who would trace and stop leaks by using wire taps and other illegal methods. Nicknamed "the plumbers," this clandestine group made its priority the discrediting of Daniel Ellsberg and indirectly the entire antiwar movement. As a first step, they broke into the office of Ellsberg's psychiatrist in search of damaging evidence. That burglary was just the beginning.

The "no holds barred" attitude that led to creation of the plumbers unit carried over into the 1972 presidential campaign. Nixon had convinced himself that he had been cheated out of the 1960 presidential election, and he was determined not to be cheated again. During the 1970 congressional elections, the president had suggested to his political advisers that they use "dirty tricks" to defeat the Democrats. CREEP, formed in response to Edmund Muskie's bid for the Democratic nomination, was staffed with zealots eager to do Nixon's bidding. Both Haldeman and John Mitchell, two of the president's closest advisers, served on that body, which, armed with hundreds of thousands of dollars provided by Herbert Kalmbach and Maurice Stans, was dedicated to winning in 1972 at any cost. The rumor concerning Muskie's slandering of French Canadians during the crucial New Hampshire primary was, in fact, planted by a CREEP operative named Donald Segretti.

The Break-In

In late 1971, G. Gordon Liddy, a former CIA operative and member of the plumbers team that had broken into Ellsberg's psychiatrist's office, joined CREEP as counsel to its finance committee. In January 1972, in the office of Attorney General Mitchell, with White House Counsel John Dean and Jeb Stuart Magruder, deputy director of CREEP, present, Liddy proposed a fantastic scheme of harassment against the Democrats, including wire taps, kidnappings, and hijackings. Mitchell rejected the scheme, not because it was illegal and unethical, but because it was too expensive; the estimated price tag was $1 million. In late March, the former attorney general approved a plan for wire tapping the Democratic National Committee (DNC) and provided Liddy with $10,000 to facilitate that task. CREEP and probably the president wanted to be privy to DNC Chairman Larry O'Brien's campaign strategy. In April 1972, Liddy hired E. Howard Hunt and James McCord, two former CIA agents who had been part of the plumbers team, to spy on the opposition. They in turn retained several Cuban exiles, veterans of the Bay of Pigs operation and the Nixon administration's dirty tricks campaign. After several bungled attempts, the team succeeded in bugging DNC chairman Larry O'Brien's offices. When one of the bugs failed, the burglars returned to replace it.

Early on the morning of June 17, 1972, Frank Wills, a night watchman at the Watergate office and apartment building, made his usual rounds. Upon finding the door lock to the offices of the DNC taped shut, he alerted the police. They in turn arrived in time to apprehend McCord and four of the Cubans. Among other items found on the suspects was an address book with Howard Hunt's White House phone number in it. Panicked, Liddy immediately began shredding documents at CREEP headquarters and appealed successfully to have the five burglary suspects freed.

On June 20, Nixon learned the details of the break-in from Haldeman and realized how implicated Mitchell and members of the White House staff were. Instead of ordering an investigation and disavowing the perpetrators, the president decided that "political bugging" was just part of the game and that it was possible to cover up the whole thing. Later that week, Nixon through Haldeman ordered Richard Helms, head of the CIA, and General Vernon Walters, Nixon's military aide, to tell the FBI, then investigating the Watergate burglary, that its probe, if pursued, would lead to a breach of national security. In so doing, the president of the United States participated in a conspiracy to obstruct justice, in itself a federal crime. The taping system that Nixon had installed in the Oval Office in 1969 captured the incriminating conversation and, when finally made public in 1974, would play a key role in the president's demise. During the weeks that followed, FBI chief L. Patrick Gray, a Nixon loyalist who had succeeded to J. Edgar Hoover's job following the latter's death, obeyed instructions from Ehrlichman and Dean to destroy incriminating evidence taken from Howard Hunt's safe. Gray also permitted White House Counsel John Dean to sit in at the interviews that the FBI conducted with Watergate suspects, and Dean regularly updated Nixon on the investigation.

Shortly after learning of the break-in, Ehrlichman conferred with Nixon at the presidential retreat at Key Biscayne, Florida, and ordered Dean to engineer a comprehensive cover-up that would first try to conceal any connection between the Watergate burglars and CREEP and, if that failed, to protect the White House. Dean decided that the most urgent item on the cover-up agenda was keeping the burglars quiet. Accordingly, he met with presidential bag man Herbert Kalmbach who quickly came up with $220,000, which was funneled to the burglars through their lawyers. Much of the money used to finance the Watergate cover-up was itself illegally raised. Since 1969, Kalmbach had successfully solicited tens of millions of dollars in unreported campaign contributions, and the majority of the money given to Dean and Haldeman to deal with the Watergate matter was raised after the Federal Election Campaign Act went into effect in April 1972. Kalmbach would later serve six months in prison.

As White House and CREEP spokesmen continued to downplay the Watergate incident as a case of petty thievery and deny any connection between them and the burglars, *Washington Post* reporters Carl Bernstein and Bob Woodward were tracing the flow of CREEP campaign funds through banks in Miami and Mexico to members of the plumbers unit. While White House and committee officials continued to "stonewall," that is, to deny any wrongdoing and refuse to provide any information, the *Washington Post* began to run Woodward and Bernstein's stories, which revealed not only the Watergate connection but also uncovered Segretti's campaign of dirty tricks against McGovern. By this point, the two reporters were being fed inside information by a highly placed administration official using the code name "deep throat." Noting that the *Washington Post* owned television stations with licenses that would be up for renewal, the president swore to get even with the newspaper.

To the dismay of the White House and CREEP, the wheels of justice continued to turn. In September, a Washington, D.C., grand jury indicted the five Watergate burglars along with Liddy and Hunt. A spokesman for the Justice Department told the media that "we have absolutely no evidence that anyone else should be charged." As the 1972 presidential contest neared its climax, the White House press secretary dismissed Watergate as a "third-rate burglary attempt" masterminded by overzealous underlings with no direction from above. As Nixon's overwhelming victory indicated, most voters believed him.

The Stonewall Crumbles

The trial of the Watergate Seven, so dubbed by the press in ironic reference to the Chicago Eight, got underway in January 1973. Five of the defendants pleaded guilty; two underwent a jury trial and were convicted. All the while money continued to flow to the defendants from Dean and Haldeman, and they continued to deny any connection with the White House. Presiding Judge John J. Sirica did not believe them and said so. As the date for sentencing approached, Sirica, known as "Maximum John," threatened long prison terms unless those convicted came clean. James McCord broke. On March 23, the day scheduled for sentencing, Sirica read a letter from McCord admitting that he had been acting on orders from the White House and that he and the others had been pressured to keep quiet. Sirica sentenced Liddy to six years in prison but delayed setting terms for the others in hopes that they would cooperate.

Meanwhile, the U.S. Senate, with a Democratic majority, decided to conduct its own investigation. A number of traditional donors to the Democratic Party had shut their purses in 1972. Their reluctance had more to do with aversion to McGovern. As Speaker of the House Tip O'Neill subsequently learned, the CREEP operatives had warned Democratic deep pockets that if they contributed, they faced reprisal from federal agencies. If Nixon and his subordinates were allowed to get away with this and other dirty tricks, the Democratic leadership decided, the two-party system and democracy itself might be endangered.

Accordingly, the Senate named North Carolina Democrat Sam Ervin to head a special committee to investigate the Watergate episode. The Senate Special Committee on Presidential Campaign Activities, with four Democratic and three Republican members, became known as the Watergate Committee and held almost continuous hearings for the next year and a half. The selection of Ervin to head the committee was a stroke of genius. A conservative, states' rights, strict Constructionist who had sided with the GOP on a number of issues, Ervin could help convince conservatives that the Watergate investigation was not a liberal witch hunt. Moreover, the self-styled "country lawyer" was a graduate of Harvard Law School and a veteran of North Carolina politics – more than a match for Haldeman, Ehrlichman, and Dean. During the Ervin hearings and the confirmation hearings for L. Patrick Gray to be FBI director held before the Senate Judiciary Committee, the president invoked executive privilege in an effort to prevent all current and former White House aides from testifying. The Senate took the position that executive privilege did not cover criminal activity; that is, no one was above the law. To the enragement of the White House, Gray during the course of his hearings revealed that he had interviewed Herbert Kalmbach and that the president's lawyer or lawyers had admitted funding Donald Segretti and his dirty tricks campaign.

During the months that followed, Washington, D.C., prosecutors, Judge Sirica, and the Watergate Committee worked in tacit alliance, while

Woodward and Bernstein kept the public abreast of events in the pages of the *Washington Post*, sometimes outstripping committee investigators and prosecutors in uncovering the facts. Howard Hunt, whose wife had been killed in a plane crash on her way to deliver hush money to the plumbers, demanded of Dean that he be paid $130,000 to keep quiet. Dean went to Nixon and warned him of "a cancer within, close to the presidency, that's growing"; Watergate and the subsequent cover-up could lead to the indictment of Mitchell, Haldeman, Ehrlichman, and even the president's counsel. The president was not interested in coming clean. Pay Hunt, he ordered. When told that payoffs could reach $1 million, he replied, "We could get that . . . and you could get it in cash." Dean suspected correctly that the president was setting him up to take the fall for Watergate. On advice of their lawyers, Dean and Jeb Magruder began cooperating with prosecutors in return for promises of immunity. During interviews with Watergate Committee staff in March, Dean revealed that he, Haldeman, Ehrlichman, Mitchell, and others close to the president had been involved in payoffs "and that's an obstruction of justice." Nevertheless, Nixon directed his aides to continue the cover-up and payment of hush money. "Don't you agree that you'd better get the Hunt thing?" Nixon asked Dean. "I mean, that's worth it, at the moment. . . . You've got no choice with Hunt. . . . We've got to figure out where to turn it off at the lowest cost we can, but at whatever cost it takes." Increasingly panicked, Nixon decided he would have to throw some meat to the wolves.

The Road To Resignation

On April 30, the president went on national television to announce that there had indeed been a conspiracy to conceal the facts in Watergate but that he was in no way involved. He announced that he was firing Dean and, at the same time, accepting the resignations of Haldeman and Ehrlichman, "two of the finest public servants I have ever known." The sacrifice of Nixon's top two aides failed to appease his critics. The Ervin Committee opened its hearings in May, and the Senate Judiciary Committee made it a condition of Nixon's nominee for attorney general, Elliot Richardson, that he appoint an independent special prosecutor. Richardson selected his old law school professor, Archibald Cox, and charged him with investigating crimes related to Watergate and the 1972 presidential election generally. Richardson also promised the Judiciary Committee that he would neither remove nor interfere with Cox. Nixon denied any role in Watergate and "any awareness of or participation in the cover-up."

In May, the Ervin Committee began a series of televised hearings on Watergate that would last throughout the summer and transfix the public. The committee began with low-level operatives in CREEP and the White House and worked their way up. Ehrlichman was arrogant and condescending, citing the president's authority under national security to order wire taps and break ins. Mitchell stonewalled, giving up no information, and Haldeman squirmed. The highlight of the hearings was John Dean's testimony. Promised immunity from prosecution, Dean revealed that Nixon had been intimately involved in the scheme to conceal White House complicity in the now-famous burglary. Out of "excessive concern" over antiwar demonstrations and an insatiable appetite for "political intelligence," the president and his advisers had condoned clearly illegal activity. Even more shocking, Dean revealed the presence of a secret taping system that Nixon had ordered installed in the White House and Executive Office Building. All of the president's conversations with his aides were recorded and stored. Alexander Butterfield, the presidential assistant in charge of the taping system, subsequently revealed details concerning its installation and operation.

As Judge Sirica, the Ervin Committee, and Special Prosecutor Cox moved to gain access to the tapes, Nixon – just recently released from the hospital for treatment of viral pneumonia – declared that he would never release the tapes, citing executive and lawyer–client privilege. He denounced rumors that he was considering resigning as "poppycock." "Let others wallow in Watergate," he proclaimed, "we are going to do our job." In fact, the rumors were true. On May 25, he asked newly installed chief of staff Alexander Haig if he should quit. With "the Congress being Democratic, the Republicans being weak, wouldn't it be better for the country just to check out?" Haig objected but Nixon persisted:

Well, Al, we've got to take a hard look at it because – you see, what really counts is the man. And goddamnit, the man's got to be doing his job and I'm not really doing the job because I'm so wound up in this son-of-a-bitching thing . . .

But Haig persisted and the old, defiant Nixon returned.

A year-long battle for the "Nixon tapes" then ensued. On July 23, 1973, Nixon rejected a subpoena served by the Senate panel. In October, special prosecutor Cox, a distinguished, tough-minded Harvard legal scholar, took the president to court in an effort to force him to turn over the now-famous recordings. The president's specially selected counsel, constitutional law expert Charles Allen Wright, insisted that the courts had no power to rule on the president's use of executive privilege. The Constitution made the three branches of government equal. The judiciary was not superior to the executive. Cox disagreed. "There is no exception for the President," he declared, "from the guiding principle that the public, in pursuit of justice, has a right to every man's evidence. Even the highest executive officials are subject to the rule of law." Judge Sirica agreed with Cox and, on August 29, 1973, ordered Nixon to produce the tapes. Nixon declared that he would give way only after a ruling by the Supreme Court.

In the midst of the struggle over the tapes the vice presidency was engulfed by scandal. In September, Spiro Agnew, the darling of the American right, came under investigation by a grand jury for accepting payoffs from contractors he had favored during his tenure as executive of Baltimore County and then as governor of Maryland. His lawyers argued that a vice president could not be indicted until and unless he was impeached and removed. The vice president actually asked Speaker of the House Carl Albert (D-Oklahoma) to proceed with impeachment, but Albert insisted that the House would proceed after and not before an indictment. Agnew at first swore to stay and fight, but under pressure from Nixon, who was angered and frightened by the vice president's flirtation with impeachment, he resigned in return for a Justice Department ruling that allowed him to plead nolo contendere to one count of income tax evasion. To succeed him, Nixon picked Gerald Ford, the conservative, affable House minority leader from Michigan.

On October 15, General Alexander Haig, who had replaced Haldeman as White House chief of staff, informed Attorney General Richardson that the president would submit summaries of the tapes, but not the tapes themselves. When Cox declared that only actual transcripts would satisfy the law, the White House ordered Richardson to fire Cox. He refused and resigned, as did his deputy, William Ruckelshaus. Finally, Solicitor General Robert Bork agreed to step in as acting attorney general and fire Cox. The house cleaning on Saturday, October 20, touched off in Haig's words a national "firestorm." With this action, Richardson later wrote, Nixon had abused his power "more blatantly than at any other stage in the whole sordid history of Watergate." The White House was deluged with negative mail, the *New York Times* talked of resignation, while the *Washington Post* called for impeachment. Picketers surrounded the White House carrying signs that read, "Honk for Impeachment." The American people had reelected the president by an overwhelming margin in 1972, and they were slow to admit their mistake. However, the "Saturday night massacre" seemed to be the last straw. Nixon responded to the wave of outrage by submitting some of the tapes and reopening the special prosecutor's office under Houston attorney Leon Jaworski. But the momentum touched off by the Saturday night massacre could not be stopped.

On March 1, 1974, the grand jury that had been hearing evidence against the Watergate burglars returned more indictments in the case. At that point, Special Prosecutor Jaworski asked Judge Sirica to turn over the transcripts of tapes already in his possession and to subpoena 64 more. At the same time, the Judiciary Committee subpoenaed 42 tapes on its own. The White House responded by releasing 1,300 pages of transcripts. Even though carefully edited, the transcripts repelled Congress and the American people. They exposed the president's crudeness and cynicism for all to see. "Expletive deleted" became a national joke. White House lawyers cataloguing the tapes reported to Sirica that some were missing, and there was an 18.5-minute gap in a June 20, 1972, conversation between the president and Haldeman. A subsequent check of the chief of staff's notes revealed that the two men had discussed Watergate, and the president had called for a "counterattack."

Jaworski, a Houston lawyer and Democrat who had voted for Nixon, was not satisfied with the White House's compliance. The new special prosecutor filed suit in due course and, on July 24, 1974, the Supreme Court ruled unanimously that the president must surrender the tapes. Writing on behalf of an 8-to-0 majority, Chief Justice Burger declared that executive privilege was endorsed by the Constitution, but such a claim "could not prevail over the fundamental demands of due process of law in the administration of justice." When Nixon balked, the House Judiciary Committee, chaired by New Jersey Democrat Peter Rodino, voted to recommend three articles of impeachment. The House indictment read that the president deserved to be removed from office because he had obstructed justice through the payment of "hush money" to witnesses, was defying Congress and the courts by withholding the White House tapes, and had used federal agencies to deny American citizens their constitutional rights. Thirty-five million viewers sat mesmerized before the televised hearings. "My faith in the Constitution is whole, it is complete, it is total," declared Barbara Jordan, the magisterial black congresswoman from Texas, "and I am not going to sit here and be an idle spectator to the diminution, the subversion, the destruction, of the Constitution."

On August 5, 1974, before the full House could meet to vote on impeachment, Nixon handed over the tapes. Among the conversations was the one of June 23, 1972, in which Haldeman and Nixon had discussed how to use the CIA to throw the FBI off the trail. This was the so-called "smoking gun" that would prove beyond a shadow of a doubt the president's participation in the cover-up. Fully aware that they implicated him in the cover-up, the president once again contemplated resignation. Impeachment was certain. Following release of the tapes, all the House Judiciary Committee members who had voted against the articles indicated that they would reverse themselves when they came up before the full body. Senator Barry Goldwater told Nixon that he could not count on more than 10 votes in the Senate. Concerned about the president's judgment and mental health, the secretary of defense issued orders to military commanders around the world not to obey orders from the White House without his explicit approval. On the evening of August 7, Nixon summoned Kissinger to the White House. The president seemed to have been drinking heavily and was overcome with self-pity. After a long rambling discourse in which he pondered his place in history, Nixon knelt in prayer, pulling an embarrassed Kissinger to the floor with him. On the evening of August 8, he informed the nation over television that he was leaving office the next day. In a maudlin farewell speech to his staff, Nixon paid tribute to his father and his mother – "a saint" – and implied that he was taking the blame to save his subordinates. Giving the signature Nixon "V" for victory sign, he and Pat departed for California and comfortable exile. Immediately thereafter, Gerald R. Ford was sworn in as president of the United States.

Watergate Epilogue

After repeatedly assuring press and public that he had no intention of pardoning Nixon, the new president reversed himself, granting the former president a full pardon only a month after his resignation. Ford insisted that the move was necessary to end the national nightmare, but rumors of a deal persisted throughout his tenure in office.

On matters of substance in both foreign policy and domestic affairs, Richard Nixon had proved himself capable of defining the national interest in pragmatic, nonideological terms and of acting effectively to advance that interest. The openings to China and the Soviet Union created the possibility for a new era of dialog and peaceful coexistence. Perhaps only a confirmed cold warrior like Nixon could have taken such action without subjecting the nation to an anticommunist backlash. With the United States gripped by stagflation, the president turned first to classical economic theory and then to Keynesianism, first to economic nationalism and then to modified free trade in an effort to restore prosperity to the nation. On social policy, the president proved to be more consistently conservative; most of the progress made from 1969 to 1974 in civil rights, women's liberation, and environmental health and safety were due to Congress and the federal courts rather than the executive. In the end, however, all this was overshadowed by Watergate.

In one sense, the Watergate scandal constituted America's darkest hour. Nixon was the first president in history to resign under fire. Twenty-five members of the administration, including four cabinet officers, were convicted. In 1974, in a letter to President Ford, CIA Director William Colby acknowledged that during the Nixon administration, the agency had maintained files on some 10,000 U.S. citizens and engaged in illegal domestic operations against opponents of U.S. policy in Vietnam as well as other dissidents. In short, Watergate confronted the nation with its gravest constitutional crisis since the Civil War. The burglary and revelations that followed produced a deep sense of disillusionment with what Arthur Schlesinger, Jr., would term the "imperial presidency." Following in the aftermath of Vietnam, the break-in and cover-up only deepened public cynicism toward a government that lied to its citizens and violated their constitutional rights.

At the same time, Watergate demonstrated the vitality of American democracy; the nation's institutions emerged from the crisis unscathed. Faced with a massive conspiracy by the executive – the press, the courts, and Congress had persisted and succeeded in uncovering wrongdoing that threatened the very foundations of the republic. Woodward and Bernstein kept the scandal before the public eye during the fall and winter of 1972/1973; Judge Sirica refused to accept the contention that the

Watergate Seven were acting alone; and determined to defend themselves against an escalating campaign of dirty tricks, the Democratic majority in Congress moved to defend itself and coincidentally the democratic system. Watergate prompted Congress to pass legislation to restore the balance of power within the three-branch federal system. The War Powers Act of 1973 required presidents to consult with Congress before sending American troops into combat abroad and to withdraw U.S. forces within 60 days if Congress did not specifically approve their deployment. In reaction to the pervasive Nixon claim of "executive privilege," Congress strengthened the 1966 Freedom of Information Act to ensure that government agencies responded promptly to requests for information and placing the burden of proof on them for showing why documents should remain classified. Finally, Congress passed the Federal Election Campaign Act of 1974, which established limits on campaign contributions and expenditures by candidates in federal elections, and provided for partially funded presidential elections.

The most lasting damage done to the nation by Watergate was the undermining of the public's trust in its elected officials and the political process itself. Innumerable political cartoons and talk show dialogs portrayed any and all public officials as venal, grasping, corrupt, and totally self-serving. Even sophisticated columnists and political analysts acquiesced in the mood of disillusionment, exuding in their columns and reports deep cynicism and contempt. As a result, voter turnout at national elections declined dramatically in the years after Watergate.

ADDITIONAL READINGS

De Benedetti, Charles, and Charles Chatfield, *An American Ordeal: The Antiwar Movement of the Vietnam Era* (1990).
Garthoff, Raymond L., *Detente and Confrontation: American–Soviet Relations From Nixon To Reagan* (1985).
Hersh, Seymour, *The Price of Power: Kissinger in the Nixon White House* (1983).
Isaacs, Arnold, *Without Honor: Defeat in Vietnam and Cambodia* (1983).
Kutler, Stanley I., *The Wars of Watergate* (1990).
McQuaid, Kim, *The Anxious Years: America in the Vietnam and Watergate Era* (1989).
Schulzinger, Robert D., *Henry Kissinger: Doctor of Diplomacy* (1989).
Shawcross, William, *Sideshow: Kissinger, Nixon and the Destruction of Cambodia* (1979).
Small, Melvin, *Johnson, Nixon and the Doves* (1988).
Speigel, Steven J., *The Other Arab–Israeli Conflict: Making America's Middle East Policy From Truman To Reagan* (1985).

11 From Confidence to Anxiety

American Society, 1960–1980

T he two decades following the election of John F. Kennedy were among the most tumultuous and troubling through which the United States had yet passed. The era began with the U.S. economy going full blast and the election of an activist president committed to progressive reform at home and enlightened anticommunism abroad. By the end of the 1960s, the country was deeply divided over Vietnam, over the place of minorities and women in American society and, in fact, over the basic values that would define the United States. The 1970s were punctuated by America's first defeat in a foreign war, the resignation of a president facing sure impeachment, and an economy caught in the twin grip of rising unemployment and increasing inflation. For the first time since its triumph over the Axis powers, Americans began to question the assumptions that underlay the Cold War, and particularly the nation's ability and obligation to promote prosperity and ensure stability around the world. The pervasive notion, so characteristically American, that each succeeding generation would be materially better off than its predecessor was also called into doubt. With the apparent end of significant economic growth and the possibility that poverty would become increasingly institutionalized, the threat of class conflict assumed proportions that the United States had not known since the 1930s. At the same time, popular and high culture reached levels of diversity and quality hitherto unknown, while the American system of higher education became the best in the world. Despite resistance from conservatives and reactionaries, many of the social movements of the 1960s, civil rights and feminism in particular, continued to gain momentum and bear fruit. During this period, a pervasive confidence gave way to a widespread anxiety and then to profound readjustment, a process that produced both reaction and reform, stagnation and growth.

An Economy in Transition

The Era of Prosperity

The economic boom of the late 1940s and 1950s continued unabated into the 1960s, giving rise to the confidence that in part made possible the New Frontier and Great Society programs. By 1970, the annual volume of exports from the United States to other countries was approaching $180 billion per year. The gross national product (GNP) had increased more than 100% since 1945. Between 1962 and 1968, the United States experienced a real yearly growth rate of 5%, a level unattained since the remarkable days of the Gilded Age. Inflation remained at an insignificant 1% during the first half of the 1960s, while unemployment hovered between 3% and 5%. The civilian workforce grew from 54 million workers in 1945 to 111 million in 1983, and corporate profits increased from $33 billion in 1963 to $229 billion in 1978. Per capita income in real dollars stood at $1,824 in 1960; by the 1970s, it had reached $2,000.

A number of forces and circumstances, some of them holdovers from the 1950s and some of them new, contributed to the boom of the 1960s. Federal expenditures for research and development in the private sector increased dramatically after Sputnik, reaching $15 billion a year by the mid-1960s. Meanwhile, computers were revolutionizing the manufacturing process and business operations of all types, especially banking, insurance, and utilities, activities that comprised one half of all business in the United States. The price of personal computers declined dramatically; as a result, by 1970, the number of units produced annually had increased to more than 100,000. While industry used computers to paint auto bodies and run smelting furnaces, individuals employed them to prepare tax returns, play games, monitor investments, and plan family budgets. Indeed, the design, manufacture, and sale of computers became one of America's leading industries.

In addition to chemicals, steel, and automobiles, electronics, electric power production, and aircraft manufacturing led the nonservice parade during the 1960s. Engineers and scientists touched off a technological revolution by inventing transistors and then substituting them for vacuum tubes in radios, televisions, and a whole host of other electronic devices. Transistors made possible the production of high-quality electronic calculators, microscopes, and toys that were smaller and cheaper. Production and utilization of a larger number and variety of electrical appliances and entertainment units was made possible by an ever-increasing output of electric power. Following passage of the Atomic Energy Act of 1954, nuclear power became a cheap and attractive alternative to coal and water-generated electric power. Despite intermittent concerns over health and safety, by the end of the 1970s, more than 80 nuclear power plants were in operation in the United States. In the aircraft manufacturing and aircraft production industries, the switch to jet propulsion in the late 1950s led to an explosion of air travel. Swollen with federal funds, the aircraft industry, which simultaneously produced missiles, combat aircraft, and commercial airliners, developed larger, faster, and more efficient planes.

The economic growth of the 1960s was far more notable in some areas of the United States than in others. The Pacific Coast grew faster than any other region in the nation. By 1963, California, feeding on giant aircraft industries, tourism, and commercial agriculture, and boasting a distinctive lifestyle, had surpassed New York as the richest and most populous state. The defense and space industries played an important role in the development of the economies of both Texas and Florida. In addition, Texans benefited from a huge Gulf Coast petrochemical industry, whereas Floridians relied on tourism and citrus cultivation to achieve prosperity. The states bordering the Great Lakes and comprising the Midwest managed to hold their own, although declining efficiency and productivity in the auto and steel industries boded ill for the future. Much of New England struggled to maintain living standards and to retain its population, which was increasingly attracted by opportunities in the Sun Belt. Meanwhile, poverty in Appalachia, the rural South, and the inner city remained chronic.

In agriculture, the trend toward more production by fewer people continued. Tractors, harvesters, gins, and machine pickers became larger, more efficient, and more pervasive. Modern farmers attended agricultural and mechanical colleges where they learned techniques of scientific management and absorbed the principles of genetic plant and animal breeding. When they returned to the farm they applied these principles and bought sophisticated chemicals and herbicides from giant fertilizer companies. Farms became larger, more efficient, and, above all, fewer in number. Caught in a squeeze between mounting production and falling prices, farmers had to cultivate increasingly more acreage to make a profit. As a result, the number of American farms declined from 4 million in 1960 to 2.3 million in 1980. It appeared to many by the latter date that the family farm was well on its way to extinction. In addition, consolidation put a virtual end to farm tenancy and sharecropping, driving the rural poor into urban areas, which further contributed to problems in the nation's inner cities.

America's consumer and service economy was fueled by a tremendous growth in credit. By the mid-1960s, consumer debt amounted to more than $70 billion, 8 to 10 times what it had been in 1945. Composed initially of home mortgages and installment loans, consumer debt became increasingly concentrated in credit cards. Indeed, the American credit card, accepted in most parts of the world, became a symbol of American affluence. At the same time, an entire industry grew up around the establishment and maintenance of credit information on individuals.

Although Americans spent far more than they saved, private investment increased dramatically during the 1960s and 1970s. Individual and group

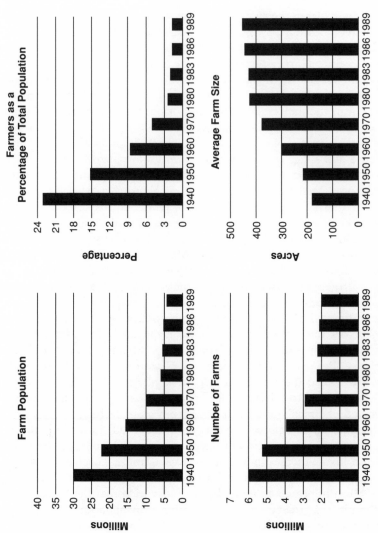

Figure 11–1. The American Farmer, 1940–1989. The postwar years saw a fundamental transformation of American agriculture. While the small family farmer joined the rural exodus to the cities, large farms prospered. *Source:* U.S. Bureau of the Census, *Statistical Abstract of the United States, 1990* (1990).

354

retirement funds grew incredibly from $44 billion in 1959 to $453 billion in 1980. The United States could boast 20 million individual stockholders by 1965, and some growth stocks such as AT&T and IBM doubled their value every two to three years. These billions of dollars pumped into the private sector proved crucial to the maintenance and expansion of America's massive economy.

"Stagflation" and Its Causes

Many of the companies that enjoyed such phenomenal growth during the 1960s did so because the United States had become a major player in the world economy in the post–World War II years. After a stuttering start, Washington officials worked with some success to reduce international trade barriers, while the United States made funds available through the International Bank for Reconstruction and Development (IBRD) and International Monetary Fund (IMF) for foreigners to buy American goods. Generous credit, a recovering world economy, and liberal tax policies for U.S. exporters resulted in a massive flow of exports. As of 1961, the United States accounted for one fourth of the world's manufactured exports and one third of its capital goods. Eleven of the top 12 American industrial concerns boasted sales in excess of $1 billion in 1970. Americans continued to invest abroad. U.S. firms built plants in Europe, Canada, south Asia, Latin America, and the Middle East; by 1967, the value of products produced by American companies abroad apporached the $100 billion mark. In addition, U.S. investors bought into foreign concerns: the British auto industry, Chilean utilities, and French communication companies. Then suddenly, in the early 1970s, dark clouds appeared on the economic horizon.

The deterioration in America's financial and commercial position was the product of several events and circumstances. First, the Johnson administration had attempted to pay for the war in Vietnam and the Great Society programs without raising taxes. The result was a rapidly mounting deficit and a steady increase in the money supply, both of which would fuel inflation in the 1970s. Second, the United States began to face stiff competition from cheap, high-quality foreign goods, principally from Germany, Japan, Taiwan, and other emerging industrial powers. Spoiled by two centuries of abundance, the United States continued to allow business and labor to go their own way. Without an industrial policy to tailor developments in domestic manufacturing and service to the changing international economy, the United States continued to lose more of its world and domestic market share. The Japanese government, for example, subsidized targeted industries and used its diplomatic clout to help Japan penetrate and dominate overseas markets. No such approach existed in the United States. As a result, the trade deficit soared. Finally, America's increasing dependence on foreign oil contributed both to the trade deficit and inflation. This dependency became especially damaging in 1973, with the outbreak of the Yom

Kippur War. When the United States continued its usual policy of aiding Israel, the Organization of Petroleum Exporting Countries (OPEC), centered in the Middle East, applied sanctions. OPEC declared that it would no longer sell oil to nations supporting Israel, and it imposed production quotas on itself with the objective of raising the price of crude oil by 400%.

Under the impact of these forces, inflation rose to 5% in 1972 and then exploded to 10% by the end of 1973. The budget deficit for 1973 was nearly $40 billion, more than 300% larger than President Nixon had forecast. Suddenly, the international economy began to take on the guise of a hawk rather than a pigeon. The booming Japanese and German economies, rebuilt with American money following World War II, began to make serious inroads into the American market. The percentage of foreign automobiles sold in the United States jumped from 4% to 17% during the 1960s and would comprise one third of the total by 1980. By 1972, the trade deficit had reached $10 billion.

The invasion of American markets by German automobiles and Japanese transistors was a gradual phenomenon, the direct pain of which was limited to a few hundred thousand displaced workers, but the OPEC price boost and Arab boycott was a different matter. By the 1970s, its once abundant petroleum resources depleted by World War II, Korea, and Vietnam as well as by a wasteful, energy-consuming domestic economy, the United States had become dependent on foreign sources, especially the oil emirates of the Middle East, for a significant percentage of its petroleum. As a result of the Arab oil embargo and OPEC price increases, gasoline and heating oil prices in the United States increased by nearly 33% during the winter of 1973/1974. As long lines formed at gas stations and the inflation rate increased, Americans railed at allegedly selfish sheiks. What was so galling to Americans about the oil crisis was that it demonstrated that the United States was no longer solely in charge of its economic destiny. With the passage of time, the new dependency only became more pronounced; expenditures for foreign oil increased from $4 billion in 1970 to $90 billion in 1990.

At the same time that the Yom Kippur War and OPEC pricing practices joined with increasingly noncompetitive industries and mounting deficits to fuel inflation, structural unemployment increased dramatically during the 1970s. Just as important as the invasion of the domestic market by cheap, high-quality foreign goods was the fact that the American economy was entering a postindustrial stage. From 1945 to 1965, blue-collar jobs had grown at a rate of 19%, while jobs as a whole grew by 32%. However, industrial productivity increased by only 1% per year from 1972 through 1978. Industrial workers, finding their jobs filled by robots or computers or eliminated altogether by foreign competition, lined up for unemployment compensation by the thousands.

By the end of the 1970s, stagflation – the name given to the twin phenomena of rising inflation and increasing unemployment – had begun to
take its toll. As real income dropped by 2% each year from 1973 through
1981, the average price of a new single-family home more than doubled,
while the cost of basic necessities rose by 110%. The accompanying defla-
tion of the nation's morale was almost palpable. The American living standard fell to fifth in the world behind Denmark, West Germany, Sweden,
and Switzerland. By 1979, two thirds of those polled expressed the belief
that "next year will be worse than this year," and nearly two thirds con-
curred in the observation that "our current standard of living may be the
highest we can hope for."

The Rebellious Generation

Hippies

The rise and decline of the counterculture and one of its components, the
student movement, paralleled the decades of boom in the 1960s and stagflation in the 1970s. Indeed, there seemed to be an ironic, even paradoxi-
cal relationship between affluence and rebelliousness in the youth culture.
Even as the "hippies" and protesters of the 1960s rebelled against the perceived materialism and complacency of the 1950s, critics were pointing out
that virtually all members of the counterculture were disaffected children
of middle- and upper-class families and that the very affluence that they
ridiculed made their "alternative lifestyles" possible. Some went further. In
1968, *Reader's Digest* concluded to its 28 million readers that "murder, rape,
disease, suicide – the dark side of the hippie moon has become increasingly
visible." This became the culture's interpretation of the counterculture. At
the close of the 1960s, an opinion poll asked citizens to identify the most
harmful groups in the United States; they named "communists, prostitutes,
and hippies." Student activists dismissed the criticism as characteristic
of the materialistic and reactionary mind-set against which they were re-
belling. Frustrated by persistent racism at home and imperialism abroad,
the nation's youth called for a fundamental reexamination of everything
from political institutions to lifestyles. Then, as the economy worsened in
the 1970s, America's youth rejected protest and political activism, seeking fulfillment instead in a rampant careerism. Meanwhile, most members
of the counterculture, baby-boom generation had made peace with conventional society, matriculated from graduate or professional schools, and
started careers and jobs. Only a few remained outside the mainstream,
seeking refuge in rural areas and maintaining the old lifestyle as a monument to the turbulent, idealistic years of their youth.

The hippie movement expanded dramatically after 1968. From some
75,000 in the autumn of 1967, the counterculture numbered 200,000 by

the end of 1968. These included "full-time hippies"; the press noted that at least another 300,000 shared some practices and beliefs. One reporter estimated that 20,000 were dropping out each year. The term hippie meant many different things. Coined by a San Francisco journalist to mean a hip, streetwise youth, the counterculture actually included everyone: "freaks," those who were too odd to be part of society; "heads," those who focused on drug use; and "seekers," those looking for spiritual meaning or philosophical truth. According to Terry Anderson, the one unifying theme in the movement was alienation. Whether it was by racism, corporate exploitation, *in loco parentis* rules at the nation's universities, the war in Vietnam, the perceived hypocrisy of mainstream religious denominations, or conventional morality, hippies were alienated. A chasm was created between generations. Youth blamed their parents for all that was wrong with society, but mostly for being hypocritical. They consumed caffeine, alcohol, and nicotine and then passed harsh laws outlawing not only hard drugs but also LSD and marijuana. While some administration officials criticized a post office stamp for making Henry David Thoreau look too much like a hippie, President Nixon was presenting Elvis Presley with a citation for his role in the "fight against drugs." By 1972, one third of college students surveyed believed that marriage was obsolete and that having children was not important. Those expressing respect for religion, patriotism, and conventional morality had dropped by 20%. The most pervasive bumper sticker on the hippies' vehicle of choice, the Volkswagen minivan, was "QUESTION AUTHORITY."

The values of the counterculture grew out of its alienation from the dominant culture. Because society was perceived to be white dominated and racist, hippies were egalitarian. Because America was seen as a warmongering, imperial world power, hippies were pacifists and isolationists. Because the larger society appeared to be obsessed with status and material gain, hippies scorned materialism. Because most Americans seemed to be carelessly polluting society, hippies were environmentalists. "Don't give me no hand me down world," The Guess Who demanded; singer Joni Mitchell lamented, "They paved paradise and put up a parking lot." Because conventional culture was perceived to be pointlessly puritanical, hippies endorsed any activity that "felt good," including sex and drugs. The path to happiness was constant experimentation. "Do anything you want as long as nobody gets hurt," was a hippie truism. "Change jobs, spouses, hairstyles, clothes; change religion, politics, values, even the personality; try everything, experiment constantly, accept nothing as given," advised one underground newspaper. "All you need is love," they sang, while another wrote, "Love is other, love is being and letting be, love is gentle, love is giving and love is dropping out, love is turning on, love is a trip, a flower, a smile, a bell."

The ultimate counterculture "happening" was the Woodstock rock festival, which unfolded in the rolling hills of upstate New York. Hundreds of thousands of young people gathered for three days of pot smoking, love making, and "rapping" (a kind of free-association-style conversation). Hard rock artist Jimi Hendrix opened the festivities with his famous dissonant, mocking rendition of the Star-Spangled Banner. He was followed by virtually every major rock group then performing in the United States. Coordinators of the festival and many participants proclaimed the achievement of mass, cultural nirvana. With no violence, no rules, no grades, no status, no careerism, and no discipline, Woodstock represented the coming of the new age, they proclaimed.

Student Protest
As the decade of the 1960s came to an end, students continued to comprise the cutting edge of the antiwar movement. A Gallup poll taken in 1969 indicated that, among those collegians queried, doves outnumbered hawks by a three-to-one margin. Indeed, the New Left served as a philosophical point of departure for more than 750,000 college-age men and women across the United States. Yet, as protests mounted and became more violent from 1968 to 1971, the student protest movement seemed to lose its way. Frustrated by their inability to elect George McGovern and other antiwar candidates and by the continued fighting in Southeast Asia, those in the forefront of the movement either became more radical or rejected political activism altogether. The 1969 Students for a Democratic Society (SDS) national convention disintegrated into bitter infighting, with the "crazies" and "motherfuckers" frankly advocating anarchy and the Revolutionary Youth Movement and Weathermen preaching armed revolution. Shortly thereafter, the Weathermen announced the "Days of Rage" in Chicago and, through isolated acts of terrorism, sought a confrontation with the police that they hoped would lead to mass insurrection. Dressed in denim or leather jackets, some with football helmets or gas masks, armed with pipes and chains, the Weathermen met in Lincoln Park and chanted, "Revolution's begun! Off the pig! Pick up the gun!" After they swept through the streets smashing windows and assaulting bystanders, the police moved in. In the ensuing melee, 50 were injured and 100 arrested. In October 1970, Angela Davis, former faculty member at UCLA, black militant, and self-proclaimed communist, was arrested in New York in connection with a courtroom shootout in San Raphael, California, in which a judge and three others were killed. Later in the year, the Reverend Philip F. Berrigan, a Catholic priest, was indicted with five others for conspiring to kidnap presidential adviser Henry Kissinger and to bomb the heating systems of the federal buildings in Washington, D.C. Similar to other adherents of the New Left, the Weathermen, Angela Davis, and the Berrigans saw the world

in terms of a struggle between a pervasive U.S. imperialism and movements of national liberation. However, unlike many of their fellows, they
believed that violence, indeed guerrilla warfare, was the only viable means
to achieve economic and social justice.

In turn, random violence by Black Power advocates and antiwar demonstrators helped discredit protest movements and activism in general. Inevitably, a backlash developed among conservatives and traditional liberals
who believed that law and order were prerequisites to a civilized society.
That reaction, coupled with the fact that the antiwar movement was increasingly dominated by the political and cultural middle of American society, left the radicals more isolated and more alienated than ever before.

Turning Inward

During the mid-1960s, protest on the left and alternative lifestyles – drug
experimentation, communal living, long hair, and nontraditional clothing –
had tended to go hand in hand, reinforcing each other, but as frustration
with the war mounted and political infighting increased, the two tended
to diverge. Similar to the alienated intellectuals during the 1920s in the
aftermath of the fight over the Treaty of Versailles, some left-wing antiwar protesters in the late 1960s and early 1970s rejected both traditional
and nontraditional political activism and sought fulfillment through experimentation with LSD, peyote, and other drugs, and through sexual promiscuity, communal living, and individual artistic endeavor. In *The Making of
the Counterculture* (1969), Theodore Roszak called on young people and
the disaffected in general to reject the scientific method and rationalism
of the enlightenment. Self-realization and wisdom was to be found in pure
feeling and intuition, and through intimate, continuous, and unstructured
association with other humans. For some, this turning away from the public sphere resulted in a religious experience. Norman Brown's *Life Against
Death: The Psychoanalytic Meaning of History* (1959) attained new popularity. Brown, a classics professor at Wesleyan University, insisted that
intuition rather than rationality was the best guide to reality. The highest
truths were not accessible through reason and rational discourse. Brown
was particularly emphatic about the need to resist socially imposed restrictions on sexual activity, calling for "polymorphous perversity." Many alienated young people turned to a life of pure feeling and rampant polygamy,
whereas some became "Jesus freaks" and others immersed themselves in
Buddhism, Hare Krishna, or other Eastern religions. "Did you ever happen to think what would happen if Jesus were to come down to earth
again?" one hippie wrote. "What would the typical American think? He
would probably be thinking, 'Look at that disgusting hippy. Probably high
on something, preaching peace, happiness and good will.'"

After 1968, an increasing number of hippies sought to isolate themselves
in enclaves called communes, cooperatives, collectives, or communities. By

1970, an estimated 2,000 rural and 5,000 urban communes provided homes to 2 to 3 million members of the counterculture. Outside San Francisco, musician Lou Gottlieb founded Morning Star and opened it to anyone who wanted to practice "voluntary primitivism." Eventually, the communal lifestyle attracted artists, spiritual seekers, environmentalists, vegetarians, and gays. Some of the early communes advocated free love and attracted residents who practiced group sex or bisexuality. Harrad West in Berkley and Talsen in Oregon featured "group marriages." Many communards used dope, and most communes grew their own marijuana. Most rural communes were set up to be self-sufficient farms, but urban collectives came in many varieties. Some were political, such as the Kate Richards O'Hare Collective near Cornell University, which was based on the principles of socialism. Others were centered on education; residents alternated between working and going to college. Soldiers returning from Vietnam organized the Veteran's Collective in San Francisco.

At its philosophical edges, the counterculture crumbled into nihilism. The Rolling Stones held a free concert at the Altamont Speedway, and the Hell's Angels, hired to maintain security, stomped one spectator to death and knifed another as Mick Jagger sang "Street Fighting Man." Medical personnel attempting to aid those suffering from drug overdoses or LSD "bad trips" were abused and harassed. In the pages of *Rampart* magazine, Eldridge Cleaver attempted to legitimize rape "as an insurrectionary act." In 1969, Charles Manson, the deeply psychotic leader of a drug cult, and several of his young followers recruited from San Francisco's Haight–Ashbury district ritually murdered actress Sharon Tate and four of her friends in her Malibu home. Although hippies hated him because he gave the counterculture a bad name, Manson fascinated the press and conventional society. He raised the horrific but titillating specter of armed hippies as sexual predators. Susan Sontag proclaimed America to be "a cancerous society." After visiting North Vietnam, she declared that "the *Reader's Digest* and Lawrence Welk and Hilton Hotels" were "organically connected" to the brutal American bombing of Vietnamese villages. Critics attacked the "politics of the absurd," but argued that it was only a symptom of a fundamental disease. From time immemorial, enduring human relationships had been based on commitment and the willingness to sacrifice for others. When relationships were reduced to transitory, random sexual encounters, much of the power went out of them, whether they were heterosexual or homosexual. In fact, the twin emphases on individual expression and self-indulgence on the one hand and communal existence on the other hand were mutually exclusive. The discipline and compromise that the counterculture found so repellant in the American political system were necessary ingredients to any form of group living.

In fact, most of those who came of age in the early 1970s found protest, communal living, and antiestablishment behavior passé. "I remember

having soybeans for breakfast, lunch and dinner, and nothing else," recalled Cynthia Bates of The Farm. "Having kids made you more sensitive
to the lack of necessities.... How long could you live in a house with 50
other people?" With unemployment and inflation on the rise, they enrolled
in business colleges by the tens of thousands and seemed destined to become the career-obsessed duplicates of the youth of the 1950s. Popular culture reflected the change. Hard rock continued, but the Who, the Doors,
Led Zeppelin, and the Rolling Stones produced music that was distinctly
apolitical. Among the most popular television programs of the 1970s were
"Happy Days" and "Laverne and Shirley," paens to the supposedly halcyon
high school days of the late 1950s. In the wake of Vietnam, the Days of
Rage, and Watergate, the United States longed for the seeming simplicity
of adolescence. Idealism did not disappear, but it became abstracted and
fantasized. The most popular movies of the period were George Lucas's
"Star Wars" trilogy, featuring a young, idealistic protagonist and a beautiful, spirited heroine battling the forces of evil against a backdrop of in-
tergalactic warfare. Public opinion polls indicated that young people were
disillusioned with politics, did not believe that the United States had any
authentic mission in world affairs, and saw college as a ticket-punching operation whose end was to secure a better-paying job rather than to develop
one's mind.

In 1979, historian Christopher Lasch penned a scathing indictment of
contemporary youth in *The Culture of Narcissism*. The driving forces behind the culture of the 1970s, he insisted, were disillusionment, pessimism,
materialism, and selfishness. The protest movement of the 1960s, designed
initially to challenge the conventionalism of the 1950s and the dominance
in American life of the military–industrial complex, had degenerated into
low theater, that is, a means for self-dramatization. In the face of institutionalized racism, militarism, political unresponsiveness, and stagflation,
the New Left withered and died, leaving in its wake college students who
could not see beyond their careers and veterans of the 1960s who immersed
themselves in health food fads, *Architectural Digest*, transcendental meditation, or music lessons.

Yet, as was true of the 1950s, there were currents of change and questioning in the 1970s, signs that the United States was attempting to heal the
wounds of Vietnam and Watergate, reidentify authentic American values,
and build a community that was worth inhabiting. Millions of Americans
tuned into the long-running television series "M*A*S*H," an antiwar
comedy/drama set in the context of the Korean War and featuring heroes
that deplored the irrationality of armed conflict and yet did their duty. In
the late 1970s, the nation began to try to come to grips with *America's
Longest War* (1979), the title of George Herring's best-selling history of the
war in Vietnam. In "The Deerhunter" (1978), a wrenching motion picture
epic about the Vietnam conflict, a group of high school friends are snatched

from their working-class environment in the coal fields of eastern Pennsylvania and set down in the jungles of Southeast Asia in the midst of a war that featured a murderous enemy but no frontlines. Their encounter with captivity, death, and drugs causes them to confront the very essence of what it meant to be a human. The acclaimed and widely viewed miniseries, "Roots" (1976), based on the best-selling novel by Alex Haley, provided many white Americans with their first realistic view of the African American experience, including slavery, peonage, and institutionalized discrimination. The ongoing success of the 1970s' most controversial television series, "All in the Family," starring Carroll O'Connor and Jean Stapleton, pointed to an increased awareness of race, class, and ideological differences. Archie Bunker, the series' antihero, is a forgotten, working-class American with all the race, class, and gender prejudices associated with the stereotype. He feels threatened by integration, the antiwar movement, college professors, feminism, the media, and liberals in general, and sets about defending his cultural bunker. Most who watched the show did not identify with Archie but rather were repelled by him. Those who had protested in the 1960s might have come to terms with mainstream culture in the 1970s, but they retained a commitment to social justice, anti-imperialism, and participatory democracy that would act as a counterweight to the conservatism of the 1980s.

Women's Liberation

Change Without Fulfillment

If the student protest movement and counterculture were passing phases, there were other social phenomena of the 1960s and 1970s that proved more enduring. In addition to civil rights, the most significant of these was women's liberation. In September 1968, when the Miss America Pageant opened in Atlantic City, the all-white event was picketed by more than 100 women. Journalist Charlotte Curtis described the scene: "Women armed with a giant bathing beauty puppet and a 'freedom trash can' in which they threw girdles, bras, hair curlers, false eyelashes, and anything else that smacked of 'enslavement' picketed the Miss America Pageant here today." Demonstrators accused the organizers of being racist, and several managed to momentarily disrupt the festivities by tossing a stink bomb. "The demonstrators," the *New York Times* wrote, "belonged to what they called the Women's Liberation Movement."

Although the content of the typical American woman's life had changed dramatically in the post–World War II years, she had made little progress in acting collectively to achieve equality, redress grievances, and define what it meant to be a woman in modern America. Cultural stereotypes continued to prevail. By 1970, 60% of all families earning $10,000 or more featured working women. Yet most of the jobs that women held were sexually segregated, heavily concentrated in low-level service areas, and not conducive to individual advancement or growth. On college campuses, advisers steered co-eds away from "male professions" such as business, science, and engineering, and toward "female occupations" such as nursing, teaching, and home economics. If women were lucky enough to secure interviews for medium- and upper-level white-collar jobs, they found themselves being asked, "Are you engaged?" and if not, "Can you type?" Indeed, most women with college degrees had three opportunities – teach, type, and take temperatures. Airline stewardesses were fired when they married or reached age 32, prompting Congresswoman Martha Griffiths to write United Airlines: "You are asking . . . that a stewardess be young, attractive and single. What are you running, an airline or a whorehouse?" The average salesman in the United States earned $8,500 per year, whereas a saleswoman made only $3,500. In addition, the culture continued to teach that women should work to be a helpmate to her spouse and to supplement the family income rather than to fulfill her own potential. Home economists, religious figures, and women's magazines persisted in urging women to glory in their own femininity, which they limited to the roles of wife, mother, and income supplementer. Her man, not herself, was the object of existence for the idealized traditional woman. "If anybody had asked me to marry them between April and September of 1962," declared future Congresswoman Elizabeth Holtzman, referring to the year she graduated from college, "I would have said yes. It appeared to solve so many problems."

Discrimination, both formal and informal, plagued the American woman in other walks of life. Eighteen states exempted only women from serving on juries. In 17 states, women could not tend bar, and in 6 they could not enter into financial agreements without a male cosigner. Schools expelled all pregnant girls, but not their boyfriends or husbands, and fired pregnant teachers. Some states prohibited not only single but even married women from obtaining contraception.

Compared with African Americans and other oppressed minority groups, women operated at a disadvantage in developing a group consciousness, and thus in organizing and affecting the political process. They suffered from the peculiar problem of being literally seduced by (husbands and lovers) representatives of the oppressor. They did not live in separate neighborhoods or belong, for the most part, to separate political and cultural organizations. There was no critical mass of protesters to articulate an ideology. Indeed, some women as well as men viewed challenges to existing gender role models as cultural heresy. Nevertheless, the sense of unease and unreality among American women was palpable by the mid-1960s.

The Feminist Conscience

With the publication of Betty Friedan's *Feminine Mystique* in 1963, many of the discontents and hopes of the American woman were at long last articulated. A graduate of Smith College, Friedan lived the life of a typical suburban housewife as she fitfully pursued a career as a freelance writer. Her articles and books addressed "the problem that has no name," the silent longing of housewives for an existence beyond den mother, cook, helpmate, bridge partner, grocery shopper, and domestic ornament. Thousands of women read and agreed with Friedan's contention that they were imprisoned by a society that told them only what they *should* be, rather than being empowered by a milieu that encouraged them to be what they *could* be. The central message of feminism, that "the personal is political," came as a revelation to many women. Indeed, the notion that the plight of individual women was caused by and linked to the institutions and mores of the larger society served as the catalyst for a movement that had for so long been atomized. At the same time, as William Chafe and others have pointed out, the civil rights movement was serving as a model and stimulus to women's liberation.

As their abolitionist forebears had a century earlier, American women who participated in the civil rights movement sensed that they, no less than African Americans, were being categorized and discriminated against on the basis of an accident of birth. Feminists quickly perceived that similar to blacks, they could make progress toward achieving equality under the law and equality of opportunity through joint action. Working in the Student Nonviolent Coordinating Committee (SNCC), the Southern Christian Leadership Conference (SCLC), and the Congress of Racial Equality (CORE), where they were routinely discriminated against and sexually harassed, a critical mass of young women acquired the tools to build a movement: a language of protest, experience in organizing meetings and demonstrations and, most important, a sense of solidarity as an oppressed group. In 1972, the first woman rabbi in the United States, Sally J. Priesand, was ordained in Cincinnati. That same year, Jean Westwood was chosen head of the Democratic National Committee, and the FBI named its first two female agents, Susan Lynn Roley, a former U.S. Marine, and Joanne E. Pierce, a former nun. The University of Miami gave the first athletic scholarship awarded to a woman to swimmer Lynn Genesko. Yet these "firsts" smacked more of tokenism than a massive, meaningful change. Title VII of the Civil Rights Act of 1964 stated that discrimination in employment on the basis of sex as well as race was prohibited, and experienced women activists – pioneers in the labor movement, political activists, and business and professional women – used the new legislation to organize and launch a national women's rights organization. The National Organization of Women (NOW), the women's rights branch of the feminist movement, brought together the older experienced groups with the new young veterans of the civil rights organizations. Through litigation, political pressure, and public information campaigns, they labored together to ensure equality under the law and equal opportunity for women. Their Bill of Rights for Women demanded equal access to education and jobs, enforcement of laws banning sex discrimination, maternity leave for working mothers, federally funded day care centers, and a woman's right to control her own reproductive life. By 1977, NOW could claim 65,000 members. In a major equal rights decision, the Supreme Court ruled that women in the armed forces were entitled to the same benefits for their spouses as those accorded male servicemen. For a short period, women in the SDS hoped that that organization could be used as a vehicle to change the way young Americans thought about gender roles and then to serve as an opening wedge for women's liberation in the larger society. In 1967, the national convention passed a resolution endorsing women's rights, but the debate was raucous and sexist. Frequently ridiculed and reduced to menial tasks within the organization, the women of the New Left departed to join NOW or to form their own organizations.

Outside the formal political sphere, women's liberation frequently took the form of "consciousness-raising" sessions, which were held with increasing frequency on campuses and in communities across the nation. Within these meetings, women enjoyed the "social space" that made it possible for them to discover that they shared common problems with sex, job discrimination, and the male's refusal to recognize female individuality. The emphasis in these meetings was on sharing and democracy, and the women who participated in them subsequently sought to transfer these themes to their own families. Challenging the traditional patriarchal model, they argued that all family members were equally valuable, and that as responsible adults, women should share in decision-making equally with men. Gradually the women's movement began to define its own goals and establish its own agenda. In 1973, a group of women who felt condescended to and infantalized by the male medical establishment authored a best-selling, women's health manual entitled *Our Bodies, Ourselves*. Gloria Steinem published *Ms.* magazine, which explored topics ranging from female sexual responsiveness to breaking the "glass ceiling" in corporations (an invisible job level above which members of a subordinated group were not allowed to rise). In *The Church and the Second Sex* (1968), feminist theologian Mary Daly made the Christian argument for equality of access to all levels of church hierarchy. A Gallup poll taken in the early 1960s revealed that fewer than one third of females questioned felt discriminated against, but by 1970 that percentage was 50% and had climbed to two thirds by the time Nixon left office.

The New Woman
The new woman was of two minds concerning sexuality. On the one hand, she embraced the revolution in morals and manners that swept the nation in the 1960s. The "pill" became available in 1961, placing birth control in the hands of women and providing them with a powerful tool to control not

only birth but also their own sexuality. Four years later, Virginia Johnson and William Masters published their classic work on human sexuality, *Human Sexual Response*. It exploded numerous myths about sexuality – that women did not enjoy intercourse as much as men, for example, and that it was difficult for women to have orgasms. Feminists insisted on their right to be sexually active with whom they wanted at a time of their choosing. Women's increasing willingness to abandon unsatisfying or abusive relationships contributed to a growth in the divorce rate from 2.2 per 1,000 of population in 1960 to 5.2 in 1980. At the same time, they were increasingly aware of and repelled by the use of women's bodies to sell things and the pervasive tendency of men to view women as objects. At Grinnell College in Iowa, female activists staged a "nude-in" when representatives of *Playboy* magazine showed up to photograph co-eds. Women must come to understand, one activist wrote, that "they are not inferior – nor chicks, nor bunnies, nor quail, nor cows, nor bitches." but individuals capable of seizing control of their own destiny. In the view of some radical feminists, virtually all heterosexual intercourse was a form of rape, nothing more or less than a continuous process of intimidation by which all men keep all women in a state of fear. One extremist urged women to liberate themselves from the biological slavery of reproducing children and create artificial wombs.

Growing self-awareness and economic conditions combined to change the pattern of family life and to continue the shift in gender roles that had begun in the 1950s. The percentage of women who were gainfully employed increased from 44% in 1970 to 51% by 1980. Married females flocked to the workforce not only out of a desire for self-realization, but also out of a need to increase family income as inflation threatened the middle-class status of tens of thousands of families. Changing patterns of work and career opportunities caused women to delay marriage or to dispense with it altogether. Married women had fewer children and bore them at a later age. From a postwar high of 25.3 births per 1,000 population in 1957, the rate dropped to 14.8 in 1975. Again, women limited the number of offspring they had in order to be freer to pursue work outside the home and also because four- and five-children families became increasingly unaffordable. It should be noted that the new psychological, gender, and career vistas opened up by the modern feminist movement created as much anxiety as satisfaction for the American woman. Some traditionalists believed themselves laggards if they shunned a career, whereas some modernists felt guilty about neglecting husbands and children or doing without them altogether. Those who sought to balance work and family experienced stress and fatigue.

For the most part, leaders of the women's movement in America defined success and achievement in political and economic terms. They emphasized gender-free hiring practices, equal pay for equal work, penetration of the traditionally white male power structure, and democratization of the family. There were those, however, who chose to affirm women's traditional roles as nurturers and defined success in terms of childbearing and home-making. A half century earlier the progressive movement had emphasized the biological and psychological differences between men and women in campaigning for the passage of special laws limiting the number of hours women might spend in the workplace and for other measures designed to protect the nuclear family and working women's health and safety. In the 1960s, a group of conservative women established the La Leche League, an organization committed to breast feeding and hence to the nonseparation of mother and child. Its popularity (it claimed nearly 2 million members at one point), according to historian Lynn Weiner, demonstrated that many American women in the 1960s and 1970s remained committed to tradi-tional gender roles and to motherhood, and were willing to organize to defend them.

Even farther to the right were antifeminist women activists. A number of black females shied away from the movement because they believed that it was a distraction from the civil rights movement, the realization of whose goals would lead to the creation of a polity that was just and equitable for all. The new feminism was, in essence, a quarrel between white men and white women, declared the editor of a black women's magazine in 1971. Many Catholic and evangelical Protestant women refused to associate with the movement because it favored abortion and opened its doors to lesbians. In 1972, Phyllis Schlafly, a conservative supporter of Barry Goldwater's 1964 presidential candidacy, formed a "Stop ERA" organization named the Eagle Forum, which at its strongest boasted 50,000 members.

In fact, by the 1970s, observers were chronicling a virulent antifeminist backlash. Economic hard times deepened antifeminist sentiment as men became resentful of women competing for scarce jobs in the workplace. Working-class women increasingly denounced the movement as a vehicle to serve only the interests of the college educated. Marabel Morgan's *The Total Woman* (1975) both reflected and stimulated antifeminism. "A total woman caters to her man's special needs," she wrote, "whether it be in salads, sex, or sports." In 1978, 20,000 feminists gathered in Houston for the National Women's Conference; Schafly managed to attract 8,000 for a counterrally. "The American people," she proclaimed, "do not want the ERA, and they do not want government-funded abortion, lesbian privileges, or . . . universal child care."

Television revealed how relative was the progress made by feminists during the 1960s and 1970s. The "Mary Tyler Moore Show" was remark-able for featuring a single, independent career woman as its heroine, but the costar was a paternalistic male who was Mary's boss and to whom in a crunch she was forced to turn for wisdom and advice. Two sex-based shows, "Three's Company" and "Charlie's Angels," featured women in their traditional screen roles as sex objects. In the former, two unmarried

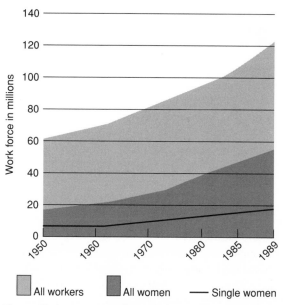

Figure 11–2. **Women in the work force, 1950–1989.** Since 1960 the proportion of American women who are gainfully employed has surged upward. As a result, young women coming of age in the 1990s have far different expectations about their lives than did their grandmothers or even their mothers. *Sources:* Statistical Abstract of the United States, *1988* (1987), 373; *World Almanac and Book of Facts, 1989* (1988), 152; *Statistical Abstract of the United States, 1991* (1991), 387, 390.

females lived with a single male and built a vapid existence based on sexual innuendo. The latter was a detective-adventure show, which featured professional women who continually put themselves in harm's way but who habitually dressed as if they were off to a wet T-shirt contest.

Perhaps the greatest blows dealt to the American women's movement by conservatives came in the area of abortion rights. In 1971, a group of women formed the National Abortion Rights Action League (NARAL) and pressured state legislatures to begin reviewing abortion laws. To help raped and battered women, they established women's crisis centers. "When we talk about women's rights," declared one activist, "we can get all the rights in the world ... and none of them means a doggone thing if we don't own the flesh we stand in." Although NOW and Planned Parenthood applauded *Roe v. Wade*, the 1973 Supreme Court decision that upheld a woman's right to terminate unwanted pregnancies during the first two trimesters, conservatives organized the National Right to Life Committee and began their unceasing campaign in the courts, at the polls, and in the streets to do away with all vestiges of legalized abortion. In 1976, led by Representative Henry Hyde (R-Illinois), Congress passed legislation barring the use of Medicare and Medicaid funds for abortion. In 1977, the Supreme Court upheld the constitutionality of the Hyde bill; in 1978, Congress extended the ban on federally funded abortions to military personnel and members of the Peace Corps.

Gay Liberation

Another group of Americans wanted to assert the distinction between human sexuality and reproduction, but for very different reasons. Gay and lesbian communities had existed since the founding of the republic, but not until the 1960s and 1970s did they begin to "come out of the closet" in significant numbers and to mobilize on behalf of political action to secure their constitutional rights. During the 1950s, the Daughters of Bilitis and the Mattachine Society broke new ground in publicly agitating for an end to discrimination against gays in the military, in the workplace, in federal and state government, and in all other areas of life. Then, out of the gay communities in San Francisco and New York City's Greenwich Village came the Society for Individual Rights and other organizations that simultaneously agitated for civil rights and supported gays and lesbians in their decisions to proclaim and defend their sexual identity.

As was the case with the black civil rights movements, specific, dramatic acts of brutality and oppression proved more important to mobilizing gays and their supporters than institutions and organizations. Early in 1966, New York Mayor John Lindsay ordered his police department to crack down on homosexual activity in the area between Times Square and Washington Square. The American Civil Liberties Union chastised the mayor for confusing "deviant social behavior with criminal activity," but the authorities persisted. In 1969, when New York City police raided a popular gay bar in Greenwich Village, the gay community rose up and staged an all-night protest. In the days that followed the "Stonewall Riot," as it was called, homosexual men and women formed the Gay Liberation Front. "We reject society's attempt to impose sexual roles and definitions of our nature," the group's manifesto read. "We are stepping outside these roles and simplistic myths. We are going to be who we are." Gay activists resorted to time-proven methods of protest, including street demonstrations and sit-ins, and established connections with other protest movements by declaring their opposition to the war in Vietnam and their support of black liberation.

"Gray Power"

During the 1960s and 1970s, Americans became aware not only of racial and gender discrimination, but also of age discrimination. *Newsweek* noted in 1971 that "an increasing number of senior groups are...joining the growing ranks of the country's demonstrators" in a movement the magazine labeled "Gray Power." Despite Medicare and Social Security, one quarter of those Americans older than 65 years of age lived in poverty. More important, perhaps, was the senior citizen's loss of status. "The old and the young have three common traits," asserted an official of the American Association of Retired Persons (AARP). "Both have no money, no power, and no identity." In Philadelphia, 600 members of the Gray Panthers organization staged demonstrations for lower mass transit fares, better bus routes, and easier access to buses. In Chicago, seniors launched a crusade for tax relief; in New York City, they pressured state legislators to abolish mandatory retirement laws. Ever the sensitive politician, President Nixon held a White House conference on aging, calling on local governments to reduce taxes for the elderly. To protect the value of Social Security payments, Congress passed and the president signed the Cost of Living Allowances (COLA), which automatically increased payments to match the rate of inflation.

The Chicano Movement

The second reconstruction served as a model and stimulus for the women's liberation movement and gay liberation and was, at the same time, part of a broader movement of ethnic minorities for equal treatment under the law and greater cultural autonomy. By far, the largest Hispanic group (the dominant white culture made no distinction between Cubans, Salvadorans, Panamanians, Puerto Ricans, or Mexicans) was Mexican Americans, which included those who had been living in the West and Southwest since before the arrival of the first white settlers. Like Native Americans, they found themselves victims of exploitation and discrimination, relegated in most cases to second-class citizenship. Stimulated by the rhetoric of the Atlantic Charter and by their contributions to the war effort, Mexican Americans began organizing after World War II in an effort to penetrate the white-dominated power structure. Similar to the civil rights movement for black Americans, the Hispanic empowerment movement stressed both pride in native culture and assimilation into the majority culture. The League of United Latin American Citizens (LULAC), founded in Texas in 1928, increased its membership after the war to 15,000. LULAC and the GI Forum, established in 1948 also in Texas, stressed English literacy, education, and exercise of the franchise. LULAC successfully guided two cases through the federal court system that anticipated *Brown*. In 1947, the Supreme Court in *Mendez v. Westminster* upheld a lower court ruling that prohibited the segregation of Mexican Americans in public facilities. In 1954, LULAC lawyers obtained an order from the high court forbidding the exclusion of Mexican Americans from Texas jury lists. These breakthroughs did not end segregation and discrimination but did establish a firm legal basis from which Mexican American activists could attack racial barriers.

The number of Mexican nationals coming to the United States increased dramatically during World War II when the American and Mexican governments cooperated in establishing the bracero program. Under this arrangement, approximately 300,000 Mexicans entered the United States as temporary laborers, primarily on farms and railroads. The labor shortage, and along with it the bracero program, continued into the postwar period. Agribusiness in the West and Southwest gradually became dependent on this cheap source of farm labor, and despite harsh working conditions, low pay, and lack of social services, immigration mounted annually. Many who came accepted citizenship, whereas others worked for a period and moved back to Mexico. Thousands of braceros and their children took up residence in urban ghettos, called barrios, in Los Angeles, Denver, San Antonio, and El Paso in search of better jobs and conditions. Despite the harshness of life in the barrios and on American farms, economic opportunity in the United States was far greater than in Mexico. As a result, during the 1950s, tens of thousands of mojados or "wetbacks" – so named because many swam the Rio Grande River to gain entry – entered the United States illegally. Beginning in 1954, the Eisenhower administration launched "Operation Wetback," and over the next few years some 3.7 million allegedly illegal immigrants were rounded up and deported. Immigration officials often ignored due process, and consequently legal aliens and even some American citizens were caught up in the deportation process. Operation Wetback broke up families, as well as left a legacy of anger and mistrust of Anglo culture and politics among Mexican Americans.

By 1960, Mexican Americans constituted the second largest ethnic group in the United States. Although numbering only 3.5 million and representing 2.3% of the national population, Hispanics made up 12% of the combined populations of California, Texas, Colorado, and New Mexico. By 1980, the number stood at 9 million for these four states, and census officials predicted that by the end of the twentieth century, Mexican Americans would surpass African Americans as the largest ethnic group in the United States. Although some Latinos penetrated the white power structure and ascended into the middle class, most did not. The unemployment rate for Hispanics remained 45% higher than that for whites. Hispanic men working full time earned only 71% of what their white counterparts made. Many public facilities and schools were segregated, and in most classrooms speaking Spanish was prohibited. Thus, educational levels for most Hispanics remained shockingly low. As of 1969, nearly 4% of Mexican American adults were functionally illiterate. In Texas, 90% had not graduated from high school. In 1968, California boasted 2 million Hispanics, but not one occupied elective state office. The U.S. Commission on Civil Rights chronicled numerous incidents in which white police singled out Hispanics for harsh treatment, physically abusing them and arresting them on insufficient grounds. One Los Angeles official declared that people of Mexican descent were "biologically crime prone." Aware of their increasing numbers and encouraged by the success of the civil rights movement, Hispanic Americans established new, more militant organizations to protest unequal treatment by local, state, and federal courts, and discrimination in hiring and public services. The pioneer in this effort was Caesar Chavez, a Mexican American farm worker who organized the National Farm Workers' Association in 1963 and between 1965 and 1969 led a series of dramatic strikes and boycotts that forced growers to recognize the union and bargain with it. His 25-day hunger strike brought national attention, including a picture on the cover of *Time* magazine. Meanwhile, in Texas, Jose Angel Guitierrez established a new political party called La Renza Unida; San Antonio Mayor (subsequently congressman) Henry B. Gonzalez led the movement to penetrate the established white power structure. A separatist cultural wing of the movement emerged that celebrated the Hispanic heritage and that lobbied for bilingualism in the schools. The Mexican American Youth Organization (MAYO) began demanding Mexican American study programs at universities from California State to the University of Texas. "Viva la revolucion" proclaimed posters on high school lockers. Young activists declared that "brown is beautiful," and movement newspapers such as *El Papel* and *La Raza* appeared in Albuquerque and Los Angeles. From San Diego to Houston, school boards were overwhelmed with Mexican American parents insisting that schools abolish "Anglo education" by hiring Hispanic teachers and counselors and by providing bilingual education and heritage classes. The programs and organizations that sprang up in the 1960s were known collectively as the Chicano movement.

Native Americans

For the millions of descendents of European immigrants that made up the bulk of the U.S. population, the Native American existed only as an historical footnote or as a staple of television westerns. Following World War II, Congress reversed policies pursued by the Roosevelt administration, which had been sensitive to the cultural independence of Native Americans and which had generally dealt with the tribes as sovereign entities. In 1953, in response to pressure from timber and mining companies, Congress passed Concurrent Resolution No. 108, which provided for the "termination" of Native American treaties and sovereignty rights. During the next eight years, the House and Senate passed 12 specific termination bills covering 60 tribes, nearly all in the West. Senator Arthur Watkins of Utah, the leader of the termination movement, declared that Congress had rejected "the concept that the Indian people exist within the United States as independent nations." Some of the tribes signed termination agreements eagerly because of one-time cash payments from the division of tribal assets, but they soon came to regret the decision. Once the money was spent, tribal members had to accept poorly compensated and unskilled jobs in hostile environments to survive. The National Congress of American

Indians condemned the termination concept in the early 1960s; as a result, the federal government modified the policy and made Native Americans eligible for antipoverty and other Great Society programs. In the end, termination affected only about 3% of federally recognized Native Americans. The demise of this dubious enterprise did not mean, however, an end to white encroachment on reservations and Native American rights.

In the midst of the energy crisis of the 1970s, it was revealed that substantial deposits of fossil fuels and fissionable materials lay beneath Native American lands. Indeed, government and corporate engineers estimated that 5% of America's untapped petroleum resources were on Native American territory, and 30% to 40% of its uranium and as much as 30% of unexploited coal veins were to be found there. Traditionally, the Federal Bureau of Land Management had leased mineral rights to private companies; royalties to the various tribes from such agreements were paltry. Then in 1973, the Northern Cheyenne of Montana won a path-breaking suit in federal court that allowed them to suspend and renegotiate mineral contracts. In 1975, the mineral-rich tribes, using OPEC as a model, formed the Council of Energy Reserve Tribes (CERT). With the aid of federal grants, CERT began a comprehensive inventory of deposits on Native American lands and initiated a program to train tribal leaders in energy resource management.

Buoyed by these successes, Native American lawyers, building on a tradition stretching back to the administration of Andrew Jackson, filed a series of suits in federal court that were designed to protect the tribes, their historic rights, and their reservations. In 1974, President Richard M. Nixon, decrying government paternalism, signed into law the Indian Self-Determination Act, a measure that restored the legal status of Native American tribes and gave them partial control over federal programs on their soil. Supported by the Native American Rights Fund established in 1946 to help settle treaty disputes, these lawyers won a landmark case in 1978, *U.S. v. Wheeler*, which reasserted the principle of "unique and limited" sovereignty for Native American tribes. In Maine, the Passamaquoddy and Penobscot tribes successfully laid claim to 12.5 million acres seized illegally in the nineteenth century. A series of court decisions handed down in 1979 required Rhode Island to return 1,800 acres to the Narragansetts and awarded the Sioux more than $100 million for "dishonorable dealing" in the government acquisition of the Black Hills of South Dakota.

Despite these courtroom victories, the plight of Native Americans, the product of more than a century of victimization by the dominant white society, remained lamentable. As of the early 1970s, some 300,000 had left the reservation in search of a better existence. What most of these "urban Indians" found was a life of toil and hardship as day laborers and menials, a life made all the harder by discrimination and separation from their native culture. For the nearly 500,000 Native Americans who remained behind, things were not much better. Chicasaws, Choctaws, Navajos, Oglala, Sioux, and countless other tribes lived on reservations that were neither autonomous nor integrated into the nation's political and social system. The Bureau of Indian Affairs (BIA) treated their charges as a kind of dependent nation, creating a situation in which Native Americans were denied complete control over their own affairs and cut off from the industries and service economy that provided jobs to other Americans. In 1976, the General Accounting Office of Congress revealed that the Indian Health Service had sterilized as much as one quarter of the Native American female population without their consent. Generally speaking, schools on most reservations were inferior, unemployment ran as high as 50%, and, not surprisingly, alcoholism and suicide rates far exceeded those for the U.S. population as a whole. A typical Native American family in the early 1960s earned only one third of the average family income in the United States.

The late 1960s and early 1970s witnessed a burgeoning of Native American militancy. In 1970/1971, Native Americans occupied Alcatraz Island off San Francisco, claiming the deserted prison site under a treaty provision making unused federal lands available to Native Americans. Russell Means and other activists founded the American Indian Movement (AIM), which began protesting the twin themes of paternalism and neglect that characterized BIA treatment of Native Americans. Various tribes brought suit against the federal government seeking to regain control of lands they claimed had been illegally seized. A spate of documentaries and historical novels such as Vin Deloria's *Custer Died for Your Sins* (1969) and Dee Brown's *Bury My Heart at Wounded Knee* (1971) created a new awareness of the historical wrongs done to the Native Americans. In February 1973, Means and a band of heavily armed activists seized the post office at Wounded Knee, South Dakota. Holding several hostages at gunpoint, they demanded free elections of tribal leaders, investigation of the BIA, and review of all U.S.–Native American treaties. Following a tense standoff with FBI agents, the militants surrendered. AIM's seizure of Alcatraz Island, hostage-taking at Wounded Knee, and the occupation of the BIA offices in Washington, D.C., did not accomplish very much in the short run, but by the end of the 1970s federal agencies were dealing with Native Americans in a much more sensitive and evenhanded manner. Furthermore, a concerted effort was underway to help descendents of the nation's original inhabitants enjoy a degree of prosperity while retaining as much of their native culture as possible. Perhaps most important, the militancy of the 1970s blunted the movement within and without the Native American nations to see Native Americans completely assimilated into the dominant white society. "Forty years ago," observed a Crow college professor, "Indians would deny their religions because they didn't want to be persecuted. But now, Crow grandparents are teaching their children the old ways." In the wake of Wounded Knee, AIM established "survival schools" to transmit cultural traditions and preserve the basic skills of hunting, fishing, and ritual purification. "A tribe is a people who live together in a special way," declared one tribal leader.

The Culture of Poverty

African Americans, women, Mexican Americans, and Native Americans learned from each other and were inspired by each others' examples. They were bound together, in addition, by the fact that they were all part of the burgeoning "culture of poverty" in America. Not all members of these groups were poor – indeed, women and members of ethnic minorities made significant economic progress in the 1960s and 1970s – but they constituted a disproportionate percentage of those Americans living below the poverty line. According to estimates, nearly three quarters of all new jobs created during the 1960s and 1970s were in the low-paying retail and service sectors. Women flooding into the job market had only these jobs to choose from; thus, although employment opportunities expanded numerically during this period, they did not grow qualitatively. The new morality that winked at casual sexual encounters and permitted divorce for often frivolous reasons may have been liberating for some women, but for others, particularly those with children, the departure of the male breadwinner spelled economic disaster. Between 1950 and 1980, the number of families receiving aid under Aid for Families with Dependent Children (AFDC) increased from 3 to 8 million. During the 1970s, the sum of poor families with a man present decreased by 25%, whereas the total of poor families headed by women increased by almost 39%. Approximately 25% of all working women who were heads of households with children earned incomes beneath the poverty level.

In addition, it was at the poverty line that race and gender seemed to intersect in America. For black and Puerto Rican women, desertion or neglect by biological fathers became epidemic. Whereas the percentage of poor white families headed by women reached 14% by 1980, that figure was 47% for black women and 40% for Puerto Ricans. One out of three black children were born to a teenage mother, and 55% of all African American babies were born out of wedlock. New sexual mores were not alone responsible. Young black men simply could not find jobs – the unemployment rate for this group ran to an astronomical 50% in the 1970s – and many state AFDC regulations stipulated that payments could not be made to households with a male present. Racism and poverty combined to create a vicious circle on which the second reconstruction seemed to have had absolutely no effect.

If the culture of poverty created a two-class society for white Americans, that was all the more true for African Americans. For some black American families, the 1960s and 1970s were decades of opportunity and upward mobility. By 1980, an estimated 35% to 45% of African American families had achieved middle-class status. The number of black elected officials sky-rocketed from 103 in 1964 to 4,311 in 1977. The infant mortality rate for African Americans declined from 40 deaths per 1,000 births in 1965 to 24.2 in 1975. On the tenth anniversary of the 1968 Kerner Commission Report, public opinion polls indicated that whites perceived themselves increasingly tolerant of blacks and comfortable with racial equality. The Mormon Church, notorious for its divinely justified racism, had a new revelation and opened the priesthood to "all worthy male members ... without regard for race or color." In a controversial book, *The Declining Significance of Race*, sociologist William Wilson argued that racial prejudice no longer explained the problems of black poverty.

There may have been a decline in overt racism, but African Americans continued to operate at a disadvantage. "Blacks as a group are still behind whites," observed historian Manning Marable; "no amount of statistical doubletalk will obscure this fundamental fact." The departure of industry from urban centers and the emergence of a service economy forced blacks to accept lower-paying jobs and to make do with part-time work in the absence of full-time employment. Most frustrating was the simple absence of jobs; unemployment rates for blacks of both genders and all ages remained twice as high as for whites.

Those upwardly mobile African Americans who earned advanced degrees, provided better lives for their children, and climbed the social ladder tended to move out of the nation's inner cities and head for the suburbs. What they left behind – some 30% of all black Americans – were deserted women, unwed mothers, drug addicts, jobless, and homeless. During the period that stretched from the Civil War through World War II, institutionalized racism – segregation and discrimination embedded in law or custom – had fused the black community together within urban ghettos. Those communities, typically stratified, boasted self-help and community action projects and, most importantly, gave a sense of belonging and identity to the great majority of their inhabitants. Ironically, the civil rights movement and the relative prosperity of the period separated the black middle class from the less fortunate, shattering inner-city communities, robbing them of black leadership, and leaving those who did not benefit from the new opportunities behind to face unemployment, crime, disease, homelessness, and hopelessness. In the past, the majority of poor families in America had lived in rural areas. As of the mid-1970s, 70% lived in the inner city, 70% were nonwhite, and 50% came from female-headed households.

The inner-city stay-behinds were hardly a mass of passive statistics, however. In the early 1970s, the city-dwelling poor, many of them African American and Hispanic, embraced community action at the political, cultural, and social levels as a way out of poverty and powerlessness. Atlanta elected a black mayor, Maynard Jackson, and by 1978 46% of black southerners compared with 57% of white southerners voted regularly. Outside the South, Coleman Young in Detroit, Richard Hatcher in Gary, Indiana, and Tom Bradley in Los Angeles were elected by putting together multiethnic coalitions formed around the theme of urban renewal.

Other racial and ethnic groups advanced at a slower pace. Mexican Americans took control of the San Antonio city council in 1978, and from Texas to southern California Hispanics developed powerful political organizations at the neighborhood and ward levels. In cities across the United States, officials elected by the new urban coalitions moved to improve city services and open public employment to minorities and women. Unfortunately, the economic downturn of the 1970s vitiated many of their efforts. Mayors and city council members found that temporary job-training programs for youth, for example, were turning out workers for factories that were shutting down.

Some urban dwellers remained in the inner city because they had to, but others did so through choice, unwilling to leave the museums, theaters, orchestras, and neighborhoods that were not available in suburbia. They banned together with residents of poorer neighborhoods to pressure state and national governments to appropriate funds for "save the city" programs. In 1974, President Ford signed the Community Development Act, which appropriated $8.4 billion over three years to fund direct grants to cities to be used as they saw fit. These community block grants encouraged citizens to participate in local planning efforts. Neighborhood committees, acting in conjunction with mayors and city managers, allocated funds for law enforcement, water treatment plants, public housing, and cultural activities. At the same time, preservationist groups organized to save historical buildings and form trusts to restore old houses and turn vacant lots into public parks.

Public Education under Fire

One of the goals that women, African Americans, and Anglo-Saxons shared was a better education for their children, but American public education between 1960 and 1980 was characterized by cycles of crisis and reform. During the 1960s, in response to Sputnik and perceived stagnation, public schools and colleges were subjected to severe criticism and to wave after wave of curriculum reform. At the same time, public education was rocked by the social movements of the day. Schools received a greater influx of public monies, but a large portion of these resources went to pay for busing, affirmative action programs, and expanded facilities for those requiring special education. Nevertheless, by the close of the 1960s, Americans believed that their system of public education was the best in the world. Then in 1975, the College Entrance Examination Board revealed that scores on the Scholastic Aptitude Test (SAT) had declined steadily since 1964. The report touched off a wave of national soul-searching and produced a spate of books including *A Nation at Risk* (1983), which decried the decline of standards in America's schools. Critics blamed the permissiveness of the 1960s and the tendency of educational "innovators" to substitute form for substance. By the 1980s, education had become a major issue in American politics. State after state passed laws mandating standards and providing funds for gifted and talented programs, while school boards sought to hammer out a core curriculum that qualified college-bound students for the best schools and prepared the vocational student for a life of skilled labor.

The explosion in higher education following World War II had produced a system of huge state-supported "multiversities" to go along with the nation's traditional liberal arts colleges and science institutes. These giant educational enterprises were heavily bureaucratized with a rigid, lecture-oriented curriculum and huge classes. The student protest movement that swept the nation's campuses in the 1960s was not only partly the result of anger against the war in Vietnam but also due to the impersonality and authoritarianism of the modern university. The Free Speech Movement spread quickly, and students succeeded in obtaining some access to the decision-making process at Michigan, Berkeley, Wisconsin, and Texas universities. New courses dealing with contemporary social issues entered the curriculum, and the number of minority students attending institutions of higher learning increased dramatically.

The scientific revolution that had begun in American education following Sputnik continued into the 1970s and 1980s. By 1965, 1 million Americans held scientific degrees and the nation's universities were turning out 8,000 Ph.D.s in science each year. A symbiotic relationship developed between business and the federal government on the one hand and science departments and engineering colleges on the other hand, with extramural organizations providing an increasing proportion of scholarship and research funds for universities. For example, in 1950 the federal government spent $973 million on research and development, whereas by the 1970s that figure had reached $15.3 billion. Americans won more than their share of Nobel Prizes in chemistry, physics, and medicine, and the domestic aircraft, computer, electronic, and nuclear industries flourished as their crack teams of research scientists kept them on the cutting edge.

Fundamentalism Versus Ecumenicalism: Religion in Modern America

The anxieties of the 1960s and 1970s stimulated a religious revival of significance in the United States. Particularly conspicuous was the continued growth of Pentecostal and evangelical movements outside and inside mainstream denominations, the popularity of televangelists, and the movement into politics by conservative religious groups. The social turmoil of the 1960s and the materialism and economic anxieties of the 1970s opened the door for evangelical groups such as the Assemblies of God. Featuring tightly knit congregations, the evangelicals and Pentecostals ministered closely to the emotional and psychological needs of their members, implying in their membership drives that mainstream denominations and congregations were more interested in social causes than in the spiritual well-being of the individual. Evangelicals and Pentecostals provided theological certainty and clear moral boundaries to a society in which traditional rules regarding sex and drug use seemed to be disappearing. A powerful clique seized control of the huge Southern Baptist convention and insisted on acceptance of a literal interpretation of the Bible as a condition of fellowship. In a 1976 poll, 22% of all Americans identified themselves as evangelicals.

To shield their children from the temptations of the world and to assert the primacy of God and the Bible, fundamentalists established thousands of private Christian academies in the 1970s. In the opinion of the religious right, the federal government, staffed by "secular humanists," was acting purposefully to undermine the moral standards of America's youth. They attributed rioting in the urban ghettos, the "loss" of Vietnam, student protests, and the persistence of the counterculture to a pervasive "permissiveness" that was as much a matter of public policy as lack of personal discipline. Nothing did more to reinforce this notion than the Supreme Court's decision in 1962 in *Engel v. Vitale*, which outlawed compulsory prayer in the public schools. School districts throughout the United States ignored the ruling until forced to comply by suits filed by individuals or groups. Fundamentalists responded by employing elaborate dodges or by switching their children to private, religiously oriented schools. Those that remained sought to force public schools to operate by "Christian" principles. In 1973, angry parents conducted a book burning in Drake, North Dakota, where 36 copies of *Slaughterhouse-Five* (1969) by Kurt Vonnegut were put to the torch as "tools of the devil."

While conservatives railed against the Supreme Court and secular humanists that they insisted controlled not only the legal system but also Congress and the educational system, liberals were immersing themselves in a new version of the Social Gospel. Black churches spearheaded the civil rights movement, providing it with much of its energy, justification, and strategy. By the 1960s, African American Christians were joined by white activists from all the major denominations. Although many fundamentalists supported the war in Vietnam, seeing it as part of the crucial struggle against "godless communism," Quakers, Methodists, Presbyterians, Baptists, Congregationalists, Catholics, and Jews also played an increasingly important role in the antiwar movement. The activists of the 1960s and 1970s were responding in particular to the "New Theology," a philosophy that originally grew out of the writings and ministry of Dietrich

Bonhoeffer, a German theologian martyred by the Nazis. Similar to Washington Gladden, C. M. Sheldon, and other participants in the turn-of-the-century social gospel movement, proponents of the new theology stressed the "immanence" rather than the "transcendence" of God. The divine was not some abstraction ruling over the world from a distant heaven, but a living, immediate presence that was actually or potentially resident in all men and women. The object of religion was to unleash the divine in man to do good in the world. Professor Thomas J. J. Altizer of Emory University in Atlanta went a step further. Altizer, who coined the phrase "God is dead," insisted that Christ was divine but that his crucifixion marked his passage from the purely transcendent to the purely immanent. There had been no resurrection and ascension; God was completely in the world. In *The Secular City*, Harvey Cox argued that the task of theology was to make religion relevant and responsive to the new forces in society. At its most extreme, the New Theology degenerated into situational ethics.

Cults

To the surprise and dismay of fundamentalists on the one hand and hardcore members of the New Left on the other hand, there was some overlap between religion and the counterculture in the 1970s. A number of American youth who rejected political activism sought release and fulfillment in spirituality. Others were attracted by the life of Christ, which exemplified the power of love and sacrifice, and called for resistance to injustice. The rock opera "Jesus Christ Superstar" both reflected and stimulated the new interest in Christianity not only among the California-based "Jesus freaks" but also among young people in general. Those who did not find solace and inspiration in traditional religion embraced Buddhism or transcendental meditation.

The 1970s witnessed the emergence of religious "cults," groups of individuals drawn together by devotion to and extravagant admiration for a principle or individual. Many were perversions of Christianity, and all featured charismatic leaders who enthralled, isolated, and usually exploited his or her followers. In September 1976, the Reverend Sun Myung Moon, head of the evangelical Unification Church, presided over a "God Bless America" rally in Washington, D.C., that drew some 50,000 people. He subsequently came under attack from parents who claimed brainwashing tactics had been used to recruit young people into the church and to persuade them to surrender their worldly goods. The converts, who solicited contributions in public places, were frequently referred to as Moonies. Two years later Jim Jones, founder and charismatic head of the People's Temple, moved his California-based cult to Guyana. His followers, many of whom were former drug addicts, convicted felons, and homeless people, were completely in thrall to him. In November, Jones led the residents of "Jonestown," the name of the settlement he had established in the South

American jungle, in a mass suicide. Upon consuming cyanide-laced purple Kool-Aid, 911 individuals died, 200 of them children.

Televangelism

A prominent feature of the religious landscape in the third quarter of the twentieth century was the influence of televangelists from Billy Graham to Oral Roberts to Jimmy Swaggert to Jim Bakker. A dynamic Baptist evangelist, Graham came to national attention by addressing huge, televised rallies in sports arenas and convention centers. Handsome, immaculately groomed, he espoused a Bible-oriented, traditional Christianity that struck a chord with Americans confronted with rapid change and an ongoing identity crisis. Roberts was a Pentecostalist and Tulsa-based evangelist who used faith-healing to build a multimillion dollar empire that included a college and, for a while, a medical school. Jimmy Swaggart, a cousin of rock star Jerry Lee Lewis, was a Church of Christ proselytizer who harangued the faithful on Sunday morning from a national television hookup in Louisiana. His fiery, emotional sermons stressed sin and salvation. Operating with the loose approval of a branch of the Assemblies of God, Jim Bakker emphasized a conservative social agenda and the spiritual benefits of contributing money to his movement. Despite its emotionalism and the self-serving motives of its stars, or perhaps because of them, television evangelism became an important means of worship for millions of Americans.

One of these televangelists, Jerry Falwell, cofounded the Moral Majority, a coalition of religious fundamentalists who bound themselves to political and legal action to advance their conservative social agenda. Working with conservative political figures and organizations, the Moral Majority dedicated itself to returning prayer to the schools, outlawing abortion, abolishing AFDC, continuing the crusade against communism at home and abroad, and reducing the power of the federal government. Falwell helped raise millions of dollars for Ronald Reagan and other conservative candidates, while the Moral Majority did much to define the political debate of the period.

Catholicism

For the huge Catholic Church in America, the years from Kennedy to Carter were ones of reform and reaction. As the 1960s opened, the liberal and much-loved Pope John XXIII convened the first Vatican Council in several centuries. Although he died in its midst in mid-1963, the assembled clergy modernized the liturgy, authorizing the substitution of modern languages for Latin, and launched an ecumenical movement that went a long way toward reconciling Catholics with other denominations and religions. No sooner had the Vatican Ecumenical Council issued decrees condemning nuclear arms and anti-Semitism, and taking a more flexible position on birth control, than the reactionary Paul VI became pope and attempted to turn back the clock. He issued a papal bull, *Humanae Vitae* (Of Human Life), which took a hard line on birth control and condemned abortion under any conditions. But the forces unleashed by John XXIII could not be quelled. Priests and nuns participated prominently in the civil rights and anti–Vietnam War movements and continued to insist that the church existed for humankind and not humankind for the church.

The Right To Life and the Right To Death

Two great issues divided religious conservatives and liberals by the late 1970s – the right to be born and the right to die. Put simply, conservatives believed that in matters of life and death, individuals should not have any choice and liberals believed that they should. Right-to-lifers insisted that from birth to death nature, that is, God's plan for his creation, must be allowed to take its course. Not surprisingly, the hierarchy of the Catholic Church, Orthodox Jews, and many evangelical Protestants were profoundly upset by *Roe v. Wade*. For more than a century, Catholic doctrine had held that life begins at the moment of conception, but the Supreme Court's 1973 decision sanctioned destruction of fetuses under certain conditions. Christians and Jews opposed to abortion argued that human intervention in the process of conception and birth was wrong because it amounted to man playing God. Satan had been thrown out of heaven for seeking to interfere with the divine plan. Similarly, they insisted that terminally ill patients, or those who were legally responsible for them, had no right to end life prematurely. Liberals, including many Methodists, Presbyterians, Baptists, Episcopalians, and Presbyterians as well as some Catholics and most Jews, believed that the mother's health and the prospects for a healthy, reasonably opportune life for the child ought to affect the decision for birth, while pain, suffering, and quality of life ought to affect the decision for death. Prochoice Christians took the position that it was not only absurd but sinful for intelligent, well-meaning people not to intervene in nature to end senseless pain, to protect the health of already viable humans, and to ensure that all humans had the opportunity to enjoy a quality life.

Most of the prochoice, prolife debate focused on the beginning of life until a dramatic court case shifted attention to its end. In 1975, the parents of a 22-year-old girl who had been irreparably injured in an auto accident sued in court to force their daughter's physician to remove her from the life support system that kept her breathing. Karen Ann Quinlan, argued her father, had a right to die with "grace and dignity." Right-to-life groups denounced the parents, who were Catholic, for seeking to substitute man's will for God's. The judge refused to grant the requested order, arguing that in the age of organ transplants and rapid technological advance, no one could say that death was inevitable. By that date, however, 18 states had passed laws declaring that cessation of meaningful brain activity rather than stoppage of the heart or lungs constituted death. An appeals court found for the parents, and the doctor duly removed Karen Ann Quinlan from her respirator. (She continued to breathe on her own for several years before dying a natural death.) The Quinlan case, however, marked the beginning and not the end of a debate that had at its poles two groups of committed Christians and Jews.

The Mainstreaming of Environmentalism

By the latter part of the 1960s, members of the American middle class were worried about their status, their children, their country, and their planet. Between 1945 and 1970, the U.S. population grew by an astounding 32%, from 140 to 205 million people. In many developing areas, the growth rate far exceeded that. In 1969, Paul Ehrlich published his widely read *The Population Bomb*, in which he predicted that by the mid-1980s the planet would be overrun with people and that the struggle for food and living space would touch off nuclear confrontations with Japan and the USSR. It was up to more advanced countries such as the United States to engage in population control. He declared that if Americans could not limit their families to two children or fewer, the government would have to step in and force them to do so through compulsory sterilization or other coercive measures. That same year, the environmentalist movement burst onto the national scene. In the wake of the massive oil spill off the coast of Santa Barbara in 1969, which killed millions of fish and covered thousands of cormorants and other shorebirds with sticky black residue, the residents of that community adopted a "Declaration of Environmental Rights" in 1970. Calling on Americans to redefine progress as "long-term quality" rather than "immediate quantity," the manifesto declared that man was a "member, not master, of the community of living things." Led by white middle-class participants in the civil rights and antiwar movements, the mass concern for clean air, clean water, and biologically degradable products captured headlines not only in the alternative press but in *Time, Newsweek,* and the *Washington Post*. The sense of guilt and anxiety generated by the civil rights movement and the war in Vietnam gave the crusade for environmental purity an almost hysterical quality. Activists began confronting local companies that polluted the air. Approximately 800 environmentalists burst into the boardroom of Commonwealth Edison Power Company in Chicago and demanded that the board cut sulfur emissions and electricity rates. Northwestern students staged an environmental teach-in that attracted 10,000. In April 1970, the first Earth Day was held. Congress adjourned for the day, and 10 million schoolchildren participated in events to mark the occasion. "It was Earth Day," reported the *New York Times*, "and like Mother's Day, no man in public office could be against it."

One of the reasons that the ecology movement gained the notice and popularity that it did was that it incorporated the antimaterialist and anti–Western Civilization ethos of the counterculture. In 1970, Charles Reich published *The Greening of America*, which was nothing less than a refurbishing of the transcendentalist notions of Ralph Waldo Emerson and Henry David Thoreau. Reich, a member of the Yale Law School faculty and a former clerk to the backpacking Supreme Court Justice William O. Douglas, divided America into money-grubbing corporate exploiters and mindless consumers on the one hand and spiritually fulfilled, selfless nature lovers on the other. He bemoaned the mechanized exploitation of the wilderness and insisted that in destroying nature America was destroying its link with humanity, higher reason, and the cosmos. Even the Sierra Club and its upper-class, well-heeled members abandoned its traditional, practical conservationism for the mystical, semireligious approach to environmentalism put forward by Reich.

In fact, many leaders of the new environmental movement were veterans of the civil rights and antiwar struggles. As such, they were deeply distrustful of the corporate power structure. Their probes into the sources of environmental pollution only made them more so. Beginning in 1965 with the publication of Ralph Nader's *Unsafe at Any Speed*, environmentalists embarked on a crusade against unchecked corporate power. Nader, a Harvard Law School graduate, demonstrated that the giant auto makers had established monopolistic conditions that allowed them to engage in superficial competition over model styles, while manufacturing automobiles that rendered their passengers vulnerable to serious injury at even the lowest-speed crashes. In 1966, partially in response to Nader's revelations, Congress enacted the National Traffic and Motor Vehicle Safety Act. The one-man public interest lobby then turned to a new topic. "Air pollution," Nader subsequently wrote, "is a new way of looking at an old American problem, concentrated and irresponsible corporate power." A believer in the Goldwater aphorism that "extremism in the pursuit of virtue is no vice," Nader and his team of consumer advocates badgered and berated corporate America for the next quarter of a century, launching one crusade after another in an effort to persuade the federal government to force corporations to respect consumers and the environment alike. "Nader's Raiders" lobbied against a variety of products, from insecticides to asbestos insulation to lead paint to sharp-pointed toys, and a host of other products they considered dangerous to the public's health.

Indeed, as the 1970s wore on, many Americans came to see corporate America as a direct as well as an indirect threat to the nation's physical well-being. In 1971, Congress passed the National Cancer Act in full expectation that millions of dollars in federal research funds would lead to eradication of the dreaded disease within the decade. Instead, the incidence of cancer for all groups increased alarmingly during the next 5 years. The National Cancer Institute had assumed initially that virulent carcinogens were the main cause of the disease, but evidence pointed increasingly to environmental pollutants as the culprits. Some enterprises acted voluntarily to eliminate dangerous substances from the world's supply of food, water, and air, but most were resistant. In 1974, evidence came to light that the Manufacturers' Chemists Association had withheld evidence for 2 years that vinyl chloride, a plastic used in bottling, was potentially cancer producing for workers involved in its manufacture. Tens of thousands of humans were thus exposed to a harmful carcinogen without their knowledge. For more than 40 years, asbestos manufacturers (asbestos was a basic fire retardant used in insulating houses and buildings) had denied the harmful effects of their product, despite evidence to the contrary. By the late 1970s, scientists and consumer advocates had developed reliable data showing that asbestos poisoning was producing at least 50,000 deaths per year. Such revelations, admitted Bendix president W. Michael Blumenthal, raised grave questions about the "moral standards or ethical behavior of the business world today."

Television and the Homogenization of America

The communications revolution that had begun with the appearance of the first televisions in the late 1940s had become a national phenomenon by 1960. Households without running water had televisions; families whose basic needs were continually in question had televisions; institutions from prisons to nursing homes to hospitals were sure to provide access to televisions. Academics, urban intellectuals, and the American intelligentsia in general blasted television programming in the 1960s and 1970s. They bemoaned the endless series of soap operas, westerns, variety shows, and sports programs and declared that "the tube" was turning America's youth into a mass of passive receptacles whose attention spans were so attenuated that they would not be able to function as independent adults. In fact, the majority of programming provided by the three major networks did consist of shows such as "I Love Lucy," "Wagon Train," "The $64,000 Question," "The Ed Sullivan Show," "General Hospital," and the NFL on CBS. Whether the critics liked it or not, television affected virtually every aspect of American life. Professional and college sports flourished as their audiences expanded from the thousands to the tens of millions, and television revenues made both big businesses. Politicians had to be adept at 30-second sound bites and televised news conferences. Governments could no longer keep the horrors of war from anxious homefronts; indeed, during the Vietnam conflict, television brought the fighting into American living rooms every night. Leaders of the civil rights movement used the medium to dramatize the plight of oppressed African Americans in the South and in the nation's inner cities. Daily visions of the affluent society presented in programming and commercials created a rising level of expectations among the disadvantaged, generating both hope and despair.

Television had its defenders as well as its critics. The medium broke down barriers between groups and cultures, and fostered a sense of community. Television provided company and comfort to the elderly and the infirm. News coverage and public service programming made education available to many whom could not otherwise have afforded it. Stimulated by a $150 million grant from the Ford Foundation, National Educational Television had become a major force in American culture and education by the 1970s. By 1980, more than 300 public television stations were operating in the United States. Vast television audiences watched the Kefauver crime hearings, the Senate Foreign Relations Committee hearings on Vietnam, and the Watergate hearings. Americans mourned the death of John F. Kennedy together and rejoiced in unison as American astronauts set foot on the moon in 1969. "Just as the printing press democratized learning," Daniel J. Boorstin observed, "so the television set has democratized experience."

Nor was all programming vacuous or superficial. Miniseries such as "Roots" and series such as "M*A*S*H" and "All in the Family" appealed to millions of Americans with a social conscience. Television was even able to make fun of itself. The most popular character of the 1976 television season was the title character in "Mary Hartman, Mary Hartman," a parody of daytime soap operas. Mary and her family were surrounded by hypocrites – a shyster lawyer who forged portions of a malpractice suit, an adulterous minister, and a brutally insensitive psychologist – and corroded by the banality of everyday life. "The hardest decision I have to make each day," observes Mary's exhibitionist grandfather, "is whether to play checkers in the park or go down to the Safeway and watch them unload melons."

The motion picture industry, which had boomed during the 1940s, was initially hard hit by television. During the 10-year period from 1948 through 1958, weekly movie attendance dropped by about 50%, and a large number of independent houses went out of business. Warner Brothers, Paramount, and the other big houses attempted to recoup their losses by producing expensive extravaganzas such as "Ben Hur," "Exodus," "The Ten Commandments," and "Cleopatra" and by making made-for-television movies. By the 1960s, the industry was on its feet again. "The Sound of Music" and "My Fair Lady" delighted music lovers, whereas Ian Fleming's James Bond thrillers attracted those with a taste for adventure and sex. "Z," "Midnight Cowboy," and "The Graduate" dealt with serious social and psychological themes, while Frederico Fellini produced a series of films that captivated American "art" audiences. With the liberalization of obscenity laws and changing mores, Hollywood became more explicit about sex. Harold Robbins's "The Dream Merchants," Jacqueline Susann's "Valley of the

Dolls," and Grace Metalious's "Peyton Place" were all turned into explicit movies. In fact, both liberals and conservatives came to bemoan the conspicuous place both sex and violence played in the films of the 1960s and 1970s. "Bonnie and Clyde," "A Clockwork Orange," and the films of Sam Peckinpah not only featured but also to an extent glorified gratuitous violence.

Music: From "Folk" to "Rock" and Beyond

Music historian Geoffrey Stokes, looking back over the 1960s, noted a distinction between rock and roll and the new form that superceded it – rock. "Black, white, folkish, psychedelic, bluesy . . . it was all rock," he observed; "and in a certain sense, the musical and social ways in which that paradox worked itself out in the 1960s is the story not only of a pop art form but of the generation that embraced it." By the late 1950s, rock and roll had become somewhat predictable; Elvis Presley was riding trends rather than setting them. The stage was set for the rise of regional innovations, the first being southern California surf music. Out of the suntanned, wave-riding subculture around Malibu came the twangy-guitar, melodic tunes of the Beach Boys. "Surf City" and "Surfin' U.S.A." promised "two girls for every boy" and tapped perfectly into the vacuous, upper middle-class youth culture of southern California.

Folk music, driven underground in the 1950s by McCarthyism (two members of the Weavers were investigated as communist sympathizers), was revived by three San Francisco Bay area college students who came on like surfers with brains. When "Tom Dooley" hit number one on the charts, the Kingston Trio was off and running. Suddenly, every college town had a coffee house. Hard-core folk enthusiasts detested Dave Guard, Bob Shane, and Nick Reynolds because they were collegiate rather than beatnik, funny rather than ideological. More authentically folk, that is, more political and beat, were Peter, Paul, and Mary and Joan Baez. A Boston University student in the late 1950s, Baez became a standard at Cambridge's Club 47; in 1961, her album "Joan Baez 2" sold 1 million copies. Baez stood in sharp contrast to folkdom's other female superstar, Mary Travers of Peter, Paul and Mary, a former acting student, blond, high energy, and charismatic. Baez, whose first big hit was the narrative ballad "Wildwood Flower," was plain looking, plain dressing, and rather stilted in performance. However, her pure soprano voice and traditional protest lyrics were stunning. In 1963, Baez began introducing Bob Dylan to her audiences.

Dylan seemed as unlikely a candidate for superstardom as Baez. Although his repertoire was almost exclusively folk, his style was neither traditional nor commercial. Dylan's voice was both harsh and nasal, the lyrics of his early tunes frequently obscure. But Dylan was ubiquitous and a fast learner. When Peter, Paul, and Mary's 1963 recording of Dylan's "Blowin' in the Wind" appeared on traditional southern rhythm and blues stations, it became the unofficial anthem of the civil rights movement, marking the alliance of folk music with the politics of protest and social justice.

Meanwhile, in the working-class seaport of Liverpool, England, a music revolution was in the making. In 1961, record producer Brian Epstein went to the Cavern Club to hear a group called the Beatles. Over the next few years, he helped transform John Lennon, Paul McCartney, George Harrison, and Ringo Star (who replaced Pete Best on drums) into England's leading rock-and-roll band. When early in 1963 the Beatles descended on the United States from Liverpool, the music scene in America changed forever. With their appearance on the "Ed Sullivan Show" in February, these English imports became the colossi of American popular music. Dubbed subsequently by one music critic as "the Mozarts of rock 'n' roll," over the next 10 years, the Beatles wrote and performed an amazing repertoire of songs from the simple but immensely popular "I Want To Hold Your Hand" to the more socially conscious and complex "Lady Madonna" to the LSD-inspired "Lucy in the Sky with Diamonds." In 1964, the group made its first film, "A Hard Day's Night." Despite a rudimentary plot posing the question, "Will the boys make it through a typical day of press conferences, fan pursuit, encounters with disapproving adults, manic playfulness, and occasional self-doubt in time to play a concert for their adoring fans?", historian and White House intellectual Arthur Schlesinger, Jr., gave it a glowing review in *Show* magazine. The group's writers, Lennon and McCartney, turned out some of the most original and enduring music that rock and roll was to produce. Working-class youths themselves, they extended and refined the blend of rhythm and blues, jazz, swing, and pure African music that Elvis Presley had synthesized in the 1950s. The Beatles attracted thousands of young female groupies because they were hip and sexy and, at the same time, pleased the critics because they created original music that was both witty and intelligent. "We're more popular than God," John Lennon remarked.

Stunned by the commercial success of the Beatles, record companies and booking agents rushed to sign rock performers who were long-haired, male, and English. Some of those who followed in the Beatles' wake were Freddie and the Dreamers, the Dave Clark Five, and the Rolling Stones. From 1964 to 1966, Dave Clark Five singles would make the American charts 18 times; seven singles, including "Over and Over," would reach the Top 10. The majority of the "first-wave" English music was pretty and melodic, but not all. In the summer of 1964, the Newcastle group the Animals, recorded "House of the Rising Sun," a long, raw rock ballad about a New Orleans brothel. The Animals opened the door for other hard rock groups.

Sensing that the Beatles, at least in image, were a bit too tame, producer Andre Oldham introduced the Rolling Stones to an American audience that preferred their rock a bit on the rough side. During their second American tour, the group cracked the Top 10 with "Time Is on My Side." They were snaggle-toothed, rough-featured, and slightly menacing. Mick Jagger snarled his way across the United States squeezing every sexual innuendo from his lyrics, while, to quote one music historian, Keith Richards appeared to be auditioning "for a role as the Big Bad Wolf." In 1967, after three of the Stones were convicted of drug possession in a British court, the group was barred from performing in the United States.

In the mid-1960s, rock began to diversify. Led by the Beatles' "Nowhere Man," the music industry produced a genre that could be described as folk rock. In 1966, Paul Simon and Art Garfunkel went to the top of the charts with "The Sound of Silence." The lyrics were private, introspective, and unsentimental: "Hello, darkness, my old friend.... A vision softly creeping ... The words of the prophet are written on the subway walls...." Simon, who wrote four more hit singles in the space of a year, including "I Am a Rock" and "Homeward Bound," was essentially a poet who sang and performed. At the same time, the success of Tommy James's "Hanky Panky" indicated that a portion of the record-buying public rejected rock's claims to high culture. Blue-collar ethnics, kids who would not go to college and who would go off to Vietnam, still preferred simple, rhythmic tunes that focused on romance and sex.

Motown

The British invasion temporarily threatened the gains made by black artists. During its pre–rock-and-roll period, the music industry had included a few African Americans popular with white audiences, such as Nat "King" Cole and the Mills brothers, but they were exceptions. The emergence of the new genre, however, based as it was on rhythm and blues, ended the isolation of black music from white. Black artists raised in gospel and rhythm and blues, such as Chuck Berry, Fats Domino, and Little Richard, delighted teens of all colors with hits such as "Long Tall Sally," "Blueberry Hill," and "Mabeline." In 1963, the last pre-Beatles year, 37 of the 106 Top 10 records were by blacks, including Sam Cooke, Marvin Gaye, and the Impressions. In the first year of the British invasion, however, only two records by African American artists made the Top 10. This set the stage for one of the postwar music scene's true geniuses.

Berry Gordy, Jr., was a member of a closely knit Detroit family that had migrated northward from Georgia for fear that its business success might attract the attention of the Ku Klux Klan. Gordy, a high school dropout who subsequently earned his equivalency degree in the Army, began in the music business as a retailer and songwriter. Soon, however, he put together the Motown group of labels and created one of America's great music business empires. Gordy bound his artists to him with complex contracts that tied their compensation to future production. He was loyal to them and expected loyalty in return. Motown stars did not have independent managers; they were represented by Gordy's International Talent Management, Inc. Motown became associated with a distinct sound and style. The Temptations, the Supremes, and Stevie Wonder created a rhythmic, precise music featuring bland lyrics and live performances famous for their exaggerated choreography and glittering costumes. In July 1964, the Supremes, whose arrangements set Ross's compelling, breathy voice against the crackling Motown cadences, started an incredible streak of five number one hits in a row.

Acid Rock

As the drug scene came to dominate the counterculture, bands such as San Francisco's the Grateful Dead and Jefferson Airplane (as well as the Beatles) produced and encouraged hallucinogenic, psychedelic music. Some of the drug culture music was mellow and melodic, if lyrically unreal, while another strain, "acid rock," was a dizzying, deafening swirl of sound. Jimi Hendrix typified the acid rock genre. Born into a middle-class family in Seattle in 1942, he began playing the guitar as a child. While working backup on "the chitlin circuit" – venues featuring black artists performing before black audiences – he began experimenting with fuzz tone and feedback on his electric guitar. Hendrix was the first to take the instrument and the studio's electronic possibilities and make them into music, music that was raucous and discordant but at the same time fluid, flexible, and melodic. His innovative first album, "Are You Experienced," sold 500,000 copies, reaching number five on the *Billboard* chart.

Disco

The narcissism of the 1970s produced its own form of music – disco. Rhythmic and glitzy, disco music was made for dancing and featured at night clubs that bore the name of the genre. The disco beat spawned a $4 billion-per-year industry, including records and tapes, dance costumes, and more than 200 specialized radio stations. Embedded in the disco milieu was a pervasive demand that its denizens conform to social convention. Disco guidebooks contained not only complicated dance steps, but also instructions on how to dress, how to comport oneself, and how to gain entrance into the most expensive clubs. Young people caught up in the materialism of the 1970s found this type of expensive conformity appealing. The ultimate disco movie was "Saturday Night Fever," which featured a young ethnic played by John Travolta who made the disco scene and embraced conventional middle-class values as a way to move up from his working-class neighborhood in Brooklyn to a new life in Manhattan.

High Culture

The affluence of the 1960s stimulated a revival in American performing and creative art. Private expenditures on symphony orchestras, art galleries, ballet troupes, and community theater increased geometrically. As the number of college graduates and per capita income for the middle and upper classes increased, the United States became a hotbed of artistic activity. Both the Kennedy and Johnson administrations actively promoted the arts and high culture. In the 1960s, public monies built the Lincoln Center for the Performing Arts in New York City and the music center pavilion in Los Angeles. To the delight of Senator J. William Fulbright, who had sponsored the legislation creating a national cultural center and spearheaded the fund-raising effort, the Kennedy Center for the Performing Arts opened in 1971. The National Arts and Humanities Act passed by Congress in 1965 provided millions of dollars in grants for innovators in the creative and performing arts.

The area of artistic endeavor in which Americans had the greatest impact was painting. Fueled by private and public funds, American artists moved away from the realism and social consciousness of the 1930s, which had featured regional art and the social themes of the Works Progress Administration (WPA) artists' project, to abstractionism and abstract expressionism in the 1960s and 1970s. Even the realist Andrew Wyeth, America's most popular postwar artist, referred to his landscapes, still lifes, and portraits as abstractionist. Although representational, his art evoked strong feeling and created new perspectives, centering as it did on universal themes of loneliness, sexuality, and the relationship between nature and humankind.

Abstract expressionists such as Jackson Pollock, Mark Rothko, and Willem de Kooning rejected representational and decorative approaches altogether. Their overriding objective was to create mood or feeling rather than the image of a figure as it actually existed or even as it was filtered through the imagination. The thing to be transmitted was the feeling at the time the paint hit the canvas. Pollock's canvasses were huge expanses of painting surface that he stretched on the floor and actually walked on as he splashed, dropped, or spread huge globs of paint amid delicate webs and indefinite planes applied more deliberately. His *Blue Poles* and de Kooning's series, *The Women*, were noteworthy for their vivid colors, while Pollock's *Echo* reminded viewers of Picasso taken to another level of abstraction. Traditionalists deplored the chaotic, discordant productions of the abstractionists and the artistically uninitiated simply refused to come to grips with them. Over time, however, the art world came to appreciate abstract expressionism as an authentic reaction to a world under constant threat of nuclear annihilation and a consumer culture that sought to raise materialism to the level of religion.

While the abstractionists participated in their art, another genre, "pop art," competed for the condemnation of traditionalists. Robert Rauschenberg, Andy Warhol, and other originators of the form painted prepared food cans, arranged worn out auto parts in sprawling sculptures, and in general portrayed the detritus of contemporary culture in a variety of interesting ways. Although critics decried their work as visually and thematically barren, the creations of the postwar pop artists contained an element of social realism and sought to make a statement about the deteriorating environment. Similar to the abstract expressionists, they saw value in the very controversy that they provoked.

Literature and American Society

The American literary tradition of portraying middle-class foibles begun by Sinclair Lewis was carried on by John Gould Cozzens, John Cheever, and John Updike. Cozzens's *By Love Possessed* (1957), which depicted two days in the life of a middle-aged lawyer, was declared the novel of the year. In *The Wapshot Chronicle* (1957), *The Wapshot Scandal* (1964), and *Bullet Park* (1969), John Cheever peeled back the layers of conventional life to reveal the enduring power of sexual lust, personal insecurity, ambition, and the psychological unconscious. His characters wandered the suburbs of New York City and Connecticut compromised, confused, and repressed. It was Cheever who coined the term "upwardly dispossessed" to refer to a material success that had seemingly removed its beneficiaries from all that was essential in life. John Updike's trilogy *Rabbit, Run* (1960), *Rabbit Redux* (1971), and *Rabbit Is Rich* (1981) focused on the life of former high school athlete and car dealer Harry "Rabbit" Angstrom. His nickname was an obvious play on Lewis's character George F. Babbitt. Rabbit was alternately bored and contented with his moderately attractive, relentlessly normal wife and continually at war with a son who appeared determined to reject the middle-class values to which his father aspired. The protagonist was caught between the reality of a typical marriage, a successful car dealership, and a country club social routine and a fantasy world in which his deeper emotional and psychological needs were met.

Books by African Americans about the black experience were a conspicuous feature of postwar American literature. Ralph Ellison's *The Invisible Man* (1952) is generally regarded as one of the most important works of the twentieth century. Although published in the 1950s, it came to prominence during the turbulent decade that followed. Set during the period of the great migration of southern blacks to northern urban centers during the second quarter of the twentieth century, *The Invisible Man* is the story of a young African American's physical journey from southern cotton fields to college to urban ghetto, as well as his emotional journey from innocence to bitter disillusionment as he encountered America's pervasive caste system. As the title implies, Ellison used the motif of invisibility to depict the dehumanizing effects of white supremacy. Toni Morrison's *Song of Solomon* (1978) and Alice Walker's *The Color Purple* (1982) portrayed the dynamics of black families struggling to survive in a racist world. Among their most memorable characters were black women caught in a double bind of racism and sexism as they raised families and fostered enduring relationships. Perhaps the most visible literary figure of the 1960s was James Baldwin, a man who combined fine literary skills with political activism. His *Go Tell It on the Mountain* (1953), a novel of the great black migration, prefigured Ellison's work. *The Fire Next Time* (1963) was an updated version of W. E. B. Dubois' *The Souls of Black Folk*, a montage of autobiography, social anthropology, anecdotes, and protest literature. Through it ran a subtle message: if white society did not resolve the dilemma of discrimination and segregation in the midst of a democracy peacefully, it would be resolved violently.

Above all, the novels of the postwar era were characterized by the presence of the antihero. In a sense, J. D. Salinger's *The Catcher in the Rye* (1951) started the trend. Holden Caulfield, an insecure, acne-ridden young student, was a not-unsympathetic character, but his search for identity and his self-absorption frequently left readers irritated and ambiguous. In 1955, a Russian émigré, Vladimir Nabokov, published *Lolita*, a tale of pathos and sexual obsession featuring a seedy, lecherous academic and his sexy, adolescent traveling companion. Katherine Anne Porter's *Ship of Fools* (1962), a novel 20 years in the writing, was set aboard a transatlantic luxury liner on the eve of World War II. The cast was a seething mass of prejudices, pretensions, and perversions. One of the most famous of the era's tarnished central characters was Yossarian in Joseph Heller's *Catch-22* (1960), an antiwar novel full of farce and black humor. The protagonist in Ken Kesey's *One Flew Over the Cuckoo's Nest* (1962) was an antisocial inmate of an insane asylum who led a wrenching and unsuccessful rebellion against institutional paternalism and conformity. The narrator was a deranged Native American who eventually met a violent end. In *Giles Goat-Boy* (1966), John Barth satirized the human condition by creating a central character who was the offspring of a woman and a computer. Truman Capote's heroes in *In Cold Blood* (1966) were two mass murderers caught in a system of criminal justice that refused to recognize that they were victims in the same sense, if not in the same degree, as the people they killed. Similar to Mailer's *The Executioner's Song* (1979), it was a compelling indictment of capital punishment.

Capote and Mailer typified the contemporary literary artist who was obsessed with man's inhumanity to man and transfixed by the ever more prominent role of violence in modern society. Dee Brown's 1971 novel, *Bury My Heart at Wounded Knee*, portrayed the virtual destruction of Native American life and culture in the Midwest between 1860 and 1890.

Kurt Vonnegut's *Slaughterhouse-Five* (1969) was a surrealistic tale centered on the Allied bombing of Dresden during World War II. In 1977, the first of a series of troubling books focusing on the Vietnam battle experience appeared. Philip Caputo's *Rumor of War* was a personalized account of a combat soldier's encounter with America's longest and most unsuccessful war.

A notable feature of the literary scene in the 1960s and 1970s was a burst of creative activity by southern writers, both old and new. William Faulkner and Robert Penn Warren continued to contribute as did Eudora Welty and Carson McCullers. One of the most striking of the newcomers was William Styron. His *Lie Down in Darkness* (1951) depicted the corrosive relationship between a father and daughter set in a small southern town. *Nat Turner's Rebellion* (1967) was a fictionalized account of the 1831 slave rebellion and its charismatic, tortured leader. Walker Percy in *Love Among the Ruins* (1971), *The Second Coming* (1980), and other works explored the folkways of the contemporary South and their intersection with larger social issues and cultural trends through a sensitive southern physician. Flannery O'Connor in *Wise Blood* (1952) and *The Violent Bear It Away* (1960) continued the tradition of southern gothic begun by Faulkner. This devout Catholic, whose career was cut short by premature death, specialized in tragicomic allegories on humanity's fall and redemption. In 1961, Harper Lee won a Pulitzer Prize for *To Kill a Mockingbird*, which told the story of a white southern lawyer who chose to defend a black man charged with raping a white woman. The twin motifs of southern civility and sensitivity on the one hand and madness and cruelty on the other hand made the book one of the most memorable of the postwar period.

Summary

As a multicultural democracy, America has always been a land of contrast and paradox. The centrifugal forces in a land so vast with so many different ethnic and cultural heritages have been great. At no time was this truer than during the 20 years following John F. Kennedy's election to the presidency. The task of preserving a republican form of government while acting as the world's leading noncommunist superpower proved taxing to the nation's institutions and values. Nevertheless, America seemed equal to the task. Politics, popular culture, foreign affairs, and economics seemed to come together during the Kennedy–Johnson years as the United States prepared to defend the peoples of the Third World from the scourge of international communism and lift its own disadvantaged out of the morass of poverty, discrimination, and sexism. Keynesian economics would pay for it all.

Then, however, Americans were reminded of the Niebuhrian maxim that all human institutions are corrupt, all intentions flawed, and that what man would perfect, he would destroy. The crusade in Vietnam went sour as Americans discovered that the country they would preserve and defend did not really exist. At home, rising levels of expectations among black Americans led to extremism and in turn to a white backlash. The Great Society programs promised not only justice and equality but also minimal prosperity for all. In many cases, they proved to be far too limited to achieve their objectives and, in a few cases, they turned out to be positively counterproductive to those objectives. As it had so often in the past, America turned to traditional values and processes in an effort to find its center. In 1968, the nation elected a moderate conservative, but he proved to be the antithesis of the political philosophy he espoused. When Richard M. Nixon proved to be not a constitutional strict constructionist but a constitutional deconstructionist, the sovereign people turned their back on politics and political life in disgust.

The economy seemed to mirror and reinforce the course of political and diplomatic history. Americans experienced unparalleled affluence in the 1960s, but by the 1970s the economy had entered a period of slow but apparently irreversible decline. Confronted with the inexplicable phenomenon of stagflation, members of the middle and upper class concluded that material existence would be worse and not better for their children. For the chronically poor who lived in America's inner cities, in the rural South, and in Appalachia, poverty became increasingly institutionalized and hence inescapable.

But Americans coped as they have always coped, and there were bright spots. Despite, or perhaps because of, the divisions of the 1960s, the United States was more democratic in 1980 than it had ever been. Women began to define their roles in society and borrow techniques from the antiwar and civil rights movements, organizing to realize their objectives. Black Power and white backlash aside, the second reconstruction moved ahead inexorably, and African Americans entered the middle class, exercised the right to vote, and penetrated the white power structure. Energized by the culture of protest that sprang up in the 1960s, other traditionally oppressed and exploited minority groups mobilized to arouse the majority's conscience and to share in the fruits of American society. The movement within these groups for cultural self-realization and autonomy was, as it had been in the past, a sign of the vigor and success of their campaigns for liberation and equality.

By the 1970s, Americans were challenging the military–industrial complex for control not only of foreign policy but also of the environment. At the same time that Congress passed the War Powers Act, it responded to pressure from environmentalists by enacting measures to clean up the nation's air and water, preserve its forests and deserts, and limit corporate America's freedom to pollute. Environmentalism was one of the great rallying points of the 1970s because it attracted both conservatives and liberals. It was also one of the most divisive issues of the 1970s because it offended liberals and conservatives. Virtually all Americans agreed on the value of a clean, toxic-free environment, but traditionalists worried about the encroachment of state power on the private sector and liberals feared that environmental restrictions would cripple the economy, denying tax monies to the state and jobs to the poor.

As always, popular and high culture reflected the materialism and idealism, the profundity and superficiality of society as a whole. On the music scene, rock and roll was pervasive from the British invasion to folk rock to hard rock to disco. To some extent changing lyrics reflected first the idealism and culture of protest that characterized the 1960s and then the disillusionment and apolitical nature of the 1970s, but for the most part, artists and their songs focused on the eternal themes of love, sex, loneliness, and joy. As it had in the 1950s, television and the movies offered escape for the frustrated and disappointed and inspiration for the involved and socially conscious – "M*A*S*H" and "All in the Family" on the one hand and "Three's Company" and "Charlie's Angels" on the other hand. Harlequin romances, formulaic potboilers featuring simplistic plots, handsome heroes, evil villains, beautiful heroines, and a lot of sex, sold millions, but so did the sophisticated social satire of John Updike and John Cheever, as well as the social protest novels of James Baldwin and Toni Morrison.

It was then a time like all times, full of idealism and cynicism, tastelessness and authenticity, heroism and cowardice, confidence and uncertainty, and beauty and astonishing ugliness. Despite its flaws and rigidities, its injustices and callowness, American society continued during the 1960s and 1970s to seethe with life, opportunity, and hope.

ADDITIONAL READINGS

Chafe, William H., *Women and Equality: Changing Patterns in American Culture* (1977).

Degler, Carl N., *At Odds: Women and the Family in America From the Revolution To the Present* (1980).

Echols, Alice, *Daring to Be Bad: Radical Feminism in America*, 1967–1975 (1989).

Gitlin, Todd, *The Sixties: Years of Hope, Days of Rage* (1987).

Isserman, Maurice, *If I Had a Hammer: The Death of the Old Left and the Birth of the New Left* (1987).

Jackson, Kenneth, *Crabgrass Frontier: The Suburbanization of the United States* (1985).

Kazin, Alfred, *Bright Book of Life: American Novelists and Storytellers From Hemingway To Mailer* (1973).

Lemann, Nicholas, *The Promised Land: The Great Black Migration and How It Changed America* (1991).

Marty, Martin E., *Pilgrims in Their Own Land* (1984).

May, Elaine T., *Homeward Bound: American Families in the Cold War Era* (1988).

Melosi, Martin V., *Coping with Abundance: Energy and Environment in Industrial America* (1985).

Miller, James, *"Democracy Is in the Streets": From Port Huron To the Siege of Chicago* (1987).

Murray, Charles, *Losing Ground: American Social Policy, 1950–1980* (1986).

Ravitch, Diane, *The Troubled Crusade: American Education, 1945–1980* (1983).

Reich, Charles, *The Greening of America* (1970).

Sitkoff, Harvard, *The Struggle for Black Equality, 1954–1981*, rev. ed. (1993).

Wilkinson, J. Harvie, *From Brown To Bakke: The Supreme Court and School Integration, 1954–1978* (1980).

12   Governing in a Malaise

The Presidencies of Gerald R. Ford and Jimmy Carter

America's ignominious withdrawal from Vietnam and the Watergate scandal created a crisis of confidence in national politics unknown since the Great Depression. The Second Indo-Chinese War brought home to Americans the truth that severe limitations existed on their nation's ability to determine the course of global events. Not only did it appear that the forces of international communism had scored a clear-cut victory, but also that in the process of defending its perceived interests, the United States had transgressed many of the values and principles for which it claimed to be fighting. The collapse of the Government of Vietnam (GVN) in 1975 left America exhausted and divided; hawks, doves, and all those in between felt betrayed and contaminated.

Americans' sense that they had been lied to and deliberately deceived during crucial periods in the Vietnam War created an attitude of deep cynicism toward government at all levels, but particularly the federal government. In the wake of the Watergate scandal, this cynicism became pervasive and acute. The president of the United States and his aides had participated in a criminal conspiracy and then obstructed justice by covering it up. Nixon had, moreover, corrupted other government agencies – the FBI, for example – and flaunted the Constitution. Although Nixon's success was only temporary, the average American's confidence in the political system and the institutions that anchored it was shaken to the core.

To make matters worse, the economic situation continued to deteriorate in the mid-1970s. The cost of living increased 7% in 1973 and skyrocketed to 11% the following year. In 1974, the gross national product (GNP) actually declined. Budget and trade deficits continued to fuel stagflation, and the culture of poverty flourished. Some Americans began to wonder if perhaps their faith in capitalism and regulated private enterprise had been misplaced. Increasingly, the political system seemed irrelevant to the nation's pressing social problems. The welfare system, no matter how well intentioned, was not doing its job. The authentically poor were falling through the cracks while "welfare cheats" and unscrupulous caregivers were ripping off the system. Following a bloody uprising at Attica in 1971, pundits, politicians, and people on the street began to question the efficacy of the judicial and penal system. Racial tensions subsided somewhat, but the civil rights movement foundered in the backlash against urban rioting, busing, and the Black Power movement. Desegregation of the nation's school systems slowed to a snail's pace, and African Americans suffered disproportionately from inflation and joblessness.

The Interim President

This was the situation that greeted President Gerald R. Ford when he took the Oath of Office on August 9, 1974. A midwesterner through and through, Ford was born in Omaha, Nebraska, on July 14, 1913, and grew up in Grand Rapids, Michigan. He attended the University of Michigan at Ann Arbor, where he started as a center for the varsity football team. After working his way through Yale Law School, Ford served in the U.S. Navy during World War II. First elected to Congress in 1948, he soon earned a reputation as a party loyalist and a conscientious if unimaginative congressman. His self-professed model was Senator Arthur H. Vandenberg; appropriately, in foreign policy matters, Ford was a cold warrior who was more an interventionist than an internationalist. That is, similar to other conservative Republicans, he distrusted the United Nations and other collective security organizations, believing that the United States could best secure its interests and those of the free world by acting unilaterally. "I am a Ford, not a Lincoln," the self-effacing congressman announced when Nixon selected him to be vice president and, in fact, up to that point the Michigan congressman's greatest ambition was to be speaker of the House of Representatives. He was an affable, open, unpretentious man, a breath of fresh air following the conspiratorial, neurotic Nixon. However, his political honeymoon with the American people was short lived.

On September 8, 1974, President Ford granted Richard M. Nixon a full pardon. Ford declared that his intention was to put the national nightmare of Watergate to rest, but his act was more than symbolic. Nixon was sure to be indicted on criminal charges for obstructing justice. Americans were appalled. A large number of the former president's aides were then serving or about to serve prison sentences for their role in obstructing justice. Was the presidency above the law? Ford added fuel to the flames subsequently by decreeing that the White House tapes and Nixon's presidential papers belonged to the former president and did not have to be turned over to the National Archives. Congress subsequently overturned that order by passing legislation superseding it. From that point on, Ford was contaminated by Watergate. His approval rate plummeted to 50% and declined steadily thereafter. The voters showed their disapproval in the 1974 midterms when nearly 60% of the voting population cast their ballots for Democrats.

In domestic affairs, Ford proved himself to be as thoroughly conservative as Nixon if not as mean spirited. He was committed to the traditional Republican virtues of free, unregulated enterprise, a balanced budget, and a reduced role for the federal government. The former Michigan congressman was, moreover, an outspoken opponent of busing to achieve racial balance, and, in fact, toward the end of his term the U.S. Civil Rights Commission declared that, by its lax enforcement of school desegregation decrees and open housing regulations, the Ford administration had actively contributed to the process of resegregation.

Ford's reaction to the worsening economic situation – increasing unemployment, rising inflation, and acute energy shortages – was almost Hooverian in its passivity. The administration reacted to the inflationary crisis with a typically Republican campaign of voluntarism. Wearing a Whip Inflation Now (WIN) button, the president called on management and labor to discipline themselves by holding wages and prices to their prevailing levels. At the same time, Ford pressured the Federal Reserve Board not to cut interest rates, and he promised a tax increase as part of an ongoing effort to balance the budget.

The Democratic Congress reacted to the economic crisis just as typically as Ford had, namely, by pushing for lower interest rates, a tax cut (particularly on lower and middle incomes), and increased spending for welfare and job programs. During his two years in office, Ford vetoed more that 40 bills, including those for health care and federal aid to education. By mid-1975, the president was fast becoming an object of public derision. On the popular television program "Saturday Night Live," comedian Chevy Chase portrayed Ford as a bumbling, simple-minded, ex-football player and elicited gales of laughter mimicking the president's frequent physical miscues – he stumbled and hit his head entering the presidential helicopter, for example, and he splayed a golf tee shot so severely that it struck a woman spectator in the head. The image of Ford as lacking the basic intellectual skills to govern became pervasive.

Despite his vetoes, Ford recognized eventually that the recession of 1975 required positive action. Reluctantly, he agreed to a tax cut and a modest increase in federal spending. This coupled with the determination of the activist 94th Congress produced some significant legislation. In addition to extending the Voting Rights Act of 1965 for another 10 years, the Democratic majorities enacted a $4 million public works measure to help blunt the effect of unemployment. The following year, Congress passed a tax bill that extended the personal and corporate income tax cuts it had made in 1975. However, the executive and legislative branches failed to come to terms in regard to a long-range energy policy, and the Energy Policy and

Conservation Act of 1975 merely continued price controls and kept in place machinery for allocation of domestically produced oil.

Denouement in Vietnam

Meanwhile, Ford was forced to preside over the final denouement of the Vietnam War. The cease-fire concluded in January 1973 ended almost before the ink could dry on the document. The government of Nguyen Van Thieu, banking on continuing support from the United States, launched an offensive against the National Liberation Front. Thieu had sadly miscalculated. Even the most bellicose members of Congress were sick of the conflict and were determined to do nothing to reinsert the United States into the "quagmire" of Southeast Asia. In the fall of 1974, Congress halved Secretary of State Kissinger's $1.5 billion aid request for the GVN. Early in 1975, the North Vietnamese Army (NVA) decided that the time had arrived for the final offensive. When several divisions of North Vietnamese regulars overran government positions in the Central Highlands, Thieu's troops fled in panic leaving their weapons behind. As Army of the Republic of Vietnam (ARVN) troops fought with panicked refugees for control of the roads, the communist offensive turned into a juggernaut.

By mid-April, it was clear that the end was near. President Ford made a halfhearted and unsuccessful effort to wring last-minute aid out of Congress and then ordered plans for evacuation of American personnel and "essential" Vietnamese to be implemented. As the public watched in horror, a giant transport carrying Vietnamese orphans to new homes in the United States crashed. The tragic end of "Operation Babylift" seemed to many to be a metaphor for America's disastrously misplaced idealism in Vietnam. On April 29, the last U.S. helicopter lifted off the roof of the American Embassy. The team in charge of evacuation had managed to take 150,000 Vietnamese officers, civilian officials, and other assorted supporters, but they had to leave hundreds of thousands more behind. The next day the remnant of the Thieu government surrendered to the NVA commander who immediately renamed Saigon Ho Chi Minh City. In the United States, an eerie calm prevailed in the months following the last battle. Although 56,000 died and another 270,000 were wounded, Americans wanted desperately to forget their longest and least successful war.

At the same time that the NVA was advancing on Saigon, the Khmer Rouge closed in on the Lon Nol regime penned up in the Cambodian capital of Phnom Penh. With the collapse of that government and the subsequent triumph of the Pathet Lao in Laos, the validity of the domino theory seemed to have been borne out. But that justification for the Indo-Chinese War had been based on the notion of a monolithic communist threat. If there was ever a doubt concerning the validity of that notion, it was dispelled in 1978 when troops from Communist Vietnam invaded Cambodia and went to war with the Khmer Rouge.

In 1975, President Ford managed to revive the spirits of American nationalists with an apparently decisive military action against the new Cambodian government. In May, the Khmer Rouge seized an American merchant vessel, the *SS Mayaguez*, in the Gulf of Siam, claiming that it had violated Cambodia's territorial waters. Without waiting for an investigation and unaware that the Cambodian government had already released the 39 Americans aboard, Ford denounced the seizure as an act of piracy and ordered U.S. Marines into a group of islands off Cambodia's coast where it was suspected the *Mayaguez* was being held. U.S. planes bombed an airbase and petroleum facility, and the U.S. Navy sank three Cambodian gunboats. The United States suffered 41 killed in action, but most Americans hailed the operation and chose to believe Ford's claim that his timely action had saved both the *Mayaguez* and its men.

Republican Détente Continued

Ford and Kissinger were committed to forging détente with the Soviet Union, but they were severely constrained by conservatives' insistence that any framework they negotiated maintain U.S. military superiority and force concessions from the Soviets on human rights. The 1972 SALT I accord had called on its signatories to conclude a comprehensive arms limitation treaty by 1977. In the fall of 1974, Ford met with Soviet President Leonid Brezhnev in the Siberian city of Vladivostok. They signed a preliminary and very modest agreement that established a ceiling of 2,400 delivery vehicles with no more than 1,320 to be armed with multiple warheads. Even that framework was unacceptable to American hawks like Senator Henry M. Jackson of Washington, who, in preparation for his run for the presidency in 1976, blasted Kissinger for considering an agreement that tolerated Soviet superiority in land-based intercontinental ballistic missiles (ICBMs) (the United States continued to enjoy a wide lead in submarine-launched missiles and bombers) and for not pressuring Moscow over human rights. The Kremlin regarded efforts by the U.S. government to link arms control with better treatment of political dissidents and Jews as meddling in its internal affairs, and, as a result, Soviet resistance to concessions stiffened.

In 1975, Ford further angered anticommunist hard-liners in the United States when he refused to meet with prominent Soviet dissident Aleksandr Solzhenitsyn, an exiled Soviet writer who had been stripped of his Soviet citizenship after his work criticizing the Soviet police state won a Nobel Prize. When Ford journeyed to Helsinki, Finland, in July 1975 to attend the Conference on Security and Cooperation in Europe, conservatives at home urged him to confront the Soviets over human rights. He proved responsive and so, to a degree, did the Soviets. In the Helsinki accords, the United States and its allies recognized the boundaries of Eastern Europe as they had been established at the end of World War II, and in return, the Soviet Union acceded to a declaration of human rights that endorsed freedom of migration, expression, and religion. Jackson and his cohorts chose to ignore the latter achievement and blasted the Ford administration for acquiescing in the permanent communization of Eastern Europe.

In the fall of 1975, President Ford survived two attempts on his life. Lynette "Squeaky" Frome – a member of the notorious Charles Manson cult, which had slaughtered actress Sharon Tate and her guests in her Malibu home in 1970 – fired at the president in September. Only weeks later, Sara Jane Moore, a deranged figure who had been at the fringes of the Patty Hearst case (the newspaper heiress who had been captured and then converted by a black nationalist organization, the Symbionese Liberation Army), also discharged a pistol at the president. Usually threats to the life of a chief executive caused the American people to rally to his side. However, the average person seemed hardly to notice the assaults on Ford. Critics declared that this indifference stemmed from the fact that they had never recognized him as a man of presidential stature.

The Election of 1976

Ford had antagonized the right wing of his own party by signing the preliminary SALT II accords and, in the fall of 1975, by firing his hawkish secretary of defense, James Schlesinger. When his wife Betty, whom had won wide respect for her poise and grace as first lady, hailed the Supreme Court's decision legalizing abortion as "a great, great decision," irate right-wing Republicans screamed for blood. *Manchester Union-Leader* editor William Loeb, Edmund Muskie's old bête noire, called for the president to repudiate his wife's statement and termed Ford gutless when he would not.

Smelling blood, conservative California Governor Ronald Reagan declared his candidacy for the Republican nomination in November 1975. He accused Ford of selling out to the powerbrokers and special interests in the U.S. government and losing touch with the average Republican. Recapitulating the political philosophy that he had developed during his 20-year transformation from liberal Democrat to conservative Republican, he declared his opposition to an activist federal government, extension of Social Security, abortion, busing, détente with the Soviet Union, and to social "permissiveness" in general. Reagan advocated lower taxes, less government, prayer in the schools, and an aggressive foreign policy that would demonstrate to the Soviets that, Vietnam aside, America had not lost its nerve. The California governor struck a responsive chord with many Americans by criticizing the ongoing effort dating from the Johnson administration to negotiate a new canal treaty with Panama. In the wake of Vietnam, the canal had become a symbol of U.S. national sovereignty.

Although Reagan defeated Ford in a series of western and southern primaries, the president, relying on established party machines in the midwest and northeast states and on the argument that it was suicidal for the GOP to repudiate a sitting president, won a narrow victory at the Republican National Convention in Kansas City. In other ways, however, the convention was a triumph for the Reagan wing of the party. Ford was forced to dump Nelson Rockefeller as his vice presidential running mate for the ultrapartisan Senator Robert Dole of Kansas. He rejected the framework he had agreed to at Vladivostok for a SALT II treaty, and he announced he was suspending negotiations on a canal treaty. The platform endorsed constitutional amendments providing for prayer in the schools and prohibiting abortion. The GOP did declare its support for the Equal Rights Amendment, a position it had taken consistently since 1940.

In the aftermath of Watergate and their sweeping victory in the 1974 midterms, the Democrats looked forward to the 1976 presidential election with great anticipation. Not surprisingly, a number of aspirants stepped forward to offer themselves to the voters. The early frontrunner was Senator Edward M. Kennedy, but, citing personal reasons, he removed himself from consideration in 1974. The field that subsequently developed included Senator Henry M. Jackson of Washington, Congressman Morris K. Udall of Arizona, Governor George C. Wallace of Alabama, and Governor James Earl Carter of Georgia. No one gave Carter, a one-term governor, much of a chance, but he surprised the experts by winning the New Hampshire primary. The Georgian had traveled the United States for the Democratic National Committee in 1974 making important contacts. A deeply religious person with a warm smile and self-effacing manner, Carter seemed an antidote to the sordidness of Watergate, an individual of traditional values who could restore the nation's trust in its institutions and political processes. Having established himself in New Hampshire, Carter went on to defeat Wallace in the important Florida primary. Dismayed by Carter's outspoken support of a balanced budget and his opposition to busing, liberals persuaded Senator Frank Church of Idaho to enter the race. Church made little headway, but California Governor Jerry Brown, another late entry, slowed Carter's momentum. Despite his personal philosophy – a blend of Catholicism and Zen Buddhism – some Democrats considered Brown's brand of populism to be more sophisticated than Carter's. Although the Georgian won no more primaries outside the South, he continued to accumulate delegates and entered the Democratic National Convention in New York with an insurmountable lead. The Georgian was duly nominated on the first ballot. To give the Democratic ticket ideological and geographical balance, Carter chose Minnesota Senator Walter Mondale, a traditional liberal, as his running mate.

When the 1976 campaign began, Carter enjoyed a seemingly insurmountable 62% to 29% advantage in the polls, but he soon saw his lead melt away. The Democratic candidate's southernness, his born-again Baptist faith, and his outsider image appealed to some Americans but not to others. Urban, suburban, and northern dwellers became increasingly put off by the "bubba" image that the Republicans succeeded in casting on the Democratic nominee, and the bland, Episcopalian Ford became by contrast increasingly attractive. Carter's eccentric family caused unease in an America seeking in that bicentennial year to once again get comfortable with itself. His mother, "Miss Lillian," had served in the Peace Corps in India after raising her family. The Democratic candidate's sister, Ruth Carter Stapleton, was a traveling evangelist, while brother Billy was an aggressive, working-class filling station owner who eventually succeeded in having a new brand of beer named for himself. With northern, urban Americans wondering about his background and qualifications, Carter proceeded to foul his own political nest by granting an interview to *Playboy* magazine in which he admitted that he had "committed adultery in my heart many times" and used such unbecoming terms as "screw."

The candidates agreed to three televised debates, which turned out to be generally dull affairs. Nevertheless, the second may have provided Carter with the edge he needed to win. In answering a question concerning Poland, the president declared that "there is no Soviet domination of Eastern Europe, and there never will be under a Ford administration." Carter reminded Ford that Poland, Hungary, Czechoslovakia, and the other nations of that region had been occupied continuously by Soviet troops since 1945. "The Blooper Heard Round the World," declared *Time* magazine. Once again, Ford's basic competence to be chief executive of the most powerful nation in the world was brought into question.

The election revealed that America was still in political and emotional transition. Carter won with 49.9% of the vote to Ford's 48%. The tally in the electoral college was 297 to 241, but Ford carried 27 states to Carter's 23 plus the District of Columbia. Carter captured the entire South, but in almost every state the margin of victory was provided by black voters, nearly 80% of whom voted for the Democratic candidate. The degree to which Americans had voted for Carter out of a reaction to Watergate rather than out of an understanding of and commitment to his philosophy and programs remained unclear.

Unfunded Liberalism: The Carter Presidency and Domestic Affairs

Jimmy Carter

Jimmy Carter was born on October 1, 1924, the oldest of four children, to Earl and Lillian Gordon Carter. His father was a successful agribusinessman, operating a peanut brokerage firm in tiny Plains, Georgia. The younger Carter graduated from high school in 1941 and, after honing his science and math skills at Georgia Tech, gained admittance to the Naval Academy, thus realizing a childhood dream. He graduated in 1946 in the top 10% of his class and immediately thereafter married Rosalynn Smith,

Table 12–1. The election of 1976				
Candidates	Parties	Electoral vote	Popular vote	Percentage of popular vote
Jimmy Carter	Democratic	297	40,827,394	49.9
Gerald R. Ford	Republican	240	39,145,977	47.9

another Plains native. To Carter's delight, he was admitted by Capt. Hyman Rickover to the U.S. Navy's newly established atomic submarine program. After much arduous training, the Georgian qualified as an atomic engineer and was selected to be chief engineer aboard the newly commissioned Seawolf.

News that Carter's father was dying changed his life forever. Following Earl's death, he decided to take Rosalynn and his three young sons and return to Plains. There he took over the family peanut business and devoted his free time to public service. From 1963 to 1966, Carter served in the state legislature where he earned a reputation as a foe of lobbyists for special interests, an enemy of corruption and inefficiency, and a champion of the underprivileged and underrepresented. In 1966, he ran unsuccessfully for governor of Georgia, finishing a close third to Lester Maddox and Governor Ellis Arnall. His distress at his defeat was assuaged by a second religious conversion – the first had come at age 11 – which transformed his public service activities from a pastime to a vocation. Carter was no simple-minded literalist who believed that mere faith would solve the world's problems, but he was sure that service to God meant service to humanity.

Being born again seemed initially to have made Jimmy Carter more rather than less opportunistic. Convinced that it was permissible to use dubious means to achieve righteous ends, he vowed that he would not be "outsegged" again, referring to Maddox's successful segregationist campaign in 1966. During the Democratic gubernatorial primary in 1970, Carter openly appealed to white supremacists, condemning busing and visiting a segregated private academy. He easily defeated his closest rival, former Governor Carl Sanders, and went on to win the general election.

As governor, Carter soon revealed that his bow to white supremacy had been nothing more than an electoral ploy. In his inaugural address, he promised to lead Georgia into a new era of racial harmony and social justice. Within two years, he had compiled an impressive record as a progressive and racial moderate. The number of black state employees increased by one third, and Carter built 111 new community health centers. Employing a fiscal philosophy that would carry over into his presidency, the former peanut farmer introduced the concept of "zero-based budgeting," a system in which every budget request was subjected to annual review to ensure accountability and efficiency. In 1971, *Time* featured Carter on its cover, touting him as one of the new breed of enlightened southern politicians. The following year, the Georgia governor began laying the groundwork for his run for the presidency.

Carter beat Gerald Ford in 1976, but the way he won and the makeup and mood of his constituency boded ill for his presidency. Different groups that had voted for him expected different things. Professional people tended to be interested in balancing the budget and reducing taxes, while blacks and organized labor, which had conducted a massive get-out-the-vote campaign for Carter, anticipated social welfare programs and employment-generating public works. Younger voters were increasingly interested in environmental and quality-of-life issues, whereas the elderly focused their attention on Social Security and health care reform. In addition, Carter had campaigned against the U.S. government without realizing that he would need the permanent civil servants and skilled bureaucrats to run the government regardless of what policies he put in place. Finally, although the Democrats maintained their two-to-one edge in the House and three-to-two margin in the Senate, most of the House members and one fifth of the senators had been newly elected since 1972 and felt no obligation to an anti-establishment president. This fact, coupled with the backlash against the Johnson–Nixon imperial presidency, did not foreshadow a close relationship between the executive and legislative branches of government.

The cabinet and White House staff were a combination of representative Democrats and close Carter associates. Included in what the press came to refer to as the "Georgia Mafia" were Chief of Staff Hamilton Jordan, Press Secretary Jody Powell, Head of the Domestic Policy Staff Stuart Eizenstat – all three were former campaign workers and gubernatorial aides – as well as Atlanta attorney Griffin Bell as attorney general and Atlanta banker Bert Lance as head of the Office of Management and Budget (OMB). For Treasury, Carter selected Michael Blumenthal, former chief operating officer at the Bendix Corporation. Former Defense Department official Cyrus Vance became secretary of state and Columbia University academic Zbigniew Brzezinski was tabbed to be national security adviser. Vance was a typical member of the foreign policy establishment; Brzezinski was not. The cabinet included two African Americans and two women – Andrew Young as ambassador to the UN, Juanita Kreps as head of commerce, and former Howard Law School Dean Patricia Harris (both female and African American) as secretary of housing and urban development.

Although *Time* and other national news publications referred to Carter as a populist, he was closer to being a traditional progressive. A stickler for detail, he championed efficiency and honesty in government and continually invoked the public well-being in his ongoing battle with special interests. Indeed, Carter saw himself as above politics, both traditional and bureaucratic, a trustee of the public welfare. He tended to attribute sordid motives to those who opposed his programs rather than seeing them as individuals who held a different view of the public interest. His initial unwillingness to compromise what he considered his principles evoked uneasy memories of Woodrow Wilson.

Any effective administrator must expend political capital, but Jimmy Carter, with the best of motives, seemed hell-bent on bankrupting himself before the end of his first year in office. In the name of national reconciliation, on his first day in office, the new president offered a "full, complete and unconditional pardon" to Vietnam-era draft resisters. Although his courageous move did in fact help Americans to put the war behind them, the head of the Veterans of Foreign Wars called the day of the announcement one of the saddest in American history. Peace activists denounced the president for not including deserters and those receiving less than honorable discharges. Shortly afterward, Carter abruptly cancelled 19 water projects located principally in the South and the West. Although the dams, river navigation projects, and irrigation systems were of questionable economic value and symbolized the "Washington insider system," which the press and public had been decrying, the move alienated important Democratic senators and congressmen and boded ill for the president's subsequent legislative initiatives.

Economic Doldrums

Out of necessity, the Carter administration first turned its attention to the faltering economy. The recovery package that the new president submitted to Congress included an across-the-board $50 tax rebate, a $900 million reduction in corporate taxes, and only modest new sums for public works and other job-creating programs. The administration's priorities reflected Carter's basic fiscal conservatism – he was more concerned about controlling inflation than reducing unemployment. Indeed, his approach reflected the contradiction that had plagued Eisenhower's "modern Republicanism" – one could not be "liberal" on social issues and "conservative" on fiscal matters. When subsequently Carter refused to support a rise in the minimum wage from $2.30 to $3.00, organized labor openly broke ranks with the administration. But the president was amenable to compromise. He was willing to countenance some spending for job-creation programs and eventually agreed to support a phased increase in the minimum wage. On May 5, 1977, Congress passed a $20.1 billion measure to increase employment through various job programs. In June, it approved a one-year extension of the Comprehensive Employment and Training Act. The administration dropped its idea of a tax rebate, but Congress reduced corporate taxes by $34 billion over a three-year period, with incentives for employers who hired new workers. A minimum wage bill provided for a phased-in increase from $2.30 to $3.35 by 1981. Unemployment declined from 7.9% in December 1976 to 6.4% the following year and dropped to less than 6% in 1978. However, Carter received little credit for the decline in joblessness. The president's initial moves had served to portray him as a fiscal conservative who would subsume social and economic justice to the goal of a balanced budget. Carter's approach to welfare reform only served to reinforce that image.

Welfare Reform – Again

Shortly after his inauguration, Carter instructed Health, Education and Welfare (HEW) Secretary-designate Joseph Califano to come up with a comprehensive scheme for welfare reform by May 1977. Califano favored a plan that would lump all welfare payments into a single cash rebate, a maximum of $4,200 for a family of four. At the urging of Labor Secretary Ray Marshall, Califano's welfare reform proposal was tied to legislation creating 1.4 million new jobs. The president, who was committed to a "zero-cost" approach to welfare reform, was appalled. "Are you telling me that there is no way to improve the present welfare system except by spending billions of dollars?" he asked his aides. "In that case, to hell with it!" He eventually relented, however, and agreed to a program that called for modest spending increases. Carter's plan provided jobs for welfare recipients who could work and a "decent income" for those who could not, such as those with disabilities and single parents with small children. Assailed in Congress by liberals and conservatives alike, the Carter welfare reform program as it finally emerged from the House and Senate did little more than provide $2.8 billion in additional spending to help the states manage their welfare systems.

Agriculture and Social Security

Farm policy was yet another area where a combination of fiscal conservatism and inexperience spelled trouble for the president. A massive grain sale to the Soviet Union in 1972, together with droughts, poor harvests, and a rising world population had cut deeply into America's traditionally gigantic farm surpluses. As a result, Congress passed legislation substituting a system of lower, flexible price supports for the high, fixed rates that had been in place. By the time Jimmy Carter took over in 1977, the farm picture had once again changed dramatically. Agricultural production, including a bumper crop in the Soviet Union, increased worldwide, and the price of a bushel of wheat, which had sold for as much as $5.32 in February 1974 was selling for $2.85. To the consternation of the agricultural community, President Carter sent a farm bill to Congress in March that included price supports even lower than existing schedules. He was attempting to balance the budget on the backs of American farmers, various farm organizations declared. The president promised to veto any measure that contributed significantly to the deficit, but, faced with an override, he signed a measure into law in September that set the target price of a bushel of wheat at a range from $3.00 to $3.05.

Warned that the Social Security fund faced bankruptcy by the end of the twentieth century if current tax rates and payment schedules remained in place, Carter and Califano made a good-faith effort to put the system on a sound financial footing. Inflation coupled with cost-of-living provisions had increased payments over the years, whereas income had remained stable. In addition, the American population was aging rapidly, meaning that the pool of people drawing old-age benefits was increasing. Califano estimated that $83 billion in new revenue over the next 5 years would be required to keep the Social Security fund solvent. Although he sensed the political fall-out that would result from his supporting a large new payroll tax, Carter reluctantly assented to a plan that would triple the maximum tax over 10 years from $965 to $2,854. After much debate, the House and Senate agreed to raise the tax rate in increments and to increase the taxable salary cap. However, Califano's suggestions for long-range reform of the program, such as raising the benefit age from 62 to 65, never gained significant support either in Congress or with the White House.

The Culture of Hostility to Government

Jimmy Carter's efforts to keep "Washington insiders" at arms length and his fundamentally conservative approach to fiscal and social matters did not reassure Americans; the wave of antigovernment sentiment that began with Watergate continued to mount. In June 1978, over the opposition of Governor Brown and virtually every other public figure in the state, Californians voted overwhelmingly to reduce their property taxes by 57%. The residents of that state were angry at the high cost of housing and the state's $4 billion budget surplus. They decided that California's system of public education (college was free for those who could meet admission standards) and its parks and highways – the finest in the nation – were simply not worth it, and they rebelled. Proposition 13, the ballot name of the tax-reduction proposal, threatened to become a national phenomenon. The measure's chief proponent, 75-year-old Howard Jarvis, who had urged Californians to "take control of the government again or it will control you," began setting up organizations in several other states.

By the fall of 1977, President Carter's approval rating in the polls began a decline from which it would never recover. In March, a Harris poll had indicated that 75% of Americans believed that the new chief executive was a man who could "inspire confidence"; by late September, that number had fallen to 50%; and, as of April 1978, Carter's approval rating stood at 29%. The Georgian was not unmindful of his growing unpopularity, and he moved to reverse the trend. He continued to try to portray himself as the "citizen president," ordering bands to dispense with the traditional "Hail To the Chief" when he entered a room; enrolling his daughter, Amy, in public rather than private school; carrying his own suit bag when he traveled; and periodically holding "town meetings" throughout the country. But paradoxically, the same people who voted for Carter because he promised not to become a Washington insider – that is, one who lived by manipulating Congress and special interests – blamed him for not being able to get his legislative initiatives enacted into law. When he did compromise, press and public, recalling his paens to principle, saw him as weak and indecisive. His handling of two issues, one involving ethics in government and the other affirmative action, particularly contributed to that impression.

Bert Lance, head of OMB, was one of Jimmy Carter's closest friends and oldest political supporters. A successful Atlanta banker with substantial holdings in the National Bank of Georgia (NBG) and several other smaller institutions, Lance agreed during his confirmation hearings to put all of his stock in a blind trust, but he then put off doing so. Worse, he obtained a $3.4 million loan from the First National Bank of Chicago in return, so the *Washington Post* alleged, for depositing $200,000 of NBG money in a non–interest-bearing account. The president repeatedly declared his OMB director innocent of any wrong-doing, even calling a press conference during which he turned to Lance and stated, "Bert, I'm proud of you." But the criticism would not go away. If Lance was not guilty of criminal conduct, he was most assuredly skirting the boundaries of ethical behavior. Finally, on September 21, 1977, which Carter termed "one of the worst days I've ever spent," the president forced his friend to resign. Clearly he had stood by Lance longer than propriety required, and his support in the face of various revelations seemed to undercut his claim to be guardian of the nation's ethical standards. Most significant, it damaged his credibility.

An equally important test case for the administration was its handling of the first reverse discrimination case to reach the Supreme Court, *Bakke v. Regents of the University of California.* Since the 1960s, various states and the federal government had passed affirmative action statues providing special hiring and advancement opportunities for minorities and women, even over employees with seniority. Colleges and universities encouraged African Americans, Chicanos, and Native Americans to apply, even setting aside slots to be filled by members of these groups alone. Inevitably, affirmative action produced a backlash among whites who claimed they were victims of "reverse discrimination." In 1973, Allan Bakke, a U.S. Marine veteran who had twice been denied admission to the University of California Medical School at Davis, filed suit in federal court claiming discrimination on the grounds that 16 minority students with college grades and MCAT scores lower than his had been admitted. A federal district court ruled in his favor, the board of regents of the University of California appealed, and the Supreme Court agreed to hear the case.

The *Bakke* case pitted important Democratic constituencies against each other. American Jewish leaders generally favored affirmative action if it did not include quotas. African American organizations were supporters of the stratagem in all its forms, whereas organized labor, jealous of its seniority system, generally opposed affirmative action. Black organizations urged the Justice Department to file an amicus curiae brief on behalf of the regents. In fact, the administration was deeply split over the *Bakke* case. Attorney General Griffin Bell wrote a brief that challenged Davis's right to operate a dual admissions system, while Califano and Vice President Mondale urged the president to use the *Bakke* case to restate his absolute commitment to affirmative action. They eventually won, and the government's brief contained a ringing endorsement of affirmative action. In its decision, not rendered until June of 1979, the high court approved affirmative action programs in a five-to-four decision, but ruled that Davis was operating an unconstitutional quota system and ordered that Bakke be admitted. The Carter administration had gotten the decision that it wanted, but the bitter wrangling centering on Bell and Califano had become public, leaving the impression of a deeply divided administration and a president who was not master of his own ship.

The Energy Crisis

Like chief executives before and after him, Jimmy Carter realized that his ability to achieve a degree of social and economic justice and to guarantee his political future depended on the economy. To the degree that he could control inflation, stimulate new investment, and increase productivity, he and his nation would prosper. No matter what his monetary policy, no matter how many new government jobs were created, no matter what reforms were made in the social welfare system, America would not prosper until and unless the energy crisis that began in 1971 was dealt with. Since the Yom Kippur War in 1973, the price of foreign oil had more than doubled from $6 a barrel to $12. At the same time, the percentage of foreign oil of the whole used by the United States had increased from 35% to 50%. During the brutal winter of 1976/1977, an estimated 400,000 workers missed a day of work because of energy shortages. With schools, hospitals, and other public facilities facing the prospect of a loss of heat, the Federal Energy Administration ordered refineries to concentrate on the production of heating oil rather than aircraft and auto fuel. Gas shipped across state lines was then regulated by the federal government and priced at $1.44 per 1,000 cubic feet, while gas sold within a producing state brought $1.90. As a result, oil- and gas-producing states had an abundant supply while those without this vital resource suffered acute shortages. President Carter asked for authority to deregulate the price of gas piped across state lines as part of an effort to promote production and sale. In the Emergency Natural Gas Act, Congress granted this authority to the president. With the temporary deregulation of interstate gas, the vital fuel would flow to those areas where it was most needed. In late April, the president sent the Hill legislation requesting the establishment of a cabinet-level Department of Energy. What was needed, however, was a long-term energy policy that would keep

Table 12–2. Trend of inflation, 1967–1981

	Consumer price index	Dollar's real value	Median family income	
			On paper	In reality
1967	100.0	$1.00	$7,974	$7,974
1968	104.2	.96	8,632	8,284
1969	109.8	.91	9,433	8,591
1970	116.3	.86	9,867	8,484
1971	121.3	.82	10,285	8,479
1972	125.3	.80	11,116	8,872
1973	133.1	.75	12,051	9,054
1974	147.7	.68	12,902	8,735
1975	161.2	.62	13,719	8,511
1976	170.5	.59	14,958	8,773
1977	181.5	.55	16,009	8,820
1978	195.4	.51	17,640	9,028
1979	217.7	.46	19,684	9,042
1980	247.0	.40	21,023	8,511
1981	272.3	.37	22,390	8,223

Source: Andrew Hacker, ed., *A Statistical Portrait of the American People* (1983), p. 159.

America from being mortgaged to the oil powers of the Middle East and Latin America.

The president and his advisers operated on the assumption that the cost of energy had to be increased to the point where Americans would conserve, and profits would be such that entrepreneurs would develop new sources of fuel. At the same time, they did not want to increase prices to the point of recession and even depression, and they had to guard against massive windfall profits for energy companies lest the new policies touch off a consumer revolt. After due deliberation, Carter's chief energy adviser, James Schlesinger, and his lieutenants came up with a complex piece of legislation that taxed all domestic oil production, created a standby gasoline tax to go into effect when consumption exceeded certain levels, imposed a "gas guzzler" tax on automobiles that used an excessive amount of fuel, required a certain number of new utilities and power plants to burn coal or other fuels instead of oil and natural gas, penalized wasteful industrial users, and established tax credits and other incentives for conservationists. President Carter unveiled his energy program before a national television audience in which he declared the energy crisis to be the "moral equivalent of war."

The president's failure to submit his program to full public review and to consult and appease the many vested interests that would be affected by his energy policies cost him dearly. Oil and gas companies favored the end of price controls but opposed heavier taxes and federal regulation. Laissez-faire conservatives insisted that the best approach to the energy crisis was for the federal government to ease environmental restrictions and remove price controls on oil and natural gas without imposing windfall profit taxes. In this climate, energy companies would be encouraged to discover and exploit new reserves. Responding to these concerns, the Senate gutted the legislative package, removing all energy taxes except that imposed on inefficient – "gas guzzling" – cars. It left in place innocuous sections providing incentives for coal and other alternative fuel use and appropriating $1.02 billion for a broad range of conservation measures. As the bill was being debated in the fall of 1977, the president added a measure to his package allowing the Department of Energy to regulate intrastate and interstate gas to bring the prices in line and hold them down. Although the price of interstate gas would increase some $0.30 over the $1.46 rate under this plan, oil and gas interests were not satisfied. The Senate voted to impose a three-year cap of $2.46 and then to permit total deregulation. In the fall of 1978, the administration's energy package, fundamentally altered, finally passed both houses.

Critics, noting that the acronym for moral equivalent of war was "meow," charged that the president had sold out to the giant oil companies and natural gas producers, and that the legislative package finally enacted would be inflationary without relieving the United States of its dependence on foreign sources. In fact, the energy bill that Congress passed attempted to conserve energy through deregulation and tax credits rather than through taxation, but it was nevertheless an important first step toward establishing a national energy policy. Moreover, deregulation of natural gas paved the way for more rational distribution of a scarce resource and prevented an ugly national polarization pitting oil- and gas-producing states against energy poor states.

There were other significant achievements in the domestic sphere. In 1979, honoring a pledge he had made to American teachers during the presidential campaign, Carter carved a separate Department of Education out of the existing Department of Health, Education and Welfare, which became the Department of Health and Human Services. The White House succeeded in introducing merit pay into the civil service system and introduced rules making it easier to fire incompetents. Environmentalists applauded when the president induced Congress to create a $1.6 billion "Superfund" designed to clean up the nation's worst toxic waste sites and when he snatched 1 million acres of Alaska wilderness from prospective developers, creating a series of new parks, national forests, and wildlife preserves. But Carter received little credit for his accomplishments. Perhaps, as television commentator Eric Sevaried observed, the problem was that the president had "the mind of an engineer" in which problems were broken down into constituent parts and solved piecemeal. There was no overarching vision or at least conceptualization that gave definition to his domestic program and that could be used to rally Congress and the public. Actually, the president had a great deal of vision, which would become obvious after he left office, but it was an idealistic, primarily religious vision that he and his advisers believed inappropriate for the head of a secular republic to articulate.

Human Rights and a Hard Line: The Carter Presidency and Foreign Affairs

In foreign affairs, Carter, similar to John F. Kennedy, intended to be his own secretary of state. The man whom he selected to head the State Department, Cyrus Vance, was a wealthy New York attorney who had served as deputy secretary of defense from 1964 to 1967 and had participated in the Paris peace talks from 1968 to 1969. Carter respected Vance but looked on him primarily as a person who could implement decisions and manage the elitist bureaucrats in the Foreign Service. If Carter was to be decision maker and Vance the implementer, Zbigniew Brzezinski would be the idea man. Carter's national security adviser was a Columbia University Soviet specialist and a former head of the Trilateral Commission. The president considered him "a first-rate thinker" who could explain complex geopolitical issues and provide a series of innovative options from which he, Carter, could choose.

The principal themes of the Carter foreign policy were human rights and open diplomacy. During the campaign, the Democratic candidate had lashed Henry Kissinger for his secrecy and balance of power approach to foreign affairs. "Our Secretary of State simply does not trust the judgment of the American people," he told the Chicago Council on Foreign Relations. Open covenants openly arrived at, he pledged, echoing Woodrow Wilson's Fourteen Points. His promise to make American foreign policy conform to its lofty principles also echoed Wilsonian rhetoric. The president declared that he would make the Helsinki accords on human rights – freedom of expression, freedom of migration, freedom from economic exploitation – the criteria for U.S. dealings with other countries. Carter and Vance were mindful of the "lessons" of Vietnam; the secretary of state understood the limits that constrained American policy and perceived correctly that for most of the developing world issues of nationalism, decolonization, and socioeconomic justice were more important than the Cold War. Nevertheless, the president insisted, the United States did not have to aid countries oppressing and exploiting their populations and should be free to condemn violation of human rights at any and every opportunity. It should be noted, too, that Carter's political advisers believed that human rights was a "no lose" issue that would not only attract liberals but also cold warriors because of its implicit attack on the Soviet Union.

The president's belief that he could make morality the basis of American foreign policy and simultaneously safeguard its strategic and economic interests was flawed. It showed a basic ignorance of history and international politics. Woodrow Wilson's dealings with Mexico from 1913 through 1917 demonstrated that, no matter how well intentioned U.S. intervention in the affairs of other countries, it was inevitably interpreted as imperialism by both friend and foe and was used by authoritarian, repressive regimes to generate nationalist support that otherwise would not have existed.

The Soviet–American Rollercoaster

Six days after his inauguration, President Carter informed Soviet Premier Leonid Brezhnev that he was deeply committed to détente. In fact, despite his national security adviser being a rabid anticommunist who saw the Soviet Union as head of an international communist conspiracy determined to dominate the world, Carter believed that the two superpowers could work out a modus vivendi that would avoid nuclear war and introduce a period of global peace and stability. He was an ardent supporter of the 1972 SALT I agreement, which placed limitations on different types of ICBMs. However, he could not see that public denunciations of the Soviet Union for violation of human rights and calls for the Kremlin to stop persecuting dissidents and allow the free emigration of Jews to Israel would infuriate Brezhnev and his cohorts, who viewed the whole human rights campaign as an effort to meddle in the Soviet Union's internal affairs. While Carter wrote to Brezhnev declaring his support for détente, the State Department publicly condemned the Soviet government for its treatment of Andrei Sakharov, and Carter wrote to the Soviet dissident pledging his undying support for human rights. Soviet Ambassador Anatoli Dobrynin filed an official protest with the White House and the Kremlin ordered two leading dissidents arrested. The brouhaha over human rights and Soviet dissidents ensured that the Soviet–American arms limitation talks that began in March would unfold in a chilly atmosphere.

Both Carter and Brezhnev wanted not only to limit further construction on ICBMs and other strategic weapons, but also to cut existing stockpiles. The 1974 SALT I agreement, scheduled to expire in October 1977, merely placed a ceiling of 2,400 missile launchers. At the same time, both heads of state were determined that their adversary not gain an advantage as a result of any accord signed. The 1977 round of talks opened in Moscow with Secretary of State Vance making a sweeping public proposal, suggesting deep cuts in land-based missiles and a moratorium on new guidance systems. The Soviets were infuriated; they had a huge lead in land-based launchers, whereas the United States was far ahead in submarine-based missiles and in guidance mechanisms. Brezhnev denounced the Vance proposal without even making a counteroffer, and the talks collapsed.

American and Russian negotiators resumed their discussions in Geneva in May in a sullen mood. Determined to come up with some agreement lest the expiration of SALT I leave a dangerous void, Vance and the administration's newly confirmed arms negotiator, Paul Warnke, accepted 2,400 strategic launchers as a starting point; in return, Soviet Foreign Minister Andrei Gromyko indicated that his country would work toward a 10% cut in both nation's strategic arsenals. The two sides also consented to a protocol that suspended plans for the development and deployment of American cruise missiles (pilotless aircraft that could fly low enough to avoid Soviet radar) and the Soviet backfire bomber, which the U.S. government believed could be modified to attack the United States. SALT II was not the drastic reduction for which many hoped, but it kept the disarmament dialog going.

The Developing Nations and Social Justice

Presidential advisers Vance and Andrew Young had little trouble convincing President Carter that large areas of the developing world were unaffected by and unconcerned with the Cold War. Problems there – poverty, social injustice, clan warfare – were indigenous and needed to be dealt with on their own terms. Thus, during the first part of his administration, Carter abjured the temptation to view every regional conflict through the prism of the East–West conflict. Despite the claims by white minority governments in Africa that their continuance in power was crucial to the success of the struggle against the forces of international communism, Carter repeatedly declared his support for black majority rule. The president backed up his call by persuading Congress in 1977 to impose economic sanctions against Rhodesia's white minority government headed by Ian Smith. Zambian President Kenneth Kaunda praised Carter, declaring that America's new chief executive had "brought a breath of fresh air to our troubled world." Right-wing Republicans in the U.S. Senate disagreed. Jesse Helms and Strom Thurmond declared that Carter's support for black nationalism was playing into the hands of the communists.

Early in 1978, Secretary of State Vance attempted to mediate between the Smith government and Robert Mugabe and Joshua Nkomo, leaders of the militant black Patriotic Front. Mugabe and Nkomo demanded immediate all-race elections, a proposal that Smith rejected. Vance withdrew from the talks, and Smith subsequently announced an "internal settlement" in which a new government would include black moderates. Smith would remain prime minister, however, and whites would be guaranteed a majority in parliament sufficient to block any constitutional change.

The proposed internal settlement touched off a heated debate within the Carter administration pitting Vance, who denounced Smith's strategy as a subterfuge for keeping whites permanently in power, and Brzezinski, who argued that the plan was a necessary first step toward rule by moderate blacks. In what many saw as a struggle between black nationalism and anticommunism, Carter sided with his national security adviser. When a proposal came before the UN Security Council condemning Smith's internal settlement, the president ordered Ambassador Young to abstain. Typically, Carter angered both sides in the controversy. Liberals were convinced that the president had betrayed his commitment to human rights, whereas conservatives such as Helms and Thurmond continued to rail at the administration for not lifting sanctions against Rhodesia.

Meanwhile, in Latin America, the U.S. government attempted to use economic aid to pressure various military strongmen to respect human rights and to take steps to reassure the republics of U.S. respect for their sovereignty. Nowhere was this latter goal more apparent and more fully realized than in U.S.–Panamanian relations.

Both the Johnson and the Nixon administrations had made a commitment in principle to the negotiation of a new Panama Canal Treaty. The original pact signed in 1903 gave control over a 10-mile-wide strip of Panamanian territory to the United States "in perpetuity" and was viewed by Panamanians as a clear infringement on their national sovereignty. In the fall of 1977, an American delegation headed by Sol Linowitz signed two agreements with Panamanian representatives. The first, the Panama Canal Treaty, stipulated that the United States would continue to operate the canal until the year 2000, at which time Panamanians would take over with the condition that Americans then employed would be retained. Under the terms of the second, the Treaty Concerning the Permanent Neutrality and Operation of the Panama Canal, the United States was authorized to "guarantee the neutrality" of the waterway permanently and Panama was committed to not discriminate against shippers. In addition, the United States reserved the right to move warships through the canal after the year 2000 and to act to defend the canal against any aggression.

For the next six months, a bitter debate raged in the United States over the wisdom of ratifying the Panama Canal treaties. Superpatriots condemned the accords in the aftermath of Vietnam as yet another U.S. defeat. They somehow linked the regime of Panamanian strongman General Omar Torrijos with the forces of international communism and declared the Carter administration's decision to relinquish control as nothing less than "appeasement." The tiny, unreliable nation of Panama would be able to hold America's economy hostage and compromise the security of the entire hemisphere. The canal zone was "sovereign United States territory" no less than Alaska and the states carved out of the Louisiana Territory, declared Governor Ronald Reagan of California.

The Carter administration fought back vigorously. In a "fireside chat" to the nation, the president pointed out that the United States had not "bought" the canal zone and therefore did not own it. What the original treaty did was give the United States the right to use it. Administration spokesmen pointed out that less than 10% of the nation's trade passed through the canal, and the Joint Chiefs of Staff declared the canal to be strategically irrelevant. America's largest warships could not use it and any nuclear submarine seeking passage would have to surface and identify itself, thus negating its effectiveness. Defenders of the treaties organized the Committee of Americans for the Canal Treaties, a prestigious body that included W. Averell Harriman and former CIA Director William Colby. Republicans Gerald Ford and Henry Kissinger endorsed the treaty and even John Wayne, having made friends with General Torrijos, advocated passage. With the help of Democrat Harry Byrd and Republican Howard Baker, the Panama Canal treaties were approved by the U.S. Senate. Latinos throughout the hemisphere hailed the new U.S.–Panamanian agreements as a major step by the United States toward recognition of the sovereignty and juridical equality of all American states.

Although the Carter administration's policy toward Nicaragua and El Salvador began on an equally high note, the relationship between the United States and these two countries quickly degenerated into a Cold War free-for-all. Since 1934, the United States had supported the anticommunist dictatorship established by General Anastasio Somoza Garcia. The U.S. government sold it arms and provided economic aid, and, in return, Nicaragua supported U.S. intervention in Guatemala in 1954, in Cuba in 1961, and in the Dominican Republic in 1965. Meanwhile, the oppressive Somozas and their brutal National Guard suppressed all dissent, jailing and torturing those who spoke out, while the economy was run for the benefit of family members and friends. By the late 1970s, the Catholic Church, working- and middle-class Nicaraguans, and many business interests had become fed up. When the Sandinista National Liberation Front (FSLN), named for Cesar Augusto Sandino, who had led a guerilla movement against American occupation forces in the 1920s, initiated a revolution against the government in 1978, most Nicaraguans supported it. After a string of defeats, Anastasio Somoza Debayle fled the country only to be assassinated in Nicaragua.

The uprising against Somoza enjoyed widespread support in the United States. Aside from offering to mediate between the besieged government and the Sandinistas, the Carter administration remained neutral during the insurrection. After the government fell, the president persuaded Congress to appropriate $75 million in aid for the new Sandinista regime to help it institute democratic reforms and maintain a degree of free enterprise in Nicaragua. Critics argued that Sandinista leader Daniel Ortega and his closest lieutenants were Marxists, but to no avail. The Carter administration continued to support the Sandinistas until 1980, when it decided that there was clear evidence that Ortega was supporting the rebels in El Salvador. Thereafter, the U.S. government cut off all aid.

Events in the tiny Central American republic of El Salvador, an impoverished, overcrowded land of 5 million souls, confronted the Carter administration with a dilemma that was inherent in the president's approach to foreign policy. The U.S. government had to choose between a government that was clearly guilty of massive human rights violations and a revolutionary movement that was certainly Marxist in orientation and probably the beneficiary of aid from not only the Sandinistas, but Castro's Cuba. Like so many other Latin American republics, El Salvador had historically been ruled by a tiny land-holding aristocracy acting in close alliance with the military and the Catholic Church. The masses, peasants and day laborers, were ignorant, exploited, and unrepresented. By the 1970s, the Catholic Church, revolutionized by its embrace of liberation theology, took up the cause of the impoverished; activist priests and nuns, together with leftist students and intellectuals, began agitating against the government.

In October 1979, a group of reformist-minded but anticommunist officers seized control of the government. They installed a new regime headed by Christian Democrat Jose Napoleon Duarte, who subsequently enraged the plutocracy by attempting to institute programs of land reform and progressive taxation. Members of the former ruling clique in league with right-wing officers in the military organized "death squads," which assassinated an estimated 13,000 Salvadoreans during Duarte's first year in office. Carter initially embraced the Christian Democratic government and persuaded Congress to vote an aid package. When, subsequently, the government failed to take action against the death squads, specifically a group of soldiers who assassinated the archbishop of El Salvador and raped and killed four female American missionaries, the U.S. government withdrew aid. As a result, civil war broke out between the government and the left-wing Democratic Revolutionary Front. Under pressure from hard-line anticommunists in and out of Congress, the Carter administration was forced to resume shipments to the government of both armaments and nonmilitary material.

To the Camp David Accords

Although Central America, and Panama in particular, dominated the front pages of U.S. newspapers at times during the first year and a half of Carter's term in office, the real focus of the new president's foreign policy was the Middle East. Carter, Vance, and Brzezinski were all committed to maintaining the security of Israel, but they were also sensitive to the needs and desires of the 4 million Arabs displaced by the 1948/1949 and 1967 wars. In addition, they were acutely aware that the United States was increasingly dependent on Middle Eastern oil and that the petroleum-rich states of the region were willing to use oil as a weapon against Israel and its allies. To them, a settlement of the Arab–Israeli conflict seemed to be manifestly in America's interests.

In an effort to demonstrate to the Arab world that the United States was not blindly pro-Israeli and could be trusted to mediate the conflict in

the Middle East, President Carter announced in March 1977 that he favored a settlement based on the establishment of fair boundaries, including a "homeland" for the Palestinians. Although he subsequently denied
that this meant support for a separate Palestinian state, American Jewish
leaders and Israelis were angry and alarmed. They feared that the administration was ready to negotiate directly with the Palestinian Liberation
Organization (PLO), which Israel regarded as nothing more than a collection of renegade terrorists. Perhaps in part as a response to these anxieties,
in the summer of 1977, Israelis voted into office the ultranationalist, right-
wing Likud party. Its head and the new prime minister was Menachem
Begin, himself a former anti-British and anti-Arab terrorist who had long
resisted any concession to the Arabs. That fall, in a joint communiqué with
the Soviet Union, the Carter administration called for a new Geneva Conference on the Middle East. The ensuing silence was deafening. Israel was
unwilling to participate in talks at which the PLO was represented, and
Syria, among other states, was unwilling to attend without a Palestinian
delegation.

In an effort to break the Middle East logjam, Egyptian President Anwar
Sadat announced that he would visit Jerusalem and meet personally with
Begin and other members of the Israeli government. Sadat, who believed
that in return for recognition and assurances regarding its security, Israel
would eventually relinquish the lands taken in the Six-Day War, addressed
the Israeli Knesset, or Parliament, and announced that "Israel has become an established fact." Thinking that this constituted a significant step
toward the Arab recognition that Israel had so long coveted, Sadat then
proposed that Israel return the lands taken in 1967 and begin the process
of turning the West Bank and Gaza into a self-governing state. Noting the
widespread condemnation among other Arab states of Sadat's visit, Begin
rejected the Egyptian proposal. He only promised withdrawal from the
Sinai Peninsula; indeed, he referred to the West Bank, which he called
by its Hebrew names, Judea and Samaria, and Gaza as liberated areas
that had become irreversibly part of Israel. Most alarming, he hinted that
the government would sponsor new Israeli settlements in the occupied
territories.

With hopes of a settlement dashed, life returned to normal in the Middle East. When PLO terrorists shot 35 Israeli civilians, the Israeli military invaded southern Lebanon, attacked fedayeen camps, and killed more
than 1,000 noncombatants in the process. Libyan President Muammar al-
Qaddafi denounced Sadat as a traitor and called for his assassination. At
this point, Carter decided that the United States would have to intervene directly. In February, he hosted Sadat at the White House to underscore America's support for the notion of trading land for recognition. The next month
Begin came to Washington, D.C., for two days of talks that Brzezinski
described as "generally unpleasant." Carter, in a fighting mood, made it

plain that the United States was Israel's only reliable ally. He insisted that Begin negotiate on the basis of UN Resolution 242. Specifically, in return for Arab recognition, Israel should withdraw all its forces from the occupied territories. For five years, during which neither Israel nor Jordan would lay claim to the West Bank, that area would be governed by an interim authority. At the end of the period, the Palestinians living there would decide for themselves whether to affiliate with Israel or Jordan, or to continue with the interim regime. Carter tried to reassure Begin that the U.S. would not support an independent Palestinian state on the West Bank, but the Israeli leader left disgruntled and defiant. To show dissatisfaction with the Israeli position, the Carter administration arranged to sell 60 F-15 fighters to Saudi Arabia. Although American Jewish leaders mounted a massive lobbying campaign, for one of the few times during his term in office, Carter asserted himself with Congress. After the administration agreed to sell 20 F-15s to Israel, the Senate and House approved the Saudi transaction.

Public opinion polls taken in the fall of 1977 indicated that only 38% of Americans approved of the way Carter was handling foreign affairs and 51% disapproved. The president's efforts to solve the Middle East riddle seemed to have no impact on the public's view of him. His ratings continued to decline. With his prestige at an all-time low, Carter decided to take the biggest risk of his presidency. He invited Sadat and Begin to Camp David, the presidential retreat in Maryland, for nearly two weeks of discussions in September 1978. With the national and international media providing minute-by-minute coverage, the Egyptian and Israeli leaders, with Carter an active participant, signed two pacts: Framework for the Conclusion of a Peace Treaty between Egypt and Israel and Framework for Peace in the Middle East. The latter was a vague document that provided for "transitional arrangements for the West Bank and Gaza" and promised "full autonomy to the inhabitants." At the same time, all due regard was to be given to the "legitimate security concerns" of Israel. The only thing that seemed clear when the meeting ended was that Egypt would have to recognize Israel before negotiations on Palestinian autonomy in the occupied territories began.

The Camp David accords did not produce the peace that Carter so desperately desired. Begin was not going to tolerate the creation of a Palestinian state in the West Bank and Gaza, in which the PLO played a dominant role. To do so, he believed, would be to expose the Israeli population to constant terrorist attacks. The most he was willing to do was to withdraw from the Sinai and include Palestinians living in the occupied territories in the Israeli political process. For their part, the other Arab states wanted nothing to do with the frameworks Sadat and Begin had hammered out. A separate peace between Egypt and Israel would make future attacks on Israel on behalf of the Palestinians almost impossible. Israel still controlled the West

Bank, Gaza, and the Golan Heights. Nevertheless, in early March 1979, Carter flew to the Middle East and persuaded Sadat and Begin to come to Washington, D.C., later that month and sign a bilateral peace treaty. That agreement provided for gradual Israeli withdrawal from the Sinai, recognition between the two countries, and negotiations on Palestinian rights in the West Bank and Gaza. Carter had achieved an important first step, but his dream of a general settlement to the bitter Arab–Israeli dispute remained unrealized.

NATO

At the outset of his administration. President Carter declared that closer relations with the North Atlantic Treaty Organization (NATO) allies would be one primary goal of his foreign policy. However, Western European–American relations in the late 1970s proved to be uneven and generally strained. Conservatives such as Chancellor Helmut Schmidt of West Germany considered Carter's human rights campaign naive and mischievous. In the spring of 1977, Carter precipitated a major crisis with the European allies when he came out against additional funding for development of an enriched radiation weapon (ERW), known commonly as the neutron bomb. This device was actually a tactical nuclear weapon with high radiation yield but low blast and heat that could be used by NATO troops against East bloc tanks without destroying nearby population centers. Proponents of the weapon pointed out that it would allow NATO to gain tactical parity with the Warsaw Pact armies without a costly and politically controversial troop buildup. But critics found the idea of a bomb that killed people but preserved property morally repugnant. Also, there was the argument that the neutron bomb made war more likely because it made survival and even victory in a nuclear conflict seem possible. Despite a firestorm of criticism at home and in Europe, Carter stuck by his decision.

The Carter Malaise

Inflation

Despite the furor over the Panama Canal treaty and the media attention devoted to the Middle East situation, the nation's attitude toward its political leaders continued, in the absence of war, to be determined by the state of the economy. Although Jimmy Carter had struggled mightily to contain federal spending, even to the point of alienating his liberal constituencies, the inflation rate continued to rise. Indeed, the administration forecast 7.5% for 1979, and most independent observers declared that figure to be far too optimistic. Because he feared recession, the president resisted applying the traditional antidotes to an overheated economy – a tighter money supply and increased interest rates. Instead, he and his advisers focused on prices and wages as the primary culprits. He agreed to scale back his proposed tax cut to $19.4 billion and postponed its implementation until January 1979. At the same time, he created the Council on Wage and Price Stability (COWPS) to try to persuade business and labor to voluntarily break the upward spiral of wages and prices. Barry Bosworth, the 35-year-old economist named to head COWPS, proposed to achieve this feat through "jawboning," a combination of entreaty and public denunciation of firms and unions that refused to follow the government's guidelines. Voluntarism worked no better under Jimmy Carter than it had under Herbert Hoover or Richard Nixon, however.

Wall Street and the international business community were particularly unimpressed with COWPS; the day following the president's speech to the nation announcing his inflation policy, panic-selling on the stock market drove the Dow-Jones average down by almost 10%. On international currency markets, the dollar plunged against gold, as well as against the pound, franc, deutschmark, and yen. The administration responded by casting fears of recession aside. Treasury Secretary Michael Blumenthall announced a full point rise in the discount rate (the rate of interest the government charged its prime customers) to 9.5%, a reduction of funds available to commercial banks for loans by $3 billion, and the purchase of $30 billion worth of foreign currencies. These strokes only momentarily halted the stock market plunge and the slide of the dollar. By December, the government was having to cut into its $30 billion reserve and the inflation rate finished the year at 9%.

The rising inflation rate vastly complicated another task President Carter had set for himself – the creation of a national health insurance (NHI) system. Although many Americans were covered by Medicare, Medicaid, or some form of private health insurance, some 40 million more – mostly the working poor and unemployed – were completely unprotected. To the delight of Senator Edward Kennedy and other liberal advocates of national health care, Carter declared his support for a comprehensive plan during the 1976 campaign. Following the election, the administration considered two options for providing every American with health care: a universal, federally funded system of health insurance and a mandatory employer-financed mechanism supplemented with federal funds for catastrophic illness. To the enragement of Senator Kennedy and organized labor, the president announced that the system Congress selected would have to be phased in over a three-year period and then only as budget constraints would allow. "The American people," Kennedy declared, "should not tolerate any delay on national health insurance." Following a series of stormy encounters at the White House, Kennedy announced that he would accept a phasing in of NHI provided the president would promise to implement the program regardless of the inflation rate and the deficit level. This Carter would not do, and thus the monumental problem of national health care remained unresolved for another four years.

The Iran Hostages

With Carter's disapproval rate hovering around 69% in the summer of 1978, many of his political advisers comforted themselves with the thought that things could not get worse. They were wrong. By the time Jimmy Carter became president, Iran had become one of America's strongest allies. Under Mohammed Reza Shah Pahlavi, the autocratic and staunchly anticommunist monarch whom the CIA had helped restore to the Peacock Throne in the 1950s, Iran served as the lynchpin in the Central Treaty Organization (CENTO). Indeed, the CIA had established listening posts along the 1,000-mile Soviet–Iranian border that were vital to the American intelligence effort. In addition, outside Saudi Arabia, Iran was the largest oil-producing nation in the noncommunist world. On New Year's Eve of 1977, President Carter visited Iran and praised that country as "an island of stability" in a sea of turmoil. In his toast, Carter declared the Shah fully deserving of "the respect and the admiration and love which your people give to you." Carter's perception of the Peacock Throne was the product of one of the most monumental intelligence failures in American history. As America was soon to learn, a large number of Iranians felt something other than love and admiration for their monarch.

The cornerstones of the Shah's rule were political autocracy, westernization and modernization, and subservience to the United States. The fundamentalist leadership of Iran's Shi'ite Muslim population (90% of the whole) were deeply offended by these principles. The mullahs resented the increasingly important role played by women in Iran's political and economic life and the secularization of society in general. Supported by the leftist fedayeen, students, and intellectuals, they clamored for the establishment of a constitutional democracy. Some merchants, peasants, and unskilled workers denounced the modernization of the economy, the so-called "white revolution," which seemed to guarantee that Iran's burgeoning wealth would be reserved only for the educated, westernized element of the population. Increasingly, popular ire focused not only on the Shah but also on the United States. Iranians were well aware of the fact that the CIA had trained the government's hated secret police (SAVAK) and that American oil companies were exploiting the nation's rich petroleum resources. The oil profits that did not go into the Shah's pockets or to the Arabian-American Oil Company (ARAMCO) went to the U.S. government in the form of huge arms purchases. By the late summer of 1978, the Iranian government was under attack by both the Islamic Revolutionary Guard loyal to fundamentalist religious leader Ayatollah Ruhollah Khomeini and Iranian fedayeen, which had close ties to the PLO. Of the two, the fundamentalists were by far the more important. Khomeini, an 81-year-old Islamic fanatic, had been living in exile in Paris for the previous 16 years. Rigid concerning goals but flexible as to means, the Ayatollah authorized his followers to resort to any extreme of violence to establish God's kingdom in Iran. When in August a theater in Abadan burned down, killing

377 people, the Shah's opponents successfully laid the blame at his doorstep. More than 100,000 people demonstrated and rioted throughout Iran. The Shah declared martial law, and his troops fired into a crowd in Tehran's Jaleh Square, killing an estimated 700 people. In January 1979, gravely ill with cancer, the Shah fled Iran. The Ayatollah flew home the next month and proclaimed the establishment of an Islamic Republic with him as its head.

The Carter administration was deeply disturbed by the overthrow of one of America's staunchest allies and the establishment in Iran of a government that seemed distinctly antiwestern. As the Shah's regime crumbled, the U.S. ambassador to Iran, William Sullivan, suggested strongly that he be allowed to meet with Khomeini and work out a modus vivendi that would protect U.S. interests. Carter, at Brzezinski's insistence, refused, considering instead a military coup against the new fundamentalist regime. Although the theocracy that the Ayatollah established was a failure by western standards – it was no more democratic than the Shah's regime and its anti-modernization campaign sent the economy into a tailspin – it enjoyed the support of the Iranian people. Thus, there was no coup. Throughout 1978, the mullahs whipped up nationalist sentiment against the "Great Satan," that is, the United States. Khomeini announced that he was cutting off oil shipments to America but not to Western Europe and Japan. The crowning blow to Iranian–American relations came in October 1979, when, against the advice of the U.S. Embassy in Teheran, President Carter granted asylum to the Shah, who was then residing temporarily and uncomfortably in Mexico City. As the gravely ill Pahlavi entered a New York hospital for treatment, Khomeini announced that Iran's former oppressor would now be able to conspire first-hand with the government of the United States. On November 4, Islamic Revolutionary Guards seized the American Embassy and took its 400 officials and workers hostage.

Khomeini's decision to violate international law and seize diplomatic personnel was more than just an impulsive reaction to Carter's decision to grant the Shah entry into the United States. He and his cohorts refused to believe that the former monarch was truly ill; they were convinced the purpose of his presence in the United States was to hatch a counterrevolutionary plot with the CIA. Seizure of the embassy would lead to a crisis with the United States that the mullahs could blame for the economic and political chaos that was then wracking Iran. By constantly invoking the threat posed by the "Great Satan," the Ayatollah could whip up nationalist support for his regime that might not otherwise have been forthcoming. As the price of the hostages' release, Teheran demanded that the international community seize and repatriate the Shah's personal wealth and that he be returned to Iran to stand trial.

The Carter administration's reaction to the seizure of the U.S. Embassy was a mixture of confusion and anxiety, a reaction that seemed symbolic of America's declining status in the world. Night after night an anguished nation watched television film of the blindfolded hostages being abused by their captors. The options available to the White House were limited. It would be unseemly and discreditable to send the Shah home to certain death. In fact, Carter had no legal right either to deport the deposed monarch or to seize his wealth. To apologize for past U.S. actions in Iran and submit to a UN investigation as Teheran demanded would have destroyed Carter politically. Any effort to free the hostages would almost certainly result in their death and a general war from which only the Soviets would benefit. The one option left was economic pressure, but the dependence of America's principal allies, Western Europe and Japan, on Middle Eastern oil boded ill for any attempt to isolate and punish the fundamentalist regime in Teheran. The United States reviewed the visas of 50,000 Iranian students living in the United States with a view to deporting them, but there were legal restraints protecting those with valid documents. The United States did freeze some $8 billion in Iranian assets in the United States and suspended the sale of arms to Teheran. None of these measures were sufficient to force the Revolutionary Guards to release their captives, however.

By the spring of 1980, the Carter administration was becoming desperate; unless and until the hostage situation was resolved, the Democrats' chances of winning the presidential election were nil. On April 7, the United States broke diplomatic relations and imposed an economic embargo. Unfortunately, America's principal allies refused to participate in these punitive measures. Meanwhile, the cutoff of Iranian shipments of oil to the United States contributed to a 130% rise in the price of gasoline and heating fuel. On April 24, the president authorized the military to carry out a dangerous and foolhardy attempt to rescue the hostages. Operation Eagle Claw called for eight helicopters from the aircraft carrier *Nimitz* to rendezvous with six C-130 Hercules transports in the Iranian desert. Marine commandos were to swoop down on the embassy, kill the captors, and rescue the hostages. When a sandstorm caused one of the helicopters to crash into a C-130, the White House called off the entire operation. Shortly afterward, Americans watched Revolutionary Guards triumphantly displaying the charred remains of those killed in the crash. The hostages were then separated and relocated, making another rescue attempt impossible.

Democratic Détente, SALT, and Afghanistan

Anxieties within and without the Carter administration were intensified by a sharp downturn in Soviet–American relations during 1979. By the end of the 1970s, the Soviet economy had entered a downward spiral. Although leading the United States in the production of oil, steel, coal, and cement, the Russians had invested badly and insisted on following collectivist principles that stunted growth and innovation. Privately owned concerns, which cultivated only 3% of Russia's arable land, produced nearly 50% of the nation's foodstuffs. Massive military and foreign aid expenditures in Vietnam and Cuba drained much-needed capital from the system. A chronic cereal shortage became still worse. Nevertheless, the Kremlin stubbornly refused to interfere with the huge collective farms. Soviet technology in computers, electronics, transportation, and communication lagged far behind the West and Japan, while the communist nation's workforce became less rather than more productive. The Carter administration wanted to use this vulnerability to force concessions from the Kremlin on arms control and human rights. However, before entering into a new round of negotiations, the White House decided to finalize the process that had begun under Nixon and normalize relations with Communist China. Such a move, the administration believed, would produce benefits in its own right but would have the additional advantage of further isolating the Soviet Union and contributing to its vulnerability.

In the spring of 1977, Secretary of State Vance visited China and met with Vice Premier Deng Xiaoping. In 1978, President Carter announced that in January 1979 the two nations would establish full diplomatic relations. As a condition for exchanging ambassadors with Beijing, the Carter administration had to sever relations with Taiwan, withdraw the few remaining American troops from that island, and acknowledge that Taiwan was "part of China." Carter pointed out the commercial benefit of rapprochement with China, but he made no secret of the fact that it would help counter an aggressive Soviet foreign policy in Southeast Asia and elsewhere. In late 1978, the communist government of Vietnam, by then a client state of the Soviet Union, invaded Kampuchea (Cambodia) in an effort to overthrow the pro-Chinese Khmer Rouge leader, Pol Pot. When the Chinese subsequently invaded northern Vietnam in retaliation, the president remained conspicuously quiet.

Nevertheless, both the United States and the Soviet Union wanted to prevent the development of new weapons systems and slow an arms race that was devastating both their economies, although the Soviets' at a faster rate than America's. As a result, despite the otherwise deplorable state of Soviet–American relations, representatives of the two nations signed a SALT II treaty in Vienna in June 1979. The total number of nuclear delivery vehicles was to be reduced to 2,250 by 1981 and MIRVed warheads were to be limited to 1,200. SALT III was to focus on reducing nuclear stockpiles. Although the agreement neither benefited one party at the expense of the other nor halted the arms race – Carter subsequently approved the MX (experimental missile), a $30 billion portable network of mobile missiles hidden in a maze of underground tunnels, and the Soviets went ahead with deployment of their SS-20 intermediate-range nuclear missiles capable of hitting Western Europe – opposition to ratification of SALT II in the United States quickly became intense.

Opponents of détente headed by former Assistant Secretary of Defense Paul Nitze, one of the coauthors of NSC 68, organized the Committee on the Present Danger. Spokesmen for that organization insisted that verification procedures were inadequate and that the Soviets could not be trusted. Meanwhile, arms control advocates argued that SALT II was all form and no substance, that the MX was too costly and would pose a threat to the environment, and that negotiations should continue until a real arms control agreement was reached. Then in the summer of 1979, with the debate over SALT II in full swing, American intelligence revealed the presence of a Soviet brigade of 2,500 combat troops in Cuba. Although the Kremlin argued that the brigade had been there for years and that its sole purpose was to train Castro's armed forces, the revelation resulted in a major furor. Chairman of the Senate Foreign Relations Committee Frank Church declared that the presence of Soviet troops in Cuba constituted a major obstacle to ratification. Reluctantly, President Carter withdrew the treaty in January 1979.

The denouement of SALT II coincided with the Soviet invasion of Afghanistan, an event that tipped the balance within the Carter administration in favor of Brzezinski and the hard-liners and caused Soviet–American relations to reach their lowest point since the Cuban missile crisis. In 1978, the Soviet Union had engineered a coup that resulted in the establishment of a Marxist regime in that remote, mountainous, but strategically important country. Under siege from Muslim fundamentalist guerrillas angry at the antireligious bent of the new regime, the pro-Soviet government grew increasingly weaker. To forestall its overthrow or co-option, and in spite of the obvious risk to the ratification of SALT II, the Kremlin sent 85,000 troops into Afghanistan during the Christmas holidays of 1979. They executed the failed Marxist leader, replacing him with another puppet, Najibullah. By the spring, more than 100,000 Soviet occupation troops were in place. Russia's Vietnam had begun.

The invasion of Afghanistan, bordering the Soviet Union, China, and Pakistan, angered and frightened Carter and his advisers. It marked the first time Soviet troops had directly intervened in a nation outside Eastern Europe. Perhaps most alarming, the Kremlin invoked the Brezhnev Doctrine, last used to justify the Czech invasion of 1968, which held that the Soviet Union had the right to use force to correct any "deviation from socialism" in Marxist states. For the Carter administration, the invasion of Afghanistan raised the specter of a Soviet military takeover of the entire Middle East. Ironically, the Kremlin was acting in part to prevent the spread of Islamic fundamentalism into the Soviet republics of central Asia, the same fundamentalism that was responsible for the holding of the American hostages in Iran. In the weeks that followed, Brzezinski became the dominant policy voice in the White House, and after the failed effort to rescue the hostages in Teheran, Vance quietly departed. Carter vehemently denounced the Afghan adventure, broadened and deepened ties with China, stopped grain sales to the Soviet Union, approved covert CIA aid to the Afghan rebels and, in his most controversial move, called for a boycott of the Olympic games scheduled for Moscow that summer. In his State of the Union address in January 1980, the president announced what came to be known as the "Carter Doctrine": "an attempt by any outside force to gain control of the Persian Gulf region will be regarded as an assault on the vital interests of the United States of America, and as such an assault will be repelled by use of any means necessary, including military force." Thus did the administration break with the Nixon Doctrine, which called for multilateral rather than unilateral action to safeguard western interests.

Carter's hard-line response to the Soviet invasion of Afghanistan merely angered friend and foe alike, without affecting the fundamental situation. West Germany and Japan then enjoyed a robust trade with the Soviet Union and Eastern Europe. More importantly, America's European allies faced a huge Soviet bloc army and dozens of warheads mounted atop the new SS-20 missiles. In any major East–West confrontation, it would be America's NATO partners that would be atomized rather than America. Led by West German Chancellor Helmut Schmidt, the Europeans declared that the invasion of Afghanistan was predictable if not praiseworthy; no nation would tolerate such instability along its border. In the United States, many in Congress and the press denounced Carter and Brzezinski for over-reacting and resurrecting the domino theory. Why not let the Soviet Union exhaust itself in Afghanistan as the United States had in Vietnam? Finally, Lord Killanin, head of the International Olympic Committee, publicly denounced the United States for using athletes "as pawns in political problems that politicians cannot solve themselves."

The "Crisis of Spirit"

Unfortunately for the president, the U.S. economy stubbornly resisted administration efforts to control inflation and stimulate growth. OPEC's fourth and largest price rise in five months sent gas prices soaring again in July 1979, and actually touched off the nation's first energy riot. In Levittown, Pennsylvania, truckers barricaded the interstate; two nights of violence left 100 people injured. Confronted with public opinion polls showing a growing perception of presidential ineptitude, Carter secluded himself for 12 days at Camp David, where he consulted with prominent individuals from business, labor, government, academia, and the religious community. The object of the conferences, according to the White House, was to deal with the "crisis of spirit" that seemed to be dragging the country down. Privately, Vice President Mondale advised the president that his low standing with the public had less to do with a crisis of spirit and more to do with inflation, the energy crunch, and unemployment. What was needed, he declared, was a thorough review of the administration. Carter reluctantly agreed and only days later, on July 16, accepted the resignation of five of his Cabinet members, including Michael Blumenthal at Treasury, Griffin Bell at Justice, Brock Adams at Transportation, Joseph Califano at HEW, and James Schlesinger at DOE. To complete the shakeup, Carter announced the appointment of Hamilton Jordan to be White House chief of staff and instructed the rest of his aides to obey Jordan's orders "as if they were the President's own."

Many liberal Democrats in Congress viewed the resignations as forced and interpreted the dismissal of Califano in particular as proof of the president's fundamental conservatism. Further eroding Carter's standing with liberals was his decision to dismiss Andrew Young as UN ambassador after the White House learned that he had held an unauthorized meeting with a PLO official in late July. The National Association for the Advancement of Colored People (NAACP) called a meeting of 200 black American leaders to protest the decision.

As 1980 began, the U.S. economy appeared to be headed for a major depression. The projected inflation rate for the year was 18.2%, and economists predicted that prices might rise at a 20%-per-year clip throughout the 1980s. Real per capita income for urban workers fell by 1.4% in February alone. The unemployment rate hovered around 7%, and interest rates stood at 18.5% headed for 20% before the year was out. Markets for the nation's two most important products, housing and automobiles, virtually collapsed. As of March, housing starts were down 42% compared with the same time the previous year.

As Americans contemplated the possibility of their economic demise, a natural disaster of ominous proportions seized the national headlines. The eruption of Mount St. Helens in southwest Washington state blew the top of the mountain into the atmosphere, leveled some 120 square miles and set off a series of fires, mudslides, and floods. Soot darkened much of the northwest sky for days. Although 400 people had been evacuated before the eruption, 15 died and 40 were missing. Mount St. Helens had been dormant since 1857.

The Election of 1980

Finding the president's political vulnerability irresistible, Senator Edward Kennedy announced that he would challenge Carter for the Democratic nomination. The popular Massachusetts senator fared well in the early primary contests, besting Carter in Connecticut and New York where Jewish voters were angry over the president's demand that Israel dismantle Jewish settlements in the occupied territories, including Jerusalem. Because most of the rest of the primaries were to be held in the South and Midwest, Carter's advisers were encouraged. What they wanted was to drive Kennedy out of the race early and present the Republicans with a united front. Unfortunately for their plans, Kennedy won narrow victories over the president in Pennsylvania and Michigan in April, convincing him to stay put and fight it out. The failure of the Iranian hostage mission on April 24 sent Carter's popularity plummeting to an all-time low. Polls indicated that 70% of Americans wanted a change in the White House and that the leading contender for the GOP nomination, Ronald Reagan, was ahead of Carter in the polls by a margin of 44% to 43%.

In response to prodding by Jordan, Powell, and other advisers, Carter hit the campaign trail, besting Kennedy in Tennessee and North Carolina. Meanwhile, on Capitol Hill, the president scored two important political victories when Congress passed the administration's $227 million windfall profits tax on oil companies and created the Synthetic Fuels Corporation with authority to spend up to $88 billion over the next 10 years to develop alternative fuels. Of the 1,666 convention votes needed for nomination, the president had accumulated 1,500. Nevertheless, Carter's approval rating on the eve of the national nominating conventions was the lowest for any chief executive in American history, lower even than for Richard Nixon during the depths of the Watergate crisis.

On July 16, Governor Ronald Reagan of California received the Republican nomination and he selected George Bush, a moderate, East Coast Republican who had served in Congress representing his adopted state of Texas, as his running mate. Reagan, who had made a name for himself as a lead actor in class B movies and as the cowboy host of television's "Death Valley Days," had been an effective, popular governor. He cultivated the image of a right-winger but was in fact a pragmatic politician who would compromise over virtually any issue while he mouthed simple conservative verities.

With his own nomination virtually assured, President Carter attempted to appease Senator Kennedy and get him out of the race. Kennedy would have none of it. He decided to stay to the bitter end and use party unity as leverage to get his planks on unemployment, health insurance, and social welfare written into the Democratic platform. Only weeks before the Democrats gathered in August, the press reported that President Carter's brother Billy was being investigated by the Senate and Justice Department. Billy, who epitomized the image of the beer-guzzling bubba, had made a highly controversial trip to Libya in 1978 and had subsequently accepted a $220,000 loan from the government of Col. Muammar al-Qaddafi. The subsequent investigations revealed that Billy had not attempted to influence government policy but had acted as intermediary between Libya and a Florida oil company in a business deal. The president's brother dutifully registered with the Justice Department as an agent of a foreign government, but "Billygate" as the Republicans termed it, was just another cross for the president to bear as he prepared for the 1980 election.

As the Democratic convention opened, Carter's forces managed to easily defeat Senator Kennedy's motion to do away with the rule binding delegates to candidates they had voted for in the caucuses and primaries. Still Kennedy refused to withdraw. Only after the president agreed to planks in the platform pledging support for a $12 billion jobs program and promising not to try to balance the budget through high interest rates and unemployment (Kennedy relinquished his demand for wage and price controls) did Kennedy succumb. His subsequent support for the Carter–Mondale ticket, however, was at best lukewarm.

As the campaign began, Carter's team faced a dilemma: how to turn America's attention away from controversial subjects and yet convince voters that there was a significant difference between the candidates. At Hamilton Jordan's suggestion, the president decided to focus on Ronald Reagan and attempt to convince Americans that he was incapable of leading a great nation in a complex world. Early in the campaign, it seemed that that stratagem would work; in fact, it appeared that Reagan would do Carter's work for him. He referred to the war in Vietnam as a "noble cause," expressed personal doubts about the theory of evolution, suggested that the New Deal was patterned after Benito Mussolini's corporate state, and proposed making Social Security voluntary. Indeed, polls taken at the end of September indicated that the president had reduced Reagan's lead to 4% with 12% undecided.

As the race heated up, the League of Women Voters pressed the president to participate in a three-way televised debate with Reagan and independent candidate John Anderson. The Illinois congressman had launched a National Unity campaign calling for gun control, passage of the Equal Rights Amendment, federal subsidies for a mass transit system, and a $0.50 per gallon tax on gasoline. Carter's handlers were willing to countenance a face-to-face debate with Reagan but refused to commit to a three-way encounter. The ensuing Reagan–Anderson debate had little appreciable impact on the race. When subsequently Anderson's ranking fell below the 15% required by the league, the way was cleared for a two-way debate. This debate, which took place a week before the election, may have been the decisive event of the campaign. Carter conducted himself well, mastering complex questions with apparent ease. But Reagan carefully avoided the gaffes that had plagued him earlier in the campaign and, toward the end of the debate, asked two crucial rhetorical questions: "Are you better off than you were four years ago?" and "Do you feel that our security is safe, that we're as strong as we were four years ago?" If the answer was no, he concluded, "Why then I think your choice is very obvious as to whom you'll vote for."

As election day approached, the GOP feared a last-minute deal freeing the American hostages in Iran that would push Carter over the top. In fact, despite warnings that an election eve emancipation might backfire, the Carter camp worked feverishly to deliver such a "surprise." In September, the Ayatollah had dropped his demand that America apologize for past

	Electoral vote	Popular vote	Percentage of popular vote
Republican Ronald Reagan	489	43,899,248	50.8
Democratic Jimmy Carter	49	35,481,435	41.0
Independent John B. Anderson	–	5,719,437	6.6
Minor parties	–	1,395,558	1.6

Map 12–1. The election of 1980.

depredations in Iran. The hostages would be freed in return for a pledge by the United States not to meddle in Iran's internal affairs, to release Iran's frozen assets, to cancel all claims by Americans against Iran, and to return the Shah's wealth. The Carter administration responded positively, and two days before the election the president announced that Iran had set realistic terms for release of the hostages. But there was no release. The whole affair left Americans feeling impotent and frustrated, and they vented their anger on Jimmy Carter.

In an election in which one out of every four voters settled on a candidate during the last week of the election, Ronald Reagan scored a landslide victory. He won 51% of the popular vote to Carter's 41%. John Anderson came in a distant third with 7%. The electoral vote was even more decisive – 489 to 49. Indeed, in addition to the District of Columbia, the Carter–Mondale ticket carried only Georgia, Minnesota, Maryland, Rhode Island, and West Virginia. Moreover, the Republicans gained control of the Senate for the first time in 28 years as George McGovern, the party's standard bearer in 1972, and seven other liberal Democrats went down to defeat.

Summary

Jimmy Carter was partly responsible for his own demise, yet in ways he was simply overtaken by events. The stagflation that plagued the American economy throughout his administration was the product of massive expenditures during the Vietnam War without corresponding tax hikes and of American dependence on ever more expensive Middle Eastern oil. Elected by a party that had traditionally stood for federal spending to cure unemployment, Social Security for the elderly and disabled, and expanded social services for all sectors of society, Carter felt constrained to balance the budget by tightening the money supply, raising the discount rate, and cutting government spending, especially in the domestic sphere. Reacting to alleged cynicism and balance of power politics during the Nixon years, Carter launched a foreign policy based on human rights without seeing that by definition such an approach constituted interference in the internal affairs of other nations. Riding on the crest of revulsion against government that came in the wake of Watergate, Carter promised to run the country while holding Congress and the bureaucracy at arm's length. When his programs bogged down or were modified out of existence, the public quickly forgot Watergate and accused the Georgian of ineptitude.

The Carter administration certainly had its triumphs. The Panama treaty and Camp David accords were significant achievements. The administration made an excellent start toward a national energy policy and initiated the debate on national health insurance. A man of unquestioned personal rectitude and good intentions, Carter restored America's faith in the integrity if not the efficacy of the political process. Carter campaigned as an enlightened southern populist, but his philosophy in practice was more progressive than populist, blending as it did fiscal responsibility with social justice. Some have argued that similar to Herbert Hoover, Jimmy Carter was simply the wrong person for his times. But it is doubtful that anyone could have dealt with stagflation, achieved détente in an anticommunist environment, solved the Middle East crisis, and dispelled public distrust of government in the aftermath of Vietnam and Watergate.

ADDITIONAL READINGS

Bill, James, *The Eagle and the Lion: The Tragedy of American–Iranian Relations* (1987).

Brzezinski, Zbigniew, *Power and Principle: Memoirs of the National Security Adviser* (1983).

Carroll, Peter N., *It Seemed Like Nothing Happened* (1982).

Carter, Jimmy, *Keeping Faith: Memoirs of a President* (1981).

Ford, Gerald R., *A Time to Heal: The Autobiography of Gerald R. Ford* (1979).

Hartmann, Robert T., *Palace Politics: An Inside Account of the Ford Years* (1980).

Kaufman, Burton I., *The Presidency of James Earl Carter* (1993).

Lasch, Christopher, *The Culture of Narcissism* (1979).

Quandt, William B., *Decade of Decision: American Policy Toward the Arab–Israeli Conflict, 1967–1976* (1977).

Reeves, Richard, *A Ford, Not a Lincoln* (1975).

Seymour, Ian, *OPEC: Instrument of Change* (1980).

Smith, Gaddis, *Morality, Reason and Power: American Diplomacy in the Carter Years* (1986).

Vance, Cyrus, *Hard Choices: Critical Years in American Foreign Policy* (1983).

Wandersee, Winnifrid D., *On the Move: American Women in the 1970s* (1988).

Wilson, William Julius, *The Truly Disadvantaged: The Inner City, the Underclass, and Public Policy* (1987).

Yergin, Daniel, *The Prize* (1991).

13 The Culture of Narcissism

The Reagan Era

In 1987, novelist Tom Wolfe published *Bonfire of the Vanities*, the tale of an affluent New York bond trader, who lusts after financial, sexual, and material fulfillment. Able to make or lose millions through split-second computer trading, the protagonist dreams of being a "master of the universe" (the name of a superhero toy figure popular at the time). A misadventure involving his BMW, his mistress, and a black teenager becomes the thread that unravels his world. Wolfe's tale of greed and self-absorption in the midst of social fragmentation, poverty, and racial and class animosity was a stereotypical but useful guide to the times. In *Habits of the Heart: Individualism and Commitment in American Life* (1985), Robert N. Bellah, a University of California sociologist, and four other scholars interviewed 200 middle-class men and women and found them alienated, isolated, and despondent. They were materially successful but psychologically and spiritually unfulfilled. The anti-intellectualism and cult of hostility to government that pervaded press and politics, Bellah and his associates observed, had left a void. For better or worse, government was a reflection of and an instrument of popular will. To denigrate it as an abstraction was to denigrate the notion of community. He called for a return to religion in its authentic, communal, self-sacrificing sense – not merely as a justification for self-aggrandizement, or for nonbelievers – and a return to the notion of republicanism, government by enlightened individuals who recognized that the individual good is always tied to the common good. Would-be masters of the universe may have dominated the 1980s, but the longing for community remained strong, restraining and softening the rampant individualism of the times.

The Emergence of the New Right

Unlike Richard Nixon's landslide victory in 1972, Ronald Reagan's thumping of Jimmy Carter seemed to signal a sea change in American politics, a major shift from a liberal to a conservative majority. Whereas the

Republicans made virtually no gains in Congress in 1972, they gained 12 seats in the Senate four years later, defeating such liberal Democratic heavyweights as Gaylord Nelson, George McGovern, and Frank Church, and 33 places in the House of Representatives. A mere six years after suffering its worst defeat since the Great Depression, the Republicans had won their greatest victory, seeming to validate Kevin Phillips's prediction of an emerging conservative majority. In fact, Reagan's victory coincided with and was in part made possible by the continuing growth and political activism of the New Right.

Neoconservatism was a blend of both old and new. It encompassed traditional positions such as anticommunism, opposition to government intervention and bureaucracy, and support for free enterprise and a balanced budget. At the same time, the New Right included Americans, many of them working-class Democrats, who were outraged at social issues they believed attacked and undermined conventional morality, the nuclear family, and religious faith. Thus, they mobilized in anger over busing to achieve racial balance, bans on prayer in public schools, the 1973 *Roe v. Wade* Supreme Court decision legalizing abortion, the extension of the First Amendment to cover pornography, the ongoing campaign to have Congress pass the Equal Rights Amendment (ERA), and the extension of antidiscrimination laws to cover homosexuals. To many Americans, the U.S. government seemed to be going in the wrong direction. At the same time, the public demanded a crackdown on crime – FBI statistics revealed a rise in violent crimes (rape, armed robbery, assault, and murder) from 738,000 in 1970 to 1,345,000 in 1980 – the Supreme Court was handing down rulings expanding the rights of arrested people and convicted felons, even for a time abolishing the death penalty. Similarly, just as the Civil Rights Division of the Justice Department, the Equal Employment Opportunity Commission, and other federal agencies were pressing affirmative action programs on the public and private sectors in an effort to compensate historic injustices done to ethnic minorities and women, many Americans, especially white males, were beginning to complain about "reverse discrimination." Those same Republican strategists who recognized the dimensions of this popular anger and who devised Nixon's "southern strategy" played prominent roles in fashioning the Reagan majority.

Demographic patterns continued to favor the Republicans. The 1980 census, which reported a population of 226,504,825, indicated a shift of 17 seats in the House of Representatives from the Northeast and Midwest to the South and West. The so-called Sun Belt was relatively white, relatively nonunion, and overwhelmingly conservative on fiscal matters and many social issues. The rise and fall of two communities illustrate the sharpness of demographic change during the 1970s and its implications for national politics.

In 1950, the area between San Jose and San Francisco, California, had consisted largely of farms and uninhabited land. By 1980, there were more than a dozen cities of 100,000 or more in this strip of America. This was the so-called Silicon Valley, the site of the new computer industry. Industries in the region produced tiny silicon microchips with imprinted circuits. These semiconductors constituted the artificial intelligence centers for computers and the basic building blocks of modern electronics. The technology was developed at Stanford Research Park in Palo Alto, and, not surprisingly, electronics and defense industries relocated to the area to be close to and take advantage of this major research facility. In the 1970s, a revolution in consumer electronic products fueled an explosive new wave of growth; by 1980, some 1,700 high-tech firms employing tens of thousands of white, educated, conservative Americans had set up shop in Silicon Valley.

Meanwhile, across the United States, one of the Democratic Party's old New Deal strongholds was falling apart. For a century, the Monongahela Valley in western Pennsylvania, which included Pittsburgh, Homestead, and Clairton, had formed the steel-making center of America. The giant mills of U.S. Steel, Bethlehem, and others employed tens of thousands of factory workers, who had, since the unionization movement of the 1930s, voted Democratic. By 1980, the area's economy was in rapid decline because of cheaply produced foreign steel and because of the decisions of steel executives to divert capital to chemical firms, shopping malls, and other operations rather than modernize their steel mills. In 1984, steel accounted for only 34% of U.S. Steel's revenues; that same year, it paid some $6 billion to acquire Marathon Oil of Ohio. Overall employment in the steel industry dropped from 400,000 in 1980 to 167,000 in 1987. Whereas U.S. Steel employed 26,500 individuals in 1979, that number had dropped to 4,000 by 1990. American factory workers in the 1980s were either unemployed or underemployed, frustrated, dispirited, and angry – fertile ground for a Republican Party pledged to represent the new "forgotten man."

Leaders of the New Right argued that American liberals had developed a master plan to break down the nuclear family, destroy the once widespread popular belief in God, and substitute government supervision for individual initiative. By removing children from the home for additional hours each day, busing not only promoted racial mixing but undermined parental authority. Similarly, conservatives alleged, *Roe v. Wade* encouraged teenagers to engage in sex by providing them with a means to terminate pregnancies that resulted from premarital intercourse. According to the New Right, liberals had seized control of governmental machinery during the 1960s and were using it to advance their own evil agenda. The conservative backlash of the 1970s and 1980s produced dozens of single-issue lobbying organizations. The National Right to Life Committee besieged "abortion" clinics and regaled legislators with gory pictures of unborn fetuses. The 50,000

Americans, mostly women, who joined Phyllis Schlafly's Eagle Forum spent millions of dollars warning Americans that passage of the ERA would mean unisex toilets, women in combat, and homosexual marriages.

Far more important than these single-issue groups in advancing the cause of neoconservatism was the growing participation in the political process by evangelical Christians. By the time Ronald Reagan was elected president, more than 50 million Americans admitted to having been "born again" and having had a "personal experience" with God. The most important correlative factor – more than class, race, region, or gender – in predicting opposition to abortion, busing, and the ERA was religious commitment. A Washington for Jesus rally brought 200,000 evangelical Christians to the nation's capital. One speaker declared the world to be "aflame in sin." Televangelists entered the political arena with a vengeance. Fundamentalist television talk shows such as the "700 Club" and the "PTL (Praise the Lord) Hour" reached millions of Americans. One of the hosts, the charismatic Pat Robertson (the son of a long-time congressman), urged his listeners to go to the polls and vote humanists, hedonists, and atheists out of office. "We have enough . . . votes to run the country," he declared. Jerry Falwell continued to harangue the nation from his "Old Time Gospel Hour" broadcast over 225 television and 300 radio stations. Falwell's Moral Majority learned which issues to focus on and which legislators to target through his sermons and mail-outs. "We're going to single out those people in government who are against what we consider to be the Bible, moralist position," Falwell proclaimed. Some respected analysts, including the pollster Lou Harris, credit the Moral Majority with Reagan's election in 1980. Working with sympathetic local ministers, it registered an estimated 5 million evangelicals who had never voted before and accounted for 10 million votes in the fall election, providing Reagan with his margin of victory.

Convinced that the national news media was controlled by the liberal, eastern establishment, the New Right adopted a new and effective technique – the direct mail campaign. The tactic was developed by a right-wing Texas lawyer-turned-political-consultant named Richard Vigurie. He established a multimillion dollar company he called RAVCO, and effectively appealed to conservatives to lend their votes and money to a variety of right-wing causes from the ERA to abortion to busing to prayer in the schools. At its peak RAVCO sent out 100 million pieces of mail on behalf of single-issue groups and conservative political candidates. These letters were generally personal appeals with a shrill message full of anger and fear. Critics of the direct mailing technique condemned it as a get-rich-quick scheme by unscrupulous political consultants, but in reality, the cost of such campaigns frequently consumed the lion's share of the funds raised. However, politically they were quite effective. The vivid language and graphic pictures virtually compelled a response. A survey conducted by the National Right to Life Committee showed that 70% of those contacted by mail voted in 1978, and another 50% donated at least $25 to a "right to life" campaign.

While Vigurie and the direct mail entrepreneurs generated grass roots support for the conservative agenda, a new group of think tanks emerged to lend intellectual legitimacy to family values, individualism, and religion. During the 1960s, liberals had controlled the national debate over socioeconomic and foreign policy issues through the Brookings Institute, the Ford Foundation, and the Rockefeller Foundation. To compete with these centers of social activist thought, well-heeled conservatives such as brewing magnate Joseph Coors and the descendents of newspaper tycoon William Randolph Hearst contributed millions of dollars to create the Heritage Foundation and the American Enterprise Institute. The Hoover Institute, associated with Stanford University, acquired new funding and new status. Conservative intellectuals at these centers produced hundreds of articles and scores of books giving constitutional, philosophical, and historical justification to the struggle against affirmative action, abortion rights, and the ERA. They were joined in their conservative crusade by newspaper columnists such as George Todt and William Safire and the *National Review's* William F. Buckley.

There was no doubt about the strength and success of the New Right. The American Conservative Union claimed 300,000 members, and the National Conservative Political Action Committee unquestionably played crucial roles in creating the Reagan majority. But, in fact, a closer look at the election statistics for 1980 reveal that massive voter apathy had as much to do with Reagan's election and GOP successes in Congress as the "conservative revolution." Ronald Reagan was elected by 28% of the voting population. The largest voting bloc in 1980 was comprised of those who did not vote, that is, 47%. This figure was particularly striking when compared with an 85% turnout in such West European countries as West Germany, Sweden, and Italy in the 1970s. The decline in voter turnout was sudden and sharp. During the Gilded Age, nearly 90% of those eligible had cast their ballots and, as late as 1960, two thirds of American voters had turned out on election day. Those who stayed away from the polls in 1980 were overwhelmingly working-class, poor, and unemployed Americans, traditional Democratic constituencies. In cities such as New York, which were proportionately overpopulated with laborers, service workers, and welfare recipients, voter turnout dropped from 63% in 1960 to 42% in 1976. In contrast, nearly 70% of those eligible to cast their ballots in the well-to-do suburbs of Chicago and Minneapolis turned out.

The causes of this voter dropout and its demographics are a matter of speculation. Disenchantment with government and politics in the wake of Vietnam and Watergate was intense. The Yankelovich polling concern ran a survey that asked questions concerning trust in government and faith in the future and compared the answers with a survey done a decade earlier. Between the 1960s and 1970s, the number of people believing that the government was run for the wealthy and influential few grew from 28% to 65%. Those who were convinced that the people governing them were basically intelligent and competent fell from 69% to 29%. Most revealing, only 29% were of the opinion that lawmakers and officials would "do what is right most of the time." Ironically, the disaffected middle and upper classes continued to vote Republican or switched parties, while the disaffected working classes and poor stopped voting, making their view that the government was controlled by a wealthy and powerful elite a self-fulfilling prophesy. Political pundits and critics of the Democratic Party claimed that its working-class constituency had abandoned it because the party had abandoned its working-class constituency. Instead of concentrating on job creation, higher wages, and increased social benefits, the Carter administration had sought to deal with the socioeconomic crisis by balancing the budget, raising interest rates, and reducing taxes. When the party returned to its New Deal roots, observers claimed, voters would return to it.

The "Me Decade"

Although social activism remained strong in American culture and society with feminists, the civil rights movement, gay liberation, and environmentalism scoring significant successes, the dominant theme of the 1980s seemed to be the self-absorbed narcissism that had sprung up in the late 1970s. Indeed, novelist Tom Wolfe termed the period the "me decade." Faced with memories of Watergate and Vietnam, with economic stagnation, and with a seemingly discredited liberalism, many Americans turned their back on civic action and social justice. That such a reaction had taken place following both world wars made it no less threatening to the democratic process.

Evidence of a pervasive narcissism was everywhere. Escapist, vacuous novels like Erich Segal's *Love Story* (1970) and Peter Benchley's *Jaws* (1974) were turned into best-selling movies. *Superman* (1978) made a comeback, and millions flocked to see Harrison Ford as Indiana Jones, the swashbuckling adventurer in *Raiders of the Lost Ark* (1981). Checkout stand tabloids such as the *National Enquirer* boomed as did daytime talk shows, which explored in great detail the private lives of the dysfunctional and deviant. "Yuppies" (young urban professionals) bought and remodeled entire inner-city blocks, creating islands of elegance and affluence in a sea of crime and poverty. The middle class worked relentlessly on their bodies, running, lifting, stretching, cycling, and dieting. Jim Fixx's *The Complete Book of Running* sold 800,000 copies; sales fell off sharply, however, when the author died of a heart attack while training. As wives joined husbands in the workforce, couples postponed childbearing and then, when they did have children, put their young ones in day care centers. Indeed, as early as 1977, 35% of all American children under five spent their days with babysitters or in day care centers. At the same time, affluent young parents spent enormous sums on special schools such as Montessori, which promised to develop their pupils' minds at an early age, thus ensuring their entry into the best prep schools and colleges.

Perhaps the most dramatic and graphic manifestation of the self-absorption of the 1980s was the "human potential movement." The leader in this field was Werner Erhard (born Jack Rosenberg, a door-to-door encyclopedia salesman) whose Erhard Seminars Training (EST) enrolled 6,000 people per month at its peak, grossing $25 million in 1980. The Erhard seminars combined pop psychology, mysticism, and self-help philosophy. Participants signed up for 60-hour intensive sessions where through role-playing, humiliation, and brainwashing, participants learned the central lesson of life, namely, "You are the one and only source of your experience. You created it." EST and similar programs taught self-esteem and the value of "power relationships," that is, relationships with those who profited one's career or built up one's ego.

Ronald Reagan

No one articulated the philosophy and desires of the "me generation" better than Ronald Reagan. The new president was born in Tampico, Illinois, and he grew up in a series of small towns in the western part of the state, along the Mississippi River. As an adult, he liked to recall that his youth was idyllic, but in reality his father was an alcoholic who had to move frequently to escape his debtors. Nevertheless, Reagan's devout mother loved him deeply and encouraged him in an amateur acting career in high school. He attended the denominational Eureka College near Peoria where he continued to act and absorbed good heartland values of individualism, free enterprise, hard work, and conventional morality. Upon graduation, he took a job at WHO radio in Des Moines, Iowa. During the next five years, Reagan enthralled audiences by giving a play-by-play reenactment of baseball games from tickertape summaries.

Although he was later to be the darling of American conservatives, Reagan voted Democratic throughout the 1930s and 1940s. Indeed, his father, Jack, eked out an existence by working for a New Deal relief agency, and Reagan idolized Franklin D. Roosevelt, memorizing segments of his most famous speeches. In 1937, while covering a Chicago Cubs baseball game Reagan wrangled a screen test with Warner Brothers. The studio signed him to a contract, and the former sports announcer moved to Hollywood where he starred in a series of grade B movies. His most memorable performance was as George Gipp in "The Knute Rockne Story." "Win one for the Gipper!" became one of Reagan's stock phrases. He also specialized in westerns, which he loved, but as one biographer has noted, he rarely seemed to get the girl. Nonetheless, in 1940, he married actress Jane Wyman. The couple subsequently had two children, one adopted and one biological.

During World War II, Reagan remained in Hollywood where he made training films for the armed forces. Nevertheless, he worshipped the military and later manufactured stories about witnessing heroic deeds at the front. In reality, he never left California. By the late 1940s, Reagan's film career appeared to be headed for decline, and he grew increasingly interested in public affairs and politics. From 1947 through 1952, he served as president of the Screen Actors Guild. The Red Scare of the 1950s made a deep impression on the handsome midwesterner, and he became convinced of the existence of a communist conspiracy to take over the film industry. He denounced and then testified against actors, directors, and writers who were subsequently blacklisted by the Federal Bureau of Investigation (FBI) and the House Un-American Activities Committee (HUAC).

In 1952, Reagan's marriage to Jane Wyman ended in divorce, but he married another actress, Nancy Davis, shortly afterward. Nancy subsequently bore Reagan two children and introduced him to the world of astrology. In 1954, he took a position with General Electric and, for the next eight years, he hosted a television program for the giant conglomerate and toured the United States speaking on its behalf to workers, executives, and local chambers of commerce. His talks invariably ended with odes to individualism, free enterprise, and middle-class values. America's businessmen and corporate executives, Reagan proclaimed, were struggling valiantly to hold back the tide of "socialism" – rising taxes, government intervention in the economy, and social welfare. In 1964, the Californian caught the attention of American conservatives by delivering a nationally televised address on behalf of Barry Goldwater. It was full of cliches and cribbed lines from Franklin D. Roosevelt, Abraham Lincoln, and Winston Churchill, but Reagan's good looks, engaging personality, and fervor brought $1 million into Goldwater's faltering campaign.

Shortly after the 1964 presidential election debacle, a group of California Republicans handpicked Reagan to challenge the popular and powerful Democratic governor Edmund G. "Pat" Brown. Reagan's political handlers prepared anecdotes, issue positions, and slogans, which they wrote on three-by-five cards for the candidate to memorize, and they kept him away from inquisitive reporters as much as possible. His Republican primary opponents and California Democrats wrote Reagan off as a lightweight. A political moderate, Brown had presided over a vast expansion of the state's social services from higher education to social welfare to transportation. Californians benefited from those services, but many, particularly conservatives in the South, resented the higher taxes that were necessary to pay for them. They were also disturbed by the antiwar movement, the counterculture, the Berkeley free speech movement, and urban unrest, which manifested itself in California in the destructive Watts ghetto riot of 1965. After winning the Republican primary, Reagan successfully portrayed the moderate Brown as a friend of "welfare cheats," "permissive" judges, and urban rioters. If elected, Reagan promised, he would discipline the state's budget and its youth, and clean up the "mess" at Berkeley, as he put it. Try as he might, Brown was unable to convince the voters that Reagan was an undereducated, ill-informed placebo, and Brown lost the election by 1 million votes.

As governor of California, Ronald Reagan foreshadowed the combination of rhetorical stridency and political compromise that was to characterize his presidency. He denounced the increasingly disorderly demonstrations at Berkeley, forcing the resignations of President Clark Kerr and several other administrators he considered too liberal. While decrying the budget deficit left to him by Governor Brown, Reagan doubled government spending from $5 billion to $10 billion a year. At the same time, his speeches changed little from the talks he had given for GE. Infuriated by Gerald Ford's selection of Nelson Rockefeller to be his vice president, Reagan nearly ousted the incumbent in 1976. Four years later, he easily captured the GOP nomination and then the White House.

The new president surprised and momentarily angered some conservatives by naming James A. Baker III as White House chief of staff. A friend of Vice President George Bush, Baker was a nondoctrinaire conservative who advised Reagan to focus his energies on his top two legislative priorities – a major tax cut and massive increases in defense expenditures. The religious right wanted Reagan to expend his political capital, pressuring Congress to pass constitutional amendments on the abortion and school prayer issues, but he wisely refused. Reagan continued to pay lip service to the conservative social agenda, but he realized that the country was deeply divided over abortion, busing, affirmative action, and separation of church and state. Americans had voted for him because he was genial, reassuring, and positive about the future. He sensed that if he was able to control inflation and limit unemployment, he would be reelected.

Supply-Side Economics

The notion of a massive tax cut was emotionally and ideologically appealing to Ronald Reagan and American conservatives. They had accumulated varying amounts of personal wealth, attributing their success to their own hard work and individual initiative. They resented a progressive tax system in which, according to their perception, the enterprising and successful paid for the slothful and unsuccessful. At the same time, the president decried welfare cheats for whom excessive public payments allegedly destroyed any initiative to work and he attacked a tax system that he claimed increasingly denied the well-to-do any incentive to work. Never mind that this was illogical; it appealed to the prejudices of his conservative constituents, and he believed it.

Reagan and his conservative budget director, David Stockman, were impressed by the writings of an obscure economist named Arthur Laffer. Laffer made the obvious observation that taxes set too high or too low would either strangle the economy or bankrupt the federal government. At 100%, all economic activity would grind to a halt; at zero, the government would cease to function. The task of the administration was to find the ideal rate, the "Laffer curve," at which business activity would be maximized and at which the government could continue to function smoothly. In the late 1970s, two ambitious Republicans, Congressman Jack Kemp of New York and Senator William Roth of Delaware, insisted that a 30% cut in personal and business taxes would achieve the ideal balance. They dubbed their philosophy "supply-side economics" in opposition to the "demand-side economics" of J. M. Keynes and J. K. Galbraith, which called for government spending to stimulate consumer demand, in turn creating jobs in the private sector. The Kemp–Roth tax cut promised to achieve the same end but in ways that would not inflate the budget or undermine individual initiative. In supply-side economics, business and industry would plow the monies that previously went to taxes back into their enterprises. Expanding industry and commerce would create new jobs and increase the tax base. Although the tax rate would decrease, government revenues would increase. The Kemp–Roth plan had languished in Congress during the Carter years, but Reagan embraced it with enthusiasm. Neither he nor Kemp nor Roth seemed aware of the fact that the Eisenhower administration had tried supply-side economics in the 1950s, and it had failed.

In his State of the Union address in January 1981, Reagan unveiled his economic program. He called for a 25% reduction in personal and corporate taxes over the next three years. The maximum tax bracket would be reduced from 70% to 50%, while both capital gains and estate and inheritance taxes would decline. The president proposed to make up the revenue shortfall by cutting spending for domestic programs. The administration's budget did not tamper with Social Security or Medicare benefits, and proposed to maintain a "social safety net" for the poor, elderly, and disabled. Rather the proposed $41.4 billion reduction in expenditures would come mainly from cuts in funding for government departments and regulatory agencies, and from elimination of social services and reductions in welfare payments in non–Social Security and Medicare programs.

Advocates for the poor and disadvantaged mobilized to fight the administration's budget. NAACP Director Benjamin Hooks predicted hardship and distress for the dependent and working poor. Liberal Democrats in Congress pushed for restoration of some proposed cuts and were partially

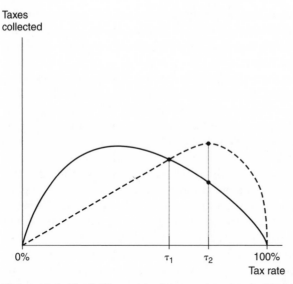

Figure 13–1. The Laffer curve relates tax rates to the total amount of taxes collected, with receipts being zero at the extremes of the rate scale and positive in between.

successful, but the Reagan tax cut, totaling nearly $280 billion, was immensely popular with the public and sailed through intact. Indeed, a large number of conservative southern Democrats, dubbed "boll weevils" by the press, enthusiastically supported the concept of supply-side economics and voted for the president's budget.

Ronald Reagan was all in favor of fiscal responsibility except when it came to the military. He named Caspar Weinberger, a Harvard-educated hawk and leading advocate for the military–industrial establishment, secretary of defense and told Budget Director Stockman and his aides, "Defense is not a budget item." Weinberger and the Joint Chiefs of Staff created a widespread impression that the Soviets had gained a massive advantage in nuclear and conventional forces during the Carter years, and successfully resisted Stockman's efforts to reign in defense spending. Weinberger proposed an annual increase of almost 10% in the Carter budget, and Reagan readily endorsed it. Over the next five years, Department of Defense (DOD) expenditures would reach almost $1.5 trillion. The Reagan defense budgets were the largest in peacetime history and helped triple the deficit by the time the "conservative" Californian left the White House.

From Social Security to the Environment

The economic situation, desperate when Ronald Reagan took the Oath of Office, did not improve appreciably in 1981 and 1982. Unemployment reached an astounding 10%, while inflation continued at a double-digit rate and the prime interest rate hovered near 20%. Despite a rash of business failures, an increase in homelessness, and substantial Democratic gains in Congress in 1982, Reagan refused to reject the concept of supply-side economics. If the United States would be patient, prosperity would return by 1984. He was right, if for the wrong reason. The tight money policies of Federal Reserve Board Chairman Paul Volker, a Carter appointee, began to pay off. The inflation rate fell from 14% in 1980 to 3.5% in 1984. Interest rates declined to 11% – high, but almost half the rate prevailing when Reagan took office. For a variety of reasons – dynamics within OPEC and discovery of new petroleum sources – the price of oil dropped precipitously and the non–energy-producing states experienced economic recovery. For 1983/1984, the gross national product (GNP) increased at a remarkable 4.3% clip. The economy expanded 6.8%, its best showing since 1951, and real income increased by 2.8%. Supply siders took credit for the return of prosperity, but in truth massive expenditures in the defense–aerospace industries stimulated growth in the Southwest, New England, and the West Coast. The projected budget deficit for 1984 was almost $200 billion.

The area in which the Reagan administration showed true fiscal responsibility was Social Security reform. Informed that the trust fund from which payments were made would be bankrupt by the year 2000, Reagan appointed a bipartisan commission headed by economist Alan Greenspan to study the problem and report. In 1982, the commission recommended, among other things, increasing the retirement age from 65 to 67, taxing Social Security benefits paid to the well-to-do, and delaying cost-of-living increases. In 1983, Congress converted those proposals into law.

In his inaugural address, Ronald Reagan had declared that "government is not the solution to our problem, government is the problem." In fact, the president and his staff considered any government regulation as anticompetitive. The budgets for the Occupational Health and Safety Administration (OSHA), the Securities and Exchange Commission (SEC), and the Environmental Protection Agency (EPA) were slashed. The justification given was to balance the budget, but the intended and actual effect was to render these agencies incapable of enforcing regulations established by Congress. Frequently, Reagan recruited individuals who were opposed to the mission of the agency or department they headed. Transportation Secretary Drew Lewis relaxed enforcement of regulations on the automobile industry for everything from stronger bumpers to reduced exhaust emissions. Environmental polluters, from chemical producers to coal-burning manufacturing plants, found an understanding friend in EPA head Anne Burford Gorsuch. Indeed, during the Reagan presidency, toxic waste dumps became an ever more conspicuous part of the American landscape. Perhaps the most controversial of the administration's new team of "regulators" was Interior Secretary James G. Watt, who had (before assuming office) represented a political lobby that favored exploiting the public domain. He attacked environmentalists as extremists and socialists. Under his rule, the Interior Department opened federal lands to exploitation by coal and timber companies, blocked the creation of new wilderness preserves, and began the process of making 1 million acres of offshore land available to private companies for drilling. So confrontational was Watt that he was forced to resign in 1983 – he referred to a public commission with which he disagreed as consisting of "a black, a woman, two Jews, and a cripple" – but the policies he had initiated remained in place.

Spending the Way to Victory: Reagan and the Cold War

The Reagan administration seemed most serious about acting in areas where the old and new right intersected: reduced taxes, less government, and confrontation with the forces of international communism. Although he blasted his predecessor for being soft on communism, for coddling the Soviets, and for pursuing a human rights policy that opened the door to left-wing revolutionaries in the developing world, Reagan actually took up where Carter had left off. Reagan's view of Soviet communism seemed frozen in the mid-1950s. The Kremlin, Reagan was convinced, was at the head of a worldwide conspiracy to export totalitarianism to all parts of the world. At his first press conference, the president declared that the Soviets were "prepared to commit any crime, to lie, to cheat" to facilitate the spread of Marxism. For Reagan, as for members of the Moral Majority, Soviet communism represented all the negative forces abroad in the world: atheism, state socialism, and immorality. Likewise, anticommunism was a crucial component of the struggle to resurrect the hallowed principles of liberty, free enterprise, patriotism, and family values. For Reagan, the Soviet Union was truly "the Evil Empire." The president's principal foreign policy advisers – Secretary of State Alexander Haig and his successor, George Shultz, Secretary of Defense Caspar Weinberger, National Security Adviser Richard Allen, and Ambassador to the United Nations Jeane Kirkpatrick – all shared their chief's fear of an overweening Soviet state, although some were far more ideological than others and they differed dramatically on how to deal with the red menace.

Like the Eisenhower administration in the 1950s, the Reagan administration soon proved that it was more willing to roll back the Iron Curtain in word than in deed. In 1980, the long-time desire for an independent trade union among Polish workers culminated in the establishment of Solidarity. After a series of strikes threatened to overturn the communist government, it recognized the union and opened a limited dialog with its leader, Lech Walesa. These concessions only led to more demands, and within a year Solidarity had become a rallying point for Catholics and nationalists, counting some 10 million Poles among its members. When it demanded a national referendum on the ruling communist clique and continued military ties to the Soviet Union, Moscow pressured the government into a crackdown. The communists arrested Walesa and outlawed his independent union. Although many Americans sympathized deeply with Solidarity, the Reagan administration's response to the wave of repression was mild indeed. The U.S. government refused either to impose a grain embargo – which would have hurt American farmers – or to call in some $25 billion in overdue debts owed by the Soviet Union and Poland.

Defenders of the Reagan administration would later claim that its huge defense budgets were deliberate attempts to spend the Soviet Union into bankruptcy. Whether this was the case, whether Reagan and Weinberger really believed their own propaganda about Soviet arms superiority, or whether the administration was simply serving its military–industrial constituency is unclear. What is certain is that the administration embarked on a massive arms buildup and rejected meaningful arms control negotiations with the Soviets. After promising to develop a "new basing mode," the administration secured congressional appropriations to begin work on the MX missile system. Reagan ordered the DOD to have 100 B-1 bombers ready to fly by 1986, despite some experts' advice to abandon the expensive B-1 for the projected Stealth bomber, a low-flying, shielded aircraft not subject to radar detection. The administration also went ahead with plans for development of the air-launched cruise missiles (ALCMs) intended for deployment in Europe.

Although Congress approved virtually all the president's defense proposals, a nationwide poll in the spring of 1982 indicated that 57% of the respondents favored an immediate freeze on the testing, deployment, and production of nuclear weapons. During the 1980 campaign, Reagan had stated that SALT should not be ratified until and unless it was completely reworked, but in 1982 in an effort to undercut mounting antinuclear sentiment, the president authorized a new round of arms control talks, the Strategic Arms Reduction Talks (START). After the death of Leonid Brezhnev in November of that year, the Reagan administration once again proposed a plan in which the United States would refrain from deploying some 572 Pershing II and cruise missiles in Europe; in return, the Soviets would remove the 613 intermediate range missiles they had stationed in Eastern Europe. The new Soviet leader, Yuri Andropov, rejected the proposal as a thinly veiled attempt by the United States to gain nuclear superiority over the Soviet Union and its allies. Moscow would have to dismantle existing missiles in return for an American promise not to build more, thus putting the Soviet Union further behind in total number of warheads. Moreover, the Kremlin pointed out that cruise and Pershing missiles could reach Moscow from Europe while Soviet intermediate missiles could not threaten Washington.

In the spring of 1983, Reagan unveiled an ambitious new defense plan that threatened the concept of mutual assured destruction (MAD) and virtually assured an escalation of the arms race. To deal with the Soviet Union's "margin of superiority," the United States would launch the Strategic Defense Initiative (SDI). Labeled "Star Wars" by its critics, the new defense system would consist of lasers and particle beams projected from ground stations and satellites in space. These "death rays" would allegedly destroy incoming enemy missiles before they entered the earth's atmosphere. Those few that slipped through would easily be taken care of by the anti-ballistic missile (ABM) system, according to the administration. Domestic critics of the plan claimed that SDI was both impractical and outrageously expensive. Andropov denounced SDI as a deliberate attempt by the United States to undermine the concept of mutually assured destruction, the basis for global peace since the late 1950s. It would, he declared, "open the floodgates of a runaway race of all types of strategic arms, both offensive and defensive."

With arms control negotiations at a standstill, Soviet–American relations took still another nosedive in September 1983, when Soviet aircraft shot down a South Korean Boeing 747 commercial airliner (KAL 007), killing 269 people, including 60 Americans. The airliner had accidentally strayed over Sakhalin Island, the site of Soviet missile sites and communications facilities, but the Kremlin claimed that the overflight had been deliberate and that KAL 007 was on an intelligence mission, and refused to apologize or express remorse. The Reagan administration vehemently denounced the atrocity and shortly thereafter began deploying Pershing II and cruise missiles in Great Britain and West Germany. In response, Soviet representatives walked out of the START talks in Geneva; according to one government official, relations between the two superpowers were "white hot."

Sandinistas and Contras: Central America and the Cold War

The Reagan administration was determined, it said, to battle international communism "on all fronts." The primary arena of struggle between the forces of democracy and totalitarianism, free enterprise and state socialism during the 1980s was Central America. Like Carter and Brzezinski, Reagan, Haig, and Kirkpatrick decided that the Sandinista regime in Nicaragua was thoroughly Marxist, an agent of Soviet imperialism, and a conduit of arms and money from Cuba to left-wing revolutionaries in El Salvador. The economic embargo of Cuba remained in place, and in 1981, the administration agreed to underwrite a land reform program in El Salvador and sent 55 military advisers to help train President Jose Napoleon Duarte's army. In the fall of that same year, Reagan secretly approved the expenditure of nearly $20 million by the CIA to train and equip a rebel army, which came to be known as "contras," to overthrow the Sandinistas in Nicaragua. By 1983, some 2,000 contras operating out of Honduras were fighting a guerrilla war in Nicaragua.

The Reagan administration's Central American policy came in for sharp and immediate criticism. The struggles in El Salvador and Nicaragua were basically civil wars springing from indigenous roots. The infusion of American aid and advisers – the administration referred to them as "trainers" – and the sponsoring of the contras could only lead to another Vietnam, critics argued. U.S. strategic and economic interests were not threatened by what transpired in those two tiny, impoverished nations. Indeed, some liberals argued that socioeconomic progress was more likely under left-wing rather than right-wing governments. Anti-administration journalists and members of Congress insisted, in addition, that military aid was irrelevant; the roots of political unrest in Central America as in other developing areas were social and economic. Finally, Washington's anticommunist policies inevitably placed the United States on the side of brutal military juntas that engaged in gross human rights violations.

In justifying its approach to Central America, the Reagan administration shamelessly invoked the domino theory and the image of a monolithic communist threat. The guerrillas in El Salvador and the Sandinistas in Nicaragua were "Soviet proxies," and their activities were examples of "international terrorism" emanating from Moscow. The United States was "the last domino," President Reagan declared. But the leading apologist for the administration's Central American policy was UN Ambassador Jean Kirkpatrick. The former Georgetown University political scientist asserted that there was a distinct difference between "authoritarian" and "totalitarian" governments. Authoritarian regimes such as that in El Salvador had to circumscribe civil liberties in times of civil war, but they were not inherently or pervasively repressive. In religion, cultural matters, family values, and economics much leeway existed in authoritarian societies, whereas every aspect of human existence was controlled in totalitarian systems. Moreover, authoritarian systems were capable of evolving into democratic, libertarian societies and totalitarian states were not. Like Jimmy Carter, Ronald Reagan found that he could not always be consistent. In 1982, when an "authoritarian" government in Argentina seized the Falkland Islands from Great Britain, the United States came to the aid of its NATO partner and, in an effort to isolate the Soviet Union, the Reagan administration strengthened its ties with the "totalitarian" regime in China. Nevertheless, the Kirkpatrick model continued as justification for a relentlessly anticommunist policy in Central America.

In the spring of 1982, El Salvador held national elections. The insurgents and their supporters refused to participate, and Duarte's Christian Democrats lost control of the National Assembly to a right-wing coalition dominated by the military. The land reform program came to an end and government-sponsored "death squads" began systematically liquidating opponents of the regime. Reagan responded by blaming the unrest on the insurgents and announcing that Salvadorian troops would be trained in the United States. If Congress refused to continue aid, the president declared, he would put even more American advisers into the country. Meanwhile, the CIA continued to funnel supplies to the contras in Nicaragua. There was a certain "symmetry" to American policy, Kirkpatrick and the State Department declared. The United States would continue to undermine the Sandinista regime as long as it plotted to overthrow the pro-U.S. government in El Salvador.

In October 1983, the Reagan administration sent troops into the tiny Caribbean island of Grenada claiming to prevent the establishment of another Soviet beachhead in the Americas. In 1979, leftists under the leadership of Maurice Bishop had overthrown the corrupt but anticommunist government in that British Commonwealth country. During the next few years, Bishop accepted help from the Castro government in building what he termed an "international airport." In the summer of 1982, he visited Moscow and declared that he had received assurances of long-term financial assistance. The following spring, Reagan displayed U-2 photographs of Cuban barracks and the airstrip on Grenada. When in October fighting broke out between Bishop and his conservative opponents, Reagan sent U.S. Marines and U.S. Army units into the island. American troops quickly "restored order" and presided over the installation of a transitional government that proved to be thoroughly anticommunist. Hungry for any kind of military triumph in the wake of Vietnam, Americans generally applauded the administration's Grenada adventure. Such was not the case with Reagan's policies toward Lebanon, however.

Disaster in Lebanon

Like its predecessors, the Reagan administration viewed the political instability in the Middle East as an open, continuing invitation to the Soviet Union to project its military and political power into the region. By mid-1982, the formerly stable and prosperous country of Lebanon teetered on the brink of chaos. The Arab–Israeli conflict and the presence of thousands of Palestinian refugees in the southern part of the country had upset the delicate balance between Christians and Muslims. Sectarian militia were fighting pitched battles for control of Beirut, Syrian troops occupied the northern part of the country, and PLO fatah fighters dominated the southern part of the country. In June, Israel invaded from the south in an effort to halt Palestinian raids and to crush the PLO. At this point, the United States arranged for a cease-fire and the peaceful evacuation of Yassir Arafat and his government-in-exile. The U.S. government subsequently contributed 800 troops to a peace-keeping force. What was intended as a 30-day stay turned out to be a year-and-a-half ordeal for the Marines involved. Caught in a cross-fire between Christian and Muslim militia, the Americans were in an impossible position. On October 23, 1983, a suicide bomber drove an explosives-laden vehicle through a check point and into a Marine barrack.

The resulting explosion killed 283 sleeping soldiers. By early the next year, Reagan had withdrawn the last remaining soldier from Lebanon. Surprisingly, the Middle East disaster seemed to have little impact on Reagan's popularity. Indeed, the press began referring to him as the "Teflon president" because nothing negative seemed to stick to him.

The "Great Communicator"

If ever a president and his advisers understood that in the age of television appearance was reality, it was Ronald Reagan, Jim Baker, Edwin Meese, and Michael Deaver (Meese and Deaver were presidential aides). Reagan's experience as a Hollywood star and television host enabled him to appear confident and relaxed in front of the camera and microphone. The White House prepared public appearances and announcements always with 30-second sound bite and camera angle in mind. With his ruddy good looks and tremulous, sincere voice, the aged president reassured the American people about themselves and their future. On college campuses where but a few years earlier students had demonstrated against Lyndon B. Johnson, Richard M. Nixon, and government in general, a new generation wore ties, skirts, and chanted "USA! USA!" in response to Reagan's oratory. The president was also a capable one-on-one persuader. Indeed, compared with Jimmy Carter, Reagan was an excellent congressional politician. Not only did his self-effacing sense of humor break down the defenses of even the most cynical of congressmen and senators, but also his willingness to compromise made him seem part of the system. Indeed, Reagan's ability to instill a sense of community in those with whom he came in contact earned him the title of "the Great Communicator" from the press.

Reagan's response to two events during his first term made him seem decisive and tough as well as humane. In 1981, the air traffic controllers' union struck for higher wages and better working conditions, thus violating a legislative ban on strikes by public employees. Reagan responded promptly by firing them all and calling in military controllers to handle commercial flights until civilian replacements could be trained. Public, press, and Congress all praised him for his action; in the midst of a deep recession, the controllers' wage demands appeared to be outrageous. That spring the president was shot and critically wounded by a deranged gunman, John Hinckley. Reagan, who remained conscious throughout, was the epitome of gallantry under fire. "Honey, I forgot to duck," he quipped to his wife, Nancy, and jokingly asked his doctor, just before he began operating, if he were a Republican. The press thought him corny, but his lack of pretension and mean-spiritedness made him irresistible. No president since John F. Kennedy received better treatment from the media.

Only in retrospect would it become apparent that Ronald Reagan was a shell, a stereotypical actor who went from one role to the next, who served as a facade for an inner core of advisers who in most respects actually ran the United States. His press conferences were disasters and were kept to a minimum. He frequently seemed unfamiliar with his own programs. Reagan's gaffes were legendary; during the 1980 campaign, he had once blamed trees for air pollution. If his speeches and answers were not strictly scripted, he became anxious and confused. Toward the end of his second term, word began to leak out that the president frequently nodded off at cabinet meetings and could not remember the names of his closest advisers. But in 1984, much of this was not apparent or did not matter. Reagan had the presence and the vision, and as he prepared to run for a second term, political prognosticators predicted that he would be almost impossible to defeat.

The Election of 1984

In retrospect, Ronald Reagan was unbeatable in 1984, but hope springs eternal in the breasts of politicians, and a bevy of Democratic aspirants entered the fray. The man who came closest to replicating the all-American image of Ronald Reagan was Senator John Glenn of Ohio. A fiscal conservative and cold warrior, the former astronaut was then in the process of having a movie made about him and his fellow space explorers. Senator Gary Hart of Colorado claimed to be the candidate with new ideas. His rugged good looks, self-effacing humor, and engaging speaking style were reminiscent of John F. Kennedy. Unfortunately for him, so was his extramarital sex life. The choice of African Americans and many McGovern Democrats was the Reverend Jesse Jackson, a protégé of Martin Luther King, Jr. Indeed, he had been on the balcony in Memphis with King when he was shot. Jackson headed what his supporters referred to as the Rainbow Coalition, a multiracial political grouping that allegedly represented Democrats of all races and ethnic groups. Nuclear freeze proponent Senator Alan Cranston of California was first among a group of minor candidates. The front runner for the Democratic nomination, however, was former Vice President Walter Mondale. Jimmy Carter had insisted that Mondale be involved in issue development and decision making throughout his presidency. The son of a minister and a piano teacher, Mondale was a compassionate man, a traditional New Deal/Great Society Democrat who could appeal to African Americans, labor unions, teachers, environmentalists, and women's groups.

The Minnesotan's candidacy received a momentary setback when he was up-ended in the New Hampshire primary by Hart, who successfully attacked Mondale for pandering to "special interest groups." Mondale rallied in the Midwest and Mid-Atlantic states, but Hart showed strength in the West and New England. Gradually, all were driven from the field but Mondale, Hart, and Jackson. Jackson's association with the Black Muslims and his intemperate racial slurs – he referred to New York as "Hymietown" – cost him dearly. By the time the Democratic National Convention met in San Francisco, Mondale had rounded up a majority of the delegates, and he was nominated on the first ballot. After some delay, he picked Congresswoman Geraldine A. Ferraro as his running mate. A bright, articulate, attractive woman, Ferraro was selected not only because she would add strength across the board but because, it was hoped, her presence on the ticket would exploit the "gender gap," which showed a 10- to 15-point difference between men and women on such issues as a nuclear freeze and social justice.

Mondale and his advisers believed that Reagan was vulnerable on a number of points. Under Reaganomics, the rich had grown richer and the poor poorer. Even the administration's budget director, David Stockman, had admitted that the president's tax policies were an update of Herbert Hoover's "trickle down" approach – if the rich did well, some of their prosperity was bound to reach the lower rungs of the socioeconomic ladder. It seemed obvious that Reagan's arms buildup not only risked a violent, possibly apocalyptic clash with the Soviet Union but was unbalancing the budget to such a degree that future generations would never be able to dig out from beneath the deficit. Opinion polls indicated that more than 70% of Americans favored a nuclear freeze. A clean, safe environment also seemed to be of growing importance to Americans, Democrats believed, and Reagan's antiregulatory stance could be portrayed as hopelessly anachronistic.

The Democrats were grasping at straws. The economy was on the upswing; except for the 20% at the bottom of the economic scale, Americans were better off than they had been four years earlier. The deficit was an abstraction that had no immediate, tangible effect on the average person's life. The census showed that seven states had 1 million or more people 65 years of age or older and that virtually all population growth had been in the South and West – both plusses for the Republicans. Reagan extolled traditional values and exuded optimism about the future. "I think there's a new feeling of patriotism in our land, a recognition that by any standard America is a decent and generous place, a force for good in the world," the president declared. In the aftermath of Watergate and Vietnam, this was just what Americans wanted to hear. From the beginning of his campaign, Mondale was on the defensive. He had to try to confront the nation with reality, that is, to focus on the issues: that America was mired in red ink, confusing selfishness with opportunity and beating up on defenseless Third World countries to move past Vietnam. This was not what Americans wanted to hear. In a famous quip, the Democratic candidate declared, "He'll raise taxes, so will I. He won't tell you, I just did." Political columnists and commentators praised him for his candor and then agreed that he had committed political suicide. Republican ideologue Jean

Table 13–1. The election of 1984

Candidates	Parties	Electoral vote	Popular vote	Percentage of popular vote
Ronald Reagan	Republican	525	54,451,521	58.8
Walter Mondale	Democratic	13	37,565,334	40.5

Kirkpatrick dubbed Mondale "bad news Fritz Mondale," accusing him of being part of the "blame-America-first crowd."

The presidential and vice presidential candidates participated in two televised debates, each in October. Ferraro held her own with George Bush; Mondale won the first and lost the second encounter with Reagan. The debates, as it turned out, did not matter. Polls showed the Republicans leading wire to wire. In a crushing defeat for Mondale, Reagan captured 49 states and 525 electoral votes. The popular vote showed 54.5 million (59%) for Reagan and 37.6 million (41%) for Mondale. There was no coattail effect for the 1984 election, however. Democrats retained their majority in the House and made small gains in the Senate. The outcome of the contest was an affirmation of Ronald Reagan's personal campaign skills and the correctness of his campaign strategy. When a reporter observed to a White House staffer that the president seemed more interested in petting dogs than addressing issues, the staffer replied: "We are not here to educate America. We are here to re-elect Ronald Reagan." The "gipper" seemed to personify America, or to embody what most Americans believed they were. To attack him was to attack the nation – its hopes and dreams, its traditions and values. Reagan's campaign slogan, "we brought America back," fell on appreciative ears. In 1980, only one fifth of Americans polled indicated they believed the United States was being run for the benefit of all; in 1984, that figure had doubled. During the depths of the Carter malaise, three quarters of those questioned indicated they believed the past would be better than the future; by the time the 1984 election results were in, 50% of those polled were looking forward rather than backward. However, the rebirth of American optimism would be short lived.

Four More Years

As Ronald Reagan began his second term, the only real cloud on the political horizon seemed to be the deficit, and that, as pragmatists such as the president knew, would not really affect the everyday lives of Americans – at least not during Reagan's remaining years in office. The only major change in the administration came when White House Chief of Staff James Baker changed places with Treasury Secretary Donald Regan. The president did not seem to notice any difference at first, but he soon would. Baker's assistant, Michael Deaver, resigned to cash in on his newfound influence as a Washington, D.C., insider. He opened a public relations firm and soon ran afoul of influence-peddling laws. Reagan's White House counselor, Edwin Meese, persuaded his chief to nominate him for the post of attorney general. Congress then uncovered the fact that the nominee had used his office to promote the interests of Wedtech, a defense contracting firm that had been defrauding the government. Meese's friend and financial adviser, E. Robert Wallach, was a major stockholder in the company. The Senate Judiciary Committee decided that Meese had been guilty only of extremely bad judgment and confirmed him. Nevertheless, at this point the "sleaze factor" was only a minor irritation for the president.

As 1986 began, the nation was shocked and saddened by the explosion of the space shuttle *Challenger* 74 seconds after takeoff. The blast killed all seven astronauts aboard, including Christa McAuliffe, a high school teacher from Concord, New Hampshire, the mother of two, and the first civilian chosen for a space shuttle flight. On June 9, a presidential commission report identified failure of a seal on the solid-fuel booster rocket as the cause of the explosion and noted that NASA officials had been warned concerning the reliability of the seals, especially in cold weather. Rumors circulated that the agency, under pressure from the White House not to postpone what was sure to be a public relations event of the first magnitude, had pushed ahead with the launch in spite of these warnings. The official report, however, merely criticized NASA for a long history of managerial and engineering mistakes.

By the summer of 1986, stock market prices had reached all-time highs. To Reagan's satisfaction, Congress passed his tax reform bill, the principal legislative initiative of his second term. The measure closed several glaring loopholes and reduced the number of tax brackets from 15 to 3: 15%, 28%, and 33%. The bill eliminated taxes for the poorest Americans, but the real beneficiaries were the wealthy who under the old system could theoretically be taxed at a maximum rate of 50%. To celebrate – Ronald Reagan loved celebrations: parades, awards, commemorations – the first couple hosted a televised Fourth of July extravaganza at the Statue of Liberty. Republican celebrities entertained America, and New York put on the largest fireworks display in history. Shortly thereafter, the illusion that Reagan and his advisers had so carefully created began to come apart.

President Reagan responded to warnings concerning the ill effects of huge deficits by blaming Congress for funding irresponsible entitlement programs and "pork barrel" legislation for their home districts. In reality, the president's budget was the real culprit. Tax cuts, coupled with a 41% real increase in defense spending, sent the deficit soaring from $90 billion in 1982 to $283 billion in 1986. That latter figure was more than 10 times higher than for any other presidential administration. To finance the deficit, the federal government had to borrow at home and abroad. When the

Federal Reserve Board raised interest rates to attract capital, billions of dollars flowed into the United States from overseas, the value of the dollar skyrocketed, imports became cheaper, and exports more expensive. The flood of goods from abroad forced some American industries to close their doors or to relocate abroad to take advantage of cheap labor and lower prices. The inability of American products to compete in foreign markets unbalanced trade with foreign nations even further – from $36 billion in 1980 to $170 billion in 1987. America was living on borrowed money; the party of fiscal responsibility was mortgaging the future of the nation's children and grandchildren. By 1987, interest service on the national debt absorbed the output of 1.5 million workers annually.

Under prodding from responsible conservatives in his own party, President Reagan endorsed a balanced budget amendment to the Constitution but insisted that it apply only to his successors. Congress did pass the Graham–Rudman–Hollings Act, which outlined steps the federal government would have to take to balance the budget, but then caved in to White House pressure to adopt accounting methods that negated the effect of the legislation. Fundamental or politically popular items were simply declared "off budget" and not counted in figuring the budget deficit.

The "Culture of Greed"

Supply-side economics both stimulated and reflected what historians have referred to as a "culture of greed," a pervasive self-centered acquisitiveness that seemed to pervade the 1980s. Financier Ivan Boesky, the co-inventor of "junk bonds" who had made millions on Wall Street buying and selling large corporations, told the graduating class at Berkeley in 1986 that "greed is healthy." The principle of unlimited acquisition was what had made America great. A whole generation of Americans, those born between 1945 and 1959, seemed to take him at his word. These young urban professionals, whom *Time* magazine termed "yuppies," rejected community action and social consciousness. They were determined to devote their lives to securing and retaining well-paying jobs and enjoying an affluent lifestyle. Most were liberal on social issues – they did not want to be burdened with unwanted children and denied the right to enjoy "recreational" drugs – but conservative on fiscal issues. They supported the Reagan administration for its low-tax, antiregulation policies. The symbols of yuppiehood were BMW automobiles, designer warm-up suits, gourmet foods, and high-tech sound equipment. They subscribed to *Architectural Digest*, jogged, lived on high-fiber diets, and wore natural fibers. To a greater or lesser extent, they did not care what happened to their fellow Americans.

The true beneficiaries of Reaganomics, however, were the super rich. Supply-side policies nearly doubled the percentage of the nation's wealth going to the top 1% of earners from 8.1% to almost 15%. The average chief executive officer of *Fortune* magazine's Top 500 corporations made 93 times what the average worker did at that company. Professional sports, flooded with revenue from lucrative television contracts, paid its athletes astronomical sums to play games for a brief period in their lives. But the real authors and symbols of the super rich were corporate raiders such as Boesky, T. Boone Pickens, Carl Ichan, Michael Milken, and Ross Perot, and real estate tycoons such as Donald Trump. In response to changes in the tax law and Reagan's virtual abandonment of the antitrust statutes, Wall Street was gripped by "merger mania" from 1981 through 1987. Huge corporations staged hostile takeovers of other giant concerns, some competitors and some not. Boesky and Milken realized that standard investors such as insurance companies and pension funds would not put up money for such high-risk ventures and they pioneered the junk bond – high-risk, high-interest bonds that reaped huge profits for their holders if the merger went through. Unfortunately, the engineers of these takeovers frequently had to sell off the most profitable sectors of their new enterprises to pay off the bondholders. Critics also complained that the mergers added dramatically to the price of stock when the productivity and competitiveness of the company in question had not really increased.

The rash of mergers drove stock prices ever upward and brought about an inevitable crash on Wall Street in 1987. During a single week in October, stocks listed on the Dow Jones averages lost 13% of their value. In one day, the market value of U.S. stocks dropped by $500 billion. Junk bond dealing and irresponsible mergers had started the nosedive, but economists at home and abroad declared that the massive decline was due in large part to the federal government's uncontrolled deficit spending and America's trade imbalance. As one Republican economist pointed out, the United States was borrowing abroad at twice the rate it had in the nineteenth century when it was industrializing. But the GNP was increasing at only a fraction of that rate. America was borrowing and consuming, and international creditors were losing faith in the nation's economy.

Adding to the nation's economic woes was the virtual collapse of the savings and loan industry, a victim of its own excesses and the Reagan administration's antiregulatory policies. During the 1970s, savings and loan (S&L) institutions, or "thrifts," languished because they could not compete with unregulated money market funds. The S&Ls were limited to low-risk, low-profit, long-term home mortgage transactions for the most part, whereas the funds could invest freely. Attracted by higher dividends, tens of thousands of depositors moved their accounts out of the thrifts. Responding to intensive lobbying efforts, at the close of the Carter administration, Congress had increased the federal insurance level on S&L deposits to $100,000. Then in 1982, President Reagan signed the Garn–St. Germain Act, which virtually deregulated the thrift industry. Declaring the measure to be the economic equivalent of a home run, Reagan predicted that it would free billions of dollars to seek their most profitable level in the economy, thus creating new enterprises and raising overall productivity. He was wrong.

Deregulation, coupled with the rise in insurance levels, meant that thrift operators could speculate with their depositors' monies without risk to themselves. They poured billions into undeveloped land, commercial property, shopping centers, and other high-risk ventures. Charles Keating's Lincoln Savings and Loan and the Denver-based Silverado Savings and Loan, which included Vice President Bush's son, Neil, among its directors, became multibillion dollar operations virtually overnight by paying top dollar for $100,000 accounts. In many areas, cheap money stimulated the construction industry and created a real estate boom that drove housing prices through the ceiling. In addition, a number of unscrupulous thrift leaders went beyond irresponsibility. They conspired with builders to drive up the price of projects, receiving kickbacks for their efforts. They made unsecured loans to business partners and "flipped" (sold back and forth) properties several times per day to drive up prices. Because the federal government – American taxpayers – would foot the bill in case deals went sour, the buccaneers of the S&L industry could proceed without fear.

Signs of impending disaster appeared on the horizon in the mid-1980s when the Penn Square S&L of Oklahoma and the Continental Illinois Bank went bankrupt and required a federal bailout. Experts within the financial community had been predicting trouble for years, but the Reagan administration had starved regulatory agencies – the Securities Exchange Commission, the Federal Deposit Insurance Corporation – of funds so that a mere handful of bank examiners were available to deal with thousands of enterprises. In addition, the largest and most corrupt S&Ls, swollen with funds, could act as heavy hitters when it came to campaign contributions. By contributing to the war chests of Senators Donald Riegle, Alan Cranston, John Glenn, John McCain, and others, Keating managed to put off the closing of Lincoln Savings and Loan for one year. By the time it went under, Keating's operation would cost the American taxpayer $2.6 billion. Clearly, the culture of greed had its victims and its victors.

Terrorism as an Issue

At the same time it was turning a blind eye to white-collar crime at home, the Reagan administration declared war on terrorism abroad, at least in some cases. Since the Iranian hostage crisis, international terrorism directed against Americans had become a major political issue. Late in November 1985, the *New York Times* reported that since 1968 U.S. citizens had been attacked by terrorists in 72 countries. In 1985, 17 Americans were killed in terrorist attacks and 154 were wounded. In June of that year, a TWA jetliner was hijacked in Athens by two Shi'ite Muslim terrorists who forced the plane to fly to Beirut and demanded the release of 766 Shi'ites held in Israel. Some of the hostages were released, but 39 Americans were removed from the plane and hidden away. Following a week of tense negotiations, during which the Israeli government reluctantly agreed to free their prisoners, the Shi'ites released their captives. On October 7, the Italian liner *Achille Lauro* was hijacked in the Mediterranean by four members of the Palestinian Liberation Front (PLO). En route to Port Said, Egypt, the terrorists shot and killed a wheelchair-bound American, 69-year-old Leon Klinghoffer, and dumped his body overboard. The number of individuals involved in these incidents was quite small, but intense media coverage, widespread popular empathy with victims, and feelings of vulnerability together with the attention both Reagan and Carter devoted to the terrorism made it one of the most visible issues of the 1980s.

Although strictly speaking Libya was not part of the Middle East, that country and its outspoken military ruler, Colonel Muammar al-Qaddafi, championed the cause of the Palestinians and railed against the West in general and the United States in particular. In 1980, a mob had burned the American Embassy to the ground while police stood by idly. After he assumed the presidency, Reagan retaliated by expelling Libyan diplomats from Washington, D.C. In August of 1981, a U.S. naval flotilla held maneuvers off the Libyan coast. Qaddafi declared that his nation's territorial waters had been violated, and he dispatched a squadron of fighters, two of which the Americans shot down. In 1982, the White House announced that Libyan terrorists were abroad in the United States with instructions to assassinate the president. The administration then embargoed trade with what Reagan termed an openly terrorist state. "We have to put Qaddafi in a box and close the lid," newly named Secretary of State George Shultz told reporters.

In the spring of 1986, relations between Libya and the United States reached crisis stage. The Reagan administration suspected correctly that Qaddafi was sheltering a Palestinian terrorist group that had bombed the Vienna and Rome airports in late 1985, killing 19 (including 5 Americans and 1 Israeli) and wounding 112. In April 1986, a bomb went off in a West Berlin discotheque, killing an American serviceman and a Turkish woman and injuring 230. Generalizing from intelligence reports indicating that Qaddafi was considering terrorist acts against Americans, the White House decided that Libya was responsible. At a news conference, Reagan denounced Qaddafi as the "mad dog of the Middle East." Later that month, 13 F-111s operating out of bases in Great Britain staged a surprise attack on Tripoli. During the 12-minute assault, the U.S. fighters destroyed the Libyan strongman's living quarters and command and communications center. They also killed a number of civilians, including one of Qaddafi's children. Whether intimidated by the attack or restrained by subsequent economic and diplomatic pressure exerted by the nations of Western Europe, the

Libyan firebrand became more restrained. Even though it subsequently became apparent that the Syrians rather than the Libyans were responsible for the West Berlin bombing, the Reagan administration continued to boast of its disciplining of Qaddafi.

There were some people who argued that the U.S. government's campaign against terrorism was hypocritical. Was it not true that America's great friend and ally in the Middle East, Israel, engaged in "state-sponsored terrorism"? With the withdrawal of American peace-keeping troops following the Beirut bombing, the buffers between the Israelis and their Christian allies were removed and one of the most savage acts of the long and already bloody Arab–Israeli conflict ensued. On September 14, Muslim terrorists assassinated the recently elected president of Lebanon, the pro-Israeli Bashir Gemayel of the Christian, or Phalangist, militia. Under the pretense of protecting the Muslim population from Phalangist retaliation, Israeli troops occupied West Beirut. On September 17, with the tacit approval of the Israeli government, the Phalangists wreaked their revenge on the Sabra-Shatilla refugee camps, machine-gunning 800 Palestinian civilians. When a subsequent investigation implicated the Begin government, the United States succeeded in persuading Israel to withdraw its army from Lebanon. But the basic issues of long-term Israeli security and a homeland for the Palestinians remained as unsettled as ever.

The Iran–Contra Affair

Meanwhile, a bloody, life-and-death struggle between Iran and Iraq had erupted in 1980. Iraq, ruled by the secular military strongman, Saddam Hussein, and Iran, still very much under the control of Ayatollah Khomeini and the mullahs, were age-old rivals. This new chapter in their ongoing struggle was the product of an intense competition for regional leadership and control of petroleum resources, refining facilities, and strategic ports. The State Department feared both and attempted to keep either from winning a decisive victory. From 1981 to 1986, the Reagan administration secretly funneled aid to Iran, but from 1987 on tilted toward Iraq. As usual, the United States coordinated its policies with Israel, but that nation with Iraq as its immediate neighbor tended consistently to favor Iran. After the U.S. began aiding Iraq, Iranian aircraft targeted Western ships in the Persian Gulf carrying cargoes to and from their enemy. At this point, Reagan ordered the U.S. Navy to begin convoying tankers in the Gulf. The intrusion of American military power may have protected the shipping lanes, but also led to two tragic cases of mistaken identity. In May 1987, the pilot of an Iraqi fighter-bomber mistook the *USS Sharp* for an Iranian warship, blasting it with a missile that killed 37 sailors. In 1988, the commander of the *USS Vincennes* mistakenly shot down an Iranian airliner, killing 290 civilians. To the U.S. government's intense annoyance, many in the international community equated the incident with the downing of KAL Flight 007.

The Iraq–Iran war, coupled with the bloody conflicts in Central America, produced one of the most bizarre incidents in contemporary diplomatic history – the Iran–Contra affair.

The contras, the anti-Sandinista army made up of Nicaraguan exiles and trained by the CIA, depended almost entirely on American aid and equipment, despite the claims of CIA Director William Casey that the force was spontaneous, indigenous, and focused primarily on cutting off the flow of supplies to the rebels in El Salvador. By 1985, the contra force numbered somewhere between 10,000 and 20,000. The hierarchy included genuine anti-Marxist democrats, but many of the field commanders had been officers in Samoza's army. Concerned over charges of U.S. intervention into Nicaraguan internal affairs and stories of atrocities committed by the contras, in 1982 Congress passed the Boland Amendment sponsored by Representative Edward P. Boland of Massachusetts, which limited CIA aid to the contras to $24 million and stipulated that none of the funds be used to overthrow the Sandinistas. Reagan, who shared Nixon's and Kissinger's views on executive control of foreign policy, directed his subordinates to circumvent the law. The Pentagon began donating "surplus" equipment to the contras, and Casey's agents trained the contras in assassination techniques and coordinated attacks on transportation and port facilities. In 1984, an angry Congress passed an updated version of the Boland Amendment that barred the CIA or "any other agency or entity involved in intelligence activities" from aiding the contras.

This new congressional initiative only strengthened the White House's determination to aid the "freedom fighters" in Nicaragua. With Reagan's approval, a team that included CIA Director William Casey, National Security Council (NSC) Adviser Robert McFarlane, and NSC aide Colonel Oliver North, began raising money from abroad from anticommunist governments and from wealthy conservatives at home. While McFarlane solicited small amounts from Israel, South Africa, South Korea, Saudi Arabia, and Taiwan, Colonel North and Republican fundraiser Carl "Spitz" Channel put together a presentation on behalf of the contras that included film of the gallant contras in action and a direct appeal by the charismatic, simple-minded North. In 1985, this "Project Democracy" raised several million dollars from such anticommunist luminaries as Nelson Bunker Hunt, Ellen Clayton Garwood, and the ever-reliable Joseph Coors. Secretary of State George Shultz warned the president that these activities constituted a possible impeachable offense, but the gipper decided to press ahead.

Meanwhile, Shi'ite Muslim terrorists bankrolled by the Iranian government had taken seven Americans hostage in Beirut. One, William Buckley, was the CIA bureau chief there; the other six were private American citizens who had chosen to stay on in Lebanon despite State Department warnings. Reagan was deeply moved by the plight of the hostages – he like other Americans watched a lot of television – and, following repeated appeals by the families of the victims, directed his subordinates to develop a plan. In the fall of 1985, despite U.S. attacks on Libya and the White House's repeated denunciations of international terrorism, the United States began selling large numbers of antitank missiles to Iran for use in its war with Iraq in an effort to secure the release of the hostages. The deal was worked out between McFarlane and an Iranian intermediary, Manucher Ghorbanifar, who claimed to represent a "moderate" faction in Tehran desirous of better relations with Washington, D.C. Despite three separate arms shipments, funneled through Israel to avoid violating the law banning arms sales to nations that supported terrorism, only one hostage, the Reverend Benjamin Weir, was set free in 1985. Another, Lawrence Jenco, was released in 1986, but by then the Iranian-backed Shi'ites had captured three additional hostages. Despite later denials, Reagan gave direct approval for the arms sales to Iran and, as subpoenaed documents subsequently revealed, there was no doubt in anyone's mind that this was an "arms-for-hostages" deal.

Shortly after the arms sales to Iran began, Colonel North developed what he believed was an ingenious plan. Why not use proceeds from the arms sales to Iran to support the contras in Nicaragua? Many in the White House saw North as a loose cannon, an anticommunist true believer – naive, undereducated, and dangerous. Not surprisingly, Reagan was beguiled by North; according to White House officials who later testified before Congress, the president knew about and approved the diversion of funds from arms sold to Iran to the contras. According to North, this method of funding did not violate the Boland Amendment. He was wrong. The weapons sold to Tehran were paid for with taxpayer funds; federal law required that proceeds be returned to the Treasury and prohibited the executive branch from expending monies not appropriated by Congress. In February 1986, North arranged for the sale of 1,000 TOW missiles to Iran. The proceeds, between $6 and $10 million, were transferred to the contras.

In October 1986, the Sandinistas shot down a plane flown by three Americans carrying aid to the contras. One of the three, Eugene Hasenfus, admitted to being a CIA agent. His subsequent statements led to the uncovering of the secret arms network the Reagan administration had set up for the contras. At the same time, an obscure Lebanese magazine, *Al Shiraa*, reported the arms-for-hostages deals that had been transpiring throughout 1985 and 1986. Tehran confirmed the stories and declared that the "moderates" with whom McFarland, North, and McFarland's successor, Admiral John Poindexter, had been negotiating were actually agents of the Ayatollah. Reagan and his subordinates denied that arms had been sold to Iran for the release of the hostages; CIA Director Casey insisted that all aid to the contras from the United States was strictly private. On November 25, following the midterm election, Attorney General Edwin Meese released the results of an internal investigation. Among other things, the report revealed that between $10 and $20 million of the Iranian arms sales proceeds had been diverted to the contras. That revelation touched off a year of congressional investigations, administration stonewalling, document shredding, and lying. Reagan again denied knowledge either of an arms-for-hostages deal or the transfer of proceeds to the contras. When his approval rating dropped below 50%, he fired both Poindexter and North.

With investigative reporters digging up details of the Iran–Contra deal daily, President Reagan was forced to name a three-member panel headed by Texas Republican Senator John Tower. The Tower Report, published in February 1987, detailed how arms sales to Iran intended to help maintain a balance in the Middle East war had degenerated into a ransom scheme to free the hostages in Beirut and then into a clandestine source of funds for anti-Sandinista forces in Central America. In the summer, a special Senate committee held televised hearings on the burgeoning scandal. The handsome, charismatic North dominated the proceedings. Taking the offensive, he declared that his and President Reagan's duty was to protect national security and that obligation transcended congressional mandates. "Olliemania" swept the country as tens of thousands of Americans deluged their representatives in Congress with letters of support for the flag-waving Marine, whom one committee staffer referred to as "the world's most powerful lieutenant colonel." In March 1988, a special prosecutor indicted North, Poindexter, Channel, and others involved in the Iran–Contra scheme. CIA Director Casey had died of a brain tumor or he almost certainly would have also been included. Eventually all involved pleaded guilty and were convicted, although the Supreme Court subsequently reversed several of the convictions on technical grounds. The picture of Ronald Reagan that emerged from the Tower Report and the congressional hearings was of a chief executive that was ill-informed, inattentive, naive, and easily manipulated. Although Poindexter and eventually North declared that Reagan was fully informed throughout on both the arms-for-hostages deal and the secret aid to the contras, Congress was unwilling to press the matter lest it incur the public's wrath for bringing down a second presidency in a decade. For its part, the American people proved eager to view Reagan as victim rather than villain in the Iran–Contra scandal.

Battling the "Evil Empire"

Ironically, it was in the area of Soviet–American relations, at an all-time postwar low in 1985, that Reagan was able to recoup his political fortunes. Many Americans who voted for Ronald Reagan in 1984 did so in spite of his confrontational posture toward the Soviet Union. They were particularly worried about the arms buildup and the Reagan administration's apparent unwillingness to negotiate. Statements alluding to the survivability of a nuclear war from various government officials sent a shiver up the nation's collective spine. A Pentagon representative declared that all an American family had to do to get through a thermonuclear blast would be to "dig a hole, cover it with a couple of doors, and then throw three feet of dirt on top." When another member of the Reagan team assured a congressional committee that the mail would go through in the wake of a nuclear exchange, one member observed that it would be difficult to deliver where there were "no addresses, no streets, no blocks, no houses." A group of antinuclear doctors and scientists refuted the notion that the world could survive and thrive in the wake of missile attack. The physicians predicted that nuclear war would bring on "the last epidemic." Scientists presented data to prove that the dust and smoke from a nuclear exchange would produce a prodigious global cloud that would obscure the sun for a year, bring on a "nuclear winter," and undermine the very basis of life on earth.

Glasnost and Perestroika

The only bright spot in this exceedingly depressing picture was a dramatic and promising change in the leadership of the Soviet Union. Andropov had died in early 1984 following a long illness and was succeeded by Konstantin Chernenko, another aging autocrat who repressed his countrymen and pursued a hard line abroad. Upon Chernenko's death in March 1985, Mikhail Gorbachev became General Secretary of the Communist Party of the Soviet Union. Gorbachev represented a new generation of Soviet leaders – educated, nonideological technocrats who had shed the paranoia of Stalin's generation. In his mid-50s, charismatic, cosmopolitan Gorbachev was, like Peter the Great, fascinated rather than fearful of western technology and culture. Steeped in philosophy, law, and agricultural economics, he was married to a woman who held a doctorate in philosophy. Gorbachev was determined to save socialism, the Communist Party of the Soviet Union (CPSU), and the Soviet Union by modernizing them. He understood that his country had fallen behind the United States, Japan, West Germany, and even some developing countries in technological innovation and economic output. The only way to reverse his country's dramatic and inevitable decline, Gorbachev reasoned, was through policies of perestroika (social and economic reform) and glasnost (democracy and openness to the international community). Specifically, economic progress would require the substitute of some free market mechanisms for collectivization in the Soviet economy. Rewards would have to be tied to productivity, certain industries decentralized, and the principle of private ownership applied to certain sectors, especially agriculture. The Soviet Union would have to cooperate with the capitalist countries. That cooperation, Gorbachev perceived, would pay dividends in two ways. It would give the Soviet Union access to western technology and markets, and allow the Kremlin to divert resources from its monstrous military machine to the civilian sector. The Soviet Union would remain a single-party state, but Russians could choose from communist candidates at certain levels, and their representatives would have authentic input into national decisions.

To create an opening to the West, Gorbachev took a number of unilateral steps. He stopped his country's nuclear testing program, halted the deployment of intermediate range missiles in Eastern Europe, and called for on-site inspection to enforce future arms control treaties. He concluded agreements with Japan and West Germany for the exchange of nonnuclear technology and he replaced his hard-line foreign minister, Andrei Gromyko, with the pragmatic, sophisticated Edward Shevardnadze. During the summer of 1985, the new Soviet leader departed for a whirlwind tour of Europe, Latin America, and the United States. His sincerity and charm particularly impressed the hard-nosed British Prime Minister Margaret Thatcher, who upon Gorbachev's departure declared him a man with whom the West could do business.

Throughout his first five years in office, Ronald Reagan had steadfastly refused to meet face to face with a Soviet chief of state. Perhaps because he sensed in Gorbachev the dawning of a new era or perhaps because his wife Nancy's astrologer advised that the time was right, the president agreed to a summit in Geneva in November 1985. The meeting was only partially successful. While Nancy Reagan and Reisa Gorbachev competed for the attention of the cameras, the two heads of state disagreed over SALT II and SDI. Although he chided Gorbachev for continuing human rights violations in the Soviet Union, Reagan was his usual cordial self and Gorbachev retained his composure, determined to keep the channels open for future negotiation. The summit ended on a high note. At dinner, the Reagans discovered that the Gorbachevs were movie buffs and regaled them with fascinating anecdotes of their life in Hollywood.

A year later with very little prior publicity, Reagan and Gorbachev met in Reykjavik, Iceland. During the previous year, the Soviet leader had taken a very aggressive stance on arms control issues. His overall goal, he stated, was the total elimination of nuclear weapons by the end of the twentieth century. As the meeting opened, Gorbachev took the initiative, proposing 50% cuts in ICBMs as a prelude to their eventual elimination. Not to be outdone, to the consternation of his advisers, Reagan suggested scrapping all American – and possibly British and French – nuclear weapons within 10 years in return for Russian acquiescence in the construction and deployment of the SDI. The Soviets were as puzzled as Reagan's top aides. Why would SDI be necessary with a full-scale nuclear build-down underway? Gorbachev, suspecting that the Americans were trying to establish clear nuclear superiority, rejected Reagan's proposal and the Reykjavik meeting broke up. Nevertheless, the two leaders departed on a friendly note. The path to disarmament was still open. As the Gorbachev–Reagan relationship ripened, individuals on both sides of the Iron Curtain began tentatively to anticipate an end to the Cold War.

The two leaders met again in Washington, D.C., in 1987, and this time signed the first concrete arms reduction pact since SALT II (still not ratified). By this point, Gorbachev had decided that SDI was probably both scientifically and politically unfeasible. He dropped his demand that the U.S. government abandon the project, clearing the way for his and Reagan's signing of the Intermediate-Range Nuclear Forces (INF) treaty. It called for the elimination of all intermediate-range missiles in Europe and contained provisions for on-site inspection. Russia and America still possessed 30,000 nuclear warheads aimed at each other, but the INF treaty was an important, concrete first step toward arms control. In the ensuing domestic debates, both Reagan and Gorbachev were criticized by conservatives. But the Soviet leader was determined to proceed with the modernization of the Soviet economy, and that required a shift of resources from the military to the civilian sector and cooperation with the western economic superpowers. In the wake of the Iran–Contra scandal, Reagan had replaced many of his hard-line advisers. Donald Regan departed to be replaced as chief of staff by Senator Howard Baker of Tennessee. William Webster moved over from the FBI to head the CIA. Frank Carlucci replaced the rapacious Caspar Weinberger at Defense and General Colin Powell headed the NSC. These moves, coupled with the widespread popular desire for arms control, paved the way for Senate ratification of the INF treaty by a vote of 93 to 5.

In 1988, the Soviet Union pulled its troops out of Afghanistan and supported efforts to end civil wars in Africa and Southeast Asia. Gorbachev, who during his trip to America had hosted a party for celebrities such as Paul Newman and Henry Kissinger, actively courted American opinion. In fact, polls showed him to be one of the country's favorite world leaders. In June, Reagan traveled to the heart of the evil empire. In Moscow, in front of Lenin's Tomb, he embraced his friend, Mikhail. "They've changed," the president announced to reporters. Nancy Reagan's dream that her husband be remembered most for arms control and détente with the Soviet Union was well on its way to realization.

Reagan the Conservative

The beginning of the end of the Cold War was certainly one of the most important legacies of the Reagan era, but there were others. In cutting government programs for the poor, President Reagan quipped that America had been making war on poverty for 20 years, and poverty had won. In a sense he was correct; the poverty rate for all Americans stood at about 13% at the beginning of the 1980s – the same rate that had prevailed in the mid-1960s. But government programs had helped. In the quarter century following World War II, the bulk of the poor was made up of the elderly and disabled. Social Security and Medicare had improved their lot appreciably. Government programs either did not exist for or did not help unemployed young males, single mothers, and young children. Given the Reagan administration's philosophy of deliberate neglect and its regressive tax policies, poverty not only persisted among these groups, but it also became worse. Although net income for the top 10% of income earners increased by 27%, it fell by 10% for the bottom. The census bureau reported that the number of Americans living substandard material lives grew from 34.4 million in 1982 to 35.3 million in 1983, boosting the poverty rate to its highest level in 18 years. The feminization of poverty continued; the percentage of children living with never-married mothers increased during the 1980s from 2.7% to 7%. By 1989, one out of four children in America were being born out of wedlock. The number of female-headed households jumped to 60% among black Americans and 50% among Hispanics. The high school dropout rate in America's inner cities approached 50% in the 1980s. Homelessness became a significant problem, with tens of thousands Americans sleeping in public parks, alleyways, and highway underpasses.

Poverty in America was a function of the culture of greed and the outgrowth of structural problems in the economy. Middle-income jobs were rapidly disappearing from America as it moved well into the postindustrial era. More jobs were created in the 1980s than were lost, but more than half those lost were in the well-paying industrial sector; half of those created were in the low-wage service sector and paid a wage insufficient to support a family of four. Without the prospect of a job with decent compensation, there was no incentive for inner-city youth to stay in school, get married, and raise a family. Drugs and crime became increasingly the favored path to affluence. Quite simply, without jobs, the institutions they traditionally reinforced seemed destined to disappear among a significant sector of the population.

Although Ronald Reagan shied away from pushing the conservative social agenda in Congress, he advanced the cause of right-to-lifers, school prayer advocates, law-and-order zealots, and affirmative action opponents by his appointments to the federal judiciary. Similar to Richard Vigurie, William F. Buckley, William Safire, and Jerry Falwell, Reagan believed that the Warren Court had tipped the balance in favor of government interventionism, undermined family values, and paved the way for a rising crime rate. At one point, he backed a constitutional amendment to outlaw busing. The administration refused to support renewal of the 1965 Voting Rights Act, and when Congress proceeded anyway, it refused to press suits that would enforce it. The president had infuriated civil rights groups by asking the Supreme Court to restore tax exempt status to segregated private schools. During his eight years in office, Reagan was able to appoint more than 400 federal judges, nearly all of them young white males. He had

the Justice Department carefully screen the appointees for any hint of liberalism. The Senate confirmed his first three Supreme Court appointees
rather easily: Sandra Day O'Connor and Antonin Scalia as associate justices and William Rehnquist as chief justice. But in 1987 the senators balked
at the nomination of Robert Bork. For a generation, Bork was the right's
leading legal intellectual. In various decisions and articles, he had denied
that there was a constitutional right to privacy (he defended a Connecticut
law that would deny contraceptives to even married couples) and insisted
that women's rights were not included in the provisions of the Fourteenth
Amendment to the Constitution. At one point, Bork had attacked the principle of racial equality that underlay the 1964 Civil Rights Act. The Senate
Judiciary Committee revealed Reagan's nominee to be an abrasive extremist, and this, coupled with memories of his role in firing Nixon Special
Prosecutor Archibald Cox, sent him down to overwhelming defeat. Undeterred, Reagan nominated Anthony Kennedy, a person equally conservative
but far less confrontational than Bork. He won nomination easily.

The Reagan administration's plan to turn the justice system over to the
New Right also called for tougher punishment for criminals, even if that
meant less concern for civil liberties. In this the administration had the
support of an overwhelming majority of American citizens. In the middle of
the Reagan administration, the Supreme Court ruled that illegally obtained
evidence could be admitted at a trial provided it could be proved that the
evidence would have been discovered by lawful means anyway. After 1984,
the Supreme Court upheld a rash of new state capital punishment statutes,
permitted the introduction of some illegally seized evidence, and cut away
at previous decisions requiring that police fully advise suspects of their
rights. The states built hundreds of new prisons, and by 1990 one million
Americans, 1 out of every 250, were incarcerated.

In 1985, the president signed a bill introducing major changes in U.S.
criminal law. It permitted, under certain conditions, detention without bail
for the first time in peacetime.

The Rehnquist Court did refuse to overturn *Roe v. Wade* and proved
reluctant to tear down the barrier between church and state, the key consideration in the school prayer issue. In 1985, the high court struck down
an Alabama law permitting one minute of prayer or meditation in public
schools, and it ruled that public school teachers could not enter parochial
school classrooms to provide remedial or enrichment instruction. That reluctance was no doubt partly due to the fact that in 1984 the Senate rejected
a school prayer amendment permitting organized spoken prayer in public
schools. The religious right won a consolation prize that same year, however, when the high court ruled that a city could include a nativity scene
as part of an official Christmas display without violating the constitutional
principle mandating separation of church and state. In 1989, the conservative majority pleased affirmative action opponents by outlawing in *City*

of Richmond v. J. A. Croson Company government "set-aside" programs, which reserved a certain portion of contracts for minority groups.

The Paradox of America

There was in the American cultural arena in the 1980s a parallel to the seeming paradox that prevailed in government and business. Just as deficits flourished under an administration committed to fiscal conservatism and corporate mergers and insider trading flourished in a climate of free enterprise, immorality and scandal blossomed in the alleged age of family values and drug use increased in the midst of a physical fitness craze. Americans in the 1980s jogged, hiked, performed aerobic exercise to videotape instruction, stopped smoking cigarettes, and consumed high-fiber diets. They followed closely periodic Surgeon General reports that warned against the dangerous effects of overeating, lack of exercise, and a polluted environment. At the same time, drug use increased geometrically. During the Reagan years, various studies indicated that as many as 40 million Americans annually consumed an illegal substance. One out of two people under the age of 45 had tried marijuana at least once. During the 1980s, the typical user was a Hispanic or African American living in the inner city. The appearance of "crack," an inexpensive cocaine derivative, made drugs available to the poor as well as the rich. In America's inner cities, a definable drug culture emerged as cocaine, marijuana, heroin, and a variety of synthetic drugs provided both a means to escape the misery of everyday life and one of the few avenues for upward social mobility. Deaths resulting from drug overdose or misuse amounted to only about 4,000 to 5,000 per year compared with 200,000 alcohol-related and 300,000 tobacco-related deaths annually, but another 8,000 were killed in turf wars and drug-related crimes.

Although the Reagan administration rhetorically attacked drug use as a cultural problem, the way in which it used its resources defined it as a criminal issue. The first lady launched a high-profile campaign against drug use with the theme "Just Say No." The administration's war on drugs was more concerned with interdicting supply routes, arresting dealers, and jailing users than it was with eliminating the poverty that spawned the drug culture or with rehabilitating users. By 1989, the federal government was spending nearly $15 billion per year on a largely futile effort to wipe out illegal drug use and trade.

Laissez-Faire in Education

A number of contemporary American presidents promised to be or declared that they were "the education president." Ronald Reagan was not one of them. Under Reagan, federal aid to education was slashed dramatically, so much so that his own secretary of education, Terrell Bell, commissioned a study to point out the deplorable state of public education in America. *A Nation at Risk* chronicled a sad tale of declining test scores, underequipped laboratories, ill-rewarded teaching staff, and a system that had produced an estimated 23 million functional illiterates. Indeed, the report declared the state of education to be so poor that it "[t]hreatens our very future as a nation and a people." Intensely aware of Japanese economic competition, Americans of all political persuasions cast an envious and fearful eye on the authoritarian but effective Japanese educational system. Conservatives blamed the lackluster performance of American school children on permissiveness, wasteful bureaucracy, deemphasis of the Western cultural tradition, and sex education. Liberals pointed to lack of funding, careerism, anti-intellectualism among the nation's leaders, and rigid and outmoded instructional techniques.

By the end of the 1980s, support for public education seemed to be at an all time low. Private schools with selective admission standards mushroomed. Some middle-class parents opted out of the system because they did not want their children associating with poor minorities, others because they feared contamination by non-Christians, and still others because they craved rigorous academic standards to prepare their offspring to enter the best colleges and universities. These parents were understandably reluctant to increase property taxes to pay for public schools, as were many working-class families whose heads lacked faith in education and were frankly anti-intellectual. Finally, a rapidly aging population included a large number of people who had paid taxes to support the education of their own children and felt no responsibility to do the same for the children of others. In this climate, school millages failed regularly and the quality of education continued to suffer.

Popular Culture

An educated populace, as observers of the social scene in America noted, was a product not merely of formal classroom instruction but of a sophisticated and informed press. During the 1980s, hundreds of independent dailies were swallowed up by huge conglomerates. As of 1986, 12 newspaper chains, including the giant concerns owned by British press tycoon Robert Maxwell and Australian entrepreneur par excellence Rupert Murdoch, accounted for almost half of the total annual sales in the United States. With the exception of the *Washington Post*, the *New York Times*, and several other national and regional publications, newspapers gave in to the perceived popular craving for human interest stories and crime news. Gone were the regional distinctiveness and editorial sharpness of an earlier time. In 1978, *USA Today*, the ultimate generic paper, first appeared. It featured multicolored exploding pie charts, a huge sports section, a multitude of pictures, and stories that were barely more than headlines.

During the 1980s, popular culture became a major national industry. As in other sectors of the economy, consolidation and the emergence of giant conglomerates were characteristic. The huge Disney Company continued to make movies, but also entered the television market and ran hugely successful theme parks in Florida and California. Gulf + Western bought Paramount Studios while Time, Inc., publisher of *Time, Life,* and a host of other magazines, acquired Warner Communications. Media entrepreneur Ted Turner entered into direct and successful competition with the major networks by booting up his Atlanta superstation through orbiting satellites. He then astounded the experts by launching a highly successful 24-hour news station, CNN (Cable News Network). Meanwhile in the publishing world, the S.I. Newhouse newspaper chain bought up *Vanity Fair, Vogue,* the *New Yorker,* and *House and Garden.* Much of the foreign capital that flowed into the United States because of high interest rates and a weak dollar went into the entertainment industry. Japan's Sony Corporation bought Columbia Pictures for $3.4 billion in 1989, the German firm Bertelsmann acquired RCA Records, and Rupert Murdoch gobbled up 20th Century Fox.

At the same time that ownership shrank in the mass culture industry, the number and variety of offerings proliferated. The advent of cable television expanded the number of channels available to viewers from 4 or 5 to 30 or 40. Ted Turner acquired movie libraries from Hollywood and began broadcasting old movies to a national audience. Programming became much more specialized, with channels focusing on sports, religion, music videos, business, and ethnic concerns. Indeed, stations catering to Hispanics and African Americans proliferated. In 1971, the federal government began funding National Public Radio (NPR) and, by the 1980s, more than 300 listener-supported stations were broadcasting jazz, classical music, and in-depth news reports. "All Things Considered" joined the *Post* and *Times* as journalists to the nation's decision makers. Direct marketing channels enabled consumers to buy everything from underwear to power tools without leaving home. A new device, the videocassette recorder (VCR), allowed viewers to record television shows for later viewing and to watch rented movies in their own dens and living rooms.

Not surprisingly, television dominated popular culture in the 1980s. Daily average viewing time increased from less than six hours in the 1970s to an astounding seven hours in the 1980s. *TV Guide,* founded in the 1950s, continued as one of America's leading magazines. Programming did not improve appreciably, with numerous sitcoms, crime shows, and made-for-TV movies, many of them dramatizations of the latest and most sensational kidnapping or murder. The arch-typical show was the nighttime soap opera "Dallas," whose protagonist, J. R. Ewing, enthralled legions of viewers with his sexual exploits and unscrupulous business dealings. The CBS news program "60 Minutes" exposed government and corporate mismanagement and shed some light on the lives of the underclass, but it stood virtually alone. Television became the primary advertising medium in the 1980s with television advertisement revenues exceeding $26 billion by 1990. Some of the nation's brightest minds devoted their energies to selling beer, cars, pet food, and antacids. Public television scored a notable success with its daily educational children's show "Sesame Street," but Saturday mornings were filled with mindless cartoons designed to sell Barbie dolls, plastic weapons, and sugar-coated cereal. Professional baseball, the National Basketball Association, the National Football League, and the National Collegiate Athletic Association (NCAA) signed billion-dollar contracts with the television networks. Sportswriters paid almost as much attention to the superstars' huge playing contracts and product endorsements as they did to their on-court and on-field achievements. By 1990, the Super Bowl, which pitted the winner of the National Football Conference against the winner of the American Football Conference, had accounted for 8 of the 10 largest television audiences in history.

That Ronald Reagan was president during the heyday of television was no accident. He was a master of the 30-second sound bite (a brief, catchy observation or summation), and the photo opportunity. Because television would make or break a candidacy, politicians tailored their appearance, their speech, and even their programs to a viewing audience whose attention span was limited to half a minute. Because of the astronomical cost of advertising on television, not only senators and representatives but also local sheriffs and county judges had to spend an inordinate amount of time fund-raising. Their need, in turn, accentuated the clout of special interests that could deliver the contributions needed to purchase air time.

Many Americans who were not parked in front of a television screen spent hours per day in front of another small box, the computer monitor. Children could play games or do their homework on their personal computers (PCs), housewives could keep family accounts on them, small businesses could store records on them, public schools and colleges could instruct through them, and writers and artists could perform their craft on them. Computer addicts spent their social time in cyberspace, making friends, exploring hobbies, or, by 1990, shopping. In 1981, 2 million Americans owned PCs; by 1988, that figure stood at 45 million. Critics worried that those who lived in television land or cyberspace were abdicating their lives, sacrificing real for vicarious experience, opting for an existence on which they could pull the plug rather than suffer the consequences. In general, they overestimated the impact of electronically conveyed mass culture and the world of cyberspace. Americans continued to live, love, work, and die in the real world. Arguably, neither the civil rights nor the anti–Vietnam War movements would have had the impact they did without television.

Despite the distractions offered by PCs and television, Americans continued to attend the movies in record numbers. Vietnam continued to be a powerful theme. "Platoon" (1986) and "Born on the Fourth of July" (1989) continued where "The Deerhunter" had left off, exploring the trauma of a nation and its soldiers caught up in a conflict that they only dimly understood and could not win. The most popular of the Vietnam genre, however, was Sylvester Stallone's "Rambo" series, featuring a Special Forces superhero who returns to Vietnam to wreak vengeance on the local communists and their Sino–Soviet handlers. The message implicit in every "Rambo" movie was that America's fighting men could have won the war in Southeast Asia had they not been betrayed by feckless politicians and cowardly armchair generals. George Lucas continued his "Star Wars" series with "Return of the Jedi" (1983) and Steven Spielberg his anthropology-adventure series with "Indiana Jones and the Temple of Doom" (1984). Well-disposed critics hailed "E.T.: The Extraterrestrial" (1981), the story of a friendship between a small boy and a grotesque if lovable alien, as a paen to interracial understanding. Michael Douglas starred with Glenn Close in one of the decade's hottest films, "Fatal Attraction" (1987). Close played an obsessed career woman who is rejected after a weekend fling with Douglas and responds by trying to murder him in various horrific ways. The ever-popular Robert DeNiro and Al Pacino played various Italian American gangster roles, while Sylvester Stallone raked in millions with his "Rocky" series, the tale of a down-and-out prize fighter who rises to the top of his brutal profession through a combination of willpower, resourcefulness, courage, and patriotism.

Rock and roll in its various guises continued to dominate the popular music scene. Perhaps the 1980s' two most remarkable music personalities were Michael Jackson and Madonna. Jackson, the most precocious member of the Jackson Five – "a diminutive dervish . . . irresistibly cute," declared one critic – entered adulthood either determined to shock the public or confused about his identity. He straightened his hair, bleached his skin, and reconstructed his face to make it as aquiline as possible. His pelvic gyrations and androgynous demeanor became the stuff of daily conversations as he thrilled and baffled crowds throughout America and around the world. His 1982 album "Thriller" produced six number-one singles, including "Billie Jean" and "Beat It." Madonna (Madonna Louise Ciccione), a self-made Marilyn Monroe update, hit the charts with "Like a Virgin" in 1984. Sporting a belt buckle reading "Boy Toy," the former professional dancer seduced millions with her spectacularly sexy music videos. She followed "Virgin" with "Material Girl" and a dozen other hits. In 1992, Madonna would publish a volume of soft porn photos, personal remembrances, and erotica appropriately titled *Sex*.

Had it not been for the popular culture industry, the United States would have suffered a much larger trade deficit than it did during the 1980s. Ford Motor Company may not have been able to compete with the Germans and Japanese, but Madonna could. The music industry earned 70% of its revenue from sales abroad. Proceeds from movie, television, and music royalties amounted to $5.5 billion annually by the end of the 1980s. Cabbies in London, Paris, and Hong Kong followed J. R. Ewing's philanderings as closely as the denizens of the American heartland.

A Penchant for Hypocrisy

Some social commentators argued that the 1980s were not only the decade of greed but also of hypocrisy. Although he rarely attended church, Ronald Reagan openly and successfully courted the religious right. He championed the cause of prayer in the schools and criticized the federal courts for not permitting the teaching of creationism – a Biblical account of the earth's creation and the origin of the species – as a scientific alternative to the theory of evolution. He assured a gathering of fundamentalist ministers that he was "born again," and he declared that all the world's ills could be cured by reliance on the Bible.

The president was attempting in part to plug into the huge audience created by the televangelists whose popularity continued to grow throughout the 1980s. Those who were best at fund-raising were able to go on prime-time television and put on the most impressive extravaganzas, and in turn those in prime time were able to raise the lion's share of the funds. As in other walks of American life, the rich got richer. The televangelists of the 1980s seemed to have been divided into two broad groups – those that preached fire and brimstone and hell and damnation, and those that equated spiritual redemption with material affluence. From New Orleans, Jimmy Swaggert fulminated against abortion, extramarital sex ("fornication"), communism, and secular humanism (an ill-defined concept that included the notion that rational humans were capable of leading a moral life without the guidance of a Supreme Being). Jim and Tammy Faye Bakker's PTL show featured a well-coiffed optimistic and apparently pious couple that preached the doctrine of unlimited accumulation. Unfortunately, these two ministries crashed on the rocks of personal sin in 1987. Jim Bakker was indicted for bilking financial contributors out of $158 million in connection with a religious theme-park scheme called Heritage USA. It was also revealed that he forced a church worker to have sex with him and then paid her hush money with church contributions. After uncovering her pastor's sins, the worker, Jessica Hahn, cashed in by posing nude for *Penthouse* magazine. Swaggert was also a victim of the flesh. After he confessed to buying sex from prostitutes in a seedy Louisiana motel, he too was forced to relinquish his ministry. Not all televangelists were unscrupulous charlatans, and, despite the sins of the most outrageous, media religion continued to be immensely popular.

Despite the fact that Ronald Reagan had been divorced, that his two wives were professional women, and that he had difficult relationships

with two of his four children, the president held up the traditional, nuclear family as the norm. In fact, it had never been the norm in America
and became even less so during the 1980s. Divorces in 1981 hit a record
1.21 million in 1981. In 1970, 40% of American families featured married
heterosexual couples and one or more children under 18; in 1980, that figure had dropped to 31%; in 1990, 26%. During Reagan's presidency, the
percentage of women employed full time outside the home exceeded 50%.
So-called "pro-family values" continued to be at odds with feminist objectives – affordable, publicly subsidized child care; passage of the ERA; and
access to abortion for both rich and poor. When the deadline for state ratification of the ERA amendment passed in 1982, Republicans in Congress
blocked reenactment. Reagan appointees to the Supreme Court made it
more rather than less difficult for women to sue their employers for gender
discrimination. The president persuaded Congress to outlaw Medicare- and
Medicaid-funded abortions for poor women. He favored instead "chastity
clinics" in which girls and unmarried women were counseled to avoid sex
if they wanted to escape unwanted pregnancies.

The AIDS Epidemic

Many Americans anticipated that the election of Ronald Reagan, with his
strong fundamentalist constituency, marked the end of the sexual revolution in America. Sexual mores changed, but not because of a moral awakening. Shortly after the former actor took the Oath of Office, the nation
was swept by a fear of genital herpes. The Surgeon General estimated that
20 million Americans had the disease, and that 300,000 to 500,000 new
cases were occurring every year. The herpes scare, however, paled in comparison to a terrible new sexually transmitted disease – acquired immune
deficiency syndrome (AIDS). Apparently originating in Africa, the disease
was transmitted by the exchange of bodily fluids, especially blood and semen. It eroded the body's natural defense system, making it vulnerable
to any and all sorts of diseases. Because AIDS struck male homosexuals
and intravenous drug users who shared needles, it was linked by the religious right and middle-class America with deviant behavior. Although the
Surgeon General insisted that the chief weapon against AIDS short of an
outright cure must be a widespread sex education campaign emphasizing the need to use condoms, Reagan refused even to speak out on the
subject much less go to Congress and ask for the massive funding that
was required. By the middle of the 1980s, AIDS had found its way into
the nation's blood banks and from thence into hemophiliacs. Eventually,
the heterosexual population began to suffer. By the end of 1990, 100,000
people had died of the disease. In response, some Americans had fewer
sexual partners and tended to opt for "safe" or protected sex with greater
frequency.

Summary

It is perhaps fitting to measure Ronald Reagan's presidency by the question he asked American voters in 1980: "Are you better off than you were four [eight] years ago?" Some were and some were not. Members of the upper class definitely benefited from supply-side economics, while the middle class essentially ran in place, and those on the lower rungs of the socioeconomic ladder lost ground. Women and minorities felt the sting of government neglect or even hostility toward their efforts to attain equal opportunity, while white, male business leaders enjoyed a return to official favor. In foreign policy, Americans benefited psychologically from the new sense of confidence and optimism that the president imparted. Following a prolonged period of bitter confrontation, the president displayed his pragmatism – and political deftness – by presiding over the most significant rapprochement in postwar Soviet–American relations. His self-proclaimed tactic of spending communism into oblivion may or may not have worked, but the Reagan defense buildup created massive, unprecedented budget deficits in the United States that would plague generations to come. In the end, however, it must be said that his pragmatic conservatism was an accurate reflection of the mood of the times.

ADDITIONAL READINGS

Blumenthal, Sidney, *The Last Campaign of the Cold War* (1990).
Blumenthal, Sidney, and Thomas B. Edsall, eds., *The Reagan Legacy* (1988).
Chace, James, *The Consequences of the Peace: The New Internationalism and American Foreign Policy* (1992).
Ehrenreich, Barbara, *Fear of Falling* (1989).
Gaddis, John Lewis, *The United States and the End of the Cold War: Implications, Reconsiderations, Provocations* (1992).
Johnson, Haynes, *Sleepwalking Through History* (1991).
Kennedy, Paul, *The Rise and Fall of the Great Powers* (1987).
Reagan, Ronald, *An American Life* (1990).
Regan, Donald T., *For the Record* (1988).
Rogers, Everett M., and Judith K. Larsen, *Silicon Valley Fever* (1984).
Schaller, Michael, *The Reagan Record: America and Its President in the 1980s* (1992).
Schwartz, Herman, *Packing the Courts* (1988).
Serrin, William, *Homestead* (1991).
Shilts, Randy, *And the Band Played On: Politics, People, and the AIDS Epidemic* (1987).
Stewart, James B., *Den of Thieves* (1991).
Stockman, David, *The Triumph of Politics* (1986).
Wills, Garry, *Reagan's America* (1987).

14 In Search of Balance

America into the Twenty-First Century

$\mathbf{A}$s Americans emerged from the crisis of confidence and narcissism of the post-Vietnam/post-Watergate era, they sought to balance competing philosophies and tendencies in foreign affairs, domestic policy, and cultural endeavors. Determined simultaneously not to become bogged down in regional conflicts and indigenous disputes, the United States wisely stood back as the Soviet Union and Warsaw Pact disintegrated. Post–Cold War administrations sought to encourage democracy and free market economies in the former communist countries of Eastern Europe, without threatening their security or sense of national sovereignty. As far as Communist China was concerned, the byword was watchful waiting. Policymakers did not deny that regional conflicts posed a threat to international stability and hence to the national interest, but in areas geographically remote from the United States or conflicts tangential to its interests, the U.S. government sought to work through international organizations and nations more proximate. However, in situations closer to home, as with Panama and Haiti, and in conflicts in which the United States was directly threatened, such as in the Iraqi invasion of Kuwait, the United States took the lead. The object of American policy was to assert leadership without seeking hegemony.

In domestic affairs, the New Right continued its attacks on liberalism, whereas liberals scrambled to define and identify with the political center. America remained generally conservative without being ideological. The average person favored a balanced budget, workfare instead of welfare, lower taxes, and an emphasis on private enterprise. At the same time, they supported a social safety net for the elderly, infirm, disabled, and poor. Despite the fact that many people found abortion personally repugnant, the majority favored freedom of choice and the decisions of the conservative Supreme Court reflected that position. Similarly, most Americans supported constitutional protection for gays and lesbians, although resisting their identification as a protected minority. Even though it was statistically but a fraction of the whole, the traditional nuclear family continued to be held in high regard by the majority. Americans supported equality of opportunity and political empowerment for women, while insisting that gender distinctions be maintained and that love and romance not go by the boards. Despite persistent strains of racism, the United States was a society that was willing to afford its black, Hispanic, and Asian citizens an equal opportunity to advance educationally, vocationally, and politically, as long as they did not play the "politics of victimization" to seek unfair advantage. The common American man and woman were willing to tolerate multiculturalism as long as it did not become a centripetal force and destroy the common language, political institutions and process, and ideas that made them Americans. As the twenty-first century approached, the citizenry strove for the same ideals it had striven for as the eighteenth and nineteenth century impended – equality of opportunity, individual freedom, fair play, and compassion.

Brave New Conservatism: The Presidency of George H. W. Bush

The Election of 1988

Grateful that the Twenty-Second Amendment prevented Ronald Reagan from running for a third term, Democrats looked to 1988 with cautious hope. When the Republicans nominated Vice President George Bush, this hope escalated into anticipation. "If we can't beat Bush," one Democratic politico declared, "we'd better find another country." These were words he would live to regret. The United States was at peace and prosperous in 1988, and the Democratic Party was an organization without a sense of constituency. Mondale had run as a traditional New Deal liberal and been soundly trounced. Indeed, the Republicans had succeeded in making liberalism a dirty word in the 1980s, forcing liberals to hide behind such terms as "progressive" and "populist."

The early frontrunner for the Democratic nomination was Gary Hart, the self-proclaimed heir to John F. Kennedy, the man of still-to-be-defined "new ideas." Hart was attractive, self-effacing, and a media favorite. He promised to pursue conservative fiscal policies while keeping New Deal/Great Society programs in place. Echoing a theme that would reverberate throughout the Democratic effort in 1988, Hart promised competent management and preparation for the competition of the twenty-first century. Richard Gephardt of Missouri centered his candidacy on an appeal to economic nationalism, a campaign directed none too subtly at the Japanese. Traditional liberal Paul Simon made a brief splash on the campaign trail and then faded into the background. Michael Dukakis, the serious, intelligent, "high-tech" governor of Massachusetts, promised to bring to the national scene the expertise that had turned his home state's economy around. The only Democratic aspirant who directly addressed the issues of racial discrimination, poverty, and war was Jesse Jackson.

The media had previously delved into the private lives of presidential candidates in an effort to make "character" a central campaign issue, but never to the extent it did in 1988. Rumors had circulated for years that Hart, who was married with children, was a womanizer. In May 1987, in the midst of the primary season, the *Miami Herald* reported that Hart had spent a weekend in his Washington, D.C., townhouse with model Donna Rice. Shortly thereafter, the *National Enquirer* published a photo of Rice sitting in Hart's lap while the two sailed to Bimini aboard a yacht named, incredibly, *The Monkey Business*. Hart's candidacy was over. Several weeks later, Delaware Senator Joseph Biden withdrew from the Democratic primaries when members of the media revealed that he had cribbed part of a speech from a British politician. Public figures and some commentators declared that what individuals did with their private lives was irrelevant to their competence to hold public office. The media disagreed, criticized their predecessors for covering up for politicians who favored them, and insisted that dishonesty in one sphere was sure to produce dishonesty in others. Perhaps most important, scandal sold newspapers and magazines.

Between April and June, Dukakis defeated Jackson in a majority of the primary races and finished a strong second in those he did not win. Jackson was a legitimate candidate, winning in Michigan and South Carolina, but voters still thought of him as a racist because of his derogatory remarks made regarding Jews in 1984. In addition, his old fashioned, New Deal liberalism was outdated. In his acceptance speech in Atlanta, Dukakis achieved an atypical eloquence. Competence not ideology was the key issue in the upcoming campaign, he declared. Taking Neil Diamond's *Coming To America* as his theme song, Dukakis emphasized his immigrant roots and his ability to govern an increasingly pluralistic America. His vision of the American Dream, of a land of racial and ethnic tolerance and equal opportunity, was compelling, but questions remained about his sensitivity, vision, and political skills, particularly after it became known that he had let Jesse Jackson find out from reporters that Senator Lloyd Bentsen of Texas, rather than Jackson, was his choice for a running mate.

In May, public opinion polls showed George Bush trailing Dukakis 54% to 38%. Democratic strategists viewed the Republican candidate as an inarticulate, unfocused "wimp" with no program and no political acumen. They were mistaken. Although he enjoyed Ronald Reagan's endorsement, Bush had had to fend off a challenge from the peppery, sharp-tongued Robert Dole of Kansas. A disabled veteran of World War II, Dole was a hard-nosed conservative and Republican partisan with a surprisingly good civil rights record and an apparent grasp of foreign policy issues. Yet, after trouncing Bush in the Iowa caucuses, Dole foundered in New Hampshire, and his campaign quickly fell apart.

To many, George Bush appeared to be a child of privilege who had relied on his father's money and influence to achieve high office. The son of
Prescott Bush, an investment banker and U.S. senator, Bush grew up in affluence in Connecticut, attending prep school and then Yale. After serving
in World War II, he had transplanted to Texas where he made a fortune in
the oil business. Before becoming vice president, Bush had been elected
to office only twice – to the House of Representatives from his Houston
district in 1966 and 1968. He ran unsuccessfully for the Senate twice (1964
and 1970) and, in 1980, for the Republican nomination for president. But
Bush had held a number of responsible positions – ambassador to the
United Nations (UN), chairman of the Republican National Committee,
ambassador to China, and head of the Central Intelligence Agency (CIA) –
in addition to the vice presidency. He was, moreover, no "wimp," a term
applied to him by *Newsweek* magazine. Bush had quit school to join the
armed forces during World War II. He was the youngest fighter pilot in the
Pacific theater and was shot down by enemy fire.

As the race began, Bush puzzled both experts and laypeople by choosing 41-year-old Senator Dan Quayle to be his running mate. The son of
an Indiana publisher and a wealthy mother, Quayle was singularly undistinguished. He was something of a joke in the Senate, once having read
a speech given him by an aide that had nothing to do with the topic being debated at the time. But even after it became known that Quayle had
used family influence to gain entry into the National Guard and thus avoid
serving in Vietnam, Bush stuck by him. Critics charged that Bush wanted
an ineffectual "yes" man in the number two spot so that he would not be
upstaged, just as he had not upstaged Ronald Reagan.

As the general election campaign got underway, Michael Dukakis attempted to focus the electorate's attention on the future – on how the
Republicans had undermined it and how he would save it. Blaming the
deficit on "discredited Bush–Reagan policies," the Democratic candidate
promised to reduce the deficit through better management rather than
through raising taxes. Meanwhile, Republican strategists decided to go for
"gut" issues, ones that appealed to the nation's emotions and prejudices,
that would increase Dukakis's "negatives," to use the term of the day. Early
in the campaign, Bush's handlers assembled a small but representative
group of voters that were leaning toward Dukakis. The GOP team revealed
that while governor of Massachusetts, the Democratic candidate had vetoed a bill compelling public school teachers to lead the Pledge of Allegiance
each day and had signed a weekend furlough bill for convicted criminals.
The team learned to their delight that these facts struck strongly discordant notes with their sample group. Here were campaign issues with which
to conjure. Lee Atwater and his Republican campaign team took out 30-
and 15-second advertisements linking Dukakis's vetoing of the pledge bill
with his membership in the American Civil Liberties Union, implying that

Bush's opponent was not only unpatriotic but also "permissive," playing on popular beliefs that defense of the civil liberties of all, including criminals and hate groups, was undermining the republic.

The centerpiece of the GOP's negative public relations campaign was the Willy Horton case. Horton was a Massachusetts inmate convicted of rape and assault. Freed on the furlough program, he fled the state to Maryland where he terrorized a couple and raped the wife. "If I can make Willy Horton a household name, we can win the election," Atwater told his lieutenants. Subsequent ads showed a revolving door letting people out of prison and accusing Dukakis of permissiveness. Most of the individuals pictured were black. Horton was black. The crime was rape. The Horton ads were designed not only to play on popular fears of crime, but also on the racism of some whites. Bush, who was fond of Clint Eastwood western and detective movies, declined to remain above the fray. Dukakis's slogan for convicts was not "make my day" (an invitation by Eastwood's Dirty Harry character to armed robbers to have a shootout with him), he declared, but "have a nice weekend."

To the frustration of his advisers, Dukakis did attempt to remain above the fray. While the Bush camp smeared him, he stayed home in Massachusetts conducting state business during the early stages of the contest. By the time he hit the campaign trail in late September, it was too late. When Bush did address substantive issues, he wrapped it in Hollywood hype. "Read my lips," he declared, "No new taxes." In fact, the 1988 election was a media-dominated event from beginning to end. Building on the Reagan heritage, both candidates concentrated on camera angles and a quote of the day that would be short and sensational enough to make the evening news. The average "sound bite" had declined from 30 seconds to 9 seconds. In this sort of competition, Dukakis (who remained ambivalent about running for president throughout) did not stand a chance. George Bush won 53% of the popular vote and carried 40 states. The final tallies were 48,886,000 for Bush and 41,809,000 for Dukakis in the popular vote and 426 to 112 in the electoral college.

George Bush

George Bush proved to be a surprisingly popular president during his first year and a half in office. Much of that had to do with the widespread sense of relief at the winding down of the Cold War, but also, when compared with Reagan, Bush seemed to be a man of compassion who was willing to acknowledge that in the postindustrial age government had certain obligations to its citizens. In his inaugural address, he appealed for national unity and bipartisan cooperation. He promised "to make kinder the face of the nation and gentler the face of the world." Bush expressed sympathy for the homeless, unwed mothers, deprived children, and the poor in general. But he also acknowledged the deficit and its corrosive long-term effect on the

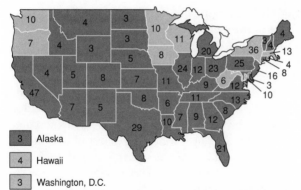

	Electoral vote	Popular vote	Percentage of popular vote
Republican George H. Bush	426	48,886,000	54
Democratic Michael S. Dukakis	112	41,809,000	46

Map 14–1. The election of 1988.

economy and the quality of life in America. Reagan had replaced the picture of Harry Truman hanging in the White House with a portrait of Calvin Coolidge. Bush replaced that with the likeness of Theodore Roosevelt. In many ways it was a symbolic move – an eastern, patrician president with a western patina. Moreover, like Theodore Roosevelt, the new chief executive would pursue an aggressive foreign policy. That is where the comparison stopped. There would be no vigorous new initiative in domestic affairs analogous to progressivism.

If the American people were willing to give George Bush the benefit of the doubt at the outset, the same was not true of Congress and government in general. Indeed, as the new administration assumed control, opinion polls indicated public faith in those who governed them and "the system" in general was at an all-time low. Not without some reason, Americans blamed Congress for the savings and loan (S&L) debacle. The implication of five senators in the Lincoln S&L scandal directly linked public officials with the irresponsibility and greed that seemed to pervade Wall Street and the thrifts. Late in 1989, Speaker of the House James Wright, a Democrat from Texas, resigned amid charges that he had sought special favors for a Texas S&L that had made improper loans in the 1980s, and that he had exerted influence on behalf of a wealthy businessman from whom he had accepted gifts. In 1990, investigative journalists revealed that no fewer than 12 congressmen and senators had taken money from those seeking special favors from the government. These stories, coupled with a brief, ill-advised effort by Congress to raise salaries by 50% in 1989, touched off an orgy of Congress-bashing by Common Cause (a public interest lobby), Ralph Nader, and the national media.

Like every president since Lyndon Johnson, George Bush faced the dilemma of how to care for the disadvantaged and maintain a strong national defense while reducing the budget. Cleaning up after the thrifts put the administration in a financial hole before it really got started. By 1989, hundreds of thrifts had failed, and thousands of depositors were clamoring for their money. Bush responded by securing congressional approval of a plan that closed fatally damaged S&Ls and created a new agency, the Resolution Trust Corporation, to sell off and distribute their assets. At the same time, Congress pumped funds into a new bail-out agency created out of the Federal Deposit Insurance Corporation (FDIC), which previously had taken care of only banks, and into the S&L fund. The estimated cost to taxpayers over 30 years was $300 to $500 billion. Perhaps George Bush's most concrete pledge during the campaign had been his "read my lips" promise not to raise taxes. The problem was that the deficit stood at $2.6 trillion at the end of the Reagan years and the anticipated shortfall for 1991 was $260 billion. As pressure on the administration to take action mounted, Bush huddled repeatedly with congressional leaders throughout 1990. Reluctantly, on June 26, Bush announced that "both the size of the deficit . . . and the need for a package that can be enacted" required "tax revenue increases." He and the leaders of the House and Senate put forward a proposal that upped excise and income taxes and cut popular programs such as Medicare and unemployment insurance. With midterm congressional elections looming, a coalition of conservative Republicans, angry over the president's broken pledge not to raise taxes, and liberal Democrats, distressed at cuts in entitlement programs, blocked passage. At that point, an aroused public demanded that the government act; in October, Congress and the administration cooperated in passing a measure that raised taxes on the top 2% of earners by eliminating certain deductions that increased taxes on alcohol, gasoline, and expensive consumer goods, and that raised Medicare payroll taxes for workers. The budget office predicted savings of $40 billion for fiscal 1991 and $490 billion over the next five years. However, a sharp downturn in the economy sent tax collections tumbling; as a result, the deficit for 1991 was $300 billion, the largest in history.

Education and Environment
During the 1988 campaign, Bush promised to be both the "education president" and the "environment president." In both areas, however, the burgeoning budget limited the administration to largely symbolic actions. In education, the White House promised more learning for the buck. In consultation with the nation's governors, the president ostentatiously set a number of impressive goals: dramatically higher achievement scores in science and math, an increase in the high school graduation rate from 60% to 80%, and a coordinated attack on the nation's appalling illiteracy rate. However, rhetoric would not suffice. The fact was that there were no new education dollars; with women no longer having to settle for low-paying

teaching jobs, many regions suffered from a shortage of qualified instructors. Compounding the problem was the tendency over time for colleges of education to become self-contained empires and to substitute general education courses in teacher training curricula for the basic arts and sciences courses that provided the substance to public school instruction. It became possible for students earning a degree in secondary education and who were going to teach math or history in the high schools to take as few as 12 hours of math and history. The typical arts and sciences major in these fields required an average of 33 hours. In addition, public education was unable to solve the dilemma of simultaneously teaching the gifted and well-prepared and the disadvantaged and disabled, without seeming to stigmatize the latter. As a result, scores refused to rise, and the crisis of American education continued.

Bush's term in office was punctuated by a series of environmental disasters; the most visible and controversial of these involved the *Exxon Valdez*. The vessel ran aground in Alaska's picturesque Prince William Sound, spilling millions of gallons of crude oil and spoiling a hundred miles of coastline, including fisheries and animal habitats. The Coast Guard investigated and found the captain of the tanker had been operating while under the influence of alcohol. Exxon was subsequently forced to pay $2 billion to clean the seashore and wash the fur and feathers of those birds and mammals that had managed to survive. The Bush administration condemned this and other spills and called for responsible corporations to clean up toxic waste dumps scattered across the United States. But after voters in California and New York defeated tax initiatives to pay for costly cleanups, the administration proceeded warily.

For years, scientists had warned that the massive burning of petroleum products was creating a carbon dioxide buildup in the upper atmosphere. This blanket was trapping heat on the earth's surface and creating a "greenhouse effect," a global warming that if not checked would melt the polar ice caps, inundating the world's coastal areas and withering its arable lands. There were those in the scientific community who denounced this scenario as alarmist. The administration sided with the skeptics and announced that significant restrictions on gasoline use would have to await further studies.

Nonetheless, Bush, unlike his predecessor, acknowledged that an environmental problem existed and that it was the responsibility of the government to act. The twentieth anniversary of the first Earth Day was held on April 20, 1990, and Congress approved major revisions in the Clean Air Act requiring city governments to take action to reduce smog and setting stiffer emission standards for automobiles. The measure addressed the growing problem of "acid rain" endemic to the Northeast and Midwest and caused by industries burning coal high in sulphur content. The amount of sulphuric acid falling from the sky did decrease, but the growing

obsolescence of coal-burning plants had more to do with this trend than
government regulation.

The Supreme Court and the Conservative Social Agenda

Members of the New Right anticipated that during the Bush administra-
tion they would begin to reap the judicial harvest that Ronald Reagan had
sowed by his appointments to the federal judiciary. In that hope, they were
generally disappointed. In a 1989 decision, the high court ruled that the
First Amendment guaranteeing free speech protected those who burned the
American flag in acts of protest. Amid cries of anguish from the American
Legion, the Veterans of Foreign Wars (VFW), and the Heritage Foundation,
President Bush denounced the decision and promised support for a constitutional amendment specifically outlawing flag burning. Opponents argued
that such provisos trivialized the nation's charter. When subsequently the
Supreme Court struck down an act of Congress outlawing desecration of
the flag, sentiment for an amendment quickly waned. If the flag remained
vulnerable, one commentator observed, at least the Constitution – then on
the eve of its 200th birthday – remained unsullied.

The same year that the court acted to protect civil liberties in one area, it
restricted them in another. In *Webster v. Reproductive Services of Missouri*,
the justices ruled in a five-to-four decision that states could deny access to
public facilities to women seeking abortion. Writing for the majority, Chief
Justice Rehnquist declared that "nothing in the Constitution requires states
to enter or remain in the business of performing abortions." Although conservatives predicated a wave of laws prohibiting public hospitals and public employees from participating in abortions, this was not the case. Only
Utah, Pennsylvania, and Louisiana enacted such measures. Webster did
not overturn *Roe v. Wade*, but abortion rights activists were apprehensive.
"[T]he signs are very ominous and a chill wind blows," mused Justice Harry
Blackmun, author of the *Roe* decision.

Experienced politicians sensed correctly that no clear consensus existed
on the abortion issue, and they acted accordingly. Prochoice and right-
to-life advocates labored to make their cause the determining factor in
elections during the Bush presidency, but to no avail. Republicans and
Democrats took positions on both sides of the issue and as many candidates as could waffled. To the intense disappointment of the New Right,
the usually ideological Lee Atwater declared that there was room for both
opponents and advocates of abortion rights under the Republican "tent."

The president did his best to avoid the issue. Early in his career, he
had seemed prochoice, but during the presidential campaign he had declared "abortion is murder." When Justice William Brennan retired from
the Supreme Court, the Moral Majority fully expected Bush to reward them
for their support. Instead, he picked David Souter of New Hampshire. A
former state Supreme Court justice, Souter had served briefly on the federal

bench. His views on the abortion issue were unknown, and he refused to discuss them during his confirmation hearings. Liberal organizations such as the National Organization for Women (NOW) and the National Women's Political Caucus insisted that the privacy principle was so important that potential justices could not refuse to address it. But Souter did refuse, and the Senate, relieved at not having to come down on one side or the other, overwhelmingly approved him.

When another vacancy appeared on the high court, however, Bush felt free to be more aggressive with his appointment because he had the opportunity to cloak a conservative social agenda with a black skin. In mid-1991, the distinguished civil rights lawyer and Supreme Court justice Thurgood Marshall announced his retirement. To replace him, Bush selected Clarence Thomas, a black federal court judge who had grown up impoverished in the segregated South. After attending Catholic elementary and secondary schools, Thomas matriculated at Yale Law School. He served as an aide to a Republican senator and then head of the Equal Employment Opportunity Commission (EEOC) under Reagan before being appointed to the U.S. Court of Appeals. The American Bar Association, pointing out that Thomas had served on the federal bench for only 16 months before being nominated to the high court, was less than enthusiastic about his selection. Undeterred, Bush defended him as the "best person" to fill Marshall's shoes. Two things made him attractive to the administration. First, in speeches, articles, and decisions, Thomas had expressed reservations about a woman's right to abortion, criticized the concept of a minimum wage, questioned the efficacy of busing and affirmative action as mechanisms for achieving racial justice (even though he had been admitted to Yale under an affirmative action program), and urged African Americans to rely on their own resources and intelligence to advance in a multicultural world. Second, Thomas was black. Liberals opposed to his conservative political and judicial philosophy ran the risk of being labeled as racists if they opposed his nomination.

Thomas confirmation hearings would have been controversial and inflammatory under any circumstances, but they escalated to the sensational when Anita Hill, a University of Oklahoma law professor, testified that Thomas had sexually harassed her when both worked for the EEOC. The televised Judiciary Committee hearings attracted a national audience as Hill quietly but graphically detailed her allegations. Republican committee members subjected Hill to a biting, sometimes brutal cross-examination, to them and their party's ultimate regret. Thomas's appearance was a study in righteous indignation. He denied all of Hill's charges and claimed that she had been put up to her assault on his character by civil rights leaders whom he had previously written off as habitual whiners and moaners. The hearings, he declared, were a "high-tech lynching for uppity blacks."

Despite going through "living hell," he would "rather die than withdraw," Thomas declared.

The Bush administration's choice to succeed Thurgood Marshall neither died nor withdrew. Following a stormy floor debate, the Senate voted to confirm Thomas by a vote of 52 to 48. Somewhat ironically, Thomas's nomination had the effect of galvanizing the temporarily moribund feminist movement. In 1975, pioneer feminist Betty Friedan had abandoned NOW, claiming that it was becoming antimale, antifamily, and antifeminine, and that it was concentrating on gay/lesbian issues to the exclusion of the overriding concern of equal rights and opportunities for all women. Anita Hill's ordeal before the Senate Judiciary Committee angered women of all political and sexual persuasions. A revived feminism rallied around the pervasive problem of sexual harassment. Republicans, Democrats, lesbians, heterosexuals, blacks, and whites supported laws and regulations, particularly on college campuses, that banned unwanted sexual approaches, abusive language, and even "suggestive" sounds and motions. Feminists, gay activists, and civil rights leaders thus placed themselves in uneasy alliance with social conservatives who had long pressed for restriction of the free speech amendment. But they argued that sexual harassment, similar to racial epithets, made life so uncomfortable for their objects that the majority would have to accept some infringement on its rights. More significant, women's frustration with the male-dominated political power structure led to an unprecedented number of female candidates for local, state, and national office in 1992.

The Drug Crisis
Public opinion polls taken during the 1988 election indicated that the American people continued to be deeply worried about the drug problem. So, along with promising to be the education and environment president, George Bush announced to his countrymen that he would make drug abuse his top domestic priority. Shortly after his election, Bush named William Bennett, Reagan's controversial education secretary, to be his "drug czar." As such, Bennett would head the Office of National Drug Control Policy, a cabinet-level position without a department. The drug problem was indeed immense; in 1989, 375,000 babies were born addicted to cocaine or heroin, and the drug traffic was serving as a massive capital formation mechanism for organized crime and inner-city street gangs. The Bush–Bennett approach was, however, essentially a retread of the Reagan approach. The emphasis was on law enforcement and interdiction rather than prevention and rehabilitation. The administration began pressuring employers to institute testing in the workplace, and it spent several billion dollars strengthening the Drug Enforcement Agency (DEA), increasing border patrols and subsidizing antidrug police activities in countries ranging from

Columbia to Peru. Indeed, 70% of the $7.9 billion earmarked for the war on drugs went toward the construction of new prisons, additional DEA agents, and new prosecutors.

The End of the Cold War

In foreign affairs, it was Bush's good fortune to be president when the Cold War came to an end. From late 1945 until the latter part of the Reagan administration, world politics had been dominated by an armed standoff between the United States and the Soviet Union. Every brushfire war and every confrontation over spheres of interest and World War II occupation zones threatened to escalate into a nuclear holocaust. George Kennan, J. William Fulbright, Walter Lippmann, and other sophisticated cold warriors had envisioned a scenario whereby the United States through alliances and aid would contain Soviet communism within its post-1948 borders until it should collapse under the weight of its own contradictions. They antici-pated correctly that collectivization, state control, and a closed society and economy would eventually render the Soviet Union incapable of competing in a postindustrial world and that a new generation of leaders would trans-form Lenin's creation into a social democracy. With the advent of Mikhail Gorbachev, glasnost, and perestroika, their vision began to materialize.

George Bush and his team were well qualified to deal with these earth-shaking events. Similar to his hero Theodore Roosevelt, Bush was a prag-matic imperialist, determined to safeguard American interests, econom-ically and strategically defined, short of armed conflict if possible but through force of arms if necessary. His foreign policy team was formidable and experienced. For secretary of state, he selected fellow Texan and for-mer Treasury Secretary James Baker II. National Security Adviser Brent Scowcroft had served in the same capacity under Reagan. For chairman of the Joint Chiefs of Staff, Bush selected General Colin Powell, Reagan's Na-tional Security Council (NSC) adviser during the last months of his admin-istration. Secretary of Defense Richard Cheney had served as a high-level official in the Ford administration and then gone on to be a powerful mem-ber of the House of Representatives. Bush and his advisers were keenly aware of the limitations both material and political on American power, and they would resist calls that the United States participate actively in the demise of the Warsaw Pact and the fall of communism in the Soviet Union. Their approach, one that would become familiar in the post–Cold War era, was one of watchful waiting.

Shortly after George Bush took the Oath of Office, the first democratic elections since 1917 were held in the Soviet Union. The results indicated that the citizens of the USSR believed that Gorbachev was going too slow in opening up the nation to democracy and free market economics. Non-communist nationalists and reformers won a number of seats in the na-tional legislature. Encouraged by glasnost and perestroika, anticommunist, nationalist elements in the Baltic states of Estonia, Latvia, and Lithuania began challenging their puppet regimes and demanding the departure of Soviet occupation troops. Meanwhile, in Poland, under the leadership of Lech Walesa, Solidarity had risen from the ashes and, through demonstrations and boycotts, was pressuring the communist dictatorship of General Voitech Jaruzelski into holding free elections. After it was clear that the Kremlin would not intervene militarily to save him, Jaruzelski agreed to a coalition government and elections. Then in July, Gorbachev made an astounding announcement. In a direct repudiation of the Brezhnev doctrine, which had been used to justify sending Soviet troops into Czechoslovakia in 1968, the Soviet leader announced to a meeting of Warsaw Pact leaders that his country would respect the national sovereignty of all nations and that in effect the Kremlin no longer cared how its neighbors conducted their internal affairs. "There is no universal road to socialism," he proclaimed.

Gorbachev's pronouncement unleashed the forces of democracy, nationalism, and economic liberalism in Eastern Europe that had been contained since World War II by Soviet occupation. The Hungarian government, long the most liberal of the Warsaw Pact regimes, tore down barbed wire fencing along a 150-mile stretch of its border with Austria. At once, thousands of East Germans circumvented their country's sealed-off border, flooding into West Germany first by way of Hungary and then Austria. A massive, peaceful uprising in Czechoslovakia toppled the communist regime there and eventually produced a democratically elected government headed by playwright Vaclav Havel. In Bulgaria, the communist-dominated regime survived only by changing its name and promising to institute reforms. Only in Rumania was there significant bloodshed. The tyrannical Nicolae Ceaucescu, who had completely corrupted his country – an estimated 40% of the population were or had been at one time government informers – refused to go peacefully. When troops loyal to him fired into crowds of demonstrators, an enraged populace intimidated the military and arrested Ceaucescu. He and his wife were executed following a hasty trial.

The most dramatic events of 1989 occurred in Germany, the overriding symbol of the Cold War and a divided Europe. As thousands of East German citizens fled via Hungary and Austria, those that stayed behind demonstrated against the repressive government of long-time dictator and Kremlin puppet, Erich Honniker. Aware that Soviet troops would not be forthcoming, Honniker resisted the urge to use police and troops to crush the demonstrators. On November 9, the government announced that the border between East and West Germany was open. On November 15, wrecking crews moved in and began destroying the Berlin Wall, the 12-foot high concrete and barbed wire symbol of oppression in the German Democratic Republic (GDR). East and West Germans joined by Americans and other Europeans held giant celebrations on Christmas and New Year's Eve on the remnants of the barrier. In parliamentary elections in March 1990, the Christian Democrats swept to victory on the momentum of Chancellor Helmut Kohl's promise to unify the two Germanies. Then on October 2, 1990, the GDR merged with the German Federal Republic into a single capitalist, multiparty state.

Throughout this process, the Bush administration wisely stood on the sidelines giving quiet encouragement. Once it became clear that Gorbachev was truly committed to limited privatization and demilitarization of the Soviet economy and to the principle of self-determination for Eastern Europe, the U.S. government tried not to take steps that would antagonize nationalists and hard-line communists opposed to Gorbachev's program. Thus did Bush at first oppose German reunification, and he rejected suggestions that he fly to Berlin to celebrate the destruction of the wall. Gorbachev opposed reunification initially, then when it was clear that the two halves would be joined, he supported its inclusion in the North Atlantic Treaty Organization (NATO). Carefully, the U.S. government mediated between its European partners and the Soviets. The Kremlin finally accepted NATO membership for a united Germany in return, ironically, for the continued presence of American troops in Europe, which the Soviets believed would act as a guard against a revived German militarism. An $8 billion credit from the new Germany to the Soviet Union also eased the pain of reunification.

Liberals and conservatives criticized the Bush administration for not furnishing massive economic aid to Gorbachev as he proceeded with glasnost and perestroika. The problem facing the U.S. government, however, was that as Gorbachev's popularity in the United States and Western Europe increased, his political position eroded at home. In the spring of 1990, noncommunists won a series of elections in the Soviet Union, gaining control of the municipal governments in Moscow and Leningrad. That summer, Gorbachev's one-time protégé, Boris Yeltsin, left the Communist Party to form his own political organization. A year later in June 1991, he was elected president of the Russian Republic, which comprised two thirds of the land mass of the former Soviet Union and included nearly one half of its population. Yeltsin effectively flanked Gorbachev on the left, criticizing him and the Communist Party for not proceeding fast enough with installing a market economy in the Soviet Union and being slow in embracing true democracy. All the while, Gorbachev vacillated between reformers and hard-liners. In January 1991, he sided with the Red Army when it sought to keep the Baltic republics – annexed in 1940 – from breaking away. Soviet soldiers fired on separatist demonstrators in Vilnius, Lithuania, killing 14. At the same time, he seemed increasingly resigned to rapid liberalization of the economy and democratization within the republics of the former Soviet Union. The Bush administration continued to voice support for Gorbachev, and the president met with him six times during the 19 months between December 1989 and August 1991. But he was loath to commit the United States economically and politically to the leader of a system that seemed headed for oblivion rather than reform.

In the summer of 1991, Bush traveled to Moscow to sign a Strategic Arms Reduction Treaty with Gorbachev. The agreement committed both parties to a one-third reduction in their bombers and missiles and to cuts in conventional forces as well. Shortly thereafter, on August 18, a group of hard-liners representing the Red Army, the KGB, and the Communist Party hierarchy attempted a coup. The group acted while Gorbachev was out of Moscow. They had him placed under house arrest at the resort where he was vacationing and held incommunicado. Troops loyal to the plotters surrounded the Russian parliament building in Moscow, but Yeltsin and a majority of the legislators refused to capitulate, declaring their support for Gorbachev. When the leaders of the coup decided not to use force, the conspiracy collapsed. Eight were arrested and one committed suicide in captivity. Gorbachev rushed to the scene to take command, but Yeltsin had permanently upstaged him. The president of the former Soviet Union belatedly resigned from the Communist Party of the Soviet Union (CPSU) but to no avail. In December 1991, Yeltsin led the way in the creation of the Commonwealth of Independent States (CIS), which allied his Russian Federation with the Ukraine and Belarus (previously Bylorussia). Within a month, 11 former Soviet republics had joined the CIS. The Baltic states insisted on full independence, while Georgia, the home of Josef Stalin, remained in the grip of hard-liners and refused to join. On December 25, 1991, the hammer and sickle flag, the universal symbol of the Soviet Union, was hauled down from atop the Kremlin.

Troubled Détente: Sino–American Relations

The Bush administration was similarly circumspect in its dealings with Communist China. The president had served as American representative to that huge country in 1974/1975 and had developed close ties with its aging leadership. Ever the ideological pragmatist, Bush believed that pressure from the United States would only forestall democratization and economic reform in Maoist China. As the Chinese tasted the prosperity that trade with the West would bring, and the World War II generation of leaders passed from the scene, China would follow the path taken by the former Soviet Union. Unfortunately for the U.S. government and Beijing, militant students in China were not willing to wait. In the spring of 1989, university students staged demonstrations in China's largest cities demanding freedom of expression, political democracy, and better jobs for college graduates.

By early May, student protests became focused on Beijing. Thousands gathered in Tiananmen Square before the mausoleum containing Mao's embalmed body. Student leaders, intellectuals, workers, and a few members of the ruling Central Committee of the Communist Party made

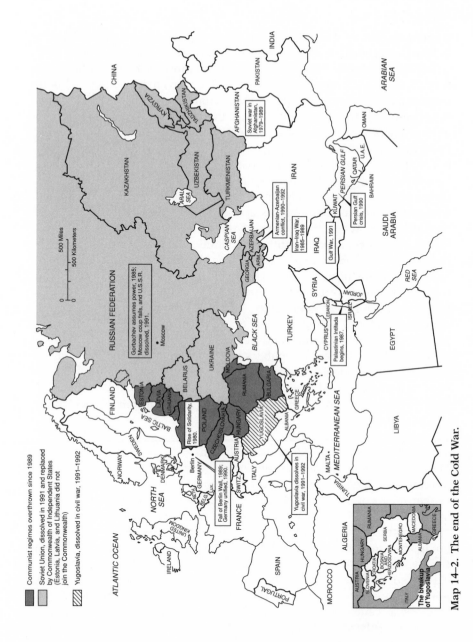

Map 14–2. The end of the Cold War.

Communist regimes overthrown since 1989

Soviet Union, dissolved in 1991 and replaced by Commonwealth of Independent States (Estonia, Latvia, and Lithuania did not join the Commonwealth)

Yugoslavia, dissolved in civil war, 1991–1992

Gorbachev assumes power, 1985; Moscow coup fails, and U.S.S.R. dissolved, 1991.

Rise of Solidarity, 1980.

Fall of Berlin Wall, 1989; Germany unified, 1990.

Yugoslavia dissolves in civil war, 1991–1992

Soviet war in Afghanistan, 1979–1989

Armenian-Azerbaijan conflict, 1990–1992

Iran-Iraq War, 1985–1989

Gulf War, 1991

Persian Gulf crisis, 1990

Palestinian Intifada begins, 1987.

The breakup of Yugoslavia

500 Miles
500 Kilometers

pro-reform speeches. The young people erected a huge paper mache "Goddess of Liberty," which bore a striking resemblance to the Statue of Liberty. Attempts by police to break up the crowd only swelled the ranks of the protesters, estimated at around 200,000. On May 15, Gorbachev arrived for a summit with Deng Xiaoping, Mao's successor. The thousands of reporters and television crew members in town for the summit provided worldwide coverage of the Tiananmen Square demonstrations.

Deng had lived through the tumultuous and destructive Cultural Revolution. He and the vast majority of his countrymen shared a deep-seated fear of social upheaval. After Gorbachev departed, the Chinese leader declared martial law, banned television crews from the square and ordered the army, which had imported peasant soldiers from the provinces for the event, to disperse the protestors. A number of reporters and photographers managed to remain on the scene, however, and beginning June 3, they recorded the Tiananmen "massacre" as government troops machine-gunned students and tanks rolled over defenseless protestors. Deng jailed the survivors and purged from his regime those who had sympathized with the prodemocracy movement. The wave of outrage that swept the United States during the Tiananmen Square massacre proved to be relatively weak. The Bush administration condemned Beijing for its repression and temporarily suspended sales of military and nonmilitary items. The following month, however, he dispatched Brent Scowcroft to China to assure Deng and his associates that relations would return to normal as soon as the controversy died down.

Cooling Off Central America

The Bush administration's pragmatism and nonideological approach to foreign policy was apparent in its approach to Central America. In 1987, Costa Rican President Oscar Arias Sanchez persuaded the four other regional presidents to approve a peace plan. It included a general cease fire, immediate negotiations between insurgents and government forces in both Nicaragua and El Salvador, an end to outside military aid to rebel forces [U.S. aid to the contras and Soviet bloc aid to the Farabundo Marti National Liberation Front (FMLN) in El Salvador], and a commitment by all countries involved to hold elections and move toward "political pluralism." Arias won the 1987 Nobel Peace Prize for the plan that took his name, but Ronald Reagan obviously did not agree with the committee's choice. The Arias Plan would permit the Soviets through Cuba to continue to aid Sandinista President Daniel Ortega's government in Nicaragua (and also permit continued U.S. support for the government in El Salvador). Reagan refused to cooperate and pressed Congress for additional aid to the contras.

Soon after his inauguration, Bush and Baker openly broke with the policies of the preceding administration. Taking the Arias Plan as a basis for action, Baker halted U.S. aid to the Contras and pressed the Sandinistas to hold free elections. He did so in part because Gorbachev gave secret assurances that the Soviet Union would withhold aid from the Nicaraguan government and insist that Ortega accept the results of a free election. At the same time, the U.S. government pressed the right-wing government of President Alfredo Cristiani in El Salvador to negotiate with the FMLN. In the Nicaraguan elections held in February 1990, Ortega and the Sandinistas were resoundingly defeated. The socialist regime had failed to revitalize Nicaragua's war-torn economy. Its collectivist policies and general ineptness, coupled with a U.S. embargo, had deepened the country's chronic poverty. The winner was Violeta Chamorro, widow of the publisher of *La Prensa*, a paper that had crusaded first against Samoza and then Ortega. In El Salvador, the Christiani government and representatives of the rebel FMLN arranged a fragile cease-fire in February 1992 and began negotiating.

George Bush's reputation as a peacemaker in Latin America was, unfortunately, overshadowed by his decision to send troops into Panama in late 1989. That small impoverished country had been ruled since the 1960s by the brutal and corrupt military dictator General Manuel Noriega. During the 1980s, Noriega had angered the Reagan administration by simultaneously funneling aid to the contras and working undercover for Fidel Castro. He also worked both sides of the street as far as drug trafficking was concerned. While cooperating with DEA agents who seized shipments of cocaine headed north from Peru, Bolivia, and Columbia, he conspired with the drug lords to let other shipments through and to launder their profits. All the while, the Panamanian dictator remained in the pay of the CIA.

In 1988, two Florida grand juries indicted Noriega on charges that he participated directly in the smuggling of drugs into the United States, that he accepted bribes for allowing Panamanian banks to launder drug money, and that he actually permitted Columbians to manufacture drugs in Panama. Under intense pressure from critics who demanded to know why Washington was providing aid to a man who was both an autocrat and a drug dealer, Reagan cut off military and economic aid, and pressured Noriega to step down, but in the tried and true tradition of Latin American dictators who incurred the wrath of the United States, Noriega wrapped himself in the Panamanian flag and posed as the defender of Panama's national sovereignty.

Not long after George Bush took the Oath of Office as president, Noriega held presidential elections. His attempts to rig the contest failed, and Guillermo Endara won. The general responded by declaring the election results null and void, and proclaiming himself "maximum leader." In October 1989, American officials in Panama encouraged dissident officers in the Panamanian Defense Force to overthrow their corrupt commander, but when they attempted a takeover, the U.S. government refused to help.

Amid their arrests and summary executions, "the wimp factor" began to plague Bush once again.

In mid-December 1989, after Noriega declared that Panama and the United States were in a "state of war," President Bush approved Operation Just Cause. On December 29, 27,000 Marines landed in Panama with the stated objective of protecting the canal, safeguarding American citizens, and interdicting the drug traffic flowing north from South America. Panamanian Defense Force (PDF) troops loyal to Noriega held off the Marines for several days but then capitulated. The U.S. command subsequently installed Endara as president. Noriega proved elusive, but the Marines eventually located him in the Vatican embassy in Panama City. After lengthy negotiations, the drug dictator agreed to surrender. He was returned to Florida to stand trial and was ultimately convicted of the drug charges brought against him. Operation Just Cause had taken the lives of 24 U.S. soldiers, 139 PDF troops, and more than 300 Panamanian civilians.

Bush's Panamanian expedition was immensely popular with the American people. It stirred their martial spirit and, together with Granada, helped erase memories of the Vietnam humiliation. The president was so confident of popular support that he had not even bothered to consult Congress. The War Powers Act technically gave the executive 60 days to conduct hostilities abroad before gaining congressional approval, but Operation Just Cause ended far short of that deadline. Nary a congressional voice was raised against the operation for fear of the political fallout. Reaction abroad was mixed. Europeans generally regretted the apparent resurrection of the Roosevelt Corollary to the Monroe Doctrine (enunciated in 1904 by Theodore Roosevelt, the corollary declared that the United States would have to act as trustee for the civilized world and intervene in any American republic defaulting on its foreign debt or succumbing to civil disorder) at a time when the Soviets were giving up the Brezhnev Doctrine. While welcoming the result, many Latin American nations shuddered at this new evidence of North America's willingness to invade its weaker neighbors to the south when matters there did not suit it. Both the Organization of American States (OAS) and the UN considered resolutions of condemnation; indeed, in the latter body, such a proposal failed only because the U.S. delegate vetoed it.

The Gulf War

If any doubt existed in the post-Vietnam era that the United States intended to defend its economic and strategic interests broadly defined, it disappeared when the Bush administration went to war with Iraq in early 1991. On August 2, 1990, Iraqi military strongman Saddam Hussein sent nearly 100,000 troops into tiny, oil-rich Kuwait. Hussein declared that Iraq was merely reclaiming what was its own. Kuwait, bordering Iraq to the south, had been part of Iraq prior to the Paris Peace Conference of 1919. The real motivations behind the invasion, however, were money and power. Hussein had run up a debt of nearly $80 billion during the bloody eight-year war with Iran. He desperately needed ready cash to rebuild his nation's economy and to sustain the vast army and police state that underpinned his dictatorship. Kuwait's prodigious output of petroleum kept world prices down and Iraqi profits from its oil sales low. With Kuwait's oil and a reequipped military, Iraq would become the dominant military power in the Middle East and an important player on the world scene.

The Bush administration responded to the invasion of Kuwait promptly and vigorously. Declaring that "this will not stand" and comparing Saddam Hussein with Adolf Hitler, President Bush began the political and military process of assembling a multinational coalition capable of driving Iraqi troops out of Kuwait. The reasons for this aggressive response were many. The Bush administration feared that, if this clear-cut case of aggression went unchecked, it would be followed by other acts of blatant imperialism. In fact, after subduing Kuwait, Saddam began massing troops along Kuwait's border with Saudi Arabia. Then there was the ever-present matter of credibility. The United States had developed close ties with Kuwait and even closer bonds with Saudi Arabia. If the U.S. government did not stand by its friends in the region, the United States would quickly lose all influence. In this same vein, a fully armed and oil-rich Iraq posed a potential threat to America's chief ally in the region, Israel. Saddam was an outspoken champion of the Palestinian cause and had frequently promised to lead a "jihad," or holy war, against Israel (although his regime was secular). Rumors were already rampant that Saddam was building nuclear weapons, and it was well known that he had used poison gas against the Kurdish minority in his own country. But the real motive force behind the war with Iraq was oil. If Saddam was allowed to keep Kuwait, he would control a quarter of the world's proven oil supplies; if he succeeded in overrunning Saudi Arabia that figure would be nearly half. At that point, he would be able to determine the price of oil, driving it through the ceiling if he wanted, destroying the economies of America, Western Europe, and Japan.

With the United States in the lead, the UN imposed a stringent economic embargo on Iraq and adopted a series of resolutions calling for Iraqi withdrawal. Carefully, Secretary of State Baker and his team cleared the way for military intervention. Most delegates to the UN General Assembly and all members of the Security Council favored military action. The Soviets who had furnished Saddam with a large portion of his armaments broke with him and quietly supported a U.S.-led army of liberation. Bush's pragmatic approach to the Tiananmen Square massacre paid dividends as China agreed not to oppose the use of force. Great Britain under Prime Minister Margaret Thatcher not only supported intervention but also agreed to play a leading role. Among Middle Eastern states, only Iran and the Palestinians in Jordan supported Saddam. The former sided with Iraq in return for Saddam's promise to return everything taken in the Iran–Iraq war and the latter because they hoped Iraq's invasion of Kuwait would ignite an Arab–Israeli war. With this wide-ranging support, the Bush administration launched "Operation Desert Shield" and within weeks had a 700,000 person army, navy, and air force stationed in northern Saudi Arabia and the waters around Kuwait. Twenty-eight nations contributed forces, and after some arm-twisting, economic superpowers such as Japan, Saudi Arabia, and Germany agreed to finance a large portion of the costs.

America's aggressive reaction to the invasion of Kuwait took Saddam aback. The U.S. government's support during the war with Iran and its fear of Islamic fundamentalism led Saddam to believe that it would sit on the sidelines while he pursued his aggressive ambitions. Indeed, shortly before the invasion, the U.S. ambassador had apologized for Voice of America criticism of Iraq's deplorable human rights record and assured the Iraqi dictator that the United States "does not intervene in inter-Arab border disputes." But, in reality, his failure to anticipate the reaction of the United States and the rest of the world was testimony to the profound isolation in which he lived.

In November 1990, President Bush doubled the size of the U.S. contingent in and around Saudi Arabia to more than 500,000 and shifted the focus of its mission. The White House announced that Operation Desert Storm had as its goal nothing less than the liberation of Kuwait, and the UN Security Council set a date of January 15, 1991, for Saddam to evacuate his troops or face attack. While the military buildup continued, Bush sought consensus at home. Initially, an overwhelming majority of Americans favored the sending of American troops to the Middle East. But when the objective of the operation shifted from protection of Saudi Arabia to liberation of Kuwait, support dwindled to a bare majority. Remembering Vietnam, Bush went to Congress and asked for authority to go to war in accordance with the Security Council's resolutions. A long, thoughtful congressional debate on the situation in the Middle East and American foreign policy in general ensued. On January 12, Congress rejected a Democrat-sponsored resolution asking the administration to refrain from the use of force and give economic sanctions more time to work. Both houses then voted to authorize military operations. Virtually all Republicans supported the administration, whereas a majority of Democrats opposed it. The vote in the Senate was 42 to 42, with the tie being broken by Vice President Quayle.

The deadline for an Iraqi pullout from Kuwait came and went. Chairman of the Joint Chiefs of Staff Colin Powell authorized the commander of Desert Storm, General H. Norman Schwarzkopf, to initiate hostilities. For a month, American fighter bombers attacked strategic targets within Kuwait and Iraq. On February 24, 1991, some 550,000 allied troops, 250,000 of them from the United States, crossed into Kuwait. Saddam promised the "Mother of All Battles," but the Iraqi army and air force were no match for allied technology and firepower. After liberating Kuwait, Schwarzkopf drove into southern Iraq. In less than 100 hours, the battle was over. At the cost of 136 American lives, the coalition had smashed the Iraqi war machine, killing an estimated 100,000 soldiers in the process. In a desperate effort to fend off defeat, Saddam had rained Scud missiles on Israel in hopes of drawing them into the war. Such an eventuality would, he believed, cause Saudi Arabia, Egypt, and other Arab members of the coalition Baker, Powell, and Schwarzkopf had so carefully put together to break away and join with him. But Israel either refused to be baited or was restrained by threats and promises from the U.S. government. Jerusalem held its hand. As a parting shot, the retreating Iraqi army set fire to 650 Kuwaiti oil wells, a holocaust that took nine months to extinguish.

In the wake of this rather easy victory, pressure mounted on the Bush administration, the United Nations, and the coalition to "finish the job," that is, to move into Baghdad and depose Saddam Hussein. Stories concerning the brutality of Iraqi troops in Kuwait coupled with Saddam's well-known offenses against his own people – the gassing of Kurdish tribesmen and the sacrifice of tens of thousands of young soldiers in suicide attacks against Iran – created a groundswell of anger in the United States and other coalition nations. But President Bush wisely ordered Schwarzkopf to remain within the perimeter that had been set up in southern Iraq. If the coalition went into Baghdad, it would become involved in house-to-house fighting and probably a prolonged guerrilla war. Moreover, Saddam, entrenched with his Republican Guard in bunkers deep beneath the city, would be hard to capture. Moreover, the president and his advisers realized that Iraq's total destruction would at once make Iran the dominant power in the region. The administration anticipated that the Iraqis themselves would rise up and overthrow their dictator, but it was wrong. To be sure, there was an insurrection: in the south, a large minority belonging to the Shi'ite division of Islam – predominant in Iran – took up arms against the government, while in the north Kurdish tribesmen fought for autonomy. Although crippled, Saddam still had enough power to dominate his rebellious countrymen, and American troops stood by helplessly on the southern shore of the Euphrates, while his Republican Guards slaughtered the opposition.

The Gulf War succeeded in safeguarding the West's Middle Eastern oil supplies, and it demonstrated that America – deficits, Vietnam legacy, and all – was still a superpower capable of rapidly projecting its power into any and every region of the world. It restored to America much of the self-confidence that had been lost during Vietnam. Also, the conflict demonstrated that the United States had "learned the lessons" of America's longest war. The military command demanded that the political and military objectives of the conflict be clearly spelled out before the battle was joined and that it have more than sufficient force in the field to accomplish those objectives. The Bush administration was upfront with Congress and the American people about what it intended to do, but once hostilities started, kept a tight rein on the press. In a sense, the Gulf War was irrelevant to the Arab–Israeli conflict, but the Israeli government was somewhat reassured by the fact that Arabs were willing to fight Arabs on behalf of regional security. Shortly after the end of the war, Washington persuaded Jews and Arabs to enter yet another round of peace talks. This time the Israelis agreed to the inclusion of Palestinians – albeit in the Jordanian delegation – and the United States agreed to Soviet participation.

"It's the Economy, Stupid": The Election of 1992

Not surprisingly, the coalition victory in the Gulf War sent George Bush's popularity soaring. It proved shockingly short lived. Within a year, a sharp economic downturn and the growing impression that the president did not know anything or care much about domestic affairs sent his prestige tumbling. A prolonged economic recession began in July 1990, the sharpest if not the longest since the Great Depression. In December alone, the nation's largest corporations – Xerox, General Motors, and IBM – cut their workforce by 100,000. By 1992, the economy had lost more than 2 million jobs, and 19 states were technically in a depression. The problems of the Reagan years – a ballooning deficit, the S&L bailout, the mounting trade imbalance, and the lack of an industrial policy – had created a massive crisis of confidence. Nowhere was this more apparent than in the declining rate of investment. While the Japanese were reinvesting 31% of their gross domestic product (GDP), Americans were plowing only 15% of theirs back into the economy.

The more the nation sank into the economic doldrums, the more confused George Bush seemed to become. At one point, he acknowledged that "people are hurting" and then in the next breath declared that "this is a good time to buy a car." As he and the Democratic-controlled Congress squabbled over a recovery plan, commentators began to compare George Bush with Herbert Hoover, the Depression-era president who had first insisted that there was no real problem and then assured his countrymen that the crisis would be short and self-correcting. The Federal Reserve Board dropped the prime lending rate in an effort to jump-start the economy, but to no avail. All that George Bush could do as he headed into the 1992 election was hold his military trophies high, hoping that his triumphs in Panama and the Middle East would be enough to carry him to a second term.

Bush's tax compromise with Democratic congressional leaders coupled with his soft approach to the New Right's social agenda opened the door to

a challenge from Pat Buchanan, a former Nixon speech writer and a pug-
nacious conservative. He accused the president of abandoning "the principles of the Republican Party." He was, Buchanan declared, "the biggest
spender in American history." During the Nixon administration, Buchanan
had proved himself to be one of the most partisan and ideological men in
America. There was in his blend of pre–World War II isolationism and
fiscal conservatism a mean-spiritedness that smacked of nativism if not
anti-Semitism. He called for an end to foreign aid, the withdrawal of all
U.S. troops from Europe, and the closing of America's frontiers to further
immigration. Buchanan entered the New Hampshire primary in February
1992, with guns blazing. His campaign workers spread out across the state
and uncovered a surprising amount of support, primarily among young
white males who did indeed believe that George Bush the conservative was
essentially a fraud. Buchanan won an impressive 37% of the vote and, in
the primaries that followed, garnered a consistent 20% to 30%. The Bush
camp alternately threatened and pleaded in an effort to persuade Buchanan
to withdraw, but he would not.

Clinton
Democratic chances for recapturing the White House were dimmed when
the only candidate of truly national stature, Mario Cuomo, decided not to
run. That left the door open for 45-year-old William Jefferson Clinton, the
governor of Arkansas. Clinton, who began envisioning himself as president
as an adolescent, possessed gold-plated educational credentials, something
that he realized was politically essential for a politician from the hinter-
lands with national ambitions. After graduating from Georgetown University in Washington, D.C., where he supported himself by working in the
mailroom of Senator J. William Fulbright, Clinton secured a Rhodes Scholarship to Oxford and then matriculated at Yale Law School. While there, he
persuaded one of his brightest classmates, Hillary Rodham, to forsake the
power corridors of the Northeast and return with him to Arkansas. At 32
years of age, in 1979, Clinton became the youngest governor in the country,
and he served continuously in that capacity with one two-year hiatus until
his nomination for the presidency in 1992.

Clinton's oft-stated admiration for John F. Kennedy and his opposition
to the war in Vietnam caused him to be branded as a liberal early in his political career. As his prospects for election or appointment to a national post
increased, Clinton worked to position himself as a "centrist." He promised
to cut the defense budget, but he had supported the Gulf War and frequently
stated his determination to defend U.S. strategic and economic interests by
whatever means necessary. The United States, Clinton declared, should reward the republics of the former Soviet Union for political and economic
reform with a massive aid package. He rejected the Reagan–Carter contention that "government was the problem" and argued that it simply had

to be made more responsible to the needs of the people. During the general election campaign, the Arkansan called for reform of the welfare system making benefits terminable and tying them to work, and he promised a new health care system that would be based on universal coverage. In addition, under his administration there would be tax relief for the middle class and a restructuring of the student loan program. In part, he captured the Democratic nomination by convincing party leaders that he would do anything to win, which was true, and that he could reattach lost constituencies, such as the South and ethnic, working-class, middle Americans to the party, which was only partially true.

Bill Clinton was a tireless, indeed voracious, campaigner. He was handsome, witty, and a superb speaker. He had the Kennedy knack of self-effacement, going on the "Johnny Carson Show" in 1988 to play the saxophone and make jokes about himself after having delivered a disastrous nominating speech on behalf of Michael Dukakis at the Democratic convention. His wife, Hillary, was independent, intelligent, and well-informed, specializing in health care and family abuse issues. But Clinton was vulnerable. For his efforts to be all things to all people and for his periodic lack of candor, he earned the sobriquet "Slick Willie" from his enemies. Tales of his womanizing dogged him as governor and followed him on the presidential campaign trail. His forthright opposition to the war in Vietnam probably won him more support than it lost, but evidence that he had dodged the draft damaged him with veterans' groups and conservatives in general.

Perot

With Clinton's "negatives" and Bush's apparent unwillingness or inability to address the economic downturn, the way was open for the independent candidacy of H. Ross Perot. Perot's data processing company had computerized Social Security and Medicare during the 1960s and 1970s, in the process making its CEO a multimillionaire. A friend of Richard Nixon's, Perot was an increasingly strident critic of the executive branch, Congress, and both political parties for not addressing real issues such as deficit reduction and instead focusing on their own political futures and pork-barrel projects for constituents. His self-made image, his credentials as a political outsider, and his attacks on Congress and the president struck a responsive chord with a public tired of a government mired in perpetual gridlock. In February 1992, during a televised call-in talk show, Perot was asked if he would consider running for president. He would, he said, if enough "volunteers" emerged to get his name on the ballot in all 50 states. Over the next two weeks, Perot's corporate headquarters was deluged with more than 2 million calls.

By July, Perot was pulling even with the two major party candidates in the polls. The Clintons generally treated the east Texas tycoon with kid gloves in hopes that he would eventually withdraw and throw his support

to them. The Republicans attacked. Perot was no conservative, GOP leaders declared. He had opposed the Gulf War, was prochoice on the abortion
issue, and supported gun control. Telling an aide, "I'm not having fun any-
more," Perot abruptly quit. Two months later, stung by bitter criticism from
his disillusioned supporters, he reentered the race, but his credibility had
been irreparably damaged.

The last stages of the presidential contest unfolded at a furious pace.
Clinton was everywhere, campaigning sometimes 24 hours per day, deflecting questions about his personal life and struggling to focus voter attention
on vital issues. Without a viable social program or economic recovery plan,
the Bush campaign spent most of its time lashing out at Clinton and Perot.
The independent candidate spent millions of dollars of his own money on
"infomercials" broadcast over the major networks. Most were 30-minute
talking head productions featuring Perot waving a pointer and delivering confusing harangues on the economy and social policy. The League
of Women Voters sponsored a series of three-way debates, which showed
Clinton at his best.

James Carville, Clinton's chief campaign strategist, had posted signs
in Democratic campaign headquarters proclaiming, "It's the economy,
stupid!" He was right. The voters made Bill Clinton the first baby-boomer
president, and they did so by a wide margin. He captured 43% of the popular vote to Bush's 38% and won in the electoral college by a vote of 370
to 168. Perot failed to carry any states but tallied 19% of the popular vote,
the best showing by a third-party candidate since 1912. Clinton won because he and his wife, who it was clear would be a major player in any
Clinton administration, appeared to be smart, competent, and devoted to
the public interest. He was right on the social issues. Despite the fervency
of right-to-lifers, a majority of Americans were prochoice. Women played
a major role in the election of 1992, helping elect the Clintons and placing four new women in the Senate: Carol Moseley Braun of Illinois (the
first African American woman), Diane Feinstein and Barbara Boxer from
California, and Patty Murray from Washington. Clinton attracted a large
number of Americans who had voted Republican for the previous 12 years.
He ran strongly in the Northeast, industrial Midwest, and Far West, becoming the first Democrat since Lyndon Johnson to capture California.
With large Democratic majorities in both houses, the stage was set for the
United States to address social and economic issues that had gone begging
for a quarter century.

America the Diverse

The America that entered the 1990s was more than ever a multicultural
society. Between 1985 and 1990, 5 million immigrants entered the country, creating a populace that was more than 8% foreign born. This figure

compared with 4.7% in 1970. More than one fifth of all people living in California in 1990 had been born in another country.

In the eternal tension between pressures for acculturation and the drive to maintain ethnic identity, ethnicity seemed to be winning out. As of 1990, more than 1.7 million citizens identified themselves as Native Americans, a figure that reflected natural increase and also a growing willingness by Americans to include themselves in that category. Although rates of disease, poverty, and alcoholism continued to be high on Native American reservations, tribes took advantage of the 1961 law permitting them to buy land and set up business enterprises to establish resorts, trading posts, and giant bingo parlors.

Asian Americans emerged as a important minority as immigrants from Korea, Vietnam, the Philippines, and Indonesia joined already well-established Chinese and Japanese communities. The West Coast continued to be the focus of Asian American life and settlement, but communities sprang up all across the nation. With their traditional emphasis on education, close-knit families, and self-discipline, Asian Americans did disproportionately well at school and business, but there were also tensions. Many second- and third-generation members of this subculture suffered as they sought to shed the rigidities and traditionalism of the old ways in favor of the fluid individualism of American life.

The 1990 census showed a total of 20 million Hispanics living in the United States, and demographers predicted that they would surpass African Americans as the largest minority by 2000. Some 14 million of these were Mexican Americans, most of them living in the Southwest. By 1990, both Los Angeles and Miami were one-third Hispanic as were 23% of all Texans. Despite a 1991 law making it more difficult for illegal aliens to cross the 1,000-mile border with Mexico and imposing stiff penalties on employers hiring undocumented workers, an estimated 12 million Hispanics lived in the United States illegally. While third- and fourth-generation members of this ethnic group managed to penetrate the white power structure and achieve middle-class status, newcomers were generally forced to accept work as fruit and vegetable pickers, day laborers, or domestics. As of 1990, one third of Puerto Ricans and one fifth of Mexican Americans lived at or below the poverty line.

The quality of life for many African Americans improved, but for a substantial minority it declined. Indeed, if there was one striking characteristic about black America in 1990, it was the widening gap between the affluent middle class and impoverished underclass, most of whose members dwelt in the nation's inner cities. African Americans continued to make political gains as the nation elected its first black governor, L. Douglas Wilder of Virginia. The census indicated that 12% of all college students were African American, a figure close to their percentage of the population as a whole. Almost half of the black workers in the labor force held white-collar jobs. The inner city featured strong black institutions – the church, fraternal organizations, neighborhood associations, and labor unions – but they generally fought a losing battle against poverty, and violence. Ten times more black youths were murdered than whites. By 1990, one out of four black males ages 20 to 30 were either in prison or on parole. As of that year, two thirds of all African American births were to single women, many of them young, uneducated, and poor. As a result, two thirds of all black children had been on the welfare rolls by age 18. Denied any opportunity for upward social mobility or any kind of better life, young black inner-city dwellers turned to crime and drugs: in hundreds of cities, gangs battled with each other over turf – the right to sell drugs from a particular locale to a regular clientele. Attracted by the money, clothes, and extravagant automobiles of the drug dealers, children as young as nine and ten were drawn into the subculture.

The Persistence of Racism

Racism continued to be a dominant undercurrent in American life. It had become unfashionable for politicians to appeal directly to racial prejudice, but there were subtler ways. While most politicians of both parties courted and won over black voters, some Republicans and some Democrats catered to whites by railing against welfare cheats, high crime, and high taxes. Because African Americans constituted a disproportionate percentage of the welfare rolls and prison populations, the message was that they were responsible for most of society's ills. For all of the progress made in the area of civil rights, the United States seemed always on the verge of a racial explosion.

On March 3, 1991, members of the Los Angeles police department arrested a 25-year-old exconvict named Rodney King for speeding. When he showed signs of resisting arrest, the officers stunned him with a cattle prod and, while he lay on the ground, kicked him and beat him with fists and truncheons. The assault continued for more than 20 minutes while 11 other officers watched. King's skull was repeatedly fractured and he also suffered a shattered cheekbone and broken ankle. Unbeknownst to the police, a nearby resident had caught the brutality on videotape. Within days, images of King's beating were being broadcast on the nightly news all across the United States. The four police officers directly involved were arrested and charged with assault, while leaders in the African American community denounced the King beating as part of a persistent pattern of police brutality. In the spring of 1992, despite the videotape, the officers were acquitted by an all-white jury in Simi Valley, an upper middle-class suburb of Los Angeles. Immediately, an angry mob took to the streets, rampaging through south central Los Angeles. Black youths attacked motorists, severely beating a white trucker; broke windows; and looted shops. A particular target of the rioters were Korean shopkeepers, whom inner-city Hispanics and blacks had long accused of exploiting them. Entire city blocks went up in flames. When police and National Guardsmen had restored order, 44 people lay dead with another 1,800 injured.

In the wake of the Rodney King verdict, African Americans in Los Angeles were more than ever convinced that they could not receive justice at the hands of a system controlled by whites. When they saw an opportunity, they retaliated.

Clearly, the decline of Jim Crow in the South and the gains of the civil rights movement in general since 1950 had not solved fundamental problems in the black community of crime, poverty, illegitimacy, and powerlessness. When in 1965 Daniel Patrick Moynihan had decried the disintegration of the black family as responsible for the ills that plagued African Americans, he had been denounced for blaming the victims of racism for the wrongs that had been inflicted on them by the white majority. Indeed, the logic of the civil rights movement was that once white racism was defeated or at least contained, crime, joblessness, ignorance, and family dysfunction would disappear.

The 1990s witnessed widespread attacks on the old assumptions. Sociologists, social critics, and political conservatives, both black and white, pointed out that racial attitudes among the white majority had changed appreciably. Not only were blacks being elected to office in record numbers by multiracial constituencies, but also African American celebrities such as comedian Bill Cosby and basketball star Michael Jordan had become integral parts of the national identity. In *The Scar of Race*, Paul Sniderman and Thomas Piazza noted a decline in what they termed "unembarassed racism" and a tendency among whites to view blacks more in terms of class and behavior than skin color. Still the ghettos seethed and the black family continued to disintegrate. Some stepped forward to argue that government programs, such as busing, welfare, and affirmative action, were not only irrelevant but also harmful. Others such as historian Raymond Wolters charged that busing led to white flight and racial backlash without any compensatory rise in educational levels among black youth. Conservatives continued to insist that welfare locked African Americans into a cycle of dependency and encouraged black males to remain unmarried and jobless. In its extreme form, which included informal quotas and set-asides in the awarding of government contracts, affirmative action discriminated. In so doing, it violated the hallowed American principle of equality of opportunity and threatened the very premise on which the civil rights movement had been founded. In 1996, two white university professors operating, ironically, out of an office on the University of California, Berkeley, campus launched the California Civil Rights Initiative. That measure, which was subsequently enacted, prohibited the state of California from using "race, sex, color, ethnicity or national origin as a criterion for either discriminating against or granting preferential treatment to, any individual or group." Thus did the most populous state in the union outlaw the concept of "compensatory discrimination" that had been adopted during Lyndon B. Johnson's presidency and supported, at least in name, by every succeeding administration.

No consensus on the best approach to solving problems of the black community emerged. Philosophical heirs of Malcolm X, such as Nation of Islam leader Louis Farrakan and film maker Spike Lee, called on black males to take responsibility for their actions, to exercise discipline, to support their wives and children, and to stand up to white oppression. Lee lauded Malcolm as a martyr and role model, "a strong Black man with backbone, with conviction." The Reverend Jesse Jackson, who had stood with Martin Luther King, Jr., on the balcony in Memphis when he was shot, continued to advocate government programs to obliterate discrimination and achieve a moderate redistribution of wealth, while preaching and modeling self-help. Black studies programs featuring Afrocentric curricula continued to proliferate, but at the same time leaders of the black community continued to insist on the right to integrate.

The O. J. Simpson Case

In June 1994, television newscasters broke into regularly scheduled programming to report that former Buffalo Bills superstar and sports analyst O. J. Simpson was being pursued by police as a suspect in the brutal stabbing deaths of his estranged wife, Nicole Brown Simpson, and her friend, Ronald Goldman. A national television audience watched mesmerized as police cruisers surrounded and followed Simpson and a friend over miles of Los Angeles freeway. Finally, after arriving back at the Simpson home, O. J. surrendered. The case drew worldwide attention as Simpson, a multimillionaire, assembled one of the finest and highest-paid legal teams in history. By December 1994, jury selection was complete. The men and women who would hear the case included eight blacks, two Hispanics, one white, and one person identified as half white and half Native American. What made the case so sensational was not only the brutality of the murders – Brown Simpson and Goldman's throats had been cut, their heads almost severed from their bodies – but also that O. J. was black and Nicole was white.

As the proceedings unfolded, it became clear that O. J. had a history of wife abuse. Eight times police had been called to the Simpson home. Protected by his celebrity status, however, the former football star had never been charged.

The evidence in the case seemed to point to a conviction. Simpson's blood had been found on the gate near the murdered couple, traces of Goldman's blood were in Simpson's Bronco, Nicole's blood was on a sock found in the defendant's bedroom, and several strands of Simpson's hair were discovered adhering to Ron Goldman's shirt. Confronted with these damaging facts, Simpson's lawyer, Johnny Cochran, who had during his career earned an estimated $45 million by attacking racism in the Los Angeles

Police Department (LAPD), decided to play the race card. He manipulated the jury selection process so that as many blacks without a college education as possible were chosen. He then concentrated on indicting the LAPD as a racist institution and convincing the jury that officer Mark Fuhrman had planted the evidence pointing to his client's guilt. Cochran did indeed prove that the LAPD had a history of racism, but not that its officers framed Simpson. Nevertheless, to the outrage of whites and women's groups, the jury acquitted O. J. Simpson.

Johnny Cochran's strategy grew out of a philosophy called critical race theory that began to take root in the legal community in the mid-1980s. Its proponents rejected the achievements of the civil rights movement as superficial. White society remained fundamentally racist, and African Americans continued to be chronically disadvantaged. Because, critical race theorists argued, the white majority could never transcend its racist perspectives, formally neutral laws would continue to fuel white domination. The most radical of these scholars suggested that black jurors should nullify certain laws if sending guilty black defendants to prison would not serve the goals of the African American community. For these individuals, black lawbreaking was a form of black self-help, a legitimate way of adjusting the scales after centuries of racial oppression.

The Female Dilemma

The dawning of the 1990s witnessed dramatic advances by American women. Comprising 42% of the workforce in 1970, women had increased that proportion to 57% by 1991. Females were employed in all walks of life from construction laborers to police officers to fire fighters to bankers. By 1991, women made up 41% of all executive and managerial positions, up from 32% in 1983. Only 20% of lawyers and doctors were female, but that marked a significant increase over previous levels. Women made spectacular gains in academia. From novelist Joyce Carol Oates to historian Barbara Tuchmann, female writers flourished. Toni Morrison, a black woman, won the Pulitzer Prize in 1987 for her novel *Beloved* and the Nobel Prize for literature in 1993. Women in the workplace still did not demonstrate the earning power that men did, bringing in 74 cents to a dollar for men by the 1990s. Some question existed, however, as to whether the difference in wage scales was due to sexism by employers or to choices by women who opted to interrupt careers to devote full time to child-rearing or to select jobs that allowed them to be part-time homemakers.

Women's relationship to the family changed as their place in the economy and society changed. As the divorce rate continued to climb, and single women bore a larger portion of the nation's children, single-parent households, usually headed by women, became the norm. Indeed, as of 1995, only 25% of the nation's households were married with children. The proportion of children living in homes with two parents fell from 85% in 1970 to 72% in 1991. For blacks, the figure was 42%; for whites, 80%. The birthrate remained low, with women marrying later and having fewer children. Because women lived longer than men, they were more isolated. The number of households with just one person grew from 17.1% of the whole in 1970 to 24.6% in 1990 and to 25% in 1995. Most of these were women; nearly half of the females living alone were 65 or older, and 44% were widows.

As women grew in self-awareness, and their economic and political power increased, their tolerance of exploitation decreased. They were particularly sensitive to rape and sexual harassment. Businesses, federal bureaucracies, and the military were rocked by harassment scandals. This was true not because harassment and rape were more pervasive, but because women were more willing to report it and society to judge it. Business and academic institutions enacted strict regulations prohibiting unwanted sexual contact. Critics, some of them feminists, argued that sensitivity was going too far, however, portraying every male as at best a brutish boor and at worst a rapist. One ironical result of radical feminism was to portray women as nothing but sex objects. Inevitably, some young women internalized the putative male perception. In *A Nation of Victims* (1993), the conservative social critic Charles Sykes denounced some feminists for practicing "the politics of victimization."

The 1990s witnessed the advent of so-called "second-stage" feminism. First-stage feminism had concentrated on ensuring equality under the law and in the workplace for women. NOW and other groups continued to file lawsuits under the Fourteenth Amendment and Title VII of the Civil Rights Act and to win significant victories. A number of corporations, large and small, were forced to pay restitution to women who proved that they had been discriminated against. By the early 1990s, six states had enacted "comparable worth" or "pay equity" laws. Some in the women's movement lauded these advances but urged feminists to look beyond simply making women into successful men. In a highly controversial book titled *In a Different Voice* (1982), psychologist Carol Gilligan argued that women were biologically (some would say culturally) different from men. The female persona was nurturing, compassionate, and altruistic, whereas men were competitive, abstract, and generally less sensitive, especially to the plight of individuals. Building on her work, radical feminists such as Suzanne Gordon called for the movement to shift its focus away from government programs designed simply to replace males with females in the workplace, academia, and politics. Women were morally superior to men and had a duty to transform the very bases of society moving it away from competitive capitalism to a caring, nurturing social order.

In reality, the radical feminists were few in number and received more attention from the media and conservatives than they perhaps deserved.

A majority of feminists, Betty Friedan being a prime example, did believe that women ought to move beyond first-stage feminism, while lauding its accomplishments. But the next level should not involve rejection of males or the traditional family but an accommodation between family and career. The current generation's daughters would ask, Friedan wrote, "How can I have it all...the career I want, and the kind of marriage I want, and be a great mother?" Thus did the women's movement in its institutional, organized form increasingly focus on better child care facilities in the workplace, extended pregnancy and postnatal leave for both men and women, and harsher penalties for "deadbeat dads," divorced men who did not pay child support. In her 1992 book, *The Revolution From Within*, Gloria Steinem argued that the issues confronting women were not political, institutional, or even external. A better life could only be realized from individual inquiry into family history, the nature of women, and one's particular characteristics and resources.

The Culture Wars

As ethnic and gender awareness grew, formerly disadvantaged groups demanded that higher education alter its curricula to correct past injustices and reflect new realities. Since the 1960s, African Americans had been demanding that history and literature give a larger place to the contributions of black soldiers, sailors, politicians, and workers. By the 1990s, most universities boasted well-developed African American studies programs. Chicanos made some headway in the West and Southwest and, by the 1990s, women's studies programs were being found on college campuses across the country. Affirmative action opened academia's doors to minorities and women, most of whom had been victimized by the white power structure and who saw the established curriculum as an instrument of oppression.

Gradually, the movement for inclusion of formerly disregarded groups turned into denunciation of "elites." In English and history departments, young radicals debated their traditionalist elders over whether to alter the canon to reduce or eliminate the formerly pervasive influence of "dead white European males." Some literary scholars embraced deconstructionism, the notion that one text had as much value or relevance as another and that there were no universal standards in literary criticism. The new social history stressed the role of the common, inarticulate, frequently powerless man and woman over politicians, generals, bankers, and established literati. Some curricula became obsessed with Native Americans, uneducated women, powerless blacks, and developing nations.

Critics denounced the new wave as cultural nihilism, arguing that universal notions about beauty and truth had always guided the study of literature, and that forms and structures had become accepted because they had proved themselves over time. Historians insisted that institutions and powerful people were worthy of study because they had had the greatest impact on the greatest number of people. History was history, not cultural anthropology, however worthy that field might be. In 1987, University of Chicago classicist Alan Bloom, a self-confessed elitist, published the best selling *The Closing of the American Mind*, in which he bemoaned the erosion of standards and called for a return to basics, meaning the traditional canon of Western Civilization. Efforts to increase the self-esteem of women and minorities were admirable, but they should not be allowed to distort the historical record, argued Arthur Schlesinger, Jr., in *The Disuniting of America* (1991). Predictably, he urged a new effort to define and cultivate a common culture and past.

Soon the "culture wars" spilled over into politics. In Miami, Los Angeles, and other cities Hispanics pushed for bilingualism. In 1996, the Oakland city school board temporarily mandated the teaching of "ebonics" (street English spoken by some urban blacks), along with standard English. Conservatives struck back. Lynne Cheney, who headed the National Endowment for the Humanities under Ronald Reagan, declared war on multiculturalism and sponsored a program to define and preserve the classics of Western literature and history. The Republican secretary of education, William Bennett, decried the deterioration of standards in the nation's schools, a process, he charged, that was being caused by the abandonment of a core curriculum and by the notion that learning was a relative thing. Unfortunately, extremists on both sides of the "political correctness" argument tended to act in ways that stifled freedom of inquiry and expression, the very lifeblood of academia and of a healthy democracy.

The Presidency of William Jefferson Clinton

In the midst of a gala inaugural celebration, Bill Clinton delivered his maiden address as president. Black poet and Arkansas native Maya Angelou preceded him and spoke of a "new day." In his well-received speech, Clinton promised to end the "deadlock and drift" in government; he emphasized the need for change and called for "a new season of American renewal." The government, he declared, should be returned to "those to whom it belongs," that is, to those who lived outside the Washington, D.C., beltway. "Today a new generation raised in the shadow of the Cold War assumes new responsibilities in a world warmed by the sunshine of freedom but threatened still by ancient hatreds and new plagues," he observed. The nation should act to redress social and economic grievances at home and protect its legitimate interests abroad, but it should move cautiously, carefully, and wisely. Clinton would prove to be more cautious than anyone anticipated. Within two years, political cartoonist Gary Trudeau would portray him in his comic strip, *Doonesbury*, as a waffle.

Environmentalism As a Global Issue

The Bush–Quayle administration's insensitivity to environmental matters had played a role in the election. Even those who wanted to use the nation's natural resources for fun and profit feared the laissez-faire approach the Republican Party had followed during the 1980s. Clinton's vice president, Albert Gore of Tennessee, was the author of the environmental manifesto *Earth in the Balance* and was named to head the administration's "green team." Gore and company promised to do nothing less than reverse federal policy and in the process boost energy efficiency, preserve wetlands, and reduce global warming. This proved to be a worthy but empty promise.

Not all was gloom and doom on the environmental scene, however. America's well-being in the short term was dependent in part on the state of renewable resources. By the 1990s, the oil panic of the 1970s seemed a distant memory. With gasoline selling at $1.20 to $1.40 per gallon, fuels for home and auto consumption were in real dollars cheaper than they had been since World War II. Estimates of global petroleum reserves had actually grown from 615 billion barrels in 1985 to 917 billion barrels in 1990. Americans chose not to remember that 70% of the world's proven oil reserves lay under the sands of the Middle East and that the United States had been forced to fight the Gulf War to preserve that source.

As a renewable resource, America's forests were actually in as good a condition as they had been in the 1920s, despite urbanization and spectacular population growth. The number of trees growing was actually greater. But much of America's forest land had been converted into lumber plantations where trees were systematically planted and harvested. This constant human activity subverted the forests as ecosystems capable of nurturing biodiversity. Because the United States was as much a part of the natural global environment as it was the political, the degradation of the tropical rain forests, which supported 90% of the world's biological species, posed a long-term threat to the nation's well-being. The UN Food and Agriculture Organization estimated that at 1990 rates of cutting and burning, virtually all the original tropical forests would be destroyed within a generation. Agricultural scientists pointed out that much of the world's food supply was threatened by these developments. Despite genetic engineering, the major source of new strains of corn, wheat, and rice resistant to disease were the "wild relatives" of domesticated plants, the same wild relatives that lived in the tropics.

Humanity's intervention into and pollution of the environment continued to threaten existing animal species in the United States. The number of entries on the endangered species list established by the Endangered Species Act of 1973 had grown from 150 to 190. Through a concerted effort, environmentalists, by preserving and enhancing natural habitats, had actually increased the numbers of whooping cranes, bald and golden eagles, beaver, bison, deer, and wild turkey, but these were token achievements.

The draining of wetlands and human intrusion into forests affected migratory bird populations dramatically. Fishing grounds around the world were being overworked, and those off the coast of North America were no exception. High-tech fishing fleets competed to feed an ever-expanding population. The take of blue-fin tuna and cod in the Atlantic and red snapper in the Gulf of Mexico declined precipitously. In the Pacific Northwest, the salmon population, once 16 million strong, dropped to 1 million.

Nothing contributed more to the decline of wildlife and the organisms that supported them than environmental pollution. The 1993 Toxic Release Inventory showed that for the first time American manufacturers had cut their toxic waste releases. Toxic emissions and dumps still totaled an awesome 33.5 billion pounds per year, but almost half of that was being internally recycled. Individual households that produced 195 million tons of trash per year also began recycling in a serious way, sending 17% of disposable waste back to municipal plants for processing and reuse. There was no advance on the sewage front, however. Overburdened sewage systems overflowed into rivers, lakes, and oceanfronts forcing the temporary closing of more than 2,000 beaches in 1991 alone. During the 1980s, more than 68,000 hazardous waste spills had been reported. The rate only increased as the 1990s progressed, and no wonder. The *Los Angeles Times* estimated that every day 500,000 individual shipments of hazardous wastes totaling 2 to 4 million tons moved across the American landscape.

In 1987, the leading manufacturing nations of the world had sent representatives to a gathering in Montreal to discuss ways in which the depletion of the ozone layer over Antarctica could be halted. They pledged to phase out the use of chlorofluorocarbons (CFCs), the nontoxic, odorless chemical compounds used to make aerosol sprays, refrigerator coolants, and plastics. Initially, some scientists and the political representatives of the chemical industry had challenged the notion that CFCs were causing ozone depletion or that the thinning of the ozone layer that surrounded the earth was harmful. By the 1990s, however, no one was denying that erosion of ozone was harmful. Not only did it lead to skin cancer among humans, but it killed microrganisms in the oceans and damaged commercial crops. The hope was that the Montreal Protocol would have reversed the depletion process, but in 1992 research scientists discovered that the hole over Antartica had expanded by 25 percent, to over 9 million square miles.

The great environmental fear of the 1990s, however, was global warming. The continued release into the atmosphere of carbon dioxide, created primarily by the massive burning of fossil fuels, threatened to raise the average global temperature anywhere from 1.5 degrees to a disastrous 4.5 degrees centigrade. Such a trend would melt glaciers, inundate coastlines, and disrupt ecosystems. According to one scenario, Chicago would be as warm as New Orleans by 2020. Equally appalling were the costs of solutions to the problem. Industrial nations such as the United States, which was responsible for 21% of greenhouse gas emissions, would have to move away from the automobile almost completely as a means of transportation. Industries would have to modify production techniques in a fundamental way. Alternative fuels, electric cars, and strict population control would be politically unpopular in no small part because the changes would cost an estimated $95 billion per year. Even if the United States made the necessary changes, what of the rest of the world? Europe and the former Soviet Union contributed 14% each to carbon dioxide emissions. Would they be willing to make the sacrifices and bear the costs? Nor would the developing world be spared. The methane given off by cattle trapped reradiated heat at a rate 70 times higher than carbon dioxide. The trees that were rapidly being cut down in the rain forests of the tropic zone were prime consumers of CO_2. Ending the greenhouse effect would require sacrifices and changes so fundamental as to seem impossible.

President Clinton and Vice President Gore addressed these and other environmental issues at a series of national and international meetings. The administration enthusiastically supported the Energy Policy Act of 1992, which included incentives for renewable energy, established efficiency standards for appliances, and experimented with nonpetroleum fuels in government vehicles. The Department of Energy established goals for the reduction of ozone depleting and greenhouse emissions. In 1993, President Clinton named biologist Jack Ward Thomas to head the U.S. Forest Service, which regulated logging in national forests. Environmentalists were delighted because Thomas had once headed a scientific team that had called for banning timber cutting in some federal forests in the Northwest to protect the spotted owl. But these were drops in the bucket. Nothing short of massive action at the international level to control population growth and regulate economic development in both the developing and postindustrial world would save the environment.

"Don't Ask, Don't Tell"

During the campaign, Clinton and his wife, Hillary, had made no effort to hide their liberalism on the major social issues of the day: gay rights, abortion, and equal rights for both women and African Americans. No issue was more emotional or controversial than that of gays in the military. On political, if not moral and philosophical, grounds the issue was a no-win affair. Gays and lesbians constituted less than 5% of the total population according to a 1994 study, and some of those who normally would support gay rights as a civil liberty were troubled by what they perceived to be an environment that subjected individuals to involuntary intimacy. Instead of waiting until the end of his administration to take up the issue of gays in the military, Clinton led off with it. On January 21, 1993, the president instructed Secretary of Defense Les Aspin to draw up an executive order lifting the ban on homosexuals within the armed forces. The Joint

Chiefs of Staff, supported by organizations such as the Veterans of Foreign Wars and the American Legion, protested vigorously. After President Clinton met with Senator Sam Nunn (D-Georgia), chairman of the Armed Services Committee, the administration announced what it termed "an honorable compromise." Under the "don't ask, don't tell" policy, recruiters were prohibited from inquiring about an individual's sexual orientation. Homosexuals could not be banned from the military for being homosexuals as long as they remained celibate while they were in the service. The honorable compromise was a political disaster, offending both liberals and conservatives.

Clinton was equally forthright and politically more astute in championing abortion rights. Two days after the inauguration the president signed a series of executive orders reversing his predecessor's policies. No longer were doctors working in federally funded clinics forbidden to give advice on abortion; military hospitals were allowed to perform abortions; and funds for UN population programs that encompassed abortion were restored.

The election of a prochoice president, coupled with opinion polls showing that a majority of Americans were prochoice if not proabortion, seemed to galvanize radicals in the prolife movement. On March 8, 1993, the Supreme Court declined to revive an invalidated Louisiana law that would have prohibited almost all abortions in the state. Following the firebombing in February of an abortion clinic in Texas, David Gunn, a gynecologist, was shot to death by a prolife activist outside an abortion clinic in Pensacola, Florida. The director of Rescue America, Don Treshman, described the shooting as "unfortunate" but added, "The fact is that a number of mothers would have been put at risk by him and over a dozen babies would have died at his hands." The realization that isolated individuals perceived abortion as murder and were willing to kill to prevent it sent a chill through the health care profession and intimidated physicians who were willing to give women a choice.

Gridlock over Healthcare

One of Clinton's first acts as president was to appoint his wife, Hillary, to head a task force charged with reform of the health care system. Following a period of intense study and debate, the administration unveiled its plan to the public in September 1993. In a televised address, the president announced that universal health insurance was "the most urgent priority" facing the United States. At the center of the Clintons' proposals was the formation of regional health alliances, which would purchase high-quality health care at low cost. In the months that followed, an administration team headed by Mrs. Clinton lobbied the public and Congress on behalf of a system that extended federally guaranteed medical coverage to all citizens. The American Medical Association, insurance companies, and conservatives in general countered with a plan calling for a privately funded system to which all participants were required to contribute. By 1994, the debate – frequently confused, sometimes misleading, always complex – had reached a crescendo. In the end, Congress and the White House proved unable to reach a compromise, even though the Clintons agreed to a privately operated system if it involved universal coverage. Commentators spoke of the "failure of the Clinton plan," and the perceived inability of the president to deliver on one of his primary campaign pledges helped drive down his popularity in the polls.

America the Violent

America in the 1990s seemed to be a nation enthralled with violence. Motion pictures and television made murder and mayhem seem commonplace. In the nation's inner cities, drug lords killed each other and innocent bystanders with heedless abandon, while gangs battled over turf and bragging rights. Middle-class youths in small towns began purchasing guns for protection and as status symbols. For years, the issue of gun control had polarized the nation. Advocates pointed to the rising level of violent crime, the casual possession and use of every type of firearm by teens and even subteens, and to the emergence of a culture devoid of respect for human life. Opponents, citing the constitutional right of all citizens to bear arms, insisted that criminals rather than guns committed crimes. Law-abiding Americans had a right to defend themselves; the only thing the criminal underclass respected was the threat of retaliation.

The movement for gun control received an unwelcome boost from a series of violent acts that marred 1993. In September, a British tourist was held up and shot dead near Tallahassee, Florida, making him the ninth visitor to be murdered in the state that year. In February, four agents of the federal Bureau of Alcohol, Tobacco and Firearms (BATF) died during a raid on the Waco, Texas, headquarters of a religious sect called the Branch Davidians. Following a 51-day siege, federal authorities stormed the cult's complex; the inhabitants set fire to their buildings and themselves. In all, 72 people died. In the midst of the siege, President Clinton had taken the unprecedented step of speaking out against the National Rifle Association's opposition to gun control. Then on November 30, he signed the Brady Bill, named after James Brady, the former White House press secretary wounded in the assassination attempt on President Reagan in 1981. The legislation imposed a five-day waiting period to enable background checks to be made on would-be gun purchasers. The previous week, the Senate had approved a $22 billion anticrime program that prohibited the sale of handguns to juveniles, banned the sale of semiautomatic assault weapons, and provided for the recruitment of 100,000 additional police officers. Despite these breakthroughs, however, guns and violent crime continued to proliferate, threatening to turn America into an armed camp by the end of the century.

Cold War Dividend

Responding to deep-seated public resentment toward bureaucracies and taxes, the Clinton administration moved to cut spending by slimming down the federal government and eliminating wasteful programs. At the same time, the new president attempted to take advantage of the end of the Cold War by shifting funds from defense to essential social, educational, and anticrime programs. Shortly after taking office, Clinton announced a 25% reduction in the White House staff and called on other agencies to follow suit. His 1994 budget promised to reduce the federal deficit $140 billion by 1997. This target was to be achieved by raising the tax rate on couples making $140,000 and more and single people earning $115,000 and up, and by raising the corporate income tax. The administration's economic program envisaged cuts in the defense budget of $123.9 billion between 1994 and 1998. Secretary Aspin announced the scrapping of Star Wars, and the administration began dismantling or scaling down 92 overseas bases and 129 domestic installations. The Clinton budget marked the first decline in defense spending since the Cold War began.

Clinton Abroad: Foreign Affairs in the 90s

In foreign affairs, Bill Clinton had promised, in rather vague terms, to address the problems of the post–Cold War era. The United States, he said, should provide aid to the former Soviet Union to help it down the road to democracy and free enterprise. Indeed, there were Wilsonian overtones to his foreign policy statements. Advancing democracy should be the object of "a long-term Western strategy," he said. At the same time, the president emphasized that the focus of future foreign policy would be the global economy. America would have to learn how to compete peacefully with Japan and the German-led European community. Finally, Clinton seemed to echo former President Jimmy Carter in calling for an American-led campaign to ensure respect for human rights. Indeed, during the campaign he had blasted the Bush administration for not doing more to stop the sectarian conflict then raging in the former Yugoslavia.

Bosnia

In 1991, the Yugoslav republic had splintered along ethnic and religious lines. With the collapse of the communist regime, Yugoslavia, a federation that included the states of Serbia, Montenegro, Croatia, Bosnia-Hercegovina, Slovenia, and Macedonia, broke apart. Slovenia and Croatia declared their independence. When Bosnia-Hercegovina attempted to break away from Yugoslavia, war erupted between the Serb and Croatian minorities in Bosnia on the one hand and the Bosnian government, which was largely dominated by Muslims, on the other hand. The Croats wanted to merge with Croatia and the Serbs with Serbia. Both groups were

Christian. Neither wanted to be part of an independent Bosnia ruled by Muslims. For the next three years, tens of thousands of people died as first the Croats and then the Serbs, aided by the army of the Serbian Republic under the leadership of nationalist Slobodan Milosovic, secured control of large parts of Bosnia. During these campaigns, the Serbs engaged in "ethnic cleansing" in which thousands of Muslims were raped, tortured, and killed. The Muslims and Croats conducted their own ethnic cleansing campaigns but on a much smaller scale. The United Nations inserted some 24,000 peace-keeping troops into the combat zones and negotiated one cease-fire after another, only to see all of them collapse in the face of the blood-and-soil nationalism of the Balkans.

As President Clinton came into office, the pressure on him to intervene militarily to relieve the Serbian siege of Sarajevo and to stop the bloodshed in general became intense. He insisted, however, that the Bosnian nightmare was a matter for NATO and the United Nations, and that the members of those organizations in closest physical proximity to Bosnia, namely France and Germany, should take the lead. Privately, the Clinton administration had decided that it would intervene in Bosnia only when and if the parties involved showed a willingness for peace. In 1995, after years of bloody fighting and ethnic cleansing, and a crushing economic embargo imposed on Yugoslavia by the United Nations, the Serbs (pressured by Milosovich, who had been forced by international pressure to do a turnabout), Croats, and Muslims agreed to a cease-fire and to Bosnia-wide elections for a parliament and a three-person presidency. The Dayton Accords (named for the Ohio city where the negotiations took place) were to be backed by a 60,000-person NATO force, including 20,000 American troops.

Despite its professed sympathy for human rights, the Clinton administration was afraid of becoming bogged down in another Vietnam-type conflict, thus its reluctance to intervene in Bosnia. The new regime inherited another situation, however, in which the United States was already deeply involved. Late in 1992, the Bush administration authorized a U.S.-led but UN-sanctioned military intervention into the East African state of Somalia. During the 1980s, first Moscow, then Washington, D.C., had poured weapons into this poor but strategically located nation of 5 million people in an effort to win the support of dictator Mohamed Siad Barre. When the Cold War ended, he fled, but Somalia teemed with weapons. What ensued was a civil war between rival clan leaders President Ali Mahdi Mohammed and General Mohammed Farah Aydid that impoverished and brutalized the country, creating hundreds of thousands of refugees and mass starvation. Although a similar situation existed in Sudan, the American media focused on the swollen bellies and fly-covered corpses in Somalia. The Bush administration caved into public pressure and, on December 3, received UN Security Council approval for military intervention. A week later, 28,000 U.S.

troops landed in Mogadishu, the capital and scene of much of the fighting. The expeditionary force set up a relief network but did not disarm the clansmen who withdrew to await events.

President Clinton pledged to stay the course in Somalia, and he proved as good as his word. In June 1993, a price of $25,000 was placed on General Aydid's head, but he remained at large. When a U.S. helicopter was shot down by Somali militiamen, killing many of its occupants, and a further 18 Americans died in a firefight in October, the United States began to lose heart. During spring 1995, the last of the U.S. and UN troops withdrew. The military situation remained unresolved, but mass starvation had ended, and the semblance of a national economy had once again emerged in Somalia.

Haiti
Like most of its predecessors, the Clinton administration perceived Latin America, and specifically the Caribbean basin, as the area most vital to U.S. national interest. The poorest republic in the Western Hemisphere, Haiti had suffered under one military strongman after another throughout the nineteenth and twentieth centuries. With the support of a tiny business and planting elite, these brutal dictators had exploited and oppressed the nation's peasantry. In 1991, the cycle appeared to be broken with the election of Jean-Bertrand Aristide, a Catholic priest and social activist. Aristide, however, soon ran afoul of the military and the plutocracy. Late in the year, he was driven into exile in the United States.

For three years, the military regime of General Raul Cedras imposed a reign of terror on Haiti. Paramilitary thugs tortured and killed Aristide supporters and those suspected of opposition to the government. The United States imposed a blockade in an effort to bring down Cedras and restore Aristide to power, but the embargo only further impoverished rural peasants and the urban poor. Finally, President Clinton ordered military intervention. Before U.S. troops could land, however, former President Jimmy Carter persuaded Cedras to voluntarily step down. As a consequence, American troops occupied the country without resistance. Late in 1994, President Aristide returned to Haiti, and that unfortunate republic once again started haltingly down the path toward democracy and reform.

NAFTA
As far as international economics was concerned, Bill Clinton was as committed to free trade and American participation in a global economy as his Republican predecessors. With a great deal of effort, he pushed through Congress the North American Free Trade Agreement (NAFTA), which provided for the gradual elimination of tariffs and other trade barriers between the United States on the one hand and Canada and Mexico on the other. What was envisioned was a vast North American free trade zone in which

goods and capital would flow freely across borders, allowing Mexico, the United States, and Canada to produce and export those goods and services that they produced most efficiently. Mexican petroleum, agricultural products, and cheaply produced manufactured goods would enjoy new access to U.S. markets, while Mexico would be open to North American technology. Protectionists in the United States complained that U.S. manufacturers would move their operations to Mexico to take advantage of cheap labor, thus increasing unemployment in the United States. The Clinton administration replied that every blue-collar job lost in the United States would be replaced by a new white-collar one. That argument prevailed.

In fact, the world was increasingly divided into three major economic blocs: the 12-nation European Community (EC), the U.S.–Canada–Mexico free-trade area, and a more fluid Asian development area powered by Japanese capital and featuring minieconomic superpowers such as South Korea, Singapore, and Taiwan. While Clinton facilitated creation of the North American bloc, he turned America increasingly away from Europe and toward the Pacific as American corporations positioned themselves to furnish economic infrastructure to such emerging giants as Communist China and Indonesia.

Revolt of the Middle Class

Americans voted for Clinton because they wanted movement. But after two years in office, the president had failed to persuade the electorate that he had the will or the vision to change, much less overturn, the status quo. That this was more a matter of public perception rather than reality made no difference. American voters went to the polls for the midterm elections in 1994 in an angry and defiant mood. The result was a Republican landslide. The GOP captured control of both houses of Congress for the first time in 40 years. Speaker of the House Thomas Foley lost, the first holder of that office to lose an election since 1862. Not a single Republican incumbent was ousted. Eleven Democratic governors went down to defeat, including Mario Cuomo of New York, arguably the nation's foremost liberal spokesman.

Underlying the antigovernment sentiment that culminated in America in 1994 was the decline of the American middle class. During the period between 1945 and 1973, the rich had gotten richer in America but so had the poor. During this period when worker productivity grew by an annual rate of 3%, incomes for all working Americans doubled – corporate executives, mail carriers, construction workers, and street cleaners. The vast American middle class could anticipate owning a split-level home in the suburbs complete with spacious backyard and barbecue. Then stagnation set in.

Between 1979 and 1992, the person earning the exact median-level income in America suffered a wage cut of about $100 a month. That is, after

13 years of hard labor, the typical member of the middle class in the United States made 4% less money. At the same time, the rich grew richer. The typical full-time worker in the top third of income earners earned 7% more than they had in 1979, while the richest 5% enjoyed an increase of 29%. It was not that America was that much poorer, although productivity did decline during these years, but that income was being unevenly distributed. Inability to realize the American Dream bred frustration among the American middle class, and it vented their anger at the polls, not only voting for conservative candidates for Congress but also for legislation limiting immigration.

In the 1880s, California workers, feeling their livelihoods and families threatened by competition from waves of Chinese immigrants, had formed the American Workingman's Party, which succeeded in pushing through Congress the Chinese Exclusion Act. In the 1990s, California was once again the staging ground for a revolt by those who felt their standards of living threatened by immigration. In 1994, a group of citizens in Orange County launched a drive on behalf of Proposition 187, which would prohibit the widespread practice of allowing illegal aliens access to public education and welfare services. Opponents of the measure, which seemed to include most of the state's civic leaders, labeled its supporters racists and spent millions to defeat it. Republican Governor Pete Wilson, who had once sued the federal government to recover the costs of public monies spent on illegal aliens, endorsed Proposition 187, and both he and it swept to victory in the 1994 elections.

Newt

The leader of the new Republican majority in Congress was Representative Newt Gingrich from suburban Atlanta. With a Ph.D. in history and a penchant for futurism, Gingrich had made his way in the world as a partisan hatchetman. By the early 1990s, however, he was being hailed by some journalists as a modern-day populist as he attacked, in his words, "the counter-cultural, redistributionist, bureaucratic welfare state model." He, like right-wing radio and television personality Rush Limbaugh, had a flair for couching his program in simplistic, emotion-laden language. "It is impossible to maintain civilization," he declared, "with 12-year-olds having babies, 15-year-olds killing each other, 17-year-olds dying of AIDS, and 18-year-olds receiving diplomas they cannot read." Gingrich, who was slated to be the next speaker of the House; Bob Dole, the Senate majority leader designate; and the rest of the GOP had campaigned on their "Contract with America." That document, signed ostentatiously on the Capitol steps in September 1991, promised tax cuts for the "middle class" – everyone making $200,000 or less – and a reduction in the capital gains tax. It called for an increase rather than a decrease in defense spending. All this was to be paid for by reductions in the federal bureaucracy and elimination of "nonessential" social programs. In this same vein, the GOP promised to propose an amendment to the Constitution requiring the federal government to present a balanced budget each year. The Contract called for term limits for political office holders, although after their landslide win, the victors announced that they had promised merely to bring the issue to a vote in Congress and not necessarily to support it.

It took only weeks, however, for the electorate to sour on the abrasive Gingrich. Many recoiled from the Contract with America, moreover, when they began to realize that it was their programatical ox that was to be gored and when they perceived that proposed GOP cuts would be only a monetary drop in the bucket compared with the costs of a tax cut and increased defense spending. There was, moreover, a fundamental philosophical and cultural cleavage in the new Republican majority, pitting moralizers concerned about family values and willing to countenance an intrusive government to safeguard those values against traditional conservatives who championed civil liberties, laissez-faire in a pluralistic society, and pragmatic problem solving. Bill Clinton, the most relentless and successful political campaigner since Franklin D. Roosevelt, was down but not out.

With Newt Gingrich and the Republicans riding high after their success in the 1994 midterm elections, President Clinton wisely decided to occupy the political middle ground. Sensing that the American people in the end would tire of ideologues and extremists and that they desperately longed for bipartisan cooperation, he set about coopting the Republican program. Clinton pushed through Congress a crime bill, which appropriated federal funds for the hiring of 100,000 additional police and shortened the appeals period for death-row inmates. The White House worked with Speaker Gingrich and Senate Majority Leader Bob Dole to hammer out a welfare reform bill that effectively ended Aid for Families with Dependent Children (AFDC), requiring welfare recipients to work after two years and terminating all welfare payments after five years. Clinton reduced the federal workforce by 250,000, and, partially as a result, the federal deficit fell by 60%. Although the president joined with Republicans in pledging to balance the budget by 2002, he locked horns with them over the fiscal 1996 budget, which they attempted to use to reduce federal entitlement programs. The deadlock twice caused a temporary shutdown of the government, but in the end the administration won both substantively and politically. It protected Social Security, Medicare, and other benefits and succeeded in portraying the Republicans as insensitive to the needs of the poor and elderly.

The Election of 1996

There was no question about Clinton's renomination. After 1992, he and Al Gore had gone out of their way to conciliate various factions in the party and to appear to the public as humble listeners rather than as "Boy

Princes," to quote *Time* magazine. The Republicans struggled as usual with their right wing – the fundamentalists and states' righters who somewhat contradictorily pushed for an absolute ban on abortions and the right to die, prayer in public schools, funding for parochial schools, the unfettered right to bear arms, and an end to affirmative action. Representing the GOP center, Senator Bob Dole of Kansas beat back a bid from the ultraconservative Pat Buchanan. Dole, a decorated veteran of World War II who had been severely wounded, was an experienced Washington, D.C., insider, a skilled negotiator, but a man with little charisma and no distinctive program. During the campaign, Dole called for a massive tax cut and attempted to capitalize on the personal shortcomings of the president. The Republicans made some headway when it was revealed that Democratic National Committee fundraiser John Huang had solicited millions from an Indonesian business consortium. Rumors that the White House offered a night's lodging in the Lincoln Room to anyone contributing $100,000 or more to the campaign did not help Clinton either.

In the end, however, the public answered Bob Dole's constant campaign refrain "Who Do You Trust?" with "Clinton." The incumbent won with 50% of the popular vote and 379 electoral votes to Dole's 41% and 159 electoral votes. Ross Perot, heading his Reform Party, captured only 9% and did not score in the electoral college. Clinton won because he appeared to be moderate, effective, and responsive, and because the economy was booming; inflation, interest rates, and unemployment were the lowest for any presidential administration since 1968. He also benefited from the "gender gap"; women voted for the president 54% to 38%. Bill Clinton became the first two-term Democrat since Roosevelt, but the Republicans retained control of both houses of Congress. The message that voters apparently sent in 1996 was that they wanted the bridge to the twenty-first century to be built on bipartisanship.

Four More Years

The Clinton Scandals

It had become apparent as early as the 1992 election campaign that a Clinton administration would be periodically buffeted by charges of personal wrongdoing. Aside from rumors concerning Clinton's womanizing and draft dodging, by the 1990s, partisan congressional investigations into the personal lives of national candidates and office holders had become accepted practice. The press, both tabloid and mainstream, seemed to have an insatiable appetite for the alleged financial and sexual wrongdoings of political figures. That opinion polls indicated that the public did not really care as long as the country was at peace and prosperous seemed not to matter.

No sooner did the Clinton administration take office than the White House became embroiled in a scandal the press dubbed "travelgate." The

Clintons engineered the firing of most of the staff of the White House travel office, allegedly for incompetence but probably because most were Republicans. The president opened himself to charges of nepotism and favoritism when he appointed a distant cousin to run the office. Moreover, the new team directed the lion's share of executive travel to an agency owned by television producer Harry Thomasson, an Arkansan and Clinton intimate. Amid a firestorm of controversy, the White House rehired most of the fired staffers and reassigned the president's cousin.

Whitewater

Much more significant than "travelgate" was the Whitewater investigation. In 1978, the Clintons had joined with James B. McDougal and his wife, Susan, in a failed real estate scheme. The development, situated on a tract of land southwest of Little Rock, was to be known as Whitewater. The president and first lady insisted that Whitewater was just a business venture gone bad, one in which they had lost a considerable sum of money. But a subsequent investigation into the failure of Madison Guaranty Savings and Loan, owned and operated by Jim McDougal, led to charges that Madison had channeled funds to Clinton's gubernatorial campaign, that the Clintons had acted to protect Madison from federal investigators after the election, and that Hillary Clinton had benefited financially from the thrift's mismanagement. The president and first lady at first did not respond to the charges, then sought to dismiss them, and then argued that Whitewater was the work of Republican right-wingers in Arkansas and nationally. Suspicions of wrongdoing were heightened when, in January 1994, the Justice Department subpoenaed White House records, thus making them off limits to congressional investigators. Responding to the ensuing uproar, the president asked Attorney General Janet Reno to appoint an independent counsel to look into the Whitewater affair. She first selected Robert Fiske, but he was subsequently replaced by Kenneth Starr, a former Bush administration official. Starr was a conservative and member of the religious right who had at one time attended Harding College in Searcy, Arkansas. During the 1960s, this Church of Christ–affiliated school had been a major source of anticommunist propaganda, and its president, George Benson, had raised millions of dollars for right-wing causes. Subsequent investigations by Starr's team, which by 1998 had spent more than $10 million of taxpayer money, lead to the indictment and imprisonment of several Arkansas business people and administration officials, but not to evidence of criminal activity by the first couple. To help cover the cost of their legal defense, which exceeded $4 million by 1998, the Clintons created a legal defense fund, the first ever to be established by a sitting president.

Sex and the Married President

If Whitewater were not enough, the Clinton presidency was repeatedly rocked by charges of sexual misconduct. During Clinton's 1992 campaign, administration supporters had hoped that accusations by Gennifer Flowers that she and Clinton had had a long-term affair while he was governor (which turned out to be true) marked the last of such incidents. They were to be sadly disappointed. In 1994, Paula Jones, a former Arkansas state employee, filed suit against the president, claiming that he made sexual advances to her in a Little Rock hotel room when he was governor. Jones claimed that she could and would identify the chief executive's genitals. The president denied the encounter and sought to postpone litigation. In 1997, a federal court delivered a setback to the Clinton White House when it rejected the president's claim of temporary immunity and ruled that even though he was the nation's chief executive, he could not avoid trial on sexual harassment charges and that he would have to testify if subpoenaed. The administration gained a reprieve when in March 1998, federal Judge Susan Webber Wright threw out Jones's case for lack of evidence either that she had been coerced or that she had suffered job discrimination. But this was only a reprieve.

By the time Wright made her decision, Clinton was involved in another sex scandal centering on White House intern Monica Lewinsky. Starr, who had expanded his investigation to include the Jones case, persuaded Defense Department employee Linda Tripp, a friend of Lewinsky's, to wire herself to record conversations with the young intern concerning a relationship she claimed to be having with Clinton. During those conversations, which were subsequently made public, Lewinsky talked of engaging in oral sex with the president on several occasions in the Oval Office. After some delay, Clinton publicly denied that he had ever had sex with "that woman . . . Miss Lewinsky." Lewinsky, the daughter of a well-to-do Los Angeles businessman and Democratic campaign contributor, had denied having an affair with Clinton during interviews with Paula Jones's lawyers, and then after the Tripp revelations, insisted that the relationship had been consensual. Starr's investigators interrogated then subpoenaed Lewinsky, threatening to indict her for lying under oath. The president's defenders continued to insist that he was the victim of a right-wing political hatchet job, pointing out that the ultraconservative Rutherford Foundation had bankrolled the Paula Jones suit to the tune of several million dollars. Critics pointed out that Jones aside, the president had had several affairs, had continued to engage in adulterous behavior while in office, and was in fact morally bankrupt.

Impeachment

Then, in the fall of 1997, Paula Jones's legal team sought to bolster its case by seeking testimony from women rumored to have had illicit sexual contact with Clinton. In early 1998, Starr's office provided the Jones lawyers with tapes of conversations secretly recorded by Linda Tripp, an erstwhile "friend" of Monica Lewinsky. When asked about Lewinsky in his deposition on January 17, Clinton appeared evasive, relying on quibbles and contorted definitions to convey the misleading impression that he and Lewinsky were little more than casual acquaintances. Shortly thereafter, the White House launched an offensive to discredit Starr, sending out cabinet members to back up the president's story.

After securing immunity from prosecution, in 1998, Lewinsky provided investigators with details concerning dozens of phone conversations and meetings with the president and of gifts they had exchanged. The impetus toward an impeachment inquiry built in the summer, after word leaked that Lewinsky had given prosecutors a dress with a semen stain – physical evidence that could prove she and the president had had sexual contact. Clinton acknowledged on August 17 that he had misled his family, his staff, the public, and Jones's lawyers, although he insisted that his testimony had been "legally correct." Indeed, in a televised speech the same day, he seemed to be more combative than contrite. The threat to the Clinton presidency as a result of "the Affaire Lewinsky," as the newspapers had begun referring to it, soon heightened when Starr submitted to Congress a 445-page summary of his investigation, which, he asserted, contained "substantial and credible information ... that may constitute grounds for impeachment." The principal offenses cited were perjury and obstruction of justice. To the consternation of Starr and his supporters, the president's approval ratings (of his job performance, not his personal conduct) soared, hovering between 65% and 70%.

Despite the polls, Republicans in the House, with some Democratic support, voted on October 8, 1998, to conduct a full-scale impeachment inquiry into Starr's charges against the president. That proved to be a political error. Although GOP leaders, including the irrepressible Newt Gingrich, predicted that their party would gain 20 seats in the House and as many as 5 in the Senate, the Republicans actually lost 5 congressional positions and failed to pick up a single seat in the Senate. It marked the first time the party controlling the White House had gained seats in the House in an off-year election since 1934, when Franklin D. Roosevelt was laboring to pull the country out of the Great Depression. On November 6, Gingrich announced that he was not only giving up the speakership but also his seat in the House.

The Clinton White House hoped the midterm election results and a subsequent decision to settle the Paula Jones lawsuit for $850,000 would end the impeachment drive. They were mistaken. Led by Representative Henry Hyde (R-Illinois), the House leadership declared that their constitutional duty to hold the president accountable transcended political considerations. The Judiciary Committee opened hearings that featured testimony by Starr and White House lawyers who did not dispute the facts of the case against the president but denied that he had committed impeachable offenses. "As surely as we all know that what he did is sinful," White House Counsel Gregory Craig argued, "we also know it is not impeachable." Hyde and his colleagues disagreed. With Democrats pushing for a vote of censure rather than impeachment, the Republican-dominated committee passed and sent to the floor of the House four impeachment articles; the charges were two counts of perjury, obstruction of justice, and abuse of power.

On the eve of the debate, the House and the nation were rocked by two new developments. Angered by Saddam Hussein's ongoing refusal to cooperate with UN arms inspectors, President Clinton authorized massive air strikes against one of Saddam's residences and a host of other targets. Then, with Republicans charging the White House with trying to divert the nation's attention by manufacturing a foreign crisis, House Speaker-designate Robert Livingston (R-Louisiana) admitted that charges by *Hustler* magazine publisher Larry Flynt that he had several times committed adultery were true. Only days later, he resigned both the speakership and his House seat. Livingston called on Clinton to follow suit, but to no avail. In January 1999, the House, by an almost straight party-line vote (228–206), impeached the president for lying to the grand jury and for abuse of power.

Facing mounting demands for his resignation and a sure trial in the Senate, Clinton announced that he intended to serve "until the last hour of the last day of my term" and called for a quick end to the impeachment proceedings. There was no quick end. In January, Chief Justice William Rehnquist solemnly swore in each of the 100 senators. Henry Hyde and his team of prosecutors presented the case for impeachment while the president's lawyers and Arkansas Senator Dale Bumpers, who argued eloquently that the punishment did not in this case fit the crime, spoke for the defense. In the end, however, impeachment forces failed even to muster an absolute majority (a two-thirds vote is required for conviction), and America was spared the trauma of a forced removal of a sitting president.

Sexual Harassment

The Clinton scandals forced the more serious students of the American political and social scene to focus on the two most important legislative and legal issues involved – sexual harassment statutes and the independent counsel law. Legally there are two kinds of sexual harassment. The first is called quid pro quo. If an employee's boss docks her pay or fires her or otherwise punishes her for rebuffing an advance, he is clearly guilty. Not until the 1960s was even blatant quid pro quo harassment illegal; most judges deemed such matters "personal." The 1964 Civil Rights Act opened the door to antidiscrimination suits by including sex on the list of protections. It was not until 1977, however, that a federal court ruled that quid pro quo harassment violated the act. In 1991, following the Anita Hill–Clarence

Thomas incident, President Bush signed a law granting sexual harassment plaintiffs the right to jury trials and to big money damages.

Quid pro quo cases were difficult to prove because the accused boss could claim that his employee was fired or demoted because she was incompetent. Feminists began to argue that harassers could create a hostile environment even if they did not demand sex in exchange for something. One such victim was Mechelle Vinson, who began dating her boss at Meritor Savings Bank and eventually admitted to having sex with him 40 or 50 times. She claimed that she felt pressured into the relationship and that he made unwanted advances to her in the workplace. Vinson did not suffer at her boss's hands when she objected, however. A lower court threw out her case, but in 1986, the Supreme Court ruled that speech or conduct itself can create a "hostile" environment. Unwelcome verbal or physical behavior, if "severe or pervasive" enough, was deemed to be discriminatory, even when there was no quid pro quo. In the wake of that ruling, there was a huge surge in sexual harassment cases. In 1995, 9 out of 10 human resources managers reported that they handled at least one sexual harassment charge. Many employers, fearing lawsuits, instituted zero-tolerance polices banning just about any speech or conduct with sexual undertones. The problem was that the legal principle of harassment hinges on impossibly ambiguous terms such as "unwelcome" and "pervasive." A municipal courthouse employee who claimed that the exhibition of an impressionist nude painting by a local female artist constituted sexual harassment won her case. By 1998, a backlash appeared to have set in. In a Time/CNN poll, just 26% of those surveyed described sexual harassment of women as a "big problem," down from 37% in 1991. More importantly, 57% of men and 52% of women agreed that "we have gone too far in making common interactions between employees into cases of sexual harassment."

Above the Law
The independent counsel mechanism was the product of a conflict of interest inherent in the office of attorney general. That person is to be an impartial enforcer of the law and, at the same time, like every other cabinet member, an instrument of the president's political will. When the necessity arises for investigating wrongdoing by the president, vice president, or high-ranking administration official, as was increasingly true in the wake of Watergate, the attorney general faces a dilemma. The clash between law and politics that has always confronted the Justice Department was thrown into sharp relief during Watergate when President Nixon forced the resignation of Independent Prosecutor Archibald Cox, who had been appointed by then–Attorney General Elliot Richardson. In an effort to protect the independence of such investigators, in 1978, Congress enacted the independent counsel law. Under its terms, which cover some 50 officials of the executive branch, the attorney general conducts a preliminary

investigation, and, if there are sufficient grounds, he or she asks a three-judge panel to name a special prosecutor. The decision by an attorney general to appoint a special counsel is final and not reviewable by the courts. A modified version of the act was repassed in 1994.

Democrats and Republicans have differed over the wisdom of the independent counsel law, depending on which party has been in control of the White House. The apparent excesses of the Starr team, however, have caused unease on both sides of the aisle in Congress and among the general populace. What has become clear is that the counsel is beyond the federal system of checks and balances. Virtually every time Starr had gone to Reno asking for permission to expand his investigation, she had acceded. The independent counsel is empowered to call grand juries and to seek indictments against virtually any citizen. Those subpoenaed to testify before such grand juries are not entitled to be accompanied by counsel and are not immune from further prosecution unless such immunity is specifically granted by the prosecutor. A competent prosecutor, so the saying goes in the legal community, can obtain a grand jury indictment against a ham sandwich. Once an indictment is obtained, the independent counsel can pressure witnesses to give evidence on virtually any subject. Those who refused are subject to contempt charges. Indeed, Susan McDougal spent more than a year in jail for refusing to answer Starr's questions. Former Associate Attorney General and Clinton friend Webster Hubbell was sentenced to a lengthy prison term for overbilling clients at his law firm, an offense that has hardly been at the top of law enforcement agendas in recent years. Some legal experts argue that the whole approach embodied in the independent counsel mechanism is contrary to the U.S. system of justice. "I always told my prosecutors to go where the evidence leads," Republican Richard Thornburgh, attorney general under Presidents Reagan and Bush, has said. "Under this statute you pick a target and try to find the evidence to make a case against him." The Clinton scandals and the manner in which they have been investigated and publicized have just added to the list of reasons why qualified people will be reluctant to enter public service in the twenty-first century.

Prosperity

As previously noted, many Americans were willing to overlook President Clinton's personal shortcomings because the economy, presumably under his direction, was booming. During 1998, the monthly jobless rate fell to just 4.3% of the civilian workforce, the lowest rate since the early 1970s. Indeed the proportion of the population employed rose to what Kathrine Abraham, commissioner of the Bureau of Labor Statistics, claimed was a historically high level of 64.2% with 131.38 million individuals employed. This meant that employment had grown by an astounding 2 million workers in one year. Home ownership rose to an all-time high of 66.8%

as 30-year mortgage rates dipped below 7%. A breakdown of statistics showed that blacks and Hispanics, although still lagging behind in home ownership, were among the biggest gainers. The misery index, a combination of the jobless and inflation rates, fell to its lowest level since it was first invoked in the 1970s. During the third quarter of 1998, the real – 1992 dollars rather than current dollars – GDP rose to an annual rate of $7.56 trillion, nearly $250 billion more than during the previous 12-month period.

Both fueling and reflecting this growth was an unprecedented boom on the stock market. In the spring of 1998, the DowJones Industrial average topped 8,000 for the first time. On August 31, strongly influenced by debt defaults in Indonesia and the former Soviet Union, and by economic stagnation in Japan, Korea, and other formerly prosperous Asian countries, the stock market fell a record 512 points. However, it soon rallied, and in the spring of 1999, the Dow surpassed the 10,000 mark. Investing in the stock market became, much as it had in the 1920s, the national pastime. In June 1999, *Forbes* magazine reported that there were some 465 billionaires among the "working rich," a large majority of them Americans. Critics noted that America's trade deficit continued to mount and that, in an age of increasing global economic interdependence, depression in Brazil, Japan, Indonesia, and elsewhere spelled trouble for the United States. President Clinton's advisers admitted that this was so but reveled in the fact that the nation faced a huge budget surplus rather than deficit for the foreseeable future.

War and Peace in the Middle East
Bill Clinton's second inauguration in January 1997 took place amid increasing tensions in the Middle East. In Israel, Prime Minister Benjamin Netanyahu headed a political coalition, which included the right-wing Likud party and was dedicated to implementing as little of the peace accord with the Palestinians as possible. With armed clashes between Israeli security forces and Palestinian youth on the increase once again, the Clinton administration came under intense pressure from human rights activists to force the Israelis to halt new settlements in occupied territory and to implement the peace accords, and from American Zionists to lend all aid and support to Netanyahu in his struggle against Palestinian nationalists. After months of nerve-wracking diplomacy, the U.S. government persuaded Netanyahu and PLO Chairman Yasser Arafat to attend a conference at the Wye River Plantation in Maryland. There in October the parties signed the Wye River Memorandum, which promised the further redeployment of Israeli forces from 13% of the West Bank, which would put 18.8% of the region under Palestinian control. Future withdrawals were to be negotiated in the final status talks, which were set to be concluded by May 1999. For their part, the Palestinian authority promised renewed efforts to

control terrorism and to nullify provisions in the Palestinian charter that
called for Israel's destruction.

While the United States wielded the olive branch in the Arab–Israeli
conflict, it was forced to employ the thunderbolt in its ongoing confrontation with Iraq. In January 1998, Saddam Hussein denied UN inspectors
access to a number of suspected weapons sites. U.S. forces were sent to the
region, but a military strike was averted when UN Secretary-General Kofi
Annan worked out an agreement in February so that so-called "presidential
sites" – locations Saddam had declared off-limits to foreigners – would be
open to inspection.

Mindful of past deceptions by Baghdad, Clinton warned that if Iraq
reneged on the agreement, "then the United States . . . would have the unilateral right to respond at a time, place, or manner of our own choosing."
His resolve was tested in late fall, when Saddam again refused to cooperate with the inspectors in an attempt to pressure the United Nations to end
crippling economic sanctions on Iraq. After failed negotiations, the United
States and Great Britain unleashed a major air bombardment. American
and British planes blasted several presidential sites. However, the bombing
seemed to have little effect on Baghdad's intransigence. Meanwhile, France,
Russia, and China, anxious for trade with Iraq, led the way in calling for a
lifting of UN sanctions.

Kosovo

Observers of the Bosnian crisis of the mid-1990s predicted that the wave
of nationalism and ethnic cleansing could not be contained within that
province. They were right. The increasingly autocratic Slobodan Milosevic was able to retain power in the former Yugoslavia, now reduced to
Serbia and Montenegro, primarily by appealing to Serbian ultranation-
alists, propagandizing, and isolating his countrymen from the outside
world. Shortly after coming to power, he ended the autonomous status
of Kosovo, a province in the southwest part of Serbia made up of 90%
ethnic Albanians and 10% ethnic Serbs. As Serb military police continued to harass the Albanian majority, intellectuals, youths (many of them
jobless), and farmers grew increasingly disenchanted with the peaceful approach of the Democratic League of Kosovo (LDK) headed by Ibrahim
Rugova. Following bloody Serb crackdowns in the central Drenica region,
Albanian nationalists turned to the burgeoning Kosovo Liberation Army
(KLA), which was pledged to winning independence for the province
through force of arms.

In July 1998, Serbian police and the Yugoslav army launched a massive
attack on rural areas in an attempt to destroy the KLA's base of support.
Thousands of homes in more than 400 villages were looted and burned,
approximately 350,000 people were displaced, and at least 1,000 Kosovar
Albanians killed. Religious differences made the violence particularly

ferocious. The Albanian Kosovars were Muslim, while the Serbs were Orthodox Christian; the latter were determined to protect the numerous historic and religious sites in Kosovo.

By September, NATO, concerned about instability on its southeastern flank and under increasing pressure from human rights advocates, decided to intervene. Under threat of air assault, Milosevic signed an agreement with U.S. envoy Richard Holbroke, which provided for the stationing of 2,000 unarmed foreign observers in the troubled province and the gradual withdrawal of Serb police and military personnel. But instead of pulling his forces out, in early 1999, Milosevic decided that the only way the KLA could be destroyed and Kosovo be preserved for Serbians was to drive out a majority of the Albanian population, thus creating more of an ethnic balance. In March and April, some 60,000 Serb police and soldiers systematically rounded up and expelled ethnic Albanians from Kosovar, driving them into Albania or Macedonia, and in the process threatening to destabilize those countries. In April, after Milosevic refused NATO's repeated demands to cease and desist, the alliance, led by the United States, launched around-the-clock air attacks on Serb positions in Kosovo and on Serbia itself. The assault only hardened Belgrade's resolve.

The Clinton administration, supported by Germany and France, refused pleas to introduce ground troops. That Russia, a traditional ally of Serbia, was adamantly opposed to the bombing but particularly the deployment of NATO ground forces had much to do with the alliance's position. While NATO bombers destroyed much of Yugoslavia's infrastructure, Serb forces drove more than 1 million of Kosovo's 2 million ethnic Albanians out of the province. But expulsion was only part of the ordeal the Kosovar Albanians had to endure. Serb forces systematically robbed the refugees, burned or shelled their houses, selectively raped the women, and executed some 10,000 young men. In late May 1999, the Hague international tribunal indicted Milosevic as a war criminal. In June, Belgrade finally admitted defeat and began pulling its troops out of Kosovo. The Allies divided the region into five districts and prepared occupation forces. As the regime in Belgrade teetered on the brink of collapse and Kosovo's more than 1 million refugees prepared to return, the Clinton administration was receiving grudging approval from even its harshest Republican critics. Not a single American life had been lost in the operation.

Thus did the end of the Cold War prove to be a mixed blessing. Although authoritarian and oppressive, communism and Sino–Soviet hegemony had imposed a kind of order on a large part of the world. In only a very few cases, the disintegration of this empire was replaced with democracy and a free market system. Without a viable middle class, trained technocrats, capital, and an economic infrastructure, most former communist states found it impossible to move from socialism to capitalism. The attempted transition left huge voids filled by inflation and unemployment. Inevitably, the peoples of Eastern Europe and the former Soviet Union turned to nationalism and state socialism if not totalitarianism in a search for minimal security. The task that faced the Clinton administration during its remaining years was formidable: how to use shrinking American power and diminishing resources to combat totalitarianism, promote democracy, and foster human rights, while protecting the nation's strategic and economic interests in an increasingly chaotic world.

Election 2000

Although most residents of the planet considered the end of the twentieth century and the beginning of the new millennium to be January 1, 2000, scholars reiterated again and again that under the Judeo-Christian calendar, the new period in human history did not begin until the arrival of 2001. Regardless, most people marked the coming of 2000 in grand style. Worldwide, scenes of bread and circuses marked the arrival of the new year, even in countries that used other calendar systems. Extensive fireworks displays welcomed 2000 in many cities, from Hong Kong to Berlin, from Moscow to Paris, from Bethlehem to New York, from Beijing to London. The British even built an immense exposition hall and entertainment center, the Millennium Dome, to usher in 2000. A year later, many of these same revelers, anxious for an excuse to celebrate again, declared correct those scholars who had been proclaiming the advent of 2001 as the true beginning of the new millennium – and partied all over again. Americans responded to the turning of the twentieth century and the coming of second millennium by immersing themselves in trivial history, reading avidly an endless number of retrospective lists about the past. *Life* magazine published two such works, one ranking the 100 most important events and people of the past 1,000 years, proudly titled "The Life Millennium," and one featuring a pictorial history of the twentieth century. Four scholars and journalists collaborated on *1000 Years, 1000 People* (New York: Kodansha International, 1998), a book ranking the 1,000 most important individuals of the second millennium.

The coming of the new age was not without anxiety. No account of the advent of the twenty-first century would be complete without the story of "Y2K," the "millennium bug." Those societies that had become increasingly dependent on computers became consumed with the fear that the arrival of the year 2000 would result in a technological disaster as computers attempted to revert to the year 1900. The problem, first identified in the early 1990s, involved the realization that most early computers were designed with two-digit number recognition programs, so that 1987, for example, would register as "87." Programmers feared that when 1999 became 2000, the older computers would translate the date as "00" and shut down, confused at having to start again at the beginning of their numerical

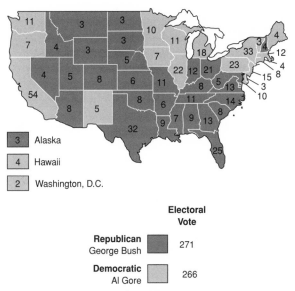

Map 14–3. The election of 2000.

sequence. With concerns ranging from the failure of electric and sewer systems to the unintentional launch of nuclear warheads, governments and businesses worked throughout the late 1990s to make their systems "Y2K compatible." The United States offered assistance to other nations who did not possess the technological expertise to protect networks whose failure could pose a threat to themselves or to Americans. As December 31, 1999, approached, individuals prepared for a collapse in social order resulting from the computer chaos. The more paranoid filled bunkers with water and food. Survivalist groups buried barrels of propane across the landscape in case of a disaster; not all of them have been recovered yet. But as 2000 arrived across the globe, upgraded computer systems performed the changeover effortlessly, so much so that some individuals considered the whole Y2K scare an invention of a greedy computer industry interested in selling more products.

The Clinton impeachment trial had left the nation exhausted and more disillusioned than ever with domestic politics. Despite the very real achievements of the Clinton presidency, the man and his legacy would be forever marred by the scandals surrounding his sexual excesses and particularly his lying to Congress and the public. Fairly or unfairly, his misbehavior opened the Democratic party to charges by the superrighteous within the Republican party that the Democrats were not only soft on defense, agents of big government, and tax-and-spenders but also purveyors of immorality. In this atmosphere of political tension, the candidates for the 2000 presidential election built up steam for their campaigns, all pledging to restore order and dignity to national politics. Former basketball star and United States Senator Bill Bradley challenged Vice President Gore for the Democrat nomination in 2000, but the latter experienced little real competition for his party's bid. A number of candidates vied for the spot on the Republican ticket, with Senator John McCain of Arizona and Governor George W. Bush of Texas leading the pack. Popular distaste for congressional Republicans coupled with the Bush team's hardball tactics (particularly the change that he would not stand up to the "secular humanists" who were allegedly corrupting American society) contributed to McCain's eventual defeat, though his record as a prisoner of war in Vietnam and his championing of campaign finance reform inspired a fair amount of support. By the summer of 2000, Governor Bush and Vice-President Gore had secured their parties' nominations for the presidency, with former Congressman and Haliburton executive Dick Cheney and Senator Joe Lieberman, respectively, selected as vice presidential nominees. Republicans and Democrats alike promised to move beyond the partisan bickering that had characterized national politics in the recent past.

Governor Bush focused on his desire to return a sense of moral leadership to Washington, D.C., and actively courted the rapidly growing Hispanic population. Relatively fluent in Spanish, Bush was able to gain some ground with that traditionally Democratic constituency (31% ended up voting for him). That Hispanics would surpass African Americans as the largest minority group in the country in 2000 made these inroads particularly significant. Debates over immigration policy, especially the status of illegal immigrants who were pouring into the United States in search of work, served as one of the backdrops to the presidential contest. The Democratic party had traditionally been pro-immigration and the Republican anti, but the appetite of Wal-Mart, Tyson Foods, and other business for cheap labor led to the emergence of a pro-immigration faction within the GOP. Although Bush courted the burgeoning Hispanic constituency, the 2000 Republican party platform advocated continuing English as the dominant national language and stressed the need to prevent illegal immigration by assisting Latin American countries in strengthening their own economies. Characteristically, Bush and the GOP paid lip service to the cause of small business while planning a massive tax cut that would benefit primarily large corporations and the superrich. In an initiative labeled No Child Left Behind, the GOP promised to introduce "accountability" in the nation's school systems, in part by allowing vouchers for taxpayers who chose private over public schools and in part by mandating uniform testing of school children at every level. Not surprisingly, the Republicans sought to take advantage of the Clinton scandals by promising to return an aura of respectability and morality to the presidency. The Democratic Party platform in 2000, conversely, praised the Clinton administration and called for a continuance of three themes: prosperity, progress, and peace.

The Democrats contrasted economic development under Clinton with the recession of the early 1990s under the Bush senior administration, warning repeatedly that the nation dare not return to the disastrous fiscal policies of yesteryear and urging voters to continue to recognize that "It's the economy, stupid" by choosing Vice President Gore. Ralph Nader, a consumer rights advocate, ran on the ticket of the Green Party, whose platform included pledges to support social justice and economic sustainability with a focus on protecting the natural environment. Polls taken in the run-up to November 7 promised a close election.

As Election Day unfolded and states released their vote tallies, Gore displayed strength in urban areas and among minorities, whereas Bush held sway in rural areas. *USA Today* published a map that showed the national vote, county by county, in the days after the election, that reflected this rural–urban split. The Republican ticket ran well among white males, management and business, and married white women, whereas Gore and Liebrman scored with labor, recent immigrants, minorities, and single white women. Democrats unsatisfied with their party's environmental policies and with the Clinton administration's conservative fiscal and welfare policies voted with the Green Party, which contributed to Republican victories in several states. With the contest a dead heat, allegations of voting inconsistencies in several counties in Florida held up the completion of the national count. Overeager media anchorpersons called the state for Gore but then embarrassingly had to retract their statements as contested votes were counted for Bush. A later report put Florida in the Bush column, inspiring a victory celebration at the State Capitol in Austin, Texas, but that ceremony also proved premature. By the early hours of November 8, nearly all of the nation's ballots had been certified except those from the Sunshine State, and it quickly became clear that the awarding of the disputed votes in Florida would tip the balance in the electoral college for one candidate or the other.

Over the course of the next six weeks, legal challenges to the Florida voting system flooded state and federal courts, as lawyers and judges tried to determine exactly what constituted a vote for a candidate. Florida's contested counties, including Miami-Dade, Volusia, Palm Beach, and Broward, used punch-card ballot systems, and arguments arose about how much of the "chad," the small circle of paper produced when the voting machine responded to a voter's choice by perforating the ballot, had to be detached for a ballot to count. Terms like "hanging chad," "pregnant chad," and "dimpled chad" filled the media's reports of these court battles, as did images of volunteers staring endlessly at individual ballots trying to decide whether a citizen had appropriately cast his or her vote. Some local officials demanded the right to hold the election in their precincts again, but the courts rejected this option as untenable. Many Americans, exhausted by the partisan bickering of the Clinton impeachment drama, expressed disgust as the deadlock persisted, and both Gore and Bush refused to concede. The Republican secretary of state in Florida, Katherine Harris, worked with her fellow partisans to ensure that any recount would be favorable to Governor Bush, whereas Democrat lawyers instigated lawsuits in support of recounts that would favor Gore. The Democrat-dominated Florida State Supreme Court made several rulings in Gore's favor, prompting Republicans to appeal to the United States Supreme Court for a final decision. In a personification of the tenseness of the situation, vice presidential candidate Dick Cheney suffered a minor heart attack. Republicans paraded around centers for recounting disputed ballots bearing signs reading "Sore Loser" in reference to the Gore–Lieberman Democratic ticket. The United States Supreme Court, with seven of nine members having been appointed by Republican presidents, ruled five-to-four in Bush's favor and ended the recount process. In the words of Justice John Paul Stevens, "Although we may never know with complete certainty the identity of the winner of this year's presidential election, the identity of the loser is perfectly clear. It is the nation's confidence in the judge as an impartial guardian of the rule of law." Judicial experts predicted that the Court's decision to intervene in the 2000 presidential election would earn it the reputation as the most politicized in American history.

9/11 and the War on Terror

Thirty-six days after the 2000 presidential election, then, following prolonged court fights over ballot procedures and conflicting sets of Florida representatives to the electoral college, and after a final defeat in the United States Supreme Court, Vice President Gore conceded defeat, and Governor Bush assumed the title "President elect." George W. Bush, quickly dubbed "W" by some journalists to distinguish him from his father, is the eldest son of George Herbert and Barbara Bush. He was born in Connecticut but was raised in the West Texas oil town of Midland. Like his father, George W. attended Philips Academy and Yale. After serving in the Air National Guard, he returned to West Texas, where he failed in two businesses before using his father's connection in the oil industry to create Arbusto, which succeeded. Shortly before his fortieth birthday the former party animal found Jesus Christ and gave up alcohol. He subsequently became part owner of the Texas Rangers baseball club, but when he failed in his bid to be chosen commissioner of baseball, he entered politics. Bush defeated Democrat Ann Richards for the Texas governorship in 1994 and gradually gained national recognition as a moderate-to-conservative Republican. He had campaigned for the presidency as a "compassionate conservative," promising tax cuts, welfare reform, and partial privatization of Social Security while at the same time pledging more money for education, job training, and drug rehabilitation. Noting Bush's lack of interest in books, other cultures, science, the environment, or really any other topic of current interest, pundits argued that he would prove to be a mere puppet of Dick Cheney and other members of the first Bush administration, who had been so unceremoniously turned out of office by Bill Clinton.

With a Senate evenly divided between the two major parties and Republicans in control of the House of Representatives, the GOP readied itself to shape the national agenda for the next four years. On January 20, 2001, Bush took the Oath of Office on the west front of the United States Capitol, ending one of the most contentious and drawn-out political battles in the nation's history. Senator Strom Thurmond of South Carolina, the only centenarian to serve in Congress, provided a bit of comic relief when he replied to a reporter's inquiry as to how many presidential inaugurations he had attended by answering, "All of them." Many historians predicted that, like former President Rutherford B. Hayes, who had been elected in 1776 with a minority of the popular votes, that Bush would be hamstrung. But, despite Gore having won the popular vote, the new president's days were not filled with bickering over the election results. Sensing that such carping would be counterproductive, Democrats chose to contest with the new president over the substance of his policies, not the legitimacy of his reign. Gore supporters among the general population, especially blacks, were not so forgiving. In an attempt to deflect their ire and to broaden his political base, Bush appointed several African Americans to influential posts in his administration, including secretary of state and national security adviser. But there were to be no concessions by the new administration in the ideological field. Bush's fervent religious convictions appealed to many Christians in the United States, and he unabashedly acknowledged the dominant role faith would play in his decision-making both as chief executive and commander-in-chief. The president's principal political adviser, Karl Rove, also a strong conservative and devout Christian, went out of his way to tell liberals that there would be no compromising on issues such as prayer in the schools, school choice, abortion rights, and other hot-button social issues. In part, the political wounds of 2000 were healed and the ongoing culture wars submerged by one of the most horrendous events in the nation's history, a terrorist attack on the World Trade Center in New York, the symbol of America's dominance in the global economy. That tragedy brought the nation together with a common sense of resolve and served to legitimize the presidency of George W. Bush in the eyes of many who had previously doubted.

As the nation prepared for the new millennium, the threat of terrorism, of attacks by fringe groups on United States interests at home and abroad, ranked as perhaps the most significant security issue facing the nation since the collapse of the Soviet Union. When Timothy McVeigh detonated a bomb outside a federal building in Oklahoma City in 1995, he had demonstrated that the American heartland was no longer safe from depredations by violent extremists. Meanwhile, shootings at schools across the country, particularly the April 1999 killings of twelve high school students and one teacher at Columbine High School in Colorado, had parents, children, and teachers all across the nation on edge. Other domestic episodes of terrorism included snipers killing people at random around the nation's capital in the fall of 2002 and the capture of the so-called "Unabomber," who had sent explosive devices through the mail and killed and injured several people over a period of years. In 1993, international terrorists had struck a direct blow at the United States by detonating a bomb in the basement of the World Trade Center in New York City. The explosion failed to bring down the twin towers but killed a number people and inflicted substantial structural damage. Several individuals of Middle Eastern descent were convicted of the plot and sentenced to life imprisonment at the federal Supermax penitentiary in Colorado, the same facility housing the Unabomber and Terry Nichols, a coconspirator of McVeigh's. Thus was fear of terrorism a constant concern for the federal government and for many individuals throughout the 1990s, but no one dreamed of the ends that Muslim extremists were willing to go to compel the "infidel" United States to withdraw from the Middle East, especially Saudi Arabia, the family-run kingdom that is home to Islam's two holiest cities, and to withdraw support from Israel in its ongoing conflict with the Palestinians.

It was true, however, that during the 1990s a low-level conflict had developed between the United States and those in the Arab world who sought to use religion as a vehicle to maintain or gain power and to reduce American influence in the Middle East. Saddam Hussein, whose ruling Baathist part was aggressively secular, invoked "jihad," or holy war, in his ongoing struggles with Washington. The Clinton and Bush administrations considered him not only a threat to the balance of power in the Middle East but also a financial sponsor of terrorism against the West in general and the United States in particular. As a result of the peace imposed on Saddam in 1991, United Nations inspectors periodically investigated his nation's military stockpiles and searched for illegal weapons of mass destruction. Convinced that the dictator on the Euphrates was not fully complying with the international regulations, both Bush, Sr., and Clinton had authorized military strikes on targets within Iraq as punishment. The 1998 air assault, named "Operation Desert Fox," had outraged other nations with an interest in the area, none of whom had been consulted by the United States prior to the attack.

In 1998, President Clinton authorized military strikes against those countries other than Iraq suspected of harboring terrorists. After attacks on the American embassies in Kenya and Tanzania, the president ordered troops to fire missiles at terrorist camps in Sudan and Afghanistan, the latter home to a new political faction, the Taliban. The Taliban had emerged from the war between Afghanistan and the Soviet Union in the 1980s, and by the middle of the 1990s it had become a state within a state, espousing a national unity based on a strict interpretation of the teachings of the Koran, the Islamic holy scripture. By 1996 the Taliban controlled most of Afghanistan, including the capital of Kabul. Under its rule, women lost many of their freedoms, including the right to attend school, and the state outlawed any images, from paintings to television broadcasts, that supposedly distracted Afghanis from the teachings of Islam. Through connections with other terrorist organizations and with the support of the government of neighboring Pakistan, Taliban militia swept the Afghan government and the nation's warlords before it and threatened to become a power in the region.

Concerns about terrorism increased as the year 2000 approached, but New Year's Eve celebrations came and went without incident. Later in the year, however, in a symbolic attack against the United States military, a small boat manned by suicide bombers sailed up to the *U.S.S. Cole*, and then anchored in a Yemeni port, and detonated a large explosive device. While the *Cole* remained afloat, the bomb killed 19 crew members. The al-Qaeda terrorist network claimed responsibility for the attack on the vessel. The organization was not unfamiliar to United States security officials who had linked it to the World Trade Center bombing in 1993 in addition to other incidents of violence. Al-Qaeda, which translates as "the base," emerged in the early 1990s from terrorist splinter factions in Saudi Arabia, Algeria, and Egypt that had sought to overthrow governments in their respective states. Gradually the target changed from individual regimes to what al-Qaeda leaders considered the principal support for the authorities that they detested, the United States. Osama bin Laden, a wealthy Saudi dissident, emerged as the acknowledged leader of al-Qaeda. Under his direction, the organization developed a number of principles, including an unquestioning support of jihad against enemy cultures, particularly the United States. Al-Qaeda insisted that true believers in Islam were financially and personally obligated to support terrorist attacks against the West and promoted a perversion of Islamic beliefs that changed peace and understanding into hatred, bloodlust, and violence. Some observers insisted that bin Laden was a religious fanatic who was deeply offended by the continuing presence of American military personnel on the sacred soil of the Arabian Peninsula. Others claimed that he was merely interested in power, in deposing and replacing Saudi Arabia's ruling family. Despite Koranic bans on suicide and violence against innocents, bin Laden and al-Qaeda used individuals willing to trade their lives for the promise of a glorious afterlife as homicide bombers to blow up infidel targets, including the *Cole*. Bin Laden appeared in videotapes broadcast on Arabic news networks praising the *Cole* attack and pledging to use his funds to train more terrorists and continue attacks on American targets. For much of the year following, however, little was heard from al-Qaeda and its leader. Gradually, public concerns about terrorism lessened.

Then, on September 11, 2001, for the first time since the War of 1812, the mainland United States came under direct attack from an external force when al-Qaeda terrorists hijacked four passenger jetliners and turned them into missiles. In a well-orchestrated plan, 19 individuals of Arabic descent boarded airplanes (in New York, Boston, and Washington, D.C.), all of which were full of jet fuel, ready for transcontinental journeys. At some point during the flights, teams of militants took over the airplanes using small knives, box cutters, and similar weapons. The passengers apparently believed that the hijackers would keep them safe to use as bargaining chips for whatever political or social aims they had in mind. But the al-Qaeda operatives had no intention of making demands from the United States or indeed of witnessing the end of the day. At approximately 8:45 Eastern time on the morning of September 11, one of the four planes crashed into the north tower of the World Trade Center in New York. Immediately, television news crews began covering the incredible event, which appeared initially to be an innocent, if horrific, accident. Fifteen minutes after the first crash, millions across the globe watched live as a second plane streaked into the south tower, creating an immense ball of flame and smoke, producing matching wounds on the twin buildings. Reports trickled in of a crash and fire at the Pentagon, the Virginia home of the United States military, just across the Potomac River from Washington, D.C. Slowly word spread that that incident had been deliberate as well; a third airliner had crashed, gouging a huge hole in the world's largest office building. Rumors ran rampant about other attacks, including a false alarm about a bomb at the State Department. A fourth plane went down in Pennsylvania, likely intended for a target in the federal capital. Passengers on board tried to wrest control back from the terrorists, who then crashed the plane.

Officials ordered the evacuation of the United States Capitol, the White House, and other federal nerve centers. President Bush, in Florida to visit with elementary school children, boarded Air Force One and traveled to one military base after another in various parts of the country to throw would-be assassins off the trail. Vice President Dick Cheney and other executive officials hunkered down in the White House emergency command structure, desperate for word on other possible attacks. Helicopters carried congressional leaders and executive branch members to secure locations in case of a breakdown in the political institutions of the nation. For the first time in history, immense Cold War–era blast doors, designed to protect against a nuclear explosion, closed shut to seal the nation's most secure military installation, the North American Air Defense Command (NORAD), buried deep in Colorado's Cheyenne Mountain. The Federal Aviation Administration ordered the skies cleared of all commercial flights, ending 98 years of continuous passenger travel over the United States. Uncertainty and fear prevailed, while federal officials waited and wondered and Americans everywhere clustered around televisions and looked over their shoulders, worried that the terrorists would strike them next.

By the late afternoon of September 11, 2001, fear began to subside; the United States had avoided mass panic. People all over the world watched again and again on television as the twin towers of the World Trade Center collapsed, covering the southern tip of Manhattan in clouds of dust, smoke, and sheets of office paper. Eventually one of the smaller buildings at the base of the complex collapsed, adding to the mountain of rubble and bodies. The Pentagon had been heavily damaged, but with far fewer casualties, primarily because the section of the building that had been hit had been emptied for renovation. The people's representatives, forced out of the Capitol for fear it would be attacked, returned briefly to pass unanimous memorials rallying the country. They then gathered on the steps of the east front and sang "God Bless America" in a symbolic display of unity. Eventually, President Bush returned to Washington, D.C., but he did so in defiance of senior security officials who still considered the city a target. He spoke to the nation and the world from the Oval Office that night, insisting that the United States was down but not out and that the events of the day "shattered steel, but they cannot dent the steel of American resolve."

In the weeks that followed the terrorist attacks, which killed approximately three thousand people, federal investigators determined that Osama bin Laden's al-Qaeda terror network had been the culprit. New York City Mayor Rudolph Giuliani emerged as a heroic figure, strong and defiant in the face of his city's darkest hour. *Time* would name him the 2001 "Person of the Year." Cleanup of the World Trade Center destruction lasted well into the next summer. Meanwhile, the attacks and President Bush's calm, resolute reaction to the crisis transformed him from a sometimes comical figure whose claim to his office had been uncertain at best to an eminently presidential figure, fully capable of uniting the nation in times of extraordinary crisis. Though Bush took his Oath of Office in January 2001, one could argue that he did not truly become president until the night of September 20, 2001, when he addressed a joint session of Congress and outlined the United States' official reaction to the terrorist attacks. Bush proclaimed what pundits subsequently termed the "Bush Doctrine," that the United States would use its military might to crush not only the terrorists responsible for the terrible attacks but also any government that supported or aided in any way those terrorist organizations. The president promised to bring the perpetrators of the September 11 attacks to justice, but warned his countrymen and women not to view the crisis as a holy war:

The enemy of America is not our many Muslim friends, it is not our many Arab friends; our enemy is a radical network of terrorists and every government that supports them. . . . These terrorists kill not merely to end lives but to disrupt and end a way of life. With every atrocity they hope that America grows fearful, retreating from the world and forsaking our friends. They stand against us because we stand in their way. We are not deceived by their pretenses to piety. We have seen their kind before. They are the heirs of all the murderous ideologies of the twentieth century; by sacrificing human life to serve their radical visions, by abandoning every value except the will to power, they follow in the path of fascism, Nazism, and totalitarianism, and they will follow that path all the way to where it ends: in history's unmarked grave of discarded lies.

President Bush warned that a war against terrorism would not be easy and would not be short. It did not involve a struggle against any one specific country, but instead an ideology. There was one country, however, that had been consumed by that ideology and that consequently provided bin Laden and his minions with a home base. That country was Afghanistan.

On October 7, 2001, American forces, allied with those of several other countries, launched Operation Enduring Freedom against the Taliban regime; hostilities opened with an intense missile barrage against the Afghani capital and other cities. Over the course of the next few weeks, U.S. ground troops, aided increasingly by warlords and other Afghans who had suffered at the hands of the repressive clerics, advanced on Taliban strongholds. Americans watched the news, struggling to learning the names of strange new places such as Kabul, Kandahar, Mazar-i-Sharif, Kunduz, and the Tora Bora Mountains. With the exception of Saddam Hussein's Iraq and the increasingly conflicted regime in Pakistan, no world government paid much attention to the complaints of the Taliban leadership, which grew more constricted and endangered with every passing day. While a growing number of Taliban fighters defected to the lines of American and British troops, some Pakistani radicals tried to enter Afghanistan to fight for the remnants of what they considered a valiant Muslim society under attack by the Western world. The search for Osama bin Laden, whom most sources placed somewhere in the Tora Bora Mountains, proved unsuccessful, but the Taliban government finally collapsed in early December 2001. After a conference in Bonn, Germany, a new Afghani government under Hamad Karzai took control of the nation and began laying the groundwork for a constitutional democracy that protected the rights of minorities and women. American forces remained in the country to stamp out the remaining terrorists and Taliban loyalists and to continue the hunt for bin Laden.

Meanwhile, in the United States, the Bush administration was working to put the nation on a war footing. Shortly after the attacks, Congress passed the Uniting and Strengthening America by Providing Appropriate Tools Required to Intercept and Obstruct Terrorism (USA PATRIOT) Act, intended to enhance the federal government's ability to preempt and respond to attacks against the nation. The measure gave the Justice Department increased authority to tap telephones and engage in other eavesdropping methods to search for terrorists. It also established a means of providing electronic security for Internet functions and gave the Treasury and other agencies the power to prevent financial institutions and charitable organizations from being used to raise funds for al-Qaeda and other terror-ist groups. Civil libertarians complained about the new authority granted to Attorney General John Ashcroft, a puritanical conservative who had had the bare breasts of the statues fronting the Justice Department draped. They warned that the First Amendment freedoms of speech and action were about to be sacrificed to the war on terror, but their complaints fell on deaf ears. To coordinate the domestic fight against terror, President Bush authorized the creation of the Office of Homeland Security, which subsequently became a cabinet-level agency.

The new obsession with security was everywhere apparent. Government buildings across the country experienced a drastic increase in security mea-sures, which often limited the public's access to their institutions and politi-cal leadership. The Idaho State Capitol, for example, received the nickname "Fort Kempthorne," in recognition of that state's governor, who authorized substantial closures at the statehouse in the interest of protecting the Gem State's legislature and state offices. Similar developments took place in Colorado, which led *Rocky Mountain News* reporter Peter Blake to comment:

Before, you were assumed to be harmless when you went to the Statehouse, interested only in observing or participating in the process. There was security, but it kept a low profile and was responsive rather than proactive. Now the assumption is you're a terrorist who wants to blow the place up. And patrol officers are all over the place. Perhaps we're lucky the Capitol's age of innocence lasted as long as it did.

For months the State Capitol resembled what lawmakers called "Fortress Colorado," until early in the 2002 legislative session, after security mea-sures failed to stop a thief from stealing a state senator's truck parked in the circle around the building. The General Assembly insisted on returning to a state approximating normality; regular police patrols and surveillance cameras, but no more metal detectors and cavity searches of schoolchil-dren on field trips.

Adding to the atmosphere of uncertainty and danger in the weeks and months after the terrorist attacks, an individual for unknown reasons placed into the United States mail several samples of the deadly virus anthrax. Spores spread through the air and infected a number of postal workers and other mailhandlers, killing several. Media personalities, in-cluding National Broadcasting Company anchor Tom Brokaw and several national political figures, received threatening letters and mail laced with anthrax, leading to the closure of several federal office buildings. During the weeks that followed, office staff sometimes refused to open mail, partic-ularly if they worked for influential people; pranksters added to the popular contagion by putting laundry detergent, sugar, and salt into envelopes and posting them. When the anthrax mailings suddenly stopped, the panic over chemical terrorism subsided.

One of the few positive effects of the September 11, 2001, terrorist attacks was an increased interest in history and commemoration. On the anniversary of the event, Arthur Schlesinger, Jr., wrote a column comparing the attacks to the destruction of the *USS Maine* in 1898 and the Pearl Harbor attack in 1941, both seen as seminal events by their contemporaries but interpreted in different ways by modern historians. Almost three months after the terrorist attacks, the nation focused more attention than usual on the anniversary of the surprise attack on Pearl Harbor. Veterans of that battle and the countless others that had fought in World War II basked in newfound attention as the nation celebrated their sacrifice along with that of the hundreds of firefighters and police who had perished trying to save those trapped in the World Trade Center. Indeed, donations to the construction of a World War II memorial in Washington, D.C., increased, as did visitor attendance at other war monuments. Tourists flocked solemnly to Manhattan to see the ruins of the World Trade Center, which crews were painstakingly sifting through looking for human remains and then slowly hauling away. So many visitors came to the site that New York officials built four large platforms for them to view the rubble; the platforms into which visitors had carved messages of hope and strength were later dismantled and preserved as historical items themselves. And all over the United States, stores sold out of American flags as patriotic citizens hung the stars and stripes from their porches and car windows.

As 2002 began, security concerns continued to top other issues in the national list of concerns. The Winter Olympics took place as scheduled in Salt Lake City, Utah, without incident, though the massive police presence lent a note of somberness to the games. President Bush participated in the opening ceremony that featured a delegation of Americans carrying a banner that had flown from one of the World Trade Center towers. Public spaces closed to visitors across the country after the attacks gradually reopened, including Liberty Island in New York Harbor (but not the statue itself) and the United States Capitol, although tourists could no longer wander unescorted through the building. The Department of Homeland Security established a color-coded gauge to inform the public of the current level of terrorist threat, from the lowest, blue, to the highest, red. In the months that followed, the warning level hovered around the yellow or "guarded" level, occasionally rising to the orange or "elevated" level during particularly important national holidays or international gatherings. The electorate signaled its approval of the way the Bush administration was handling the post-9/11 world by handing Republicans victories in the 2002 midterm congressional elections. In so doing they returned the country to single-party rule and convinced Bush and his advisers that voters wanted them to proceed with their conservative-to-radical domestic agenda.

With the situation in Afghanistan considered well in hand, the White House turned its attention to other perceived threats to the general peace. President Bush had identified an "axis of evil" during his 2002 State of the Union message comprising Iran, Iraq, and North Korea. All three powers, he insisted, were innately hostile to the United States and its allies; Iran and Iraq because they were in the grasp of radical Islamic fundamentalists and a power-mad dictator, respectively; and North Korea because it was ruled by a clique of fanatical communists. All three, Bush told the nation, were busily building arsenals of atomic, chemical, and biological weapons, "weapons of mass destruction" (WMDs), for use against the West. Iran – gripped by an ongoing struggle between radical clerics and reform-minded modernizers – attempted to placate the United States. North Korea remained consistently belligerent, however, occasionally publicizing its plans for developing nuclear weapons and the missiles to deliver them. Kim Jong Il, the country's reclusive leader who ruled his impoverished, frequently starving population with the fifth largest army on earth, hurled threats and taunts at the United States and its client state, South Korea. But it was Iraq that topped the Bush administration's list of diplomatic and military priorities. Since the Persian Gulf War of the early 1990s, when the United States and other countries forced Saddam Hussein out of Kuwait, that nation had stood as a symbol of defiance and opposition to American influence in the Middle East. Consistently ignoring orders from the United Nations to destroy any weapons of mass destruction, Hussein barred its inspectors from touring his military facilities. Many within Bush's circle of advisers, especially Vice President Dick Cheney, who had been secretary of defense during the first Gulf War, had concluded that it had been a mistake not to remove Saddam as part of Operation Desert Storm. A reputed plot by Iraqi security personnel to assassinate Bush, Sr., added fuel to the flames.

The United States and Great Britain, who remained America's closest and most constant ally in the war against terrorism, appealed several times to the United Nations Security Council to adopt strong measures that would compel Iraq turn over its weapons of mass destruction. Lest there be any doubt as to their existence, Secretary of State Colin Powell appeared before that body and presented evidence, subsequently discredited, demonstrating that Saddam was in fact secretly producing WMDs. Some nations, including France, Germany, and Russia, opposed any military action in Iraq, favoring instead additional sanctions and strongly worded UN resolutions. Despite Powell's charts, graphs, and photos, their representatives argued that there was still no conclusive proof that Saddam was in possession of WMDs. As early as October 2001, Secretary of Defense Donald Rumsfeld publicly acknowledged the possibility of United States's military action in Iraq to force a "regime change." If the UN would not act to save the world, the United States must.

In his 2003 State of the Union address, President Bush chastised North Korea and encouraged the establishment of democratic reforms in Iran, but he focused most of his attention on Iraq, detailing that nation's incessant disregard for international security and particularly its flouting of United Nations resolutions concerning its weapons programs. Intelligence reports provided clear proof, he insisted, that Saddam possessed the ability to produce and deploy weapons of mass destruction. He demanded that the Iraqi leader step down and told the Iraqi people that they should consider the dictator in Baghdad their enemy, not the United States, a friend who was simply trying bring liberal reforms to the cradle of civilization. After a not very successful effort to tie the ruling clique in Baghdad to the Taliban, Bush argued persuasively that for the betterment of the Middle East in general and the terrorized Iraqi people in particular, the despotic murderer of the Euphrates needed to go. On March 19, 2003, after Hussein failed to comply with an ultimatum to leave Iraq, a "coalition of the willing" composed of 45 nations, including the United States and Great Britain, over the objection of some European allies, opened fire on Iraqi targets. With images hauntingly similar to those of the 1991 conflict, a massive, primarily American ground force invaded Iraq from the south and west. The Second Gulf War had begun.

The regular Iraqi Army melted away before the coalition juggernaut, and after putting up token resistance, Saddam's Republican Guard surrendered. The dictator, his two brutal offspring, and top Baathist party leaders went into hiding. In May 2003 President Bush landed aboard an American aircraft carrier and proclaimed the war officially over. The pacification of Iraq proved far more difficult than defeating Saddam, however. The nation was an artificial creation of the 1919 Paris Peace Conference. Comprising a Kurdish minority living primarily in the north, a Sunni Muslim minority generally loyal to Saddam, and a Shiite Muslim majority, Iraq lacked ethnic and religious (Turkmen, Kurds, Arabs) cohesion and had had absolutely no experience with democracy. Although coalition forces were able to kill Saddam's two sons and capture the dictator himself before the year was out, they were subjected to an increasing number of mortar attacks and roadside bombings carried out by Saddam loyalists and foreign fighters associated with al-Qaeda. In the spring of 2004 pitched battles erupted between coalition forces and the al-Mahdi militia, a guerrilla band loyal to the radical Shi'ite cleric Muqtada al-Sadr. A year following the official end of the second Gulf War more than 700 American military personnel had died in Iraq, the majority since the official end of hostilities, and critics began comparing the conflict to Vietnam. Citing Vice President Cheney's ties to Haliburton, a huge Texas-based firm that was awarded without competition billions of dollars in contracts to supply U.S. troops and rebuild Iraq's shattered infrastructure, plus the Bush administration's close ties to the oil industry, some even charged that the war was nothing more than an effort to further enrich corporate America.

America's decision to invade Iraq and oust Saddam took place and indeed was partially the result of the ongoing Arab–Israeli conflict. In an effort to build on the Wye River Accords, a new Israeli prime minister, Ehud Barak, had in 1999 entered into direct negotiations with the Palestinian authority, nominally led for many years by Yassar Arafat, and also with Syria, still smarting over the territory it had lost in the 1967 War. But to no avail. Incidents such as 9/11, although on a much smaller scale, had become commonplace to the citizens of Israel and Palestine. Groups like Hamas and Islamic Jihad carried out bloody suicide bombings on Tel Aviv discotheques and Jerusalem buses, prompting Israeli forces to retaliate with missile strikes on Palestinian targets in Gaza and the West Bank. Although Yassir Arafat rushed to condemn the September 11 attacks, Americans were treated to television scenes of wild celebration in sectors of the Palestinian territory. It became increasingly clear in the months that followed that Arafat had little or no control over Hamas and other radical elements in Palestine. Even his own party, Fatah, spawned a terrorist subgroup, the al-Aqsa Martyrs' Brigade. In 2001, the Likud party, this time headed by the hard-line Ariel Sharon, came to power once again in Israel. Sharon had promised to extend rather than reduce Israeli settlements in occupied territory, and the general situation went from bad to worse. Eventually President Bush announced that he would no longer negotiate with Yassar Arafat if the Palestinian leader could not end the attacks on Israeli citizens, and despite Washington's promulgation of a new plan for settling the Arab–Israeli conflict, the "Roadmap to Peace," chances of a negotiated settlement receded sharply.

The war on terror directly affected America's relations with its former Cold War foe, Russia. President Boris Yeltsin, leader of the Russian federation since the collapse of communism in the early 1990s, resigned on the last day of 1999, and Vladimir Putin, the pragmatic, moderately reform-minded former head of the KGB, took over the government. On the one hand, Russia sympathized with the United States in the wake of 9/11, primarily because it suffered from periodic bombings and assassinations carried out by rebels from Chechnya, the predominantly Muslim province that had been attempting to break away ever since the demise of communism. On the other hand, Putin opposed the war in Iraq, seeing it as just a trumped-up conflict to enable the United States to control that nation's oil resources. In the aftermath of the 2001 terrorist attacks, Bush pulled the United States out of a 1972 treaty designed to limit and then reduce the major powers' stocks of intercontinental ballistic missiles, a step many viewed as leading to a new effort to create a missile defense shield to protect the United States from a nuclear assault. Washington claimed that a retooled SDI was needed to protect the country from rogue powers like North Korea, but the Russians felt the move was directed at them. Nevertheless, although Putin termed the withdrawal a mistake, the Russian government did not make any substantive statements of disapproval, nor did it move to erect its own shield.

Further east, the United States continued to build on its modern relationship with China, most famously established during the presidency of Richard Nixon. The bonds between the world's most populous communist state and the world's most powerful capitalist country were not without their problems, however. Most notably, in early 2001 an American plane engaging in surveillance accidentally collided with a Chinese fighter jet shadowing it, an act that killed the Chinese pilot. The severely damaged American plane landed in China, where angry government representatives detained and interrogated the crew for a week and a half while the United States, embarrassed at its diplomatic gaffe, negotiated for the crew's release. In the two years that followed, President Bush worked to cultivate a stronger relationship with the Chinese government, including a visit to that country in late 2002 to shore up diplomatic support for the expected conflict in Iraq. As globalization progressed, trade ties between the former enemies increased dramatically. A new generation of communist leaders labored to combine communist totalitarianism in the political sphere with free market competition in the economic realm. America not only bought an ever-increasing amount of cheaply produced consumer goods from China, but itself sought to exploit the abundance of cheap labor there to produce certain U.S. commodities.

The steady march forward of globalization during the second Bush administration coupled with the war on terrorism subjected the domestic economy to a roller-coaster ride. As the 1990s drew to a close, the "dot com" industry, dominated by high-tech companies tied to the rapidly expanding Internet, provided the fuel for a bull market on Wall Street, a market that was based on dramatically overvalued stocks. Throughout 1999 the stock market climbed ever upward, reaching record highs with each new day while the United States enjoyed one of the biggest boom periods in its economic history. But Newtonian physics asserted itself; in 2000 the "dot com" bubble burst when a saturated market could no longer maintain the phenomenal rate of growth, and the bull market turned bear. Internet businesses went bankrupt, and enterprises across the board suffered substantial losses. Former millionaires and billionaires found themselves broke overnight, and individuals who had placed retirement portfolios in the hands of get-rich-quick stockbrokers discovered that they had little or no money left to fall back on. The terrorist attacks of 2001 and the wars in Afghanistan and Iraq only prolonged the painful downturn; indeed, in the wake of the collapse of the World Trade towers, stock prices declined by as much as 25%. The Bush adminstration's response to the economic decline

was to push through Congress a $900 billion tax cut that benefited dispro-
portionately the very rich and increased the national deficit to Reagan-era
levels.

A string of corporate scandals in the early 2000s exacerbated the recession. The Justice Department continued to prosecute antitrust suits, first
initiated during the Clinton administration, against Microsoft, the world's
largest computer software company, whose owner, Bill Gates, topped the
list of the world's wealthiest individuals. An effort to break up the company,
which some saw as monopolistic, into smaller organizations failed, and the
attention of federal regulators soon shifted to other businesses who were
guilty of offenses far worse than attempted monopoly. Firestone Tires and
Ford Motor Cars engaged in an embarrassing public debate about each
other's product when several Ford vehicles equipped with Firestone tires
rolled over and burst into flames. Then, in 2002 a slew of corporations
folded, accompanied by accusations of fraud at the highest levels; among
other things, guilty executives had sold off millions of dollars of their own
stock, taking advantage of inside information of forthcoming profit–loss
reports or arranged so-called golden parachutes, multimillion-dollar sev-
erance packages, before the companies they had mismanaged actually had
to declare bankruptcy. Corruption and greed at the highest levels of corporations such as Enron, WorldCom Inc., and Qwest infuriated rank-and-file
employees, who often found themselves without a job, a dime of sever-
ance pay, or a retirement fund. A number of companies such as Enron
had required their employees to take their retirement in company stock,
now virtually worthless. Indeed, Enron, the giant energy conglomerate,
became the symbol of the new corporate buccaneer. It collapsed into the
nation's largest bankruptcy ever when whistleblowers uncovered an accounting scandal that hid the company's substantial debt and overinflated
profits. The scandal sent Enron stock plummeting from $82 a share to a few
pennies in less than a year. WorldCom Inc. neglected to reveal almost $4
billion in debt to its shareholders and was charged with fraud by the federal
Securities and Exchange Commission. The accounting firm Arthur Ander-
sen, employed by Enron and WorldCom Inc., among other companies, was
accused of covering up more than $4.4 billion of debt for at least seven ma-
jor corporations, resulting in federal charges of obstruction of justice.

The airline industry suffered more than most, particularly after the terrorist attacks of 2001 in which their liners were turned into missiles aimed
against American civilian targets. Security concerns among the general
populace caused travel to drop off sharply, with many families staying home
or driving for vacations. To make matters worse business men and women
curtailed travel during the economic downturn. Despite federal subsidies,
United Airlines, one of the world's largest carriers, had to reorganize after declaring Chapter 11 bankruptcy. By extension, the tourism industry
(hotels, restaurants, theme parks, rental car agencies, etc.) also suffered.

British Prime Minister Tony Blair went so far as to appear on British Airways advertisements in the United States, encouraging vacationers to return to England. Meanwhile, stringent security measures put in place by Homeland Security and a new federalized airport security authority discouraged many foreign travelers from coming to the United States.

When they were not scanning newspapers and television for the latest terror alert and stock market report, Americans allowed themselves to be distracted by other events and interests in the first years of the new millenium. The American space program and its devotees thrilled to the return of John Glenn to space in 1998 and then grieved at the disintegration of the space shuttle *Columbia* during reentry in 2003. The subsequent investigation determined the cause of the destruction to be a piece of insulation that had dislodged from the fuselage and damaged the shuttle's heat deflecting tiles, making the Columbia vulnerable to the superhigh temperatures created when it attempted to reenter the earth's atmosphere. It found, more disturbingly, that political pressure on the National Air and Space Administration to perform delicate and complex missions with aging technologies and limited budgets had contributed indirectly to the loss of seven astronauts. Meanwhile, fires in the tinder-dry West destroyed millions of acres of forests and prairies, killing firefighters and destroying millions of dollars worth of property every summer from 1999 to 2003. Debates over sexual orientation filled the airwaves after the murder of a homosexual University of Wyoming student in 1998, the Episcopal church's ordination of its first openly gay bishop, and the marriage of gay and lesbian couples by San Francisco city officials. Sports continued to obsess many Americans, particularly the national pastime of baseball, which saw season record high home run totals by Mark McGwire in 1999 and Barry Bonds in 2001, while Cal Ripken, Jr., retired in 2001 with a remarkable, perhaps unbeatable, record of consecutive games played. The New York Yankees won an emotional World Series victory in 2001 shortly after the terrorist attacks that destroyed the World Trade Center. Indeed, what was perhaps most remarkable about 9/11 was that despite the death and destruction and the knowledge that a powerful and secretive terrorist organization had dedicated itself to making war on the United States, Americans carried on much as usual. The evening of the attack restaurants in Manhattan continued to serve meals and tourists attended the Broadway shows they had come to town to see. The fabric of American life had barely been rent.

In many respects the problems and controversies that confronted America as it entered the twenty-first century were the same as those that had confronted it throughout its history. What role should government play in the economy and society? How would it be possible preserve a national identity while guaranteeing cultural autonomy for a multitude of ethnic groups? What were the proper mechanisms for ensuring equality of opportunity and political democracy? How far could and should society go in providing food, clothing, and shelter to the disadvantaged? Is dependency an inevitable by-product of the welfare state? How far should the United States go in relinquishing its sovereignty in the name of collective security, in expending its blood and treasure to maintain peace and stability in the far reaches of the globe? Or does the nation's traditional commitment to social justice require it to align itself with revolutions directed against the status quo? One major difference facing those in charge of the nation's foreign relations is that instead of focusing primarily on relations with other nation-states, the United States will have to focus on intranational problems and transnational entities such as al-Qaeda. They will also have to take religion into account in their deliberations to a degree unmatched in the nation's history.

What will differentiate the twenty-first century from previous eras is that the world will have to reconcile an ever-expanding population with diminishing and degraded resources. The debate that has raged since the 1970s between individuals such as Paul Ehrlich, who predicted a disastrous population growth to the 12- to 14-billion level by the middle of the twenty-first century, and "cornucopians" such as Ben Wattenberg, who argued that either population control would ensure a leveling off at 11.5 billion in 2150 or that the earth's resources coupled with technological advances would provide plenty for all, was by the 1990s being resolved in favor of the pessimists. More than 1,500 scientists from around the world issued a press release warning that the pressure of increasing population on shrinking and contaminated resources would lead to a planet that was "irretrievably mutilated." As the Clinton administration came to recognize, the United States could not insulate itself from the implications of this process. The teeming masses of Latin America, still largely resistant to modern methods of birth control, would move northward in search of living space and the necessities of life. If the United States did not help their neighbors to the south help themselves, it would be overwhelmed. Indeed, as Vice President Al Gore frequently pointed out, global overpopulation was of direct strategic concern to the United States. Twice in 1994 the United States intervened in countries where governmental collapse and civil war were prompted in part by overpopulation and environmental degradation. Appearing in *Atlantic Monthly* in March of that year, an article by Robert Kaplan titled "The Coming Anarchy" depicted a global scenario in which overpopulation and deterioration of the environment coupled with ethnic strife led to a series of "failed states" and massive refugee problems that threatened the political and material bases of Western society. As has been true since its founding, America will have to pursue its goals of social justice, equality of opportunity, and individual liberty at home while recognizing that its survival depends on its ability to facilitate at least a partial realization of these objectives abroad.

Index